DATA MINING AND KNOWLEDGE DISCOVERY APPROACHES BASED ON RULE INDUCTION TECHNIQUES

DATA MINING AND KNOWLEDGE DISCOVERY APPROACHES BASED ON RULE INDUCTION TECHNIQUES

Edited by

EVANGELOS TRIANTAPHYLLOU
Louisiana State University, Baton Rouge, Louisiana, USA

GIOVANNI FELICI
Consiglio Nazionale delle Ricerche, Rome, Italy

 Springer

Library of Congress Control Number: 2006925174

ISBN-10: 0-387-34294-X   e-ISBN: 0-387-34296-6

ISBN-13: 978-0-387-34294-8

Printed on acid-free paper.

Printed in the United States of America.

9 8 7 6 5 4 3 2 1

springer.com

I gratefully dedicate this book to my new life's inspiration, my mother Helen and late father John (Ioannis), my late Grandfather (Evangelos), and also to my beloved Ragus and Ollopa ("Ikasinilab"). It would had never been prepared without their encouragement, patience, and unique inspiration. —*Evangelos Triantaphyllou*

I wish to dedicate this book to la Didda, le Pullalle, and Misty—four special girls who are always on my side—and to all my friends, who make me strong; to them goes my gratitude for their warm support. —*Giovanni Felici*

TABLE OF CONTENTS

Chapter 3

AN INCREMENTAL LEARNING ALGORITHM FOR INFERRING LOGICAL RULES FROM EXAMPLES IN THE FRAMEWORK OF THE COMMON REASONING PROCESS, by X. Naidenova

Chapter 4

Chapter 5
LEARNING LOGIC FORMULAS AND RELATED ERROR DISTRIBUTIONS, by G. Felici, F. Sun, and K. Truemper

Chapter 6
FEATURE SELECTION FOR DATA MINING

Chapter 7
TRANSFORMATION OF RATIONAL AND SET DATA
TO LOGIC DATA, by S. Bartnikowski, M. Granberry,

Chapter 9
RULE INDUCTION THROUGH DISCRETE SUPPORT
VECTOR DECISION TREES, by C. Orsenigo and C. Vercellis

Chapter 10
MULTI-ATTRIBUTE DECISION TREES AND
DECISION RULES, by J.-Y. Lee and S. Olafsson

Chapter 11

Chapter 16
DATA MINING FROM MULTIMEDIA PATIENT RECORDS,

Chapter 17
LEARNING TO FIND CONTEXT BASED SPELLING

Chapter 18

LIST OF FIGURES

LIST OF TABLES

Chapter 4
DISCOVERING RULES THAT GOVERN MONOTONE
PHENOMENA, by V.I. Torvik and E. Triantaphyllou   149

Chapter 20
FUTURE TRENDS IN SOME DATA MINING AREAS,
by X. Wang, P. Zhu, G. Felici, and E. Triantaphyllou   **695**

FOREWORD

As the information revolution replaced the industrial age an avalanche of massive data sets has spread all over the activities of engineering, science, medicine, finance, and other human endeavors. This book offers a nice pathway to the exploration of massive data sets.

The process of working with these massive data sets of information to extract useful knowledge (if such knowledge exists) is called knowledge discovery. Data mining is an important part of knowledge discovery in data sets. Knowledge discovery does not start and does not end with the data mining techniques. It also involves a clear understanding of the proposed applications, the creation of a target data set, removal or correction of corrupted data, data reduction, and needs an expert in the application field in order to decide if the patterns obtained by data mining are meaningful. The interpretation of the discovered patterns and the verification of their accuracy may also involve experts from different areas including visualization, image analysis and computer graphics.

The book *Data Mining and Knowledge Discovery Approaches Based on Rule Induction Techniques* edited by Evangelos Triantaphyllou and Giovanni Felici is comprised of chapters written by experts in a wide spectrum of theories and applications. The field of knowledge discovery in data sets is highly interdisciplinary, and the editors have made an outstanding job in bringing together researchers from many diverse areas to contribute to this volume. The book's coverage and presentation of topics is outstanding. It can be used as complimentary material for a graduate course in data mining and related fields. I have found the contents of the book refreshing and consistently very well written.

The last couple of decades have witnessed an awesome development of novel mathematical and algorithmic theories focusing on knowledge discovery. What is remarkable about these theories is their unified effects in real-world applications. Books that capture these exciting interdisciplinary activities in data mining and knowledge discovery in an efficient way are extremely important for the education and training of the next generation of researchers. The present book has exactly done that.

It gives me a particular pleasure to welcome this edited volume into this series and to recommend it enthusiastically to all researchers, educators, students, and practitioners interested in recent developments in data mining and knowledge discovery.

Panos M. Pardalos, Ph.D.

Professor and Co-Director
Center for Applied Optimization
Industrial & Systems Engineering (ISE) and Biomedical Engineering Depts.
University of Florida
Gainesville, FL
U.S.A.

Webpage: *http://www.ise.ufl.edu/pardalos*

PREFACE

The recent advent of effective and efficient computing and mass storage media, combined with a plethora of data recording devices, has resulted in the availability of unprecedented amounts of data. A few years ago we were talking about mega bytes to express the size of a database. Now people talk about giga bytes or even tera bytes. It is not a coincidence that the terms *"mega," "giga,"* and *"tera"* (not to be confused with *"terra"* or earth in Latin) mean in Greek *"large," "giant,"* and *"monster,"* respectively.

This situation has created many opportunities but also many challenges. The new field of data mining and knowledge discovery from databases is the most immediate result of this explosion of information and availability of cost effective computing power. Its ultimate goal is to offer methods for analyzing large amounts of data and extracting useful new knowledge embedded in such data. As K.C. Cole wrote in her seminal book *The Universe and the Teacup: The Mathematics of Truth and Beauty*, "... nature bestows her blessings buried in mountains of garbage."

Another anonymous author stated poetically that "today we are giants of information but dwarfs of new knowledge."

On the other hand, the principles that are behind most data mining methods are not new to modern science: the danger related with the excess of information and with its interpretation already alarmed the medieval philosopher William of Occam (Okham) and convinced him to state its famous "razor," *entia non sunt multiplicanda prater necessitatem (*plurality should not be assumed without necessity*)*. Data mining is thus not to be intended as a new approach to knowledge, but rather as a set of tools that make it possible to gain from observation of new complex phenomena the insight necessary to increase our knowledge.

Traditional statistical approaches cannot cope successfully with the heterogeneity of the data fields and also with the massive amounts of data available for analysis. Since there are many different goals in analyzing data and also different types of data, there are also different data mining and knowledge discovery methods, specifically designed to deal with data that are crisp, fuzzy, deterministic, stochastic, discrete, continuous, categorical, or any combination of the above. Sometimes the goal is just to use historic data to predict the behavior of a natural or artificial system; in other cases the goal is to extract easily understandable knowledge that can assist us to better understand the behavior of different types of systems, such as a mechanical apparatus, a complex electronic device, a weather system or the symptoms of an illness.

Thus, there is a real need to have methods which can extract new knowledge in a way that is easily verifiable and also easily understandable by a very wide array of domain experts. Such domain experts may not have the computational and mathematical expertise to fully understand how a data mining approach extracts new knowledge. However, they may easily comprehend newly extracted knowledge, if such knowledge can be expressed in an intuitive manner.

The present book contains a comprehensive compilation of methods that aim at deriving new knowledge in a way that is easily understood by a wide array of domain experts and end users. Thus, the focus is on discussing methods which are based on rules when they express new knowledge. The most typical form of such rules is a decision rule expressed as: IF *<some condition is true>* THEN *<another condition will also be true>*.

It presents the combined research experience of its 40 authors. This collective experience was gathered during a long search for methods capable of gleaning new knowledge from data. The last page of each chapter has a brief biographical statement about its contributors, who are world renowned experts from Australia, Belarus, Belgium, Brazil, China, Italy, Russia, Singapore, Spain, the United Kingdom, and the U.S.A.

This book provides a unique perspective into the core of data mining and knowledge discovery (DM&KD), combining many theoretical foundations for the behavior and capabilities of various DM&KD methods. It also presents a rich collection of examples, many of which come from real-life applications. A truly unique characteristic of this book is that almost all theoretical developments are accompanied by an extensive empirical analysis which often involved the solution of a very large number of simulated test problems. The results of these empirical analyses are tabulated, graphically depicted, and analyzed in depth. In this way, the theoretical and empirical analyses presented in this book are complementary to each other, so the reader can gain both a deep theoretical and practical insight of the covered subjects.

Another unique characteristic of this book is that at the end of each chapter there is a description of some possible research problems for future research. It also presents an extensive and updated bibliography and references of all the covered subjects. These are very valuable characteristics for people who wish to get involved with new research in DM&KD theory and applications.

Therefore, *Data Mining and Knowledge Discovery Approaches Based on Rule Induction Techniques* can provide a useful insight for people who are interested in obtaining a deep understanding of some of the most frequently used DM&KD methods: it can be used as a textbook for senior undergraduate or graduate courses in data mining in engineering, computer science, and business schools. It can also provide a panoramic and systematic exposure of related methods and problems to researchers. Finally, it can become a valuable guidance for practitioners who wish to take a more effective and critical approach to the solution of real-life DM&KD problems.

The arrangement of the chapters follows a natural exposition of the main subjects in rule induction for DM&KD theory and practice. All chapters are intended to be self-contained, each providing the necessary background and definitions for its comprehension.

The first chapter is written by Dr. Zakrevskij, a member of the National Academy of Science of Belarus. The algorithms described in this chapter deal with the solution of some key data mining and pattern recognition problems. The proposed approaches are based on Boolean logic. More specifically, these approaches are based on inductive inference when solving data mining problems, while for solving pattern recognition problems they are based on deductive inference. This chapter also discusses some general schemes for representing real world environments. Such environments use binary (Boolean) variables to describe entities of interest (observations grouped into different classification classes) and also more abstract concepts, such as the classification classes. Next, the extracted new knowledge can easily be described in terms of these binary variables.

The second chapter is written by Professor Triantaphyllou, one of the editors of this book. It describes his research in inferring classification rules in the form of *if—then* type of decision rules. As data one considers binary observations which are grouped into disjoint classes. Such binary data may be derived from continuous observations when one performs certain data transformations. The algorithmic developments are based on some optimization models, formulated in terms of special forms of the well-known set covering problem and solved by branch-and-bound approaches. Given certain performance metrics, these algorithms can be optimal or semi-optimal and also easily scalable. Thus, their complexities can be NP-complete or just polynomial on the size of the input data. This is done by employing a graph theoretic approach. Both theoretical and empirical results are described. Some empirical results indicate the high potential of these methods.

Chapter 3 is written by Dr. Naidenova, a distinguished member of the Military Medical Academy in Saint Petersburg, Russia. This chapter discusses some methods for solving data mining and pattern recognition problems. These methods are based on common sense reasoning. For the data mining problems an approach is described for inferring implicative logical rules from observations grouped into different classes. Other related developments deal with the problems of incremental and non-incremental learning and also with problems related to the design of good diagnostic tests.

Chapter 4 is written by Professors Torvik and Triantaphyllou. This chapter deals with the use of monotonicity for solving certain types of interesting data mining problems. Roughly speaking, monotonicity in the data means that the dependent variable (or class indicator) tends to point to a certain value when the value of an independent variable (or variables) increases (or decreases). It seems like many real-life phenomena exhibit, to a certain degree, this kind of property. From the algorithmic point of view, the utilization of the monotonicity property offers many exciting advantages in the development of optimal or semi-optimal data mining algorithms and also for solving many complex real life data mining and knowledge discovery problems. Often the latter is possible with the use of nested monotone Boolean functions and also with the use of hierarchically organized monotone Boolean functions. Some potential applications are discussed as well.

Chapter 5 is written by Drs. Felici and Sun and Professor Truemper. The problem considered in this chapter is how to analyze training data (i.e., observations about the behavior of a system of interest) and infer a Boolean function which accurately classifies observations grouped into two classes. A special sub-sampling technique is proposed to enhance the quality of the inferred rules and to evaluate and control their precision. This technique is based on a voting scheme that combines the formulas obtained from different samples of the training data to determine the class membership of new data points. Probabilistic considerations add to this scheme the capability of predicting, with a high level of precision, the error in recognizing a new data point by using only the information contained in the training data. Such logic functions can next easily be translated into classification rules for the construction of intelligent systems. This chapter presents many theoretical issues related to this rule inference problem and also discusses many application possibilities.

The sixth chapter is written by Dr. Felici, also an editor of this book, together with Professor de Angelis and Dr. Mancinelli. It treats the problems of feature selection arising in the solution of data mining problems. When the number of variables, or features, that describe the data to be analyzed is large, it may be necessary to apply these techniques to select only those features that are relevant to the purpose of the data mining application of interest, while discarding those that are redundant or nonsignificant. It also provides an overview of the literature. This overview outlines the main components of a feature selection procedure, and then it provides several examples of the two main approaches to this problem. These two approaches are: Filter methods and Wrapper methods. The authors propose a Filter method based on a modification of a well-known graph theoretical model, the *k-lightest subgraph* problem. The model is then applied to a number of test instances to evaluate its performance, and also is applied to a real application. This application is concerned with the use of a logic data miner to a database derived from the questionnaires of a survey on urban mobility.

Chapter 7 is written by Bartnikowski, Granberry, Mugan, and Professor Truemper. A common problem with almost all methods that infer logical rules from data is that the data must be in binary form. The problem now is how to represent data that initially have rational and/or nominal values in terms of data that are defined on binary variables. Such a transformation, if not properly directed, may lead to an explosion of the dimensions of the data without providing additional information useful to the data mining task under consideration. For this reason, the authors propose a new procedure to map rational and nominal values into logic variables. This procedure tries to maximize the information which is useful for the final objective while containing the dimensions of the new space. Once the original data are transformed into binary data, next various data mining techniques may be employed.

Chapter 8 is written by Professor Kusiak, and deals with a critical issue in many data mining and knowledge discovery applications: how to best describe the information embedded in the observations. Determining the features of the data is the main focus of the emerging "data farming" discipline. This chapter presents the basic notions of this discipline and also uses a number of illustrative examples.

Chapter 9 is written by Dr. Orsenigo and Professor Vercellis and describes an approach for inferring rules in terms of decision trees for classification and prediction accuracy. This decision tree inference approach is based on a particular type of support vector machines, called *discrete* support vector machines. Their characteristic is that they aim at minimizing the number of misclassified instances rather than the total misclassification distance. Such a problem is modeled as a mixed integer programming problem. Good solutions are found by a scheme based on a sequence of linear programming problems (LP). Some computational results demonstrate the high potential of this approach.

Chapter 10 is written by Dr. Lee and Professor Olafsson, and presents the development of a classification approach which is based on the induction of top-down decision trees. It studies multi-attribute decision tree induction and methods for improving their accuracy and simplicity. The authors also discuss a recently proposed algorithm which uses conjunctive and disjunctive combinations of two attributes for induction of better decision trees. Their method is called SODI, for second order decision tree induction. They also present some promising empirical results.

Chapter 11 is written by Drs. Zhai, Kho, and Fok. This chapter studies rule inference problems from observations grouped into different classes when the data are imprecise and/or incomplete. A number of related approaches, such as fuzzy logic and the Dempster-Shafer theory of belief functions are described. However, the main developments in this chapter are based on rough set theory, a powerful modeling approach. Some illustrative applications are also described.

Chapter 12 is written by Professors Noda and Freitas. This chapter studies the inference of prediction rules which are not only accurate and comprehensible, but also interesting. By "interesting" the authors mean that the rules are surprising. Thus they offer some quantitative measures to capture this notion of interestingness. This measure is used to guide a search which considers both the prediction accuracy and the degree of interestingness of candidate rules. A specially tailored genetic algorithm, according to some empirical results provided in this chapter, seems to be highly effective in discovering interesting rules or "knowledge nuggets."

Chapter 13 is written by Drs. Kirley, Abbass, and McKay. Here they discuss the development of classifier systems which are based on genetic algorithms (GAs). Different algorithmic issues are explored in order to determine what GA characteristics are important. More precisely, this chapter studies Pitt-style evolutionary classifier systems. Different performance measures and different computing platforms (sequential and parallel) are explored as well.

Chapter 14 is written by Professors G. Chen, Wei, and Kerre. This chapter studies different settings in inferring association rules from databases. Such rules can capture interesting patterns in the way items of interest occur simultaneously in database records. Thus, they have found a wide application in analyzing consumer market behaviors. This chapter pays particular attention to the presence of impression or fuzziness in the description of the pertinent data. Besides typical association rules the authors also study the inference of functional dependencies and pattern associations.

Chapter 15 is written by Professor Liao, and contains a rather wide literature review of methods that mine decision rules from fuzzy data. It considers a variety of fuzzy data mining approaches such as fuzzy clustering, fuzzy-neural networks, and fuzzy decision trees. It also considers genetic algorithms, and traditional neural networks. The results are very effectively summarized in extensive tables, where more than 100 literature references are classified and compared on the basis of some particularly interesting parameters.

Chapter 16 deals with the case of analyzing data for medical applications. Many data mining and knowledge discovery approaches for medical applications require the use of certain data preprocessing and feature extraction techniques. Such techniques may, for instance, enhance the contrast in medical images. Another related issue is how to process patient records that are based on textual and multimedia information. All the above and other related issues are discussed in detail in this chapter, which is written by Professors Elmaghraby, Kantardzic, and Wachowiak.

Chapter 17 is written by Professors Al-Mubaid and Truemper. It deals with a very interesting problem in developing a spelling checker for word processing systems. Traditional spelling checkers are very good at identifying spelling errors. However, they are weak at identifying the misuse of words that sound similar but are spelled differently. An example is the words "sight" versus "site." Unfortunately, most systems cannot identify such errors and oftentimes text may contain embarrassing errors. The approach proposed in this chapter offers high hope for successfully dealing with this computational challenge. The proposed method is based on the use of some training data (text documents) which are analyzed only once to extract information about the use of certain words. Such information is extracted in the form of Boolean functions. Once this phase is executed, new documents can be checked for this kind of spelling errors rather quickly.

Chapter 18 is written by Professors J. Chen, Kraft, Martin-Bautista, and Vila. These authors present their research findings on the induction and inference of fuzzy rules for textual information retrieval. Applications of these findings can be used when dealing with web related problems such as those where one performs a search based on some keywords of interest to the user. The empirical results provided at the end of this chapter provide solid experimental evidence of the high potential of these approaches.

Chapter 19 is written by Dr. Judson from the U.S. Census Bureau, and treats a critical problem in databases: how to link records of one database with records of another database. This is known as the record linkage problem (or RLP). When properly solved, such a linking offers the possibility to better describe entities of interest for which we have fragmented information stored in different databases. Solving the RLP involves solving a classification problem. Classes describe the "match" and "do not match" decision to be made when one considers a pair of records taken from each one of two databases. In turn, this classification problem is solved by means of Bayesian logistic regression and also by the application of the well-known Fellegi-Sunter model for the record linkage problem.

Finally, chapter 20 provides some reflections about the future of some data mining and knowledge discovery areas. These areas are in web mining, text mining, visual mining, and distributed mining. As is often the case with the advent of highly promising computer technologies, at the beginning there is lots of hype in the expectations of what such methods can accomplish and what they cannot. This is also true with the data mining and knowledge discovery fields, and especially with methods which are based on the inference of rules. This chapter is written by Wang, Zhu, Felici, and Triantaphyllou.

If one wishes to summarize the potential of these methods in one sentence, then most experts would agree that, despite some promotional hype, data mining and knowledge discovery methods will become even more important in the future as data storage, acquisition, and processing hardware systems become more cost effective and efficient. In other words, one may assert that data mining will establish itself as a necessity for all those who, for science, for business, or for the most various reasons, desire to increase their knowledge by discovering new opportunities hidden deeply in vast amounts of seemingly confusing data.

ACKNOWLEDGEMENTS

The two editors wish to express their sincere gratitude to all authors that contributed to the writing of the Chapters, for the quality of their work, for the efforts spent and for their great patience which had been challenged many times during the course of this project. Many special thanks are also given to the Editor Mr. John Martindale at Springer for his encouragement and patience, to his helpful and cheerful former Assistant Editor Ms. Angela Quilici-Burke, and also to his current Assistant Editor Mr. Robert Saley.

The editing of this book would never have been accomplished without the help and inspiration from a number of people to which *Evangelos Triantaphyllou* is deeply indebted. His most special thanks go to his first M.S. Advisor and Mentor, Professor Stuart H. Mann, currently the Dean of the W.F. Harrah College of Hotel Administration at the University of Nevada. He would also like to thank his other M.S. Advisor Distinguished Professor Panos M. Pardalos currently at the University of Florida and his Ph.D. Advisor Professor Allen L. Soyster, currently the Dean of Engineering at the Northeastern University for his inspirational advising and assistance during his doctoral studies at Penn State. Special thanks also go to his great neighbors and friends; Janet, Bert, and Laddie Toms for their multiple support during the development of this book and beyond.

Most of the research accomplishments on data mining and optimization described in the work by Dr. Triantaphyllou would not had been made possible without the critical support by Dr. Donald Wagner at the Office of Naval Research (ONR), U.S. Department of the Navy. Dr. Wagner's contribution to this success is greatly appreciated.

Many thanks go to his colleagues at LSU. Especially to Dr. Pius J. Egbelu; former Dean of Engineering and current Dean of the NSF Academy, Dr. Kevin Carman; Dean of the College of Basic Sciences at LSU for his great leadership and support to all of us especially during the challenging times when Hurricanes Katrina and Rita hit our area in the fall of 2005, Dr. S.S. Iyengar; Distinguished Professor and Chairman of the Computer Science Department who leads and inspires by example, and Dr. T. Warren Liao; his good neighbor, friend and distinguished colleague at LSU.

Dr. Triantaphyllou would also like to acknowledge his most sincere gratitude to his graduate and undergraduate students, which have always provided him with unlimited inspiration, motivation and joy.

Giovanni Felici is particularly grateful to his friend and mentor Klaus Truemper, Distinguished Professor at the University of Texas at Dallas. Besides providing a large and significant contribution to the chapters of this book, he has always inspired and stimulated Dr. Felici's work, sharing his ideas and work with the greatest generosity.

Amongst the many people who oriented his work, Dr. Felici wants to address a special thank to professor Giacomo Patrizi of the University of Rome "La Sapienza", who, many years ago, as Ph.D. Advisor, seeded the interest for research on Data Mining and Learning in the mind of his young student.

Profound gratitude is also expressed to Professor Giovanni Rinaldi, current "direttore" of the IASI - Istituto di Analisi dei Sistemi ed Informatica – of the Italian National Research Council (CNR). He has always provided the greatest support and has made all efforts to realize a pleasant and productive working environment, while sharing with Dr. Felici his profound knowledge in all fields of Operations Research and Optimization.

Most of the recent work and experience of Dr. Felici in Data Mining has been generated by close interaction with colleagues within the framework of the Optimization Laboratory for Data Mining of IASI (OLDAM), a young project that is significantly contributing to the advance of research and to the consolidation of a strongly connected research community. Many thanks are thus addressed to all the people who have been part of OLDAM, and in particular to Dr. Marco Sciandrone, researcher in IASI and co-founder of the Lab.

Chapter 1 [1]

A COMMON LOGIC APPROACH TO DATA MINING AND PATTERN RECOGNITION

Arkadij D. Zakrevskij
United Institute of Informatics Problems
of the National Academy of Sciences of Belarus
Surganova Str. 6, 220012 Minsk, Belarus
E-mail: zakr@newman.bas-net.by

Abstract: In this chapter a common logical approach is suggested to solve both data mining and pattern recognition problems. It is based on using finite spaces of Boolean or multi-valued attributes for modeling of the natural subject areas. Inductive inference used for extracting knowledge from data is combined with deductive inference, which solves other pattern recognition problems. A set of efficient algorithms was developed to solve the regarded problems, dealing with Boolean functions and finite predicates represented by logical vectors and matrices.

An abstract world model for presentation of real subject areas is also introduced. The data are regarded as some information concerning individual objects and are obtained by the experiments. The knowledge, on the contrary, represents information about the qualities of the whole subject area and establishes some relationships between its attributes. The knowledge could be obtained by means of inductive inference from some data presenting information about elements of some reliable selection from the subject area. That inference consists of looking for empty (not containing elements of the selection) intervals of the space, putting forward corresponding hypotheses (suggesting emptiness of the intervals in the whole subject area), evaluating their plausibility and accepting the more plausible ones as *implicative regularities*, represented by elementary conjunctions.

These regularities serve as axioms in the deductive inference system used for solving the main recognition problem, which arises in a situation when an object is contemplated with known values of some attributes and unknown values of some others, including goal attributes.

Key Words: Data Mining, Data and Knowledge, Pattern Recognition, Inductive Inference, Implicative Regularity, Plausibility, Deductive Inference.

---

[1] Triantaphyllou, E. and G. Felici (Eds.), **Data Mining and Knowledge Discovery Approaches Based on Rule Induction Techniques**, Massive Computing Series, Springer, Heidelberg, Germany, pp. 1-43, 2006.

1.   INTRODUCTION

1.1   Using Decision Functions

There exist a great variety of approaches to data representation and data mining aimed at knowledge discovery [Frawley, Piatetsky-Shapiro, *et al.*, 1991], and only some of them are mentioned below. The most popular base for them is perhaps using the Boolean space M of binary attributes constituting some set $X = \{x_1, x_2, ..., x_n\}$.

When solving pattern recognition problems, the initial data are frequently represented by a set of points in the space M presenting positive and negative examples [Bongard, 1970], [Hunt, 1975], [Triantaphyllou, 1994]. Every point is regarded as a Boolean vector with components corresponding to the attributes and taking values from the set $\{0, 1\}$. The problem is considered as finding rules for recognizing other points, i.e. deciding which of them are positive and which are negative (in other words, guessing the binary value of one more attribute, called a goal attribute). To solve that problem, some methods were suggested that construct a Boolean function f separating the two given sets of points. This function is used as a *decision function* dividing the Boolean space into two classes, and so uniquely deciding for every element to which class does it belong. This function can be considered as the knowledge extracted from the two given sets of points.

It was suggested in some early works [Hunt, 1975], [Pospelov, 1990] to use threshold functions of attributes as classifiers. Unfortunately, only a small part of Boolean functions can be presented in such a form. That is why disjunctive normal forms (DNF) were used in subsequent papers to present arbitrary Boolean decision functions [Bongard, 1970], [Zakrevskij, 1988], [Triantaphyllou, 1994]. It was supposed that the simpler function f is (the shorter DNF it has), the better classifier it is.

For example, let the following Boolean matrix A show by its rows the positive examples, and matrix B – the negative ones (supposing that $X = (a, b, c, d)$).

$$A = \begin{array}{c} a\ b\ c\ d \\ \begin{bmatrix} 0\ 0\ 0\ 1 \\ 0\ 1\ 0\ 0 \\ 0\ 1\ 1\ 1 \\ 1\ 1\ 1\ 0 \end{bmatrix} \end{array}, \qquad B = \begin{array}{c} a\ b\ c\ d \\ \begin{bmatrix} 0\ 0\ 1\ 0 \\ 1\ 1\ 1\ 1 \\ 1\ 0\ 0\ 0 \\ 1\ 0\ 0\ 1 \end{bmatrix} \end{array}.$$

No threshold function separating these two sets exists in that case. However, a corresponding decision function f can be easily found in DNF by the visual minimization method based on using the Karnaugh maps: rectangular tables with 2^n squares which represent different elements of the space M and are ordered by the Gray code [Karnaugh, 1953], [Zakrevskij, 1960]. This order is indicated by the lines on the top and left sides of the table. They show columns and rows where corresponding variables take value 1. Some of the table elements are marked with 1 or 0 – the known values of the represented Boolean function. For example, four top elements in Figure 1 (scanned from left to right) correspond to inputs (combinations of values of the arguments a, b, c, d) 0000, 0010, 0011, and 0001. Two of them are marked: the second with 0 (negative example) and the fourth with 1 (positive example).

It is rather evident from observing the table that all its elements which represent positive examples (marked with 1) are covered by two intervals of the space M over X, that do not contain zeros (negative examples).

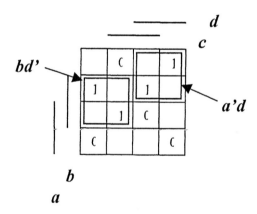

Figure 1. Using a Karnaugh Map to Find a Decision Boolean Function.

The characteristic functions of those intervals are bd' (b and not d) and $a'd$ (not a and d), hence the sought-for decision function could be

$$f = bd' \vee a'd.$$

In general, to find a decision Boolean function with minimum number of products is a well-known hard combinatorial problem of incompletely specified Boolean functions minimization. Nevertheless, several practically efficient methods were developed for its solution, exact and approximate ones [Zakrevskij, 1965], [Zakrevskij, 1988], some of them oriented towards large databases [Triantaphyllou, 1994].

It is worthwhile to note a weak point of recognition techniques aimed at binary decision functions. They produce too much categorical classification, when sometimes the available information is not sufficient for that and it would be more appropriate to answer: "I do not know". Generally speaking, for these techniques there appear to be some troubles connected with plausibility evaluation of the results of recognition. Because of it, new approaches have been developed, overcoming this drawback.

A special approach was suggested in [Piatetsky-Shapiro, 1991], [Agrawal, Imielinski, *et al.*, 1993], [Matheus, Chan, *et al.*, 1993], [Klösgen, 1995] for very big databases. The whole initial data are presented by one set of so called transactions (some subsets A_i from the set of all attributes A), and association rules are searched defined as condition statements "if V, then w", where $V \subset A$ and usually $w \in A$. They are regarded valid if only the number of transactions for which $V \cup \{w\} \subseteq A_i$ (called the *support*) is big enough, as well as the percentage of transactions where $V \cup \{w\} \subseteq A_i$ holds taken in the set of transactions where relation $V \subseteq A_i$ is satisfied (called the *confidence level*). The boundaries on the admissible values of these characteristics could be defined by users.

One more approach is suggested below. It is based on introducing a special symmetrical form of knowledge (called implicative regularities) extracted from the data. That form enables us to apply powerful methods of deductive inference, which was developed before for mechanical theorem proving [Chang and Lee, 1973], [Thayse, Gribomont, *et al.*, 1988] and now is used for solving pattern recognition problems.

1.2   Characteristic Features of the New Approach

The following main properties of the suggested common approach to data mining and pattern recognition should be mentioned next.

First, the concepts of data and knowledge are more strictly defined [Zakrevskij, 1988], [Zakrevskij, 2001]. The data are considered as some information about separate objects, while the knowledge is information about the subject area as a whole. According to this approach, we shall believe that the data present information about the existence of some objects with definite combinations of properties (attribute values), whereas the knowledge presents information about existing regular relationships between attributes, and these relationships are expressed by prohibiting some combinations of properties.

Second, no attributes are regarded *a priori* as goal ones. All attributes are included into the common set $X = \{x_1, x_2, ..., x_n\}$ and have equal rights there. Hence, the data are presented by only one set of selected points from the Boolean space over X, and there is no need to represent them, for instance, by two sets of examples (positive and negative).

Third, the knowledge consists of some known regularities. The key question is to choose a proper model for them. Starting from general assumptions the following statements are accepted. Any regarded regularity defines a logical connection between some attributes. This means that some combinations of attribute values are declared impossible (prohibited). In the simplest case such a regularity can be expressed by the logical equation $k_i = 0$ or by the equation $d_i = 1$, where k_i is a conjunct formed of some attributes (in direct or inverse mode) from the set X, d_i is a disjunct, and $d_i = \neg k_i$. For instance, the equations $ab'c = 0$ and $a' \vee b \vee c' = 1$ represent the same regularity, which prohibits the following combination: $a = 1$, $b = 0$, $c = 1$. A regularity of this kind is called *implicative regularity* (more general than functional one) [Zakrevskij, 1982, 1987]. It prohibits a set of attribute value combinations forming an interval in the Boolean space M over X – the characteristic set of the conjunct k_i. As it is shown below, regularities of the considered type could be rather easily extracted from the data, and it is not difficult to evaluate their strength and plausibility, which is very important for their further application.

Fourth, no decision functions for some separate attributes are found and used. Instead, the recognition problem is solved individually in every concrete situation, when an object with known values of some attributes is observed and the value of some other attribute (regarded as goal one in that situation) should be found. Different result types are foreseen by that [Zakrevskij, 1982]:

success – the value is found, since the knowledge is sufficient for that,

failure – the knowledge is not sufficient, and that is why the unique value of the attribute cannot be defined,

inconsistency – the object contradicts the knowledge, so either it does not belong to the subject area or the knowledge is not reliable.

Fifth, some results of the theory of Boolean functions were generalized for finite predicates [Zakrevskij, 1990]. That enabled us to extend the methods developed for dealing with data and knowledge in the case of binary attributes onto the case of multi-valued ones.

To characterize the suggested approach, it is necessary to define also the concept of the *world model*.

Not declining far from the tradition, we shall use an abstract artificial world into which many natural subject areas can be mapped without any essential detriment. Suppose this world is a set W of some objects. Objects can differ in values of attributes, where attributes compose the set $X = \{x_1, x_2, ..., x_n\}$. Each one of the attributes x_i is characterized by the corresponding finite set V_i of its alternative values, and the Cartesian product of these sets $V_1 \times V_2 \times ... \times V_n$ constitutes the space of multi-valued attributes M. Elements from W are identified with some elements of M and may be considered as abstract models of real objects of a natural subject area.

Hence, the world is represented by a relation $W \subseteq M$ or by a corresponding finite predicate $\varphi (x_1, x_2, ..., x_n)$ taking value 1 on the elements of the set W. In case of two-valued attributes this predicate degenerates into a Boolean function $f(x_1, x_2, ..., x_n)$. The world is trivial when $W = M$, and in this case the problems discussed below have no sense. However, it turns out in the majority of practical interpretations that the number of different world objects is essentially less than the number of all elements in the space M: $|W| << |M|$.

This chapter is organized as follows. The basic notions of data and knowledge are discussed in the second section, and some modes of data and knowledge representation by logical matrices are proposed, both for cases of Boolean and multi-valued attributes. The problem of extracting knowledge from data is regarded in the third section, where implicative regularities are introduced to present the knowledge, and the rules for estimating their plausibility are suggested. In the fourth section, a method for testing the knowledge matrices for consistency is proposed. Also, some algorithms of knowledge matrices equivalence transformations are described, leading to their useful simplification. The fifth section is devoted to the concluding stage of the pattern recognition process, of which the aim is to calculate the values of the goal attributes of an observed object. A method of deductive inference is suggested, which uses the previously found knowledge and the partial information about the object. Special attention is paid to the deductive inference in finite predicates. The last section contains a brief enumeration of some practical applications of the suggested approach.

2.   DATA AND KNOWLEDGE

2.1   General Definitions

Any research in the pattern recognition problem is inevitably connected with data and knowledge processing. The question about decomposing information into data and knowledge appears when developing systems of artificial intelligence defined usually as knowledge based systems.

Both data and knowledge are basic concepts, and that is why it is difficult to define them strictly formally. A number of definitions were suggested reflecting different aspects of these concepts but touching rather forms of representation of data and knowledge and the rules of their using than their essence. For instance, knowledge was regarded as "a form of computer representation of information" [Pospelov, 1990], and was defined as "information which is necessary for a program for its intellectual behavior" [Waterman, 1986]. Such attempts suggest the idea of impossibility of differentiation between data and knowledge, strict and universal at the same time, for any situation. According to a more universal definition the knowledge is regarded as some useful information derived from the data [Frawler, Piatetsky-Shapiro, *et al.*, 1991].

In this chapter, a working definition is proposed, intended for use in logical inference. Proceeding from the general suppositions, it is natural to define the data as any information about individual objects, and the knowledge about the world W as a whole. According to this assumption, we shall consider the *data* presenting information about the existence of some objects with definite combinations of properties (P), and consider the *knowledge* presenting information about the existence of regular relationships between attributes, prohibiting some other combinations of properties (Q) by equations $k_i = 0$, where k_i is a conjunction over the set of attributes X. In other words, the knowledge is regarded as the information about the non-existence of objects with some definite (now prohibited) combinations of attribute values.

Reflecting availability of the mentioned combinations by the predicates P and Q, one can present the data by the affirmations

$$\exists w \in W\colon P(w),$$

with the existential quantifier $\exists$ (there exists) and the knowledge – by affirmations

$$\neg\, \exists w \in W\colon Q(w),$$

with its negation $\neg\, \exists$ (there does not exist). The latter ones could be easily transformed into affirmations

$$\forall w \in W\colon \neg\, Q(w),$$

with the generality quantifier $\forall$ (for every).

When natural subject areas are investigated, the data present initial information obtained by discovering some objects and revealing their qualities via attribute value measurements. The result of data processing, their generalization, could be regarded as the knowledge. The classical example of the data are the Tycho Brahe tables of how the planets of our solar system move across the sky, whereas the Kepler laws, induced from them, can serve as an excellent example of the knowledge.

Suppose that the data present a complete description of some objects where for each attribute its value for a considered object is shown. Usually not all the objects from some world W could be described but only a relatively small part of them which forms a random selection $F : |F| << |W|$. Selection F can be represented by a set of selected points in the space M.

The distribution of these points reflects the regularities inherent in the world: every prohibition generates some empty, i.e. free of selected points, region in the space M. The reverse affirmation suggests itself: empty regions correspond to some regularities. But such an affirmation is a hypothesis which could be accepted if only it is plausible enough. The matter is that an empty region can appear even if there are no regularities, for instance when $W = M$ (everything is possible) and elements of the set F are scattered in the space M quite at random obeying the law of uniform distribution of probabilities. Evidently, the probability of such an event depends only on the character and the size of the empty region as well as on parameters of the space M and the cardinality of the set F. It is pertinent to remember the Ramsey theorem which asserts that in each structure consisting of n elements some regular substructures having m elements are arising if m is considerably less than n. That means that for any m a corresponding n can be found for which this assertion holds [Boolos and Jeffrey, 1989], [Graham and Spencer, 1990].

The data are obtained usually experimentally, while the knowledge is obtained from an expert, or by means of inductive inference from some data presenting information about elements of some reliable selection from the subject area. The knowledge asserts the non-existence of objects with some definite combinations of properties, declaring bans on them. The inductive inference consists in looking for empty (not containing elements of the selection) intervals of the space M, putting forward corresponding hypotheses (suggesting emptiness of the intervals in the whole subject area), evaluating plausibility of these hypotheses and accepting the more plausible of them as implicative regularities.

A set of regularities forms the contents of a knowledge base and can be subjected to equivalence transformations in order to increase the efficiency of using it when solving various problems of recognition.

The main recognition problem relates to the situation when an object is contemplated with known values of some attributes and unknown values of some others, including goal attributes. The possible values of the latter ones are to be calculated on the base of the knowledge. Sufficiently high plausibility of the forecasting should be guaranteed by that. This problem could be solved by means of deductive inference of the theorem proving type. The problem of minimizing inference chains could be solved additionally, that arises when explanatory modules of expert systems are worked out.

2.2 Data and Knowledge Representation – the Case of Boolean Attributes

Using Boolean (two-valued) attributes to describe an object, we suppose that the value 1 means that the object has the corresponding property and the value 0 means that it has not.

Consider first the problem of data representation.

If the information about some object is complete (in as much as our world model allows), it can be represented by a point in the Boolean space or by a corresponding Boolean vector indicating with 1s in some positions which properties belong to the object. For example, if $X = \{x_1, x_2, x_3, x_4\}$, the vector 1001 means that the described object possesses the properties x_1 and x_4, but not x_2 or x_3.

When the information about the object is incomplete, a ternary vector could be used for its representation. For example, the vector 10-1 means that it is not known if the object has the property x_3.

A selection of elements from W can be presented by a Boolean matrix K (or a ternary one, in case of incomplete information about the regarded elements). Let us call it a *conjunctive matrix*, meaning that its rows are interpreted as products. It could be regarded as a *data matrix* and looks as follows:

$$K = \begin{matrix} a\ b\ c\ d\ e\ f\ g\ h \\ \begin{bmatrix} 0\ 1\ 1\ 1\ 0\ 0\ 1\ 0 \\ 1\ 1\ 0\ 0\ 1\ 0\ 1\ 0 \\ \cdot\ \ \cdot\ \ \cdot \\ 1\ 1\ 1\ 1\ 0\ 1\ 0\ 0 \end{bmatrix} \begin{matrix} 1 \\ 2 \\ \cdot \\ m \end{matrix} \end{matrix}$$

Note that the number of rows m in this matrix should be large enough, otherwise it would be practically impossible to extract any useful knowledge from the data.

By contrast, when presenting knowledge it is more convenient for future operations to use *disjunctive ternary matrices* in which all rows are interpreted as elementary disjunctions, called also simply *disjuncts*.

Suppose that $X = \{a, b, c, d, e, f\}$ and consider the implicative regularity $ab'e = 0$ forbidding the combination 101 of values of the attributes a, b, e, accordingly. The corresponding empty interval of the space M contains eight elements: 100010, 100011, 100110, 100111, 101010, 101011, 101110 and 101111. The equation $ab'e = 0$ may be changed for the equivalent equation $ab'e \rightarrow 0$ with the implication operator $\rightarrow$ (if... then...), known as the *sequent* (its left part is always a conjunction, and the right part is a disjunction). The latter equation may be subjected to equivalence transformations consisting of transferring arbitrary literals between the left part (conjunction) and the right one (disjunction), changing each time their type (positive for negative or *vice versa*). In such a way it is possible to obtain the following set of the equivalent equations $ae \to b$ (if $a = 1$ and $e = 1$, then $b = 1$), $ab' \to e'$, $a \to b \vee e'$, ..., $1 \to a' \vee b \vee e'$. The last one could be changed for the disjunctive equation $a' \vee b \vee e' = 1$.

A set of regularities given in such a form can be presented by a ternary disjunctive matrix D, called below a *knowledge matrix*. For example, the knowledge matrix

$$D = \begin{bmatrix} a & b & c & d & e & f & g & h \\ 1 & - & - & 0 & - & - & 0 & - \\ - & - & - & 1 & - & 1 & - & - \\ 0 & 1 & - & - & - & - & - & - \end{bmatrix}$$

affirms that every object of the regarded area must satisfy the equations

$$a \vee d' \vee g' = 1, \quad d \vee f = 1 \quad \text{and} \quad a' \vee b = 1.$$

In other words, in the considered Boolean space there exists no object which has any of the following combinations of attribute values: ($a = 0$, $d = 1$, $g = 1$), ($d = 0, f = 0$) and ($a = 1, b = 0$).

The set of these equations can be reduced to one equation $D = 1$ where D is a CNF (conjunctive normal form) represented by matrix D. In our case:

$$D = (a \vee d' \vee g')(d \vee f)(a' \vee b).$$

2.3 Data and Knowledge Representation – the Case of Multi-Valued Attributes

In the general case of multi-valued attributes, it is more convenient to use sectional Boolean vectors and matrices introduced for the representation of finite predicates [Zakrevskij, 1990], [Zakrevskij, 1993]. A *sectional Boolean vector* consists of some sections (domains) corresponding to attributes and each section has several binary digits corresponding to the attribute values indicating definite properties. For example, the section corresponding to the attribute *color*, which has the values *blue, red, green, yellow, brown, black* and *white*, should have 7 bits.

Suppose that $X = \{x, y, z\}$, and the attributes x, y, z select their values from the corresponding sets $V_1 = \{a, b, c\}$, $V_2 = \{a, e, f, g\}$, $V_3 = \{h, i\}$ (note that these sets may intersect). Then vector 010.1000.01 describes an object with the value b of the attribute x, the value a of the attribute y and the value i of the attribute z. If a vector represents some element of the space M of multi-valued attributes, it has the only 1 in each section. The situation is different in the case of having some fuzziness. Vector 011.1001.01 can be interpreted as presenting a partial information about the object, when we know only that $x \neq a$, $y \neq e$, $y \neq f$ and $z \neq h$. Note, that each of these inequalities serves as an *information quantum* and is marked by a zero in the corresponding component of the vector.

In the case of finite predicates, generalized conjuncts and disjuncts can be used to present the knowledge [Zakrevskij, 1994]. Any interval in the space of multi-valued attributes is defined as a direct product of non-empty subsets α_i taken by one from each set V_i. Its characteristic function is defined as a conjunct, and the negation of the latter is a disjunct.

Considering the previous example, suppose that $\alpha_1 = \{a\}$, $\alpha_2 = \{a, e, g\}$, and $\alpha_3 = \{h, i\}$. The interval $I = \alpha_1 \times \alpha_2 \times \alpha_3$ presented by the vector 100.1101.11 has the characteristic function (conjunct)

$$k = (x = a) \wedge ((y = a) \vee (y = e) \vee (y = g)) \wedge ((z = h) \vee (z = i)),$$

which could be simplified to:

$$k = (x = a) \wedge ((y = a) \vee (y = e) \vee (y = g)),$$

in as much as $(z = h) \vee (z = i) = 1$. If this product enters the equation $k = 0$ reflecting a regular connection between x and y, then $I \cap W = \varnothing$, i.e. interval I turns out to be empty. The regularity can be represented by the equation

$$(x = a) \wedge ((y = a) \vee (y = e) \vee (y = g)) = 0.$$

As it can be seen from the above example, the structure of a conjunctive term in the finite predicate algebra is more intricate compared with that of the binary case – the two-stage form of the type $\wedge \vee$ is inherent in it. One can avoid that complexity changing the equation $k = 0$ for the equivalent equation $\neg k = 1$ and transforming $\neg k$ into a one-stage disjunctive term d. Such transformation is based on the de-Morgan rule and changes expressions $\neg (x_i \in \alpha_i)$ for equivalent expressions $x_i \in V_i \backslash \alpha_i$. This is possible since all sets V_i are finite.

For the considered example we have:

$$d = \neg k = (x \neq a) \vee ((y \neq a) \wedge (y \neq e) \wedge (y \neq g)) =$$
$$= (x = b) \vee (x = c) \vee (y = f).$$

Hence, the same regularity can be expressed in a more compact form, as follows:

$$(x = b) \vee (x = c) \vee (y = f) = 1.$$

Suppose that the knowledge about the world obtained either from experts or by induction from data is represented by a set of disjuncts d_1, d_2, ..., d_m. The corresponding equations $d_i = 1$ are interpreted as conditions which should be satisfied for any objects of the world, and it is possible to reduce these equations to a single equation $D = 1$ the left part of which is presented in the conjunctive normal form (CNF) $D = d_1 \wedge d_2 \wedge ... \wedge d_m$. It follows from here that in the finite predicate algebra the CNF has some advantage over the disjunctive normal form (DNF) $K = k_1 \vee k_2 \vee ... \vee k_m$ which is used in the equivalent equation $K = 0$. Indeed, DNF has three stages $(\vee \wedge \vee)$, whereas CNF has only two $(\wedge \vee)$.

Suppose for instance, that $X = \{a, b, c\}$, $V_1 = \{1, 2, 3\}$, $V_2 = \{1, 2, 3, 4\}$ and $V_3 = \{1, 2\}$. Then the knowledge matrix

$$
\begin{array}{ccc}
a & b & c
\end{array}
$$

$$
D = \begin{bmatrix}
0\ 0\ 1 & .\ 0\ 0\ 1\ 0 & .\ 0\ 0 \\
1\ 1\ 0 & .\ 0\ 0\ 1\ 1 & .\ 0\ 1 \\
0\ 1\ 0 & .\ 1\ 1\ 0\ 0 & .\ 1\ 0 \\
0\ 0\ 1 & .\ 0\ 1\ 0\ 0 & .\ 0\ 1
\end{bmatrix}
$$

may be interpreted as a set of disjunctive equations as follows:

$(a = 3) \vee (b = 3) = 1,$
$(a = 1) \vee (a = 2) \vee (b = 3) \vee (b = 4) \vee (c = 2) = 1,$
$(a = 2) \vee (b = 1) \vee (b = 2) \vee (c = 1) = 1,$
$(a = 3) \vee (b = 2) \vee (c = 2) = 1$

or as one equation with a CNF in the left part:

$((a = 3) \vee (b = 3)) \wedge ((a = 1) \vee (a = 2) \vee (b = 3) \vee (b = 4) \vee (c = 2)) \wedge$
$\wedge ((a = 2) \vee (b = 1) \vee (b = 2) \vee (c = 1)) \wedge ((a = 3) \vee (b = 2) \vee (c = 2)) = 1.$

3.   DATA MINING – INDUCTIVE INFERENCE

3.1   Extracting Knowledge from the Boolean Space of Attributes

A very important part of the pattern recognition problem is obtaining knowledge from data [Frawler, Piatetsky-Shapiro, *et al.*, 1991]. The data could be represented by a *sampling population* F – a set of some randomly selected elements from the regarded world W.

As it was formulated above, we solve that problem by analyzing the distribution of elements of set F in the Boolean space M and revealing implicative regularities which are reflected by empty intervals (not intersecting with F). That operation can be reduced to observing a Boolean data matrix K and looking for such combinations of attribute values which do not occur in the matrix.

The number of attributes coming into an implicative regularity is called its rank. It coincides with the rank of the corresponding interval. The less attributes are tied with a regularity, the stronger is the tie, as will be shown below. So, it is worthwhile to look for regularities of smaller rank. Consider, for example, the following data matrix:

$$
\begin{array}{cccccc}
a & b & c & d & e & f
\end{array}
$$

$$
\begin{bmatrix}
1 & 0 & 0 & 1 & 1 & 0 \\
0 & 1 & 1 & 1 & 0 & 0 \\
1 & 1 & 0 & 1 & 0 & 1 \\
0 & 0 & 0 & 1 & 1 & 0 \\
0 & 1 & 0 & 1 & 1 & 0 \\
0 & 0 & 1 & 0 & 1 & 0 \\
1 & 1 & 1 & 1 & 0 & 0 \\
1 & 0 & 0 & 0 & 1 & 1
\end{bmatrix}
$$

There are no empty intervals of rank 1, because each column contains 1s and 0s. So we look further for empty intervals of rank 2 and find five of them, corresponding to the following combinations: $(a = 0, f = 1)$, $(b = 1, d = 0)$, $(b = 0, e = 0)$, $(c = 1, f = 1)$, $(d = 0, e = 0)$. In a more compact form these intervals may be represented by conjuncts $a'f, bd', b'e', cf, d'e'$. Can we consider that these found empty intervals reflect real regularities inherent in the world from which the data were extracted? Such conclusions could be accepted if only they are plausible enough.

Consider the general case of n binary attributes and m elements in the sampling population (selection) F. Suppose, we have found an empty interval of rank r (comprising 2^{n-r} elements of the Boolean space M) and put forward the corresponding hypothesis, affirming that this interval is free of any elements from the regarded world W. May we rely on it and derive with its help some logical conclusions when recognizing an object with the unknown value of the goal attribute? The problem is to estimate the *plausibility* of that hypothesis.

We should take into account that the regarded interval could be empty quite accidentally, as in reality the selection F is taken by random from the whole space M. In that case there could be no regularities in the disposition of the elements from F in M.

It would be useful to find the probability p of such an event as a function $p(n, m, r)$ of the parameters n, m, r. The hypothesis can be accepted and used further in procedures of deductive inference only if this probability is small enough. Its calculation is rather difficult, so it was proposed in [Zakrevskij, 1982] to approximate it by the mathematical expectation $E(n, m, r)$ of the number of empty intervals of rank r.

That value can be calculated by the formula

$$E(n, m, r) = C_n^r \, 2^r \, (1-2^{-r})^m \,, \tag{1}$$

where C_n^r is the number of r-element subsets of an n-element set, $C_n^r \, 2^r$ is the number of intervals of rank r in the space M, and $(1-2^{-r})^m$ is the probability of some definite interval of rank r being empty, not containing any elements from F.

Some empty intervals could intersect, hence $E(n, m, r) \geq p(n, m, r)$. The question is how big could be the difference $E(n, m, r) - p(n, m, r)$? It was shown, that it becomes negligible small for small values of $E(n, m, r)$. But that is just the case of interest for us.

It turns out that the value of the function $E(n, m, r)$ grows very rapidly with rising r. That is evident from Table 1 of the dependence E on r under some fixed values of the other parameters: $n = 100$ and $m = 200$.

Table 1. The Dependency of E on r Under Fixed n and m.

R	1	2	3	4	5	6
$E(100, 200, r)$	1.24×10^{-58}	2.04×10^{-21}	3.26×10^{-6}	1.56×10^2	4.21×10^6	3.27×10^9

It is clear that searching for empty intervals and putting forward corresponding hypotheses can be restricted in this case by the relation $r < 4$. If an empty interval of rank $r < 4$ is found, we have good reasons to formulate the corresponding regularity, but there are no grounds for that if $r \geq 4$. So, when $n = 100$ and $m = 200$, there is no sense in looking for empty intervals of ranks more than 3. The search for regularities could be strongly restricted in that case by checking for emptiness only intervals of rank 3, which number is $C_{100}^3 \times 2^3 = 1{,}293{,}600$. This is not much, compared to the number 3^{100} of all intervals in the Boolean space of 100 variables, approximately 5.15×10^{47}.

A threshold ω may be introduced to decide whether it is reasonable to regard an empty interval as presenting some regularity: the positive answer should be given when $E < \omega$. Its choice depends on the kind of problems to be solved on the base of found regularities.

Suppose $\omega = 0.01$. Then the maximum rank r_{max} of intervals which should be analyzed when looking for regularities could be found from Table 2, showing its dependence on n and m :

Table 2. The Dependency of the Maximum Rank r_{max} on the Parameters n and m.

$n \setminus m$	20	50	100	200	500	1,000
10	1	2	3	4	5	6
30	1	2	2	3	4	5
100	1	1	2	3	4	5

Two conclusions, justified for the regarded range of parameters, could follow from this table. First, in order to increase r_{max} by one it is necessary to double the size of the experiment, measured by the number m of elements in F. Second, approximately the same result could be achieved by reducing by a factor of 10 the number of attributes used for the description of the regarded objects.

Suppose $r_{max} = 2$ which is justified when the selection F is rather small. In that case we have to pay attention only to pairs of attributes, looking for some forbidden combinations of their values. This task can be executed by an incremental algorithm. Such an algorithm analyzes the elements of the selection F consecutively, one by one, and fixes such two-element combinations which have occurred. This is done by using a symmetrical square Boolean $2n \times 2n$ matrix S for that, with rows and columns corresponding to the values $x_1 = 0$, $x_1 = 1$, $x_2 = 0$, $x_2 = 1$, etc. This matrix is presented in a convenient form in Tables 3 and 4. Its elements corresponding to occurring combinations are marked with 1. The rest of the combinations (not occurring) are presented by zero (empty) elements and are accepted as forbidden. The regularities presented by them connect some attributes in pairs and are called *syllogistic regularities* [Zakrevskij, 1988].

For example, let us consider the following selection of data F from the world W (only to illustrate the algorithm, despite the fact that the selection is too small for $r_{max} = 2$):

$$
\begin{array}{c}
a\ b\ c\ d\ e \\
\begin{bmatrix}
0\ 1\ 0\ 0\ 1 \\
1\ 1\ 0\ 1\ 1 \\
1\ 0\ 0\ 1\ 1 \\
0\ 1\ 1\ 0\ 0 \\
1\ 0\ 0\ 1\ 1 \\
0\ 1\ 1\ 0\ 0
\end{bmatrix}
\begin{matrix}
1 \\ 2 \\ 3 \\ 4 \\ 5 \\ 6
\end{matrix}
\end{array}
$$

Begin with its first element 01001 and fix occurring combinations of values for $C_5^2 = 10$ different pairs of attributes, marking with 1s corresponding elements of matrix S (Table 3). Note that they are presented there in symmetric pairs, besides, to facilitate further operations, additional formal pairs $(x_i = 1, x_i = 1)$ and $(x_i = 0, x_i = 0)$ are included into that set and have found their place on the main diagonal. So the whole set $(5^2 = 25$ pairs) is presented by a minor produced by the vector multiplication of definite rows and columns corresponding to argument values in the vector 01001.

By considering in the same way other elements of the selection F and by taking into account new pairs generated by them we can find all occurring pairs of attribute values obtained by the analysis of the selection F. The result is shown in Table 4.

Table 3. Finding All the Occurring Pairs of the Attribute Values Generated by the Element 01001.

	a		b		c		d		e	
a	1			1	1		1			1
b										
	1			1	1		1			1
c	1			1	1		1			1
d	1			1	1		1			1
e										
	1			1	1		1			1

Table 4. Finding All the Occurring Pairs of the Attribute Values Generated by the Selection F.

	a		b		c		d		e	
a	1			1	1	1	1		1	1
		1	1	1	1		1	1		1
b		1	1		1			1		1
	1	1		1	1	1	1	1	1	1
c	1	1	1	1	1		1	1	1	1
	1			1		1	1		1	
d	1	1		1	1	1	1		1	1
		1	1	1	1			1		1
e	1			1	1	1	1		1	
	1	1	1	1	1		1	1		1

The zero elements of the resulting matrix point to the found syllogistic regularities. These regularities can be presented in another form, by the following ternary knowledge matrix **D**.

$$
\begin{array}{c}
\quad a\ b\ c\ d\ e \\
D = \begin{bmatrix}
0 & 0 & - & - & - \\
0 & - & - & 1 & - \\
1 & - & 1 & - & - \\
1 & - & - & - & 0 \\
- & 0 & 1 & - & - \\
- & 0 & - & 0 & - \\
- & 0 & - & - & 0 \\
- & - & 1 & 1 & - \\
- & - & 1 & - & 1 \\
- & - & - & 1 & 0
\end{bmatrix}
\end{array}
$$

When the selection F is noticeably bigger compared with the number of attributes, the maximum rank r_{max} of implicative regularities could be 3, 4 or even more. The run-time for their finding swiftly increases. Nevertheless it is restricted, because the number of intervals to be checked could be approximated by $C_n^3\, 2^3$, $C_n^4\, 2^4$, etc.

3.2   The Screening Effect

Assume that we have found an empty (not intersecting with F) interval of the Boolean space M, and the mathematical expectation E corresponding to it is small enough. Then the logic of reasoning given above enables us to reject (according to the *modus tollens* rule, i.e. by means of finding contradictions) the supposition that this interval is empty accidentally, when in reality no regularity exists in the subject area W. In that case the probability of selecting elements from M for including them into W is evenly distributed, as well as the probability of using them as elements of the selection F and elements of intervals of the given rank. The hypothesis about the existence of an implicative regularity corresponding to a found empty interval is compared with the hypothesis confirming the absence of any regularities, and as a result of that comparison, the first hypothesis is accepted.

The character of probability distribution could be changed substantially when a set of existing regularities is known *a priori* and when as a result of the selection F analysis additional hypotheses are put forward, based on 'experimentally' proved emptiness of some intervals. In this case the known regularities forbid some s combinations of attribute values and that leads to reducing the number of possible combinations from 2^n (admitted by the hypothesis of the absence of any regularities) to $w = 2^n - s$.

Let us consider a conjunct of rank r corresponding to an interval of the space M which intersects with the subject area W. Suppose that a large part of this interval (comprised of u elements) belongs to the forbidden region formed by the union of intervals corresponding to known regularities. As a result the number of possible elements of the interval is reduced from 2^{n-r} to $q = 2^{n-r} - u$. It follows from here that the probability of a random hit of some definite (not forbidden) point of the space M into the considered interval changes from 2^{-r} to q/w, which could sometimes perceptibly reduce the probability of this interval intersection with the random selection F. Such an effect is called a *screen effect*. It is equivalent to a conventional rise of the rank of the analyzed conjunct and, consequently, could lead to a considerable increase of the value E. In turn, that increase can distort the results of inductive inference, and that leads to obtaining some fictitious regularities.

Consider for example the Boolean space of four attributes a, b, c, d. Suppose that the subject area is characterized by three conjunct-regularities $a'bd'$, $a'cd$ and acd'. The corresponding intervals are shown in Figure 2.

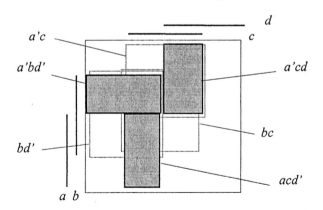

Figure 2. Illustrating the Screening Effect.

Look at the interval corresponding to conjunct $a'c$. It contains four elements presented by vectors 0010, 0011, 0110 and 0111. The three last elements belong to the forbidden region (they are screened by the given conjuncts), and only the first one does not contradict them. In this case

$r = 2$, $p = 10$, $q = 1$. As a result, the above probability decreases from 1/4 to 1/10, and that is equivalent to raising the rank of the regarded conjunction (in comparison with the case of absence of any regularities) to more than one. Similar conclusions follow from considering two other intervals which correspond to conjuncts bd' and bc.

Experimental research has confirmed that the effect of generating fictitious regularities during inductive inference could be rather big. One can compensate that screening effect by increasing the volume m of selection F or by putting an additional restriction on the rank r of the analyzed intervals.

3.3   Inductive Inference from Partial Data

It was supposed above that all objects of an experimental selection are described by their complete abstract models, with defined values of all attributes. A more general case of *partial data* presenting incomplete information about these objects was investigated in [Zakrevskij and Vasilkova, 1997]. For instance, we can know that some object has the attribute a and has not b, but we do not know if it has c.

Next suppose that the selection contains m objects which should be represented by some points of the Boolean space of n attributes, in other words by Boolean vectors with n components. However, as a result of a certain fuzziness of the data the values of several attributes (different for diverse objects) could remain unknown. It follows from here that the disposition of those points is defined to approximation of some intervals, and it is confirmed only that these intervals are not empty.

Suppose also that the *degree of fuzziness* is given by the parameter u, the same for all objects and attributes probability of the event "the value of a current attribute of a current object is unknown".

Such uncertainty can be marked by the symbol "-" in corresponding components of the vectors describing the regarded objects, changing in such a way the Boolean vectors for ternary ones. However, it is more convenient, from the computer point of view, to use sectional Boolean vectors with two-component sections in the case of binary attributes.

As a result, the information about the experimental data set is presented by a Boolean data matrix K of size $m \times 2n$, in which columns are divided into sections, two columns in each. The regularities are extracted just from this matrix.

During inductive inference, disjuncts presented by $2n$-component Boolean vectors are checked one by one, and those of them which are satisfied by every element of the given selection are accepted. The search begins with disjuncts of the minimum rank (1) and terminates by disjuncts of a certain "critical" rank. The current disjunct is compared with all rows of matrix K and, if it does not contradict with any of them (that is, if the component-wise conjunction of the compared vectors differs from the vector $\mathbf{0}$), it is considered as satisfied. Then it can be accepted as a regularity on the condition that the probability of its accidental origin is small enough.

Computation of that probability is rather complicated, but in the case of small values it can be well approximated by the mathematical expectation $E(m, n, r, u)$ of the number of disjuncts of rank r, which are satisfied by every element of the data. Note that the latter is a random selection from M represented by the corresponding $m \times 2n$ Boolean matrix K eroded according to the parameter u.

The value of E is defined as the product of the number $C_n^r 2^r$ of different disjuncts of rank r in the space of n binary attributes and the probability $(1 - \dfrac{(1-u)^r}{2^r})^m$ that one of them (arbitrarily chosen) does not contradict the data presented by the matrix K:

$$E(m,n,r,u) = C_n^r 2^r (1 - \frac{(1-u)^r}{2^r})^m. \qquad (2)$$

It is evident, that E swiftly increases with rising the rank r. The strong dependence of E on r facilitates finding the critical rank $r*$ for disjuncts checked during inductive inference. Knowing that value restricts the volume of computations performed while looking for regularities: it is defined by the number N of checked disjuncts for which ranks must not exceed $r*$. This number can be obtained by the formula

$$N = \sum_{r=1}^{r*} C_n^r 2^r. \qquad (3)$$

3.4   The Case of Multi-Valued Attributes

It is a little more difficult to extract knowledge from the space of n multi-valued attributes $x_1, x_2, \ldots, x_n$, see for example [Zakrevsky, 1994]. To begin with, define the probability p that a disjunct will be satisfied by an accidentally chosen element of the space. It could be calculated by the formula

$$p = 1 - \prod_{i=1}^{n} \frac{r_i}{s_i}, \qquad (4)$$

where s_i is the number of all values of the attribute x_i, and r_i is the number of those of them which do not enter this disjunct. For instance, for the disjunct 00.1000.101 $p = 1 - (2/2) \times (3/4) \times (1/3) = 3/4$. Let us divide all disjuncts into classes D_j, forming them from disjuncts with the same value of p. Next let us number these classes in order of increasing p and introduce the following conventional signs: q_j is the number of disjuncts in the class D_j, p_j is the value of p for elements from D_j.

Find now the mathematical expectation E_j of the number of disjuncts from the class D_j, which do not contradict the random m-element selection from the regarded space:

$$E_j = q_j\,(p_j)^m \,, \tag{5}$$

and introduce the analogous quantity E_k^+ for the union of classes D_1, D_2, ..., D_k:

$$E_k^+ = \sum_{i=1}^{k} E_j. \tag{6}$$

Inductive inference is performed by consecutively regarding classes D_j in order of their numbers and summarizing corresponding values E_j until the sum surpasses a threshold t, which is introduced by taking into account the specific of the considered subject area. All disjuncts belonging to these classes are accepted as regularities if they do not contradict the data, i.e. if they are satisfied by any element of the selection F.

An expert may fix several thresholds and assign accordingly different levels of plausibility to the found regularities. For example, regularities obtained by thresholds 10^{-10}, 10^{-6}, 10^{-3} could be estimated as *absolutely plausible, usually, most likely*, respectively. This differentiation gives some flexibility to recognition procedures. Choosing a proper level of plausibility one can use only some of regularities contained in the knowledge base and vary in such a way the plausibility of the logical conclusions obtained during recognition. For example, using only the most plausible regularities can result in obtaining a small number of logical conclusions, but more reliable ones, while extending the used part of the knowledge base extends the set of obtained logical conclusions, at the expense of their plausibility.

4. KNOWLEDGE ANALYSIS AND TRANSFORMATIONS

4.1   Testing for Consistency

Any disjunctive knowledge matrix D is *consistent* if the corresponding conjunctive normal form (CNF) D is *satisfiable*, i.e. if there exists at least one solution of the equation $D = 1$. Checking D for consistency is a hard combinatorial problem [Cook, 1971]. In the general case it involves an unavoidable exhaustive procedure, which could be significantly reduced by a tree searching technique, taking into account the specific features of the regarded problem.

In the case of binary attributes the knowledge matrix D could be presented as a ternary matrix, and checking it for consistency is equivalent to looking for a Boolean vector, which satisfies every row d_j of matrix D, either having 1 in some component where d_j has 1 or having 0 in some component where d_j has 0.

This task is equivalent to another one, over a ternary matrix C that represents the disjunctive normal form (DNF) of the characteristic Boolean function V for the prohibited area of the Boolean space M (taking value 1 on the area elements). That function V is called a *veto function*. Evidently, the equations $D = 1$ and $V = 0$ are equivalent, and matrix C could be easily obtained from matrix D by the component-wise inversion illustrated below.

$$D = \begin{bmatrix} 0 & - & 1 & 1 & - \\ - & 1 & 0 & - & - \\ 1 & - & - & - & 0 \\ - & 1 & - & - & 1 \\ 0 & - & - & 0 & - \end{bmatrix}, \qquad C = \begin{bmatrix} 1 & - & 0 & 0 & - \\ - & 0 & 1 & - & - \\ 0 & - & - & - & 1 \\ - & 0 & - & - & 0 \\ 1 & - & - & 1 & - \end{bmatrix}.$$

$$0 \ 1 \ 0 \ 0 \ 0 \qquad\qquad 0 \ 1 \ 0 \ 0 \ 0$$

In this case the function V should be checked for identity (the relation $V \equiv 1$ is verified by that), and that corresponds to checking C for degeneration. Matrix C is called *degenerate ternary matrix* if and only if no Boolean vector exists orthogonal to every row of the matrix. Remind that two vectors are orthogonal if a component exists where one vector has the value 0 and the other has the value 1. For the regarded example we can find such a vector (it is shown under C), and the same vector (shown under D) satisfies matrix D. That proves the consistency of the latter.

The discussed problem is well known; it is enough to say that it lies in the base of the theory of computational complexity. Many methods and algorithms were developed for its solution, for example [Davis, Longemann, *et al.*, 1962], [Zhang, 1997], so we shall not go here in detail.

A rather efficient method of checking a ternary matrix C for degeneration has been suggested in [Zakrevskij, 1988]. It realizes the idea "to try and find a Boolean vector w orthogonal to every row of matrix C" and uses the tree searching technique described in [Nilsson, 1971]. By that the tree vertices present current situations and edges proceeding from them point to possible choices of some component values. The sought-for vector w is constructed by assigning definite values to its components (when moving forward) one by one, and reassigning them (after it moves backward). So during the search process it is a variable ternary vector changing with time. A current situation is presented by a current value of the vector w and a minor T of matrix C obtained from C by deleting the satisfied rows (orthogonal to w) and columns which correspond to the variables having accepted some values. To reduce calculations some rules are used that allow avoiding alternative situations as much as possible.

That method implements the deductive inference of the *modus tollens* rule, illustrated with the following example of a matrix C and a search tree (see also Figure 3) which shows that matrix C is degenerate.

$$
\begin{array}{cccccc}
a & b & c & d & e & f
\end{array}
$$

$$
\begin{bmatrix}
1 & - & - & - & - & 0 \\
1 & - & 1 & - & 1 & - \\
1 & 0 & - & - & 1 & 1 \\
1 & - & - & - & 0 & 1 \\
1 & 1 & 0 & - & - & 1 \\
0 & 1 & - & - & - & 1 \\
0 & - & - & - & 0 & 1 \\
0 & 0 & - & - & 1 & - \\
0 & - & - & 0 & 1 & 0 \\
0 & 1 & - & 1 & 1 & 0 \\
0 & 1 & - & - & 0 & 0 \\
0 & - & 1 & - & 0 & 0 \\
0 & 0 & 0 & - & 0 & 0
\end{bmatrix}
\begin{array}{l}
1 \\
2 \\
3 \\
4 \\
5 \\
6 \\
7 \\
8 \\
9 \\
10 \\
11 \\
12 \\
13
\end{array}
$$

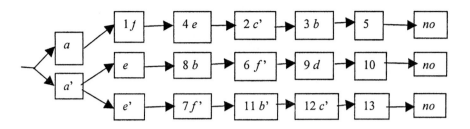

Figure 3. A Search Tree.

The tree presents the following reasoning. Suppose that a vector w exists orthogonal to every row of matrix C. Consider the variable a corresponding to the most defined column (i.e., the one with the minimum number of *don't care* elements). It could have the value either 1 or 0. If $a = 1$, then the rows from 6 to 13 are satisfied. Now in order to satisfy row 1 it is necessary for w to have $f = 1$, otherwise w cannot be orthogonal to that row. For the same reason it is necessary to accept $e = 1$ (look at row 4), then $c = 0$ (row 2), then $b = 1$ (row 3). After that it becomes impossible to satisfy row 5, so we have to return to the beginning of the produced chain and try the other value of the variable a.

If $a = 0$, then the rows from 1 to 5 are satisfied and we have to satisfy the remaining rows, from 6 to 13. Consider now the variable e. If $e = 1$, then from necessity $b = 1$ (row 8), $f = 0$ (row 6) and $d = 1$ (row 9), after which it is impossible to satisfy row 10. Else if $e = 0$, then follow $f = 0$ (row 7), $b = 0$ (row 11), $c = 0$ (row 12), after that it is impossible to satisfy row 13.

So, we have to admit that the value 0 of the variable a is also invalid, and it is impossible to construct a vector w orthogonal to every row of matrix C. Hence, that matrix is degenerate.

In the case of multi-valued attributes the knowledge is presented by a sectional disjunctive Boolean matrix D. Any solution of the equation $D = 1$ corresponds to a column minor, which includes exactly one column from each domain and has at least one 1 in every row. Checking D for consistency is more difficult now. The tree searching technique is necessary here. To facilitate the regarded task some rules formulated below can be used for reducing the size of matrix D.

Let u and v be some rows of matrix D, while p and q are some of its columns. Consider vectors a and b be satisfying the relation $a \geq b$ if the latter is satisfied component-wise. Let us say in this case that a covers b.

The following reduction rules enable us to simplify matrix D by expelling some rows or columns.

Rule 1: If u covers v, then row u is expelled.

Rule 2: If a column p is empty (not having 1s), then it is expelled.

Rule 3: If there exists a row u having 1s only in one domain, then all columns of that domain which have 0 in row u are expelled.

These rules define the equivalence transformations of D which do not change the set of solutions of equation $D = 1$. When checking D for consistency two more rules may be added. Their application can change the set of roots but does not violate the property of consistency: any consistent matrix remains consistent, and any inconsistent matrix remains inconsistent.

Rule 4: If p covers q and these columns belong to the same domain, then column q is expelled.

Rule 5: If a row u has a section without 0s, then it can be expelled.

Rules 1 and 4 are the most useful. For example, regarding the knowledge matrix

$$D = \begin{array}{cc} \begin{matrix} a_1a_2a_3 & b_1b_2b_3 & c_1c_2c_3c_4 \end{matrix} & \\ \begin{bmatrix} 0\ 1\ 1\ .\ 0\ 0\ 1\ .\ 0\ 0\ 0\ 0 \\ 1\ 0\ 0\ .\ 1\ 0\ 1\ .\ 0\ 1\ 0\ 0 \\ 1\ 0\ 1\ .\ 0\ 1\ 0\ .\ 1\ 0\ 0\ 1 \\ 1\ 0\ 0\ .\ 0\ 1\ 0\ .\ 1\ 0\ 1\ 0 \\ 0\ 1\ 1\ .\ 0\ 1\ 0\ .\ 0\ 1\ 0\ 1 \\ 0\ 1\ 0\ .\ 1\ 0\ 1\ .\ 1\ 0\ 0\ 0 \end{bmatrix} & \begin{matrix} d_1 \\ d_2 \\ d_3 \\ d_4 \\ d_5 \\ d_6 \end{matrix} \end{array}$$

we can use these rules for deleting one by one the following columns and rows: column b_1 (covered by b_3), column c_3 (covered by c_1), row d_3 (covering now d_4), column c_4 (covered by c_2), column a_3 (covered by a_2) and row d_6 (covering d_1 after deleting a_3). Executing these operations, we get a more compact matrix shown below:

$$\begin{array}{cc} \begin{matrix} a_1a_2 & b_2b_3 & c_1c_2 \end{matrix} & \\ \begin{bmatrix} 0\ 1\ .\ 0\ 1\ .\ 0\ 0 \\ 1\ 0\ .\ 0\ 1\ .\ 0\ 1 \\ 1\ 0\ .\ 1\ 0\ .\ 1\ 0 \\ 0\ 1\ .\ 1\ 0\ .\ 0\ 1 \end{bmatrix} & \begin{matrix} d_1 \\ d_2 \\ d_4 \\ d_5 \end{matrix} \end{array}$$

It is not difficult now to be convinced of the consistency of this matrix. For instance, it is satisfied by vector 10.01.01, presenting one of the solutions of the regarded system of disjunctive equations.

4.2 Simplification

Using a disjunctive knowledge matrix D in some expert system of logical recognition, it is natural to simplify it beforehand in order to facilitate subsequent repeated computations on its base. The simplification can consist in reducing the number of disjuncts as well as the number of 1s in the matrix in such a way that does not change the set of the matrix roots. So, there arises the problem of practical importance to look for a minimum disjunctive matrix equivalent to the given one.

That is the well-known problem of minimization of Boolean functions (or their DNFs, to be more correct), and hundreds of publications were devoted to it [Quine, 1952], [Karnaugh, 1953], [Nelson, 1955], [McCluskey, 1956], [Urbano and Mueller, 1956], [Zakrevskij, 1965], etc. We have no place to discuss them here. However, we would like to note that this problem was expanded onto finite predicates, which is vital for solving combinatorial tasks in the space of multi-valued attributes.

The problem of Boolean function minimization could be regarded both in exact and approximate formulations. Of course, looking for minimum DNFs is rather time-consuming, but suboptimal solutions could be very often quite satisfactory for practical purposes. For example, much less run-time is necessary to find some irredundant DNF which could serve as a good approximation to a minimum DNF. One can obtain it from an arbitrary DNF deleting from it some terms. Besides, some terms could be simplified by deleting some literals from them. The following algorithm for checking a ternary matrix for degeneration is very useful for these operations.

Let us regard the ternary matrix C presenting the DNF

$$acf' \vee be'f \vee a'd'e \vee de'f \vee b'c'f \vee b'df \vee c'e'f \vee b'c'd'.$$

$$
C =
\begin{matrix}
 & a\ b\ c\ d\ e\ f \\
\begin{bmatrix}
1 & - & 1 & - & - & 0 \\
- & 1 & - & - & 0 & 1 \\
0 & - & - & 0 & 1 & - \\
- & - & - & 1 & 0 & 1 \\
- & 0 & 0 & - & - & 1 \\
- & 0 & - & 1 & - & 1 \\
- & - & 0 & - & 0 & 1 \\
- & 0 & 0 & 0 & - & -
\end{bmatrix}
\end{matrix}
$$

Checking its terms one by one we can see that some of them are implicants of the remaining part of the DNF and so can be deleted. Suppose the term represented by a row c_i of matrix C should be checked. Then this operation is reduced to checking for degeneration of a certain minor of matrix C. That minor (denoted as $C : c_i$) is obtained by deleting from C row c_i together with all rows orthogonal to c_i and also columns where c_i has definite values (1 or 0). If the minor $C : c_i$ turns out to be degenerate, then row c_i (and corresponding term) should be deleted.

For example, the row (- - - 1 0 1) can be deleted from C but the row (- 1 - - 0 1) cannot, because the minor $C : (- - - 1 0 1)$ is degenerate and the minor $C : (- 1 - - 0 1)$ is not.

$$C:(- - - 1\ 0\ 1) = \begin{array}{c} a\ b\ c \\ \begin{bmatrix} - & 1 & - \\ - & 0 & 0 \\ - & 0 & - \\ - & - & 0 \end{bmatrix} \end{array}, \qquad C:(- 1 - - 0\ 1) = \begin{array}{c} a\ c\ d \\ \begin{bmatrix} 0 & 1 & - \\ - & - & 1 \\ - & 0 & 1 \end{bmatrix} \end{array}.$$

Checking all rows one by one, we find that three rows can be deleted from C. As a result, we get an irredundant matrix C^*. The corresponding irredundant knowledge disjunctive matrix D^* is easily obtained from C^* by the component-wise inversion.

$$C^* = \begin{array}{c} a\ b\ c\ d\ e\ f \\ \begin{bmatrix} 1 & - & 1 & - & - & 0 \\ - & 1 & - & - & 0 & 1 \\ 0 & - & - & 0 & 1 & - \\ - & 0 & - & 1 & - & 1 \\ - & 0 & 0 & 0 & - & - \end{bmatrix} \end{array}, \qquad D^* = \begin{array}{c} a\ b\ c\ d\ e\ f \\ \begin{bmatrix} 0 & - & 0 & - & - & 1 \\ - & 0 & - & - & 1 & 0 \\ 1 & - & - & 1 & 0 & - \\ - & 1 & - & 0 & - & 0 \\ - & 1 & 1 & 1 & - & - \end{bmatrix} \end{array}.$$

5.   PATTERN RECOGNITION – DEDUCTIVE INFERENCE

5.1   Recognition in the Boolean Space

The recognition problem can be formulated as the problem of a closer definition of qualities of some observed object not belonging to the experimental selection from the subject area [Zakrevskij, 1999]. Suppose that we know the values of s from n attributes of this object. That is equivalent to locating the object in a certain interval of the Boolean space M presented by the corresponding elementary conjunction k of rank s. The problem is to define by logical reasoning, as well as possible, the values of the remaining $n - s$ attributes, using for that the information contained in the knowledge ternary matrix D and in the corresponding veto function V.

Let us regard the set X_k of attributes with known values and the set of all forbidden combinations of values of the remaining attributes – for the considered object. The latter set can be described by a proper Boolean veto function $V(k)$ that could be easily obtained from V. Indeed, it is sufficient for that to transform the formula representing the function V by changing symbols of attributes presented in k for values (0 or 1) satisfying the equation $k = 1$. Denote this operation as $V(k) = V{:}k$.

Suppose that we want to know the value of an attribute x_i which does not come into X_k. The necessary and sufficient condition for the prohibition of the value 1 of that attribute is presented by the formal implication $kx_i \Rightarrow V$, i.e. belonging of the interval presented by conjunction kx_i to the prohibition region described by the function V. Analogously, the necessary and sufficient condition for the prohibition of the value 0 is presented by $kx_i{}' \Rightarrow V$.

It is not difficult to deduce from here forecasting rules to define the value of the goal attribute x_i of the object characterized by k. These rules are shown in a compressed form in Table 5 presenting the decision (a set of possible values of x_i, the bottom row) as a function of predicates $kx_i \Rightarrow V$ and $kx_i{}' \Rightarrow V$.

Table 5. Forecasting the Value of the Attribute x_i .

$kx_i \Rightarrow V$	0	0	1	1
$kx_i{}' \Rightarrow V$	0	1	0	1
x_i	$\{0, 1\}$	$\{1\}$	$\{0\}$	$\varnothing$

Note that four outcomes could appear at this approach. On a level with finding the only value (0 or 1) for the attribute x_i, such situations could be met when both values are acceptable or neither of them satisfies the veto function V. At the later case the existence of the object α characterized by k contradicts the knowledge base, and that could stimulate some correction of the latter. However, the probability of such an event is low enough, taking into account the way of forming the knowledge base.

For example, if

$$V = acf' \vee be'f \vee a'd'e \vee b'df \vee b'c'd'$$

and $k = abf$, then $V(k) = V{:}abf = e'$. It could be concluded from this that the regarded object α has value 1 in attribute e, but there are no restrictions on the other attributes (c and d). If by the same function V the object α is characterized by $k = c'e'f$, then

$$V(k) = b \vee b'd \vee b'd' = 1 \text{ (all are forbidden)},$$

and that means that the object contradicts the knowledge.

Predicates $kx_i \Rightarrow V$ and $kx_i' \Rightarrow V$ are accordingly equivalent to predicates $V{:}kx_i = 1$ and $V{:}kx_i' = 1$, and that allows reducing their calculation by checking the corresponding submatrices of the knowledge matrix D for consistency. Fixing the values of some attributes in function V is changed for selecting a corresponding minor of matrix D by deleting some rows and columns, which could be followed by further possible simplification.

Suppose that we regard the same (already minimized) knowledge matrix D corresponding to the veto function $V = acf' \vee be'f \vee a'd'e \vee b'df \vee b'c'd'$ and know that for the observed object $a = 1$ and $c = 1$. Taking into account this new information we transform matrix D as follows. First we delete from it the columns marked with a and c because these variables became constant, and delete also the rows 3 and 5 now satisfied by these constants. Further simplification is rather evident, by using the following rule: $x\,(x' \vee H) = x\,H$, where x is a Boolean variable and H is an arbitrary Boolean formula.

$$
D* =
\begin{array}{c}
\begin{array}{cccccc} a & b & c & d & e & f \end{array} \\
\left[
\begin{array}{cccccc}
0 & - & 0 & - & - & 1 \\
- & 0 & - & - & 1 & 0 \\
1 & - & - & 1 & 0 & - \\
- & 1 & - & 0 & - & 0 \\
- & 1 & 1 & 1 & - & -
\end{array}
\right]
\begin{array}{c} 1 \\ 2 \\ 3 \\ 4 \\ 5 \end{array}
\end{array}
\qquad
\begin{array}{c}
\begin{array}{cccc} b & d & e & f \end{array} \\
\left[
\begin{array}{cccc}
- & - & - & 1 \\
0 & - & 1 & 0 \\
1 & 0 & - & 0
\end{array}
\right]
\end{array}
\qquad
\begin{array}{c}
\begin{array}{cccc} b & d & e & f \end{array} \\
\left[
\begin{array}{cccc}
- & - & - & 1 \\
0 & - & 1 & - \\
1 & 0 & - & -
\end{array}
\right]
\end{array}
$$

We can conclude now that $f = 1$, by necessity. As to the remaining attributes, their values cannot be forecasted uniquely. They obey the next two conditions: $b' \vee e = 1$ and $b \vee d' = 1$. This system of logical equations has two solutions. Either $b = d = 0$ (with an arbitrary value of e), or $b = e = 1$ (with an arbitrary value of d).

Suppose the values of all attributes are known except the goal one. In that case solving the recognition problem could be facilitated by preliminary partitioning the Boolean space of attributes into four regions. After that it would be sufficient only to conclude to which of them the regarded object belongs and make the corresponding conclusion.

The characteristic Boolean functions of these regions are obtained on the base of the rules shown in Table 5. The region where the value of the attribute x_i remains unknown is described by the function $V(x_i) =$

$(V:x_i)'\wedge(V:x_i')'$, the region where x_i receives the value 1 is presented by the function $V^1(x_i) = (V:x_i)'\wedge(V:x_i')$, the region where x_i receives the value 0 – by the function $V^0(x_i) = (V:x_i)\wedge(V:x_i')'$, and the region of contradiction – by the function $V^*(x_i) = (V:x_i)\wedge(V:x_i')$.

By using the same example we obtain:

$$V = acf' \vee be'f \vee a'd'e \vee b'df \vee b'c'd',$$

$$V:f = be' \vee a'd'e \vee b'd \vee b'c'd',$$

$$V:f' = ac \vee a'd'e \vee b'c'd',$$

$$V(f) = (be' \vee a'd'e \vee b'd \vee b'c'd')' \wedge (ac \vee a'd'e \vee b'c'd')',$$

$$V^1(f) = (be' \vee a'd'e \vee b'd \vee b'c'd')' \wedge (ac \vee a'd'e \vee b'c'd'),$$

$$V^0(f) = (be' \vee a'd'e \vee b'd \vee b'c'd') \wedge (ac \vee a'd'e \vee b'c'd')',$$

$$V^*(f) = (be' \vee a'd'e \vee b'd \vee b'c'd') \wedge (ac \vee a'd'e \vee b'c'd').$$

5.2 Appreciating the Asymmetry in Implicative Regularities

So far it was silently assumed that every implicative regularity is symmetrical for all attributes included in it. In other words, all these attributes have equal rights. It was assumed, for example, that the disjunct $a \vee b \vee c$ can be transformed into any of the sequents $a'b' \to c$, $a'c' \to b$ and $b'c' \to a$, which could be used under recognition. It was assumed, therefore, that all these expressions are equivalent.

However, sometimes the symmetry of implicative regularities could be subjected to doubt. More accurate means may be suggested for their representation as well as the appropriate rules for using them in deductive inference.

Denote by $w(k)$ the number of elements from selection F which have sets of attribute values satisfying the equation $k = 1$ with a conjunctive term k (for example, the vector 10011 of values of the attributes a, b, c, d, e satisfies the equation $c'e = 1$).

Let us consider some irredundant disjunct, $a \vee b \vee c$ for instance, representing a regularity obtained as a result of the selection analysis fulfilled according to the formulated above rules. Evidently, $w(a'b'c') = 0$, but it could be that $w(ab'c') \neq 0$, $w(a'bc') \neq 0$ and $w(a'b'c) \neq 0$. Admit that the three last quantities can greatly differ by taking either too large or too small values, which is represented by the corresponding linguistic constants L and S.

Suppose that some object is observed and it is established that it has neither attribute a nor b. If it is known also that $w(a'b'c) = L$, there are rather weighty reasons for the logical conclusion that the subject possesses the attribute c. Indeed, there are many subjects in the selection that also have neither a nor b and all of them have c. In other words, the hypothesis following from the observation has many confirmations and no refutation, hence it can be accepted as a regularity. But if $w(a'b'c) = S$, the reasons for accepting this hypothesis seems to be flimsy and unconvincing, because the number of confirming examples is too small in this case. It can be said that the regarded situation itself has a low probability.

Hence, the transformation of the disjunct $a \vee b \vee c$ into the sequent $a'b' \rightarrow c$ seems to be reasonable when $w(a'b'c) = L$ and not reasonable when $w(a'b'c) = S$. Let us say that in the first case c is derived in the disjunct $a \vee b \vee c$ and the sequent $a'b' \rightarrow c$ is valid, and in the second case c is not derived and the sequent $a'b' \rightarrow c$ is not valid.

All that resembles the formalism of association rules [Agrawal, Imielinski, et al., 1993]. However, unlike the latter, arbitrary (not only positive) conjunctive terms k are regarded. Besides, a set of formal transformations is suggested below for deriving new valid sequents from the given ones.

Consider a multiplace disjunct-regularity D, and choose in it a literal x^*, meaning that x^* could be either x or x'. Splitting D represent it as $x^* \vee D_l$. Let K_l be the conjunctive term equal to the inversion of D_l. For instance, if $D_l = a' \vee b$, then $K_l = ab'$.

Affirmation 1. A literal x^* is derived in the disjunct $D = x^* \vee D_l$ if and only if $w(K_l) = L$.

Characterize any disjunct by a list of derived literals marking them by an appropriate underlying in the formula. For example, $a \vee \underline{b} \vee \underline{c}$ is a disjunct that can be transformed into the sequents $a'b' \rightarrow c$ and $a'c' \rightarrow b$, but not into $b'c' \rightarrow a$. A disjunct is called *complete* if all its literals are derived.

According to the well-known resolution rule [Chang and Lee, 1973] it is possible under certain conditions to draw from some two disjuncts a third one that is their logical conclusion. This rule can be fully applied to complete disjuncts, but demands more precise definition in the general case.

Affirmation 2. The disjunct $D_3 = b \vee c$ follows logically from $D_l = a \vee b$ and $D_2 = a' \vee c$. By that the literal c is derived in D_3 if and only if a is derived in D_l, and b is derived in D_3 if and only if a' is derived in D_2.

Proof: It follows from the existence of the disjuncts D_1 and D_2 that $w(a'b') = 0$ and $w(ac') = 0$. If a is derived in D_1, then $w(ab') = L$. This follows from the obvious equality $w(ab') = w(ab'c) + w(ab'c')$ and the above obtained $w(ac') = 0$, that $w(ab'c) = L$ and $w(b'c) = L$, i.e. c is derived in $D_3 = b \vee c$. On the other hand, if c is derived in D_3, then $w(b'c) = L$, and it follows from $w(a'b') = 0$ and $w(b'c) = w(ab'c) + w(a'b'c)$ that $w(ab'c) = L$ and $w(ab') = L$, i.e. a is derived in D_1. The proof of the second part of the theorem, concerning derivability of b in D_3, is quite similar. **End of proof.**

Corollary. The complete disjunct $\underline{b} \vee \underline{c}$ follows from the disjuncts $\underline{a} \vee b$ and $\underline{a}' \vee c$.

More complicated disjuncts can be characterized by lists of derived fragments – individual literals present only at a specific case. For the general case these fragments are represented by the right parts of valid sequents $K_1 \rightarrow D_2$ which could be generated by the corresponding disjuncts $D = D_1 \vee D_2$.

Affirmation 3. The sequent $K_1 \rightarrow D_2$ generated by the disjunct $D_1 \vee D_2$ is valid if and only if $w(K_1) = L$.

For example, $acd' \rightarrow b' \vee e$ generated by $a' \vee b' \vee c' \vee d \vee e$ is valid if and only if there are rather many subjects in F that have attributes a, c and have not d.

Affirmation 4. If the sequent K_1 is valid, then any other sequent obtained from it by transferring (with inversion) some literals from K_1 into D_2 is also valid.

For instance, if the sequent $a'b'c' \rightarrow d \vee e$ is valid, then $a'b' \rightarrow c \vee d \vee e$, $a'c' \rightarrow b \vee d \vee e$, $b' \rightarrow a \vee c \vee d \vee e$, etc. (called derivatives of $a'b'c' \rightarrow d \vee e$) are also valid.

It follows from Affirmation 4 that it is sufficient to mark in the characteristic of a disjunct only the minimum derived parts, because their arbitrary extensions will also be derived. For example, if $a \vee b$, $b \vee c \vee d$ and $c \vee d \vee e \vee f$ are marked in the disjunct $a \vee b \vee c \vee d \vee e \vee f$, then $a \vee b \vee e$, $b \vee c \vee d \vee f$, $a \vee c \vee d \vee e \vee f$, etc. are derived too. In this case only the sequents $c'd'e'f' \rightarrow a \vee b$, $a'e'f' \rightarrow b \vee c \vee d$ and $a'b' \rightarrow c \vee d \vee e \vee f$ as well as their derivatives are valid according to this marking.

Affirmation 5. The set of possible characteristics of a disjunct is isomorphic to the set of all monotonic Boolean functions of the disjunct literals.

Affirmation 6. For any disjuncts $D^* = x \vee D_1$ and $D^{**} = x' \vee D_2$ the disjunct $D = D_1 \vee D_2$ follows from them. By that D_1 is derived in D if and only if x' is derived in D^{**}, and D_2 is derived in D if and only if x is derived in D^*.

This affirmation can be regarded as a generalization of Affirmation 2 and can be proved in a similar way.

So, any system of implicative regularities constructed in accordance with the suggested definitions can be represented by boundary sequents, when it is not allowed to transfer symbols from the right part into the left one. In such a form it can be used in a system of deductive inference, facilitating the fulfillment of its procedures. Then the recognition of any observed subject is carried out by inserting into these sequents the values of some attributes obtained while observing the subject and by appropriate reducing the system.

5.3   Deductive Inference in Finite Predicates

In the case of multi-valued attributes the disjunctive knowledge matrix D turns out to be a sectional Boolean matrix presenting a finite predicate. There are some specifics in dealing with it as described in [Zakrevskij, 1990], [Zakrevskij, 1993].

Let us state the central problem of deductive inference: a disjunctive matrix D and a disjunct d mated with D (that means defined on the same pattern) are given, the problem is to find out whether d is a logical consequence of D. In other words, the question is if the conjunctive term d is derived in CNF D? That is, does it become equal to 1 on all elements of the space M where CNF D takes value 1?

Two ways for solving such problems are known: the direct inference and the back inference.

When the direct inference is executed, the initial set of disjuncts is expanded consecutively by including new disjuncts following from some pairs of disjuncts existing already in the set. This procedure continues until the disjunct d is obtained or the set expansion is exhausted without obtaining d – in the last case it is proved that d does not follow from D.

Any pair of disjuncts u and v can generate several disjuncts-consequents w_i, obtained formally by the operation $w_i = u<x_i>v$ which may be called the resolution in regard with the variable x_i and which can be considered as the generalization of the well-known in the theory of Boolean functions resolution operation onto finite predicates. It is defined as follows: the domain (section) of w_i corresponding to the variable x_i equals the component-wise conjunction of the corresponding domains from u and v (this can be considered as the unification by the variable x_i), and the rest domains equal the component-wise disjunction of the corresponding domains from u and v.

However, not every disjunct obtained in such a way deserves subsequent consideration. There is no sense in including into the regarded set a disjunct which follows from some other disjunct belonging to the set, because it represents only some expansion of the latter one. For example, disjunct 110.0111.00 follows from disjunct 010.0110.00. It is reasonable to look only for non-trivial consequents. Such is a disjunct which follows from some pair of disjuncts u and v but does not follow from u or v taken separately. Let us call it a *resolvent* of disjuncts u and v, and determine the rules for its obtaining.

Disjuncts u and v are called *adjacent* by the variable x_i if and only if the corresponding domains are incomparable (their component-wise disjunction differs from each of these domains) and there exists in each of the remaining domains a component with the value 0 in both vectors. Note that by violating the first condition a disjunct is obtained which follows either from u or from v, whereas by violating the second condition a trivial (identical to 1) disjunct is found, which follows from any other disjunct.

Affirmation 7. If disjuncts u and v are adjacent by the variable x_i and $w = u<x_i>v$, then the disjunct w is a resolvent of the disjuncts u and v.

For example:

$$
\begin{array}{lccc}
 & a & b & c \\
u = & 1\,0\,0\,.1\,0\,.0\,0\,1\,1 \\
v = & 0\,1\,0\,.0\,0\,.0\,1\,1\,0
\end{array}
$$

It is easy to see that these disjuncts are adjacent by a and also by c, but not by b. Hence, they give rise to the following two resolvents

$$
\begin{array}{l}
u<a>v = 0\,0\,0\,.1\,0\,.0\,1\,1\,1 \\
u<c>v = 1\,1\,0\,.1\,0\,.0\,0\,1\,0
\end{array}
$$

The direct inference is simple but time-consuming because the number of obtained consequents could be very large. The back inference is more efficient. It solves the problem by transforming the initial system of disjuncts into such a system which is consistent if and only if d does not follow from D. So, the problem is reduced to the regarded above problem of checking some disjunctive matrix for consistency.

Denoting by $\neg d$ the vector obtained from d by its component-wise negation, and by $D \wedge \neg d$ the matrix obtained from D by the component-wise conjunction of each of its rows with vector $\neg d$, the following rule may be formulated.

Affirmation 8. A disjunct d follows from a disjunctive matrix D if and only if the disjunctive matrix $D \wedge \neg d$ is not consistent.

Checking this condition is rather easy: 1s are expelled from all columns of D which correspond to components of the vector d having value 1, then the obtained disjunctive matrix is checked for consistency. For instance, if

$$D = \begin{bmatrix} 0\ 0\ 1\ .\ 0\ 0\ 1\ 0\ .\ 0\ 0 \\ 1\ 1\ 0\ .\ 0\ 0\ 1\ 1\ .\ 0\ 1 \\ 0\ 1\ 0\ .\ 1\ 1\ 0\ 0\ .\ 1\ 0 \\ 0\ 0\ 1\ .\ 0\ 1\ 0\ 0\ .\ 0\ 1 \end{bmatrix}$$

and

$$d = \quad 0\ 1\ 1\ .\ 1\ 0\ 0\ 0\ .\ 0\ 0$$

then the following disjunctive matrix should be checked for consistency

$$D \wedge \neg d = \begin{bmatrix} 0\ 0\ 0\ .\ 0\ 0\ 1\ 0\ .\ 0\ 0 \\ 1\ 0\ 0\ .\ 0\ 0\ 1\ 1\ .\ 0\ 1 \\ 0\ 0\ 0\ .\ 0\ 1\ 0\ 0\ .\ 1\ 0 \\ 0\ 0\ 0\ .\ 0\ 1\ 0\ 0\ .\ 0\ 1 \end{bmatrix}$$

This matrix is not consistent. Hence, the disjunct d follows from D.

5.4   Pattern Recognition in the Space of Multi-Valued Attributes

Let us describe a typical situation, where the problem of recognition arises, and some ways to solve it [Zakrevskij, 1992], [Zakrevskij, 1994], [Zakrevskij, 2001].

Suppose that an object from the world W is considered and some partial information about it is known, which can be represented by a set S of elementary prohibitions that are simplest information quanta of the type $x_i \neq v_j$: the value of attribute x_i in the object differs from v_j. In particular, this value is determined uniquely if all values except one are prohibited by such quanta. Suppose also that some definite attribute called a goal attribute is indicated, and its value should be found, without immediate measurement. This means that it must be calculated on the basis of the given information about the object and the known regularities inherent in the world W, to which the object belongs. Remember that these regularities are presented in the matrix D.

Let us represent the partial information about the object by a vector-conjunct r, where all elementary prohibitions are mapped as 0s in the corresponding components. This vector can be regarded as the interval of an initial localization of the object in the space M. Taking into account the regularities of the world W, one can make it more precise by reducing the area of the possible location of the object in the space of attributes.

It is easy to see that this area is defined as the intersection of the interval r with the set of solutions of the disjunctive matrix D.

Affirmation 9. Let a vector-conjunct r present an object from the world W the regularities of which are represented by a disjunctive matrix D. Then the area of possible location of the object is equal to the set of solutions of the disjunctive matrix $D^* = D \wedge r$.

The disjunctive matrix D^* is found rather easily by deleting from matrix D all 1s in the columns which correspond to the elementary prohibitions. Getting matrix D^*, we in a sense completely solve the recognition problem, by converting the knowledge about the world as a whole to the knowledge about a definite object. The latter knowledge can be reduced to a more compact form by the reduction rules described above. The values of some attributes, including the goal one, could be determined by that uniquely.

Rather general seems to be the formulation of the recognition problem as the problem of maximal expansion of the set of elementary prohibitions S. This problem can be interpreted as the interval localization of the object under recognition, the essence of which is that the area of its possible location should remain an interval after the reduction. It is convenient to decompose the process of such localization into the search for separate elementary prohibitions $x_i \neq v_j$, following from matrix D^*.

Let us put in correspondence to the elementary prohibition $x_i \neq v_j$ the sectional Boolean vector $s(i, v_j)$, in which all components of the domain i, except those which correspond to the value v_j, have value 1 and all components of the other domains have value 0.

Affirmation 10. The prohibition $x_i \neq v_j$ follows from matrix D^* if and only if the disjunctive matrix $D^* \wedge \neg s(i, v_j)$ is not consistent.

It can happen that matrix D^* is not consistent itself. That would testify the existence of some contradictions between regularities inherent in the set W and a partial information about the object. Otherwise solving the problem of the set S expansion leads to obtaining the minimum interval containing the area of possible location of the observed object, and this solution is always unique.

For example, if it is known that some object possesses value 1 of the attribute c, then by using vector $r = 111.1111.10$ we transform D into D^* and by simplifying the latter we get an equivalent matrix:

$$
\begin{array}{ccc} a & b & c \end{array}
$$

$$
D = \begin{bmatrix} 0\ 0\ 1 & . & 0\ 0\ 1\ 0 & . & 0\ 0 \\ 0\ 0\ 0 & . & 0\ 0\ 1\ 1 & . & 0\ 1 \\ 0\ 1\ 0 & . & 1\ 1\ 0\ 0 & . & 1\ 0 \\ 0\ 0\ 1 & . & 0\ 1\ 0\ 0 & . & 0\ 1 \end{bmatrix}, \quad D* = \begin{bmatrix} 0\ 0\ 0 & . & 0\ 0\ 1\ 1 & . & 0\ 0 \\ 0\ 0\ 0 & . & 0\ 0\ 0\ 0 & . & 1\ 0 \\ 0\ 0\ 1 & . & 0\ 0\ 0\ 0 & . & 0\ 0 \end{bmatrix}.
$$

It follows from here that the initial vector-conjunct r transforms into 001.0011.10, which means that the regarded object is located in the space M to an accuracy of only two elements.

Sometimes expert systems of logical recognition must not only give correct logical conclusions but also provide them with clear explanations of some form. One such form can be a chain of consecutively executed resolutions leading to a sought-for disjunct-consequent. Of course, it can be found via direct inference of the regarded consequent, but in this case the chain as a rule turns out to be too long and inconvenient for visual perception. The problem of looking for minimized chains of logical inference arises in connection with that. A proper method for solving it was suggested in [Zakrevskij and Vasilkova, 1998]. It uses information contained in the search tree constructed when checking for consistency corresponding minors of the knowledge matrix D.

6.   SOME APPLICATIONS

Several expert systems were constructed based on the suggested approach. For example, the system DIES was developed for running diagnostic tests on various engineering objects [Zakrevskij, Pechersky, *et al.*, 1988]. It uses the technique of logical inference in finite predicates.

The instrumental system EDIP was developed, based on the previous results and intended for running diagnostic tests on electric devices used in everyday life, for instance an iron [Zakrevskij, Levchenko, *et al.*, 1991]. It works in the dialogue mode: it first asks for some measurements and then it uses the results (together with knowledge provided by experts and presented by sectional Boolean matrices) to decide what is wrong with the device.

An experimental system for recognition of spoken words was developed in [Zakrevsky and Romanov, 1996]. The data for it are given in digital form and present the distribution of energy in the space "time × frequency" (see also Figure 4).

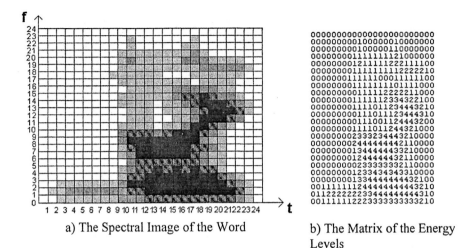

a) The Spectral Image of the Word   b) The Matrix of the Energy Levels

Figure 4.   The Energy Distribution of the Pronunciation of the Russian Word "*nool*" (meaning "*zero*").

The information given by that distribution is reflected preliminary into a space of binary attributes, which present some specially selected geometrical characteristics of the image.   That enables to apply the procedures of inductive and deductive inference described above.

The experimental system EXSYLOR for logical recognition in different areas was constructed [Zakrevskij, 1992].   That system is modeling subject areas in a finite space of multi-valued attributes. It can be tuned to any subject area (*World*) by enumerating names of essential attributes and their values and by forming in such a way a World model.   Information about separate objects composing a representative selection from the World can be introduced into the system and fill a database.   Description of regular connections between attributes represents information about the World as a whole; it is regarded as knowledge and constitutes the contents of a knowledge base.   The knowledge is given in the form of sequents (if..., then...), prohibitions or disjuncts introduced into the system by an expert or deduced from the data.   It is used in deductive procedures of computing values of the goal attributes of the objects under recognition.

The system EXSYLOR analyses data, produces and optimizes knowledge, extrapolates partial information about observed objects, and helps in planning measurements. If asked, it prepares information explaining its decisions.   It is also provided with expert and recognizer interfaces.

The complete cycle of solving the problem of logical recognition by that system includes the following procedures:
- constructing the attribute space (defining all attributes and all their values);

- obtaining a representative selection of data, describing some set of objects from the investigated "World";
- executing inductive inference which enables to find some regularities inherent in the "World", revealing them from that selection;
- fulfilling deductive inference, that is, finding possible values of goal attributes from the revealed regularities and partial description of the regarded object;
- demonstrating the chain of logical inference conducted by the system during computation of a logical conclusion.

7.   CONCLUSIONS

The proposed common logical approach to solving problems of data mining and pattern recognition combines two powerful tools of modern logic: the inductive inference and the deductive inference. The first one is used for extracting knowledge from data. The second is applied when that knowledge is used for calculation of the goal attribute values.

In a simple case the data are given as a set of points in the space M of Boolean attributes. This set is considered as a small part of some larger set defining a subject area. In the suggested method, the knowledge is presented by implicative regularities, as are called equations $k = 0$ with elementary conjunctions k. The search for knowledge is reduced to looking for empty (not containing data points) intervals of M and putting forward corresponding hypotheses which suggest that the revealed intervals do not contain any other elements of the subject area. Such hypotheses can be accepted as implicative regularities if they are plausible enough. There have been proposed some formulas for plausibility evaluation. The accepted regularities are presented by ternary vectors constituting a knowledge matrix.

That form of knowledge representation is convenient for use in the second stage of the problem, when the values of goal attributes should be found from the partial information about the observed object. This task is reduced to solving a system of logical equations.

In the more complicated case of multi-valued attributes finite predicates are used instead of Boolean functions, and sectional Boolean vectors and matrices are suggested for their representation.

The proposed means were used when constructing several expert systems of various purposes where the pattern recognition problem was the central one. The computer experiments testified a high efficiency of the proposed approach.

REFERENCES

R. Agrawal, T. Imielinski and A. Swami. "Mining association rules between sets of items in large databases", *Proceedings of the 1993 ACM SIGMOD Conference*, Washington, DC, May 1993.

M. Bongard. *Pattern recognition*, Spartan Books, New York, 1970.

G. S. Boolos and R. C. Jeffrey. *Computability and logic*, Cambridge University Press, 1989.

C. L. Chang and R. C. T. Lee. *Symbolic logic and mechanical theorem proving*, Academic Press, New York - San Francisco - London, 1973.

S. A. Cook. "The complexity of theorem proving procedures", *Proc. 3rd ACM symposium on the theory of computing*, ACM, pp. 151-158, 1971.

M. Davis, G. Longemann and D. Loveland. "A machine program for theorem proving", *Communications of the ACM*, v. 5, pp. 394-397, 1962.

W. J. Frawley, G. Piatetsky-Shapiro and C. J. Matheus. "Knowledge discovery in databases: an overview", *Knowledge discovery in data bases* (G. Piatetsky-Shapiro and W.J. Frawley, Editors), Cambridge, Mass: AAAI/MIT Press, pp. 1-27, 1991.

R. L. Graham and J. H. Spencer. "Ramsey theory", *Scientific American*, Vol. 263, No. 1, July 1990.

E. B. Hunt. *Artificial intelligence*, Academic Press, New York - San Francisco - London, 1975.

M. Karnaugh. "The map method for synthesis of combinatorial logic circuits", *Transactions AIEE, Communications and Electronics*, v. 72, pp. 593-599, 1953.

W. Klösgen. "Efficient discovery of interesting statements in databases", *The Journal of Intelligent Information Systems*, 4(1), pp. 53-69, 1995.

C. J. Matheus, P. Chan and G. Piatetsky-Shapiro. "Systems for knowledge discovery in databases", *IEEE Transactions on knowledge and data engineering*, Vol. 5, No. 6, pp. 903-913, 1993.

E. J. McCluskey, Jr. "Minimization of Boolean functions", *Bell System Technical Journal*, v. 35, No 6, pp. 1417-1444, 1956.

R. L. Nelson. "Simplest normal truth functions", *Journal of Symbolic Logic*, Vol. 20, No. 2, pp. 105-108, 1955.

N. J. Nilsson. *Problem-solving methods in artificial intelligence*, McGraw-Hill Book Company, New York, 1971.

G. Piatetsky-Shapiro. "Discovery, analysis, and presentation of strong rules", *Knowledge discovery in databases* (G. Piatetsky-Shapiro and W.J. Frawley, Editors), Menlo Park, Calif.: AAA Press, pp. 229-248, 1991.

D. A. Pospelov, ed. *Artificial intelligence. V. 2. Models and methods*, Moscow, Radio i swyaz (in Russian), 1990.

W. V. Quine. "The problem of simplifying of truth functions", *American Mathematical Monthly*, Vol. 59, No. 8, pp. 521-531, 1952.

A. Thayse, P. Gribomont, P. Gochet, E. Grégoire, E. Sanchez and P. Delsarte. *Approche logique de l'intelligence artificielle*, Dunod informatique, Bordas, Paris, 1988.

E. Triantaphyllou. "Inference of a minimum size Boolean function from examples by using a new efficient branch-and bound approach", *Journal of Global Optimization*, Vol. 5, No. 1, pp. 64-94, 1994.

R. Urbano and R. K. Mueller. "A topological method for the determination of the minimal forms of a Boolean function", *IRE Trans., EC-5*, No. 3, pp. 126-132, 1956.

D. Waterman. *A guide to expert systems*, Addison-Wesley Publishing Company, 1986.

A. D. Zakrevskij. "Visual-matrix method of minimization of Boolean functions", *Avtomatika i telemekhanika*, Vol. 21, No. 3, pp. 368-373 (in Russian), 1960.

A. D. Zakrevskij. "Algorithms for minimization of weakly specified Boolean functions", *Kibernetika*, No. 2, p. 53-60 (in Russian), 1965.

A. D. Zakrevskij. "Revealing of implicative regularities in the Boolean space of attributes and pattern recognition", *Kibernetika*, No. 1, pp. 1-6 (in Russian), 1982.

A. D. Zakrevsky "Implicative regularities in formal cognition models", *Abstracts of the 8-th International Congress of Logic, Methodology and Philosophy of Science*, Moscow, Vol. 1, pp. 373-375, 17-22 August 1987.

A. D. Zakrevskij. *Logic of recognition*, Minsk, Nauka i tekhnika (in Russian), 1988.

A. D. Zakrevskij, Yu. N. Pechersky and F. V. Frolov. *DIES - expert system for diagnostics of engineering objects*, Preprint of Inst. Math. AN Mold. SSR, Kishinev (in Russian), 1988.

A. D. Zakrevskij. "Matrix formalism for logical inference in finite predicates", *Philosophical bases of non-classical logics*, Institute of Philosophy AN SSSR, Moscow, pp. 70-80 (in Russian), 1990.

A. D. Zakrevskij, V. I. Levchenko and Yu. N. Pechersky. "Instrumental expert system EDIP, based on finite predicates", *Applied systems of artificial intelligence. Mathematical researches*, issue 123, Inst. Math. AN Mold. SSR, Kishinev, pp. 24-40 (in Russian), 1991.

A. D. Zakrevskij. "EXSYLOR - expert system for logical recognition", *Upravlyayushchie sistemy i mashiny*, No. 5/6, pp. 118-124 (in Russian), 1992.

A. D. Zakrevskij. "Logical recognition by deductive inference based on finite predicates", *Proceedings of the Second Electro-technical and Computer Science Conference ERK'93*, Slovenia Section IEEE, Ljubljana, Vol. B, pp. 197-200, 1993.

A. D. Zakrevskij. "Method of logical recognition in the space of multi-valued attributes", *Proceeding of the Third Electro-technical and Computer Science Conference ERK'94*, Slovenia Section IEEE, Ljubljana, Vol. B, pp. 3-5, 1994.

A. D. Zakrevskij. "Logical recognition in the space of multivalued attributes", *Computer Science Journal of Moldova*, Vol. 2, No. 2, pp. 169-184, 1994.

A. D. Zakrevskij and V. I. Romanov. "Implementation of the logical approach to the recognition of spoken words", *Upravljajushchie sistemy i mashiny*, No. 6, pp. 16-19 (in Russian), 1996.

A. D. Zakrevskij and I. V. Vasilkova. "Inductive inference in systems of logical recognition in case of partial data", *Proceedings of the Fourth International Conference on Pattern Recognition and Information Processing*, Minsk-Szczecin, Vol. 1, pp. 322-326, May 1997.

A. D. Zakrevskij and I. V. Vasilkova. "Minimization of logical inference chains in finite predicates", *Proceedings of the International Conference on Computer Data Analysis and Modeling*, Minsk, Vol. 2, pp. 161-166, 1998.

A. D. Zakrevskij. "Pattern recognition as solving logical equations", *Special Issue 1999 - SSIT'99 (AMSE)*, pp. 125-136, 1999.

A. D. Zakrevskij. "A logical approach to the pattern recognition problem", *Proceedings of the International Conference KDS-2001 "Knowledge - Dialog - Solution"*, Saint Petersburg, Russia, Vol. 1, pp. 238-245, June 2001.

H. Zhang. SATO: "An efficient propositional prover", *Proceedings of the International Conference on Automated Deduction*, pp. 272-275, July 1997.

AUTHOR'S BIOGRAPHICAL STATEMENT

Dr. Arkadij D. Zakrevskij graduated in 1956 from the Tomsk State University (Russia) with the BS degree in Radio-physics and Electronics. In 1960 he earned the Ph.D. degree also from at Tomsk State University. His dissertation title was "A matrix method for synthesis of digital systems". In 1967 earned the Dr.Sc. degree from the Institute of Automatics and Remote Control (Moscow). The title of that dissertation was "Programming language LYaPAS and automation of discrete automata synthesis".

During the years 1956-1971 he was a postgraduate student, Assistant, Associate and Full Professor at Tomsk State University - Siberian Physical-Technical Institute. He also served as the Head of the Chair of mathematical logic and programming. He taught courses on the theory of digital systems, programming, logical foundation of computers, mathematical logic, theory of probabilities, theory of Boolean functions, automata theory, and other related subjects.

Since 1971 he is the Head of the laboratory of logical design and a principal researcher at the Institute of Engineering Cybernetics (now the United Institute of Informatics Problems) of the National Academy of Sciences of Belarus. He is also a Professor at the Belarussian State University and at Belarussian State University of Informatics and Radioelectronics, Minsk, Belarus. He has taught courses on Boolean functions, graph theory, logical design of digital systems, discrete mathematics with application to CAD systems, and on the theory of logical control devices.

His research areas are on the logical theory of digital devices, theory of Boolean functions, programming automation, hard logical-combinatorial problems, logical recognition, solving logical equations, and parallel algorithms for logical control. He has published 11 books (see list below) in the above areas and also over 400 research papers. In 1972 Dr. Zakrevskij was elected a member of the National Academy of Science (NAS) of Belarus.

Chapter 2 [1]

THE ONE CLAUSE AT A TIME (OCAT) APPROACH TO DATA MINING AND KNOWLEDGE DISCOVERY

Evangelos Triantaphyllou[2]
Louisiana State University
Department of Computer Science
298 Coates Hall
Baton Rouge, LA 70803
U.S.A.
Email: trianta@lsu.edu
Web: *http://www.csc.lsu.edu/trianta*

Abstract: This chapter reviews a data mining and knowledge discovery approach called OCAT (for One Clause At a Time). The OCAT approach is based on concepts of mathematical logic and discrete optimization. As input it uses samples of the performance of the system (or phenomenon) under consideration and then it extracts its underlying behavior in terms of a compact and rather accurate set of classification rules. This chapter also provides ways for decomposing large scale data mining problems, and a way of how to generate the next best example to consider for training. The later methods can be combined with any Boolean function learning method and are not restricted to the OCAT approach only.

Key Words: Inductive Inference, Knowledge Discovery, Data Mining, Rule Extraction, Learning from Examples, CNF/DNF, Boolean Functions, Discrete Optimization, Maximum Clique, Connected Components in Graphs, Machine Learning.

---

[1] Triantaphyllou, E. and G. Felici (Eds.), **Data Mining and Knowledge Discovery Approaches Based on Rule Induction Techniques**, Massive Computing Series, Springer, Heidelberg, Germany, pp. 45-87, 2006.

[2] The author is very appreciative for the support by the U.S. Navy, Office of Naval Research (ONR), research grants N00014-95-1-0639 and N00014-97-1-0632.

1.   INTRODUCTION

In many scientific and engineering problems one often needs to study the operation of some system or phenomenon of interest. As input data we consider observations regarding the performance of this system under different situations. Moreover, we assume that these observations belong to disjoint classes. These observations may describe the different states of nature of the system under consideration. That is, each observation is comprised by a set of variables or attributes along with their corresponding values. Often there are only two types of states of nature or classes of observations. The first class may correspond to failures of the system and similarly, the second class may correspond to its successes. Then, a central problem is to utilize the above information (i.e., the observations grouped into different classes) and construct a set of classification rules (also known as decision rules or just rules) which can explain the behavior of the system.

Such situations may arise in many settings. For instance, the system of interest may be some kind of a mechanical device. Then observations are descriptions of the operation of this device. Such descriptions may provide information on the noise level, vibration level, temperature of different parts of the device, fluid levels, revolution speed of certain parts, etc. The different classes may be the properly functioning and malfunctioning states of this device. Then one may be interested in studying data that describe different conditions when the device is functioning properly and also when it is malfunctioning and extract any patterns that might be embedded in these data. Such patterns may be used later to accurately predict the state of this device when one has not determined yet if it is functioning properly or not, but has information on some key performance characteristics as described above.

As another example, one may wish to consider observations that describe certain clinical and non-clinical characteristics associated with studies to determine whether a given patient has a certain medical condition such as breast cancer. Observations may now describe family history facts, the presence or not of lesions in mammographic images, blood analysis results, etc. The two disjoint classes, roughly speaking, may be the benign or malignant nature of any lesions present in a patient's breasts. Usually, such final diagnosis takes place after a specimen from the lesion is analyzed in a lab (i.e., by performing a biopsy). In such cases one may wish to identify any patterns in collections of such observations which may lead to an accurate diagnosis without having to perform an invasive and costly procedure such as a biopsy.

Similar situations, like the ones described above, may arise when one studies other medical conditions, the reliability of mechanical and electronic systems, weather phenomena, characterization of images into different classes (for digital image analysis), prediction of financial events (for example, for investing type of decision-making), prediction of buying behaviors of consumers, and so on.

Until recently such inference problems have been studied by statistical models, such as regression and factor analysis. However, the proliferation of effective and efficient computing power, along with the easy availability of magnetic storage media and new ways for gathering data fast and efficiently, created the need for developing new methods for analyzing large amounts of data. Moreover, data may now be highly heterogeneous and also highly unstructured. The later is the case more and more now with the advent and proliferation of the World Wide Web (WWW).

The above are the main reasons for the emergence of the new computational discipline called *data mining and knowledge discovery from databases (DM&KDD)* [Fayyad, *et al.*, 1996]. This new discipline is based on the use of many computational methods formally known as *artificial intelligence* (AI) classification methods. Currently, such classification methods include standard back-propagation neural networks, nearest neighbor methods, discriminant analysis, cluster analysis, and linear programming based methods. Such techniques attempt to generalize from collections of available classified data. Therefore, they rely on the supposition that the more representative the data are, the more accurate the performance of these methods is.

However, there are some basic weaknesses in using these techniques. For example, according to Johnson [1991] the use of Bayesian models may be controversial, if not unethical (for instance, in medical diagnosis), because the fundamental requirement of strict randomness rarely occurs in reality. Also, standard back-propagation neural networks techniques are problematic because they do not provide an explanation of their decision-making process [Fu, 1993]. In summary, there are two closely related fundamental weaknesses with most of the existing classification methods:

First weakness:
> The way these classification methods work and produce recommendations may not be appealing to domain experts. For instance, the decision-making process inside a standard back-propagation neural network might be awkward to many users with no engineering or computer science background.

Second weakness:
> The available training data are often insufficient to guaranty statistically significant results. This is especially true for data which

describe applications in diagnostic systems. As result these methods may be unreliable for some of the real life applications or their reliability cannot be scientifically guaranteed.

The severity of the first weakness is increasingly recognized lately and some hybrid systems try to combine rule based systems with neural network techniques. Such hybrid systems produce a set of decision rules which in turn can be used for the classification of new instances. Newly developed intelligent hybrid systems, and in particular knowledge based neural networks [Fu, 1993, Galant, 1988; Bradshaw, *et al*, 1989; Hall and Romanyuk, 1990; Towell, *et al.*, 1990; and Sun and Alexandre, 1997], appear to be more promising. Unfortunately, these systems have the potential to create an exponential number of rules [Shavlik, 1994]. Moreover, they may even produce contradictory rules because they are not built in a complete logic-based framework.

The second weakness is usually treated by a brutal force approach. That is, by collecting huge amounts of training data. However, this may be a too time and cost consuming remedy. More importantly, when one considers the number of all possible states of nature, then millions, or even billions, of observations may represent only a tiny fraction of the entire state space. This may cause severe concerns regarding the reliability of the extracted knowledge, especially for medical diagnostic systems (see, for example, [Kovalerchuk, *et al.*, 2000]). For instance, a system described on 50 binary attributes corresponds to $2^{50} = 1.12589 \times 10^{15}$ different states of nature. In that case, even a few billions of observations may be considered as been statistically too few.

This chapter presents some developments for inferring a compact Boolean function from collections of positive and negative examples and also some related subjects. This chapter is organized as follows. The next section describes the main problems to be examined and some related developments from the literature. Section 3 defines the notation to be used throughout this chapter. Section 4 focuses on the problem of inferring a small number of classification rules from two collections of training (positive and negative) examples. These rules are first extracted in the form of a compact Boolean function. Some optimal algorithms and fast heuristics are described. It also describes a data transformation method for converting multi-valued data into binary ones. Section 5 describes a guided learning approach. Section 6 presents the notion of a special graph which can be easily built from the training examples. Section 7 describes how that graph can be used to decompose a large size data mining problem. A detailed illustrative example is presented in Section 8. Section 9 is the last one and describes some conclusions and possible future research topics.

2. SOME BACKGROUND INFORMATION

We assume that some observations are available and they describe the behavior of a system of interest. It is also assumed that the behavior of this system is fully described by a number, say n, of *attributes* (also known as *atoms, parameters, variables, characteristics, predicates,* or just *features*). Thus, each observation is defined by a vector of size n. The i-th (for $i = 1, 2, 3, ..., n$) element of such a vector corresponds to the value of the i-th attribute. These attributes may be of any data type. For instance, they may take continuous, discrete, or binary (i.e., 0/1) values. Each observation belongs to one and only one of K distinct classes. It is assumed that the observations are *noise free*. Furthermore, it is also assumed that the class membership associated with each observation is the correct one.

One may assume that some observations, say m, are already available. New observations (along with their class membership) may become available later but the analyst has no control on their composition. In addition to the previous scenario, the analyst may be able to define the composition of new observations (i.e., to set the values of the n attributes) and then perform a test, or ask an expert or *"oracle"*, to determine the class membership of a new observation. The main goal is to use the available classified observations to extract the underlying behavior of the target system in terms of a pattern. Next, this pattern is used to, hopefully, accurately infer the class membership of unclassified observations.

The extraction of new knowledge in the form of a set of logical decision rules from collections of classified data is a particular type of learning from examples. The related literature is vast and is increasing rapidly and thus it will not be exhaustively discussed. One of the most recent contributions is the book by Truemper [2004] which discusses methods for inferring the logic of a system of interest from sampled observations and then use it towards building intelligent systems. Complexity issues of this type of learning can be found in [Valiant, 1984; and 1985], [Kearns, *et al.*, 1987], and [Pitt and Valiant, 1988].

A considerable amount of related research is today known as the *PAC* (for Probably Approximately Correct) learning theory (see, for instance, [Angluin, 1988] and [Haussler and Warmuth, 1993]). Conjunctive concepts are properly PAC learnable [Valiant, 1984]. However, the class of concepts in the form of the disjunction of two conjunctions is not properly PAC learnable [Pitt and Valiant, 1988]. The same is also true for the class of existential conjunctive concepts on structural instance spaces with two objects [Haussler, 1989]. The classes of k-DNF, k-CNF, and k-decision lists are properly PAC learnable for each fixed k [Valiant, 1985; Rivest, 1987; and Kearns, *et al.*, 1987], but it is unknown whether the classes of all DNF, or CNF functions are

PAC learnable [Haussler and Warmuth, 1993] and [Goldman, 1990]. In [Mansour, 1992] an $n^{O(\log\log n)}$ algorithm is given for learning DNF formulas (however, *not* of minimal size) under a uniform distribution using membership queries.

Another issue is the sample complexity of a learning algorithm. That is, the number of examples needed to accurately approximate a target concept. The presence of bias in the selection of a hypothesis from the hypothesis space can be beneficial in reducing the sample complexity of a learning algorithm. Usually the amount of bias in the hypothesis space H is measured in terms of the *Vapnik-Chernovenkis dimension*, denoted as *VCdim(H)* [Haussler, 1988].

There are many reasons why one may be interested in inferring a Boolean function with the minimum (or near minimum) number of terms. In a circuit design environment, a minimum size Boolean representation is the prerequisite for a successful VLSI application. In a learning from examples environment, one may be interested in deriving a compact set of decision rules which satisfy the requirements of the input examples. This can be motivated for achieving the maximum possible simplicity (Occam's razor) and easy validation of the derived new knowledge.

Since the very early days it was recognized that the problem of inferring a Boolean function with a specified number of clauses is NP-complete (see, for instance, [Brayton, *et al.*, 1985] and [Gimpel, 1965]). Some early related work in this area is due to [Bongard, 1970]. The classical approach to deal with this Boolean function inference problem as a minimization problem (in the sense of minimizing the number of CNF or DNF clauses) was developed in [Quine, 1952 and 1955] and [McCluskey, 1956]. However, the exact versions of the Quine-McCluskey algorithm cannot handle large scale problems. Thus, some heuristic approaches have been proposed. These heuristics include the systems MINI [Hong, *et al.*, 1974], PRESTO [Brown, 1981], and ESPRESSO-MV [Brayton, *et al.*, 1985]. Another widely known approach in dealing with this problem is the use of *Karnaugh maps* [Karnaugh, 1953]. However, this approach cannot be used to solve large scale problems [Pappas, 1994]. Another application of Boolean function minimization can be found in the domain of multicast [Chang, *et al.*, 1999] where one needs a minimum number of keys.

A related method, denoted as SAT (for satisfiability), has been proposed in [Kamath, *et al.*, 1992]. In that approach one first pre-assumes an upper limit on the number of clauses to be considered, say k. Then a clause satisfiability (SAT) model is formed and is solved by using an interior point method developed by Karmakar and his associates [Karmakar, Resende, and Ramakrishnan, 1992]. If the clause satisfiability problem is feasible, then the conclusion is that it is possible to correctly classify all the examples with k or fewer clauses. If this SAT problem is infeasible, then one must increase k until feasibility is reached. In this manner, the SAT approach yields a system with the minimum number of clauses. It is important to observe at this point that from the computational point of view it is much harder to prove that a given SAT problem is infeasible than to prove that it is feasible. Therefore, trying to determine a minimum size Boolean function by using the SAT approach may be computationally too difficult. Some computational results indicate that the branch-and-bound (B&B) approach proposed in [Triantaphyllou, 1994] is significantly more efficient than the previous satisfiability based approach (5,500 times faster on the average for those tests).

In [Felici and Truemper, 2002] the authors propose a different use of the SAT model. They formulate the problem of finding a clause with maximal coverage as a minimum cost satisfiability (MINSAT) problem and solve such problem iteratively by using the logic SAT solver *Leibniz*, which was developed by Truemper [Truemper, 1998]. That method is proved to be computationally feasible and effective in practice. The same authors also propose several variants and extensions to that system, some of which are discussed in Chapter 6 of this book. Further extensions on this learning approach are also discussed in [Truemper, 2004].

A closely related problem is to study the construction of a partially defined Boolean function (or pdBf), not necessarily of minimal size, given disjoint sets of positive and negative examples. That is, now it is required that the attributes of the function be grouped according to a given scheme (called a decomposition structure) [Boros, *et al.*, 1994]. Typically, a pdBf may have exponentially many different extensions.

In summary, the most recent advances in distinguishing between observations in two or more classes can be classified into six distinct categories. These developments are; the clause satisfiability approach to inductive inference by Kamath, *et al.* [1992; and 1994]; some B&B and heuristic approaches of generating a small set of logical decision rules developed in [Triantaphyllou, *et al.*, 1994], and [Triantaphyllou, 1994]; some improved polynomial time and NP-complete cases of Boolean function decomposition by [Boros, *et al.*, 1994]; some MINSAT formulations [Felici and Truemper, 2002]; decision tree based approaches [Quinlan, 1979; and 1986]; linear programming based approaches by [Wolberg and Mangasarian, 1990], [Mangasarian, *et al.*, 1990] and [Mangasarian, *et al.*, 1995]; some approaches which combine symbolic and connectionist machines (neural networks) as proposed by [Sun and Alexandre, 1997], Shavlik [1994], Fu [1993], Goldman and Sloan [1994] and Cohn, *et al.* [1994] and finally, some nearest neighbor classification approaches by Hattori and Torri [1993], Kurita [1991], Kamgar-Parsi and Kanal [1985].

The main challenge in inferring a target set of discriminant decision rules from positive and negative examples is that the user can *never* be absolutely certain about the correctness of the decision rules, unless he/she has processed the entire set of all possible examples which is of size 2^n in the binary case. In the general case this number is far higher. Apparently, even for a small value of n, this task may be practically impossible to realize.

Fortunately, many real life applications are governed by the behavior of a *monotone* system or they can be described by *a combination of a small number of monotone systems.* In data mining and knowledge discovery research monotonicity offers some unique computational advantages. By knowing the value of certain examples, one can easily infer the values of more examples. This, in turn, can significantly expedite the learning process. This chapter discusses the case of inferring general Boolean functions from disjoint collections of training examples. The case of inferring a monotone Boolean function is discussed in Chapter 4 of this book as written by Torvik and Triantaphyllou [2006].

3.   DEFINITIONS AND TERMINOLOGY

Let $\{A_1, A_2, A_3, ..., A_t\}$ be a set of t Boolean *attributes*. Each attribute A_i ($i = 1, 2, 3, ..., t$) can be either true (denoted by 1) or false (denoted by 0). Let F be a *Boolean function* over these attributes. For instance, the expression $(A_1 \vee A_2) \wedge (A_3 \vee \bar{A}_4)$ is such a Boolean function, where "$\vee$" and "$\wedge$" stand for the logical "*OR*" and "*AND*" operators, respectively. That is, F is a mapping from $\{0,1\}^t \rightarrow \{0,1\}$ which determines for each combination of truth values of the attributes $A_1, A_2, A_3, ..., A_t$ of F, whether F is true or false (denoted as 1 or 0, respectively).

For each Boolean function F, the *positive examples* are the vectors $v \in \{0,1\}^t$ such that $F(v) = 1$. Similarly, the *negative examples* are the vectors $v \in \{0,1\}^t$ such that $F(v) = 0$. Therefore, given a function F defined on the t attributes $\{A_1, A_2, A_3, ..., A_t\}$, then a vector $v \in \{0,1\}^t$ is either a positive or a negative example. Equivalently, we say that a vector $v \in \{0,1\}^t$ is *accepted* (or *rejected*) by a Boolean function F if and only if the vector v is a positive (or a negative) example of F. For instance, let F be the Boolean function $(A_1 \vee A_2) \wedge (A_3 \vee \bar{A}_4)$. Consider the two vectors $v_1 = (1,0,0,0)$ and $v_2 = (1,0,0,1)$. Then, it can be easily verified that $F(v_1) = 1$. That is, the vector v_1 is a positive example of the function F. However, the vector v_2 is a negative example of F (since $F(v_2) = 0$).

At this point some additional definitions are also introduced. Let $e \in \{0,1\}^t$ be an example (either positive or negative). Then, $\hat{e} \in \{0,1\}^t$ is defined as the *complement of the example e.* For instance, if $e = (0,1,1,0,0,0)$, then $\hat{e} = (1,0,0,1,1,1)$. Similarly, let E be a collection of examples. Then, $\hat{E}$ is defined as the *complement of the collection E.* A Boolean expression is in CNF or DNF if it is in the form (*i*) or (*ii*), respectively:

$$\bigwedge_{j=1}^{k} (\bigvee_{i \in \rho_j} a_i), \tag{i}$$

$$\text{and} \quad \bigvee_{j=1}^{k} (\bigwedge_{i \in \rho_j} a_i), \tag{ii}$$

where a_i is either A_i or $\bar{A}_i$ and ρ_j is the set of indexes.

In other words, a CNF expression is a conjunction of disjunctions, while a DNF expression is a disjunction of conjunctions.

It is known [Peysakh, 1987] that any Boolean function can be transformed into the CNF or DNF form. The following theorem proved in [Triantaphyllou and Soyster, 1995a] states an important property which exists when CNF and DNF systems are inferred from collections of positive and negative examples.

Theorem 1:
Let E^+ and E^- be the sets of positive and negative examples, respectively. A CNF system given as (i) satisfies the constraints of the E^+ and E^- sets if and only if the DNF system given as (ii) satisfies the constraints of $\hat{E}^-$ (considered as the positive examples) and $\hat{E}^+$ (considered as the negative examples).

This theorem is stated here because the graph theoretic developments throughout this chapter assume that a system is derived in CNF form. However, since a clause inference algorithm which derives DNF expressions (such as, for instance, the SAT approach described in [Kamath, *et al.*, 1992; and 1994]) can also derive CNF expressions (by applying the previous theorem), the methods in this chapter are applicable both to CNF and DNF cases.

In summary, a set of positive examples is denoted as E^+ and a set of negative examples is denoted as E^-. Given these two sets of positive and negative examples, the constraints to be satisfied by a system (i.e., a Boolean function) are as follows. In the CNF case, each positive example should be accepted by all the disjunctions in the CNF expression and each negative example should be rejected by at least one of the disjunctions. In the case of DNF systems, any positive example should be accepted by at least one of the conjunctions in the DNF expression, while each negative example should be rejected by all the conjunctions.

4. THE ONE CLAUSE AT A TIME (OCAT) APPROACH

The main ideas are best described via a simple illustrative example. Suppose that the data in Table 1 represent some sampled observations of the function of a system of interest. Each observation is described by the value of two *continuous* attributes denoted as A_1 and A_2. Furthermore, each observation belongs to one of two classes, denoted as Class 1 and Class 2. A number of problems can be considered at this point. The main problem is how to derive a pattern, in the form of a set of rules, that is consistent with these observations. As set of rules we consider here logical clauses in the CNF (conjunctive normal form) or DNF (disjunctive normal form). That is, we seek the extraction of a Boolean function in CNF or DNF form.

Although, in general, many such Boolean functions can be derived, the focus of the proposed approach is the derivation of a function of *minimum size*. By minimal size we mean a Boolean function which consists of the minimum number of CNF or DNF clauses. We leave it up to the analyst to decide whether he/she wishes to derive CNF or DNF functions. The proposed methodology can handle both cases when Theorem 1, as described in the previous section, is used.

Table 1. Continuous Observations for Illustrative Example.

Example No.	A_1	A_2	Class No.	Example No.	A_1	A_2	Class No.
1	0.25	1.50	1	12	1.00	0.75	1
2	0.75	1.50	1	13	1.50	0.75	1
3	1.00	1.50	1	14	1.75	0.75	2
4	0.50	1.25	1	15	0.50	0.50	1
5	1.25	1.25	2	16	1.25	0.50	2
6	0.75	1.00	1	17	2.25	0.50	2
7	1.25	1.00	1	18	2.75	0.50	2
8	1.50	1.00	2	19	1.25	0.25	2
9	1.75	1.00	1	20	1.75	0.25	2
10	2.25	1.00	2	21	2.25	0.25	2
11	0.25	0.75	1				

4.1 Data Binarization

Next it is demonstrated how the continuous data depicted in Table 1 can be represented by equivalent observations with only binary attributes.

This is achieved as follows. First we start with the first continuous attribute, i.e., attribute A_1 in this case, and we proceed until we cover all the attributes. It can be observed from Table 1 that the *ordered* set, denoted as $Val(A_1)$, with all the values of attribute A_1 is defined as the following ordered list:

$$Val(A_1) = \{V_i(A_1), \text{ for } i = 1, 2, 3, ..., 9\} =$$
$$= \{0.25, 0.50, 0.75, 1.00, 1.25, 1.50, 1.75, 2.25, 2.75\}.$$

Obviously, the cardinality of this set is less than or at most equal to the number of all available observations. In this instance, the cardinality is equal to 9. Next, we introduce 9 binary attributes $A_{1,i}'$ (for $i = 1, 2, 3, ..., 9$) as follows:

$$A_{1,i}' = \begin{cases} 1, & \textit{iff } A_1 \leq V_i(A_1), \textit{ for } i = 1,2,3,...,9, \\ 0, & \textit{otherwise.} \end{cases}$$

In general, the previous formula becomes for any multi-valued attribute A_j:

$$A_{j,i}' = \begin{cases} 1, & \text{iff } A_j \leq V_i(A_j), \text{ for } i = 1,2,3,...,M, \\ 0, & \textit{otherwise.} \end{cases}$$

For instance, by using the above introduced binary attributes, from the second observation (i.e., vector (0.75, 1.50)) we get:

$$\{A_{1,1}', A_{1,2}', A_{1,3}', A_{1,4}', A_{1,5}', A_{1,6}', A_{1,7}', A_{1,8}', A_{1,9}'\} = \{1, 1, 1, 0, 0, 0, 0, 0, 0\}.$$

Similarly, for the second continuous attribute A_2 the set $Val(A_2)$ is defined as follows:

$$Val(A_2) = \{V_i(A_2), \text{ for } i = 1, 2, 3, ..., 6\} =$$
$$= \{0.25, 0.50, 0.75, 1.00, 1.25, 1.50\}.$$

Working as above, for the second observation we have:

$$\{A_{2,1}', A_{2,2}', A_{2,3}', A_{2,4}', A_{2,5}', A_{2,6}'\} = \{1, 1, 1, 1, 1, 1\}.$$

The above transformations are repeated for each one of the non-binary attributes. In this way, the transformed observations are defined on *at most* $m \times n$ binary attributes (where m is the number of observations and n is the original number of attributes). The precise number of the transformed attributes can be easily computed by using the following formula:

$$\sum_{i=1}^{n} |Val(A_i)|,$$

where $|s|$ denotes the cardinality of set s.

The binary attributed observations which correspond to the original data (as presented in Table 1) are presented in Table 2 (parts (a) and (b)).

Table 2 (a).   The Binary Representation of the Observations in the Illustrative
Example (first set of attributes for each example).

Example No.	First set of attributes: $A_{1,i}'$, for $i = 1, 2, 3, ..., 9$.								
	$A_{1,1}'$	$A_{1,2}'$	$A_{1,3}'$	$A_{1,4}'$	$A_{1,5}'$	$A_{1,6}'$	$A_{1,7}'$	$A_{1,8}'$	$A_{1,9}'$
1	1	0	0	0	0	0	0	0	0
2	1	1	1	0	0	0	0	0	0
3	1	1	1	1	0	0	0	0	0
4	1	1	0	0	0	0	0	0	0
5	1	1	1	1	1	0	0	0	0
6	1	1	1	0	0	0	0	0	0
7	1	1	1	1	1	0	0	0	0
8	1	1	1	1	1	1	0	0	0
9	1	1	1	1	1	1	1	0	0
10	1	1	1	1	1	1	1	1	0
11	1	0	0	0	0	0	0	0	0
12	1	1	1	1	0	0	0	0	0
13	1	1	1	1	1	1	0	0	0
14	1	1	1	1	1	1	1	0	0
15	1	1	0	0	0	0	0	0	0
16	1	1	1	1	1	0	0	0	0
17	1	1	1	1	1	1	1	1	0
18	1	1	1	1	1	1	1	1	1
19	1	1	1	1	1	0	0	0	0
20	1	1	1	1	1	1	1	0	0
21	1	1	1	1	1	1	1	1	0

Table 2 (b). The Binary Representation of the Observations in the Illustrative
Example (second set of attributes for each example).

Example No.	Second set of attributes: $A_{2,i}'$, for $i = 1, 2, 3, ..., 6$.						Class No.
	$A_{2,1}'$	$A_{2,2}'$	$A_{2,3}'$	$A_{2,4}'$	$A_{2,5}'$	$A_{2,6}'$	
1	1	1	1	1	1	1	1
2	1	1	1	1	1	1	1
3	1	1	1	1	1	1	1
4	1	1	1	1	1	0	1
5	1	1	1	1	1	0	2
6	1	1	1	1	0	0	1
7	1	1	1	1	0	0	1
8	1	1	1	1	0	0	2
9	1	1	1	1	0	0	1
10	1	1	1	1	0	0	2
11	1	1	1	0	0	0	1
12	1	1	1	0	0	0	1
13	1	1	1	0	0	0	1
14	1	1	1	0	0	0	2
15	1	1	0	0	0	0	1
16	1	1	0	0	0	0	2
17	1	1	0	0	0	0	2
18	1	1	0	0	0	0	2
19	1	0	0	0	0	0	2
20	1	0	0	0	0	0	2
21	1	0	0	0	0	0	2

From the way the binary attributes have been defined, it follows that
the two sets of observations are equivalent to each other. However, the
observations in Table 1 are defined in continuous attributes while the
observations in Table 2 are defined in binary ones.

Given the above considerations, it follows that the original problem
has been transformed into the binary problem depicted in Table 2 (parts (a)
and (b)). This problem has the following two sets of positive and negative
examples, denoted as E^+ and E^-, respectively.

$$
E^+ = \begin{bmatrix}
1 & 0 & 0 & 0 & 0 & 0 & 0 & 0 & 0 & 1 & 1 & 1 & 1 & 1 & 1 \\
1 & 1 & 1 & 0 & 0 & 0 & 0 & 0 & 0 & 1 & 1 & 1 & 1 & 1 & 1 \\
1 & 1 & 1 & 1 & 0 & 0 & 0 & 0 & 0 & 1 & 1 & 1 & 1 & 1 & 1 \\
1 & 1 & 0 & 0 & 0 & 0 & 0 & 0 & 0 & 1 & 1 & 1 & 1 & 1 & 0 \\
1 & 1 & 1 & 0 & 0 & 0 & 0 & 0 & 0 & 1 & 1 & 1 & 1 & 0 & 0 \\
1 & 1 & 1 & 1 & 1 & 0 & 0 & 0 & 0 & 1 & 1 & 1 & 1 & 0 & 0 \\
1 & 1 & 1 & 1 & 1 & 1 & 1 & 0 & 0 & 1 & 1 & 1 & 1 & 0 & 0 \\
1 & 0 & 0 & 0 & 0 & 0 & 0 & 0 & 0 & 1 & 1 & 1 & 0 & 0 & 0 \\
1 & 1 & 1 & 1 & 0 & 0 & 0 & 0 & 0 & 1 & 1 & 1 & 0 & 0 & 0 \\
1 & 1 & 1 & 1 & 1 & 1 & 0 & 0 & 0 & 1 & 1 & 1 & 0 & 0 & 0 \\
1 & 1 & 0 & 0 & 0 & 0 & 0 & 0 & 0 & 1 & 1 & 0 & 0 & 0 & 0
\end{bmatrix}, \text{ and}
$$

$$
E^- = \begin{bmatrix}
1 & 1 & 1 & 1 & 1 & 0 & 0 & 0 & 0 & 1 & 1 & 1 & 1 & 1 & 0 \\
1 & 1 & 1 & 1 & 1 & 1 & 0 & 0 & 0 & 1 & 1 & 1 & 1 & 0 & 0 \\
1 & 1 & 1 & 1 & 1 & 1 & 1 & 1 & 0 & 1 & 1 & 1 & 1 & 0 & 0 \\
1 & 1 & 1 & 1 & 1 & 1 & 1 & 0 & 0 & 1 & 1 & 1 & 0 & 0 & 0 \\
1 & 1 & 1 & 1 & 1 & 0 & 0 & 0 & 0 & 1 & 1 & 0 & 0 & 0 & 0 \\
1 & 1 & 1 & 1 & 1 & 1 & 1 & 1 & 0 & 1 & 1 & 0 & 0 & 0 & 0 \\
1 & 1 & 1 & 1 & 1 & 1 & 1 & 1 & 1 & 1 & 1 & 0 & 0 & 0 & 0 \\
1 & 1 & 1 & 1 & 1 & 0 & 0 & 0 & 0 & 1 & 0 & 0 & 0 & 0 & 0 \\
1 & 1 & 1 & 1 & 1 & 1 & 1 & 0 & 0 & 1 & 0 & 0 & 0 & 0 & 0 \\
1 & 1 & 1 & 1 & 1 & 1 & 1 & 0 & 1 & 0 & 0 & 0 & 0 & 0 & 0
\end{bmatrix}.
$$

Finally, it should be stated here that Chapter 7 of this book [Bartnikowski, *et al.*, 2006] presents a detailed study of the binarization problem.

4.2   The One Clause At a Time (OCAT) Concept

As it was mentioned in the previous section, the problem of deriving a Boolean function from sets of observations has been extensively studied in the literature. In our setting each example was a binary vector of size n (number of binary attributes). The proposed method employs an approach which constructs one clause at a time, called the OCAT (for One Clause At a Time) approach. That approach is greedy in nature in the sense that the first clause (in the CNF case) accepts all the positive examples while it rejects as many negative examples as possible. The second clause also accepts all positive examples, but rejects as many negative examples from the ones not rejected so far. Consecutive clauses are generated in a similar manner until all the derived clauses reject the entire set of negative examples. The operation of the OCAT approach is best described in Figure 1. In this figure E^+ represents the set with the positive examples while E^- is the set with the negative ones.

The core of the OCAT approach is step 2, in Figure 1. In Triantaphyllou, *et al.* [1994] a branch-and-bound (B&B) based algorithm is presented which solves the problem posed in step 2. A more efficient B&B algorithm, along with other enhancements, are described in Triantaphyllou [1994]. The OCAT approach returns the set of desired clauses (i.e., the CNF system) as set C.

$i = 0$; $C = \emptyset$; {initializations}
DO WHILE ($E^- \neq \emptyset$)
       Step 1: $i \leftarrow i + 1$;
       Step 2: Find a clause c_i which accepts all members of E^+
                while it rejects as many members of E^- as possible ;
       Step 3: Let $E^-(c_i)$ be the set of members of E^- which are
                rejected by c_i ;
       Step 4: Let $C \leftarrow C \wedge c_i$;
       Step 5: Let $E^- \leftarrow E^- - E^-(c_i)$;
REPEAT;

Figure 1. The One Clause At a Time (OCAT) Approach (for the CNF case).

4.3   A Branch-and-Bound Approach for Inferring Clauses

This B&B algorithm is best described in [Triantaphyllou, 1994]. The basic steps are described next in terms of an illustrative example. Consider the following two sets of positive and negative examples:

$$E^+ = \begin{bmatrix} 0 & 1 & 0 & 0 \\ 1 & 1 & 0 & 0 \\ 0 & 0 & 1 & 1 \\ 1 & 0 & 0 & 1 \end{bmatrix} \text{ and } E^- = \begin{bmatrix} 1 & 0 & 1 & 0 \\ 0 & 0 & 0 & 1 \\ 1 & 1 & 1 & 1 \\ 0 & 0 & 0 & 0 \\ 1 & 0 & 0 & 0 \\ 1 & 1 & 1 & 0 \end{bmatrix}$$

These examples are defined on four attributes (and their negations). Recall that for the CNF case, the requirement is that the clause to accept all the positive examples, while rejecting as many negative examples as possible. Next, define as $POS(A_i)$ the set of the positive examples which are accepted by a CNF clause when the attribute A_i is included in that clause. For instance, for the previous examples, one has (please note that for simplicity only the indexes of these examples are used): $POS(A_2) = \{1,2\}$, $POS(\bar{A}_3) = \{1,2,4\}$, etc. That B&B algorithm also uses the concept of the $NEG(A_i)$ set which is defined in a similar manner.

The *search states* are described in terms of *two sets*. The first set refers to the *positive examples* which are accepted by the attributes which correspond to the arcs which connect that state (node) with the root node. Similarly, the second set refers to the *negative examples* which are accepted by the attributes which correspond to the arcs which connect that state with the root node. Suppose that we are at state $S_i = [P_i, N_i]$ (where P_i, N_i correspond to the previous two sets of positive and negative examples, respectively). Now assume that the search considers the state (node) which is derived by following the arch which corresponds to attribute A_k. Then, the new state is: $S_j = [P_j, N_j]$, where the new sets P_j and N_j are defined as follows:

$$P_j = P_i \cup POS(A_k), \text{ and}$$
$$N_j = N_i \cup NEG(A_k).$$

Therefore, the search continues until terminal states are reached. A state $S_i = [P_i, N_i]$ is a *terminal state* if and only if: $P_i = E^+$ (i.e., it refers to *all positive* examples). Apparently, a terminal state with a *minimum cardinality* of the set N_i is *optimal* (in the OCAT sense). In the light of the previous considerations, the problem (for the CNF case) to be solved by the B&B search can be summarized as follows (where a_i is either A_i or $\bar{A}_i$):

Find a set of attributes S such that the following two conditions are true:
$$\left| \bigcup_{a_i \in S} NEG(a_i) \right| = minimum,$$

and
$$\left| \bigcup_{a_i \in S} POS(a_i) \right| = E^+.$$

The attributes in the S set are the ones that correspond to the attributes of the CNF clause to be constructed. Given the above definitions some useful derivations are possible. We say that a state S_i *absorbs* another state S_j if by expanding the state S_j, we cannot reach any better terminal state than the ones derived by expanding the state S_i. In such a case we call that the state S_j is an *absorbed state*. From the previous considerations it becomes obvious that once a state can be identified to be an absorbed state, then it can be dropped from further consideration. Then the following two theorems [Triantaphyllou, 1994] are applicable (only) when a CNF clause is to be generated and they provide some conditions for identifying absorbed states.

Theorem 2:
The state $S_i = [P_i, N_i]$ absorbs the state $S_j = [P_j, N_j]$ if the following condition is true: $P_j \subseteq P_i$ and $N_i \subseteq N_j$.

Theorem 3:
Suppose that $S_i = [P_i, N_i]$ is a terminal state. Then, any state $S_j = [P_j, N_j]$, such that $|N_j| \geq |N_i|$, is absorbed by the state S_i.

From the previous considerations it follows that there is a great advantage to reach terminal nodes early in the search process. In this way, the minimum size of their N_i sets can be used to effectively fathom search states. For these reasons that B&B search can be applied in *two phases*. During the first phase only a very small number (say, 10) of active states is maintained. If there are more than 10 active states, then they are ranked according to their P_i and N_i sizes. In this way, the states with the highest potential of being optimal are kept into memory. This is the principle of *beam search* in artificial intelligence (see, for instance, [Dietterich and Michalski, 1983]). At the end of phase one, a terminal state of small cardinality becomes available. Next, phase two is initiated. During the second phase a larger number (say, 50) of active states is allowed. However, states now can be fathomed more frequently because the size of a small N_i set of a terminal state is known.

An important issue with the previous two phases is to be able to decide when a terminal state is optimal (in the OCAT sense). As it was mentioned above, memory limitations may force the search to drop states which are not absorbed by any other state. Therefore, *there is a possibility to drop a state which could had lead to an optimal state (and thus to determine an optimal clause)*.

Suppose that L non-absorbed states had to be dropped because of memory limitations. Let $K_1, K_2, K_3, ..., K_L$ represent the cardinalities of their corresponding N_i sets. Next, define the quantity K_{MIN} as the minimum of the previous L numbers. Similarly, suppose that the B&B process has identified N terminal states. Let $Y_1, Y_2, Y_3, ..., Y_N$ represent the cardinalities of their corresponding N_i sets. Define as Y_{MIN} the minimum of the previous N cardinalities. Then, the previous considerations lead to the proof of the following theorem [Triantaphyllou, 1994] which states a condition for establishing optimality.

Theorem 4:
A terminal state $S_i = [P_i, N_i]$ *is also an **optimal state** if the following two conditions are true:*
$$|N_i| = Y_{MIN}, \quad and \quad K_{MIN} \geq Y_{MIN}.$$

Note that this theorem can be applied after each one of the two phases. Obviously, if it is applicable after the first phase, then the second phase does not need to be initiated. The following lemma states a condition when optimality is not provable.

Lemma 1:
If $K_{MIN} < Y_{MIN}$, *then an optimal clause accepts no less than* K_{MIN} *negative examples.*

This lemma indicates that if optimality cannot be proven, then it is still possible to establish a *lower limit* on the number of negative examples which can be accepted by an optimal clause (or, equivalently, an upper limit on the number of negative examples which can be *rejected* by an optimal clause).

4.4   Inference of the Clauses for the Illustrative Example

When the OCAT algorithm, with the B&B approach described in [Triantaphyllou, 1994] is used in step 2, two Boolean functions can be derived. The first function is derived when the examples in set E^+ are used as the positive examples while the examples in set E^- are used as the negative examples. We call the set of these clauses the *positive rules* (because the positive examples evaluate these clauses as true).

The Boolean function derived from the previous E^+ and E^- examples has the following form (note that the attribute names have been slightly altered to reflect the adjusted notation):

$$(\bar{A}_{1,8}' \wedge A_{2,2}' \wedge \bar{A}_{1,5}') \vee (A_{2,3}' \wedge \bar{A}_{1,8}' \wedge \bar{A}_{2,5}' \wedge \bar{A}_{1,6}') \vee$$
$$(A_{2,3}' \wedge A_{1,6}' \wedge \bar{A}_{1,8}' \wedge A_{1,7}' \wedge A_{2,4}') \vee (\bar{A}_{1,7}' \wedge A_{1,6}' \wedge \bar{A}_{2,4}').$$

Similarly, the second function is derived when the examples in set E^- are used as the positive examples while the examples in E^+ are used as the negative examples. Thus, we call these clauses the *negative rules*. The Boolean function derived from the previous E^- and E^+ examples is:

$$(A_{1,5}' \wedge \bar{A}_{2,3}') \vee (A_{1,5}' \wedge A_{1,6}' \wedge A_{1,7}' \wedge A_{1,8}') \vee$$
$$(A_{1,5}' \wedge A_{2,5}') \vee (A_{1,6}' \wedge A_{1,7}' \wedge \bar{A}_{2,4}') \vee (A_{1,6}' \wedge \bar{A}_{1,7}' \wedge A_{2,4}').$$

When the definitions of the Boolean attributes $A_{1,i}'$ (for $i = 1, 2, 3, ..., 9$) and $A_{2,j}'$ (for $j = 1, 2, 3, ..., 6$) are used, then it is easy to verify that the previous two functions yield the following two sets of rules defined on the two original continuous attributes A_1 and A_2:

(i) **Positive Classification Rules:**

$(A_1 \leq 1.00$ and	$A_2 \geq 0.5)$	(Rule $R^+{}_1$)
$(A_1 \leq 1.25$ and $1.00 \geq A_2 \geq 0.75)$		(Rule $R^+{}_2$)
$(A_1 = 1.75$ and	$A_2 \geq 1.00)$	(Rule $R^+{}_3$)
$(A_1 = 1.50$ and $0.75 \geq A_2$	$)$	(Rule $R^+{}_4$)

(ii) **Negative Classification Rules:**

$(A_1 \geq 1.25$ and $0.50 \geq A_2$	$)$	(Rule $R^-{}_1$)
$(A_1 \geq 2.25$ $)$		(Rule $R^-{}_2$)
$(A_1 \geq 1.25$ and	$A_2 \geq 1.25)$	(Rule $R^-{}_3$)
$(A_1 \geq 1.75$ and $0.75 \geq A_2$	$)$	(Rule $R^-{}_4$)
$(A_1 = 1.50$ and	$A_2 \geq 1.00)$	(Rule $R^-{}_5$)

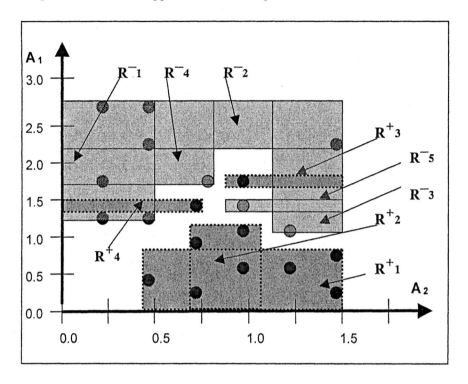

Figure 2. Continuous Data for Illustrative Example and Extracted Sets of
Classification Rules.

When dealing with DNF clauses (as is the previous case), decision rules can be derived by observing that for an example to be positive, it must satisfy at least one clause. Thus, for the first of the previous clauses (i.e., for clause $(\bar{A}_{1,8}' \wedge A_{2,2}' \wedge \bar{A}_{1,5}')$ and by noting that: $\bar{A}_8' \leftarrow \bar{A}_{1,8}'$, $A_{11} \leftarrow A_{2,2}'$, and $\bar{A}_5' \leftarrow \bar{A}_{1,5}'$) the corresponding decision rule is:

> **IF** $(\bar{A}_8$ and A_{11} and $\bar{A}_5$ are all true),
> **THEN** (this example is a positive one).

For the CNF case, a conjunction can be transformed into an equivalent logical decision rule by observing that the following two expressions are equivalent:
$$(A_1 \vee A_2) \text{ is equivalent to: } (\bar{A}_1 \rightarrow A_2).$$

From the above discussion it follows that any CNF or DNF expression with k clauses (conjunctions or disjunctions) can be described in terms of the same number k of decision rules. In the CNF case the attribute(s) which compose the "**IF**" parts of these rules are not uniquely determined. Therefore, it is the task of the field expert to decide which attributes are allowed to be present in the "**IF**" part of a rule (or *antecedent* part) or in the "**THEN**" part of a rule (or *consequent* part). It can be easily shown that given two classes of observations, then one can derive as many CNF conjunctions as the number of negative examples [Triantaphyllou, Soyster, and Kumara, 1994; or Triantaphyllou, 1994] (similar results hold for the DNF case). Therefore, for cases in which the negative examples are numerous one may be interested in determining a minimal (or at least very small) number of such logical decision rules. This is an issue of significant practical importance, since compact sets of decision rules are easier to validate and use.

The previous two sets of rules, along with the positive and negative examples (as defined in terms of the two continuous attributes A_1 and A_2) are depicted in Figure 2. The same figure also indicates some of the reasons why the proposed approach, at least for the binary case, delivered more accurate results when it was compared in [Deshpande and Triantaphyllou, 1998] with some other approaches (neural networks and separating planes via the LP approach developed by Mangasarian and his associates [Mangasarian, *et al.*, 1991]). When both sets of decision rules are used, then for a new observation to be classified as positive, it must be both accepted by the positive rules and also rejected by the negative rules (analogously for an observation to be classified as negative).

However, many existing classification techniques consider only one set of rules. Therefore, in the proposed approach there are three different classification decisions: *"Positive," "Negative,"* and *"Undecided."* Many traditional approaches do not consider the third type (i.e., *"Undecided"*). By forcing the derived sets of decision rules to be as compact as possible, the proposed approach has a tendency to isolate and *"close-in"* observations into compact groups defined in the same class. Many methods simply try to determine separating planes (borders) of some sort which are in the middle of some type of distance. Usually, such a distance reflects how apart the two classes of observations are. In this chapter the population space is actually partitioned into four types of areas: *"positive areas," "negative areas," "areas of conflict"* between the two sets of rules, and *"areas not covered"* by any rules. In Figure 2 the case *"areas of conflict"* between the two sets of rules does not occur (by coincidence).

To offset the drawback of the exponential time complexity of the B&B algorithm in step 2 of the OCAT approach, in [Deshpande and Triantaphyllou, 1998] a heuristic of polynomial time complexity is proposed. Under that heuristic the clause which is formed during a single iteration rejects *many* (as opposed to *as many as possible*) negative examples. This heuristic seems to offer an alternative approach when the problem size is very large. It can also be combined with the previous B&B approach and is also randomized as a GRASP (Greedy Random Adaptive Search Procedure [Feo and Resende, 1995]) approach.

4.5 A Polynomial Time Heuristic for Inferring Clauses

To offset the drawback of the exponential time complexity of the B&B algorithm in step 2 of the OCAT approach, in this heuristic clauses are formed in a manner such that each clause accepts all the examples in the E^+ set while it attempts to reject *many* (as opposed to *as many as possible* in the B&B approach) examples in the E^- set. Note that this is the main procedural difference between the B&B algorithm and the proposed heuristics. In the proposed heuristic this is achieved by choosing the attributes to form a clause based on an evaluative function (to be described later). Only attributes with high values in terms of the evaluative function are included in the current clause. A single clause is completely derived when all the examples in the E^+ set are accepted. The clause forming procedure is repeated until all the examples in the E^- set are rejected by the proposed set of clauses. As some computational results in [Deshpande and Triantaphyllou, 1998] indicate, this strategy may often result in Boolean functions with a small number of clauses.

Observe that if always the attribute with the *highest value* of the evaluative function is included in the clause, then there is an inherent danger of being trapped in a local optimal point. To prevent this undesirable behavior, a *randomized* approach is used. In this randomized approach, instead of a single attribute being included in a clause due to its highest value of the evaluative function, a candidate list is formed of attributes whose values in terms of the evaluative function are close to the highest value as derived from the evaluative function. Next, an attribute is *randomly* chosen out of the candidate list and is included in the CNF clause being derived.

Please note that it is possible for a CNF clause to reject as many negative examples as possible (and, of course, to accept all positive examples) but the entire system not to have a small (ideally minimum) number of clauses. Recall that the proposed heuristics follow the OCAT approach (see also Figure 1). That is, sometimes it may be more beneficial to have a less *"effective"* clause which does not reject a large number of negative examples, and still derive a system with very few clauses. Such systems are possible to derive with the use of randomized algorithms. A randomized algorithm, with a sufficiently large number of random replications, is more difficult to be trapped by a local optimal point.

A heuristic approach, termed **RA1** (for *Randomized Algorithm 1*), was proposed in [Deshpande and Triantaphyllou, 1998] to solve the first research problem considered in this chapter. Before the RA1 heuristic is formally presented, some new definitions and terminology are summarized next.

Definitions:

$C =$ The set of attributes in the current clause (disjunction).

$A_k =$ An attribute such that $A_k \in A$, where A is the set of all attributes $A_1, ..., A_n$.

$POS(A_k) =$ The number of all positive examples in E^+ which would be accepted if attribute A_k is included in the current clause.

$NEG(A_k) =$ The number of all negative examples in E^- which would be accepted if attribute A_k is included in the current clause. Please note that the last two definitions are slightly different from the previous definitions of POS and NEG as sets of examples. Now we are interested in the sizes of these sets only.

$l =$ The size of the candidate list.

$ITRS =$ The number of times the clause forming procedure is repeated.

As an illustrative example of the above definitions, consider the following sets of positive and negative examples (which were also given in Section 3.3).

$$E^+ = \begin{bmatrix} 0 & 1 & 0 & 0 \\ 1 & 1 & 0 & 0 \\ 0 & 0 & 1 & 1 \\ 1 & 0 & 0 & 1 \end{bmatrix} \quad \text{and } E^- = \begin{bmatrix} 1 & 0 & 1 & 0 \\ 0 & 0 & 0 & 1 \\ 1 & 1 & 1 & 1 \\ 0 & 0 & 0 & 0 \\ 1 & 0 & 0 & 0 \\ 1 & 1 & 1 & 0 \end{bmatrix}$$

The set A of all attributes for the above set of examples is:

$$A = \{A_1, A_2, A_3, A_4, \bar{A}_1, \bar{A}_2, \bar{A}_3, \bar{A}_4\}.$$

Therefore, the $POS(A_k)$ and the $NEG(A_k)$ values are:

$POS(A_1) = 2$	$NEG(A_1) = 4$	$POS(\bar{A}_1) = 2$	$NEG(\bar{A}_1) = 2$
$POS(A_2) = 2$	$NEG(A_2) = 2$	$POS(\bar{A}_2) = 2$	$NEG(\bar{A}_2) = 4$
$POS(A_3) = 1$	$NEG(A_3) = 3$	$POS(\bar{A}_3) = 3$	$NEG(\bar{A}_3) = 3$
$POS(A_4) = 2$	$NEG(A_4) = 2$	$POS(\bar{A}_4) = 2$	$NEG(\bar{A}_4) = 4$

DO for *ITRS* number of iterations
BEGIN;
    DO WHILE $(E^- \neq \emptyset)$
      $C = \emptyset;$ *{initialization}*
        DO WHILE $(E^+ \neq \emptyset)$

Step 1:	Rank in descending order all attributes $a_i \in a$ *(where a_i is either A_i or $\bar{A}_i$)* according to their $POS(a_i)/NEG(a_i)$ value. If $NEG(a_i) = 0$, then $POS(a_i)/NEG(a_i) = 1{,}000$ (i.e., an arbitrarily high value);
Step 2:	Form a candidate list of the attributes which have the l top highest $POS(a_i)/NEG(a_i)$ values;
Step 3:	Randomly choose an attribute a_k from the candidate list;
Step 4:	Let the set of attributes in the current clause be $C \leftarrow C \vee a_k$;
Step 5:	Let $E^+(a_k)$ be the set of members of E^+ accepted when a_k is included in the current CNF clause;
Step 6:	Let $E+ \leftarrow E^+ - E^+(a_k)$;
Step 7:	Let $a \leftarrow a - a_k$;
Step 8:	Calculate the new $POS(a_i)$ values for all $a_i \in a$;

        REPEAT

Step 9:	Let $E^-(C)$ be the set of members of E^- which are rejected by C;
Step 10:	Let $E^- \leftarrow E^- - E^-(C)$;
Step 11:	Reset E^+;

      REPEAT
  END;

CHOOSE the final Boolean system among the previous *ITRS* systems which has the smallest number of clauses.

Figure 3. The RA1 Heuristic [Deshpande and Triantaphyllou, 1998].

The problem now is to derive a small set of logical clauses which would correctly classify all the above examples. Suppose that there exists a *"hidden"* system given by the following Boolean function:

$$(A_2 \vee A_4) \wedge (\bar{A}_2 \vee \bar{A}_3) \wedge (A_1 \vee A_3 \vee \bar{A}_4).$$

It can be easily seen that the above Boolean function correctly classifies all the previous examples. Therefore, the first problem is to accurately estimate the above *"hidden"* system. This is accomplished by using heuristic RA1, as described in Figure 3.

The following theorem [Deshpande and Triantaphyllou, 1998] states an upper bound on the number of clauses which can be inferred by RA1 (where m_2 is the number of negative examples).

Theorem 5:
The RA1 approach terminates within at most m_2 iterations.

Next, let n be the number of attributes in the data set, m_1 be the number of examples in the E^+ set and m_2 be the number of examples in the E^- set. Then Theorem 6 [Deshpande and Triantaphyllou, 1998] states the time complexity of the RA1 algorithm.

Theorem 6:
The RA1 algorithm has a polynomial time complexity of order
$O(n(m_1+m_2)m_1\ m_2\ ITRS).$

From the way the $POS(A_k)$ and $NEG(A_k)$ values were defined, some critical observations can be made. When an attribute with a rather high value of the POS function is included in the CNF clause being formed, then chances are that some additional positive examples will be accepted by that clause as result of the inclusion of that attribute. Similarly, attributes which correspond to low NEG values, are likely not to cause many new negative examples to be accepted as result of the inclusion of that attribute in the current clause. Therefore, it makes sense to include as attributes in the CNF clause under formation, the ones which correspond to high POS values and, at the same time, to low NEG values.

In this chapter the notations $POS(a_i)/NEG(a_i)$ and $POS(A_k)/NEG(A_k)$ will be used interchangeably to denote the same concept. For the current illustrative example, the values of the $POS(A_k)/NEG(A_k)$ ratios are:

$$POS(A_1)/NEG(A_1) = 0.5 \qquad POS(\bar{A}_1)/NEG(\bar{A}_1) = 1.0$$
$$POS(A_2)/NEG(A_2) = 1.0 \qquad POS(\bar{A}_2)/NEG(\bar{A}_2) = 0.5$$
$$POS(A_3)/NEG(A_3) = 0.33 \qquad POS(\bar{A}_3)/NEG(\bar{A}_3) = 1.0$$
$$POS(A_4)/NEG(A_4) = 1.0 \qquad POS(\bar{A}_4)/NEG(\bar{A}_4) = 0.5$$

The above discussion illustrates the motivation for considering as possible candidates for the evaluative function, the functions: *POS/NEG*, *POS-NEG*, or some type of a weighted version of the previous two expressions. Some exploratory computational experiments indicated that the evaluative function *POS/NEG* was the most effective one. That is, it led to the formation of Boolean functions with less clauses than when the other evaluative functions were considered.

The randomization of the RA1 algorithm is done as follows. In step 2, the first *l* attributes with the highest value of the $POS(A_k) / NEG(A_k)$ ratio are chosen as the members of the candidate list and an attribute in the list was randomly chosen out of the candidate list in step 3. This is done in order to obtain different solutions at each iteration and prevent the system from being trapped by a locally optimal point.

In choosing a fixed value for the size *l* of the candidate list, there is a possibility that an attribute with a very low value of $POS(A_k) / NEG(A_k)$ ratio could be selected if the value of *l* is large enough (how large depends on the current data). That could occur if there are not *l* attributes with a sufficiently high value of the $POS(A_k) / NEG(A_k)$ ratio. If an attribute with a low value of $POS(A_k) / NEG(A_k)$ is chosen to be included in the clause, then the clause would accept less examples from the E^+ set or accept more examples from the E^- set, or both. All these three situations should be avoided as it would lead to an increase in the number of attributes in a clause (if it accepts less examples from the E^+ set) or, to an increase in the number of clauses (if the attribute accepts more examples from the E^- set), or both. To prevent the above situation from happening, a candidate list is formed of attributes, each of whose $POS(A_k) / NEG(A_k)$ value is within a certain percentage, say α %, of the highest value of the $POS(A_k) / NEG(A_k)$ value in the current candidate list. This ensures that the attribute (randomly chosen out of the candidate list) to be included in the clause has a value close to the highest value of the $POS(A_k) / NEG(A_k)$ ratios.

The above idea of using randomization in a search algorithm has been explored recently by other researchers as well. For instance, Feo and Resende in [1995] have successfully used randomization to solve clause satisfiability (SAT) problems. Also, in a book Motwani and Raghavan [1995] provide a comprehensive presentation of the theory on randomized algorithms. Randomization also offers a natural and intuitive way for implementing *parallelism* in algorithms.

To obtain a system with a very small number of clauses, the whole procedure is subjected to a certain number of iterations (denoted by the value of the *ITRS* parameter) and the system which has the least number of disjunctions is chosen as the final inferred Boolean system.

Referring to the previous illustrative example, if *l* = 3, then the values of the 3 best $POS(A_k) / NEG(A_k)$ ratios are: {1.0, 1.0, 1.0} (note that it is a coincidence that the three values are identical) which correspond to the attributes $\bar{A}_1$, A_2 and A_4, respectively. Let attribute A_2 be the randomly selected attribute from the candidate list. Note that attribute A_2 accepts examples number 2 and 3 from the current E^+ set. Therefore, at least one more attribute is required to complete the formation of the current clause. The whole process of finding a new attribute (other than attribute A_2 which has already been selected) with a very high value of *POS/NEG* is repeated. Now, suppose that the attribute with a high *POS/NEG* value happened to be A_4. It can be observed now that, when attributes A_2 and A_4 are combined together, they accept all the elements in the E^+ set. Therefore, the first clause is $(A_2 \vee A_4)$.

This clause fails to reject examples number 2, 3 and 6 in the E^- set. Therefore, examples number 2, 3 and 6 in the original E^- set constitute the reduced (and thus new) E^- set. The above process is repeated until a set of clauses are formed which, when combined together, reject all the examples in the original E^- set. Therefore, a final Boolean function for this problem could be as follows (recall that the algorithm is a randomized one and thus it may not return the same solution):

$$(A_2 \vee A_4) \wedge (\bar{A}_2 \vee \bar{A}_3) \wedge (A_1 \vee A_3 \vee \bar{A}_4).$$

5.   A GUIDED LEARNING APPROACH

The above partitioning of the population of all possible examples into the previous four disjoint regions (also recall Figure 2), suggests a natural way to select the next example to classify by the expert (*"oracle"*) when new examples are selected for training. If the new (and thus unclassified) example is selected from the region which represents *"areas of conflict,"* then when it is classified by the expert it will indicate that at least one of the positive or negative sets of rules needs to be changed (since it has to be either positive or negative). Similarly, when the new example is selected from the region which represents *"areas not covered,"* then again when it is classified by the expert it will indicate that at least one of the positive or negative sets of rules needs to be changed. This realization is in direct agreement with the guided learning approach recommended in [Triantaphyllou and Soyster, 1995b].

The above observations are better formalized as follows. Let us consider two sets of positive and negative examples, denoted as E^+ and E^-, respectively, defined on t (binary or multi-valued) attributes. Let S_{SAMPLE} denote the set of rules (systems) derived from the sample data, i.e. when the examples in E^+ are classified as positive and the examples in E^- are classified as negative. Similarly, define as $S_{R\text{-}SAMPLE}$ the set of rules (system) derived when E^- is used as the positive examples while E^+ as the negative examples.

That is S_{SAMPLE} is the set with the positive rules while $S_{R\text{-}SAMPLE}$ is the set with the negative rules. Also, define S_{HIDDEN} as the *"hidden logic"* system and $\hat{S}_{HIDDEN}$ (please note the "^" symbol on top of "S") as the complement of S_{HIDDEN}. The guided learning strategy proposed in [Triantaphyllou and Soyster, 1995b] is based on the following theorem (which is valid for the binary and also the multi-valued case):

Theorem 7:
Suppose that there exists an example v such that:
$$S_{SAMPLE}(v) \; + \; S_{R\text{-}SAMPLE}(v) \; = \; 0, \; or: \tag{1}$$
$$S_{SAMPLE}(v) \; + \; S_{R\text{-}SAMPLE}(v) \; = \; 2. \tag{2}$$
Furthermore, suppose that the example v is classified by the expert as either positive or negative. Then, one and only one of the following is true :
   a) If (1) holds and v is a positive example,
       then system S_{SAMPLE} is not valid.
   b) If (1) holds and v is a negative example,
       then system $S_{R\text{-}SAMPLE}$ is not valid.
   c) If (2) holds and v is a positive example,
       then system $S_{R\text{-}SAMPLE}$ is not valid.
   d) If (2) holds and v is a negative example,
       then system S_{SAMPLE} is not valid.

Therefore, the overall strategy, starting with two sets of rules, is to attempt to generate a sequence of new examples $v_{k+1}, v_{k+2}, v_{k+3}, ..., v_m$, where each example is appropriately classified. Each additional example should have the property that it invalidates either S_{SAMPLE} or $S_{R\text{-}SAMPLE}$, i.e. one of the two sets of rules must be modified. In doing so, it is expected that S_{SAMPLE} and $S_{R\text{-}SAMPLE}$ become more closely aligned with S_{HIDDEN} and $\hat{S}_{HIDDEN}$, respectively. Finally, as it was shown in [Triantaphyllou and Soyster, 1995b], the next example can be determined by solving a clause satisfiability problem.

During this guided learning approach one may observe that the current Boolean functions need to be modified only when a new training example indicates that a Boolean function is inaccurate (by misclassifying it). In [Nieto Sanchez, *et al.*, 2002] some algorithms are proposed which modify a Boolean function in a way that the new function correctly classifies the new example (and also all the previous training examples) and does so by performing a minimal (kind of *"surgical"*) modification. That is, these algorithms select a clause of the current function and modify it. The algorithms in [Triantaphyllou and Soyster, 1995b] and [Nieto Sanchez, *et al.*, 2002] have the potential to expedite the guided learning process both in terms of the number of the new training examples needed to accurately infer a *"hidden"* logic but also in terms of the time required to update the inferred Boolean functions.

6. THE REJECTABILITY GRAPH OF TWO COLLECTIONS OF EXAMPLES

This section presents the motivation and definition of a special graph which can be easily derived from positive and negative examples. To understand the motivation for introducing this graph, consider a situation with $t = 5$ attributes. Suppose that the vector $v_1 = (1,0,1,0,1)$ is a *positive example* while the two vectors $v_2 = (1,0,1,1,1)$ and $v_3 = (1,1,1,0,1)$ are *negative examples*. For the positive example v_1, note that A_1, $\bar{A}_2$, A_3, $\bar{A}_4$, and A_5 are true (or, equivalently, $\bar{A}_1$, A_2, $\bar{A}_3$, A_4 and $\bar{A}_5$ are false). Similar interpretations exist for the remaining two examples v_2 and v_3.

6.1 The Definition of the Rejectability Graph

Denote by *ATTRIBUTES(v)* the set of the attributes that are true (have value "1") for a particular (either positive or negative) example v. With this definition, one obtains from the above data:

$$ATTRIBUTES(v_1) = ATTRIBUTES((1,0,1,0,1)) = \{A_1, \bar{A}_2, A_3, \bar{A}_4, A_5\}$$
$$ATTRIBUTES(v_2) = ATTRIBUTES((1,0,1,1,1)) = \{A_1, \bar{A}_2, A_3, A_4, A_5\}$$
$$ATTRIBUTES(v_3) = ATTRIBUTES((1,1,1,0,1)) = \{A_1, A_2, A_3, \bar{A}_4, A_5\}.$$

Next consider a single CNF clause (i.e., a disjunction), denoted as C, of the general form:

$$C = \bigvee_{i=1}^{M} a_i \quad \text{(where } a_i \text{ is either } A_i \text{ or } \bar{A}_i).$$

The clause C *accepts* an example v (i.e., v is a positive example of C) if and only if at least one of the attributes in the set *ATTRIBUTES(v)* is also one of the attributes in the expression:

$$\bigvee_{i=1}^{M} a_i.$$

Otherwise, the example v is *not accepted* (i.e., v is a negative example of C). For instance, if the clause C is defined as: $C = (\bar{A}_2 \vee A_4)$, then the examples v_1 and v_2 are accepted by C, while the example v_3 is *not* accepted.

Now observe that there is no *single CNF clause* which can *simultaneously* reject the two negative examples v_2 and v_3, while at the same time accept the positive example v_1. This is true because any clause which simultaneously rejects the two examples v_2 and v_3, should not contain any of the attributes in the *union* of the two sets given as *ATTRIBUTES(v_2)* and *ATTRIBUTES(v_3)*. But, if none of the attributes of the set $\{A_1, A_2, \bar{A}_2, A_3, A_4, \bar{A}_4, A_5\}$ = *ATTRIBUTES(v_2) U ATTRIBUTES(v_3)* is present in the clause, then it is *impossible* to accept the positive example $v_1 = (1,0,1,0,1)$. Therefore, given any clause which accepts the positive example v_1, the previous two negative examples v_2 and v_3 cannot also be *rejected* by such clause.

From the above considerations it follows that given three examples v_1, v_2, and v_3, then the examples v_2 and v_3 are rejectable by a single clause (disjunction), subject to the example v_1, if and only if the following condition is true:

$$ATTRIBUTES(v_1) \not\subseteq ATTRIBUTES(v_2) \cup ATTRIBUTES(v_3).$$

In general, given a set of positive examples E^+, then two negative examples v_1 and v_2 are rejectable by a single clause if and only if the condition in the following theorem [Triantaphyllou and Soyster, 1996] is satisfied:

Theorem 8:
Let E^+ be a set of positive examples and v_1, v_2 be two negative examples. There exists a CNF clause which accepts all the positive examples and rejects both negative examples v_1 and v_2 if and only if:

$$ATTRIBUTES(v_i) \not\subseteq ATTRIBUTES(v_1) \cup ATTRIBUTES(v_2),$$
for each positive example $v_i \in E^+$.

The above theorem follows directly from the previous considerations. Given two collections of positive and negative examples, denoted as E^+ and E^-, respectively, Theorem 8 motivates the construction of a graph $G = (V, E)$ as follows:

$$V = \{ V_1, V_2, V_3, ..., V_{M_2} \},$$

where M_2 is the cardinality of E^- (i.e., each vertex corresponds to one negative example in E^-), and

$$e \in E, \text{ where } e = (V_i, V_j),$$

if and only if the i-th and the j-th examples in E^- are rejectable by a single clause (subject to the examples in E^+).

We denote this graph as the *rejectability graph* (or *the R-graph*) of E^+ and E^-. The previous theorem indicates that it is computationally straightforward to construct this graph. If there are M_2 negative examples, then the maximum number of edges is $M_2(M_2 - 1)/2$. Therefore, the rejectability graph can be constructed by performing $M_2(M_2 - 1)/2$ simple rejectability examinations.

An Illustrative Example
Consider the following E^+ and E^- sets (given earlier and repeated here):

$$E^+ = \begin{bmatrix} 0 & 1 & 0 & 0 \\ 1 & 1 & 0 & 0 \\ 0 & 0 & 1 & 1 \\ 1 & 0 & 0 & 1 \end{bmatrix} \quad and \quad E^- = \begin{bmatrix} 1 & 0 & 1 & 0 \\ 0 & 0 & 0 & 1 \\ 1 & 1 & 1 & 1 \\ 0 & 0 & 0 & 0 \\ 1 & 0 & 0 & 0 \\ 1 & 1 & 1 & 0 \end{bmatrix}$$

Since there are 6 negative examples, there are $6(6 - 1)/2 = 15$ possible pairwise comparisons (i.e., single rejectability tests). For instance, the first (v_1) and third (v_3) negative examples correspond to the vertices V_1 and V_3, respectively. Next one can observe that because:

$ATTRIBUTES(v_1) \cup ATTRIBUTES(v_3) = \{A_1, A_2, A_3, A_4, \bar{A}_2, \bar{A}_4\}$,

and $ATTRIBUTES(v_i) \nsubseteq \{A_1, A_2, A_3, A_4, \bar{A}_2, \bar{A}_4\}$, for each $v_i \in E^+$,

it follows that there is an edge which connects the vertices V_1 and V_3 in the rejectability graph. The rejectability graph G, which corresponds to this illustrative example, is presented in Figure 4. ∎

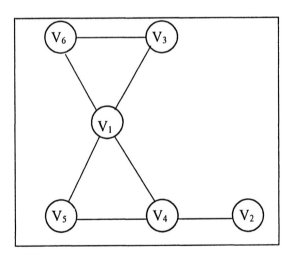

Figure 4. The Rejectability Graph for E^+ and E^-.

6.2   Properties of the Rejectability Graph

The rejectability graph G of a set of positive and a set of negative examples possesses a number of interesting properties. Two of these properties refer to the cliques of the rejectability graph. A *clique* of a graph is a subgraph in which all the nodes are connected with each other. The *minimum clique cover number* (denoted as *k(G)*) is the smallest number of cliques needed to cover the vertices of *G* (see, for instance, [Golumbic, 1980] and [Bollobás, 1979]). The following theorem [Triantaphyllou and Soyster, 1996] refers to any clique of the rejectability graph.

Theorem 9:
Suppose that the two sets E^+ *and* E^- *are given and* β *is a subset of k negative examples from* E^- *(k ≤ size of set* E^- *) with the property that the subset can be rejected by a single CNF clause which also accepts each one of the positive examples in* E^+*. Then, the vertices corresponding to the k negative examples in the rejectability graph G form a clique of size k.*

The previous theorem states that any set of negative examples which can be rejected by a single clause corresponds to a clique in the rejectability graph. However, *the converse is not true*. That is, not every clique in the rejectability graph corresponds to a set of negative examples which can be rejected by a single clause. To see this consider the following illustrative example.

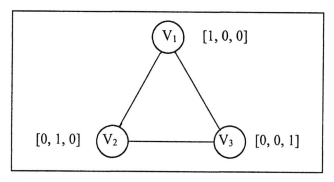

Figure 5.   The Rejectability Graph for the Second Illustrative Example.

An Illustrative Example
Consider the following sets E^+ and E^-:

$$E^+ = \begin{bmatrix} 1 & 1 & 1 \end{bmatrix}, \text{ and } E^- = \begin{bmatrix} 1 & 0 & 0 \\ 0 & 1 & 0 \\ 0 & 0 & 1 \end{bmatrix}$$

It can be easily verified that any pair of the three negative examples in E^- can be rejected by a single clause which also accepts the positive example in E^+. For instance, the first and second negative examples are rejected by the clause (A_3), which also accepts the positive example in E^+. Similarly, the first and third negative examples can be rejected by (A_2), while (A_1) rejects the second and third examples. In all cases, these clauses accept the single example in E^+. Therefore, the corresponding rejectability graph is a triangle (i.e., a clique with three nodes, see also Figure 5). However, a clause which would reject all the three negative examples should *not include* any attributes from the following set:

$$ATTRIBUTES(v_1) \cup ATTRIBUTES(v_2) \cup ATTRIBUTES(v_3) =$$
$$= ATTRIBUTES((1, 0, 0)) \cup ATTRIBUTES((0, 1, 0)) \cup$$
$$\cup \ ATTRIBUTES((0, 0, 1)) =$$
$$= \{A_1, A_2, A_3, \bar{A}_1, \bar{A}_2, \bar{A}_3\}.$$

Obviously, no such clause exists when $n = 3$.   Therefore, a minimum size set of CNF clauses which satisfy the requirements of the current examples is: $(A_3) \vee (A_2)$, which is of size 2. ■

6.3   On the Minimum Clique Cover of the Rejectability Graph

Consider two sets of positive and negative examples E^+ and E^-, respectively. Let $\hat{G}$ be the *complement* of the rejectability graph G of the two sets of examples. Recall that the complement of a graph is constructed as follows: The complement graph has exactly the same vertices as the original graph. There is an edge between any two vertices if and only if there is no edge between the corresponding vertices of the original graph. Next, define $\omega(\hat{G})$ as the *size of the maximum clique* of the graph $\hat{G}$ and $k(G)$ as the minimum clique cover number of the rejectability graph G. Let r be the minimum number of CNF clauses required to reject all the examples in E^-, while accepting all the examples in E^+. Then, the following theorem [Triantaphyllou and Soyster, 1996]] states a *lower bound* (i.e., the minimum clique cover $k(G)$) on the *minimum number* of clauses required to reject all the negative examples in E^-, while accepting all the positive examples in E^+.

Theorem 10:
Suppose that E^+ and E^- are the sets of the positive and negative examples, respectively. Then, the following relation is true: $r \geq k(G) \geq \omega(\hat{G})$.

At this point it should be stated that according to this theorem the gap between r and $k(G)$ can be positive. The same is also true with the gap between $k(G)$ and $\omega(\hat{G})$. Therefore, there is a potential for the gap between r and $\omega(\hat{G})$ to be large (since the value of $\omega(\hat{G})$ can be arbitrarily large, see for instance [Golumbic, 1980] and [Bollobás, 1979]). Results from some related computational experiments in [Triantaphyllou and Soyster, 1996] seem to indicate that when the value of $\omega(\hat{G})$ is large, then the bound is rather tight.

Although finding $k(G)$ is NP-complete, the determination of $\omega(\hat{G})$ is also NP-complete, but there are more efficient enumerative algorithms. In Carraghan and Pardalos [1990] a survey of algorithms which can find the maximum clique in any graph is presented. They also present a very efficient algorithm which uses a partial enumeration approach which outperforms any other known algorithm. In that treatment random problems with 3,000 vertices and over one million edges were solved in rather short times (less than one hour on an IBM ES/3090-600S computer). Some other related developments regarding the maximum clique of a graph can be found in [Pardalos and Xue, 1994], [Babel and Tinhofer, 1990], [Babel, 1995], [Balas and Xue, 1993], and [Balas and Niehaus, 1994].

7.   PROBLEM DECOMPOSITION

The rejectability graph provides an interesting framework for decomposing the determination of a lower bound for the number of clauses into a set of smaller problems. The decomposition is obtained through a partitioning of the rejectability graph. We consider two processes:
- *Decomposition via Connected Components, and*
- *Decomposition via the Construction of a Clique Cover.*

7.1   Connected Components

In this case, one inspects the rejectability graph for a *natural* decomposition. A *connected component* of a graph is a maximal subgraph in which there is a path of edges between any pair of vertices. Hence, the vertices of the connected components are mutually exclusive and their union is exhaustive. The following corollary is derived from Theorem 9 and illustrates the relation of the connected components of G and the clauses which can be inferred from two collections of positive and negative examples.

Corollary 1:
*Suppose that E^+ and E^- are the sets of the positive and negative examples, respectively. Then, any subset of negative examples in E^- which is rejected by a single CNF clause, subject to the examples in E^+, corresponds to a subset of vertices of the rejectability graph G which belong to the **same connected component** of the graph G.*

Pardalos and Rentala in [1990] present an excellent survey of algorithms which determine the connected components of a graph. Furthermore, they also propose a *parallel algorithm* which runs on an IBM ES/3090-400E computer (with four processors). That algorithm determines the connected components in super linear time.

The importance of Corollary 1 emerges when the sets of positive and negative examples are very large. First, one constructs the rejectability graph G. Next, one determines all the connected components of the rejectability graph by applying an algorithm (such as the one described in Pardalos and Rentala [1990]) for finding the connected components. Then, one solves the smaller clause inference problems which are formed by considering *all the positive examples* and the *negative examples which correspond* to the vertices of the individual and distinct connected components in *G*.

In other words, if a graph has two or more connected components, then one can decompose the original problem into separate problems and *the aggregation of the optimal solutions (minimum number of CNF clauses) of the separate problems is an optimal solution to the original problem.* Observe that each such sub-problem (in the CNF case) is comprised of the negative examples for that component and *all* the positive examples, i.e. the positive examples are identical for each sub-problem.

7.2   Clique Cover

The second approach is also motivated by partitioning the vertices of the rejectability graph into mutually disjoint sets. However, in this second approach, vertices are subdivided via a sequential construction of cliques.

First, the maximum clique of the rejectability graph is determined. The negative examples which correspond to the vertices of the maximum clique, along with *all* the positive examples, form the first sub-problem of this decomposition. Next, the maximum clique of the *remaining* graph is derived. The second sub-problem is formed by the negative examples which correspond to the vertices of the second clique and all the positive examples. This process continues until all the negative examples (or, equivalently, all the vertices in the rejectability graph) are considered (i.e., they are covered).

We note that this sequence of cliques does not necessarily correspond to a minimum clique cover of the rejectability graph. This procedure is simply a *greedy* approach which *approximates* a minimum clique cover. Furthermore, it is possible that a single sub-problem (in which all the vertices in the rejectability graph form a clique) may yield *more than one* clause.

It should be noted at this point that the clique cover derived by using the above greedy approach may not always yield a minimum clique cover. Therefore, the number of cliques derived in that way, *cannot* be used as a lower bound on the number of clauses derivable from positive and negative examples. Obviously, if the number of cliques is equal to $\omega(\hat{G})$, then the previous clique cover is minimal. However, even if the previous clique cover is not of minimum size, it can still be very useful as it can lead to a decomposition of the original problem into a sequence of smaller problems. Some computational tests described in Section 8, provide some insight into the effectiveness of such decomposition approach.

The two problem decomposition approaches described in this section can be combined into one approach as follows. One first decomposes the original problem in terms of its connected components. Next, a clique cover, as described above, is derived for the individual problems which correspond to the connected components of the rejectability graph. This approach is further illustrated in the demonstrative example presented in the following section.

8.   AN EXAMPLE OF USING THE REJECTABILITY GRAPH

Next we consider the following sets of positive and negative examples:

$$
E^{+} =
\begin{bmatrix}
0 & 1 & 0 & 0 & 0 & 1 & 0 & 1 & 1 & 1 \\
0 & 1 & 1 & 1 & 1 & 1 & 0 & 0 & 0 & 0 \\
0 & 0 & 1 & 0 & 1 & 1 & 1 & 0 & 1 & 0 \\
0 & 1 & 0 & 0 & 1 & 1 & 0 & 1 & 1 & 0 \\
1 & 0 & 1 & 0 & 0 & 0 & 1 & 0 & 1 & 1 \\
1 & 1 & 1 & 0 & 0 & 0 & 0 & 0 & 1 & 1 \\
1 & 1 & 0 & 0 & 0 & 0 & 0 & 1 & 1 & 1 \\
1 & 0 & 0 & 1 & 0 & 0 & 1 & 1 & 0 & 1 \\
0 & 1 & 1 & 0 & 1 & 1 & 0 & 0 & 1 & 0 \\
0 & 0 & 1 & 1 & 0 & 1 & 1 & 0 & 0 & 1 \\
1 & 1 & 1 & 1 & 0 & 0 & 0 & 0 & 0 & 1 \\
1 & 0 & 1 & 0 & 1 & 0 & 1 & 0 & 1 & 0 \\
1 & 1 & 1 & 0 & 1 & 0 & 0 & 0 & 1 & 0
\end{bmatrix}, \text{ and}
$$

$$
E^{-} =
\begin{bmatrix}
1 & 0 & 0 & 1 & 1 & 0 & 1 & 1 & 0 & 0 \\
0 & 0 & 0 & 1 & 1 & 1 & 1 & 1 & 0 & 0 \\
1 & 0 & 1 & 1 & 0 & 0 & 1 & 0 & 0 & 1 \\
0 & 0 & 0 & 0 & 1 & 1 & 1 & 1 & 1 & 0 \\
1 & 1 & 0 & 1 & 1 & 0 & 0 & 1 & 0 & 0 \\
1 & 1 & 0 & 0 & 1 & 0 & 0 & 1 & 1 & 0 \\
0 & 0 & 0 & 0 & 0 & 1 & 1 & 1 & 1 & 1
\end{bmatrix}
$$

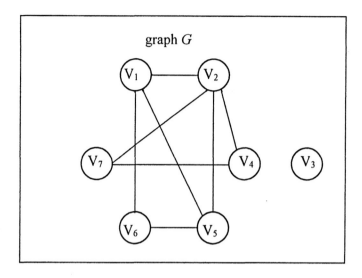

Figure 6. The Rejectability Graph for the New Sets E^+ and E^-.

One may use **any method** for inferring clauses from two disjoint classes of examples. An application of the OCAT approach in this illustrative example yields the following CNF system of four clauses:

$$(A_2 \lor A_3 \lor \bar{A}_5) \land (\bar{A}_1 \lor A_3 \lor \bar{A}_5) \land (A_1 \lor A_2 \lor A_4 \lor A_5) \land$$
$$\land (\bar{A}_1 \lor A_2 \lor \bar{A}_3 \lor \bar{A}_4).$$

Of course the question addressed in this section is whether it is possible to derive another system with *fewer* clauses.

To help answer the previous question, we apply Theorem 8 to this illustrative example. Since there are 13 positive and 7 negative examples, the construction of the rejectability graph requires 21 simple rejectability examinations. When Theorem 8 is applied to these data, the rejectability graph shown in Figure 6 is derived. For instance, there is an edge between vertices V_1 and V_6 because the first and sixth negative examples can be rejected by a single disjunction without violating the constraints imposed by the positive examples in E^+. A similar interpretation holds for the remaining edges in graph G.

The rejectability graph in the current illustrative example has *two connected components* (see also Figure 6). One component is comprised by the vertices V_1, V_2, V_4, V_5, V_6, V_7 and the second component has only the vertex V_3. Therefore, the original problem can be partitioned into *two independent* clause inference sub-problems.

Both sub-problems have the same positive examples. The first sub-problem has the same negative examples as in E^- *except* for the *third* negative example. The second problem has *only* the third negative example. The lower bound for the minimum number of CNF clauses required to appropriately classify the 20 examples is derived from the sum of the lower bounds for the two separate components. Since the rejectability graph of the second sub-problem contains only a single vertex, the size of the minimum clique cover is one. A minimum clique cover is also obvious for the first sub-problem, namely, the two sets $\{V_1, V_5, V_6\}$ and $\{V_2, V_4, V_7\}$. Hence, a minimum clique cover is two for the second sub-problem. Thus, an overall lower bound for the minimum number of CNF clauses required is three. Hence, it may well be possible that only three clauses are needed to appropriately classify all 20 examples.

As it was also mentioned in Section 2 of this chapter there is another clause inference approach which can be used to determine a minimum size set of clauses. This method, denoted as SAT (for satisfiability), has been proposed in Kamath, *et al.* [1992]. In that approach one first specifies an upper limit on the number of clauses to be considered, say k. That is, the value of k must be *pre-assumed.* Next a clause satisfiability (SAT) model is formed and solved using an interior point method developed by Karmakar and his associates [1992]. If the clause satisfiability problem is satisfied, it is possible to correctly classify all the examples with k or fewer clauses. If this SAT problem is infeasible, then one must increase k until feasibility is reached. In this manner, the SAT approach yields a system with the minimum number of clauses. It is very important one to observe at this point that computationally it is much harder to prove that a given SAT problem is infeasible than it is feasible. Therefore, trying to determine a minimum size Boolean function by using the SAT approach may be computationally too difficult. In this illustrative example, the SAT approach with $k = 3$, is feasible and returns the Boolean function with the following 3 clauses:

$$(A_2 \vee A_2 \vee A_3) \wedge (\bar{A}_1 \vee A_2 \vee \bar{A}_3 \vee \bar{A}_4) \wedge (\bar{A}_1 \vee A_3 \vee \bar{A}_5).$$

However, when the value $k = 2$ is used, then the corresponding SAT formulation is infeasible. Therefore, this set of clauses is optimal in the sense of this chapter. The last statement also follows from Theorem 10 since there exists a clique cover of 3 and a set of clauses has been derived with exactly this number of members.

9.   CONCLUSIONS

This chapter presented an approach for inferring a Boolean function from two classes of disjoint observations. The observations can be defined on multi-valued or binary valued attributes. A straightforward binarization approach is described as well. A minimization algorithm based on a branch-and-bound approach and a fast heuristic are also described.

A graph based approach for decomposing a large data mining problem into a series of smaller problems is described too. This graph based approach can also provide some bounds on the size of the inferred Boolean functions (when they are expressed in CNF or DNF format). A method for guided learning is also discussed.

Some of the results are specific to the proposed approach, termed OCAT (for One Clause At a Time) and other results can be combined with *any* data mining and knowledge discovery method. The presented methods have been tested on simulated and actual data as described in the cited papers with highly promising results.

Of particular interest are some extensions into *text mining* as described in [Nieto Sanchez, Triantaphyllou and Kraft, 2002]. Another interesting extension is the application of the OCAT approach to the mining of association rules [Yilmaz, Triantaphyllou, *et al.*, 2003]. In the later paper the application of a modified version of the OCAT approach significantly alleviates some computational problems that are caused by the huge number of the association rules that are usually returned by traditional methods. Finally it should be stated that some extensions into cases of having data with noise (stochastic data) seem to be possible with the use of monotone Boolean functions as discussed in Chapter 4 of this book authored by Torvik and Triantaphyllou [2006]. A recent book by the author [Triantaphyllou, 2006] describes in great detail all the previous issues, and much more, on data mining and knowledge discovery by means of a logic-based approach.

Future research in this area may be related to new ways for decomposing large size problems and also on the development of specialized methods for particular applications of data mining and knowledge discovery from databases. Another possible research direction might be the use of fuzzy logic and also on how to do all the above with multi-valued data directly without having to go through the binarization process first. Inferring Boolean functions from examples is a prominent area in data mining and knowledge discovery methods and more research in the future is almost guaranteed to be a hot area.

REFERENCES

Angluin, D., (1987), "Learning Propositional Horn Sentences With Hints," *Technical Report*, YALE/DCS/RR-590, Department of Computer Science, Yale University, Connecticut, U.S.A.

Babel, L. and G. Tinhofer, (1990), "A Branch and Bound Algorithm for the Maximum Clique Problem," *Methods and Models of Operations Research*, Vol. 34, pp. 207-217.

Babel, L., (1991), "Finding Maximum Cliques in Arbitrary and in Special Graphs," *Computing*, Vol. 46, pp. 321-341.

Babel, (1995), "A Fast Algorithm for the Maximum Weight Clique Problem," *Computing*, Vol. 10, pp. 12-23.

Balas, E. and J. Xue, (1993), "Weighted and Unweighted Maximum Clique Algorithms with Upper Bounds From Fractional Coloring," *Management Science Research Report #MSRR-590*, Carnegie Mellon University, Pittsburgh, PA 15213, U.S.A., 19 pages.

Balas, E. and W. Niehaus, (1994), "Finding Large Cliques by Bipartite Matching," *Management Science Research Report #MSRR-597*, Carnegie Mellon University, Pittsburgh, PA 15213, U.S.A., 11 pages.

Bartnikowski, S., M. Granberry, J. Mugan, and K. Truemper, (2006), "Transformation of Rational Data and Set Data to Logic Data," Chapter 7 in: "Data Mining and Knowledge Discovery Approaches Based on Rule Induction Techniques," Triantaphyllou, E. and G. Felici (Eds.), Massive Computing Series, *Springer*, Heidelberg, Germany, pp. 253-278.

Bollobás, B., (1979), "Graph Theory, An Introductory Course, " *Springer*, Berlin, Germany.

Bongard, M., (1970), "Pattern Recognition," *Spartan Books*, New York, NY, U.S.A.

Boros, E., P.L. Hammer, and J.N. Hooker, (1994), "Predicting Cause-Effect Relationships from Incomplete Discrete Observations," *SIAM Journal on Discrete Mathematics*, Vol. 7, No. 4, pp. 531-543.

Bradshaw, G., R. Fozzard, and L. Cece, (1989), "A Connectionist Expert System that Really Works," *Advances in Neural Information Processing*, Morgan Kaufman, Palo Alto, CA, U.S.A.

Brayton, R., G. Hachtel, C. McMullen, and A. Sangiovanni-Vincentelli, (1985), "Logic Minimization Algorithms for VLSI Minimization," *Kluwer Academic Publishers*, Norwell, MA, U.S.A.

Brown, D., (1981), "A State-Machine Synthesizer-SMS," *Proceedings of the 18-th Design Automation Conference*, pp. 443-458.

Carraghan, R. and P.M. Pardalos, (1990), "An Exact Algorithm for the Maximum Clique Problem," *Operations Research Letters*, Vol. 9, No. 11, pp. 375-382 (1990).

Chang, I., R. Engel, D. Kandlur, D. Pendarakis, D. Saha, (1999), "Key Management for Secure Internet Multicast using Boolean Function Minimization Techniques," *Proceedings of IEEE Infocomm, 1999*. Also available as a PDF file from the Citeseer website.

Cohn, D., L. Atlas and R. Ladner, (1994), "Improving Generalizing with Active Learning," *Machine Learning*, Vol. 15, pp. 201-221.

Deshpande, A.S., and E. Triantaphyllou, (1998), "A Greedy Randomized Adaptive Search Procedure (GRASP) for Inferring Logical Clauses from Examples in Polynomial Time and some Extensions," *Mathematical and Computer Modelling*, Vol. 27, No. 1, pp. 75-99.

Dietterich, T.C., and R.S. Michalski, (1983), "A Comparative Review of Selected Methods for Learning from Examples," R.S. Michalski, J.G. Carbonell, and T.M. Mitchell (eds.). *Machine Learning: An Artificial Intelligence Approach*, Tioga Publishing Company, Palo Alto, CA, U.S.A., pp. 41-81.

Fayyad, U.M., G. Piatetsky-Shapiro, P. Smyth, and R. Uthurusamy, 996, Advances in Knowledge Discovery and Data Mining, *MIT Press,* Cambridge, MA, U.S.A.

Felici, G., and K. Truemper, (2002), "A Minsat Approach for Learning in Logic Domains," *INFORMS Journal on Computing,* Vol. 14, No. 1, Winter 2002, pp. 20-36 .

Feo, T.A. and M.G.C. Resende, (1995), "Greedy Randomized Adaptive Search Procedures," *Journal of Global Optimization,* Vol. 6, pp. 109-133.

Fu, L.M., (1993), "Knowledge-Based Connectionism for Revising Domain Theories," *IEEE Transactions on Systems, Man, and Cybernetics*, Vol. 23, No. 1, pp. 173-182.

Galant, S., (1988), "Connectionist Expert Systems," *Commun. of the ACM*, Vol. 31, No. 2, pp. 152-169.

Goldman, S.A., (1990), "Learning Binary Relations, Total Orders, and Read-Once Formulas," *Ph.D. Thesis*, Massachusetts Institute of Technology, September 1990. Available as *Technical Report MIT/LCS/TR-483,* MIT Laboratory for Computer Science.

Goldman, S., and R.H. Sloan, (1994), "The Power of Self-Directed Learning," *Machine Learning*, Vol. 14, pp. 271-294.

Golumbic, M.C., (1980), Algorithmic Graph Theory and Perfect Graphs, *Academic Press*, New York, NY, U.S.A.

Gimpel, J., (1965), "A Method of Producing a Boolean Function Having an Arbitrarily Prescribed Prime Implicant Table," *IEEE Trans. on Computers,* Vol. 14, pp. 485-488.

Hall, L., and A. Romaniuk, (1990), "A Hybrid Connectionist, Symbolic Learning System," *Proceedings of the AAAI '90*, Boston, MA, U.S.A., pp. 783-788.

Hattori, K. and Y. Torri, (1993), "Effective Algorithms for the Nearest Neighbor Method in the Clustering Problem," *Pattern Recognition*, Vol. 26, No. 5, pp. 741-746.

Haussler, D. 1989, "Learning conjunctive concepts in structural domains," *Machine Learning*, Vol. 4, pp. 7-40.

Haussler, D., (1988), "Quantifying inductive bias: AI learning algorithms and Valiant's learning framework," *Artificial Intelligence*, Vol. 36, pp. 177-221.

Haussler, D., and M. Warmuth, (1993), "The Probably Approximately Correct (PAC) and Other Learning Models," Chapter in: *Foundations of Knowledge Acquisition: Machine Learning,* A.L. Meyrowitz and S. Chipman (Eds.), Kluwer Academic Publishers, Norwell, MA, U.S.A., pp. 291-312.

Hong, S., R. Cain, and D. Ostapko, (1974), "MINI: A Heuristic Approach for Logic Minimization," *IBM J. Res. Develop.*, pp. 443- 458.

Johnson, N., (1991), "Everyday Diagnostics: A Critique of the Bayesian Model," *Med. Hypotheses*, Vol. 34, No. 4, pp. 289-96.

Quine, W., (1952), "The Problem of Simplifying Truth Functions," *Am. Math. Monthly*, Vol. 59, pp. 102-111.

Quine, W., (1955), "A Way to Simplify Truth Functions," *Am. Math. Monthly*, Vol. 62.

Quinlan, J.R., (1986), "Induction of Decision Trees," *Machine Learning,* Vol. 1, No. 1, pp. 81-106.

Quinlan, J.R., (1979), "Discovering Rules by Induction from Large Numbers of Examples: A Case Study," D. Michie (ed.), *Expert Systems in the Micro-Electronic Age*. Edinburgh University Press, Scotland, UK.

Kamath, A.P., N.K. Karmakar, K.G. Ramakrishnan, and M.G.C. Resende, (1992), "A

Continuous Approach to Inductive Inference," *Math. Progr.*, Vol. 57, pp. 215-238.

Kamath, A.P., N.K. Karmakar, K.G. Ramakrishnan, and M.G.C. Resende, (1994), "An Interior Point Approach to Boolean Vector Synthesis," *Proceedings of the 36-th MSCAS*, pp. 1-5.

Kamgar-Parsi, B. and L.N. Kanal, (1985), "An Improved Branch-And-Bound Algorithm for Computing k-Nearest Neighbors," *Pattern Recognition Letters*, Vol. 3 pp. 7-12.

Karmakar, N.K., M.G.C. Resende, and K.G. Ramakrishnan, (1992), "An Interior Point Algorithm to Solve Computationally Difficult Set Covering Problems," *Math. Progr.*, Vol. 52, pp. 597-618.

Karnaugh, M., (1953), "The Map Method for Synthesis of Combinatorial Logic Circuits," *Transactions of the AIEE, Communications and Electronics*, Vol. 72, pp. 593-599.

Kearns, M., M. Li, L. Pitt, and L.G. Valiant, (1987), "On the Learnability of Boolean Formulae," Journal of the Association for Computing Machinery, No. 9, pp. 285-295.

Kovalerchuk, B., E. Triantaphyllou, J.F. Ruiz, V.I. Torvik, and E. Vityaev, (2000), "The Reliability Issue of Computer-Aided Breast Cancer Diagnosis," *Computers and Biomedical Research,* Vol. 33, No. 4, August, pp. 296-313.

Kurita, T., (1991), "An Efficient Agglomerative Clustering Algorithm Using a Heap," Pattern *Recognition,* Vol. 24, No. 3, pp. 205-209.

Mangasarian, O.L., W.N. Street, and W.H. Woldberg, (1995), "Breast Cancer Diagnosis and Prognosis Via Linear Programming," Operations *Research*, Vol. 43, No. 4, pp. 570-577.

Mangasarian, O.L., R. Setiono, and W.H. Woldberg, (1991), "Pattern Recognition Via Linear Programming: Theory and Application to Medical Diagnosis," Large-*Scale Numerical Optimization,* T.F. Coleman, and Y. Li, (Eds.), SIAM, pp. 22-30.

Mansour, Y., (1992), "Learning of DNF Formulas," *Proceedings of the Fifth Annual Workshop on Computational Learning Theory,* pp. 53-59.

McCluskey, E., (1956), "Minimization of Boolean Functions," Bell *Syst. Tech. J.*, Vol. 35, pp. 1417-1444.

Motwani, R, and P. Raghavan, (1995), Randomized Algorithms, *Cambridge University Press,* 1995.

Nieto Sanchez, S., E. Triantaphyllou, J. Chen, and T.W. Liao, (2002), "An Incremental Learning Algorithm for Constructing Boolean Functions From Positive and Negative Examples," *Computers and Operations Research*, Vol. 29, No. 12, pp. 177-1700.

Nieto Sanchez, S., E. Triantaphyllou, and D. Kraft, (2002), "A Feature Mining Approach for the Classification of Text Documents Into Disjoint Classes," *Information Processing and Management*, Vol. 38, No. 4, pp. 583-604.

Pappas, N.L, (1994), Digital Design, *West Publishing Co.*, Minneapolis/St. Paul, MN, U.S.A.

Pardalos, P.M. and J. Xue, (1994), "The Maximum Clique Problem," *Journal of Global Optimization*, Vol. 4, pp. 301-328.

Pardalos, P.M. and C.S. Rentala, (1990), "Computational Aspects of a Parallel Algorithm to Find the Connected Components of a Graph," Technical *Report*, Dept. of Computer Science, Pennsylvania State University, PA, U.S.A.

Peysakh, J., (1987), "A Fast Algorithm to Convert Boolean Expressions into CNF," *IBM Comp. Sci. RC 12913 (#57971)*, Watson, NY.

Pitt, L. and L.G. Valiant, (1988), "Computational Limitations on Learning from Examples," *Journal of the Association for Computing Machinery,* Vol. 35, No. 4, pp. 965-984.

Rivest, R.L., (1987), "Learning Decision Trees," *Machine Learning*, Vol. 2, No. 3, pp. 229-

246.

Shavlik, J.W., (1994), "Combining Symbolic and Neural Learning," *Machine Learning*, Vol. 14, pp. 321-331.

Sun, R. and F. Alexandre (Eds.), (1997), "Connectionist-Symbolic Integration: From Unified to Hybrid Approaches," *Lawrence Erilbaum Associates, Publishers,* Mahwah, NJ, U.S.A.

Torvik, V.I., and E. Triantaphyllou, (2006), "Discovering Rules that Govern Monotone Phenomena," Chapter 4 in: "Data Mining and Knowledge Discovery Approaches Based on Rule Induction Techniques," Triantaphyllou, E. and G. Felici (Eds.), Massive Computing Series, *Springer*, Heidelberg, Germany, pp. 149-192.

Towell, G., J. Havlic, and M. Noordewier, (1990), "Refinement Approximate Domain Theories by Knowledge-Based Neural Networks," *Proceedings of the AAAI '90 Conference*, Boston, MA, U.S.A., pp. 861-866.

Triantaphyllou, E., (2006), "Data Mining and Knowledge Discovery Via a Logic-Based Approach," Massive Computing Series, *Springer,* Heidelberg, Germany.

Triantaphyllou, E., and A.L. Soyster, (1996), "On the Minimum Number of Logical Clauses Which Can be Inferred From Examples," *Computers and Operations Research,* Vol. 23, No. 8, pp. 783-799.

Triantaphyllou, E., and A.L. Soyster, (1995a), "A Relationship Between CNF and DNF Systems Derivable from Examples," *ORSA Journal on Computing*, Vol. 7, No. 3, pp. 283-285.

Triantaphyllou, E., and A.L. Soyster, (1995b), "An Approach to Guided Learning of Boolean Functions," *Mathematical and Computer Modeling,* Vol. 23, No. 3, pp. 69-86.

Triantaphyllou, E., (1994), "Inference of A Minimum Size Boolean Function From Examples by Using A New Efficient Branch-and-Bound Approach," *Journal of Global Optimization*, Vol. 5, No. 1, pp. 69-94.

Triantaphyllou, E., A.L. Soyster, and S.R.T. Kumara, (1994), "Generating Logical Expressions From Positive and Negative Examples Via a Branch-and-Bound Approach," *Computers and Operations Research*, Vol. 21, No. 2, pp. 185-197.

Truemper, K., (2004), Design of Logic-based Intelligent Systems, *John Wiley & Sons, Inc.,* New York, NY, U.S.A.

Truemper, K., (1998), Effective Logic Computation, *Wiley-Interscience,* New York, NY, U.S.A.

Woldberg, W.W., and O.L. Mangasarian, (1990), "A Multisurface Method of Pattern Separation for Medical Diagnosis Applied to Breast Cytology," *Proceedings of the National Academy of Sciences of the USA*, Vol. 87, No. 23, pp. 9193-9196.

Valiant, L.G., (1984), "A Theory of the Learnable," *Comm. of ACM,* Vol. 27, No. 11, pp. 1134-1142.

Valiant, L.G., (1985), "Learning Disjunctions of Conjunctives," *Proceedings of the 9th IJCAI*, pp. 560-566.

Yilmaz, E., E. Triantaphyllou, J. Chen, and T.W. Liao, (2003), "A Heuristic for Mining Association Rules In Polynomial Time," *Mathematical and Computer Modelling*, No. 37, pp. 219-233.

AUTHOR'S BIOGRAPHICAL STATEMENT

Dr. Triantaphyllou did his graduate studies at Penn State University from 1984 to 1990. While at Penn State, he earned a Dual M.S. degree in Environment and Operations Research (OR), an M.S. degree in Computer Science and a Dual Ph.D. degree in Industrial Engineering and Operations Research. Since the spring of 2005 he is a Professor in the Computer Science Department at the Louisiana State University (LSU) in Baton Rouge, LA, U.S.A., after he has served for 11 years as an Assistant, Associate, and Full Professor in the Industrial Engineering Department at the same university. He has also served for one year as an Interim Associate Dean for the College of Engineering at LSU.

His research is focused on decision-making theory and applications, data mining and knowledge discovery, and the interface of operations research and computer science. Since the years he was a graduate student, he has developed new methods for data mining and knowledge discovery and also has explored some of the most fundamental and intriguing subjects in decision making. In 1999 he has received the prestigious IIE (Institute of Industrial Engineers), OR Division, Research Award for his research contributions in the above fields. In 2005 he received an LSU Distinguished Faculty Award as recognition of his research, teaching, and service accomplishments. Some of his graduate students have also received awards and distinctions including the Best Dissertation Award at LSU for Science, Engineering and Technology for the year 2003. In 2000 Dr. Triantaphyllou published a bestseller book on multi-criteria decision-making. Also, in 2006 he published a monograph on data mining and knowledge discovery, besides co-editing a book on the same subject.

He always enjoys sharing the results of his research with his students and is also getting them actively involved in his research activities. He has received teaching awards and distinctions. His research has been funded by federal and state agencies, and the private sector. He has extensively published in some of the top refereed journals and made numerous presentations in national and international conferences.

Dr. Triantaphyllou has a strong inter-disciplinary background. He has always enjoyed organizing multi-disciplinary teams of researchers and practitioners with complementary expertise. These groups try to comprehensively attack some of the most urgent problems in the sciences and engineering. He is a strong believer of the premise that the next round of major scientific and engineering discoveries will come from the work of such inter-disciplinary groups. More details of his work can be found in his web site (_http://www.csc.lsu.edu/trianta/_).

Chapter 3 [1]

AN INCREMENTAL LEARNING ALGORITHM FOR INFERRING LOGICAL RULES FROM EXAMPLES IN THE FRAMEWORK OF THE COMMON REASONING PROCESS

Xenia Naidenova
Military Medical Academy, Saint Petersburg
196046 Lebedev Street, 6, Russia
Email: naidenova@mail.spbnit.ru

Abstract: In this chapter we present a model of common sense reasoning that combines a pattern recognition and learning of logical rules from examples. The class of rules is implicative but these rules can be represented in different forms. The model of knowledge base and an example of the reasoning process based on knowledge are considered. An approach is proposed for inferring implicative logical rules from examples. The concept of a good diagnostic test for a given set of positive examples lies in the basis of this approach. The process of inferring good diagnostic tests is considered as a process of inductive common sense reasoning. The incremental approach to learning algorithms allows revealing the interdependence between two fundamental components of human thinking: pattern recognition (deductive inference) and knowledge acquisition (inductive inference).

Key Words: Incremental and Non-Incremental Learning, Learning from Examples, Machine Learning, Common Sense Reasoning, Inductive Inference, Good Diagnostic Test, Lattice Theory.

---

[1] Triantaphyllou, E.   and G. Felici (Eds.), **Data Mining and Knowledge Discovery Approaches Based on Rule Induction Techniques**, Massive Computing Series, Springer, Heidelberg, Germany, pp. 89-147, 2006.

1.   INTRODUCTION

The incremental approach in developing machine learning algorithms is one of the most promising directions for creating intelligent computer systems. Two main considerations determine the interest of researchers to the incrementality as an instrument for solving learning problems.

The first consideration is related to the nature of tasks to be solved. In a wide range of problems, a computer system must be able to learn incrementally for adapting to changes of the environment or user's behavior. An example of incremental learning can be found in (Maloof and Michalski, 1995) where a dynamic knowledge-based system for computer intrusion detection is described. Incremental clustering for mining in a data-warehousing environment is another interesting example of incremental learning (Ester, et al., 1998).

The second consideration is related to the intention of researchers to create more effective and efficient data mining algorithms in comparison with non-incremental ones. This goal implies the necessity to answer the following questions: how to select the next training example in order to minimize the number of steps in the learning process? How to select the relevant part of hypotheses already induced in order to bring them in agreement with a certain training example? The problem of how to best modify an induced Boolean function when the classification of a new example reveals that this function is inaccurate is considered in (Nieto et al., 2002). In this paper, the problem is solved by minimizing the number of clauses that must be repaired in order to correctly classify all available training examples. An efficient algorithm for discovering frequent sets in incremental databases is given in (Feldman, 1997).

The distinction between an incremental learning task and an incremental learning algorithm is clarified in (Giraud-Carries, 2000). A learning task is incremental if the training examples used to solve it become available over time, usually one at a time. A learning algorithm is incremental if for given training examples e_1, e_2,..., e_i, e_{i+1},..., e_n it produces a sequence of hypotheses h_1, h_2,..., h_i, h_{i+1},..., h_n, such that h_{i+1} depends only on h_i and current example e_i. As it has been shown in (Giraud-Carries, 2000), it is possible to use an incremental algorithm for both non-incremental and incremental tasks.

The analysis of existing learning algorithms shows that non-incremental data processing can be a part of an incremental algorithm (see the example in (Nieto, et al., 2002)) while incremental data processing can be embodied in a non-incremental algorithm. From the more general point of view, the incrementality is a mode of inductive reasoning for creating learning algorithms.

Induction allows extending the solution of a sub-problem with lesser dimension to the solution of the same problem but with greater dimension (forward induction) and vice versa (backward induction). There does not exist only one way of applying induction to the same problem, but many different ways that lead to different methods of constructing algorithms.

Traditionally, the inductive hypothesis in machine learning problems is described as follows: we know how to solve a learning problem for the training set of n-1 examples, thus we know how to solve the same problem for the training set of n examples. But another induction hypothesis might be the following: we know how to solve a learning problem with n/k training examples where k is the number of subsets into which the set of training examples is partitioned. Therefore, we can solve the same task with n training examples. Namely this inductive hypothesis is used in (Wu and Lo, 1998) for a multi-layer induction algorithm. The initial data set in this algorithm is divided into a number of subsets of equal size. In the first step, a set of rules is learned from the first subset of examples by the help of a generalization operation. The rules thus obtained (which might be redundant) are refined with the use of the other subsets of data. Successive application of the generalization and reduction operations allows for more accurate and more complex rules to be constructed.

In the present chapter, the following inductive hypothesis (backward induction) is used: we know how to solve a learning problem for the training set of n examples, thus we know how to solve the same problem for the training set of n-1 examples.

We focus on the incrementality as a technique of human thinking. Common sense human reasoning is by its nature an incremental process. It combines deductive and inductive steps of thinking. Deductive steps consist of using already known facts and statements of the form "if-then" for inferring consequences from them. For this goal, deductive rules of reasoning are applied. The main form of deduction is syllogism, for which are known four forms: modus ponens, modus tollens, modus ponendo tollens, and modus tollendo ponens. Inductive steps consist of using already known facts and statements, observations and experience for inferring new statements or correcting those that turn out to be false. For this goal, inductive rules of reasoning are applied. The main forms of induction are the canons of induction that have been formulated by English logician Mille (1900). These canons are known as the five induction methods of reasoning: method of only similarity, method of only distinction, joint method of similarity-distinction, method of concomitant changes, and method of residuum.

In real human reasoning, deductive and inductive steps alternate and support each other. The following mental acts are revealed in applying any reasoning rule (deductive or inductive): formulating new statements, choosing a new relevant part of knowledge or/and data for future steps of reasoning and choosing a new reasoning rule (deductive or inductive). It is difficult to consider this process to be algorithmic. It is impossible to plan a control mechanism in advance. But it is possible to speak about some preference of applying certain rules under certain conditions.

Modeling of on-line human reasoning is a key problem in creating intelligent computer systems. However, any attention is hardly paid to this topic in computer science. Knowledge engineering has arisen from a paradigm in which knowledge is considered as something to be separated from its bearer and to function autonomously with a problem solving application. This paradigm ignores the very essential feature of intelligence, namely, its continuous cognitive activity. Knowledge is corrected constantly. This means that the mechanism of using knowledge cannot be separated from the mechanism of discovering knowledge. Figure 1 illustrates the thesis that deductive reasoning (extending data about a situation) and inductive reasoning (modifying or extending knowledge) might be realized with the use of one and the same inference mechanism.

The idea to integrate two complementary processes - inductive learning from examples and deductive reasoning - has been advanced in (Giraud-Carrier and Martinez, 1995). That paper introduces an Incremental Learning Algorithm (ILA). The ILA stores its knowledge in the nodes of a network that is a balanced binary tree. Data are presented incrementally and the system adapts by dynamically adding nodes to the network. The execution part of the algorithm implements a simple form of rule-based reasoning augmented with similarity-based reasoning. The ILA's inductive learning is similar to the Nearest Hyperrectangle Learning Method (NGE) (Salzberg, 1991). A brief comparison of the ILA with other related models is given too.

A fruitful approach is incorporating data mining procedures into object-oriented databases (OODB). There are many research issues on knowledge discovery in OODBs (see, for example, (Han, et al., 1998), (Han, 1998)). The main goals of these contributions are the substantial enhancement of the power and flexibility of browsing a database, and organizing effective querying on data and knowledge. The technology of on-line analytical mining (OLAM) is based on the Data Cube technology (Han, 1998), (Han, et al., 1998) for efficient representation and processing data in OODBs. The OLAM approach requires a good data mining query language. A data mining language, called DMQL (Han, et al., 1996), has been proposed and partially implemented in the DBMiner system. The language adopts a SQL-like syntax and provides primitives for specification of different data mining tasks.

A well-known researcher, Michalski, proposed a new type of knowledge representation, called Dynamic Interlaced Hierarchies (DIH), which is relevant to the development of multi-strategy task-adaptive learning and facilitates all kinds of inference.

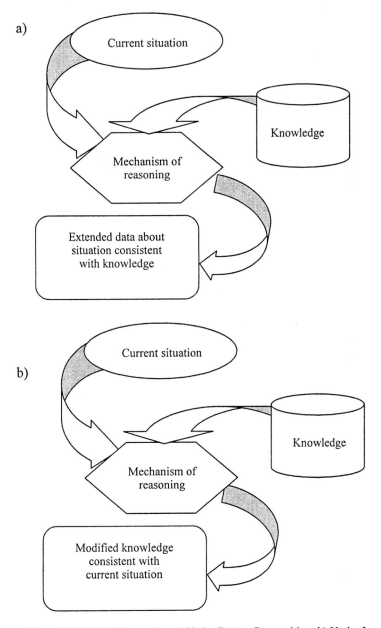

Figure 1. Model of Reasoning a) Under Pattern Recognition, b) Under Learning.

This type of knowledge representation is given in (Alkharaouf and Michalski, 1996), (Michalski and Ram, 1995). Statements or facts are stored as links between concepts and they are considered to be dynamic, as these links are constantly being created and modified.

These approaches to data mining are very promising. However, none of them possesses all the main features of human reasoning. No one of them considers any subtask of machine learning (ML) or data mining as a model of human reasoning.

In order to transform ML methods into a model of common sense reasoning it is necessary to do the following:

- Decompose ML algorithms into operations and subtasks that can be, by their content, considered as operations of high level conceptual reasoning including various kinds of reasoning rules: diagnostic rules, generalization rules, classification rules, association rules, rules involving known regularities, rules of refuting hypotheses, rules resolving contradictions, rules of inferring possible consequences or causes, and so on;
- Create a multilevel inference control mechanism that must provide the interaction between all types of rules and data in reasoning.

Our approach to machine learning problems is based on the concept of a good diagnostic (classification) test. This concept has been advanced firstly in the framework of inferring functional and implicative dependencies from relations (Naidenova and Polegaeva, 1986). But later the fact has been revealed that the task of inferring all good diagnostic tests for a given set of positive and negative examples can be formulated as the search of the best approximation of a given classification on a given set of examples and that it is this task that all well known machine learning problems can be reduced to (Naidenova, 1996). It is interesting that, on the one hand, the problem of inferring implicative logical rules from examples turns out to be equivalent to the problem of finding good diagnostic tests. On the other hand, the process of finding good diagnostic tests realizes one of the induction canons of reasoning – a joint method of similarity-distinction given in (Mille, 1900).

We have chosen the lattice theory as a model for inferring good diagnostic tests from examples from the very beginning of our work in this direction. We believe that it is the lattice theory that must be the mathematical theory of common sense reasoning. One can come to this conclusion by analyzing both the fundamental work in the psychological theory of intelligence (Piaget, 1959), and the experience of modeling thinking processes in the framework of artificial intelligence. The process of objects' classification has been considered in (Shreider, 1974) as an algebraic idempotent semi group with the unit element. An algebraic model of classification and pattern recognition based on the lattice theory has been advanced in (Boldyrev, 1974). A lot of experience has been obtained on the application of algebraic lattices in machine learning: the works of Finn and his disciples (Finn, 1984), (Kuznetsov, 1993), the model of conceptual knowledge of Wille (1992), the works of the French group (Ganascia, 1989). The following works are devoted to the application of algebraic lattices for extracting classifications, functional dependencies and implications from data: (Demetrovics and Vu, 1993), (Mannila and Räihä, 1992), (Mannila and Räihä, 1994), (Huntala, et al., 1999), (Cosmadakis, et al., 1986), (Naidenova and Polegaeva, 1986), (Megretskaya, 1988), (Naidenova, et al., 1995a), (Naidenova, et al., 1995b), and (Naidenova, 1992).

An advantage of the algebraic lattices approach is based on the fact that an algebraic lattice can be defined both as an algebraic structure that is declarative and as a system of dual operations with the use of which the elements of this lattice can be generated. This approach allows us to investigate the processes of inferring good classification tests as inductive reasoning processes. In the following part of this chapter we shall describe our decomposition of the inductive inferring process into subtasks and operations that conform with the operations and subtasks of the natural human reasoning process.

This chapter is organized as follows. Section 2 describes the forms of an expert's rules (rules of the first type) and the structure of the conceptual knowledge base in which an expert's rules are stored. Then we describe reasoning operations or rules of the second type, also providing an example of executing rule-based reasoning for inferring the value of a target attribute.

In Section 3, the concept of a good diagnostic test is introduced and the problem of inferring all good diagnostic tests for a given classification on a given set of examples is formulated. Section 3 also contains the description of a mathematical model underlying algorithms of learning reasoning. In order to transform inductive learning algorithms into the common sense reasoning process we propose a decomposition of learning algorithms into operations and subtasks that are in accordance with human reasoning operations. The concepts of an essential value and an essential example are also introduced.

Section 4 describes the proposed non-incremental and incremental learning algorithms: NIAGaRa, DIAGaRa, and INGOMAR. The chapter ends with a brief summary section.

2.   A MODEL OF RULE-BASED LOGICAL INFERENCE

Here we describe a model of common reasoning that has been acquired from our numerous investigations on the human reasoning modes used by experts for solving diagnostic problems in diverse areas such as pattern recognition of natural objects (rocks, ore deposits, types of trees, types of clouds e.t.c.), analysis of multi-spectral information, image processing, interpretation of psychological testing data, medicine diagnosis and so on. The principal aspects of this model coincide with the rule-based inference mechanism that is embodied in the KADS system (Ericson, et al., 1992), (Gappa and Poeck, 1992). More details related to our model of reasoning and its implementation can be found in (Naidenova and Syrbu, 1984), (Naidenova and Polegaeva, 1985a), and (Naidenova and Polegaeva, 1985b).

We need the following three types of rules in order to realize logical inference:

INSTANCES or relationships between objects or facts really observed. Instance can be considered as a logical rule with the least degree of generalization. On the one hand, instances serve as a source of an expert's knowledge. On the other hand, instances can serve as a source of a training set of positive and negative examples for inductive inference of generalized rules.

RULES OF THE FIRST TYPE. These rules describe regular relationships between objects and their properties and between properties of different objects. The rules of the first type can be given explicitly by an expert or derived automatically from examples with the help of some learning process. These rules are represented in the form "if-then" assertions. They accumulate generalized knowledge in a problem domain.

RULES OF THE SECOND TYPE or inference rules with the help of which rules of the first type are used, updated and inferred from data (instances). The rules of the second type are reasoning rules.

Using the rules of the first type is artificially separated from the learning process. But it is clear that there is no reason to separate the process of learning rules from the process of using these rules for class identification or pattern recognition problems: both processes are interdependent and interconnected. Anyone of these processes can require executing the other. Anyone of these processes can be built into the other.

Any model of reasoning must also include STRATEGIES or the sequences of applying rules of all types in reasoning. The application of rules is conditioned by different situations occurring in the reasoning process and it is necessary to identify these situations. Strategies have a certain freedom as so it is possible to apply different rules in one and the same situation and the same rule in different situations. The choice of a strategy determines the speed, completeness, deepness and quality of reasoning.

2.1   Rules Acquired from Experts or Rules of the First Type

An expert's rules are logical assertions that describe the knowledge of specialists about a problem domain. Our experience in knowledge elicitation from experts allows us to analyze the typical forms of assertions used by experts. As an example, we give the rules of an expert's interpretation of data obtained with the use of Pathological Character Accentuation Inventory for Adolescents. This psycho-diagnostic method was elaborated by Lichko (1983) and is a classical example of an expert system.

Some examples of the expert's rules are:

"If (D - F) ≥ 4, then DISSIMULATION decreases the possibility to reveal any character accentuation and completely excludes the CYCLOID and CONFORM types of character".

"If the index E > 4, then the CYCLOID and PSYCHASTENOID types are impossible".

"If the type of character is HYPERTHYMIA, then ACCENTUATION with psychopathies is observed in 75%, with transit disturbances – in 5%, and with stable adaptation – in 5% of all cases".

"If the index A > 6 and the index S > 7 and the index Con = 0 and the index D > 6, then the LABILE type is observed".

"If the index E ≥ 6, then the SCHISOID and HYSTEROID types are observed frequently".

"If after the application of rules with the numbers x, y, z the values of at least two indices are greater than or equal to the minimal diagnostic threshold, then the mixed types are possible with the following consistent combinations of characters: Hyp - C, Hyp - N, Hyp - Hyst, C - L, L - A, L - S, and L - Hyst".

We used the following abbreviations: Hyp - hyperthymia, C - cycloid, L - labile, A – asthenia, N – neurotic, S - schizoid, Con - conformable, Hyst - hysteroid, Sens - sensitive, D - dissimulation, F - frankness, E - emancipation, and P - psychasthenia.

It is clear that an expert's assertions can be represented with the use of only one class of logical rules, namely, the rules based on implicative dependencies between names.

Implication: a, b, $c \rightarrow d$. This rule means that if the values standing in the left side of the rule are simultaneously true, then the value in the right side of the rule is always true.

An implication $x \to d$ is satisfied if and only if the set of situations in which x appears is included in the set of situations in which d appears.

Interdiction or forbidden rule (a special case of implication) $a, b, c \to false$ (*never*). This rule interdicts a combination of values enumerated in the left side of the rule. The rule of interdiction can be transformed into several implications such as $a, b \to$ not c; $a, c \to$ not b; and $b, c \to$ not a.

Compatibility: $a, b, c \to rarely$; $a, b, c \to frequently$. This rule says that the values enumerated in the left side of the rule can simultaneously occur rarely (frequently). The rule of compatibility presents the most frequently observed combination of values that is different from a law or regularity with only one or two exceptions.

Compatibility is equivalent to a collection of assertions as follows:

$a, b, c \to rarely$	$a, b, c \to frequently$,
$a, b \to c \ rarely$	$a, b \to c \ frequently$,
$a, c \to b \ rarely$	$a, c \to b \ frequently$,
$b, c \to a \ rarely$	$b, c \to a \ frequently$.

Diagnostic rule: $x, d \to a$; $x, b \to$ not a; $d, b \to false$. For example, d and b can be two values of the same attribute. This rule works when the truth of 'x' has been proven and it is necessary to determine whether 'a' is true or not. If '$x \& d$' is true, then 'a' is true, but if '$x \& b$' is true, then 'a' is false.

Rule of alternatives: a or $b \to true$ (*always*); $a, b \to false$. This rule says that 'a' and 'b' cannot be simultaneously true, either 'a' or 'b' can be true but not both.

2.2   Structure of the Knowledge Base

We describe a very simple structure of a knowledge base that is sufficient for our illustrative goal. The knowledge base (KB) consists of two parts: the Attribute Base (*AtB*), containing the relations between problem domain concepts, and the Assertion Base (*AsB*), containing the expert's assertions formulated in terms of the concepts.

The domain concepts are represented by the use of names. With respect to its role in the KB, a name can be one of two kinds: name of attribute and name of attribute value. However, with respect to its role in the problem domain, a name can be the name of an object, the name of a class of objects and the name of a classification or collection of classes. A class of objects can contain only one object hence the name of an object is a particular case of the name of a class. In the KB, names of objects and of classes of objects become names of attribute values, and names of classifications become names of attributes.

For example, let objects be a collection of trees such as asp, oak, fir-tree, cedar, pine-tree, and birch. Each name calls the class or the kind of trees (in a particular case, only one tree). Any set of trees can be partitioned into the separate groups depending on their properties. *'Kind of trees'* will be the name of a classification, in which *'asp'*, *'oak'*, *'fir-tree'*, *'cedar'*, *'pine-tree'*, and *'birch'* are the names of classes. Then, in the KB, *'kind of trees'* will be used as the name of an attribute the values of which are *'asp'*, *'oak'*, *'fir-tree'*, *'cedar'*, *'pine-tree'*, and *'birch'*. The link between the name of an attribute and the names of its values is implicative. It can be expressed by the following way:

(<name of value$_1$>, <name of value$_2$>, ... , <name of value $_k$>) → <name of attribute>,

where the sign "→" denotes the relation "is a".
In our example (*asp, oak, fir-tree, cedar, pine-tree, birch*) → *kind of trees*, and, for each value of *'kind of trees'*, the assertion of the following type can be created: "*asp* is a *kind of trees*".

The set of all attributes' names and the set of all values' names must not intersect. This means that the name of a classification cannot simultaneously be the name of a class. However, this is not the case in natural languages: the name of a class can be used for some classification and vice versa. For example, one can say that *'pine-tree'*, *'fir-tree'*, *'cedar'* are *'conifers'*. But one may also say that *'conifers'*, *'leaf-bearing'* are *'kinds of trees'*. Here the word *'conifers'* serves both as the name of a classification and as the name of a class. In this setting, class is a particular case of classification like object is a particular case of class.

By using names in the way we do in real life we permit the introduction of auxiliary names for the subsets of the set of an attribute's values. Let A be an attribute. The name of a subset of values of A will be used as the name of a new attribute which, in its turn, will serve as the name of a value with respect to A.

The *AsB* (Assertion Base) contains the expert's assertions. Each assertion links a collection of values of different attributes with a certain value of a special attribute (*SA*) that evaluates how often this collection of values appears in practice. The values of a special attribute are: *always, never, rarely,* and *frequently*. Assertions have the following form:

(<name of value>, <name of value>, ... , <value of SA>) = *true*.

For simplicity, we omit the word '*true*', because it appears in any assertion. For example, the assertion "pine-tree and cedar can be found frequently in the meadow type of forest" will be expressed in the following way: (*meadow, pine-tree, cedar, frequently*). We also omit the sign of conjunction between values of different attributes and the sign of disjunction (separating disjunction) between values of the same attribute. For example, the assertion in the form (*meadow, pine-tree, cedar, often*) is equivalent to the following expression of formal logic: P((type of forest = *meadow*) & ((kind of trees = *pine-tree*) V (kind of trees = *cedar*)) & (*SA = frequently*)) = *true*.

Only one kind of requests to the KB is used: SEARCHING VALUE OF <name of attribute> [,<name of attribute>,...] IF (<name of value>, <name of value>, ...), where "name of value" is the known value of an attribute, "name of attribute" means that the value of this attribute is unknown. For example, the request "to find the type of forest for a region with plateau, without watercourse, with the prevalence of pine-tree" will be represented as follows: SEARCHING VALUE OF the type of forest IF (*plateau, without watercourse, pine-tree*).

2.3   Reasoning Operations for Using Logical Rules of the First Type

The following rules of the second type (operations) lie in the basis of the reasoning process for solving diagnostic or pattern recognition tasks. Let x be a collection of true values observed simultaneously.

Using implication. Let r be an implication, left(r) be the left part of r and right(r) be the right part of r. If left(r) $\subseteq x$, then x can be extended by right(r): $x \leftarrow x \cup$ right(r).

For example, $x =$ '*a, b, c, d*', $r =$ '*a, d* $\rightarrow k$', $x \leftarrow x \cup k$.

Using implication is based on modus ponens: if A, then B; A; hence B.

Using interdiction. Let r be an implication $y \rightarrow$ not k. If left(r) $\subseteq x$, then k is a forbidden value for all the extensions of x.

Using interdiction is based on modus ponendo tollens:

either A or B (A, B – alternatives); A; hence not B;

either A or B; B; hence not A.

Using compatibility. Let $r =$ '*a, b, c* $\rightarrow k$, *rarely* (*frequently*)'.

If left(r) $\subseteq x$, then k can be used for an extension of x with the value of *SA* equal to '*rarely*' ('*frequently*'). The application of several rules of compatibility leads to the appearance of several values '*rarely*' and/or '*frequently*' in the extension of x. Computing the value of *SA* for the extension of x requires special consideration. In any case, the appearance of at least one value '*rarely*' means that the total result of the extension will have the value of *SA* equal to '*rarely*'. Two values equal to '*frequently*' lead to the result '*less frequently*', three values equal to '*frequently*' lead to the result '*less less frequently*' and hence the values '*rarely*' and '*frequently*' must have the ordering scale of measuring.

Using compatibility is based on modus ponens.

Using diagnostic rules. Let *r* be a diagnostic rule such as '*x, d* → *a*; *x, b* → not *a*', where '*x*' is true, and '*a*', 'not *a*' are hypotheses or possible values of some attribute. There are several ways for refuting one of the hypotheses: to infer either *d* or *b* with the use of knowledge base (*AtB, AsB*); to involve new instances from the database and/or new assertions from the knowledge base for inferring new diagnostic rules distinguishing the hypotheses '*a*' and 'not *a*'; or, eventually, ask an expert which of the values *d* or *b* is true.

Our experience shows that generally the experts have in their disposal many diagnostic rules corresponding to the most difficult diagnostic situations in their problem domain.

Using a diagnostic rule is based on modus ponens and modus ponendo tollens.

Using rule of alternatives. Let '*a*', '*b*' be two alternative hypotheses about the values of some attribute. If one of these hypotheses is inferred with the help of reasoning operations, then the other one is rejected.

Using a rule of alternatives is based on modus tollendo ponens: either *A* or *B* (*A, B* – alternatives); not *A*; hence *B*; either *A* or *B*; not *B*; hence *A*.

The operations enumerated above can be named as "forward reasoning" rules. Experts also use implicative assertions in a different way. This way can be named as "backward reasoning".

Generating hypothesis. Let *r* be an implication *y* → *k*. Then the following hypothesis is generated "if *k* is true, then it is possible that *y* is true".

Using modus tollens. Let *r* be an implication *y* → *k*. If 'not *k*' is inferred, then 'not *y*' is also inferred.

Natural diagnostic reasoning is not any method of proving the truth. It has another goal: to infer all possible hypotheses about the value of some target attribute. These hypotheses must not contradict with the expert's knowledge and the situation under consideration. The process of inferring hypotheses is reduced to extending maximally a collection *x* of attribute values such that none of the forbidden pairs of values would belong to the extension of *x*.

2.4   An Example of the Reasoning Process

Let x be a request to the KB equal to:

SEARCHING VALUE OF type of woodland IF (*plateau, without watercourse, pine-tree*).

Let the content of the Knowledge Base be the following collection of assertions:

AtB:

1. (*meadow, bilberry wood, red bilberry wood ....*) → *types of woodland*;
2. (*pine-tree, spruce, cypress, cedars, birch, larch, asp, fir-tree*) → *dominating kinds of trees*;
3. (*plateau, without plateau*) → *presence of plateau*;
4. (*top of slope, middle part of slope, ...*) → *parts of slope*;
5. (*peak of hill, foot of hill*) → *parts of hill*;
6. (*height on plateau, without height on plateau*) → *presence of a height on plateau*;
7. (*head of watercourse, low part of watercourse, ...*) → *parts of water course*;
8. (*steepness ≥ 4°, steepness ≤ 3°, steepness < 3°, ...*) → *features of slope*;
9. (*north, south, west, east*) → *the four cardinal points*;
10. (*watercourse, without watercourse*) → *presence of a watercourse*.

AsB:

11. (*meadow, pine-tree, larch, frequently*);
12. (*meadow, pine-tree, steepness ≤ 4°, never*);
13. (*meadow, larch, steepness ≥ 4°, never*);
14. (*meadow, north, west, south, frequently*);
15. (*meadow, east, rarely*);
16. (*meadow, fir-tree, birch, asp, rarely*);
17. (*meadow, plateau, middle part of slope, frequently*);
18. (*meadow, peak of hill, watercourse heads, rarely*);
19. (*plateau, steepness ≤ 3°, always*);
20. (*plateau, watercourse, rarely*);
21. (*red bilberry wood, pine-tree, frequently*);
22. (*red bilberry wood, larch, rarely*);
23. (*red bilberry wood, peak of hill, frequently*);
24. (*red bilberry wood, height on plateau, rarely*);
25. (*meadow, steepness < 3°, frequently*).

The process of reasoning evolves according to the following sequence of steps:

Step 1. Take out all the assertions t in *AsB* containing at least one value from the request, i.e. $t \in AsB$ and $t \cap x \neq \varnothing$, where x is the request. These are assertions 1, 2, 7, 9, 10, 11, and 14.

Step 2. Delete (from the set of selected assertions) all the assertions that contradict the request. Assertion 10 contradicts the request because it contains the value of attribute '*presence of water course*' which is different from the value of this attribute in the request. The remaining assertions are 1, 2, 7, 9, 11, and 14.

Step 3. Take out the values of attribute '*type of woodland*' appearing in assertions 1, 2, 7, 9, 11, and 14. We have two hypotheses: '*meadow*' and '*red bilberry*'.

Step 4. An attempt is made to refute one of the hypotheses (the application of a diagnostic rule). For this goal, it is necessary to find an assertion that has the value of *SA* equal to '*never*' and contains one of the hypotheses, some subset of values from the request and does not contain any other value. There is only one assertion with the value of *SA* equal to '*never*'. This is assertion 2: (*meadow, pine-tree, steepness* $\leq 4°$, *never*). However, we cannot use this assertion because it contains the value '*steepness* $\leq 4°$' which is not in the request.

Step 5. An attempt is made to find a value of some attribute that is not in the request (in order to extend the request). For this goal, it is necessary to find an assertion with the value of *SA* equal to '*always*' that contains a subset of values from the request and one and only one value of some new attribute the values of which are not in the request. Only one assertion satisfies this condition. This is assertion 9: (*plateau, steepness* $\leq 3°$, *always*).

Step 6. Forming the extended request:

SEARCHING VALUE OF *the type of woodland* IF (*plateau, without watercourse, pine-tree, steepness* $\leq 3°$).

Steps 1, 2, and 3 are repeated. Assertion 15 is involved in the reasoning.

Step 4 is repeated. Now assertion 2 can be used because the value '*steepness* $\leq 4°$ is in accordance with the values of '*feature of slope*' in the request. We conclude now that the type of woodland cannot be '*meadow*'. The non-refuted hypothesis is "*the type of woodland = red bilberry*".

The process of pattern recognition can require inferring new rules of the first type from data, when it is impossible to distinguish inferred hypotheses. In general, there exist two main cases to learn rules of the first type from examples in the process of pattern recognition: i) the result of reasoning contains several hypotheses and it is impossible to choose one and only one of them (uncertainty), and ii) there does not exist any hypothesis.

3. INDUCTIVE INFERENCE OF IMPLICATIVE RULES FROM EXAMPLES

3.1 The Concept of a Good Classification Test

Our approach for inferring implicative rules from examples is based on the concept of a good classification test. A good classification test can be understood as an approximation of a given classification on a given set of examples (Naidenova, 1996). On the other hand, the process of inferring good tests realizes one of the known canons of induction formulated by J. S. Mille, namely, the joint method of similarity-distinction.

A good diagnostic test for a given set of examples is defined as follows. Let R be a table of examples and S be the set of indices of examples belonging to R. Let $R(k)$ and $S(k)$ be the set of examples and the set of indices of examples from a given class k, respectively.

Denote by $FM = R/R(k)$ the examples of the classes different from class k. Let U be the set of attributes and T be the set of attributes values (values, for short) each of which appears at least in one of the examples of R. Let n be the total number of examples of R. We denote the domain of values for an attribute Atr by $dom(Atr)$, where $Atr \in U$.

By $s(a)$, $a \in T$, we denote the subset $\{i \in S: a$ appears in $t_i, t_i \in R\}$, where $S = \{1, 2, .., n\}$.

Following (Cosmadakis, et al., 1986), we call $s(a)$ the interpretation of $a \in T$ in R. It is possible to say that $s(a)$ is the set of indices of all the examples in R which are covered by the value a.

Since for all $a, b \in dom(Atr)$, $a \neq b$ implies that the intersection $s(a) \cap s(b)$ is empty, the interpretation of any attribute in R is a partition of S into a family of mutually disjoint blocks. By $P(Atr)$, we denote the partition of S induced by the values of an attribute Atr. The definition of $s(a)$ can be extended to the definition of $s(t)$ for any collection t of values as follows: for $t, t \subseteq T$, if $t = a_1 a_2 ... a_m$, then $s(t) = s(a_1) \cap s(a_2) \cap ... \cap s(a_m)$.

Definition 1. A collection $t \subseteq T (s(t) \neq \varnothing)$ of values, is a diagnostic test for the set $R(k)$ of examples if and only if the following condition is satisfied: $t \not\subset t^*$, $\forall t^*, t^* \in FM$ (the equivalent condition is $s(t) \subseteq S(k)$).

To say that a collection t of values is a diagnostic test for the set $R(k)$ is equivalent to say that it does not cover any example belonging to the classes different from k. At the same time, the condition $s(t) \subseteq S(k)$ implies that the following implicative dependency is true: 'if t, then k' and, consequently, a diagnostic test, as a collection of values, makes up the left side of a rule of the first type.

It is clear that the set of all diagnostic tests for a given set $R(k)$ of examples (call it '$DT(k)$') is the set of all the collections t of values for which the condition $s(t) \subseteq S(k)$ is true. For any pair of diagnostic tests t_i, t_j from $DT(k)$ only one of the following relations is true: $s(t_i) \subseteq s(t_j)$, $s(t_i) \supseteq s(t_j)$, $s(t_i) \approx s(t_j)$, where the last relation means that $s(t_i)$ and $s(t_j)$ are incomparable, i.e. $s(t_i) \not\subset s(t_j)$ and $s(t_j) \not\subset s(t_i)$. This consideration leads to the concept of a good diagnostic test.

Definition 2. A collection $t \subseteq T (s(t) \neq \varnothing)$ of values is a good test for the set $R(k)$ of examples if and only if the following condition is satisfied:

$s(t) \subseteq S(k)$ and simultaneously the condition $s(t) \subset s(t^*) \subseteq S(k)$ is not satisfied for any t^*, $t^* \subseteq T$, such that $t^* \neq t$.

Good diagnostic tests possess the greatest generalization power and give a possibility to obtain the smallest number of implicative rules of the first type for describing examples of a given class k.

3.2   The Characterization of Classification Tests

Any collection of values can be irredundant, redundant or maximally redundant.

Definition 3. A collection t of values is irredundant if for any value $v \in t$ the following condition is satisfied: $s(t) \subset s(t/v)$.

If a collection t of values is a good test for $R(k)$ and, simultaneously, it is an irredundant collection of values, then any proper subset of t is not a test for $R(k)$.

Definition 4. Let $X \rightarrow v$ be an implicative dependency which is satisfied in R between a collection $X \subseteq T$ of values and the value v, $v \in T$. Suppose that a collection $t \subseteq T$ of values contains X. Then the collection t is said to be redundant if it contains also the value v.

If t contains the left and the right sides of some implicative dependency $X \rightarrow v$, then the following condition is satisfied: $s(t) = s(t/v)$. In other words, a redundant collection t and the collection t/v of values cover the same set of examples.

If a good test for $R(k)$ is a redundant collection of values, then some values can be deleted from it and thus obtain an equivalent good test with a smaller number of values.

Definition 5. A collection $t \subseteq T$ of values is maximally redundant if for any implicative dependency $X \rightarrow v$ which is satisfied in R the fact that t contains X implies that t also contains v.

If t is a maximally redundant collection of values, then for any value $v \notin t$, $v \in T$ the following condition is satisfied: $s(t) \supset s(t \cup v)$. In other words, a maximally redundant collection t of values covers the number of examples greater than the collection $(t \cup v)$ of values.

Any example t in R is a maximally redundant collection of values because for any value $v \notin t$, $v \in T$ $s(t \cup v)$ is equal to $\varnothing$.

If a diagnostic test for a given set $R(k)$ of examples is a good one and it is a maximally redundant collection of values, then by adding to it any value not belonging to it we get a collection of values which is not a good test for $R(k)$.

For example, in Table 1 the collection '*Blond Bleu*' is a good irredundant test for class 1 and simultaneously it is maximally redundant collection of values. The collection '*Blond Embrown*' is a test for class 2 but it is not good test and simultaneously it is maximally redundant collection of values.

Table 1. Example 1 of Data Classification (this example is adopted from (Ganascia, 1989)).

INDEX OF EXAMPLE	HEIGHT	COLOR OF HAIR	COLOR OF EYES	CLASS
1	Low	Blond	Bleu	1
2	Low	Brown	Bleu	2
3	Tall	Brown	Embrown	2
4	Tall	Blond	Embrown	2
5	Tall	Brown	Bleu	2
6	Low	Blond	Embrown	2
7	Tall	Red	Bleu	1
8	Tall	Blond	Bleu	1

The collection '*Embrown*' is a good irredundant test for class 2. The collection '*Red*' is a good irredundant test for class 1. The collection '*Tall Red Bleu*' is a maximally redundant collection of values and it is a good test for class 1.

It is clear that the best tests for pattern recognition problems must be good irredundant tests. These tests allow construction of the shortest rules of the first type with the highest degree of generalization.

3.3   An Approach for Constructing Good Irredundant Tests

Let R, T, $s(t)$, $t \subseteq T$ be as defined earlier.

PROPOSITION 1:

The intersection of maximally redundant collections of values is a maximally redundant collection.

Proof: Let X, $Y \subseteq T$ be maximally redundant collections of values and $Z = X \cap Y$. Suppose that Z is not maximally redundant. Then there exists a value $v \in T$, $v \notin Z$ such that

$$s(Z\ v) = s(Z). \tag{1}$$

We can write $X = Z X'$ and $Y = Z Y'$.

Therefore, we have $s(Z X') = s(Z) \cap s(X')$ and $s(Z Y') = s(Z) \cap s(Y')$.

By (1), we get $s(Z X') = s(Z\ v) \cap s(X') = s(Z X'\ v)$. Hence, by $X = ZX'$, we get that $s(X) = s(X\ v)$ and X is not a maximally redundant collection of values. Similarly we get that $s(Y) = s(Y\ v)$ and Y is not a maximally redundant collection of values. Thus we have a contradiction. **End of Proof.**

Every subset $X \subseteq T$ of values generates one and only one interpretation $s(X)$ in R which follows from the definition of interpretations for a value and for a collection of values. It is clear that every collection of values is contained in one and only one maximally redundant collection of values with the same interpretation.

PROPOSITION 2:

Every collection of values is contained in one and only one maximally redundant collection with the same interpretation.

Proof: Let $X \subseteq T$ be a collection of values and $s(X)$ be the interpretation of X in R. Suppose that there are two different maximally redundant collections of values Y_1, $Y_2 \subseteq T$ such that $s(Y_1) = s(Y_2) = s(X)$. Construct the intersection t of the examples of R of which the indices belong to $s(X)$. We know that the examples of R are maximally redundant collections of values (see Section 3.2). Thus t must be a maximally redundant collection of values (Proposition 1). Y_1 is included in all the examples of which the indices belong to $s(X)$, therefore, $Y_1 \subseteq t$. Similarly $Y_2 \subseteq t$. But if Y_1 and Y_2 are the proper subsets of t, then they are not maximally redundant collections of values containing X with the interpretation equal to $s(X)$. Consequently, Y_1 must be equal to Y_2 and to t. **End of Proof.**

One of the possible ways for searching for good irredundant tests for a given class of examples is the following: first, find all good maximally redundant tests; second, for each good maximally redundant test, find all good irredundant tests contained in it. This is a convenient strategy as each good irredundant test belongs to one and only one good maximally redundant test with the same interpretation.

A good maximal redundant test for $R(k)$ either belongs to the set $R(k)$ or it is equal to the intersection of q examples from $R(k)$ for some q, $2 \le q \le nt$, where nt is the number of examples in $R(k)$.

3.4 Structure of Data for Inferring Good Diagnostic Tests

The structure of data given in Table 2 underlies algorithms of searching for good diagnostic tests. Here $S = \{1, 2, \dots, n\}$ – the set of indices of examples, $T = \{A_1, A_2, \dots, A_j, \dots A_m\}$ – the set of values of attributes. An example is a collection of values of T represented by a row of the data table.

Table 2. Structure of the Data.

S/T	A_1	A_2	...	A_J	...	A_M
1	...	...	...	...	...	...
...	...	...	...	...	...	...
N	...	...	...	...	...	...

In order to construct algorithms for finding good diagnostic tests for a given class of examples we use correspondences of Galois G on $S \times T$ and two relations $S \rightarrow T$, $T \rightarrow S$ (Ore, 1944), (Riguet, 1948). Let $s \subseteq S$, $t \subseteq T$. We define the relations as follows:

$S \rightarrow T$: $t(s) = \{$intersection of all t_i: $t_i \subseteq T$, $i \in s\}$ and
$T \rightarrow S$: $s(t) = \{i$: $i \in S$, $t \subseteq t_i\}$.

Operations $t(s)$, $s(t)$ have the following properties (Birkhoff, 1948):

$s_i \subseteq s_j \Rightarrow t(s_j) \subseteq t(s_i)$ for all s_i, $s_j \subseteq S$;
$t_i \subseteq t_j \Rightarrow s(t_j) \subseteq s(t_i)$ for all t_i, $t_j \subseteq T$;
$s \subseteq s(t(s))$ & $t(s) = t(s(t(s)))$ for all $s \subseteq S$;
$t \subseteq t(s(t))$ & $s(t) = s(t(s(t)))$ for all $t \subseteq T$;
$t(\cup s_j) = \cap t(s_j)$ for all $s_j \subseteq S$; $s(\cup t_j) = \cap s(t_j)$ for all $t_j \subseteq T$.

Extending s by an index j^* of some new example leads to receiving a more general feature of examples:

$(s \cup j^*) \supseteq s$ implies $t(s \cup j^*) \subseteq t(s)$.

Extending t by a new value A leads to decreasing the number of examples possessing the general feature 'tA' in comparison with the number of examples possessing the general feature 't':

$(t \cup A) \supseteq t$ implies $s(t \cup A) \subseteq s(t)$.

We introduce the following generalization operations (functions):

generalization_of(t) = $t' = t(s(t))$;
generalization_of(s) = $s' = s(t(s))$.

As a result of the generalization of s, the sequence of operations $s \rightarrow t(s) \rightarrow s(t(s))$ gives that $s(t(s)) \supseteq s$. This generalization operation gives all the examples possessing the feature $t(s)$.

As a result of the generalization of t, the sequence of operations $t \rightarrow s(t) \rightarrow t(s(t))$ gives that $t(s(t)) \supseteq t$. This generalization operation gives the maximal general feature for examples the indices of which are in $s(t)$.

These generalization operations are not artificially constructed operations. One can perform mentally a lot of such operations during a short period of time. We give some examples of these operations. Suppose that somebody has seen two films (s) with the participation of Gerard Depardieu $(t(s))$. After that he tries to know all the films with his participation $(s(t(s)))$. One can know that Gerard Depardieu acts with Pierre Richard (t) in several films $(s(t))$. After that he can discover that these films are the films of the same producer Francis Veber $t(s(t))$.

3.5   The Duality of Good Diagnostic Tests

We implicitly used two generalization operations in all the considerations of diagnostic tests (see Sections 3.1, 3.2, and 3.3). Now we define a diagnostic test as a dual object, i.e. as a pair (SL, TA), $SL \subseteq S$, $TA \subseteq T$, $SL = s(TA)$ and $TA = t(SL)$.

The task of inferring tests is a dual task. It must be formulated both on the set of all subsets of S, and on the set of all subsets of T.

Definition 6. Let $PM = \{s_1, s_2, ..., s_m\}$ be a family of subsets of some set M. Then PM is a Sperner system (Sperner, 1928) if the following condition is satisfied: $s_i \not\subset s_j$ and $s_j \not\subset s_i$, $\forall(i,j)$, $i \neq j$, $i, j = 1, ..., m$.

Definition 7. To find all *Good Maximally Redundant Tests* (GMRTs) for a given class $R(k)$ of examples means to construct a family PS of subsets $s_1, s_2, ..., s_{np}$ of the set S such that:

1) $s_j \subseteq S(k)$, $\forall j = 1, ..., np$;

2) PS is a Sperner system;

3) each s_j is a maximal set in the sense that adding to it the index i of the example t_i such that $i \notin s_j$, $i \in S$ implies $(s_j \cup i) \not\subset S(k)$. Putting it in another way, $t(s_j \cup i)$ is not a test for the class k, so there exists such example t^*, $t^* \in FM$ that $t(s_j \cup i) \subseteq t^*$.

The set of all GMRTs is determined as follows:

$\{t: t(s_j), s_j \in PS, \forall j, j = 1, ..., np\}$.

Definition 8. To find all GMRTs for a given class $R(k)$ of examples means to find a family PT of subsets $t_1, t_2, ..., t_{nq}$ of T such that:

1) $t_j \not\subset t$ $\forall j, j = 1, ..., nq, \forall t, t \in FM$ and, simultaneously, $\forall t_j, j = 1, ...,$ nq, $s(t_j) \neq \varnothing$ there does not exist such a collection $s^* \neq s(t_j)$, $s^* \subseteq S$ of indices for which the following condition is satisfied $s(t_j) \subset s^* \subseteq S(k)$;

2) PT is a Sperner system;

3) each t_j is a maximal set in the sense that adding to it any value $A \notin t_j$, $A \in T$ implies $s(t_j \cup A) \subset s(t_j)$.

Definition 9. To find all *Good Irredundant Tests* (GITs) for a given class $R(k)$ of examples means to find a family PRT of subsets $t_1, t_2,..., t_{nq}$ of the set T such that:

1) $t_j \not\subset t$ $\forall j, j = 1,..., nq$, $\forall t, t \in FM$ and, simultaneously, $\forall t_j, j = 1,..., nq$, $s(t_j) \neq \emptyset$ there does not exist such a collection $s^* \neq s(t_j)$, $s^* \subseteq S$ of indices for which the following condition is satisfied $s(t_j) \subset s^* \subseteq S(k)$;

2) PRT is a Sperner system;

3) each t_j – a minimal set in the sense that removing from it any value A belonging to it implies $s(t_j \text{ without } A) \supset s(t_j)$.

3.6   Generation of Dual Objects with the Use of Lattice Operations

Let MUT be the set of all dual objects, that is, the set of all pairs (s, t), $s \subseteq S$, $t \subseteq T$, $s = s(t)$ and $t = t(s)$. This set is partially ordered by the relation $\leq$, where $(s, t) \leq (s^*, t^*)$ is satisfied if and only if $s \subseteq s^*$ and $t \supseteq t^*$.

The set $\Psi = (MUT, \cup, \cap)$ is an algebraic lattice, where operations $\cup, \cap$ are defined in the following way (Wille, 1992):

$$(s^*, t^*) \cup (s, t) = ((s^* \cup s), (t^* \cap t)),$$
$$(s^*, t^*) \cap (s, t) = ((s^* \cap s), (t^* \cup t)),$$

for all pairs (s^*, t^*), $(s, t) \in MUT$.

The unit element and the zero element are $(S, \emptyset)$ and $(\emptyset, T)$, respectively.

Inferring good tests requires inferring for any element $(s^*, t^*) \in MUT$ all the elements nearest to it in the lattice with respect to the ordering $\leq$, that is, inferring all (s, t), that $(s^*, t^*) \leq (s, t)$ and there does not exist any (s^{**}, t^{**}) such that $(s^*, t^*) \leq (s^{**}, t^{**}) \leq (s, t)$, or inferring all (s, t), that $(s^*, t^*) \geq (s, t)$ and there does not exist any (s^{**}, t^{**}) such that $(s^*, t^*) \geq (s^{**}, t^{**}) \geq (s, t)$. Inferring the chains of lattice elements ordered by the inclusion relation lies in the foundation of generating all types of diagnostic tests:

(1) $s_0 \subseteq ... \subseteq s_i \subseteq s_{i+1} \subseteq ... \subseteq s_m$ $(t(s_0) \supseteq t(s_1) \supseteq ... \supseteq t(s_i) \supseteq t(s_{i+1}) \supseteq ...$ $\supseteq t(s_m))$,

(2) $t_0 \subseteq ... \subseteq t_i \subseteq t_{i+1} \subseteq ... \subseteq t_m$ $(s(t_0) \supseteq s(t_1) \supseteq ... \supseteq s(t_i) \supseteq s(t_{i+1}) \supseteq ... \supseteq s(t_m))$.

The process of generating chains of form (1) is defined as an ascending process of generating lattice chains. The process of generating chains of form (2) is defined as a descending process of generating lattice chains.

3.7   Inductive Rules for Constructing Elements of a Dual Lattice

Let R be a table of examples and S be the set of indices of examples belonging to R. Let T be the set of attributes values each of which appears at least in one of the examples of R. By $s_q = (i_1, i_2, ..., i_q)$, we denote a subset of S, containing q indices from S. By $t_q = (A_1, A_2, ..., A_q)$, we denote a subset of T, containing q values from T. It should be more convenient in the following considerations to denote the set $R(k)$ as $R(+)$ (the set of positive examples) and the set $R/R(k)$ as $R(-)$ (the set of negative examples).

There are four possible variants of inductive transition from one element of a chain to its nearest element in the lattice:

(i)   from $s_q = (i_1, i_2, ..., i_q)$ to $s_{q+1} = (i_1, i_2, ..., i_{q+1})$;

(ii)   from $t_q = (A_1, A_2, ..., A_q)$ to $t_{q+1} = (A_1, A_2, ..., A_{q+1})$;

(iii)   from $s_q = (i_1, i_2, ..., i_q)$ to $s_{q-1} = (i_1, i_2, ..., i_{q-1})$;

(iv)   from $t_q = (A_1, A_2, ..., A_q)$ to $t_{q-1} = (A_1, A_2, ..., A_{q-1})$.

Variant (i) can be used for inferring GMRTs for a given set $R(+)$ of examples. Variant (ii) is a way for inferring GITs for a given set $R(+)$ of examples directly from the set T without previously constructing the set GMRTs. Variants (iii) and (iv) are linked with variants (i) and (ii) by the duality relation.

Consider the variant (i) for inferring GMRTs.

Let S(test) be the partially ordered set of elements $s = \{i_1, i_2, ..., i_q\}$, $q = 1, 2, ..., nt$, obtained as a result of chain construction and satisfying the condition that $t(s)$ is a test for $R(+)$. Here nt denotes the number of positive examples. Let $STGOOD$ be the partially ordered set of elements s satisfying the condition that $t(s)$ is a good test for $R(+)$.

Next we will use an inductive rule for extending elements of S(test) and constructing $\{i_1, i_2, ..., i_{q+1}\}$ from $\{i_1, i_2, ..., i_q\}$, $q = 1, 2, ..., nt-1$. This rule relies on the following consideration: if the set $\{i_1, i_2, ..., i_{q+1}\}$ corresponds to a test for $R(+)$, then all its proper subsets must correspond to tests too and, consequently, they must be in S(test). Thus the set $\{i_1, i_2, ..., i_{q+1}\}$ can be constructed if and only if S(test) contains all its proper subsets. Having constructed the set $s_{q+1} = \{i_1, i_2, ..., i_{q+1}\}$, we have to determine whether it corresponds to the test or not. If $t(s_{q+1})$ is not a test, then s_{q+1} is deleted, otherwise s_{q+1} is inserted in S(test). Each element s of S(test) can have several extensions. If all the extensions of s do not correspond to tests (the set of extensions of s is empty), then s corresponds to a GMRT and it is inserted in the set $STGOOD$.

Consider variant (ii) for inferring GITs. Let $TGOOD$ be the partially ordered set of elements t satisfying the condition that t is a good irredundant test for $R(+)$. We will use a rule of inductive transition from an element

$t_q = (A_1, A_2, ..., A_q)$ of a chain to another element $t_{q+1} = (A_1, A_2, ..., A_{q+1})$. But now each element of the chain is an irredundant collection of values and not a test for $R(+)$. If $t_{q+1} = (A_1, A_2, ..., A_{q+1})$ is irredundant, then all its proper subsets must be irredundant too.

Having constructed the set $t_{q+1} = (A_1, A_2, ..., A_{q+1})$, we have to determine whether it is an irredundant collection of values or not. If t_{q+1} is redundant, then it is deleted, if t_{q+1} is a test, then t_{q+1} is inserted in the set $TGOOD$. If t_{q+1} is irredundant but not a test, then it is a candidate for extension.

Using inductive rules for generating extensions of collections of indices or values requires the implementation of special reasoning operations as shown next.

3.8   Special Reasoning Operations for Constructing Elements of a Dual Lattice

The special reasoning operations are operations that help to perform inductive extension rules effectively. These operations are described in detail in the following subsections.

3.8.1   The Generalization Rule

Consider the variant (i) (see Section 3.7) for inferring GMRTs. The inductive extension rule requires generating for each element s in $S(test)$ the set of all its subsets. The generalization rule must provide a method that allows for each element s the following:
−   To avoid constructing the set of all its subsets,
−   To avoid the repetitive generations of it.
Some different variants of this rule are possible but any of them must contain a way for choosing indices admissible for extending s. Consider one of the possible generalization rules.

Suppose that $S(test)$ and $STGOOD$ are not empty and $s \in S(test)$. We construct the set V: $V = \{\cup s', s \subseteq s', s' \in \{S(test) \cup STGOOD\}\}$.

The set V is the union of all the collections of indices in $S(test)$ and $STGOOD$ containing s, hence s is in the intersection of these collections. If we want to get an extension of s which will not be in any element of $\{S(test) \cup STGOOD\}$, then we have to use for extending s the indices which do not appear simultaneously with s in the set V. The set of indices − candidates for extending s − is the set $CAND(s) = nt/V$.

An index $j^* \in CAND(s)$ can be deleted from $CAND(s)$ if at least for one index i from s the pair $\{i, j^*\}$ either does not correspond to a test or it corresponds to a good test (it belongs to $STGOOD$).

Let Q be the set of forbidden indices for extending s:

$Q = \{\{i,j\}: t(\{i,j\})$ is not a test for $R(+)\}$.

Then the set of admissible indices will be equal to the set

$select(s) = \{i, i \in CAND(s): (\forall j)(j \in s), \{i,j\} \notin \{STGOOD$ or $Q\}\}$.

Table 1 contains a small collection of data to be classified. Consider an example of using the generalization rule.

Suppose that $STGOOD$ contains an element $s = \{2,3,5\}$ such that $t(s)$ is a test for the second class. Suppose that $S(\text{test}) = \{\{3,4\},\{3,5\},\{3,6\},\{4,6\}\}$ and $Q = \{\{2,4\},\{2,6\},\{4,5\},\{5,6\}\}$. We try to extend $s = \{3,4\}$ in order to get a new test for the second class. The set $select(s)$ of indices for extending s is $\{5, 6\}$. But only index 6 is an admissible one. The collection $\{3,4,6\}$ corresponds to a good test – '*Embrown*'.

The extending of s results in obtaining the subsets of positive examples of more and more power with more and more generalized features (set of values). This operation is analogous to the generalization rule applied for star generation under conceptual clustering (Michalski, 1983). The theoretical framework and an algorithm for partitioning data into conjunctive concepts can be found in (Michalski, 1980).

The generalization rule with searching only admissible variants of generalization is not an artificially constructed operation. A lot of examples of using this rule in human thinking can be given. For example, if your child were allergic to oranges, then you would not buy not only these fruits but also orange juice and also products that contain orange extracts. A good gardener knows the plants that cannot be adjacent in a garden. A lot of problems related to placing personnel, appointing somebody to the post, finding lodging for somebody e.t.c., deal with partitioning a set of objects or persons into groups by taking into account forbidden pairs of objects or persons.

3.8.2   The Diagnostic Rule

The diagnostic rule is intended for getting a collection of values $t_{i+1} = \{A_1, A_2, \ldots A_q, A_{q+1}\}$ from a collection $t_i = \{A_1, A_2, \ldots, A_q\}$ such that t_i is not a test but t_{i+1} is a test for a given class of positive examples.

In the general case, the extended set t_{i+1} is not a GIT, so we use the ascending process $t_{i+1} \supseteq \ldots \supseteq t_m$ $(s(t_{i+1}) \subseteq \ldots \subseteq s(t_m))$ for inferring GITs contained in t_{i+1}.

Consider an example of the diagnostic rule (see also Table 1).

Let s be equal to $\{1,2,5,7,8\}$, then $t(s) = $ '*Bleu*', where $t(s)$ is not a test for both classes 1 and 2. We can extend $t(s)$ by choosing values which appear simultaneously with it in the examples of the first class and do not appear in any example of the second class and vice versa. These values are to be said essential ones.

The set of essential values for class 1 is {*Blond, Red*}, the set of essential values for class 2 is {*Brown*}. The values '*Low*' and '*Tall*' can be deleted from consideration because they occur with the value '*Bleu*' in the examples of both classes. We have two tests containing the value '*Bleu*' for class 1 - '*Bleu Red*' (good but redundant one) and '*Bleu Blond*' (good and irredundant one), and only one test (although not a good one) for class 2 - '*Bleu Brown*'.

This diagnostic rule is the rule of the second type with the help of which the diagnostic rules of the first type are inferred. In our previous example, the following diagnostic rules of the first type have been inferred:
'*Bleu, Brown*' → '*class 2*', '*Bleu, Blond*' → '*class 1*',
'*Bleu, Red*' → '*class 1*', '*Red, Brown*' → '*false*', and
'*Blond, Brown*' → '*false*'.

The diagnostic rule for extending a collection of values is analogous to the specialization rule already defined in (Michalski, 1983), (Ganascia, 1989). If a newly presented training example contradicts an already constructed concept description, the specialization rule is applied to generate a new consistent concept description. A specialization method has been given in (Michalski and Larson, 1978).

The diagnostic rule can be applied also for searching essential values in a collection t of values that is a test for positive examples. In this case we are interested in determining such values in t whose deletion from it implies that the remaining collection of values will not be a test for positive examples. With this point of view, we will use the following definition of an essential value.

Definition 10. Let t be a collection of values that is a test for a given class of positive examples. We say that the value A in t is essential if (t/A) is not a test for a given class of positive examples.

3.8.3   The Concept of an Essential Example

By analogy with an essential value, we define an essential example.

Definition 11. Let s be a subset of indices of positive examples; assume also that $t(s)$ is not a test. The example $t_j, j \in s$ is to be said an essential one if $t(s/j)$ proves to be a test for a given class of positive examples.

For instance, the set $s = \{1,7,8\}$ contains the indices of examples of the first class (Table 1). However, $t(s)$ that is equal to the value '*Bleu*' is not a test for the first class. Deleting index 7 of example t_7 from s implies that $t(s/7)$ equal to '*Blond Bleu*' is a test for the first class. So example t_7 is found to be an essential one in the collection of examples $\{t_1, t_7, t_8\}$. The index 7 in s is the index of an essential example.

4.   ALGORITHMS FOR CONSTRUCTING ALL GOOD MAXIMALLY REDUNDANT TESTS

4.1   NIAGaRa: A Non-Incremental Algorithm for Constructing All Good Maximally Redundant Tests

Consider one of the possible non-incremental algorithms for inferring all GMRTs for a given set of positive examples. We use the ascending process $s_0 \subseteq \ldots \subseteq s_i \subseteq s_{i+1} \subseteq \ldots \subseteq s_m$ ($t(s_0) \supseteq \ldots \supseteq t(s_i) \supseteq t(s_{i+1}) \supseteq \ldots \supseteq t(s_m)$). This process is a sequence of applications of the generalization rule (see Section 3.8.1) for generating dual elements $(s_i, t(s_i))$, beginning with two initial sets $R(+) = \{t_1, t_2, \ldots, t_i, \ldots, t_{nt}\}$ and $S(+) = \{s(t_1), s(t_2), \ldots, s(t_i), \ldots, s(t_{nt})\} = \{\{1\}, \{2\}, \ldots,\{i\}, \ldots, \{nt\}\}$, where nt is the number of positive examples.

The procedure DEBUT (see also Figure 2) produces the extensions of elements of the initial set $S(+) = \{\{1\}, \{2\}, \ldots,\{i\}, \{j\},\ldots, \{nt\}\}$ and, as result, constructs the set $\{s_{12}, s_{13}, \ldots, s_{ij}, \ldots, \}$, where $s_{ij} = \{i, j\}$, $1 < i < j < nt$.

Every element $s_{ij} = \{i, j\}$, such that $t(s_{ij})$ is not a test for a given set of positive examples, is recorded in the set Q of forbidden pairs of indices. Every element $s_{ij} = \{i, j\}$, such that $t(s_{ij})$ is a test for a given set of positive examples, is generalized by the use of the function generalization_of (s_{ij}) and after that the result s = generalization_of(s_{ij}) is inserted in the set S(test).

When DEBUT terminates, it is possible to check whether an element s of S(test) corresponds to a GMRT for a given set of positive examples or not. For this goal, we use the following rule: if some index j, for $j = 1, \ldots, nt$, belongs to one and only one element s of S(test), then s can not be extended and, consequently, s corresponds to a GMRT and it is deleted from S(test) and is inserted into *STGOOD*.

In its main part, the algorithm NIAGaRa infers, for every s in S(test), the set $ext(s)$ of all possible extensions of s which correspond to tests for a given set of positive examples. The algorithm realizes a directional choice of indices for extending s with the use of the generalization rule considered in Section 3.8.1. The procedure SELECT(s) (see also Figure 3) serves this goal. It returns the set $select(s)$ of indices that are admissible to produce extensions of s corresponding to tests.

The Procedure DEBUT

Input: $R(+)$, $R(-)$, nt, $S(+) = \{\{1\},.....,\{nt\}\}$.
Output: S(test) - the set of collections of indices to be extended,
      Q - the set of forbidden pairs of indices, *STGOOD*.

  Begin
  $STGOOD \leftarrow \varnothing$; $Q \leftarrow \varnothing$; S(test) $\leftarrow \varnothing$;
  for $i = 1$, , nt: $sum(i) \leftarrow 0$;
  begin do
  $i = S[1],..., S[nt]$
  $j = S[i+1], ..., S[nt]$
  if to_be_test $(t(\{i,j\}))$ = false **then** $Q \leftarrow Q \cup \{i,j\}$;
    else s' $\leftarrow$ generalization_of($\{i,j\}$);
    for $(\forall i)$, $i \in s'$: $sum(i) \leftarrow sum(i) + 1$;
    insert s' into S(test) under lexicographic order;
  end j
  end i
  end
  begin do
  $(\forall i)$ $(i = 1, nt)$ **if** $sum(i) = 1$ **then** find s, $i \in s$, $s \in S$(test);
  insert s into *STGOOD* under lexicographic order; /* s is a GMRT */
  Delete s from S(test);
  end
  $nts \leftarrow (\cup s, s \in S$(test));
  end

Figure 2. The Beginning of the Procedure for Inferring GMRTs.

The following sets are used in this procedure: s, $not(s)$, V, $CAND(s)$, Q, S(test), and *STGOOD*.

S(test) is the partially ordered set containing all $s = \{i_1, i_2, ..., i_q\}$, $q = 1,2, ..., nt$, satisfying the condition that $t(s)$ is a maximally redundant test for a given set of positive examples but not a good one.

STGOOD is the partially ordered set containing all $s = \{i_1, i_2, ..., i_q\}$, $q = 1,2, ..., nt$, satisfying the condition that $t(s)$ is a GMRT for a given set of positive examples.

The Procedure SELECT(s)

Input: s, nts, Q, S(test), $STGOOD$.
Output: the set $select(s)$ of indices for possible extension s.

$not(s) = \{i: i \in nts, i >$ "the last index of the collection s"$\}$;
  Begin do
    if $not(s) = \varnothing$ **then** $select(s)$ ← $\varnothing$;
    else
      $V = \{\cup s', s \subseteq s', s' \in \{S(\text{test}) \cup STGOOD\}\}$;
      if $V = \varnothing$ **then** $CAND(s)$ ← $not(s)$;
    else
      $CAND(s)$ ← $not(s) \backslash V$;
      if $CAND(s) = \varnothing$ **then** $select(s)$ ← $\varnothing$
    else
      $select(s) = \{i, i \in CAND(s): (\forall j)(j \in s),$
      $\{i,j\} \notin \{STGOOD$ or $Q\}\}$,
      where $Q = \{\{i,j\}:$ to_ be_ test $(t(\{i,j\})) =$ false$\}$;
  end

Figure 3. The Procedure for Determining the Set of Indices for Extending s.

Let nts be the union of all s in S(test). Under lexicographically ordering the elements of S(test), the restricted range of searching is the set

$$not(s) = \{i: i \in nts, i > \text{"the last index of the collection } s\text{"}\}.$$

The set V is determined as the set of indices which must be deleted from nts in order not to repeat the generation of the same tests:

$$V = \{\cup s', s \subseteq s', s' \in \{S(\text{test}) \cup STGOOD\}\}.$$

The set of indices $CAND(s)$ of candidates for extending s is equal to $not(s)/V$. If V is empty, then $CAND(s)$ is equal to $not(s)$. Finally, we have that $select(s) = \{i, i \in CAND(s): (\forall j)(j \in s), \{i,j\} \notin \{STGOOD$ or $Q\}\}$.

The procedure EXTENSION(s) (see also Figure 4) takes $select(s)$ and returns the set $ext(s)$ of all possible extensions of s in the form $(s \cup j)$ for all $j, j \in select(s)$. This procedure executes the function generalization_of (s).

The Procedure EXTENSION(s)

Input: *s*, *select*(*s*), *S*(test), *STGOOD*.
Output: *ext*(*s*) – the set of all extensions *s'* of *s* such that
t(*s'*) is a test and $||s'|| = ||s|| + 1$.
snew – a current extension of *s*.

  Begin
  ext(*s*) = ∅;
  while *select*(*s*) ≠ ∅
  snew ← *s* ∪ *j*, *j* ∈ *select*(*s*);
  if to_be_test(*t*(*snew*)) = false **then** eliminate *snew*; **else**

  Begin do
  snew ← generalization_of(*snew*);
  insert *snew* into *ext*(*s*) under lexicographic order;
  end
  end while

  end

Figure 4. The Procedure for Generating All Possible Extensions of *s*.

The procedure ANALYSIS_OF_EXTENTIONS(*s*) (see also Figure 5) checks the set *ext*(*s*). If *ext*(*s*) is empty and *V* is empty, then *s* corresponds to a GMRT and *s* is transferred from *S*(test) to *STGOOD*. If *ext*(*s*) contains one and only one element *snew*, then *snew* corresponds to a GMRT, *snew* is inserted into *STGOOD* and *s* is deleted from *S*(test). In all other cases, the set *ext*(*s*) substitutes *s* in *S*(test).

The set *nts* is modified during the process of inferring GMRTs and it may happen that the function to_be_test(*t*(*nts*)) = *true*. This condition indicates that the process of inferring GMRTs is over. The task also stops when *S*(test) is empty.

Finally, the set *TGOOD* of all GMRTs for a given set of positive examples is formed as follows: *TGOOD* = {*t*(*s*): *s* ∈ *STGOOD*}.

The procedure NIAGaRa (see also Figure 6) uses the procedures DEBUT, SELECT(*s*), ESTENSION(*s*), and ANALYSIS_ OF_ EXTENSION(*s*).

The Procedure ANALYSIS_OF_EXTENSION (s)
Input: $ext(s)$, S(test), $STGOOD$.
Output: the modified sets S(test) and $STGOOD$.

Begin
if $ext(s) = \varnothing$ and $V = \varnothing$ then
    Begin   /* s corresponds to a GMRT */;
    do
    insert s into $STGOOD$ under lexicographic order;
    end
if $\|ext(s)\| = 1$ then
    Begin do /* $snew$ corresponds to a GMRT */;
    insert $snew$ into $STGOOD$ under lexicographic order;
    end
Begin do
($\forall$ $snew$) ($snew \in ext(s)$)
insert $snew$ into S(test) under lexicographic order;
end
S(test) $\leftarrow S$(test)$/s$;
end

Figure 5. The Procedure for Analyzing the Set of Extensions of s.

The following Tables 3 and 4 illustrate the work of the procedure NIAGaRa for inferring all the GMRTs for the examples of class 2 (see also Table 1). In this example, the set $STGOOD$ is empty after the procedure DEBUT is over. We give the other example of how the algorithm NIAGaRa works in the Appendix. Next we turn to consider the computational complexity of the algorithm and procedures described.

The problem of generating all GMRTs for a given set of positive examples is NP-complete because the number of GMRTs may be exponentially large. In the worst case, the number of GMRTs is $O(2^{|T|}/|T|^{1/2})$.

The algorithm NIAGaRa is optimal in the sense that it generates each element s only once.

In essence, the number of elements of the set Q determines "virtually" the computational complexity of the algorithm. The increase of this number is equivalent to the decrease of the number of positive examples. Since class 2 contains 5 positive examples (lines 2, 3, 4, 5, and 6 in Table 1), it is possible to generate only 10 pairs of examples of this class. But 4 of these pairs are forbidden ones (Q has 4 elements). Therefore, only 6 pairs of positive examples determine the number of dual lattice elements to be generated by the algorithm. Thus, we have a "virtual" set of positive examples with 4 elements (6 pairs can be generated by four elements). As $C_4^3 = 4$, it is possible to construct only 4 triples from the set of four elements.

This estimation is very rough because we deal with the sets S(test) and Q which are not compact. Actually only two triples have been constructed in the illustrative example (Table 3).

The Procedure NIAGaRa

Input: $R(+)$, $R(-)$, nt, $S(+) = \{\{1\},....,\{nt\}\}$.
Output: the set $TGOOD$ of all GMRTs
for positive examples.

DEBUT;
Begin do
while S(test) $\neq \varnothing$ or to_be_test($t(nts)$) = false **do**

SELECT(s);
EXTENSION(s);
ANALYSIS_OF_EXTENSION(s);

$nts ::= (\cup \ s, s \in S(\text{test}))$;

end while
construct $TGOOD$ from $STGOOD$;
end

Figure 6. The Main Procedure NIAGaRa for Inferring GMRTs.

Table 3. The Results of the Procedure DEBUT for the Examples of Class 2 (see also Table 1).

S	t(s)	Test?	Generalization_of(s)	Q	S(test)
{2,3}	Brown	Yes	{2,3,5}		{2,3,5}
{2,4}	∅	No		{2,4}	
{2,5}	Brown Bleu	Yes	{2,5}		{2,5}
{2,6}	Low	No		{2,6}	
{3,4}	Tall Embrown	Yes	{3,4}		{3,4}
{3,5}	Tall Brown	Yes	{3,5}		{3,5}
{3,6}	Embrown	Yes	{3,4,6}		{3,4,6}
{4,5}	Tall	No		{4,5}	
{4,6}	Blond Embrown	Yes	{4,6}		{4,6}
{5,6}	∅	No		{5,6}	

In our illustrative example in the Appendix, the initial set S(test) contains 25 elements (admissible pairs of indices of positive examples). It roughly corresponds to decreasing the number of positive examples from 14 to 8.

Table 4. The Result of Inferring GMRTs for the Examples of Class 2 (see also Table 1).

S	not(s)	V	CAND(s)	select(s)	ext(s)	Results
{2,3,5}	{6}	∅	{6}	∅	∅	{2,3,5} → STGOOD
{2,5}	{6}	{2,3,5}	{6}	∅	∅	{2,5} → delete
{3,4}	{5,6}	{3,4,6}	{5}	∅	∅	{3,4} → delete
{3,4,6}	∅	∅	∅	∅	∅	{3,4,6} → STGOOD
{3,5}	{6}	{2,3,5}	{6}	∅	∅	{3,5} → delete
{4,6}	∅	{3,4,6}	∅	∅	∅	{4,6} → delete

If we know the number of pairs of elements of some set with N elements, then we can compute the number of subsets of this set with 3, 4, ... , N-1 elements as follows: $C_N^3 = C_N^2 (N - 2)/3$; $C_N^4 = C_N^2 [(N-3)/4][(N - 2)/3]$; ......; $C_N^K = C_N^2 2 (N - 2)!/[(N-k)!k!]$. Table 5 shows the number of combinations C_N^2, C_N^3, C_N^4 as a function of N. For the set of N elements when $N = 14$ the number of pairs of its elements is equal to 91, the number of triples of its elements is equal to 364 and the number of its subsets containing 4 elements is equal to 1001. Decreasing the number of pairs by 2 times (which is equivalent to decreasing N from 14 to 10) implies decreasing the number of triples by 3 times and the number of subsets containing 4 elements – by 5 times.

Table 5. The Number of Combinations C_N^2, C_N^3, C_N^4 as a Function of N.

N	4	5	6	7	8	9	10	11	12	13	14
C_N^2	6	10	15	21	28	36	45	55	66	78	91
C_N^3	4	10	20	35	56	84	120	165	220	286	364
C_N^4	1	5	15	35	70	126	210	330	495	715	1001

The computational complexity of the procedures DEBUTE, SELECT(s), ESTENSION(s) and ANALYSIS_OF_EXTENSION(s) depends on the computational complexity of the functions generalization_of (s), to_be_test($t(s)$) and the operation which inserts an element s into one of the sets ext(s), S(test) or STGOOD.

The function generalization_of (s) is of time complexity of order O(nt), where nt is the number of positive examples. The function to_be_test($t(s)$) can be reduced to checking whether $s(t)$ contains at least one index of negative example or not. It can be implemented by the use of radix sorting which sorts n integers in time O(n) (Aho et al., 1974). Therefore, the function to_be_test($t(s)$) is of time complexity of order O($nt + nf$), where nt and nf the number of positive and negative examples, respectively.

The operation of inserting an element s into the sets $ext(s)$, $S(test)$ or *STGOOD* under lexicographically ordering of these sets is reduced to lexicographically sorting a sequence of k-element collections of integers (element s is considered as a collection of integers). A sequence of n collections, the components of which are represented by integers from 1 to m, is sorted in time of $O(m + L)$, where L is the sum of lengths of all the collections of this sequence (Aho et al., 1974). Consequently, if *Lext*, *Lstest*, *Lgtest* are the sums of lengths of all the collections s of $ext(s)$, $S(test)$ and *STGOOD*, respectively, then the time complexity of inserting an element s into $ext(s)$ is of order $O(|T| + Lext)$, the time complexity of inserting an element s into $S(test)$ is of order $O(|T| + Lstest)$, and the time complexity of inserting an element s into *STGOOD* is of order $O(|T| + Lgtest)$.

The procedure DEBUT has a polynomial time complexity of order $O(nt^2(nt + nf) + nt^3) + O(nt^2 (|T| + Lstest)) + O(nt (|T| + Lgtest))$. The procedure SELECT($s$) has a polynomial time complexity of order $O((mt+mg) + nt^2)$, where mt – the number of elements of $S(test)$, mg – the number of elements of *STGOOD*.

The procedure EXTENSION(s) has a polynomial time complexity of order $O(nt (nf + nt)) + O(nt^2) + O(nt (|T| + Lext))$. The procedure ANALYSIS_OF_EXTENSION(s) has a polynomial time complexity of order $O(nt (|T| + Lstest + Lgtest))$.

The algorithm NIAGaRa finds all the GMRTs for a given set of positive examples but the number of these GMRTs can be exponentially large. In this case, this algorithm will be not realistic. Now we consider some decompositions of the problem that provide the possibility to restrict the domain of searching, to predict, in some degree, the number of tests, and to choose tests with the use of essential values and/or examples.

4.2   Decomposition of Inferring Good Classification Tests into Subtasks

We consider two kinds of subtasks: for a given set of positive examples (1) given a positive example t, find all GMRTs contained in t; (2) given a non-empty collection of values X (maybe only one value) such that it is not a test, find all GMRTs containing X. Each example contains only some subset of values from T, hence each subtask of the first kind is simpler than the initial one. Each subset X of T appears only in a part of all examples, hence each subtask of the second kind is simpler than the initial one.

4.2.1   Forming the Subtasks

The subtask of the first kind. We introduce the concept of an example's projection $proj(R)[t]$ of a given positive example t on a given set $R(+)$ of positive examples. The $proj(R)[t]$ is the set $Z = \{z:$ (z is non empty intersection of t and t') & ($t' \in R(+)$) & (z is a test for a given class of positive examples)$\}$.

If the $proj(R)[t]$ is not empty and contains more than one element, then it is a subtask for inferring all GMRTs that are in t. If the projection contains one and only one element equal to t, then t is a GMRT.

To make the operation of forming a projection perfectly clear we construct the projection of t_2 = '*Low Brown Bleu*' on the examples of the second class (Table 1). This projection includes t_2 and the intersections of t_2 with the other positive examples of the second class, i.e. with the examples t_3, t_4, t_5, t_6 (Table 6).

Table 6. The Intersections of Example t_2 with the Examples of Class 2.

INDEX OF EXAMPLE	HEIGHT	COLOR OF HAIR	COLOR OF EYES	TEST?
2	Low	Brown	Bleu	Yes
3		Brown		Yes
4				No
5		Brown	Bleu	Yes
6	Low			No

In order to check whether an element of the projection is a test or not we use the function to_be_test(t) in the following form:

to_be_test(t) = if $s(t) \subseteq s(+)$ then true else false,

where $s(+)$ is the set of indices of positive examples, $s(t)$ is the set of indices of all positive and negative examples containing t. If $s(-)$ is the set of indices of negative examples, then $S = s(+) \cup s(-)$ and $s(t) = \{i: t \subseteq t_i, i \in S\}$.

Table 7. The Projection of the Example t_2 on the Examples of Class 2.

INDEX OF EXAMPLE	HEIGHT	COLOR OF HAIR	COLOR OF EYES	TEST?
2	Low	Brown	Bleu	Yes
3		Brown		Yes
5		Brown	Bleu	Yes

The intersection $t_2 \cap t_4$ is the empty set. Hence the row of the projection with the number 4 is empty. The intersection $t_2 \cap t_6$ is not a test for the second class because $s(Low) = \{1,2,6\} \not\subset s(+)$, where $s(+)$ is equal to $\{2,3,4,5,6\}$. Finally, we have the projection of t_2 on the examples of the second class in Table 7.

The subtask turns out to be very simple because the intersection of all the rows of the projection is a test for the second class: $t(\{2,3,5\}) = $ '*Brown*', $s(Brown) = \{2,3,5\}$ and $\{2,3,5\} \subseteq s(+)$.

The subtask of the second kind. We introduce the concept of an attributive projection $proj(R)[A]$ of a given value A on a given set $R(+)$ of positive examples.

The projection $proj(R)[A] = \{t: (t \in R(+)) \ \& \ (A$ appears in $t)\}$. Another way to define this projection is: $proj(R)[A] = \{t_i: i \in (s(A) \cap s(+))\}$. If the attributive projection is not empty and contains more than one element, then it is a subtask of inferring all GMRTs containing a given value A. If A appears in one and only one example, then A does not belong to any GMRT different from this example.

Forming the projection of A makes sense if A is not a test and the intersection of all positive examples in which A appears is not a test too, i.e. $s(A) \not\subset s(+)$ and $t' = t(s(A) \cap s(+))$ is not a test for a given set of positive examples.

Denote the set $\{s(A) \cap s(+)\}$ by $splus(A)$. In Table 1, we have:
$s(+) = \{2,3,4,5,6\}$, $splus(Low) \rightarrow \{2,6\}$, $splus(Brown) \rightarrow \{2,3,5\}$, $splus(Bleu) \rightarrow \{2,5\}$, $splus(Tall) \rightarrow \{3,4,5\}$, $splus(Embrown) \rightarrow \{3,4,6\}$, and $splus(Blond) \rightarrow \{4,6\}$.

For the value '*Brown*' we have:
$s(Brown) = \{2,3,5\}$ and $s(Brown) = splus(Brown)$, i.e. $s(Brown) \subseteq s(+)$.

Analogously for the value '*Embrown*' we have: $s(Embrown) = \{3,4,6\}$ and $s(Embrown) = splus(Embrown)$, i.e. $s(Embrown) \subseteq s(+)$.

Table 8. The Result of Reducing the Projection after Deleting the Values '*Brown*' and '*Embrown*'.

INDEX OF EXAMPLE	HEIGHT	COLOR OF HAIR	COLOR OF EYES	TEST?
2	Low		Bleu	No
3	Tall			No
4	Tall	Blond		No
5	Tall		Bleu	No
6	Low	Blond		No

These values are irredundant and simultaneously maximally redundant tests because $t(\{2,3,5\}) = $ '*Brown*' and $t(\{3,4,6\}) = $ '*Embrown*'. It is clear that these values cannot belong to any test different from them. We delete '*Brown*' and '*Embrown*' from further consideration with the following result as shown in Table 8.

Now none of the remaining rows of the second class is a test because $s(Low, Bleu) = \{1,2\}$, $s(Tall) = \{3,4,5,7,8\}$, $s(Tall, Blond) = \{4,8\}$, $s(Tall, Bleu) = \{5,7,8\}$, $s(Low, Blond) = \{1,6\} \not\subset s(+)$. The values '*Brown*' and '*Embrown*' exhaust the set of the GMRTs for this class of positive examples.

4.2.2   Reducing the Subtasks

The following theorem gives the foundation for reducing projections both of the first and the second kind.

THEOREM 1:

Let A be a value from T, X be a maximally redundant test for a given set R(+) of positive examples and s(A) ⊆ s(X). Then A does not belong to any maximally redundant good test for R(+) different from X.

Proof: Case 1. X is a good maximally redundant test (GMRT) for $R(+)$. Suppose that A appears in Y, Y is a GMRT for $R(+)$ different from X. Then $s(Y)$ is a proper subset of $s(A)$. However, we have that $s(A) \subseteq s(X)$ and hence $s(Y)$ is a proper subset of $s(X)$. However, it is impossible as the set of GMRTs is a Sperner system and hence $s(Y)$ and $s(X)$ does not contain each other.

Case 2. X is a maximally redundant test for $R(+)$ but not a good one. Suppose that there exists a GMRT Y such that A appears in Y. Next observe that $s(Y)$ is a proper subset of $s(A)$ and $s(Y)$ is a proper subset of $s(X)$. Then $X \subseteq Y$ and X is not a maximally redundant test. We have a contradiction. **End of Proof.**

Table 9. Example 2 of a Data Classification.

INDEX OF EXAMPLE	HEIGHT	COLOR OF HAIR	COLOR OF EYES	CLASS
1	Low	Blond	Bleu	1
2	Low	Brown	Bleu	1
3	Tall	Brown	Embrown	1
4	Tall	Blond	Embrown	2
5	Tall	Brown	Bleu	2
6	Low	Blond	Embrown	2
7	Tall	Red	Bleu	2
8	Tall	Blond	Bleu	2

To illustrate the way of reducing projections, we consider another partition of the rows of Table 1 into the sets of positive and negative examples as shown in Table 9.

Let $s(+)$ be equal to $\{4,5,6,7,8\}$. The value '*Red*' is a test for positive examples because $s(Red) = splus(Red) = \{7\}$. Delete '*Red*' from the projection. The value '*Tall*' is not a test because $s(Tall) = \{3,4,5,7,8\}$ and it is not equal to $splus(Tall) = \{4,5,7,8\}$. Also $t(splus(Tall)) =$ '*Tall*' is not a test. The attributive projection of the value '*Tall*' on the set of positive examples is in Table 10.

Table 10. The Projection of the Value '*Tall*' on the Set $R(+)$.

INDEX OF EXAMPLE	HEIGHT	COLOR OF HAIR	COLOR OF EYES	CLASS
4	Tall	Blond	Embrown	2
5	Tall	Brown	Bleu	2
7	Tall		Bleu	2
8	Tall	Blond	Bleu	2

In this projection, $splus(Bleu) = \{5,7,8\}$, $t(splus(Bleu)) =$ '*Tall Bleu*', $s(Tall\ Bleu) = \{5,7,8\} = splus(Tall\ Bleu)$ hence '*Tall Bleu*' is a test for the second class. We have also that $splus(Brown) = \{5\}$, but $\{5\} \subseteq \{5,7,8\}$ and, consequently, there does not exist any good test which contains simultaneously the values '*Tall*' and '*Brown*'.

Delete '*Bleu*' and '*Brown*' from the projection as shown in Table 11.

Table 11. The Projection of the Value '*Tall*' on the Set $R(+)$ without the Values '*Bleu*' and '*Brown*'.

INDEX OF EXAMPLE	HEIGHT	COLOR OF HAIR	COLOR OF EYES	CLASS
4	Tall	Blond	Embrown	2
5	Tall			2
7	Tall			2
8	Tall	Blond		2

However, now the rows t_5 and t_7 are not tests for the second class and they can be deleted as shown in Table 12.

The intersection of the remaining rows of the projection is '*Tall Blond*'. We have that $s(Tall\ Blond) = \{4,8\} \subseteq s(+)$ and this collection of values is a test for the second class.

Table 12. The Projection of the Value '*Tall*' on the Set $R(+)$ without the Examples t_5 and t_7.

INDEX OF EXAMPLE	HEIGHT	COLOR OF HAIR	COLOR OF EYES	CLASS
4	Tall	Blond	Embrown	2
8	Tall	Blond		2

As we have found all the tests for the second class containing '*Tall*' we can delete '*Tall*' from the examples of the second class as shown in Table 13. Next we can delete the rows t_5, t_7, and t_8. The result is in Table 14.

The intersection of the remaining examples of the second class gives a test '*Blond Embrown*' because

$s(Blond\ Embrown) = splus(Blond\ Embrown) = \{4,6\} \subseteq s(+).$

The choice of values or examples for forming a projection requires special consideration.

In contrast to incremental learning, where the problem is considered of how to choose relevant knowledge to be best modified, here we come across the opposite goal to eliminate irrelevant knowledge not to be processed.

Table 13. The Result of Deleting the Value '*Tall*' from the Set $R(+)$.

INDEX OF EXAMPLE	HEIGHT	COLOR OF HAIR	COLOR OF EYES	CLASS
1	Low	Blond	Bleu	1
2	Low	Brown	Bleu	1
3	Tall	Brown	Embrown	1
4		Blond	Embrown	2
5		Brown	Bleu	2
6	Low	Blond	Embrown	2
7			Bleu	2
8		Blond	Bleu	2

Table 14. The Result of Deleting t_5, t_7, and t_8 from the Set $R(+)$.

INDEX OF EXAMPLE	HEIGHT	COLOR OF HAIR	COLOR OF EYES	CLASS
1	Low	Blond	Bleu	1
2	Low	Brown	Bleu	1
3	Tall	Brown	Embrown	1
4		Blond	Embrown	2
6	Low	Blond	Embrown	2

4.2.3   Choosing Examples and Values for the Formation of Subtasks

Next it is shown that it is convenient to choose essential values in an example and essential examples in a projection for the decomposition of the main problem of inferring GMRTs into the subtasks of the first or second kind.

An Approach for Searching for Essential Values:

Let t be a test for positive examples. Construct the set of intersections $\{t \cap t': t' \in R(-)\}$. It is clear that these intersections are not tests for positive examples. Take one of the intersections with the maximal number of values in it. The values complementing the maximal intersection in t is the minimal set of essential values in t.

Return to Table 9. Exclude the value '*Red*' (we know that '*Red*' is a test for the second class) and find the essential values for the examples t_4, t_5, t_6, t_7, and t_8. The result is in Table 15.

Consider the value '*Embrown*' in t_6:

$splus(Embrown) = \{4,6\}$, $t(\{4,6\}) = $ '*Blond Embrown*' is a test.

The value '*Embrown*' can be deleted. But this value is only one essential value in t_6 and, therefore, t_6 can be deleted too. After that $splus(Blond)$ is modified to the set $\{4,8\}$.

Table 15. The Essential Values for the Examples t_4, t_5, t_6, t_7, and t_8.

INDEX OF EXAMPLE	HEIGHT	COLOR OF HAIR	COLOR OF EYES	ESSENTIAL VALUES	CLASS
1	Low	Blond	Bleu		1
2	Low	Brown	Bleu		1
3	Tall	Brown	Embrown		1
4	Tall	Blond	Embrown	Blond	2
5	Tall	Brown	Bleu	Bleu, Tall	2
6	Low	Blond	Embrown	Embrown	2
7	Tall		Bleu	Tall, Bleu	2
8	Tall	Blond	Bleu	Tall	2

We observe that $t(\{4,8\}) = $ '*Tall Blond*' is a test. Hence the value '*Blond*' can be deleted from further consideration together with the row t_4. Now the intersection of the rows t_5, t_7, and t_8 produces the test '*Tall Bleu*'.

An Approach for Searching for Essential Examples:

We need the set *STGOOD* to find indices of essential examples in some subset s^* of indices for which $t(s^*)$ is not a test. Let $s^* = \{i_1, i_2, \ldots, i_q\}$. Construct the set of intersections $\{s^* \cap s': s' \in STGOOD\}$. Any obtained intersection $s^* \cap s'$ corresponds to a test for positive examples. Take one of the intersections with the maximal number of indices. The subset of s^* complementing in s^* the maximal intersection is the minimal set of indices of essential examples in s^*. For instance, $s^* = \{2,3,4,7,8\}$, $s' = \{2,3,4,7\}$, $s' \in STGOOD$, hence 8 is the index of essential example t_8.

In the beginning of inferring GMRTs, the set *STGOOD* is empty. Next we describe the procedure with the use of which a quasi-maximal subset of $s*$ that corresponds to a test is obtained.

We begin with the first index i_1 of $s*$, then we take the next index i_2 of $s*$ and evaluate the function to_be_test ($t(\{i_1, i_2\})$). If the value of the function is "true", then we take the next index i_3 of $s*$ and evaluate the function to_be_test ($t(\{i_1, i_2, i_3\})$). If the value of the function is "false", then the index i_2 of $s*$ is skipped and the function to_be_test ($t(\{i_1, i_3\})$) is evaluated. We continue this process until we achieve the last index of $s*$.

For example, in Table 9, $s(+) = \{4,5,6,7,8\}$. The value '*Red*' is a test for positive examples because of $s(Red) = splus(Red) = \{7\}$. Delete '*Red*' from the projection. Find the quasi-minimal subset of indices of essential examples for $s(+)$. Using the procedure described above we get that $t(\{4,6\}) = $ '*Blond Embrown*' is a test for the second class and 5,7,8 are the indices of essential examples in $s(+)$. Consider row t_5. We know that '*Bleu*' is essential in it. We have $t(splus\{Bleu\}) = t(\{5,7,8\}) = $ '*Tall Bleu*', and, consequently, '*Tall Bleu*' is a test for the second class of examples. Delete '*Bleu*' and t_5. Now t_7 is not a test and we delete it. After that $splus(Tall)$ is modified to be the set $\{4,8\}$, and $t(\{4,8\}) = $ '*Tall Blond*' is a test. Hence the value '*Tall*' together with row t_8 cannot be considered for searching for new tests. Finally $s(+) = \{4,6\}$ corresponds to the test already known.

4.2.4   An Approach for Incremental Algorithms

The decomposition of the main problem of inferring GMRTs into subtasks of the first or second kind gives the possibility to construct incremental algorithms for this problem. The simplest way to do it consists of the following steps: choose example (value), form subproblem, solve subproblem, delete example (value) after the subproblem is over, reduce $R(+)$ and T and check the condition of ending the main task. This process involves deductive reasoning as its inherent part: one must choose examples or values for a subproblem by using different criteria or considerations.

A recursive procedure for using attributive subproblems for inferring GMRTs has been described in (Naidenova et al., 1995b). Some complexity evaluations of this algorithm can be found in (Naidenova and Ermakov, 2001). In the following part of this chapter, we give an algorithm for inferring GMRTs the core of which is the decomposition of the main problem into the subtasks of the first kind combined with searching essential examples.

4.3   DIAGaRa: An Algorithm for Inferring All GMRTs with the Decomposition into Subtasks of the First Kind

The algorithm DIAGaRa for inferring all the GMRTs with the decomposition into subproblems of the first kind is briefly described in Figure 7.

4.3.1   The Basic Recursive Algorithm for Solving a Subtask of the First Kind

The initial information for the algorithm of finding all the GMRTs contained in a positive example is the projection of this example on the current set $R(+)$. Essentially the projection is simply a subset of examples defined on a certain restricted subset t^* of values. Let s^* be the subset of indices of examples from $R(+)$ which have produced the projection.

$$s^* \leftarrow s(+) = \{1, \, , nt\};$$
$$t^* \leftarrow T;$$
$$\textbf{D o}$$
$$\textbf{B e g i n}$$

Find all the GMRTs for a given set of positive examples with the use of the basic algorithm of solving subtask of the first kind;

$$\textbf{E n d}$$

Figure 7. The Algorithm DIAGaRa.

It is useful to introduce the characteristic $W(t)$ of any collection t of values named by the weight of t in the projection: $W(t) = \|s^* \cap s(t)\|$ is the number of positive examples of the projection containing t. Let $WMIN$ be the minimal permissible value of the weight.

The basic algorithm consists of applying the sequence of the following steps:

Step 1. Check whether the intersection of all the elements of projection is a test and if so, then s^* is stored in $STGOOD$ if s^* corresponds to a good test at the current step; in this case the subtask is over. Otherwise the next step is performed.

Step 2. For each value A in the projection, the set $splus(A) = \{s^* \cap s(A)\}$ and the weight $W(A) = \|splus(A)\|$ are determined and if the weight is less than the minimum permissible weight $WMIN$, then the value A is deleted from the projection. We can also delete the value A if $W(A)$ is equal to

WMIN and *t*(*splus*(*A*)) is not a test − in this case *A* will not appear in a maximally redundant test *t* with *W*(*t*) equal to or greater than *WMIN*.

Step 3. The generalization operation is performed: $t' = t(splus(A))$, $A \in t^*$; if t' is a test, then the value *A* is deleted from the projection and *splus*(*A*) is stored in *STGOOD* if *splus*(*A*) corresponds to a good test at the current step.

Step 4. The value *A* can be deleted from the projection if $splus(A) \subseteq s'$ for some $s' \in STGOOD$.

Step 5. If at least one value has been deleted from the projection, then the reduction of the projection is necessary. The reduction consists of deleting the elements of projection that are not tests (as a result of previous eliminating values). If, under reduction, at least one element has been deleted from the projection, then Step 2, Step 3, Step 4, and Step 5 are repeated.

Step 6. Check whether the subtask is over or not. The subtask is over when either the projection is empty or the intersection of all elements of the projection corresponds to a test (see Step 1). If the subtask is not over, then the choice of an essential example in this projection is performed and the new subtask is formed with the use of this essential example. The new subsets s^* and t^* are constructed and the basic algorithm runs recursively. The important part of the basic algorithm is how to form the set *STGOOD*.

4.3.2   An Approach for Forming the Set *STGOOD*

Let *L*(*S*) be the set of all subsets of the set *S*. *L*(*S*) is the set lattice (Rasiova, 1974). The ordering determined in the set lattice coincides with the set-theoretical inclusion. It will be said that subset s_1 is absorbed by subset s_2, i.e. $s_1 \le s_2$, if and only· if the inclusion relation is hold between them, i.e. $s_1 \subseteq s_2$. Under formation of *STGOOD*, a collection *s* of indices is stored in *STGOOD* if and only if it is not absorbed by any collection of this set. It is necessary also to delete from *STGOOD* all the collections of indices that are absorbed by *s* if *s* is stored in *STGOOD*. Thus, when the algorithm is over, the set *STGOOD* contains all the collections of indices that correspond to GMRTs and only such collections. Essentially the process of forming *STGOOD* is an incremental procedure of finding all maximal elements of a partially ordered set. The set *TGOOD* of all the GMRTs is obtained as follows: $TGOOD = \{t: t = t(s), (\forall s) (s \in STGOOD)\}$.

4.3.3   The Estimation of the Number of Subtasks to Be Solved

The number of subtasks at each level of recursion is determined by the number of essential examples in the projection associated with this level.

The depth of recursion for any subtask is determined by the greatest cardinality (call it 'CAR') of set-theoretical intersections of elements $s \in STGOOD$ corresponding to GMRTs:

$$CAR = \max (\|s_i \cap s_j\|, \forall(s_i, s_j)\, s_i, s_j \in STGOOD).$$

In the worst case, the number of subtasks to be solved is of order $O(2^{CAR})$.

4.3.4   CASCADE: Incrementally Inferring GMRTs Based on the Procedure DIAGaRa

The algorithm CASCADE serves for inferring all the GMRTs of maximal weight. At the beginning of the algorithm, the values are arranged in decreasing order of weight such that $W(A_1) \geq W(A_2) \geq\ \geq W(A_m)$, where $A_1, A_2,\ , A_m$ is a permutation of values. The shortest sequence of values $A_1, A_2,\ A_j, j \leq m$ is defined such that it is a test for positive examples and $WMIN$ is made equal to $W(A_j)$. The procedure DIAGaRa tries to infer all the GMRTs with weight equal to $WMIN$. If such tests are obtained, then the algorithm stops. If such tests are not found, then $WMIN$ is decreased, and the procedure DIAGaRa runs again.

4.4   INGOMAR: An Incremental Algorithm for Inferring All GMRTs

In this section, we consider an incremental learning algorithm useful when a new portion of observations or examples becomes available over time. Suppose that each new example comes with the indication of its class membership. The following actions are necessary with the arrival of a new example:

– Check whether it is possible to perform generalization of some existing GMRTs for the class to which the new example belongs (class of positive examples), i.e., whether it is possible to extend the set of examples covered by some existing GMRTs or not.
– Infer all the GMRTs contained in the new example.
– Check the validity of the existing GMRTs for negative examples, and if it necessary:
– Modify tests that are not valid (test for negative examples is not valid if it is included in a positive example, i.e., in other words, it accepts an example of positive class).

Thus the process of inferring all the GMRTs is divided into three subtasks.

These three subtasks conform to three acts of reasoning:

1)   pattern recognition or using already known rules (tests) for determining the class membership of a new positive example and generalization of these rules (deductive reasoning);

2)   inferring new rules (tests) that are generated by a new positive example (inductive reasoning a new knowledge);

3)   diagnostic operation or correcting rules (tests) of alternative (negative) classes that accept a new positive example (these rules do not permit to distinguish a new positive example from some negative examples).

The first act is performed by the procedure GENERALIZATION $(STGOOD, j*)$ (Figure 8).

The second act is reduced to the subtask of the first kind. The procedure FORMSUBTASK$(j*)$ is intended for preparing initial data for inferring all the GMRTs contained in the example with the index $j*$: the set S(test)(+) - the set of collections of indices to be extended and the set Q(+) - the set of forbidden pairs of indices. This procedure is presented in Figure 9. The procedure NIAGaRa can be used for inferring all the GMRTs contained in the example with the index $j*$.

The Procedure
GENERALIZATION $(STGOOD(+), j*)$

Input: $j*$, the set $STGOOD(+)$ of known GMRTs for the class of positive examples, the set $R(-)$ of negative examples.
Output: $STGOOD(+)$
modified by the generalization.

Begin
$(\forall s)\ (s \in STGOOD(+))$
   if to_be_test$(t(s \cup j*))$ = true **then**
   $s \leftarrow$ generalization $(s \cup j*)$;
end

Figure 8. The Procedure for Generalizing the Existing GMRTs.

The Procedure FORMSUBTASK(*j)

Input: *j**, $R(+)$, $R(-)$, $s(+)$, $STGOOD(+)$.
Output: $S(\text{test})(+)$; the set of collections of indices
to be extended, and $Q(+)$; the set of forbidden
pairs of indices.

    Begin
    $S(\text{test})(+)$ ← $\{j^*\}$; $Q(+)$ ← ∅; nts ← $s(+)$;
    $(\forall i)\ i \in nts,\ i \neq j^*$
      if to_be_test($\{j^*, i\}$) = true **then do**

      Begin
      s = generalization_of($\{j^*, i\}$);
      insert s into $S(\text{test})(+)$ under
      lexicographic order;
      end
    else $Q(+)$ ← $Q(+) \cup \{j^*, i\}$;
    end

Figure 9.   The Procedure for Preparing the Data for Inferring the GMRTs
               Contained in a New Example.

The third action of incremental learning is reduced either to the diagnostic rule (please, see Section 3.8.2) and the subtask of the first kind or to the subtask of the second kind. We may use the algorithm NIAGaRa or the algorithm DIAGaRa (like any non-incremental algorithm) for solving subtasks of both the first and the second kind. Next we use the procedure NIAGaRa.

The Procedure INGOMAR

Input : j^*, R, S, *STGOOD*, Q. **Output:** R, S, *STGOOD*, Q.
begin
$k \leftarrow$ class(j^*); $S(+) \leftarrow S(k)$; $R(+) \leftarrow R(k)$; $R(-) \leftarrow R/R(+)$;
$N \leftarrow N + 1$; $j^* \leftarrow N$, where N is the number of examples;
$S(+) \leftarrow j^* \cup S(+)$; $R(+) \leftarrow t_{j^*} \cup R(+)$;
STGOOD$(+) \leftarrow$ *STGOOD*(k);
STGOOD$(-) \leftarrow \cup$ *STGOOD*(kl), $\forall kl$, $kl \neq k$;
if $N = 1$ **then** *STGOOD*$(+) \leftarrow \{j^*\} \cup$ *STGOOD*$(+)$; **else**
if $N \neq 1$ and $\|S(+)\| = 1$ **then**

begin
STGOOD$(+) \leftarrow \{j^*\} \cup$ *STGOOD*$(+)$;
if $(\exists s)$, $s \in$ *STGOOD*$(-)$, $t(s) \subseteq t_{j^*}$
then CORRECT($t(s)$); **end**
else
if $N \neq 1$ and $S(-) = \varnothing$ **then**

CONCEPTGENERALIZATION $[j^*](S(+)$, *STGOOD*$(+))$;
else /* $N \neq 1$ and $\|S(+)\| \neq 1$ and $S(-) \neq \varnothing$ */
begin
if *STGOOD*$(+) \neq \varnothing$ **then**
GENERALIZATION(*STGOOD*$(+)$, j^*); **end**
FORMSUBTASK (j^*);
NIAGaRa $[j^*]$ (S(test)$(+)$, R, S, *STGOOD* $(+)$, $Q(+)$);
if $(\exists s)$, $s \in$ *STGOOD* $(-)$, $t(s) \subseteq t_{j^*}$
then CORRECT ($t(s)$);
end

Figure 10. The Incremental Procedure INGOMAR.

Let t be an invalid test for some negative example. Correcting t consists of two steps:

1)   Apply the diagnostic rule in order to find the set of essential values with the use of which t can be extended and constructing the extensions of t;

2)   Form a subtask of the first kind for each extension *tnew* of t in order to find all the GMRTs for the negative examples contained in *tnew* and solving the subtask with the use of the procedure NIAGaRa. Let CORRECT(t) be the procedure for correcting the invalid test t and finding new tests for negative examples.

We must consider four possible situations that can take place when a new example comes to the learning system:

a) The knowledge base is empty and does not contain any example of the class to which a new example belongs and any alternative example;

b) The knowledge base contains only examples of the positive class to which a new example belongs;

c) The knowledge base contains only examples of the negative class;

d) The knowledge base contains examples both of the positive and the negative classes.

Case 2 conforms to the generalization process taking into account only the similarity relation between examples of the same class. This problem is known in the literature as inductive inference of generalization hypotheses or unsupervised generalization. An algorithm for solving this problem in the framework of a mathematical model based on Galois's connections can be found in (Kuznetzov, 1993).

Table 16. The Data for Processing by the Incremental Procedure INGOMAR.

INDEX OF EXAMPLE	OUTLOOK	TEMPERATURE	HUMIDITY	WINDY	CLASS
1	Sunny	Hot	High	No	1
2	Sunny	Hot	High	Yes	1
3	Overcast	Hot	High	No	2
4	Rain	Mild	High	No	2
5	Rain	Cool	Normal	No	2
6	Rain	Cool	Normal	Yes	1
7	Overcast	Cool	Normal	Yes	2
8	Sunny	Mild	High	No	1
9	Sunny	Cool	Normal	No	2
10	Rain	Mild	Normal	No	2
11	Sunny	Mild	Normal	Yes	2
12	Overcast	Mild	High	Yes	2
13	Overcast	Hot	Normal	No	2
14	Rain	Mild	High	Yes	1

Let CONCEPTGENERALIZATION $[j*](S(+), STGOOD(+))$ be the procedure of generalization of positive examples in the absence of negative examples.

The procedure INGOMAR (for INcremental inferring GOod MAximal Redundant tests) is presented in Figure 10.

The data in Table 16 are intended for processing by the incremental learning procedure INGOMAR. This table is adopted from (Quinlan and Rivest, 1989).

In Tables 17a and 17b, $Q(1)$ and $Q(2)$ are the sets of forbidden pairs of indices for the examples of class 1 and class 2, respectively.

The sets $STGOOD(1)$ and $STGOOD(2)$ in these tables accumulate the collections of indices that correspond to the GMRTs for the examples of class 1 and class 2, respectively, at each step of the algorithm.

Table 17a. The Records of the Step-by-Step Results of the Incremental Procedure INGOMAR (part *a*).

J*	CLASS(J*)	Q(1), Q(2)	STGOOD(1), STGOOD(2)
{1}	1	Q(1) =EMPTY	STGOOD(1): {1}
{2}	1	Q(1) =EMPTY	STGOOD(1):{1,2};
{3}	2	Q(2) =EMPTY	STGOOD(2):{3}
{4}	2	Q(2) ∪{{3,4}}	STGOOD(2):{3}, {4}
{5}	2	Q(2) ∪{{3,4}, {3,5}}	STGOOD(2):{3}, {4,5};
{6}	1	Q(1) ∪{{1,6}, {2,6}}	STGOOD(1):{1,2}, {6}
{7}	2	Q(2) ∪ {{4,7},{5,7}}	STGOOD(2):{3,7},{4,5}
{8}	1	Q(1) ∪ {{6,8}}	STGOOD(1):{1,2,8}, {6}
{9}	2	Q(2) ∪ {{3,9},{4,9}, {7,9}}	STGOOD(2):{3,7},{4,5},{5,9}

Table 17b. The Records of the Step-by-Step Results of the Incremental Procedure INGOMAR (part *b*).

J*	CLASS(J*)	Q(1), Q(2)	STGOOD(1), STGOOD(2)
{10}	2	Q(2) ∪ {{3,10},{7,10}}	STGOOD(2):{3,7},{4,5,10},{5,9,10}
{11}	2	Q(2)∪ {{3,11}, {4,11}, {5,11},{7,11}}	STGOOD(2):{3,7},{4,5,10}, {5,9,10},{10,11},{9,11}
{12}	2	Q(2) ∪ { (4,12), (5,12), (9,12), (10,12)}	STGOOD(2): {3,7,12},{4,5,10}, {5,9,10},{10,11},{9,11},{11,12};
{13}	2	Q(2) ∪ {{4,13}, {11,13}}	STGOOD(2): {3,7,12,13},{4,5,10}, {5,9,10,13},{10,11},{9,11},{11,12}
{14}	1	Q(1) ∪ {{1,14}, {2,14}, {8,14}}	STGOOD(1):{1,2,8}, {6,14}
		{11,12} is invalid for the class 2	STGOOD(2): {3,7,12,13},{4,5,10}, {5,9,10,13},{10,11},{9,11},

Table 18. The Sets $TGOOD(1)$ and $TGOOD(2)$ Produced by the Procedure INGOMAR.

TGOOD(1)	TGOOD(2)
Sunny High	Rain No
Rain Yes	Normal No
-	Mild Normal
-	Sunny Normal
-	Overcast

5.   CONCLUSIONS

The chapter is an attempt to show that both deductive reasoning based on acquired knowledge and inductive reasoning for learning new knowledge from examples proceed with the use of the same common sense reasoning operations. The main operations involved in deductive and inductive reasoning are the following: generalization, refinement (specialization), diagnostics, searching essential values and examples, eliminating values, cutting off examples, choosing values or examples for subtasks, extending or narrowing collections of values, extending or narrowing collections of examples, using forbidden rules, forming subtasks and some others.

We proposed a unified model for combining inductive reasoning with deductive reasoning in the framework of inferring and using implicative logical rules. The key concept of our approach is the concept of a good diagnostic test. We define a good diagnostic test as the best approximation of a given classification on a given set of examples. The task of inferring good diagnostic tests from examples serves as an ideal model of inductive reasoning because this task realizes one of the canons of induction that has been originally formulated by English logician J.-S. Mille.

We have given some examples of the decomposition of inferring all good maximally redundant tests for a given set of examples into operations and subtasks that are in accordance with main human common sense reasoning operations. This decomposition allows, in principle, to transform the process of inferring good tests into a "step by step" reasoning process. Incremental algorithms of inferring good classification tests from examples demonstrate the possibility of this transformation in the best way.

We have used the lattice theory as the mathematical model for the construction of good classification tests. We have described some inductive algorithms for inferring good maximally redundant tests. These algorithms are: NIAGaRa, DIAGaRa, and INGOMAR. We did not focus on the efficiency of our algorithms, although we understand that the questions of computational complexity of reasoning are very important. We intend to give more attention to the complexity problems in future contributions.

The development of full on-line model integrating deductive and inductive reasoning is of great interest but it requires the cooperative efforts of many researchers. The main problem in this direction is the choice of a data structure underlying the algorithms of inferring good diagnostic tests.

Acknowledgements

The author is very grateful to Professor Evangelos Triantaphyllou (Louisiana State University) who inspired and supported this chapter, and to

Dr. Giovanni Felici (IASI – Italian National Research Council), for his invaluable advice concerning all the parts of this chapter.

APPENDIX:

The data to be processed are in Table 19 (the set of positive examples) and in Table 20 (the set of negative examples). Tables 21, 22, and 23 contain the results of the procedure DEBUT, i.e. the sets Q, S(test), and $STGOOD$ respectively. Table 24 presents the extensions of the elements of S(test). Table 25 contains the results of the procedure NIAGaRa, i.e. the sets $STGOOD$ and $TGOOD$.

Table 19. The Set of the Positive Examples $R(+)$.

INDEX OF EXAMPLE	$R(+)$
1	$A_1 A_2 A_5 A_6 A_{21} A_{23} A_{24} A_{26}$
2	$A_4 A_7 A_8 A_9 A_{12} A_{14} A_{15} A_{22} A_{23} A_{24} A_{26}$
3	$A_3 A_4 A_7 A_{12} A_{13} A_{14} A_{15} A_{18} A_{19} A_{24} A_{26}$
4	$A_1 A_4 A_5 A_6 A_7 A_{12} A_{14} A_{15} A_{16} A_{20} A_{21} A_{24} A_{26}$
5	$A_2 A_6 A_{23} A_{24}$
6	$A_7 A_{20} A_{21} A_{26}$
7	$A_3 A_4 A_5 A_6 A_{12} A_{14} A_{15} A_{20} A_{22} A_{24} A_{26}$
8	$A_3 A_6 A_7 A_8 A_9 A_{13} A_{14} A_{15} A_{19} A_{20} A_{21} A_{22}$
9	$A_{16} A_{18} A_{19} A_{20} A_{21} A_{22} A_{26}$
10	$A_2 A_3 A_4 A_5 A_6 A_8 A_9 A_{13} A_{18} A_{20} A_{21} A_{26}$
11	$A_1 A_2 A_3 A_7 A_{19} A_{20} A_{21} A_{22} A_{26}$
12	$A_2 A_3 A_{16} A_{20} A_{21} A_{23} A_{24} A_{26}$
13	$A_1 A_4 A_{18} A_{19} A_{23} A_{26}$
14	$A_{23} A_{24} A_{26}$

Table 20a. The Set of the Negative Examples $R(-)$ (part a).

INDEX OF EXAMPLE	$R(-)$
15	$A_3 A_8 A_{16} A_{23} A_{24}$
16	$A_7 A_8 A_9 A_{16} A_{18}$
17	$A_1 A_{21} A_{22} A_{24} A_{26}$
18	$A_1 A_7 A_8 A_9 A_{13} A_{16}$
19	$A_2 A_6 A_7 A_9 A_{21} A_{23}$
20	$A_{10} A_{19} A_{20} A_{21} A_{22} A_{24}$
21	$A_1 A_{10} A_{20} A_{21} A_{22} A_{23} A_{24}$
22	$A_1 A_3 A_6 A_7 A_9 A_{10} A_{16}$
23	$A_2 A_6 A_8 A_9 A_{14} A_{15} A_{16}$
24	$A_1 A_4 A_5 A_6 A_7 A_8 A_{11} A_{16}$
25	$A_7 A_{10} A_{11} A_{13} A_{19} A_{20} A_{22} A_{26}$
26	$A_1 A_2 A_3 A_5 A_6 A_7 A_{10} A_{16}$
27	$A_1 A_2 A_3 A_5 A_6 A_{10} A_{13} A_{16}$

Table 20b. The Set of the Negative Examples $R(-)$ (part b).

INDEX OF EXAMPLE	$R(-)$
28	$A_1 A_3 A_7 A_{10} A_{11} A_{13} A_{19} A_{21}$
29	$A_1 A_4 A_5 A_6 A_7 A_8 A_{13} A_{16}$
30	$A_1 A_2 A_3 A_6 A_{11} A_{12} A_{14} A_{15} A_{16}$
31	$A_1 A_2 A_5 A_6 A_{11} A_{14} A_{15} A_{16} A_{26}$
32	$A_1 A_2 A_3 A_7 A_9 A_{10} A_{11} A_{13} A_{18}$
33	$A_1 A_5 A_6 A_8 A_9 A_{10} A_{19} A_{20} A_{22}$
34	$A_2 A_8 A_9 A_{18} A_{20} A_{21} A_{22} A_{23} A_{26}$
35	$A_1 A_2 A_4 A_5 A_6 A_7 A_9 A_{13} A_{16}$
36	$A_1 A_2 A_6 A_7 A_8 A_{10} A_{11} A_{13} A_{16} A_{18}$
37	$A_1 A_2 A_3 A_4 A_5 A_6 A_7 A_{12} A_{14} A_{15} A_{16}$
38	$A_1 A_2 A_3 A_4 A_5 A_6 A_9 A_{11} A_{12} A_{13} A_{16}$
39	$A_1 A_2 A_3 A_4 A_5 A_6 A_{14} A_{15} A_{19} A_{20} A_{23} A_{26}$
40	$A_2 A_3 A_4 A_5 A_6 A_7 A_{11} A_{12} A_{13} A_{14} A_{15} A_{16}$
41	$A_2 A_4 A_5 A_6 A_7 A_9 A_{10} A_{11} A_{12} A_{13} A_{14} A_{15} A_{19}$
42	$A_1 A_2 A_3 A_4 A_5 A_6 A_{12} A_{16} A_{18} A_{19} A_{20} A_{21} A_{26}$
43	$A_4 A_5 A_6 A_7 A_8 A_9 A_{10} A_{11} A_{12} A_{13} A_{14} A_{15} A_{16}$
44	$A_3 A_4 A_5 A_6 A_8 A_9 A_{10} A_{11} A_{12} A_{13} A_{14} A_{15} A_{18} A_{19}$
45	$A_1 A_2 A_3 A_4 A_5 A_6 A_7 A_8 A_9 A_{10} A_{11} A_{12} A_{13} A_{14} A_{15}$
46	$A_1 A_3 A_4 A_5 A_6 A_7 A_{10} A_{11} A_{12} A_{13} A_{14} A_{15} A_{16} A_{23} A_{24}$
47	$A_1 A_2 A_3 A_4 A_5 A_6 A_8 A_9 A_{10} A_{11} A_{12} A_{14} A_{16} A_{18} A_{22}$
48	$A_2 A_8 A_9 A_{10} A_{11} A_{12} A_{14} A_{15} A_{16}$

Next we provide the results of applying the algorithm NIAGaRa on the training set of examples (Tables 19 and 20).

Input: $S = \{\{1\}, \{2\}, \ldots, \{14\}\}$; $T = \{A_1, \ldots, A_{26}\}$; $STGOOD = \varnothing$; $S(\text{test}) = \varnothing$; $Q = \varnothing$.

Output: After implementation of the procedure DEBUT we have the following sets $S(\text{test})$, $STGOOD$ and Q (Tables 21, 22, 23).

Table 21. The Content of $S(\text{test})$ after the DEBUT of the Algorithm NIAGaRa.

1,4	1,4,7	1,5	1,5,12	1,12	2,3,4	2,7	2,8
2,10	3,7	3,7,12	3,8	3,10	3,11	4,6,8,11	4,6,11
4,7	4,8	4,11	4,12	7,8	7,11	7,12	8,10
8,11							

Table 22. The Contents of $STGOOD$ after the DEBUT of the Algorithm NIAGaRa.

1,2,12,14	9,11	13

Table 23. The Set Q after the DEBUT of the Algorithm NIAGaRa.

1,3	1,6	1,8	1,9	1,10	1,11	1,13	2,5	2,6
2,9	2,11	2,13	3,5	3,6	3,9	3,13	3,14	4,5
4,9	4,10	4,13	4,14	5,6	5,7	5,8	5,9	5,10
5,11	5,13	5,14	6,7	6,9	6,10	6,12	6,13	6,14
7,9	7,10	7,13	7,14	8,9	8,12	8,13	8,14	9,10
9,13	9,14	10,11	10,12	10,13	10,14	11,12	11,13	11,14
12,13	12,14	13,14						

Next, Table 24 presents the extensions of the elements of S(test).

Table 24. The Extensions of the Elements of S(test).

S	Not(s)	V	cand(s)	select(s)	Result
1,4,	5,6,7,8,10, 11,12	1,4,7	5,6,8,10, 11,12	12	Delete s
1,4,7	8,10,11,12	$\varnothing$	8,10,11,12	12	s - GMRT
1,5	6,7,8,10,11,12	1,5,12	6,7,8,10,11	$\varnothing$	Delete s
1,5,12	$\varnothing$	$\varnothing$	$\varnothing$	$\varnothing$	s - GMRT
1,12	$\varnothing$	$\varnothing$	$\varnothing$	$\varnothing$	Delete s
2,3,4	6,7,8,10,11,12	$\varnothing$	6,7,8,10, 11,12	7,8,12	{2,3,4,7} - GMRT
2,7	8,10,11,12	2,3,4,7	8,10,11, 12	8,12	{2,7,8} - GMRT
2,8	10,11,12	2,7,8	10,11,12	10	Delete s
2,10	11,12	$\varnothing$	11,12	$\varnothing$	s - GMRT
3,7	8,10,11,12	2,3,4,7,12	8,10,11	8,11	Delete s
3,7,12	$\varnothing$	$\varnothing$	$\varnothing$	$\varnothing$	s - GMRT
3,8	10,11,12	$\varnothing$	10,11,12	10,11	s - GMRT
3,10	11,12	$\varnothing$	11,12	$\varnothing$	s - GMRT
3,11	12	$\varnothing$	12	$\varnothing$	s - GMRT
4,6,8,11	12	$\varnothing$	12	$\varnothing$	s - GMRT
4,6,11	12	4,6,8,11	12	$\varnothing$	Delete s
4,7	8,10,11,12	2,3,4,7	8,10,11, 12	8,11,12	{4,7,12} - GMRT
4,8	10,11,12	4,6,8,11	10,12	$\varnothing$	Delete s
4,11	12	4,6,8,11	12	$\varnothing$	Delete s
4,12	$\varnothing$	4,7,12	$\varnothing$	$\varnothing$	Delete s
7,8	10,11,12	2,7,8	10,11,12	11	{7,8,11} - GMRT
7,11	12	7,8,11	12	$\varnothing$	Delete s
7,12	$\varnothing$	3,4,7,12	$\varnothing$	$\varnothing$	Delete s
8,10	11,12	$\varnothing$	11,12	$\varnothing$	s - GMRT
8,11	12	4,6,7,8,11	12	$\varnothing$	Delete s

In the following Tables, A_+ denotes the collection of values A_{14}, A_{15} and A_* denotes the collection of values A_8, A_9.

Table 25. The Sets *STGOOD* and *TGOOD* for the Examples in Tables 19 and 20.

№	STGOOD	TGOOD	№	STGOOD	TGOOD
1	13	$A_1 A_4 A_{18} A_{19} A_{23} A_{26}$	9	2,7,8	$A_{\bullet} A_{22}$
2	2,10	$A_4 A_{\bullet} A_{26}$	10	1,5,12	$A_2 A_{23} A_{24}$
3	3,10	$A_3 A_4 A_{13} A_{18} A_{26}$	11	4,7,12	$A_{20} A_{24} A_{26}$
4	8,10	$A_3 A_6 A_{\bullet} A_{13} A_{20} A_{21}$	12	3,7,12	$A_3 A_{24} A_{26}$
5	9,11	$A_{19} A_{20} A_{21} A_{22} A_{26}$	13	7,8,11	$A_3 A_{20} A_{22}$
6	3,11	$A_3 A_7 A_{19} A_{26}$	14	2,3,4,7	$A_4 A_{12} A_{+} A_{24} A_{26}$
7	3,8	$A_3 A_7 A_{13} A_{+} A_{19}$	15	4,6,8,11	$A_7 A_{20} A_{21}$
8	1,4,7	$A_5 A_6 A_{24} A_{26}$	16	1,2,12,14	$A_{23} A_{24} A_{26}$

Table 26. The Set *SPLUS* of the Collections *splus(A)* for all A's in Tables 19 and 20.

$SPLUS = \{splus(A_i): s(A_i) \cap s(+), A_i \in T\}$:

$splus(A_{\bullet}) \rightarrow \{2,8,10\}$	$splus(A_{22}) \rightarrow \{2,7,8,9,11\}$
$splus(A_{13}) \rightarrow \{3,8,10\}$	$splus(A_{23}) \rightarrow \{1,2,5,12,13,14\}$
$splus(A_{16}) \rightarrow \{4,9,12\}$	$splus(A_3) \rightarrow \{3,7,8,10,11,12\}$
$splus(A_1) \rightarrow \{1,4,11,13\}$	$splus(A_4) \rightarrow \{2,3,4,7,10,13\}$
$splus(A_5) \rightarrow \{1,4,7,10\}$	$splus(A_6) \rightarrow \{1,4,5,7,8,10\}$
$splus(A_{12}) \rightarrow \{2,3,4,7\}$	$splus(A_7) \rightarrow \{2,3,4,6,8,11\}$
$splus(A_{18}) \rightarrow \{3,9,10,13\}$	$splus(A_{24}) \rightarrow \{1,2,3,4,5,7,12,14\}$
$splus(A_2) \rightarrow \{1,5,10,11,12\}$	$splus(A_{20}) \rightarrow \{4,6,7,8,9,10,11,12\}$
$splus(A_{+}) \rightarrow \{2,3,4,7,8\}$	$splus(A_{21}) \rightarrow \{1,4,6,8,9,10,11,12\}$
$splus(A_{19}) \rightarrow \{3,8,9,11,13\}$	$splus(A_{26}) \rightarrow \{1,2,3,4,6,7,9,10,11,12,13,14\}$

An Example of Using the Algorithm DIAGaRa

We use the algorithm DIAGaRa for inferring all the GMRTs having a weight equal to or greater than *WMIN* = 4 for the training set of the examples represented in Table 19 (the set of positive examples) and in Table 20 (the set of negative examples).

We begin with $s^* = S(+) = \{\{1\}, \{2\}, ..., \{14\}\}$, $t^* = T = \{A_1, A_2, ..., A_{26}\}$, $SPLUS = \{splus(A_i): A_i \in t^*\}$ (see *SPLUS* in Table 26).

Please observe that $splus(A_{12}) = \{2,3,4,7\}$ and $t(\{2,3,4,7\})$ is a test, therefore, A_{12} is deleted from t^* and $splus(A_{12})$ is inserted into *STGOOD*. Then $W(A_8)$, $W(A_9)$, $W(A_{13})$, and $W(A_{16})$ are less than *WMIN*, hence we can delete A_8, A_9, A_{13}, and A_{16} from t^*. Now t_{10} is not a test and can be deleted. After modifying $splus(A)$ for A_5, A_{18}, A_2, A_3, A_4, A_6 A_{20}, A_{21}, and A_{26} we find that $splus(A_5) = \{1,4,7\}$ and $t(\{1,4,7\})$ is a test, therefore, A_5 is deleted from t^* and $splus(A_5)$ is inserted into *STGOOD*. Then $W(A_{18})$ turns out to be less than *WMIN* and we delete A_{18} which implies deleting t_{13}. Next we modify $splus(A)$ for A_1, A_{19}, A_{23}, A_4, A_{26} and find that $splus(A_4) = \{2,3,4,7\}$. A_4 is deleted from t^*. Finally, $W(A_1)$ turns out to be less than *WMIN* and we delete A_1.

We can delete also the values A_2, A_{19}, and A_6 because $W(A_2)$, $W(A_{19})$, and $W(A_6)$ are equal to 4, $t(splus(A_2))$, $t(splus(A_{19}))$, and $t(splus(A_6))$ are not tests and, therefore, these values will not appear in a maximally redundant test t with $W(t)$ equal to or greater than 4. After deleting these values we can delete the examples t_9, t_5 because A_{19} is essential in t_9, and A_2 is essential in t_5. Next we can observe that $splus(A_{23}) = \{1,2,12,14\}$ and $t(\{1,2,12,14\})$ is a test, thus A_{23} is deleted from t^* and $splus(A_{23})$ is inserted into $STGOOD$. Now t_{14} and t_1 are not tests and can be deleted. We can delete the value A_{22} because $W(A_{22})$ is now equal to 4, $t(splus(A_{22}))$ is not a test and this value will not appear in a maximally redundant test with weight equal to or greater than 4.

Now choose t_6 as a subtask because this positive example is more difficult to be distinguished from the negative examples. By resolving this subtask we find that t_6 produces a new test t with $s(t)$ equal to $\{4,6,8,11\}$. Delete t_6. We can also delete the value A_{21} because $W(A_{21})$ is now equal to 4, $t(splus(A_{21}))$ is not a test and this value will not appear in a maximally redundant test with weight equal to or greater than 4.

Now choose t_8 as a subtask because it is essential in the current projection with respect to the subset $\{2,3,4,7\}$ that corresponds to one of the GMRTs already obtained. By resolving this subtask we find that t_8 does not produce any new test. Delete t_8. After that we can delete the values A_+, A_7, A_3, and A_{20} and these deletions imply that all of the remaining rows t_2, t_3, t_4, t_7, t_{11}, and t_{12} are not tests.

The list of all the GMRTs for the training set of positive examples is given in Table 25.

REFERENCES

N. W. Alkharaouf and R. S. Michalski, "Multi-Strategy Task-Adaptive Learning Using Dynamic Interlaced Hierarchies: Methodology and Initial Implementation of InterLACE", *Proceedings of the Third International Workshop on Multistrategy Learning (MSL-96)*, Harpers Ferry, WV, USA, pp. 117-124, 1996.

A. V. Aho, J. E. Hopcraft, J. D. Ullman, *The Design and Analysis of Computer Algorithms*, Publishing Company "Mir": Moscow, USSR, 1979.

G. Birkhoff, *Lattice Theory*, second edition, Amer. Math. Soc., Providence, R. I., 1948 (Russian edition: Moscow, "Foreign Literature", 1954).

N. G. Boldyrev, "Minimization of Boolean Partial Functions with a Large Number of "Don't Care" Conditions and the Problem of Feature Extraction", *Proceedings of International Symposium "Discrete Systems"*, Riga, Latvia, pp. 101-109, 1974.

S. Cosmadakis, P. C. Kanellakis, N. Spyratos, "Partition Semantics for Relations", *Journal of Computer and System Sciences*, Vol. 33, No. 2, pp. 203-233, 1986.

J. Demetrovics and D. T. Vu, "Generating Armstrong Relation Schemes and Inferring Functional Dependencies from Relations", *International Journal on Information Theory & Applications*, Vol. 1, No. 4, pp.3-12, 1993.

H. Ericson, A. R. Puerta, and M. A. Musen, "Generation of Knowledge Acquisition Tools from Domain Ontologies", *International Journal of Human Computer Studies*, Vol. 41, pp. 425-453, 1992.

M. Ester, H. P. Kriegel, J. Sander, M. Wimmer, X. Xu, "Incremental Clustering for Mining in a Data Warehousing Environment", *Proceedings of the 24th VLDB Conference*, New York, NY, USA, pp. 323-333, 1998.

R. Feldman, Y. Aumann, A. Amir, H. Mannila, "Efficient Algorithms for Discovering Frequent Sets in Incremental Databases", *Proceeding of ACM SIGMOD Workshop on Research Issue on Data Mining and Knowledge Discovery*, Tucson, AZ, USA, pp. 59-66, 1997.

V. K. Finn, "Inductive Models of Knowledge Representation in Man-Machine and Robotics Systems", *Proceedings of VINITI*, Vol. A, pp.58-76, 1984.

J.- Gabriel. Ganascia, "EKAW - 89 Tutorial Notes: Machine Learning", *Third European Workshop on Knowledge Acquisition for Knowledge-Based Systems*, Paris, France, pp. 287-296, 1989.

U. Gappa, and K. Poeck, "Common Ground and Differences of the KADS and Strong Problem Solving Shell Approach", *EKAW – 92, Lecture Notes in Artificial Intelligence*, No. 599, pp. 52-73, 1992.

C. Giraud-Carrier, "A Note on the Utility on Incremental Learning", *AI Communication*, ISSN 0921-7126, IOS Press, Vol. 13, No. 4, pp. 215-223, 2000.

C. Giraud-Carrier, and T. Martinez, "ILA: Combining Inductive Learning with Prior Knowledge and Reasoning", *Technical report*, No. CSTR-95-03, University of Bristol, Department of Computer Science, Bristol, UK, 1995.

J. Han, R. T. Ng, Y. Fu, Y., "Intelligent Query Answering by Knowledge Discovery Techniques", *IEEE Trans. on Knowledge and Data Engineering*, Vol. 8, pp.373-390, 1996.

J. Han, S. Nishiro, H. Kawano, W. Wang, "Generalization-Based Data Mining in Object-Oriented Databases Using an Object Cube Model", *Data and Knowledge Engineering*, Vol. 25, No. 1-2, pp. 55-97, 1998.

J. Han, "Towards On-Line Analytical Mining in Large Databases", *ACM SIG MOD RECORD*, Vol. 27, No. 1, pp. 97-107, 1998.

Y. Huntala, J. Karkkainen, P. Porkka, and H. Toivonen, "TANE: An Efficient Algorithm for Discovering Functional and Approximate Dependencies", *The Computer Journal*, Vol. 42, No. 2, pp. 100-111, 1999.

S. O. Kuznetsov, "Fast Algorithm of Constructing All the Intersections of Finite Semi-Lattice Objects", *Proceedings of VINITI*, Series 2, No. 1, pp. 17-20, 1993.

A. E. Lichko, *Psychopathies and Accentuations of Character of Teenagers*, second edition, Leningrad, USSR, "Medicine", 1983.

M. A. Maloof, R. S. Michalski, "A Method for Partial Memory Incremental Learning and its Application to Computer Intrusion Detection", *Proceedings of the 7th IEEE International Conference on Tools with Artificial Intelligence*, Washington, DC, USA, pp. 392-397, 1995.

H. Mannila, and K. – J. Räihä, "On the Complexity of Inferring Functional Dependencies", *Discrete Applied Mathematics*, Vol. 40, pp. 237-243, 1992.

H. Mannila, and K. – J. Räihä, "Algorithm for Inferring Functional Dependencies". *Data & Knowledge Engineering*, Vol. 12, pp. 83-99, 1994.

I. A. Megretskaya, "Construction of Natural Classification Tests for Knowledge Base Generation", in: *The Problem of the Expert System Application in the National Economy*, Kishinev, Moldavia, pp. 89-93, 1988.

R. S. Michalski, and J. B. Larsen, "Selection of Most Representative Training Examples and Incremental Generation of VL_1 Hypotheses: the Underlying Methodology and the Description of Programs ESEL and AQII", *Report No. 78-867*, Dep. of Comp. Science, Univ. of Illinois at Urbana-Champaign, IL, USA, 1978.

R. S. Michalski, "Knowledge Acquisition through Conceptual Clustering: a Theoretical Framework and an Algorithm for Partitioning Data into Conjunctive Concepts", *Int. J. Policy Anal. Inform. Systems*, Vol. 4, No. 3, pp. 219-244, 1980.

R. S. Michalski, "A Theory and Methodology of Inductive Learning", *Artificial Intelligence*, Vol. 20, pp.111-161, 1983.

R. S. Michalski, and A. Ram, "Learning as Goal-Driven Inference", in: *Goal-Driven Learning*, Ram, A., and Leake, D. B. (Eds), MIT Press/Bradford Books, Cambridge, MA, USA, 1995.

J. S. Mille, *The System of Logic*, Russian Publishing Company "Book Affair": Moscow, Russia, 1900.

X. A. Naidenova, V. N. Syrbu, "Classification and Pattern Recognition Logic in Connection with the Problem of Forming and Using Knowledge in Expert Systems", *Theses of Papers of Republican Scientific-Technical Conference "Interactive Systems and Their Practical Application"*, Mathematical Institute with Computer Center, Kishinev, Moldavia, pp. 10-13, 1984.

X. A. Naidenova, J. G. Polegaeva, "A Model of Human Reasoning for Deciphering Forest's Images and its Implementation on Computer", *Theses of Papers and Reports of School-seminar "Semiotic Aspects of the Formalization of Intellectual Activity"*, Kutaisy, Georgia Soviet Socialist Republic, pp. 49-52, 1985a.

X. A. Naidenova, J. G. Polegaeva, "The Project of Expert System GID KLARA – Geological Interpretation of Data Based on Classification and Pattern Recognition", *Report I-A VIII.2 10-3/35, "Testing and Mastering Experimental Patterns of Flying (Aircraft) and Surface Spectrometry Apparatus, Working out Methods of Automated Processing Multi-Spectral Information for Geological Goals"*, All Union Scientific Research Institute of Remote Sensing Methods for Geology, 1985b.

X. A. Naidenova, J. G. Polegaeva, "An Algorithm of Finding the Best Diagnostic Tests", *The 4-th All Union Conference "Application of Mathematical Logic Methods"*, Theses of Papers, Mintz, G; E, Lorents, P. P. (Eds), Institute of Cybernetics, National Acad. of Sciences of Estonia, Tallinn, Estonia, pp. 63-67, 1986.

X. A. Naidenova, "Machine Learning As a Diagnostic Task", in: *"Knowledge-Dialogue-Solution"*, Materials of the Short-Term Scientific Seminar, Saint-Petersburg, Russia, editor Arefiev, I., pp.26-36, 1992.

X. A. Naidenova, J. G. Polegaeva, J. E. Iserlis, "The System of Knowledge Acquisition Based on Constructing the Best Diagnostic Classification Tests", *Proceedings of International Conference "Knowledge-Dialog-Solution"*, Jalta, Ukraine, Vol. 1, pp. 85-95, 1995a.

X. A. Naidenova, M. V. Plaksin, V. L. Shagalov, "Inductive Inferring All Good Classification Tests", *Proceedings of International Conference "Knowledge-Dialog-Solution"*, Jalta, Ukraine, Vol. 1, pp.79-84, 1995b.

X. A. Naidenova, "Reducing Machine Learning Tasks to the Approximation of a Given Classification on a Given Set of Examples", *Proceedings of the 5-th National Conference at Artificial Intelligence*, Kazan, Tatarstan, Vol. 1, pp. 275-279, 1996.

X. A. Naidenova, A. E. Ermakov, "The Decomposition of Algorithms of Inferring Good Diagnostic Tests", *Proceedings of the 4-th International Conference "Computer – Aided Design of Discrete Devices"* (*CAD DD'2001*), Institute of Engineering Cybernetics, National Academy of Sciences of Belarus, editor A. Zakrevskij, Minsk, Belarus, Vol. 3, pp. 61-69, 2001.

S. Nieto, E. Triantaphyllou, J. Chen, and T. W. Liao, "An Incremental Learning Algorithm for Constructing Boolean Function from Positive and Negative Examples", *Computers and Operations Researches*, Vol. 29, No. 12, pp. 1677-1700, 2002.

O. Ore, "Galois Connexions", Trans. Amer. Math. Society, Vol. 55, No. 1, pp. 493-513, 1944.

J. Piaget, La genèse des Structures Logiques Elémentaires, Neuchâtel, 1959.

J. R. Quinlan, and R. L. Rivest, "Inferring Decision Trees Using the Minimum Description Length Principle", *Information and Computation*, Vol. 80, No. 3, pp. 227-248, 1989.

H. Rasiova, *An Algebraic Approach to Non-Classical Logic*, Studies in Logic, Vol. 78, North-Holland Publishing Company, Amsterdam-London, 1974.

J. Riguet, "Relations Binaires, Fermetures, Correspondences de Galois", *Bull. Soc. Math.*, France, Vol. 76, No 3, pp. 114-155, 1948.

S. Salzberg, "A Nearest Hyper Rectangle Learning Method", *Machine Learning*, Vol. 6, pp. 277-309, 1991.

J. Shreider, "Algebra of Classification", *Proceedings of VINITI*, Series 2, No. 9, pp. 3-6, 1974.

E. Sperner, "Eine satz über Untermengen einer Endlichen Menge". *Mat. Z.*, Vol. 27, No. 11, pp. 544-548, 1928.

R. Wille, "Concept Lattices and Conceptual Knowledge System", *Computer Math. Appl.*, Vol. 23, No. 6-9, pp. 493-515, 1992.

X. Wu, and W. Lo, "Multi-Layer Incremental Induction", *Proceedings of the 5-th Pacific Rim International Conference on Artificial Intelligence*, Springer-Verlag, pp. 24-32, 1998.

AUTHOR'S BIOGRAPHICAL STATEMENT

Dr. Xenia Naidenova is a Senior Researcher at the St.-Petersburg Military Medical Academy. She was born in 1940 in Leningrad (now Saint-Petersburg). She studied computer engineering at the Electro - Technical University of Saint-Petersburg from where she received her diploma of engineer and her doctorate in computer science. She worked as an engineer, as a programmer and, at last, as a scientific researcher, but the main domains of her scientific activity were pattern recognition, machine learning, and modeling human reasoning with the use of computers.

The main direction of her work in the Military Medical Academy is in developing software technologies for creating medical and psychological diagnostic tools and systems. She is a member of the Russia Association for Artificial Intelligence founded in 1989. She is the author of several popular-scientific essays about the most famous scientists and their treatises published by "BOOK" Press, Moscow, in the annual issues of "Book Memorable Dates", 1983-1988 (for example about Robert Hooke, Simon Stevin, Ivan Sechenov and some others).

Chapter 4 [1]

DISCOVERING RULES THAT GOVERN MONOTONE PHENOMENA

Vetle I. Torvik * and Evangelos Triantaphyllou **

*: *University of Illinois at Chicago, Dept. of Psychiatry, 1601 W Taylor St, Chicago, IL 60612*
Email: vtorvik@uic.edu; Web: http://arrowsmith2.psych.uic.edu/torvik
**: *Louisiana State Univeristy, Dept. of Computer Science, 298 Coates Hall, Baton Rouge,*
LA 70803, Email: trianta@lsu.edu; Web: http://www.csc.lsu.edu/trianta

Abstract: Unlocking the mystery of natural phenomena is a universal objective in scientific research. The rules governing a phenomenon can most often be learned by observing it under a sufficiently large number of conditions that are sufficiently high in resolution. The general knowledge discovery process is not always easy or efficient, and even if knowledge is produced it may be hard to understand, interpret, validate, remember, and use. Monotonicity is a pervasive property in nature: it applies when each predictor variable has a non-negative effect on the phenomenon under study. Due to the monotonicity property, being able to observe the phenomenon under specifically selected conditions may increase the accuracy and completeness of the knowledge at a faster rate than a passive observer who may not receive the pieces relevant to the puzzle soon enough. This scenario can be thought of as learning by successively submitting queries to an oracle which responds with a Boolean value (phenomenon is present or absent). In practice, the oracle may take the shape of a human expert, or it may be the outcome of performing tasks such as running experiments or searching large databases. Our main goal is to pinpoint the queries that minimize the total number of queries used to completely reconstruct all of the underlying rules defined on a given finite set of observable conditions $V = \{0,1\}^n$. We summarize the optimal query selections in the simple form of selection criteria, which are near optimal and only take polynomial time (in the number of conditions) to compute. Extensive unbiased empirical results show that the proposed selection criterion approach is far superior to any of the existing methods. In fact, the average number of queries is reduced exponentially in the number of variables n and more than exponentially in the oracle's error rate.

Key Words: Monotone Boolean Functions, Active Learning, Data Mining.

---

[1] Triantaphyllou, E. and G. Felici (Eds.), **Data Mining and Knowledge Discovery Approaches Based on Rule Induction Techniques**, Massive Computing Series, Springer, Heidelberg, Germany, pp. 149-192, 2006.

1.   INTRODUCTION

The process of extracting new knowledge from large amounts of data is often called *Knowledge Discovery* or *Data Mining*. The general knowledge discovery process is not always easy or efficient, and even if knowledge is produced it may he hard to understand, interpret, validate, remember, and use. This chapter addresses the problem of learning monotone Boolean functions with the underlying objective to *efficiently acquire simple and intuitive knowledge that can be validated and has a general representation power.* The following key properties strengthen the argument in favor of this objective:

Key Property 1: *Monotone Boolean functions are inherently frequent in applications.*

The following three examples illustrate the versatility of the monotonicity property and how it applies to practical situations. A) Suppose a computer tends to crash when it runs a particular word processor and web browser simultaneously. Then, the computer will probably crash if it, in addition, runs other software applications. Further, suppose this computer does not tend to crash when it runs a particular CD player and web browser simultaneously. Then, it will probably not crash when it only runs the web browser (or the CD player). B) If a keyword search in a database gives interesting hits, then hits for a proper superset of these keywords is also probably going to be interesting. On the other hand, if a keyword search in a database does not give interesting hits, then hits for a proper subset of these keywords is probably not going to be interesting either. C) With all other factors constant, a student with a high Grade Point Average (GPA) is more likely to be accepted into a particular college than a student with a low GPA.

Recent literature contains a plethora of phenomena that can be modeled by using monotone Boolean functions. Such diverse phenomena include, but are not limited to, social worker's decisions, lecturer evaluation and employee selection (Ben-David, 1992), chemical carcinogenicity, tax auditing and real estate valuation (Boros *et al.*, 1994), breast cancer diagnosis and engineering reliability (Kovalerchuk *et al.*, 1996), signal processing (Shmulevich, 1997), rheumatology (Bloch and Silverman, 1997), voting rules in the social sciences (Judson, 1999), financial systems (Kovalerchuk and Vityaev, 2000b), record linkage (in administrative databases (Judson, 2001), and in bibliographic databases (Torvik *et al.*, 2004)).

Key Property 2: *Monotone Boolean functions are simple and intuitive.*

This property is perhaps the most important one when human interaction is involved since people tend to make very good use of knowledge they can easily interpret, understand, validate, and remember. Due to the increasing computational efficiency and storage capacity, the recent trend has been to increase the knowledge representation power in order to capture more complex knowledge. For example, the popular neural networks are capable of representing very complex knowledge. Unfortunately, even small neural networks can be hard to interpret and validate.

Key Property 3: *Monotone Boolean functions can represent relatively complex knowledge and still be validated.*

Validating knowledge that is generalized from a set of specific observations, which may be noisy and incomplete, is based on philosophical arguments and assumptions. Traditional statistical approaches tend to require specific modeling in small dimensions, to gain a theoretical justification for the final model. This justification is obtained at the cost of eliminating the computational feasibility of learning higher dimensional rules. On the other hand, the more general the knowledge representation is, the more one tends to lose the handle on its validation.

In practice, a great deal of time and effort is put into the knowledge discovery process. Software applications are tested, diseases are researched, database search engines are trained to be intelligent, and so on. The inference process generally involves gathering and analyzing data. Gathering the data often involves some sort of labor that far outweighs the computations used to analyze the data in terms of cost. Therefore, the main objective in this chapter is to minimize the labor associated with gathering the data, as long as it is computationally feasible.

Monotone Boolean functions lay the ground for a simple and efficient question asking strategy, where it may be easy to pinpoint questions whose answers make incomplete knowledge more general or stochastic knowledge more accurate. Due to the underlying monotonicity property, this learning strategy may significantly increase the learning rate, as an unguided learner might not receive the relevant pieces of information early enough in the inference process. Therefore, it is highly desirable not only to be able to pose questions, but also to pose "smart" questions. The main problem addressed in this chapter is how to identify these "smart" questions in order to efficiently infer monotone Boolean functions. This chapter focuses on the case when the monotone Boolean functions are defined on the set of n-dimensional Boolean vectors $\{0,1\}^n$. This does not necessarily limit the application domain as the methodology developed in this chapter can be applied to any finite set of vectors $V \subset \mathbb{R}^n$, and any monotone function can be represented by a set of monotone Boolean functions.

This chapter is organized as follows: The background information and the relevant literature is reviewed in section 2. Formal definitions of the problems and their solution methodology are given in section 3. In section 4, experimental results are provided, for which a summary and discussion is given in section 5. Section 6 concludes the paper with a few final remarks.

2.   BACKGROUND INFORMATION

2.1   Problem Descriptions

Let V denote a finite set of vectors defined on n variables. A vector $v \in V$ is said to *precede* another vector $w \in V$, denoted by $v \preceq w$, if and only if (iff) $v_i \leq w_i$ for $I = 1, 2, ..., n$. Here, v_i and w_i denote the I-th element of vectors v and w, respectively. Similarly, a vector $v \in V$ is said to *succeed* another vector $w \in V$, iff $v_i \geq w_i$ for $I = 1, 2, ..., n$. When v precedes (or succeeds) w, and the two vectors are distinct (i.e., $v \neq w$), then the vector v is said to *strictly precede* (or *strictly succeed*, respectively) w, denoted by $v \succ w$ (or $v \prec w$, respectively). If a vector v either precedes or succeeds w, they are said to be *related* or *comparable*. A Boolean function defined on the set of vectors $\{0,1\}^n$ is simply a mapping to $\{0,1\}$. A monotone Boolean function f is called *non-decreasing* iff $f(v) \leq f(w) \; \forall \; v, w \in \{0,1\}^n : v \preceq w$, and *non-increasing* iff $f(v) \geq f(w) \; \forall \; v, w \in \{0,1\}^n : v \preceq w$. This chapter focuses on non-decreasing functions, which are referred to as just *monotone*, as analogous results hold for non-increasing functions.

Monotone Boolean functions lay the ground for a simple question asking strategy, which forms the basis of this chapter. More specifically, the problem of inferring monotone Boolean functions by successive and systematic *function evaluations* (*membership queries* submitted to an oracle) is addressed. The monotone Boolean function can be thought of as a phenomenon, such as breast cancer or a computer crash, together with a set of predictor variables. The *oracle* can be thought of as an entity that knows the underlying monotone Boolean function and provides a Boolean function value in response to each membership query. In practice, it may take the shape of a human expert, or it may be the outcome of performing tasks such as running experiments or searching large databases.

This inference problem is broken down by the nature of the oracle: whether it is deterministic or stochastic, and whether it is two-valued or three-valued. The simplest variant considers the guided inference of a deterministic monotone Boolean function defined on at most n Boolean variables. This case is referred to as Problem 1 which is generalized into two different problems.

The first generalization includes a pair of nested monotone Boolean functions and is referred to as Problem 2. Since this problem includes two oracles, it is further broken down into three subproblems 2.1, 2.2, and 2.3, differing only in the manner in which these two oracles are accessed. The second generalization includes stochastic membership queries and is referred to as Problem 3.

Problem 1: Inferring a Monotone Boolean Function from a Deterministic Oracle

Initially, the entire set of 2^n Boolean vectors $\{0,1\}^n$ is considered to be unclassified. That is, the values of the underlying monotone Boolean function f are all unknown and may be 0 or 1. A vector v is then selected from the set of unclassified vectors U and is submitted to an oracle as a membership query. After the vector's function value $f(v)$ is provided by the oracle, the set of unclassified vectors is reduced according to the following monotonicity constraints: $f(w) = 0$, $\forall\ w \in U$: $w \preceq v$, when $f(v) = 0$, or the following monotonicity constraints: $f(w) = 1$, $\forall\ w \in U$: $v \preceq w$, when $f(v) = 1$. Here, the relationship $v \preceq w$ holds if and only if $v_i \leq w_i$, for $I = 1, 2, ..., n$, where v_i and w_i denote the I-th Boolean elements of the vectors v and w, respectively. Vectors are then repeatedly selected from the unclassified set until they are all classified (i.e., $U = \{\}$). Given the classification of any unclassified vector, other vectors may be concurrently classified if the underlying Boolean function is assumed to be monotone. Therefore, only a subset of the 2^n vectors need to be evaluated in order to completely reconstruct the underlying function. Thus, a key problem is to select "promising" vectors so as to reduce the total number of queries (or *query complexity*).

Problem 2: Inferring a Pair of Nested Monotone Boolean Functions from Deterministic Oracle(s)

A pair of monotone Boolean functions f_1 and f_2 are called *nested* when the following relationship holds: $f_1(v) \geq f_2(v)$ (or $f_1(v) \leq f_2(v)$) $\forall\ v \in \{0,1\}^n$. The case when $f_1 \geq f_2$ is addressed in this chapter as analogous results hold for the case when $f_1 \leq f_2$. A single monotone Boolean function does not capture the idea of a classification intermediate to 0 and 1. However, a pair of nested monotone Boolean functions can do so. For example, some vectors might belong to a class with a high probability (i.e., where $f_1 = 1$ and $f_2 = 1$), and some might belong to the other class with a high probability (i.e., where $f_1 = 0$ and $f_2 = 0$). Other instances might not be classifiable with a satisfactorily high probability. A pair of nested monotone Boolean functions allows for this intermediate classification (i.e., where $f_1 = 1$ and $f_2 = 0$) to be incorporated. This makes the monotone Boolean function model more powerful.

Since the inference of a pair of nested monotone Boolean functions may include two oracles, it is further broken down into three subproblems 2.1, 2.2, and 2.3, differing only in the manner in which the oracle(s) are accessed. These three problems were defined to capture the main inference scenarios that may arise in real world applications.

Problem 2.1: Sequentially Inferring Nested Functions from Two Oracles

For this problem the two functions are considered to be available via their two respective oracles where the inference situation dictates that, for example, function f_1 should be completely reconstructed before the inference of function f_2 begins. In other words, the two functions are to be *sequentially inferred.* This approach may simply be the only feasible or reasonable one or it may be dictated by the cost of querying the oracle associated with f_2 far surpassing the cost of querying the other oracle.

Problem 2.2: Inferring Nested Functions from a Three-Valued Oracle

For this problem the two nested monotone Boolean functions are viewed as a single function f taking on the three values 0, 1, and 2, corresponding to $(f_1, f_2) = (0,0)$, $(1,0)$ and $(1,1)$, respectively. Notice that (f_1, f_2) cannot take on the values $(0,1)$ due to the nestedness constraint $f_1 \geq f_2$. The single three-valued function is used to emphasize that the Boolean function values arrive in pairs, for each vector, from a single oracle.

Problem 2.3: Inferring Nested Functions from Two Unrestricted Oracles

This problem is similar to Problem 2.1, in that two oracles are queried separately. Unlike Problem 2.1, no restrictions are put on the manner in which the two oracles are queried. At each inference step, a vector can be submitted to either of the two oracles. In this sense, this is the least restrictive of the three problems, and it is therefore expected that this approach will be the more efficient.

Problem 3: Inferring a Monotone Boolean Function from a Stochastic Oracle

This problem is identical to Problem 1, except that the membership values are now stochastic in nature. As in Problem 1, vectors are selected from $\{0,1\}^n$ and are submitted to an oracle as membership queries. Unlike Problem 1, it is assumed that the oracle misclassifies each vector v with an unknown probability $q(v) \in (0, \frac{1}{2})$. That is, for a given monotone Boolean function f, the oracle returns 1 for vector v with probability $p(v) = q(v) \times (1 - f(v)) + (1 - q(v)) \times f(v)$, and it returns 0 with probability $1 - p(v)$. It is assumed that the oracle is not misleading the inference process and is better at classifying the vectors than completely random guessing, hence the oracle's misclassification probability is assumed to be less than one half.

The stochastic inference problem involves estimating the misclassification parameter $q(v)$ for each vector v, as well as reconstructing the underlying function f. In this chapter, these two tasks are based on a maximum likelihood framework. A monotone Boolean function that is the most likely to match the underlying function, given the observed queries, is referred to as the *inferred function* and is denoted by f^*. Associated with a function f^* are the estimated misclassification probabilities which are denoted by $q^*(v)$ for each vector v.

The inference process consists of two steps that are repeated successively. In the first step, a vector is submitted to the oracle as a query. After a vector's function value is provided by the oracle, both $q^*(v)$ and f^* may have to be updated, according to the following monotonicity property: $p(v) \leq p(w)$ if and only if $v \preceq w$, $\forall\, v, w \in \{0,1\}^n$. These two steps are repeated until the likelihood of the inferred function f^* matching the underlying function f is high relative to the likelihood of any of the other monotone Boolean functions matching f. In other words, the underlying function is considered completely inferred when the maximum likelihood ratio for the inferred function, denoted by $\lambda(f^*)$, reaches a value that is close to 1. Again, the key problem is to select "promising" vectors so as to reduce the total number of queries required in this process.

2.2   Hierarchical Decomposition of Variables

In some applications, the variables may be monotone Boolean functions defined on a set of Boolean variables at a lower level. Kovalerchuk *et al.* (1996) decomposed five breast cancer diagnostic variables in a hierarchical manner as follows. Function $f_1(v)$ describes their "biopsy subproblem" and is defined as 1 if a biopsy is recommended for a tumor with the features described by vector v, and 0 otherwise. Function $f_2(v)$ describes their "cancer subproblem" and is defined as 1 if a tumor with the features described by v is highly suspicious for malignancy, and 0 otherwise. The first variable v_1 is defined as 1 if the *amount and volume of calcifications* is "pro cancer", and 0 if it is "contra cancer". In reality, this variable was inferred (through queries to the radiologist) as the following monotone Boolean function: $v_1(x_1, x_2, x_3) = x_2 \vee x_1 x_3$. Here, the extra variables are defined as follows:

$x_1 = 1$ if the *number of calcifications/cm²* is "large", 0 if "small",
$x_2 = 1$ if the *volume of calcifications (cm³)* is "small", 0 if "large", and
$x_3 = 1$ if the *total number of calcifications* is "large", 0 if "small".

The second variable v_2 is defined as 1 if the *shape and density of calcifications* is "pro cancer", and 0 if it is "contra cancer". In reality, this variable was inferred (through queries to the radiologist) as the following monotone Boolean function: $v_2(x_4, x_5, x_6, x_7, x_8) = x_4 \vee x_5 \vee x_6 x_7 x_8$. Here, the extra variables are defined as follows:

$x_4 = 1$ if the *irregularity in the shape of individual calcifications* is "marked", 0 if "mild",

$x_5 = 1$ if the *variation in the shape of calcifications* is "marked", 0 if "mild",

$x_6 = 1$ if the *variation in the size of calcifications* is "marked", 0 if "mild",

$x_7 = 1$ if the *variation in the density of calcifications* is "marked", 0 if "mild", and

$x_8 = 1$ if the *density of calcifications* is "marked", 0 if "mild".

In general, one can construct a hierarchy of the sets of variables, where each set of variables corresponds to an independent inference problem. Figure 1 shows this hierarchy for the breast cancer diagnostic variables. The upper level consists of the set $\{v_1, v_2, v_3, v_4, v_5\}$ which is linked to the sets of variables $\{x_1, x_2, x_3\}$, and $\{x_4, x_5, x_6, x_7, x_8\}$ at the lower level. Here, the variables v_1 and v_2 have to be defined before the inference problem defined on the set variables $\{v_1, v_2, v_3, v_4, v_5\}$ can begin. In general, the inference problems at the lower level have to be completed before the inference problems at the upper levels can begin.

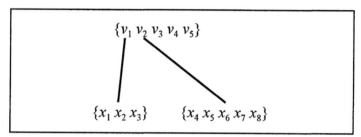

Figure 1. Hierarchical Decomposition of the Breast Cancer Diagnosis Variables.

The breast cancer inference problem is defined on the set of Boolean variables $\{x_1, x_2, x_3, x_4, x_5, x_6, x_7, x_8, v_3, v_4, v_5, f_i\}$. This problem includes a total of $2^{12} = 4,096$ vectors to choose from. However, it can be approached hierarchically, as three independent problems defined on the sets $\{x_1, x_2, x_3\}$, $\{x_4, x_5, x_6, x_7, x_8\}$, and $\{v_1, v_2, v_3, v_4, v_5, f_i\}$, respectively. These problems include a total of $2^3 + 2^5 + 2^6 = 104$ possible vectors to choose from. The hierarchical approach to this problem reduces the number of possible vectors to choose from by a factor of $4,096/104 \approx 39.4$. Please notice that a single monotone Boolean function is to be inferred for each of the sets $\{x_1, x_2, x_3\}$, and $\{x_4, x_5, x_6, x_7, x_8\}$. This corresponds to Problem 1 defined on the sets $\{0,1\}^3$ and $\{0,1\}^5$, respectively. In contrast, a pair of nested monotone Boolean functions defined on the set $\{v_1, v_2, v_3, v_4, v_5\}$ are to be sequentially inferred. This corresponds to Problem 2.1 and includes the query domain $\{0,1\}^6$.

2.3   Some Key Properties of Monotone Boolean Functions

An ordered set of related vectors $v^1 \preceq v^2 \preceq ... \preceq v^p$ is sometimes called a *chain*, while an *antichain* (or *layer*) consists of a set of mutually unrelated vectors. When a set of vectors is partitioned into as few layers as possible, a *layer partition* is formed. Similarly, when a set of vectors is partitioned into as few chains as possible, a *chain partition* is formed. For a particular layer partition, the layers can be ordered as $L^1, L^2, ..., L^r$ so that a vector $v^i \in L^i$ cannot succeed another vector $v^j \in L^j$, if $I < j$. Let $\{0,1\}^n$ denote the set of vectors defined on n Boolean variables. The layer partition for the set $\{0,1\}^n$ is unique, while its chain partition is not unique. In fact, the way one partitions $\{0,1\}^n$ into chains can be used effectively in the inference of monotone Boolean functions. An example is the symmetric chain partition used by Hansel (1966) and Sokolov (1982) as described in section 2.4.

A *directed graph* G is often written in the form (V, E), where V denotes its set of vertices, and E denotes its set of directed edges. Here, a directed edge from vertex v to vertex w is written as (v, w). A directed graph (V, E) is called *cyclic* if it has a sequence of edges that starts and ends with a vector v: (v, v^1), (v^1, v^2), ...,$(v^r, v) \in E$. Figure 2 shows a *partially ordered set* (or *poset* for short). In general, posets can be formed by a set of vectors V together with the precedence relation $\preceq$, and are written as $(V, \preceq)$.

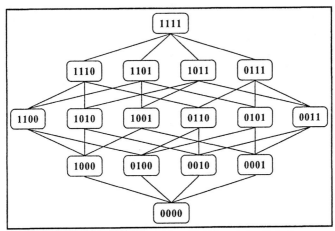

Figure 2. The Poset Formed by $\{0,1\}^4$ and the Relation $\preceq$.

A poset can be viewed as a directed graph where each vertex corresponds to a vector and each directed edge (v, w) represents the precedence relation $v \preceq w$. When drawing a poset as a directed graph, its edges' directions are often omitted without loss of information. The graph of a poset is acyclic and so all the directions can be forced upwards on a page by ordering the vertices by layers, as in Figure 2. Precedence relations that are transitively implied by other relations are considered *redundant*. For example, the precedence relation $(0000) \preceq (1100)$ is redundant because it is implied by the two precedence relations $(0000) \preceq (1000)$ and $(1000) \preceq (1100)$. For the purpose of reducing storage and simplifying the visualization of posets, redundant precedence relations are generally omitted, as in Figure 2.

Two posets P^1 and P^2 are said to be *isomorphic* if there exists a one-to-one mapping of the vectors in P^1 to the vectors in P^2, where the precedence relations are preserved. That is, if $v^1 \to v^2$ and $w^1 \to w^2$, then $v^1 \preceq w^1$ iff $v^2 \preceq w^2$, $\forall \, v^1, w^1 \in P^1$ and $v^2, w^2 \in P^2$. For example, the poset formed by the vectors $\{0000, 1001, 0100\}$ is isomorphic to the poset formed by the vectors $\{1110, 1100, 1101\}$. Here, one possible isomorphic mapping is as follows: $(0000) \to (1100)$, $(1001) \to (1110)$ and $(0100) \to (1101)$.

A vector v^* is called an *upper zero* of a Boolean function f if $f(v^*) = 0$ and $f(v) = 1 \, \forall \, v \in \{0,1\}^n : v \succ v^*$. Similarly, a vector v^* is called a *lower unit* if $f(v^*) = 1$ and $f(v) = 0 \, \forall \, v \in \{0,1\}^n : v \prec v^*$. Lower units and upper zeros are also referred to as *border vectors*. For any monotone Boolean function f, the set of lower units $LU(f)$, and the set of upper zeros, $UZ(f)$ are unique and either one of these two sets uniquely identifies f. Boolean functions are often written in Disjunctive Normal Form (DNF) or in Conjunctive Normal Form (CNF) using the AND, OR, and NOT operations, denoted by $\wedge$, $\vee$, and $\sim$, respectively. A DNF or a CNF representation is *minimal* if removing any of its clauses results in a different mapping $\{0,1\}^n \to \{0,1\}$. For any monotone Boolean function f there is a one-to-one relationship between its lower units and its minimal DNF representation, as follows:

$$f(v_1, v_2, ..., v_n) = \bigvee_{w \in LU(f)} \left(\bigwedge_{i:w_i=1} v_i \right).$$

Similarly, there is a one-to-one relationship between the upper zeros of a monotone Boolean function f, and its minimal CNF representation as follows:

$$f(v_1, v_2, ..., v_n) = \bigwedge_{w \in UZ(f)} \left(\bigvee_{i:w_i=0} v_i \right).$$

For example, the monotone Boolean function defined by its lower units $\{110, 101\}$ can be written in minimal DNF as $v_1 v_2 \vee v_1 v_3$. The corresponding upper zeros are $\{011, 100\}$ and its minimal CNF representation is $v_1(v_2 \vee v_3)$. Often the operation $\wedge$ is omitted when writing out Boolean functions, as in the previous two examples. Since the lower units and upper zeros are unique to a monotone Boolean function, so are its minimal representations in DNF and CNF. Another nice property of monotone Boolean functions is that they can be written in minimal CNF or DNF without using the NOT operation.

The set of all monotone Boolean functions defined on $\{0,1\}^n$ is denoted by M_n. For example, the set of all monotone Boolean functions defined on $\{0,1\}^2$ is given by $M_2 = \{F, v_1v_2, v_1, v_2, v_1 \vee v_2, T\}$. Here the functions T and F are defined by $f(v) = 1$, $\forall v \in \{0,1\}^n$, and $f(v) = 0$, $\forall v \in \{0,1\}^n$, respectively.

Let $m(f)$ denote the number of border vectors associated with a Boolean function f. It is well known (e.g., Engel, 1997) that $m(f)$ achieves its maximum value for a function that has all its border vectors on two of the most populous layers of $\{0,1\}^n$. That is, the following equation holds:

$$\max_{f \in M_n} m(f) = \binom{n}{\lfloor n/2 \rfloor} + \binom{n}{\lfloor n/2 \rfloor + 1}.$$

The borders of any monotone Boolean function f are the only vectors that require evaluations in order to completely reconstruct the function. Therefore, the value of $m(f)$ works as a lower bound on the number of queries for Problem 1.

The number of monotone Boolean functions defined on $\{0,1\}^n$ is denoted by $\Psi(n)$. That is, $\Psi(n)$ is equal to the dimension of the set M_n. All of the known values for $\Psi(n)$ are given in Table 1. For larger values of n the best known asymptotic is due to Korshunov (1981):

$$\Psi(n) \sim \begin{cases} 2^{\binom{n}{n/2}} e^{\binom{n}{n/2-1}\left(\frac{1}{2^{n/2}} + \frac{n^2}{2^{n+5}} - \frac{n}{2^{n+4}}\right)}, & \text{for even } n. \\[2em] 2^{\binom{n}{n/2-1/2}+1} e^{\binom{n}{n/2-3/2}\left(\frac{1}{2^{(n+3)/2}} - \frac{n^2}{2^{n+6}} - \frac{n}{2^{n+3}}\right) + \binom{n}{n/2-1/2}\left(\frac{1}{2^{(n+1)/2}} + \frac{n^2}{2^{n+4}}\right)}, & \\ & \text{for odd } n. \end{cases}$$

The number of pairs of nested monotone Boolean functions defined on $\{0,1\}^n$ is simply $\Psi(n+1)$. This fact can be observed by constructing the poset connecting two posets $P_1 = (\{0,1\}^n, \preceq)$ and $P_2 = (\{0,1\}^n, \preceq)$ associated with functions f_1 and f_2 respectively, by adding the edges corresponding to the precedence relations $f_1(v) \geq f_2(v)$, $\forall v \in \{0,1\}^n$.

Table 1. History of Monotone Boolean Function Enumeration.

$\Psi(1) = 3$, $\Psi(2) = 6$, $\Psi(3) = 20$	
$\Psi(4) = 168$	by Dedekind (1897)
$\Psi(5) = 7,581$	by Church (1940)
$\Psi(6) = 7,828,354$	by Ward (1946)
$\Psi(7) = 2,414,682,040,998$	by Church (1965)
$\Psi(8) = 56,130,437,228,687,557,907,788$	by Wiedeman (1991)

2.4   Existing Approaches to Problem 1

Let $\varphi(A, f)$ denote the number of queries performed by an algorithm A, when reconstructing the monotone Boolean function f. A *Teacher* can be thought of as an inference algorithm that knows the function ahead of time. It simply verifies that the function is correct by querying only the border vectors. Thus, $\varphi(Teacher, f) = m(f)$, $\forall f \in M_n$. Please recall that $m(f)$ denotes the number of border vectors associated with a function f.

For any monotone Boolean function inference algorithm A, the value of $m(f)$ can be considered as a lower bound on the number of queries. Thus, $\varphi(A, f) \geq m(f)$, $\forall f \in M_n$. It turns out that it is possible to achieve fewer or the same number of queries as the upper bound on $m(f)$, for all monotone Boolean functions defined on $\{0,1\}^n$. This can be achieved by partitioning the set of vectors into chains as described in Hansel (1966). In general, there are a total of $\binom{n}{\lfloor n/2 \rfloor}$ chains in n dimensions. An inference algorithm that searches these chains in increasing length is referred to as Hansel's algorithm. A key property of the Hansel chains is that once the function values are known for all the vectors in all the chains of length k, the function values are unknown for at most two vectors in each chain of the next length $k+2$. Proof of this property can be found in both Hansel (1966) and Sokolov (1982). As a result, Hansel's algorithm results in fewer or the same number of queries as the upper bound on $m(f)$ as follows. When n is odd, the shortest chains contain two vectors each, and there are a total of $\binom{n}{\lfloor n/2 \rfloor}$ chains. In this case, the maximum number of queries used by Hansel's algorithm is $2\binom{n}{\lfloor n/2 \rfloor} = \binom{n}{\lfloor n/2 \rfloor} + \binom{n}{\lfloor n/2 \rfloor+1}$. Similarly, when n is even, there are $\binom{n}{n/2} - \binom{n}{n/2+1}$ chains of length one, and $\binom{n}{n/2+1}$ chains of length greater than one. In this case, the maximum number of queries is $\binom{n}{n/2} - \binom{n}{n/2+1} + 2\binom{n}{n/2+1} = \binom{n}{n/2} + \binom{n}{n/2+1}$. That is, the following inequality holds:

$$\varphi(Hansel, f) \leq \max_{g \in M_n} m(g) = \binom{n}{\lfloor n/2 \rfloor} + \binom{n}{\lfloor n/2 \rfloor+1}, \forall f \in M_n.$$

The algorithm described in Sokolov (1982) is also based on the Hansel chains. In contrast to Hansel's algorithm, it considers the chains in the reverse order (i.e., in decreasing length) and performs the binary search within each chain. It turns out that Sokolov's algorithm is much more efficient for functions that have all their border vectors in the longer Hansel chains. As an example, consider the monotone Boolean function T. This function has only one border vector $(00...0)$, which is located in the longest chain. For this function, Sokolov's algorithm performs at most $\lfloor log_2(n) \rfloor + 1$ evaluations, while Hansel's algorithm needs at least $\binom{n}{\lfloor n/2 \rfloor}$ evaluations. For instance, when $n = 20$ this translates into at least 184,756 evaluations performed by Hansel's algorithm and at most 5 evaluations performed by Sokolov's algorithm.

Sokolov's algorithm does not satisfy the upper bound, as the following example shows. Suppose that $n > 4$ and even, and the monotone Boolean function to be inferred is defined by $f(v) = 1 \ \forall \ v \in \{0,1\}^n : |v| \geq n/2$, and 0 otherwise. Then the set of border vectors is $\{v, |v| = n/2 \text{ or } n/2\text{-}1\}$ and $m(f) = \binom{n}{\lfloor n/2 \rfloor} + \binom{n}{\lfloor n/2 \rfloor + 1}$. In Sokolov's algorithm, the first vector w^1 submitted for evaluation is a border vector since $|w^1| = n/2$. The second vector w^2 is not a border vector because $|w^2| = \lceil 3n/4 \rceil \neq n/2$ and $n/2\text{-}1$. Therefore, the following inequality holds:

$$\varphi(Sokolov, f) > \binom{n}{\lfloor n/2 \rfloor} + \binom{n}{\lfloor n/2 \rfloor + 1}, \text{ for at least one } f \in M_n.$$

In an attempt to provide a unified efficiency testing platform, Gainanov (1984) proposed to compare inference algorithms based on the number of evaluations needed for each border vector. To that end, he presented an algorithm that searches for border vectors one at a time, and we refer to this algorithm as FIND-BORDER. At the core of the algorithm is a subroutine that takes as input any unclassified vector v, and finds a border vector by successively evaluating adjacent vectors. This subroutine is also used in the algorithms of Boros *et al.* (1997), Makino and Ibaraki (1995), and Valiant (1984). As a result, any inference algorithm A that feeds unclassified vectors to this subroutine satisfies the following upper bound:

$$\varphi(A, f) \leq m(f)(n+1), \ \forall f \in M_n.$$

For the majority of monotone Boolean functions, the expression $m(f)(n+1)$ is greater than or equal to 2^n, in which cases the bound is trivial.

Earlier work on monotone Boolean function inference (such as Hansel, 1966; Sokolov, 1982; Gainanov, 1984) focuses on reducing the query complexity. More recent work (like Boros *et al.*, 1997; Makino and Ibaraki, 1997; Fredman and Khachiyan, 1996) considers both the query complexity and the computational complexity. The problem of inferring a monotone Boolean function via membership queries is equivalent to many other computational problems in a variety of fields (see, for instance, Bioch and Ibaraki, 1995; Eiter and Gottlob, 1995). In these applications, algorithms that are efficient in terms of query and computational complexity are used.

In practice, queries often involve some sort of effort, such as consulting with experts, performing experiments or running simulations. For such applications, queries far surpass computations in terms of cost. Therefore, this chapter focuses on minimizing the query complexity as long as it is computationally feasible.

2.5   An Existing Approach to Problem 2

Kovalerchuk *et al.* (1996) considered the problem of inferring a pair of nested monotone Boolean functions. Their algorithm, which exhibited a promising efficiency in their cancer diagnosis application, is an extension of Hansel's inference algorithm for a single monotone Boolean function. However, the algorithm performance analysis is far from conclusive as a single application represents a single pair of nested monotone Boolean functions.

2.6   Existing Approaches to Problem 3

The problem of guided inference in the presence of stochastic errors is referred to as sequential design of experiments in the statistics community. The field of optimal experiment design (Federov, 1972) contains various optimality criteria that are applicable in a sequential setting. The most common vector selection criterion is based on instantaneous variance reduction. Other selection criteria, such as the maximum information gain used in MacKay (1992), and Tatsuoka and Ferguson (1999), have been studied. However, no guided inference studies using a maximum likelihood framework were found in the literature.

The theory of optimal experiment design is the most extensive for simple regression models (Federov, 1972). Fortunately, efficient guided inference for more complex models have been studied, such as the feed forward neural networks in Cohn (1996), even though a sound theory has not been established. In fact, the same article reported a convergence problem for which a partial remedy was introduced in Cohn (1995).

2.7   Stochastic Models for Problem 3

Suppose a set of observed vectors $V = \{v^1, v^2, ..., v^k\}$ is given. For a given number of queries m, let $m_z(v)$ be the number of times the oracle classified vector v as z (for $z = 0$ and 1, and $v \in V$). Associated with a monotone Boolean function f, the number of errors it performs on the set of observations is given by:

$$e(f) = \sum_{i=1}^{k} (f(v^i)m_0(v^i) + (1-f(v^i))m_1(v^i)).$$

It is assumed that the oracle misclassifies each vector v with a probability $q(v) \in (0, \frac{1}{2})$. That is, for a given monotone Boolean function f, the oracle returns for vector v :

1 with probability $p(v) = q(v) \times (1 - f(v)) + (1 - q(v)) \times f(v)$, and
0 with probability $1 - p(v)$.

A key assumption is that the misclassification probabilities are all less than ½, otherwise it would not be possible to infer the correct monotone Boolean function. If the sampled values are considered fixed, their joint probability distribution function can be thought of as the likelihood of function f matching the underlying function as follows:

$$L(f) = q^{e\,(f)}(1 - q)^{m\,-\,e\,(f)}.$$

The likelihood value of a particular monotone Boolean function decreases exponentially as more observations are added and therefore this value is generally very small. However, the likelihood ratio given by:

$$\lambda(f^*) = \frac{L(f^*)}{\displaystyle\sum_{f\in F(V)} L(f)},$$

measures the likelihood of a particular function f^* relative to the likelihood of all possible monotone Boolean functions $F(V)$, defined on the set of vectors V. Note that when the set of vectors V is equal to $\{0,1\}^n$, then the set of all possible monotone Boolean functions $F(V)$ is equal to M_n.

The goal of the maximum likelihood problem is to find a monotone Boolean function $f^* \in F(V)$, so that $L(f^*) \geq L(f) \; \forall \, f \in F(V)$. Assuming that the misclassification probabilities $q(v)$ are all less than ½, this problem is equivalent to identifying a monotone Boolean function f^* that minimizes the number of errors $e(f^*)$ (Boros et al., 1995). Note that if q can take on values greater than ½, then the maximum likelihood solution may maximize the number of errors, as demonstrated by Boros et al. (1995). In this chapter, error maximization is avoided by restricting q to be less than ½; existence of such a solution is shown in Torvik and Triantaphyllou (2004).

The error minimization problem can be converted into an integer maximization problem as follows:

$$min \, e(f) = \quad\quad min\sum_{i=1}^{k} (f(v^{\,i})m_0(v^{\,i}) + (1-f(v^{\,i}))m_1(v^{\,i})) =$$

$$min(-\sum_{i=1}^{k} (f(v^{\,i})(m_1(v^{\,i}) - m_0(v^{\,i})) + \sum_{i=1}^{k} m_1(v^{\,i})).$$

Since the term $\sum_{i=1}^{k} m_1(v^i)$ is constant, it can be removed from the optimization objective. Furthermore, maximizing a particular objective function is equivalent to minimizing the negative of that objective function, resulting in the following simplified integer optimization problem:

$$max\sum_{i=1}^{k} f(v^{\,i})(m_1(v^{\,i}) - m_0(v^{\,i}))$$

$$subject\ to\ f(v^i) \leq f(v^j)\ \forall\ v^i, v^j \in V: v^i \preceq v^j,\ and$$
$$f(v^i) = 0\ or\ 1.$$

This problem is known as a maximum closure problem, which can be converted into a maximum flow problem (Picard, 1976). The most efficient algorithms developed for the maximum flow problem use the idea of preflows developed by Karzanov (1974). For example, the lift-to-front algorithm (e.g., Cormen *et al.*, 1997) takes $O(V^3)$ time. The fact that this problem can be solved in polynomial time is a nice property of the single q parameter model. For two dimensional problems (i.e., $V \subset \mathbb{R}^2$), the minimum number of errors can also be guaranteed via a dynamic programming approach (Bloch and Silverman, 1997).

A more complex error model can potentially maintain as many parameters as the size of the domain V. That is, each vector v may have an associated unique parameter $p(v)$. In this case, minimizing the weighted least squares:

$$min \sum_{i=1}^{k} (\bar{p}(v^i) - p(v^i))(m_1(v^i) + m_0(v^i))$$

$$subject\ to\ p(v^i) \leq p(v^j)\ \forall\ v^i, v^j \in V: v^i \preceq v^j,$$

where
$$\bar{p}(v^i) = \frac{m_1(v^i)}{m_1(v^i) + m_0(v^i)},\ for\ i = 1, 2, ..., k,$$

yields a maximum likelihood solution (Robertson *et al.*, 1988). This is a hard optimization problem, and several algorithms have been developed to solve it optimally and near optimally. The Pooled Adjacent Violators Algorithm (PAVA) by Ayer *et al.* (1955) only guarantees optimality when $(V, \preceq)$ forms a chain poset (also referred to as a simple order). The Min-Max algorithm developed by Lee (1983) and the Isotonic Block Class with Stratification (IBCS) algorithm by Block *et al.* (1994) guarantee optimality for the general poset but both algorithms can potentially consume exponential time. Unfortunately, no polynomial algorithm for the general poset was found in the literature.

In addition to the full parametric model, there are models of intermediate parametric complexity. One example is the logistic regression model with non-negativity constraints on its parameters, as used for record linkage in databases by Judson (2001). A monotone decision tree approach can be found in Makino *et al.* (1999), and a sequential monotone rule induction approach can be found in Ben-David (1992 and 1995).

It should be noted that the single parameter error model considered in this chapter is somewhat restrictive, in the sense that it does not estimate misclassification probabilities that vary across the vectors. However, the goal of this chapter is to efficiently uncover the underlying monotone Boolean function and not necessarily come up with accurate estimates for the individual errors. The fixed misclassification probability assumption does not affect the capability of the inference methodology as will be demonstrated in the subsequent sections. The assumption is simply used to estimate the error rate and the confidence in having inferred the correct function, and a more accurate estimate of the maximum likelihood ratio may require a substantial increase in computational complexity, as for the full parametric model described above.

3.   INFERENCE OBJECTIVES AND METHODOLOGY

3.1   The Inference Objective for Problem 1

An inference algorithm that performs fewer queries than another algorithm when reconstructing a particular deterministic monotone Boolean function is considered more efficient on that particular function. However, it has not been clear how to compare algorithms on the entire class of monotone Boolean functions defined on $\{0,1\}^n$.

The main existing algorithms by Hansel (1966), Sokolov (1982), and Gainanov (1984) focus on the upper bounds of their query complexities. Unfortunately, the worst case scenario reflects the algorithm performance on a few specific functions. It does not reflect what to expect when executing the algorithm on an arbitrary monotone Boolean function. For example, algorithms that implement Gainanov's subroutine (which we refer to as FIND-BORDER) indirectly suggest minimizing the upper bound on the number of evaluations per border vector. These algorithms greatly favor the simplest functions (which may only have a single border vector) over the complex functions (with up to $\binom{n}{\lfloor n/2 \rfloor} + \binom{n}{\lfloor n/2 \rfloor + 1}$ border vectors). Kovalerchuk et al. (1996) demonstrated promising results for a Hansel based inference algorithm on a real world application. However, their performance analysis is far from conclusive as a single application represents a single pair of monotone Boolean functions.

With no prior knowledge (other than monotonicity) about the inference application, each function is equally likely to be encountered and should therefore carry the same weight in the objective. The objective for this problem is to develop an algorithm that minimizes the average number of queries over the entire class of monotone Boolean functions defined on the set $\{0,1\}^n$. This objective can be expressed mathematically as follows:

$$Q(n) = \min_{A} \frac{\sum_{f \in M_n} \varphi(A, f)}{\Psi(n)}.$$

The objective $Q(n)$ represents the entire class of monotone Boolean functions M_n. As such, it provides a better indication of what to expect when executing an algorithm on an arbitrary monotone Boolean function.

3.2   The Inference Objective for Problem 2

The approach taken to this problem is analogous to that of Problem 1. The minimum average number of queries for Problem 2.k (for $k = 1, 2$, and 3) can be expressed mathematically as follows:

$$Q_k(n) = \min_{A_k} \frac{\sum_{f_1, f_2 \in M_n: f_2 \le f_1} \varphi(A_k, f_1, f_2)}{\Psi(n+1)}.$$

Here, $\varphi(A_k, f_1, f_2)$ denotes the number of queries performed by algorithm A_k, in reconstructing the pair of nested monotone Boolean functions f_1 and f_2 defined on the set $\{0,1\}^n$. Here, A_1, A_2, and A_3 denote algorithms designed for Problems 2.1, 2.2, and 2.3, respectively. Please recall from section 2 that the number of pairs of nested monotone Boolean functions defined on the set $\{0,1\}^n$ is equal to $\Psi(n+1)$, the number of monotone Boolean functions defined on the set $\{0,1\}^{n+1}$.

Since these three problems differ in the way the oracles are queried, it should be clarified that a query unit pertains to the membership value from one of the two functions f_1 and f_2. This definition is intuitive for Problems 2.1 and 2.3, where two oracles are accessed individually. For Problem 2.2, the membership values are provided in pairs from a single three-valued oracle. To make the definition of $Q_2(n)$ comparable to $Q_1(n)$ and $Q_3(n)$, each query to the three-valued oracle will be counted as two queries.

3.3   The Inference Objective for Problem 3

The approach taken to Problem 3 is similar to that of Problems 1 and 2. The goal is to minimize the average number of queries needed to completely reconstruct the underlying monotone Boolean function, expressed mathematically as follows:

$$\min_{A} \frac{\sum_{f \in M_n} \varphi(A, f, q)}{\Psi(n)}.$$

Here, $\varphi(A, f, q)$ denotes the expected number of queries performed by algorithm A in completely reconstructing the underlying monotone Boolean function f from an oracle with a fixed misclassification probability q. Completely reconstructing the underlying function translates into making the likelihood ratio $\lambda(f^*)$ for the inferred function f^* reach a sufficiently high value (e.g., 0.99).

It should be stressed that the misclassification probability q is unknown and ranges from 0 up to $\frac{1}{2}$. However, it is expected that the average number of queries will increase significantly with q, since, by definition, it approaches infinity as q approaches $\frac{1}{2}$, and it is finite when q is equal to 0. Therefore, the average over a large range q may not be an accurate prediction of how many queries to expect for a particular application. The average query complexity will therefore be evaluated as a function of n and q, even though q is unknown.

3.4   Incremental Updates for the Fixed Misclassification Probability Model

Suppose the error minimizing function f_{old}^* and its misclassification parameter q_{old}^*, associated with a set of vectors $V = \{v^1, v^2, ..., v^k\}$ and their $m_0(v)$ and $m_1(v)$ values, are given. When a new vector is classified by the oracle (i.e., $m_z(v) \leftarrow m_z(v) + 1$), the function f_{old}^* and its misclassification parameter q_{old}^* may have to be updated. Since the new error minimizing function is likely to be close to the old function, it may be inefficient to solve the entire problem over again.

Simply stated the incremental problem consists of finding f_{new}^* and consequently q_{new}^* when $m_z(v) \leftarrow m_z(v) + 1$. If the new classification is consistent with the old function (i.e., $f_{old}^*(v) = z$), then the old function remains error minimizing (i.e., $f_{old}^* = f_{new}^*$). Therefore, the number of errors remains the same and the misclassification estimate is reduced to $q_{new}^* = e(f_{old}^*)/(m_{old} + 1)$. Note that this case is the most likely one since it occurs with an estimated probability of $1 - q_{old}^* \geq \frac{1}{2}$. If, on the other hand, the new classification is inconsistent with the old function (i.e., $f_{old}^*(v) = 1 - z$), the old function may or may not remain error minimizing. The only case in which the old function does not remain error minimizing is when there is an alternative error minimizing function f_a^* on the old data for which $f_a^*(v) = z$. In this case f_a^* is error minimizing for the new data.

The number of possible error minimizing functions may be exponential in the size of the set V, and therefore storing all of them may not be an efficient solution to this problem. To avoid this computational burden an incremental algorithm such as the one described in Torvik and Triantaphyllou (2004) can be used.

3.5   Selection Criteria for Problem 1

When computing the optimal solutions, many different and complex posets are encountered. The optimal vectors of these posets seemed to display two general properties (Torvik and Triantaphyllou, 2002). First, the optimal vectors tend to be in the *vertical middle*. More specifically, all posets observed in the inference process when n is 4 or less have at least one optimal vector in the most populous (middle) layer. This observation alone is not sufficient to pinpoint an optimal vector. The second property observed is that the optimal vectors also tend to be *horizontal end points*.

Now consider creating a selection criterion based on the ideas of vertical middle and horizontal end points. Suppose a subset of unclassified vectors, $V = \{v^1, v^2, ..., v^p\}$ is given. Let $K_1(v^i)$ and $K_0(v^i)$ be the number of vectors that are concurrently classified when $f(v^i)$ equals to 1 and 0, respectively. Invariably selecting a vector v with the minimum $|K_1(v) - K_0(v)|$ value guarantees the minimum average number of queries for inference problems with n strictly less than 5 (Torvik and Triantaphyllou, 2002).

Unfortunately, this selection criterion is not optimal for all the posets generated for n equal to 4. It is only optimal for the subset of posets encountered when using the criterion $min|K_1 - K_0|$. Another drawback is that it is not optimal for the inference problem when n is equal to 5. However, the criterion is probably close to optimal since the larger posets eventually decompose into smaller posets.

It is important to note that what may look like intuitive criteria (without the consultation of optimal solutions) may lead to poor performance and ambiguous choices. For example, it may seem reasonable to attempt to classify as many vectors as possible for each query. The two criteria $max(K_1(v) + K_0(v))$ and $max(K_1(v)K_0(v))$ are consistent with this philosophy (see Judson, 1999). However, they are extremely counterproductive to minimizing the average query complexity and should be avoided. As an example, consider the set of vectors $\{0,1\}^4$. The criterion $max(K_1(v) + K_0(v))$ selects either the (0000) or the (1111) vector, which happens to <u>maximize</u> the average number of queries. The criterion $max(K_1(v)K_0(v))$ ties the entire set of vectors, and is therefore the choice of vector is ambiguous.

There is a logical explanation for why these two selection criteria are counterproductive. Vectors that are able to concurrently classify more vectors are also more likely to be classified by others. Following this line of thought, the selection criterion $min(K_1(v) + K_0(v))$ seems reasonable. This criterion is similar to $min|K_1(v) - K_0(v)|$, but it does not satisfy the same optimality conditions for the inference problem when n is equal to 4.

3.6   Selection Criteria for Problems 2.1, 2.2, and 2.3

The minimum average number of queries for the unrestricted problem $Q_3(n)$ is equal to that of the single function case in one dimension higher $Q(n+1)$. That is, $Q_3(n) = Q(n+1)$. To see this connection consider a pair of nested monotone Boolean functions f_1 and f_2 defined on $\{0,1\}^n$. The query domain for the nested case can be viewed as the product: $\{0,1\}^n \times \{f_2, f_1\}$. Each of the vertices in the resulting poset $(\{0,1\}^{n+1}, \preceq)$, may take on function values of 0 or 1, where the monotonicity property is preserved. In other words, a pair of nested monotone Boolean functions defined on $\{0,1\}^n$ are equivalent to a single monotone Boolean function defined on $\{0,1\}^{n+1}$.

The selection criterion $min|K_1(v)-K_0(v)|$ was shown to be very efficient in minimizing the average number of queries in Problem 1. It will therefore be used for the three nested problems with a slight modification. The query domain for the nested case is made up of the set of vectors $\{0,1\}^n \times \{f_2, f_1\}$. For a vertex labeled $(v\ f_i\ )$, let $K_z(v,\ f_i)$ be the number of vertices that are concurrently classified when the value of $f_i(v)$ is queried and the answer is $f_i(v) = z$, for $z = 0$ and 1. When the access to the oracles is unrestricted (i.e., Problem 2.3), vertices are selected based on the criterion $min|K_1(v, f_i) - K_0(v, f_i)|$. This criterion is equivalent to the criterion $min|K_1(v)-K_0(v)|$ for the single function case. The only change is in the notation since the oracle that is to provide the answer has to be identified for Problem 2.3.

For sequential oracles (i.e., Problem 2.1), queries of the form $f_2(v)$ are infeasible until all of the queries of the form $f_1(v)$ are classified. In this case, the criterion used during the first phase is $min|K_1(v, f_1) - K_0(v, f_1)|$, after which the criterion $min|K_1(v, f_2) - K_0(v, f_2)|$ is used.

For the three-valued oracle (i.e., Problem 2.2), the queries are of the form $(f_1(v), f_2(v))$ and are selected using the criterion $min|K_{11}(v)-K_{00}(v)|$. Here the value of the function $K_{zz}(v)$ equals the number of vertices concurrently classified when vertex v is queried and the result of the query is $f_1(v) = f_2(v) = z$, for $z = 0$ and 1. Once there are no pairs of vertices of the form $(f_1(v), f_2(v))$ left unclassified, the criterion $min|K_1(v, f_i) - K_0(v, f_i)|$ is used for the remaining of the query selections.

3.7   Selection Criterion for Problem 3

The status of the inference process will be considered to be in one of three stages. Stage 1 starts with the first question and lasts until a deterministic monotone Boolean function is obtained. During Stage 1 only vectors that may take on both 0 and 1 values are queried. As a result, no (identifiable) errors are observed in Stage 1, and thus the monotone Boolean function inferred during Stage 1 is deterministic. This function, however, may or may not be the correct function. In fact, the probability that it is the correct function is equal to the probability that no misclassifications were made: $(1-q)^m$, where m is the number of questions used during Stage 1 and q is the true misclassification probability. This probability decreases rapidly with m, regardless of the value of q. Therefore, the queries performed after Stage 1 will benefit greatly from a reduction in the number of Stage 1 queries. Please note that since no inconsistencies have been observed, there is no way to properly estimate q at this point.

After a deterministic monotone Boolean function is obtained in Stage 1, the inference process enters Stage 2. At this point it is unclear as to how to select queries for Stage 2, so a random selection procedure will be used for this stage. After the first error occurs in Stage 2, the inference process enters Stage 3, in which it will remain until termination. Stage 3 is the focus of this chapter, because it is the only stage in which the likelihood ratio can be properly evaluated and q can be estimated based on the observed vectors.

Please recall that the likelihood function is given by:

$$L(f) = q^{e\,(f)}(1 - q)^{m\, -\, e\,(f)},$$

and the likelihood ratio is given by:

$$\lambda(f^*) \;=\; \frac{L(\,f^*\,)}{\displaystyle\sum_{f\,\in\,F\,(V)} L(\,f\,)}.$$

As an example of the likelihood ratio computations consider the example data given in Table 2. The likelihood values for the all the possible monotone Boolean functions are given in Table 3. The function $f^* = v_1v_3 \vee v_2v_3$ produces 16 errors. Its associated estimated misclassification probability q^* is $16/36 = 4/9$, since the total number of observations is $m = 36$. Therefore, the likelihood value of this function $L(f^*)$ is $(4/9)^{16}(1 - 4/9)^{36-16} = 1.818 \times 10^{-11}$. Notice how small this value is after only 36 observations. Adding up the likelihood values the monotone Boolean functions yields $(13 \times 1.455 + 2 \times 1.536 + 5 \times 1.818) \times 10^{-11}$ $= 3.107 \times 10^{-10}$. Then the maximum likelihood ratio is computed as follows: $\lambda(f^*)$ $= 1.818 \times 10^{-11}/3.107 \times 10^{-10} = 0.0585$.

Table 2. A Sample Data Set for Problem 3.

v	$m_1(v)$	$m_0(v)$	$m_1(v) - m_0(v)$
111	0	1	-1
110	3	5	-2
101	4	1	3
11	3	1	2
100	4	5	-1
10	2	0	2
1	3	3	0
0	1	0	1

Table 3. Example Likelihood Values for All Functions in M_3.

f	$e(f)$	$q(f)$	$L(f)$	$\lambda(f)$
F	20	½	1.455×10^{-11}	0.0468
$v_1 v_2 v_3$	21	½	1.455×10^{-11}	0.0468
$v_1 v_2$	23	½	1.455×10^{-11}	0.0468
$v_1 v_3$	18	½	1.455×10^{-11}	0.0468
$v_1 v_2 \vee v_1 v_3$	20	½	1.455×10^{-11}	0.0468
v_1	21	½	1.455×10^{-11}	0.0468
$v_2 v_3$	19	½	1.455×10^{-11}	0.0468
$v_1 \vee v_2 v_3$	19	½	1.455×10^{-11}	0.0468
$v_1 v_3 \vee v_2 v_3$	16	36989	1.818×10^{-11}	0.0585
$v_1 v_2 \vee v_1 v_3 \vee v_2 v_3$	18	½	1.455×10^{-11}	0.0468
$v_1 v_2 \vee v_2 v_3$	21	½	1.455×10^{-11}	0.0468
v_2	19	½	1.455×10^{-11}	0.0468
$v_1 \vee v_2$	17	17/36	1.536×10^{-11}	0.0495
$v_2 \vee v_1 v_3$	16	36989	1.818×10^{-11}	0.0585
v_3	16	36989	1.818×10^{-11}	0.0585
$v_2 \vee v_3$	16	36989	1.818×10^{-11}	0.0585
$v_1 \vee v_2 \vee v_3$	17	17/36	1.536×10^{-11}	0.0495
$v_1 \vee v_3$	19	½	1.455×10^{-11}	0.0468
$v_3 \vee v_1 v_2$	18	½	1.455×10^{-11}	0.0468
T	16	36989	1.818×10^{-11}	0.0585

Now let us return to the vector selection (or guided inference) problem. As shown above, the probability that the correct function is inferred during Stage 1 decreases rapidly with the number of queries used during that stage. Therefore, the selection criterion $min|K_0(v) - K_1(v)|$ will be used as a standard for Stage 1, when comparing different approaches for the following Stage 3. This avoids bias in the sense that all Stage 3 approaches will benefit from using $min|K_0(v) - K_1(v)|$ during Stage 1.

One important property of the selection criterion for Stage 3 is that the maximum likelihood ratio converges to 1. It is possible to define selection criteria that do not converge. If, for example, the same vector is invariably selected, the estimated value of q will converge to its true value. In this case, the likelihood values may remain equal for several monotone Boolean functions and hence the maximum likelihood ratio will never converge to 1.

Intuition may lead to an inefficient selection criterion. For example, let $E_z(v)$

be defined by the number of errors associated with assigning the function value $f(v)$ to z, as follows:

$$E_0(v) = \sum_{w \le v} m_1(w) - m_0(w), E_1(v) = \sum_{v \le w} m_0(w) - m_1(w).$$

Then, consider defining the vector v which "contributes the most errors" by $max(E_0(v) + E_1(v))$. This vector selection criterion may lead to the same vector being invariably queried and hence it might suffer from convergence problems, as will be demonstrated empirically in section 4.

The likelihood framework seems to form a great basis for defining a Stage 3 vector selection criterion. Since the goal is to make the likelihood ratio converge to 1 as fast as possible, a reasonable approach would be to select the vector that maximizes the expected maximum likelihood ratio at each inference step. To do this, the expected maximum likelihood ratio $\Delta\lambda(v) = p(v)\lambda_1(v) + (1 - p(v))\lambda_0(v)$ has to be estimated for each vector v. Here $\lambda_z(v)$ denotes the resulting maximum likelihood ratio when $f(v) = z$ is observed. Please recall that $p(v)$ is the probability of observing $f(v) = 1$. That is, it can be estimated by $p^*(v) = q^*(1 - f^*(v)) + (1 - q^*)f^*(v)$.

As an example consider observing the vector (001). Table 4 gives the updated likelihood ratios for each monotone Boolean function when $m_z(001) = m_z(001) + 1$, for $z = 0$ and 1. For a monotone Boolean function f, and a classification z, $e_z(001, f)$ and $\lambda_z(001, f)$ here denote the updated number of errors and the likelihood ratio, respectively. The updated maximum likelihood ratios are $\lambda_1(001) = \lambda_1(001, T) = 0.0649$ and $\lambda_0(001) = \lambda_0(001, v_1v_3 \lor v_2v_3) = 0.0657$. Since the optimal function assigns the vector (001) to 0 (i.e., $f^*(001) = 0$), the estimated probability of observing $f(001) = 1$ is given by $p^*(001) = q^* = 4/9$. Therefore, the expected maximum likelihood ratio when querying vector 001 is given by $\Delta\lambda(001) = p^*(001)\lambda_1(001) + (1 - p^*(001))\lambda_0(001) = 4/9 \times 0.0649 + 5/9 \times 0.0657 = 0.0653$.

Similar computations for the other vectors yield $\Delta\lambda(000) = 0.0651$, $\Delta\lambda(010) = 0.0654$, $\Delta\lambda(011) = 0.0592$, $\Delta\lambda(100) = 0.0652$, $\Delta\lambda(101) = 0.0592$, $\Delta\lambda(110) = 0.0654$, and finally $\Delta\lambda(111) = 0.0592$. The vectors with the largest expected likelihood ratio value are (010) and (110). Since no further improvements of the selection criterion is immediately obvious, ties are broken arbitrarily.

The simulations in section 4 reveal the efficiency of the selection criterion $max\ \Delta\lambda(v)$ in terms of the query complexity. In terms of computational complexity it may take an exponential time (in the size of V) to compute $max\ \Delta\lambda(v)$. Since the computational time for incrementally finding the inferred function is of $O(V^2)$, it would be nice to find a selection criterion that does not take more time than this and still makes the likelihood converge to 1 at a faster rate than randomly selecting vectors.

Table 4. Updated Likelihood Ratios for $m_z(001) = m_z(001) + 1$.

f	$\lambda(f)$	$e_1(001, f)$	$\lambda_1(001, f)$	$e_0(001, f)$	$\lambda_0(001, f)$
F	0.0468	21	0.0462	20	0.0468
$v_1v_2v_3$	0.0468	22	0.0462	21	0.0468
v_1v_2	0.0468	24	0.0462	23	0.0468
v_1v_3	0.0468	19	0.0462	18	0.0474
$v_1v_2 \vee v_1v_3$	0.0468	21	0.0462	20	0.0468
v_1	0.0468	22	0.0462	21	0.0468
v_2v_3	0.0468	20	0.0462	19	0.0468
$v_1 \vee v_2v_3$	0.0468	20	0.0462	19	0.0468
$v_1v_3 \vee v_2v_3$	0.0585	17	0.0522	16	0.0657
$v_1v_2 \vee v_1v_3 \vee v_2v_3$	0.0468	19	0.0462	18	0.0474
$v_1v_2 \vee v_2v_3$	0.0468	22	0.0462	21	0.0468
v_2	0.0468	20	0.0462	19	0.0468
$v_1 \vee v_2$	0.0495	18	0.0469	17	0.0529
$v_2 \vee v_1v_3$	0.0585	17	0.0522	16	0.0657
v_3	0.0585	16	0.0649	17	0.0529
$v_2 \vee v_3$	0.0585	16	0.0649	17	0.0529
$v_1 \vee v_2 \vee v_3$	0.0495	17	0.0522	18	0.0474
$v_1 \vee v_3$	0.0468	19	0.0462	20	0.0468
$v_3 \vee v_1v_2$	0.0468	18	0.0469	19	0.0468
T	0.0585	16	0.0649	17	0.0529

One such possibility may be based on the inferred border vectors. For the sake of argument suppose that the underlying monotone Boolean function f to be inferred is known. Then randomly selecting vectors from its corresponding border vectors will make the maximum likelihood ratio converge to 1. As the number of queries m goes to infinity, the ratios $m_0(v)/(m_0(v) + m_1(v)) \ \forall \ v \in$ LU(f) and $m_1(w)/(m_0(w) + m_1(w)) \ \forall \ w \in$ UZ(f) all converge to q. The number of errors performed by any other monotone Boolean function g is at least $x = min\{min\{m_1(v) - m_0(v), v \in$ LU(f)$\}, min\{m_0(w) - m_1(w), w \in$ UZ(f)$\}\}$ greater than the number of errors performed by function f. Furthermore, $x \approx qm - (1-q)m = m(2q - 1)$ for large m. That is, the number of additional errors increases at least linearly with m. Then, as m goes to infinity, so does the number of additional errors performed by each of the other monotone Boolean functions. That is, the relative likelihoods $L(f)/L(g) > (q/(1- q))^x$ converge to 0 as m goes to infinity. Since the number of other monotone Boolean functions is a finite number that does not depend on m, the likelihood ratio $\lambda(f) = L(f) / (L(f) + \sum L(g))$ converges to 1 as m goes to infinity.

Focusing the queries at the border vectors of the underlying function probably allows this convergence to occur at a faster rate than randomly selecting from all the vectors. In situations where the underlying function is unknown, it may be that focusing the queries on the border vectors of the inferred function (i.e., $v \in LU(f^*) \cup UZ(f^*)$) is better than completely random selection. In the long run, an inferred border vector will not prevail if it is not an underlying border vector. Since the misclassification rate is less than ½, the rate at which the incorrectly classified inferred border vectors become correctly classified is greater than the rate at which correctly classified inferred border vectors become incorrectly classified. Therefore, in the long run all the classifications become correct when the queries are selected from the set of border vectors of the inferred function.

Notice that this convergence holds even if the misclassification probability is different for each vector, as long as they are all less than ½. Another added benefit is that finding the border vectors is easy, since they are readily available from the inferred function f^*. In fact, a simple modification of the incremental maximum flow algorithm can store each of these vectors as they are found. For each monotone Boolean function there are at most $O(V)$ border vectors in a set of vectors V. During the inference process the inferred function may take on any of these monotone Boolean functions. Therefore, randomly selecting one of the border vectors takes $O(V)$ time.

4.   EXPERIMENTAL RESULTS

4.1   Experimental Results for Problem 1

The preexisting inference algorithms described in section 2 do not specify which vector to select when there are ties. In particular, the Sokolov and Hansel algorithms may have to choose between two vectors that make up the middle of a particular chain. Furthermore, the subroutine FIND-BORDER needs to be fed unclassified vectors, of which there may be many. Even the selection criterion $min|K_1\text{-}K_0|$ may result in ties. For the purpose of comparing the algorithms on the same ground and without introducing another aspect of randomness, ties were broken by selecting the first vector in the list of tied vectors.

The results in Figure 3 are based on an exhaustive analysis (i.e., all the monotone functions were generated) for n up to and including 5. Random samples of 2,000 functions were generated for $n = 6, 7,$ and 8; while for $n = 9, 10,$ and 11 they were composed of 200 functions; the functions were generated using the algorithm described in Torvik and Triantaphyllou (2002).

The Horvitz-Thompson (1952) estimator is used to compute the averages for n greater than 5. The average number of queries is normalized by the maximum possible number of queries 2^n so that the magnitudes of the averages in Figure 3 are not overshadowed by the large values obtained for n equal to 11. As a consequence, two algorithms that result in parallel curves in such a plot, have an exponential (in n) difference in the average number of queries. Also, the gap between the curves in Figure 3 and the horizontal line *Average Number of Queries* $/ 2^n = 1$ (not shown in the figure) can be thought of as the benefit of the monotone assumption. This is due to the fact that 2^n is the number of required queries when the underlying function is not necessarily monotone.

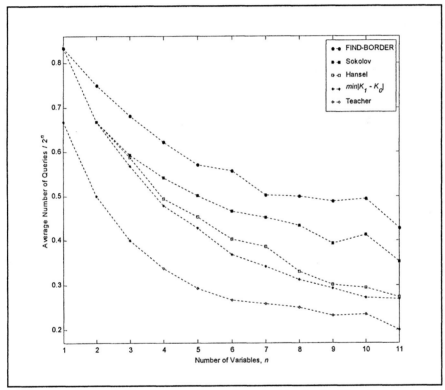

Figure 3. The Average Query Complexities for Problem 1.

The curve titled "Teacher" represents the lower bound on the number of queries for every single function. Therefore, it is expected that a few extra queries are required on the average. Since the heuristic based on the selection criterion $min|K_1-K_0|$ achieves the minimum average number of queries for n up to 4, it can be thought of as a lower bound on the average, and its gap between Teacher quantifies the benefits of knowing the actual function beforehand.

Figure 3 paints a clear picture of how the preexisting inference algorithms fare against each other. Hansel's algorithm was the best performer by far, Sokolov's came in second, and an algorithm using the subroutine FIND-BORDER (which is also used by Gainanov, 1984; Valiant, 1984; Makino and

Ibaraki, 1995; Boros *et al.*, 1997) was a distant third. In fact, since the curve differences between Hansel and Sokolov, and Sokolov and the subroutine FIND-BORDER implementation, seem to increase with n, the corresponding difference in the average number of queries increases at rate greater than exponentially with n.

The difference between the curves for Hansel and "Teacher" decreases as n increases. The algorithm based on the criterion $min|K_1-K_0|$ has a curve that is almost parallel to Hansel's curve, indicating that the selection criterion performs about 2% better than Hansel's algorithm. This decrease is especially clear in Figure 3 for n up to and including 8. For larger values of n, the high variance of our estimates makes it hard to distinguish the two curves, but the overall decreasing trends remain intact. It might seem that a 2% decrease is insignificant, but writing it as $2^n \times 0.02$ shows its real magnitude.

Another nice characteristic of this selection criterion is that it is the most consistent of all the algorithms. For example, it performs between 10 and 18 queries for 99.6% of the monotone Boolean functions in M_5. In contrast, the algorithm based on the subroutine FIND-BORDER is the least consistent with between 8 and 25 queries for 99.6% of the monotone Boolean functions.

4.2   Experimental Results for Problem 2

The results in Figures 4, 5, and 6 are based on an exhaustive analysis (i.e., all the monotone functions were generated) for n up to and including 4. For n = 4, 5, ...,12 random samples of functions were generated and the Horvitz-Thompson (1952) estimator is used to compute the averages for n greater than 4. The number of pairs of nested monotone Boolean functions generated were 2,000 for $n = 5, 6, 7$, and 200 for $n = 8, 9, 10$, and 100 for $n = 11$ and 12.

Figure 4 shows the average number of queries for Problem 2 when using the selection criteria. The lower curve corresponds to the unrestricted case (Problem 2.3), which achieves the fewest number of queries on the average. The sequential case (Problem 2.1), corresponding to the middle curve, is not as efficient as the unrestricted oracles in general, although they are very close for $n = 1, 2, 3$, and 4. The least efficient of the three types of oracles is the three-valued (Problem 2.2) corresponding to the upper curve.

The gap between the curves in Figure 4 and the horizontal line *Average Number of Queries* / $2^{n+1} = 1$ (the uppermost line of the box around the curves) can be thought of as the benefit of the monotone and nestedness assumptions together. This is due to the fact that 2^{n+1} is the number of required queries when the underlying pair of functions are neither nested or monotone. For example, when $n = 12$ in the unrestricted problem ($k = 3$) the average number of queries is reduced to about 20% of the maximum number of queries $2^{13} = 8,192$ due to the monotone and nestedness assumptions.

Figure 5 quantifies the increase in the average number of queries due to the two restrictions on the oracles for $n = 1, 2, ..., 12$. As mentioned earlier, the sequential oracles are practically unrestrictive for $n = 1, 2, 3$, and 4. For n greater than 4, the increase in average query complexity oscillates between 12% and 33% due to odd and even n, being much greater for odd n. In contrast, the three-valued oracle is much more restrictive across all the observed n, where the increase in the average number of queries oscillates between 35% and 55%, again due to odd and even n, being greater for odd n. In summary, the increases in the average number of queries for the sequential and three-valued cases are dramatic. This is probably due to the fact that the average number of queries increases exponentially with the number of variables.

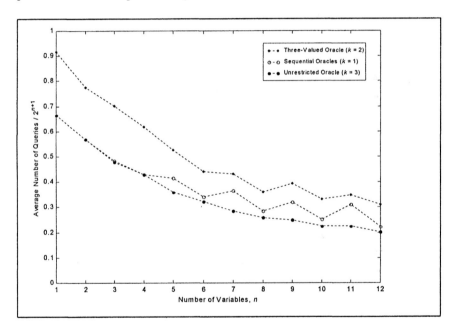

Figure 4. The Average Query Complexities for Problem 2.

If the nested property of the two functions defined on $\{0,1\}^n$ is ignored, the minimum total number of questions is, on average, $2Q(n)$. The benefit from the nestedness assumption for Problem 2 is quantified by the ratio of $Q_3(n)/2Q(n)$ which is given in Figure 6 for $n = 1, 2, ..., 12$. Therefore, the curves given in Figure 6 show the reduction in the average number of queries due to the nestedness assumption. This reduction decreases with the number of variables. It starts out at 20% for $n = 1$, and oscillates between 1% and 10% for n greater than 7.

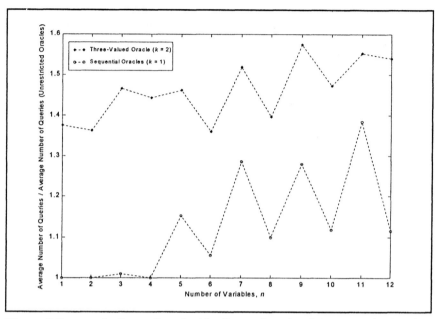

Figure 5. Increase in Query Complexities Due to Restricted Access to the Oracles.

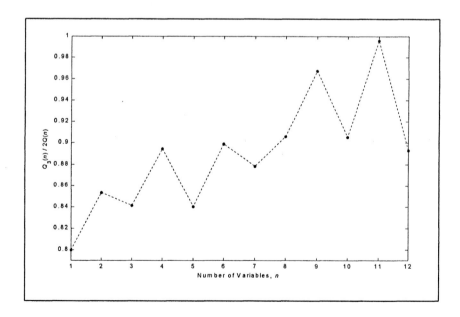

Figure 6. Reduction in Query Complexity Due to the Nestedness Assumption.

4.3   Experimental Results for Problem 3

For the purpose of comparing the efficiency of the different selection criteria for Stage 3 on the same basis, ties resulting from the selection criteria $(min|K_0(v) - K_1(v)|$ for Stage 1, and $max(E_0(v) + E_1(v))$, $max\ \Delta\lambda(v)$, and $v \in$ LU$(f^*) \cup$ UZ(f^*), the set of border vectors for Stage 3) were broken randomly. The four different inference processes using $max\ \Delta\lambda(v)$, $v \in$ LU$(f^*) \cup$ UZ(f^*), $max(E_0(v) + E_1(v))$, or random selection for Stage 3 were simulated on the set of vertices $\{0,1\}^n$. For all three Stage 3 selection criteria, the selection criterion $min|K_0(v) - K_1(v)|$ was used for Stage 1 and random selection was used for Stage 2. The resulting simulations were repeated 100, 50, 25, and 10 times for each of 6 representative functions of M_n, with misclassification probabilities 0.1, 0.2, 0.3, and 0.4, for $n = 2, 3, 4$ and 5, respectively.

The representative functions are given in Table 5. For $n = 4$ and 5, these representative functions were randomly generated from a uniform distribution with individual probabilities of $1/\Psi(n) = 1/168$ and $1/7581$, respectively. For $n = 3$, the representative functions consist of non-similar functions (one from each similar subset of M_3). These functions represent all the functions in M_3, since the average case behavior is the same for a pair of similar monotone Boolean functions.

Table 5. The Representative Functions Used in the Simulations of Problem 3.

$n = 2$	$n = 3$	$n = 4$	$n = 5$
F	F	$v_1v_2 \lor v_2v_4 \lor v_1v_3v_4$	$v_1v_4 \lor v_1v_5 \lor v_2v_4 \lor v_2v_5$
v_1v_2	$v_1v_2v_3$	$v_1v_2 \lor v_1v_3 \lor v_2v_3 \lor v_2v_4 \lor v_3v_4$	$v_1v_3 \lor v_2v_3 \lor v_2v_4 \lor v_1v_2v_5$
v_1	v_1v_2	$v_2v_3 \lor v_2v_4$	$v_2 \lor v_1v_3v_4 \lor v_1v_4v_5$
v_2	$v_1v_2 \lor v_1v_3$	$v_1v_2v_3 \lor v_1v_3v_4 \lor v_2v_3v_4$	$v_1v_3 \lor v_2v_4 \lor v_3v_5 \lor v_1v_4v_5$
$v_1 \lor v_2$	v_1	$v_1v_2 \lor v_2v_4 \lor v_3v_4$	$v_2v_4 \lor v_2v_5 \lor v_3v_5 \lor v_4v_5$
T	$v_1v_2 \lor v_1v_3 \lor v_2v_3$	$v_3 \lor v_1v_2 \lor v_1v_4$	$v_2v_5 \lor v_1v_2v_3 \lor v_1v_3v_4 \lor v_1v_4v_5 \lor v_3v_4v_5$

To compute the overall average for a given q, the individual curves were weighted by the number of similar functions the representative function has (including itself) in M_3. The individual curves for the monotone Boolean functions F, $v_1v_2v_3$, v_1v_2, $v_1v_2 \lor v_1v_3$, v_1, and $v_1v_2 \lor v_1v_3 \lor v_2v_3$, were therefore weighted by 2, 2, 6, 6, 3, and 1, respectively. For $n = 2, 4$, and 5, the overall averages were computed without weights. The overall averages for $n = 2$ and 3 benefit from a reduced variance, since no additional errors are added due to the sampling of functions as done for $n = 4$ and 5.

Figure 7 shows the resulting average maximum likelihood curves for the inference problem defined on $n = 2, 3, 4$, and 5, and $q = 0.1, 0.2, 0.3$, and 0.4. Each curve is the average of 600, 300, 150, and 60 simulated inference processes observed for $n = 2, 3, 4$, and 5, respectively. In each plot, the horizontal axis corresponds to the number of Stage 3 queries, and the vertical axis corresponds to the maximum likelihood ratio. The curves are shown for the range of Stage 3 queries where the curves corresponding to the selection criterion *max* $\Delta\lambda(v)$ has a maximum likelihood ratio that is less than 0.99.

Not only do the curves corresponding to the guided selection criteria *max* $\Delta\lambda(v)$ and $v \in LU(f^*) \cup UZ(f^*)$ converge to 1 but they do so at a much faster rate than the curves corresponding to unguided random selection. In fact, the random selection achieves a maximum likelihood ratio of only about 0.7 after the same number of queries as the criterion *max* $\Delta\lambda(v)$ uses to reach 0.99, and the criterion $v \in LU(f^*) \cup UZ(f^*)$ uses to reach about 0.9, for $n = 4$.

The difference between the curves for unguided selection and these two guided selections grows with the misclassification probability q and with the dimension n. That is, the benefits from actively selecting vectors over passively receiving observations are greater when the values of q and n are large. In other words, the higher the misclassfication probability and the dimension of the problem are, the greater become the benefits of guiding the inference process.

The curves associated with criterion $max(E_0(v) + E_1(v))$ seems to converge to a value significantly less than 1. For example, when $n = 3$ and $q = 0.3$, the maximum likelihood ratio converges to about 0.4, and this value decreases as the values of q and n increase. Therefore, the larger error rate and the vector domain is, the more important it becomes to define an appropriate vector selection criterion.

Table 6 gives the average number of queries needed by the selection criterion *max* $\Delta\lambda(v)$ to converge to a maximum likelihood ratio of 0.99 for n = 2, 3, 4, and 5, and for q = 0.1, 0.2, 0.3, and 0.4. For a given n, these numbers increase dramatically as q increases. In fact, there seems to be more than a doubling in the numbers for fixed increments of q. For a given q, these numbers do not increase in such a dramatic fashion when n increases. However, they do increase faster than linearly with n.

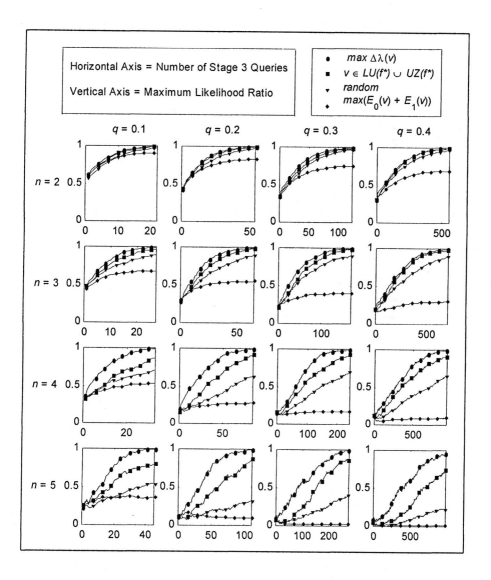

Figure 7. Average Case Behavior of Various Selection Criteria for Problem 3.

Table 6. The Average Number of Stage 3 Queries Used by the Selection Criterion *max* $\Delta\lambda(v)$ to Reach $\lambda > 0.99$ in Problem 3 Defined on $\{0,1\}^n$ with Fixed Misclassification Probability q.

	$q = 0.1$	$q = 0.2$	$q = 0.3$	$q = 0.4$
$n = 2$	22	54	125	560
$n = 3$	27	65	170	710
$n = 4$	33	85	241	951
$n = 5$	45	111	277	1167

Randomly selecting the inferred border vectors (i.e., $v \in LU(f^*) \cup UZ(f^*)$) makes the maximum likelihood ratio converge to 1, as long as the misclassification probabilities are all less than ½. That is, the misclassification probabilities do not necessarily have to be fixed. To see whether this holds for the selection criterion *max* $\Delta\lambda(v)$, consider an unrestricted model where the misclassification probability $q(v)$ is a random variable distributed uniformly on the interval $[q(1- \delta), q(1 + \delta)]$, where $\delta \in [0,1]$, for each vector $v \in \{0,1\}^n$.

The case when $\delta = 0$ corresponds to the fixed misclassification probability model, that is, when $q(v)$ is equal to q for all vectors $v \in \{0,1\}^n$. The range of values for $q(v)$ increases with δ, but the expected value of $q(v)$ is always equal to q. Therefore, the estimate of the maximum likelihood ratio based on the fixed q model is worse for larger values of δ. To compare this estimate to an unrestricted estimate, the inference process was simulated 200 times for each $\delta = 0$, 0.5, and 1, holding constant $n = 3$ and the expected $q = 0.2$. Figure 8 shows the average maximum likelihood ratio curves for the unrestricted model (dotted curves) and the fixed model (solid curves) when using the selection criterion *max* $\Delta\lambda(v)$.

The regular and the unrestricted maximum likelihood ratios both converge to 1, though at slower rates as δ increases. In other words, the selection criterion *max* $\Delta\lambda(v)$ is appropriate in situations where the misclassification probability is not necessarily fixed. In general, the unrestricted maximum likelihood ratio is much smaller than the regular one. For the case when $q(v)$ is fixed at 0.2 (i.e., $\delta = 0$), the regular maximum likelihood ratio should be used, and when $\delta > 0$ it is an overestimate of the true maximum likelihood ratio. For the case when $\delta = 1$, the unrestricted maximum likelihood ratio should be used, and when $\delta < 1$ it may be an underestimate. The true likelihood ratio lies somewhere in between the two.

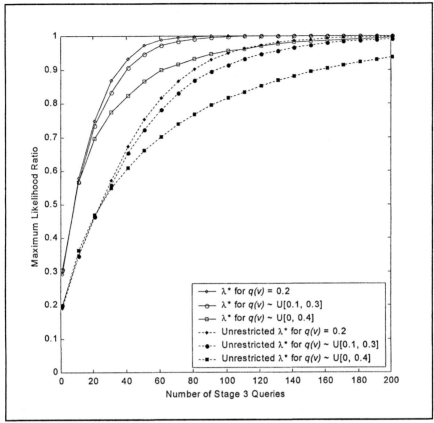

Figure 8. The Restricted and Regular Maximum Likelihood Ratios Simulated
with Expected $q = 0.2$, and $n = 3$.

5.   SUMMARY AND DISCUSSION

5.1   Summary of the Research Findings

The recent focus on the computational complexity has come at the expense
of a drastic increase in the query complexity for Problem 1. In fact, the more
recent the inference algorithm is, the worse it performs in terms of the average
query complexity. The subroutine, here referred to as FIND-BORDER, is the
most commonly used in the recent literature (Gainanov, 1984; Valiant, 1984;
Makino and Ibaraki, 1995; Boros *et al.*, 1997), and its performance was by far
the worst. Therefore, the framework for unbiased empirical comparison of

inference algorithms described in this chapter seems to be long overdue.

Even though guaranteeing the minimum average number of queries is currently only computationally feasible for relatively few variables (i.e., up to 5 or 6), the recursive algorithm used for Problem 1 revealed the non-intuitive nature of the optimal solutions. These solutions paved the way for the new selection criterion $min|K_1-K_0|$. This criterion would probably not have been developed (due to its non-intuitive nature) without the consultation of the optimal solutions.

The inference algorithm based on this selection criterion extends the feasible problem sizes to up to about 20 variables (which involves about 1 million vectors) for Problem 1. When the number of variables exceeds 20, computing the selection criterion might become intractable, while Hansel's algorithm will most likely still perform the best on the average. When creating the chain partition used in Hansel (1966) and Sokolov (1982) becomes intractable, perhaps finding border vectors one at a time by using the subroutine FIND-BORDER is still computationally feasible.

Problem 2 focused on the extension of the single monotone Boolean function inference problem to the inference of a pair of nested monotone Boolean functions. The benefits of this research are manyfold. First, it shows how the optimal and selection criterion approach to minimizing the average query complexity is extended to three different inference applications using a pair of nested monotone Boolean functions. The selection criteria seem to be good choices for the nested inference problem. They result in a slight increase in the average query complexity for the chain poset. For the poset $\{0,1\}^n$, they are optimal for $n = 1, 2, 3$ and are probably very close to optimal for n greater than 3.

Second, it demonstrates how the nested monotone Boolean function model often is sufficient (i.e., a more complex model is not needed) and necessary (i.e., simpler models are not sufficient) for a wide variety of real world applications. Suppose a simpler model, such as a single monotone Boolean function, is used for these applications. At best, the simpler model will provide a poor approximation of the phenomenon under study. At worst, it will be unable to model the phenomenon. Suppose a more complex model, such as a pair of independent monotone Boolean functions, is used for these applications. Then, at the very least, the query complexity will increase. In addition, the inferred functions may lead to conflicting knowledge and are more likely to contain errors.

Third, it quantifies the reduction in query complexity due to the nestedness assumption. The improvement due to the nestedness assumption is between 6% and 8% for larger chain posets ($h > 50$). This improvement is greater for smaller chain posets, reaching its maximum of 20% for $h = 2$. In general, the average query complexity on the chain poset is $O(log(h))$, so this improvement is not very significant. For the poset $\{0,1\}^n$, this improvement is a few percent points for $n > 8$. This improvement decreases with the number of variables, reaching its maximum of 20% for $n = 1$. The average query complexity on the poset $\{0,1\}^n$ is exponential in n. This fact makes this improvement far more dramatic than for the chain poset.

Fourth, it compares the efficiency of the three major types of oracles. The three-valued oracle provides the most significant restriction on the oracles. It causes up to 84% and 55% increase in the average number of queries for the chain poset and the poset $\{0,1\}^n$, respectively. It is interesting to observe that the sequential oracles are just as efficient as the unrestricted oracles on the chain poset and for the poset $\{0,1\}^n$ for n up to 4. This implies that the pair of nested monotone Boolean functions defined on these posets can be inferred sequentially without losing optimality. For the poset $\{0,1\}^n$ with $n > 7$, the sequential oracle causes a significant increase in the average query complexity of 12-33%.

The maximum likelihood ratio approach to modeling the inference process of Problem 3 yielded a number of benefits. It was demonstrated that an appropriately defined guided learner, such as maximizing the expected maximum likelihood ratio ($max \, \Delta\lambda(v)$) or randomly selecting inferred border vectors ($v \in LU(f^*) \cup UZ(f^*)$), allowed the maximum likelihood ratio to converge to 1, even when the misclassification probability was not fixed. This avoids the bias problems associated with the variance approach reported in Cohn (1996), and also observed with the selection criterion $max(E_0(v) + E_1(v))$ which is based on the number of errors.

For complete reconstruction of monotone Boolean functions, the guided approach showed a dramatic reduction in the average number of queries over a passive learner. The simulations also indicated that this improvement grows at least exponentially as the number of variables n and the error rate q increase. Thus, defining an appropriate and efficient selection criterion is even more beneficial for large problems and applications with a high error rate.

For large problems (i.e., $n > 5$), it may not be possible to compute the selection criterion $max \, \Delta\lambda(v)$ since it takes exponential time (in the size of the query domain V) to do so. For such problems, queries can be selected randomly from the border vectors ($v \in LU(f^*) \cup UZ(f^*)$). This only takes $O(V)$ time, and results in much fewer queries than completely random selection on the average.

Hierarchical decomposition provides a way to address a large inference problem as a set of smaller independent inference problems. Even though it was not mentioned earlier, this decomposition is applicable to all three Problems 1, 2, and 3 where it can dramatically reduce the query complexity. Perhaps the greatest benefit of this decomposition is its simplified queries. This fact may not only improve the efficiency but also reduce the number of human errors, and hence increase the likelihood of inferring the correct function.

5.2   Significance of the Research Findings

The single most important discovery described in this chapter is the near optimal selection criteria which take polynomial time to evaluate. This leads to the efficient inference of monotone Boolean functions. The significance of these criteria is further strengthened by the scope of real-life problems that can be modeled by using monotone Boolean functions. Even though only one (or a pair of nested) monotone Boolean function(s) defined on the set of Boolean vectors $\{0,1\}^n$ were studied here, the selection criterion approach to guiding the learner is appropriate for any monotone mapping $V \to F$, where the sets $V \subset \mathbb{R}^n$ and $F \subset \mathbb{R}^r$ are both finite. The query domain can be viewed as a finite poset by using the monotonicity constraints: $f_i(v) \leq f_i(w)$ iff $v \leq w$, for $I = 1, 2, ..., r$, and whatever the relationships between the functions are, such as the nestedness constraints: $f_1(v) \geq f_2(v) \ \forall \ v \in V$. The selection criteria can be evaluated for any such poset in order to pinpoint "smart" queries.

Once the border vectors have been established for each monotone function, they can be used to classify new observations. In addition, they can be represented by a (set of) monotone Boolean function(s) defined on a set of Boolean variables. Representing the inferred knowledge in this intuitive manner is perhaps the most important aspect of this problem when human interaction is involved since people tend to make better use of knowledge they can easily interpret, understand, validate, and remember.

The use of Boolean functions for analyzing fixed datasets has recently gained a momentum due their simple representation of intuitive knowledge. See Triantaphyllou and Soyster (1996b), Boros *et al.* (1995), Torvik *et al.* (1999), and Yilmaz *et al.* (2003) for example. Boolean models are also becoming more popular because methods for solving their related hard logical optimization problems are emerging (e.g., Triantaphyllou (1994), Chandru and Hooker (1999), Hooker (2000), and Felici and Truemper (2002)). Some initial studies on guided inference of Boolean functions from fixed datasets are provided in Triantaphyllou and Soyster (1996a) and Nieto-Sanchez *et al.* (2002).

The narrow vicinity hypothesis proposed by Kovalerchuk *et al.* (2000a) suggests that the use of the monotonicity assumption is often necessary and sufficient. As such, it can greatly improve upon knowledge representations that are too simple or too complex. This chapter demonstrated that the problem of guided inference in the presence of monotonicity can be of great benefit in a wide variety of important real-life applications.

5.3   Future Research Directions

As mentioned in section 5.2 the selection criterion approach to learning monotone Boolean functions defined on $\{0,1\}^n$ is applicable in the much more general monotone setting: $V \to F$, where the sets $V \subset \mathbb{R}^n$ and $F \subset \mathbb{R}^r$ are both finite. The monotone mapping $V \to F$, where the set $V \subset \mathbb{R}^n$ is infinite and the set $F \subset \mathbb{R}^r$ is finite, forms another intriguing problem. It is well known that binary search is optimal when the query domain V is a bounded subset of the real line, and $F = \{0,1\}$. However, when the set V is multidimensional and infinite (e.g., $V = [a, b]^2$), pinpointing the optimal queries is a much more complex problem. The selection criterion $min \ |K_1 - K_0|$ can be modified to accommodate this case too. Let U denote the unclassified set (i.e., a subset of V) and let the parameters $K_0(v)$ and $K_1(v)$ now denote the size of the subsets $\{w \in U: w \prec v\}$ and $\{w \in U: v \prec w\}$, respectively. For example, $K_z(v)$ is measured in terms of distance, area, volume, etc. when $n = 1, 2, 3$, etc., respectively. The selection criterion $min \ |K_1 - K_0|$ is then optimal for $n = 1$. How well this criterion performs when $n > 1$, is an open question.

For the problems considered in this chapter, the selection criteria attempt to minimize the average query costs. This objective is based on certain assumptions of the query costs (fixed cost of querying an oracle in Problems 1, 2, and 3, and highly disproportionate or equal query costs for the two oracles in Problems 2.1 and 2.3, respectively). It would be interesting to see how the dialogue with the oracle(s) changes as these assumptions are modified. When dealing with two oracles, it may be that the cost of querying the first oracle may be less than, yet of similar magnitude as, the cost of querying the second oracle. In this case, the first few queries should be directed at the first oracle. After a few queries it may be cost beneficial to begin alternating between the two oracles. It could also be that the order of the queries has an effect on the total inference cost. In some applications, additional properties may be known about the underlying function. Some applications may put a limit on the number of lower units, shifting the focus of the optimal vertices from the vertical center to the vertical edge of the poset. It may be that the underlying function belongs to a subclass of monotone Boolean functions, such as threshold functions, 2-monotonic functions, etc.

6.   CONCLUDING REMARKS

The methodologies presented in this chapter provide a framework for solving diverse and potentially very important real-life problems that can be modeled as guided inference problems in the presence of monotonicity. The benefits of these methodologies were shown to be dramatic for the specific studied here. However, these research findings are just the tip of the iceberg. The interested reader is referred to Torvik and Triantaphyllou (2002, 2003, 2004) for further details on the methodology for Problems 1, 2, and 3, respectively.

ACKNOWLEDGMENTS

The authors are very appreciative for the support by the U.S. Navy, Office of Naval Research (ONR), research grants N00014-95-1-0639 and N00014-97-1-0632.

REFERENCES

M. Ayer, H.D. Brunk, G.M. Ewing, W.T. Reid, and E. Silverman, "An Empirical Distribution Function for Sampling with Incomplete Information," *Annals of Mathematical Statistics*, Vol. 26, pp. 641-647, 1955.

A. Ben-David. "Automatic Generation of Symbolic Multiattribute Ordinal Knowledge-Based DSSs: Methodology and Applications," *Decision Sciences*, Vol. 23, No. 6, pp. 1357-1372, 1992.

A. Ben-David, "Monotonicity Maintenance in Information-Theoretic Machine Learning Algorithms," *Machine Learning*, Vol. 19, No. 1, pp. 29-43, 1995.

J.C. Bioch and T. Ibaraki, "Complexity of Identification and Dualization of Positive Boolean Functions," *Information and Computation*, Vol. 123 pp. 50-63, 1995.

D.A. Bloch and B. W. Silverman, "Monotone Discriminant Functions and Their Applications in Rheumatology," *Journal of the American Statistical Association*, Vol. 92, No. 437, pp. 144-153, 1997.

H. Block, S. Qian, and A. Sampson, "Structure Algorithms for Partially Ordered Isotonic Regression," *Journal of Computational and Graphical Statistics*, Vol. 3, No. 3, pp. 285-300, 1994.

E. Boros, P.L. Hammer, and J.N. Hooker, "Predicting Cause-Effect Relationships from Incomplete Discrete Observations," *SIAM Journal on Discrete Mathematics*, Vol. 7, No. 4, pp. 531-543, 1994.

E. Boros, P.L. Hammer, and J.N. Hooker, "Boolean Regression," *Annals of Operations Research*, Vol. 58, pp. 201-226, 1995.

E. Boros, P.L. Hammer, T. Ibaraki., and K. Makino, "Polynomial-Time Recognition of 2-Monotonic Positive Boolean Functions Given by an Oracle," *SIAM Journal on Computing*, Vol. 26, No. 1, pp. 93-109, 1997.

V. Chandru and J.N. Hooker, "Optimization Methods for Logical Inference," John Wiley & Sons, New York, NY, USA, 1999.

R. Church, " Numerical Analysis of Certain Free Distributive Structures," *Duke Mathematical Journal*, Vol. 6, pp. 732-734, 1940.

R. Church, "Enumeration by Rank of the Free Distributive Lattice with 7 Generators," *Notices of the American Mathematical Society*, Vol. 11 pp. 724, 1965.

D.A. Cohn, "Neural Network Exploration Using Optimal Experiment Design," *Neural Networks*, Vol. 9, No. 6, pp. 1071-1083, 1996.

D.A. Cohn, "Minimizing Statistical Bias with Queries," A.I. Memo No. 1552, Artificial Intelligence Laboratory, Massachusetts Institute of Technology, Cambridge, MA, USA, 1995.

T.H. Cormen, C.H. Leiserson, and R.L. Rivest, *"Introduction to Algorithms,"* The MIT Press, Cambridge, MA, USA, 1997.

R. Dedekind, R, "Ueber Zerlegungen von Zahlen durch ihre Grössten Gemeinsamen Teiler," *Festschrift Hoch. Brauhnschweig u. ges Werke II*, pp. 103-148, 1897.

T. Eiter and G. Gottlob, "Identifying the Minimal Transversals of a Hypergraph and Related Problems," *SIAM Journal on Computing*, Vol. 24, No. 6, pp. 1278-1304, 1995.

K. Engel. *Encyclopedia of Mathematics and its Applications 65: Sperner Theory,"* Cambridge University Press, Cambridge, MA, USA, 1997.

V.V. Federov, *"Theory of Optimal Experiments,"* Academic Press, New York, NY, USA, 1972.

G. Felici and K. Truemper, "A MINSAT Approach for Learning in Logic Domains," *INFORMS Journal on Computing*, Vol. 14, No. 1, pp. 20-36, 2002.

M.L. Fredman and L. Khachiyan, "On the Complexity of Dualization of Monotone Disjunctive Normal Forms," *Journal of Algorithms*, Vol. 21, pp. 618-628, 1996.

D.N. Gainanov, "On One Criterion of the Optimality of an Algorithm for Evaluating Monotonic Boolean Functions,"*U.S.S.R. Computational Mathematics and Mathematical Physics*, Vol. 24, No. 4, pp. 176-181, 1984.

G. Hansel, "Sur Le Nombre Des Foncions Booleenes Monotones De n Variables," *C. R. Acad. Sc. Paris*, Vol. 262, pp. 1088-1090, 1966.

J.N. Hooker, "Logic Based Methods for Optimization," John Wiley & Sons, New York, NY, USA, 2000.

D.G. Horvitz and D.J. Thompson, "A Generalization of Sampling without Replacement from a Finite Universe," *Journal of the American Statistical Association*, Vol. 47, pp. 663-685, 1952.

D.H. Judson, "On the Inference of Semi-coherent Structures from Data," A Master's Thesis, University of Nevada, Reno, NV, USA, 1999.

D.H. Judson, "A Partial Order Approach to Record Linkage," Federal Committee on Statistical Methodology Conference, November 14-16, Arlington, VA, USA, 2001.

A.V. Karzanov, "Determining the Maximal Flow in a Network by the Method of Preflows," *Soviet Mathematics Doklady*, Vol. 15, pp. 434-437, 1974.

A.D. Korshunov, On the Number of Monotone Boolean Functions," *Problemy Kibernetiki*, Vol. 38, pp. 5-108, 1981 (in Russian).

B. Kovalerchuk, E. Triantaphyllou, and A.S. Deshpande, "Interactive Learning of Monotone Boolean Functions," *Information Sciences*, Vol. 94, pp. 87-118, 1996.

B. Kovalerchuk, E. Triantaphyllou, J.F. Ruiz, V.I. Torvik, and E. Vitayev, "The Reliability Issue of Computer-Aided Breast Cancer Diagnosis," *Computers and Biomedical Research*, Vol. 33, pp. 296-313, 2000a.

B. Kovalerchuk, B. and E. Vityaev, *"Data Mining in Finance,"* Kluwer Academic Publishers,

Boston, MA, USA, 2000b.

C.I.C. Lee, "The min-max Algorithm and Isotonic Regression," *The Annals of Statistics*, Vol. 11, pp. 467-477, 1983.

D.J.C. MacKay, "Information-based Objective Functions for Active Data Selection," *Neural Computation*, Vol. 4, No. 4, pp. 589-603, 1992.

K. Makino and T. Ibaraki, "A Fast and Simple Algorithm for Identifying 2-Monotonic Positive Boolean Functions," *Proceedings of ISAACS'95, Algorithms and Computation*, Springer-Verlag, Berlin, Germany, pp. 291-300, 1995.

K. Makino and T. Ibaraki, "The Maximum Latency and Identification of Positive Boolean Functions," *SIAM Journal on Computing*, Vol. 26, No. 5 , pp. 1363-1383, 1997.

K. Makino, T. Suda, H. Ono, and T. Ibaraki, "Data Analysis by Positive Decision Trees. *IEICE Transactions on Information and Systems* , Vol. E82-D, No. 1, pp. 76-88, 1999.

S. Nieto-Sanchez, E. Triantaphyllou, J. Chen, and T.W. Liao, "An Incremental Learning Algorithm for Constructing Boolean Functions From Positive and Negative Examples," *Computers and Operations Research*, Vol. 29, No. 12, pp. 1677-1700, 2002.

J.C. Picard, "Maximal Closure of a Graph and Applications to Combinatorial Problems," *Management Science*, Vol. 22, pp. 1268-1272, 1976.

T. Robertson, F.T. Wright, and R.L. Dykstra, "*Order Restricted Statistical Inference*. John Wiley & Sons, New York, NY, USA, 1988

I. Shmulevich, "Properties and Applications of Monotone Boolean Functions and Stack Filters," A Ph.D. Dissertation, Department of Electrical Engineering, Purdue University, West Lafayette, IN, USA, 1997.

N.A. Sokolov, "On the Optimal Evaluation of Monotonic Boolean Functions," *U.S.S.R. Computational Mathematics and Mathematical Physics*," Vol. 22, No. 2, pp. 207-220, 1982.

C. Tatsuoka and T. Ferguson, "Sequential Classification on Partially Ordered Sets," Technical Report 99-05, Department of Statistics, The George Washington University, Washington, D.C., USA, 1999.

E. Triantaphyllou, "Inference of a Minimum Size Boolean Function by Using a New Efficient Branch-and-Bound Approach from Examples," *Journal of Global Optimization*, Vol. 5 , pp. 69-84, 1994.

E. Triantaphyllou and A.L. Soyster, "An Approach to Guided Learning of Boolean Functions," *Mathematical and Computer Modelling*, Vol. 23, No. 3, pp 69-86, 1996a.

E. Triantaphyllou and A.L. Soyster, "On the Minimum Number of Logical Clauses Which Can be Inferred From Examples," *Computers and Operations Research*, Vol. 23, No. 8, pp. 783-799, 1996b.

V.I. Torvik, E. Triantaphyllou, T.W. Liao and S.W. Waly, "Predicting Muscle Fatigue via Electromyography: A Comparative Study," *Proceedings of the 25th International Conference of Computers and Industrial Engineering*, pp. 277-280, 1999.

V.I. Torvik and E. Triantaphyllou, "Minimizing the Average Query Complexity of Learning Monotone Boolean Functions," *INFORMS Journal on Computing*, Vol. 14, No. 2, pp. 144-174, 2002.

V.I. Torvik and E. Triantaphyllou, "Guided Inference of Nested Monotone Boolean Functions. *Information Sciences*, Vol. 151, 171-200, 2003.

V.I. Torvik, M. Weeber, D.R. Swanson, and N.R. Smalheiser, "A Probabilistic Similarity Metric for Medline Records: A Model for Author Name Disambiguation," *J. of the Amer. Soc. For Info. Sci. and Tech. (JASIST)*, Vol. 56, No. 2, pp. 140-158, 2005.

V.I. Torvik and E. Triantaphyllou, "Guided Inference of Stochastic Monotone Boolean Functions", Working Paper, 2004.

L.G. Valiant, "A Theory of the Learnable," *Communications of the ACM*, Vol. 27, No. 11, pp. 1134-1142, 1984.

M. Ward, "Note on the Order of the Free Distributive Lattice," *Bulletin of the American Mathematical Society*, Vol. 52, No. 135, pp. 423, 1946.

D. Wiedemann, "A Computation of the Eight Dedekind Number," *Order*, Vol. 8, pp. 5-6, 1991.

E. Yilmaz, E. Triantaphyllou, J. Chen, and T.W. Liao, "A Heuristic for Mining Association Rules In Polynomial Time," *Mathematical and Computer Modelling*, Vol. 37, No. 1-2, pp. 219-233, 2003.

AUTHORS' BIOGRAPHICAL STATEMENTS

Dr. Torvik is a Research Assistant Professor in the Department of Psychiatry at the University of Illinois at Chicago, where he is managing a literature-based knowledge discovery project called Arrowsmith (jointly funded by the National Library of Medicine and the National Institute of Mental Health; PI: Neil R. Smalheiser, M.D., Ph.D.). He received his B.A. in Mathematics from St. Olaf College in Northfield, MN in 1995, his M.S. in Operations Research from the Oregon State University in Corvallis, OR in 1997, and his Ph.D. in Engineering Science from the Louisiana State University in Baton Rouge, LA in 2002. His Ph.D. dissertation titled "Data Mining and Knowledge Discovery: A Guided Approach Based on Monotone Boolean Functions" was awarded the 2002 LSU Distinguished Dissertation Award. His research interests include mathematical optimization and computational statistics applied to literature-based knowledge discovery and bioinformatics.

Dr. Triantaphyllou did his graduate studies at Penn State University from 1984 to 1990. While at Penn State, he earned a Dual M.S. degree in Environment and Operations Research (OR), an M.S. degree in Computer Science and a Dual Ph.D. degree in Industrial Engineering and Operations Research. Since the spring of 2005 he is a Professor in the Computer Science Department at the Louisiana State University (LSU) in Baton Rouge, LA, U.S.A., after he has served for 11 years as an Assistant, Associate, and Full Professor in the Industrial Engineering Department at the same university. He has also served for one year as an Interim Associate Dean for the College of Engineering at LSU.

His research is focused on decision-making theory and applications, data mining and knowledge discovery, and the interface of operations research and computer science. Since the years he was a graduate student, he has developed new methods for data mining and knowledge discovery and also has explored some of the most fundamental and intriguing subjects in decision making. In 1999 he has received the prestigious IIE (Institute of Industrial Engineers), OR Division, Research Award for his research contributions in the above fields. In 2005 he received an LSU Distinguished Faculty Award as recognition of his research, teaching, and service accomplishments. Some of his graduate students have also received awards and distinctions including the Best Dissertation Award at LSU for Science, Engineering and Technology for the year 2002 (by the co-author of this chapter). In 2000 Dr. Triantaphyllou published a bestseller book on multi-criteria decision-making. Also, in 2006 he published a monograph on data mining and knowledge discovery, besides co-editing a book on the same subject.

He always enjoys sharing the results of his research with his students and is also getting them actively involved in his research activities. He has received teaching awards and distinctions. His research has been funded by federal and state agencies, and the private sector. He has extensively published in some of the top refereed journals and made numerous presentations in national and international conferences.

Dr. Triantaphyllou has a strong inter-disciplinary background. He has always enjoyed organizing multi-disciplinary teams of researchers and practitioners with complementary expertise. These groups try to comprehensively attack some of the most urgent problems in the sciences and engineering. He is a strong believer of the premise that the next round of major scientific and engineering discoveries will come from the work of such inter-disciplinary groups. More details of his work can be found in his web site (*http://www.csc.lsu.edu/trianta/*

Chapter 5 [1]

LEARNING LOGIC FORMULAS AND RELATED ERROR DISTRIBUTIONS

Giovanni Felici[*], Fushing Sun[**], and Klaus Truemper[***]

[*] *Istituto di Analisi dei Sistemi ed Informatica "A. Ruberti"*

Consiglio Nazionale delle Ricerche
Viale Manzoni 30, 00185 Roma, Italy
Email: felici@iasi.cnr.it

[**] *Computer Science Department, Ball State University*

Muncie, IN 47306
Email: fsun@cs.bsu.edu

[***] *Department of Computer Science*

University of Texas at Dallas
Richardson, TX 75083-0688, U.S.A.
Email: truemper@utdallas.edu

Abstract: This chapter describes a method for learning logic formulas that correctly classify the records of a given data set consisting of two classes. The method derives from given training data certain minimum cost satisfiability problems, solves these problems, and deduces from the solutions the desired logic formulas. There are at least two ways in which the results may be employed. First, one may use the logic formulas directly as rules in application programs. Second, one may construct vote-based rules, where the formulas produce votes and where the votes are combined to a vote-total. The latter approach allows for assessment and even control of prediction errors, as follows: Once the method has produced the logic formulas, it computes from the training data estimated distributions for the vote-totals without use of any additional data. From these distributions the method estimates probabilities for prediction errors. That information supports assessment and control of errors. Uses of the method include data mining, knowledge acquisition in expert systems, and identification of critical characteristics for recognition systems.Computational tests indicate that the method is fast and effective.

Keywords: Inductive Inference, Supervised Learning, Logic Programming , Minimum Cost Satisfiability Problem, Learning vote distributions and Error Probabilities

---

[1] Triantaphyllou, E. and G. Felici (Eds.), **Data Mining and Knowledge Discovery Approaches based on Rule Induction Techniques**, Massive Computing Series, Springer, Heidelberg, Germany, pp. 193-226, 2006.

1.   INTRODUCTION

The human brain has an astonishing capacity for extracting salient features from masses of data, in particular, for identifying differences that separate one set of data from a second set of data. Much research has been done toward duplicating such capability on computers, known in the literature as *supervised learning* or *learning from examples*.

A general approach to learning problems represents the objects to be recognized by vectors in some geometric space. Here the separation of the data into sets or classes is obtained by separating surfaces; mathematical programming techniques are often used with the objective of minimizing some measure of the error in the separation ([Freed and Glover, 1981, 1986], [Mangasarian et al., 1990], [Mangasarian and Wolberg, 1990], [Mangasarian, 1993], [Bennett and Mangasarian, 1995], [Bradley et al., 1999]).

In this chapter we focus on a particular type of learning problems that are expressed in logic domains, also referred to as problems of *inductive inference* [Chandru and Hooker, 1999]. In such learning, the objects to be recognized are described by the presence or absence of certain features; the learning method uses logic formulas to express separations among groups of data, and is intended to learn logic relations connecting features with classes. Theoretical and practical interest in this type of learning is extensively discussed in [Muggleton, 1999].

The literature describes several methods that address learning in logic domains. Some of these methods solve the problem via some other combinatorial problem or technique ([Crama et al., 1988], [Kamath et al., 1992], [Triantaphyllou et al., 1994], [Felici, 1995], [Boros et al., 1996], [Triantaphyllou and Soyster, 1996], [Makino et al., 1997], and [Boros et al., 1999]). Other methods rely on special algorithms for the logic separation problem ([Breiman et al., 1984], [Valiant, 1985], [Shavlik et al., 1991], [Thrun et al., 1991], [Cohen, 1995], [Golea, 1995], [Bhargava, 1999]). The learning problem in the logic domain can also be formulated as a neural network computation problem, as described in [Nelson and Illingworth, 1990], [Domany et al., 1991], [Hertz at al., 1991].

This chapter provides a comprehensive description of the logic domain method of [Felici and Truemper, 2002]. The method has been used in diverse applications; see, for example, "Learning to Find Context-Based Spelling Errors" included in this volume, or [Di Giacomo et al., 2001]. The input for the method consists of $\{0, \pm 1\}$ vectors of two sets A and B. We call the $\{0, \pm 1\}$ vectors *records* of *logic data*. A 1 in a record means that a certain Boolean variable, say w, has the value *True*, a -1 means that w has the value *False*, and a 0 depicts the situation where the *True/False* value for w is not known.

The method deduces $\{0, \pm 1\}$ vectors that may be used to decide for each record whether it belongs to A or B. Since the $\{0, \pm 1\}$ vectors essentially separate the records of A from those of B, we call them *separating vectors*. Collectively, the separating vectors constitute a *separating set*. One may derive from any separating set an equivalent logic formula that uses the $\{0, \pm 1\}$ values of a record to compute a *True/False* value that decides membership in A or B.

The separating sets are determined in an iterative scheme. In each iteration, two logic minimization problems are solved to obtain one separating vector. The solution algorithms for the minimization problems are created with the Leibniz System (see [Leibniz System, 2000]).

Our approach is related to prior work by [Kamath et al., 1992] and [Triantaphyllou et al., 1994]. These references assume that the given logic data are complete in the sense that, in our notation, they do not contain 0s. When our problem formulation is simplified to that special case, it becomes similar to those of the two references. However, the solution methods of the references are quite different from ours.

Specifically, [Kamath et al., 1992] require an *a priori* estimate of the number of separating vectors, then formulate one logic satisfiability problem and solve it via an interior point method of linear programming to get the desired separating set. The problem size can grow substantially as the number of separating vectors increases. [Triantaphyllou et al., 1994] use the iterative approach employed here, but in each iteration solve just one satisfiability problem where the number of satisfied clauses is to be maximized, using a branch and bound method. We solve that problem as well, reformulated here as a logic minimization problem. The latter problem assures that the separating sets have a minimum number of nonzeros. We also solve a second minimization problem that produces as many nonzeros in the separating sets as possible. The two types of separating sets correspond to logic formulas with minimum and maximum number of literals respectively.

The results of the steps described so far are not symmetric in A and B. That is, if A is relabeled as B and conversely, then in general two different separating sets are produced. Thus, a total of four separating sets can be constructed from two given sets that are to be separated. We use such elaborate computations for the following reason. The sets A and B almost always are randomly chosen subsets of two populations $\mathcal{A}$ and $\mathcal{B}$, respectively. In that setting, A and B are *training sets*, and the separating vectors are used to predict membership in the populations $\mathcal{A}$ and $\mathcal{B}$ and not just in the training sets A and B. Ideally, one would desire completely accurate predictions. Of course, generally this is not possible, so instead we want predictions that involve errors in a controlled fashion. The four separating sets allow such control in a limited way. That is, two of the four separating sets tend to make few errors when predicting membership in $\mathcal{A}$, while the remaining two separations do so for $\mathcal{B}$.

So far, we have covered the basic approach, which provides for a modest amount of error control . Next, we embed that approach into a more elaborate scheme that applies the basic approach to ten subset pairs $\overline{A}$ and $\overline{B}$ taken from A and B, respectively. The scheme thus produces $4 \cdot 10 = 40$ separating sets, each of which effectively produces a vote for membership in $\mathcal{A}$ or $\mathcal{B}$. We view the vote to be $+1$ or -1. A $+1$ (resp. -1) vote predicts membership in $\mathcal{A}$ (resp. $\mathcal{B}$). Define the *vote-total* to be the sum of the 40 votes.

The scheme is so structured that the vote-total for any record of A (resp. B)

is always positive (resp. negative). Thus, the scheme correctly predicts membership for all records of A and B. Of course, that conclusion generally does not extend to the populations $\mathcal{A}$ and $\mathcal{B}$. To estimate the accuracy of predictions for the latter sets, the scheme re-uses the training data and estimates conditional probability distributions for the vote-total on $\mathcal{A}$ and $\mathcal{B}$. From these estimated distributions, the scheme estimates probabilities that are useful for error control. We emphasize that the calculations of the estimated distributions require just the training data and no additional data. This aspect is important when it is too costly or even impossible to obtain records of $\mathcal{A}$ and $\mathcal{B}$ beyond the given training data A and B.

There are at least two ways in which the results may be employed. First, one may express the separating sets as logic formulas, which are then used directly as rules in application programs. Second, one may construct rules using the vote-totals and certain thresholds. An example rule is: If the vote-total is greater that a specified threshold value, then the given record is estimated to be in $\mathcal{A}$. These rules can then be used in application programs.

How well does the scheme work? In extensive tests, it has been shown that the scheme is as accurate as the best prior methods. Without exception, those methods do not handle the case of unknown entries of records, require some manual preparation or selection of parameters, and do not estimate errors by just using the training data. In contrast, the scheme described here processes records with missing entries, does not require setting of parameters, tuning for data structure, or manual adjustment of data sets. The scheme also produces accurate estimates of the related probability distributions without use of additional data.

The chapter is organized as follows. Section 2 states some basic definitions, introduces the main ideas, and treats a simple example. Section 3 develops the iterative scheme for finding a separating set and the equivalent logic formula. Sections 4 and 5 describe the implementation of the method using the Leibniz System. In Section 6, the given logic data are viewed as training data, and the resulting logic formula is used to predict outcomes for additional logic data. We show that one may specify objective functions for the logic minimization problems so that the resulting logic formula tends to minimize errors in a desired direction. Section 7 introduces a much more elaborate method for controlling errors. The method computes a number of separation sets each of which generates one vote for membership in $\mathcal{A}$ or $\mathcal{B}$. Decisions are based on the sum of the votes. We call that sum the *vote-total*. Section 8 estimates probability distributions for the vote-total and establishes probabilities useful for error control. Section 9 discusses the results computed with our method for several learning problems. These results show that our method is a versatile, precise, and computationally efficient learning tool. Section 10 summarizes the main results of the chapter.

2. LOGIC DATA AND SEPARATING SET

We use basic concepts of propositional logic such as *Boolean variable, Boolean formulas* and their *satisfiability, conjunctive normal form system (CNF), disjunctive normal form system (DNF), satisfiability problem (SAT)*, and *minimum cost satisfiability problem (MINSAT)*. We omit for brevity the definitions of these concepts, which can be found in logic textbooks; see, for example, [Chandru and Hooker, 1999], or [Truemper, 1998].

We introduce a simple extension. An *extended (tertiary) logic variable* v may take on the value *True, False*, or 0. We interpret the three possible values as our state of knowledge about a Boolean variable, say w. That is, $v = True$ (resp. $v = False$) means that we know that w has the value *True* (resp. *False*). The case $v = 0$ depicts the situation where we do not know the *True/False* value of w.

We expand the customary evaluation of logic formulas to extended logic variables. For each variable v with value 0 that appears in a given logic formula, we replace each occurrence of v or $\neg v$ in the formula by *False*, and then evaluate it in the usual way. For example, a conjunction has the value *True* if all terms have the value *True*, and has the value *False* if there is at least one term with the value *False* or 0.

2.1   Logic Data

We define *logic data* to be vectors $r \in \{0, \pm 1\}^n$. We call such vectors *records* to differentiate them from other vectors introduced later.

In a slight abuse of notation, we associate with each record r three index sets r^+, r^-, and r^0, containing the indices i for which the elements r_i are equal to 1, -1, and 0, respectively. Evidently, the three sets are disjoint, and their union is the index set of the elements of r, which is $\{1, 2, \ldots, n\}$. We associate a *True/False outcome* with each record of given logic data. The outcome is considered to be the value of a Boolean variable t. The case $t = True$ (resp. $t = False$) typically indicates presence/absence of a certain property. We collect the records r for which the property t is absent in a set A, and those for which t is present in a set B. For ease of recognition, we usually denote a member of A by a, and of B by b. Analogously to the sets r^+, r^-, and r^0 for r, we define sets a^+, a^-, and a^0 for a, and b^+, b^-, and b^0 for b. For example, $a^+ = \{i | a_i = 1\}$.

The records r may be produced by different situations and encodings in logic variables; we sketch below the most straightforward case. Suppose that we have extended logic variables $v_1, v_2, \ldots, v_n$, and that we collect in vectors of length n *True/False/*0 values for these variables. We convert these vectors to records r by replacing *True* by 1, and *False* by -1. The 0s are not changed. We introduce an example situation that makes use of the above concepts.

Let the universe of discourse be the collection of creatures living on earth. We use the extended logic variables *walks, swims, speaks*, and the property $t = human$. Suppose we observe a cat, and note that the animal walks, does not speak, and is not human. Assume that we do not know whether the cat can swim. We encode our knowledge about that cat by the record $(1, 0, -1)$, where the 1 encodes the fact that the cat can walk; the 0 that we do not know whether that particular cat can swim; and the -1 that it cannot speak. Since the cat is not human, we declare the record $(1, 0, -1)$ to be in set A. Suppose observations about two other animals result in additional records $(1, -1, -1)$ and $(1, 1, -1)$ for A. Assume we observe three human beings, and summarize our observations in $B = \{(1, 1, 1), (1, 0, 1), (1, -1, 1)\}$. For example, the third record of B may result from us seeing a person who can walk, cannot swim, and can speak. At this point, we have

$$A = \{(1, 0, -1), (1, -1, -1), (1, 1, -1)\} \tag{1}$$

and

$$B = \{(1, 1, 1), (1, 0, 1), (1, -1, 1)\} \tag{2}$$

2.2   Separating Set

We want to differentiate the records of a given set B from the records of a given set A, by using a set S of $\{0, \pm1\}$ vectors. Such a separation makes sense only if both A and B are nonempty, and if each record of A or B contains at least one $\{\pm1\}$ entry. Hence, from now on we always assume this to be the case. Next, we introduce some definitions.

A $\{0, \pm1\}$ vector f is *nested* in a $\{0, \pm1\}$ vector g if for any entry f_i of f equal to 1 or -1, the corresponding entry g_i of g satisfies $g_i = f_i$. By this definition, f is not nested in g if and only if there is some $f_i = \pm1$ of f for which $g_i = -f_i$ or $g_i = 0$. Let A and B be sets of $\{0, \pm1\}$ records of the same length, say $n \geq 1$. For any $b \in B$, a vector $s \in \{0, \pm1\}^n$ *separates b from A* if

$$s \text{ is not nested in any } a \in A \tag{3}$$

and

$$s \text{ is nested in } b \tag{4}$$

As an example case, let b be the vector $(1, 1, 1)$ of B of (2). Then the vector $s = (0, 0, 1)$ separates b from all $a \in A$ of definition (1) since the only nonzero entry of s, which is $s_3 = 1$, corresponds to $b_3 = 1$, and since, for all $a \in A$, $a_3 = -1$. Indeed, $s = (0, 0, 1)$ separates each $b \in B$ of definition (2) from all $a \in A$ of definition (1).

One could consider other separation conditions. A seemingly appealing version is as follows. One replaces the condition (3) by the condition that, for each $a \in A$, there is an index i for which a_i and s_i are nonzero and have opposite sign. That condition is more demanding than (3) and thus may rule out the existence of a separating vector where (3) allows for one. For example, the revised condition does not admit a separating vector for $a = (1, 0)$ and $b = (0, -1)$, while (3) allows for the separating vector $s = (0, -1)$. For this reason, we prefer (3).

Since A is nonempty, condition (3) implies that s is nonzero. A set S of $\{0, \pm1\}$ vectors *separates B from A*, for short, is a *separating set*, if each $s \in S$

satisfies (3), and if, for each $b \in B$, there is at least an $s \in S$ that satisfies (4). We have seen that $s = (0,0,1)$ separates each $b \in B$ of definition (2) from all $a \in A$ of definition (1). Thus, the set $S = \{(0,0,1)\}$ separates B from A.

We establish necessary and sufficient conditions for the existence of separating sets.

Theorem 2.1. *Let A and B be sets of $\{0, \pm 1\}$ records of the same length. Then a separating set S exists if and only if no record $b \in B$ is nested in any record $a \in A$.*

Proof: For the proof of the "if" part, suppose that no $b \in B$ is nested in any $a \in A$. Take $S = B$. Any vector $s \in S$ equal to a vector $b \in B$ is nested in that b, and is not nested in any $a \in A$. Thus, such s satisfies (3) and (4), and separates b from A, and S is a separating set.

We prove the "only if" part by contradiction. Suppose that a separating set S is at hand, and that there exist $a \in A$ and $b \in B$ such that b is nested in a. The set S contains an s that separates b from A, so by (4), s is nested in b. The latter fact and the assumption that b is nested in a imply that s is nested in a, which contradicts (3). □

Note that conditions (3) and (4) for the existence of a separating set admit the case where a record $a \in A$ is nested in a record $b \in B$. The separating sets introduced later are to separate B from A or A from B. Indeed, for some subsets $\overline{A} \subseteq A$ and $\overline{B} \subseteq B$, we will determine separating sets that separate $\overline{B}$ from $\overline{A}$ or $\overline{A}$ from $\overline{B}$. By Theorem 2.1, all such separating sets exist if and only if no record of one of the two sets A and B is nested in any record of the other set. Thus, one would like to impose the latter condition on A and B. There is good reason for invoking that condition, as follows.

Suppose a record $a \in A$ is nested in a record $b \in B$. Then the information encoded in record a, by itself, cannot be sufficient to establish membership in A. Indeed, the record b, which by the nestedness of a in b contains all information of a, is in B and not in A. Accordingly, we do not want to use that $a \in A$ when we learn distinguishing characteristics that tell A from B.

These considerations motivate the following definition. Training sets A and B are *consistent* if no record of one of the two sets is nested in any record of the other set. For example, the example sets A and B of (1) and (2) are consistent. Evidently, consistency of A and B implies that, for any $\overline{A} \subseteq A$ and $\overline{B} \subseteq B$, $\overline{A}$ and $\overline{B}$ are consistent as well. Accordingly, any such $\overline{A}$ can be separated from $\overline{B}$ and vice versa. We emphasize that consistency of A and B does not rule out nestedness of records within A or within B.

We interpret the notion of separating set in terms of extended logic variables $v_1, v_2, \ldots, v_n$. Suppose A and B are sets of records of length $n \geq 1$, and S is the corresponding separating set. For each vector $s \in S$, define the index sets s^+, s^-, and s^0 analogously to the earlier definition of r^+, r^-, and r^0. For example, $s^+ = \{i | s_i = 1\}$. Derive from S the DNF system

$$\bigvee_{s \in S} \left(\bigwedge_{i \in s^+} v_i \wedge \bigwedge_{i \in s^-} \neg v_i \right) \tag{5}$$

Since each $s \in S$ is nonzero, each DNF clause of (5) is nonempty.

The next theorem links membership in A or B with *True/False* values of the DNF system (5).

Theorem 2.2. *Let r be a record that is equal to some $a \in A$ or $b \in B$. For $i = 1, 2, \ldots, n$, define*

$$v_i = \begin{cases} True & \text{if } r_i = 1 \\ False & \text{if } r_i = -1 \\ 0 & \text{if } r_i = 0 \end{cases} \tag{6}$$

If $r = a$, (resp. $r = b$), then these values of $v_1, v_2, \ldots, v_n$ produce the value False (resp. True) for the DNF system of (5).

Proof: Suppose $r = a$. Let s be any vector of S. By condition (3), s is not nested in a. Thus, there exists an index k for which $s_k = \pm 1$ and either $a_k = -s_k$ or $a_k = 0$. Define *True/False/0* values for $v_1, v_2, \ldots, v_n$ using $r = a$ in (6). Since $s_k = \pm 1$ and either $a_k = -s_k$ or $a_k = 0$, the value assigned to v_k forces the clause $\bigwedge_{i \in s^+} v_i \wedge \bigwedge_{i \in s^-} \neg v_i$ of the DNF system (5) to have the value *False*. Since the above argument applies to each $s \in S$, the DNF system (5) must have the value *False*.

Suppose $r = b$. Since S is a separating set, it contains a vector s that is nested in b. Thus, for each i, $s_i = \pm 1$ implies $b_i = s_i$. Hence, if we assign *True/False/0* to each v_i using $r = b$ in (6), then the clause $\bigwedge_{i \in s^+} v_i \wedge \bigwedge_{i \in s^-} \neg v_i$ of (5) evaluates to *True*. Thus, the DNF system (5) has the value *True*.   □

Given a set S^* that separates a nonempty set $B^* \subseteq B$ from A and which does not separate any $b \in (B - B^*)$ from A, we can use the corresponding DNF formula to classify records. That DNF formula correctly classifies the records in $A \cup B^*$ and fails on those in $B - B^*$.

We return to the example sets A and B of (1) and (2). We have seen that the set S consisting of the single vector $s = (0, 0, 1)$ separates B from A. Accordingly, the DNF system (5) consists of the single clause *speaks*, which effectively says that a creature is human if and only if it does speak. Indeed, that DNF system has the value *False* (resp. *True*) when the *True/False/0* value for the extended logic variable *speaks* is defined using any record r of A (resp. B) in (6).

3.   PROBLEM FORMULATION

Let A and B be nonempty sets of $\{0, \pm 1\}$ records of length $n \geq 1$. We decompose the problem of finding a separating set into a sequence of subproblems, each of which demands that we determine a vector s that separates a nonempty subset of B from A. For the moment, we focus on the subproblems. Later, we compose the solutions s of the subproblems to a separating set S.

3.1   Logic Variables

For $i = 1, 2, \ldots, n$, we introduce Boolean variables p_i and q_i. We link these variables with the elements s_i of the vector s to be found, by declaring $s_i = 1$ if $p_i = True$ and $q_i = False$, $s_i = -1$ if $p_i = False$ and $q_i = True$, and $s_i = 0$ if $p_i = q_i = False$. We have no interpretation for the case $p_i = q_i = True$, and rule it out by enforcing

$$\neg p_i \vee \neg q_i, \ i = 1, 2, \ldots, n \qquad (7)$$

3.2   Separation Conditions for Records in A

Condition (3) requires that s is not nested in any $a \in A$. Hence, for each $a \in A$, there must be an index i such that $s_i = \pm 1$ and either $a_i = -s_i$ or $a_i = 0$. We expand that condition for that index i to as follows: $a_i = 1$ implies $s_i = -1$; $a_i = -1$ implies $s_i = 1$; and $a_i = 0$ implies $s_i = 1$ or $s_i = -1$. In terms of our encoding of s_i by p_i and q_i, the condition becomes: $a_i = 1$ implies $\neg p_i \wedge q_i$; $a_i = -1$ implies $p_i \wedge \neg q_i$; and $a_i = 0$ implies $(\neg p_i \wedge q_i) \vee (p_i \wedge \neg q_i)$.

Since (7) requires $\neg p_i \vee \neg q_i$, we can simplify the condition to: $a_i = 1$ implies q_i; $a_i = -1$ implies p_i; and $a_i = 0$ implies $p_i \vee q_i$.

For each $a \in A$, the latter condition must hold for at least one i, so we can summarize condition (3) by the following disjunctions:

$$\left(\bigvee_{i \in (a^+ \cup a^0)} q_i \right) \vee \left(\bigvee_{i \in (a^- \cup a^0)} p_i \right) \text{ for all } a \in A \qquad (8)$$

3.3   Separation Conditions for Records in B

Let b be any record of B. By (4), if s separates b from A, then s is nested in b, that is, for all i, $s_i = \pm 1$ implies $b_i = s_i$. An equivalent condition holding for all i is: $b_i = 1$ implies $s_i \neq -1$; $b_i = -1$ implies $s_i \neq 1$; and $b_i = 0$ implies $s_i = 0$. In terms of p_i and q_i, the condition is: $b_i = 1$ implies $\neg q_i$; $b_i = -1$ implies $\neg p_i$; and $b_i = 0$ implies $\neg p_i \wedge \neg q_i$.

We introduce a Boolean variable d_b that determines whether s must separate b from A. That is, $d_b = True$ means that s need not separate b from A, while $d_b = False$ requires that separation. For the given $b \in B$, the separation condition is therefore: for all $i \in b^+$, $\neg q_i \vee d_b$; for all $i \in b^-$, $\neg p_i \vee d_b$; and for all $i \in b^0$, $(\neg p_i \wedge \neg q_i) \vee d_b$. Using the distributive law, we get

$$\begin{aligned} \neg q_i \vee d_b &\quad \text{for all } i \in (b^+ \cup b^0) \\ \neg p_i \vee d_b &\quad \text{for all } i \in (b^- \cup b^0) \end{aligned} \qquad (9)$$

Note that (9) with $d_b = False$ for at least one record $b \in B$ implies (7). As we shall see, this fact allows us to omit (7) from the MINSAT problems introduced below.

3.4   Selecting a Largest Subset

Suppose we want a vector s that separates as many $b \in B$ from A as possible. Equivalently, we want a satisfying solution for (7)–(9) that assigns the value *True* to as few variables d_b as possible. For each $b \in B$, define a cost function $c_b(d_b)$ that is equal to 1 if d_b is *True*, and equal to 0 otherwise. Using these cost functions and (8) and (9), but omitting (7), the desired s may be found by solving the following MINSAT problem, with variables d_b for $b \in B$, and p_i and q_i for $i = 1, 2, \ldots, n$.

$$
\begin{array}{ll}
\min \quad \sum_{b \in B} c_b(d_b) \\
\left(\bigvee_{i \in (a^+ \cup a^0)} q_i \right) \vee \left(\bigvee_{i \in (a^- \cup a^0)} p_i \right) & \text{for all } a \in A \\
\neg q_i \vee d_b & \text{for all } b \in B, \text{for all } i \in (b^+ \cup b^0) \\
\neg p_i \vee d_b & \text{for all } b \in B, \text{for all } i \in (b^- \cup b^0)
\end{array}
\tag{10}
$$

We argue that (7) is not needed. Suppose we have a solution for (10). Define $B' = \{b \in B \mid d_b = False\}$. If B' is empty, then the addition of (7) to (10) would not change the conclusion that no vector of b can be separated from A. If B' is nonempty, then for each $b \in B'$ we have $d_b = False$, and (7) holds due to (9).

The next theorem characterizes the situation when B' is nonempty.

Theorem 3.1. *The following statements are equivalent.*

(i) *B' is nonempty.*

(ii) *There exists a vector s that separates some $b \in B$ from A.*

(iii) *There exists an element $b \in B$ that is not nested in any $a \in A$.*

Proof: (i)$\Rightarrow$(ii): The vector s' implied by the *True/False* solution values of the p_i and q_i of (10) separates every $b \in B'$ from A.
(ii)$\Rightarrow$(iii)$\Rightarrow$(i): Use Theorem 2.1.   □

Suppose A and B are consistent. Since no vector $b \in B$ is nested in any $a \in A$, Theorem 3.1 assures that B' is nonempty. Thus, the $\{0, \pm 1\}$ vector s' derived from the solution of (10) may be one of many vectors that separate B' from A. Frequently, we have a preference among the possible choices. The issue of preference arises, for example, in situations where we want to use the vector to classify records that do not occur in A or B. We address that issue later, in Section 6. Here, we only observe that often we either want a separating vector with minimum number of nonzero entries, or want one with maximum number of nonzero entries. We say that a vector with the former (resp. latter) property has *min* (resp. *max*) *support*.

Next, we formulate the problem of selecting the appropriate separating vector as another MINSAT problem.

3.5   Selecting a Separating Vector

To identify a separating vector with the desired features, say s'', we define, for $i = 1, 2, \ldots, n$, appropriate cost functions $c_{p_i}(p_i)$ and $c_{q_i}(q_i)$. For example, if we want s'' to have min (resp. max) support, we demand that each cost function produces the value 1 (resp. 0) if the Boolean variable of its argument has the value *True*, and to have the value 0 (resp. 1) otherwise. Once the cost functions have been established, we derive the desired s'' from the solution of the following MINSAT problem, with variables p_i and q_i, $i = 1, 2, \ldots, n$. Recall that the nonempty set B' is defined from the solution of (10) by $B' = \{b \in B | d_b = \text{False}\}$.

$$
\begin{aligned}
\text{min} \quad & \textstyle\sum_{i=1}^{n} [c_{p_i}(p_i) + c_{q_i}(q_i)] \\
& \left(\bigvee_{i \in (a^+ \cup a^0)} q_i \right) \vee \left(\bigvee_{i \in (a^- \cup a^0)} p_i \right) && \text{for all } a \in A \\
& \neg q_i && \text{for all } b \in B', \text{ for all } i \in (b^+ \cup b^0) \\
& \neg p_i && \text{for all } b \in B', \text{ for all } i \in (b^- \cup b^0)
\end{aligned}
$$
$$\tag{11}$$

Arguments almost identical to those validating (10) establish that (11) has a satisfying solution, and that any optimal solution of (11) defines a separating vector s'' with the desired features. That is, s'' separates B' from A, and is of the desired kind according the chosen cost functions. In the two example cases mentioned earlier, s'' has min or max support.

We note that, by proper manipulation and scaling of the objective function coefficients, one can trivially combine the two solution steps involving (10) and (11) into one single step. In our solution approach, we choose to solve (10) and (11) in two steps; that choice is based on computational results for our solution method.

We use the above results in the following iterative algorithm for finding a separating set S^* that separates the largest possible subset B^* of B from A. It takes as input the sets A and B of $\{0, \pm 1\}$ records, and for $i = 1, 2, \ldots, n$, cost functions $c_{p_i}(p_i)$ and $c_{q_i}(q_i)$. The output is the largest subset B^* of B that can be separated from A, and a set S^* that accomplishes that separation. If A and B are consistent, we know that $B^* = B$.

Program FIND SEPARATING SET:

1. Initialize $B^* = S^* = \emptyset$.

2. Solve (10) to get a largest possible subset B' of B that can be separated from A. If $B' = \emptyset$, output B^* and S^*, and stop.

3. Solve (11). Derive from the solution a separating vector s'', and add it to S^*. Add the records of B' to B^*. Redefine B as $B - B'$, and go to Step 2.

The separating vector s'' found in the first iteration through Steps 2 and 3 separates a largest subset of the initial B from A, and thus may be regarded as the most significant explanation why the records B have the property t and those of A do not. Correspondingly, the second iteration produces the second most significant explanation given the choice of the first one, and so on.

3.6   Simplification for 0/1 Records

Suppose all records of A and B contain no -1s, and thus are $\{0, 1\}$ vectors. This case may arise when for each extended logic variable v_i, we either know that the corresponding variable w_i has value *True*, or do not know the *True/False* of w_i and permit the outcome of the record to change if the value for w_i becomes known. We emphasize that this situation is different from the case where all records are $\{\pm 1\}$ vectors.

We reduce (10) and (11) using the following observations. For any $a \in A$ and $b \in B$, $a^- = b^- = \emptyset$, which implies $a^- \cup a^0 = a^0$ and $b^+ \cup b^0 = \{1, 2, \ldots, n\}$. Assuming that at least one element in B can be separated from the elements in A, any optimal solution assigns the value *False* to at least one variable d_b. For such a d_b, the clauses $\neg q_i \vee d_b$ with $i \in (b^+ \cup b^0)$ force $q_1, q_2, \ldots, q_n$ to have the value *False*. Hence, we can eliminate $q_1, q_2, \ldots, q_n$ from (10), and get the following reduced problem.

$$\min \quad \sum_{b \in B} c_b(d_b)$$
$$\bigvee_{i \in a^0} p_i \qquad \text{for all } a \in A \tag{12}$$
$$\neg p_i \vee d_b \qquad \text{for all } b \in B, \text{ for all } i \in b^0$$

Analogously, the MINSAT problem (11) becomes

$$\min \quad \sum_{i=1}^{n} c_{p_i}(p_i)$$
$$\bigvee_{i \in a^0} p_i \qquad \text{for all } a \in A \tag{13}$$
$$\neg p_i \qquad \text{for all } b \in B', \text{ for all } i \in b^0$$

We use the solution of (13) to define s'' as follows. For $i = 1, 2, \ldots, n$, $s_i'' = 1$ if $p_i = $ *True*, and $s_i'' = 0$ otherwise.

4.   IMPLEMENTATION OF SOLUTION ALGORITHM

The MINSAT problems (10) and (11), as well as their simplified versions (12) and (13), are potentially difficult since the $\mathcal{NP}$-complete problem SET COVER (see [Garey and Johnson, 1979]) may be reduced to (12) and (13). We omit the trivial reductions.

We solve the possibly difficult problems (10) and (11) as follows. Let A, B, and the cost functions $c_{p_i}(p_i)$ and $c_{q_i}(q_i)$ be given. Note that the cost functions $c_b(d_b)$ never vary.

Consider the instance of (10) defined by the original B. It is easy to see that deletion of some clauses can reduce that instance to any instance of (10) encountered by Program FIND SEPARATING SET of Section 3.5. Indeed, the deletion involves clauses of the type $\neg q_i \vee d_b$ and $\neg p_i \vee d_b$. Equivalently, we could fix certain d_b to *True*. Hence, any MINSAT instance of (10) may be derived from the instance of (10) defined by the original B by the fixing of some variables. For this reason, we call the latter instance a MINSAT *master instance* for (10).

Suppose we delete from (11) all clauses of the form $\neg q_i$ or $\neg p_i$, getting

$$\min \quad \sum_{i=1}^{n} [c_{p_i}(p_i) + c_{q_i}(q_i)]$$
$$\left(\bigvee_{i \in (a^+ \cup a^0)} q_i \right) \vee \left(\bigvee_{i \in (a^- \cup a^0)} p_i \right) \quad \text{for all } a \in A \qquad (14)$$

Clearly, any MINSAT instance of (11) encountered by Program FIND SEPARATING SET may be derived from the MINSAT instance (14) by fixing some variables to *False*. Hence, we call (14) a MINSAT *master instance* for (11).

We emphasize that the MINSAT master instances for (10) depend on A and B, and that the MINSAT master instances for (11) depend on A, B, and the cost functions $c_{p_i}(p_i)$ and $c_{q_i}(q_i)$.

We solve the MINSAT instances encountered in the iterative algorithm with the aid of the Leibniz System, which is a software system for Logic Programming, described in the next section. The mathematics underlying the Leibniz System is described in [Truemper, 1998].

5.   LEIBNIZ SYSTEM

The Leibniz System is an advanced tool for . Next, we describe its main features. Suppose one wants to solve a class of MINSAT instances where each class member is derived from a given MINSAT master instance by the fixing of some variables. One can direct the Leibniz System to construct a solution algorithm that can solve all instances of the class. The construction is based on an analysis of the structure of the MINSAT master instance that relies on various combinatorial methods. An analogous approach is used for any class of SAT instances where each class member is derived from a given SAT *master instance* by the fixing of some variables. That is, the Leibniz System analyzes the structure of the SAT master instance, and based on that insight constructs a solution algorithm that can solve all instances of the class.

The Leibniz System also establishes a performance guarantee for the MINSAT or SAT solution algorithm, in the form of an upper time bound on the run time required for solving any one of the instances of the class. In the MINSAT case, the time bound is used by the system as follows. If the time bound exceeds a user specified value, the Leibniz System considers the solution algorithm to be too slow, and instead creates a solution algorithm that carries out approximate instead of exact minimization for the instances.

The iterative method adopted here may be viewed as a greedy algorithm that produces a separating set of small cardinality. Of course, the set S^* found may not have minimum cardinality. Clearly, if exact minimization is carried out and S^* consists of one or two vectors, then that set does have minimum cardinality. It turns our that the conclusion remains valid if approximate minimization is used, due to the way that process is done via linear programming and a certain rounding method.

Once more suppose that exact minimization is used. If the separating vector found in the first iteration separates k vectors of B from A, and if B has m vectors in total, then $\lceil \frac{m}{k} \rceil$ is a lower bound on the number of vectors required to separate B from A. [Triantaphyllou and Soyster, 1996] go beyond these elementary considerations and develop substantially tighter lower bounds on the minimum cardinality of separating sets.

The Leibniz System handles SAT or MINSAT problems with up to 10,000 variables and 10,000 clauses. That range has been ample for solving (11) in Step 3 of Program FIND SEPARATING SET of Section 3.5 for the practical problems we have processed so far. But that range has not been sufficient for solving some instances of (10) in Step 2 of Program FIND SEPARATING SET. The reason is that in (10), each entry of each record of B creates at least one clause. For example, a B with 300 records having 60 entries each creates at least 18,000 clauses, which exceeds the Leibniz System limit. We describe a simple way to overcome that difficulty.

We compile with the Leibniz System an algorithm for the SAT problem

$$\left(\bigvee_{i \in (a^+ \cup a^0)} q_i \right) \vee \left(\bigvee_{i \in (a^- \cup a^0)} p_i \right) \quad \text{for all } a \in A \tag{15}$$

and derive via a greedy method that fixes/unfixes the p_i and q_i variables, a maximal subset B' of B for which

$$\begin{array}{ll}
\left(\bigvee_{i \in (a^+ \cup a^0)} q_i \right) \vee \left(\bigvee_{i \in (a^- \cup a^0)} p_i \right) & \text{for all } a \in A \\
\neg q_i & \text{for all } b \in B', \text{ for all } i \in (b^+ \cup b^0) \\
\neg p_i & \text{for all } b \in B', \text{ for all } i \in (b^- \cup b^0)
\end{array} \tag{16}$$

has a solution. That B' is used in Step 3 of Program FIND SEPARATING SET. Of course, B' need not correspond to an optimal solution of (10). Nevertheless, one may easily verify that the modified Program FIND SEPARATING SET still finds a separating set S^* that separates the largest possible subset B^* of B from A.

6. SIMPLE-MINDED CONTROL OF CLASSIFICATION ERRORS

In almost all settings, one views the sets A and B as training sets and considers them to be randomly selected subsets of two sets $\mathcal{A}$ and $\mathcal{B}$ where $\mathcal{A}$ consists of all $\{0, \pm 1\}$ records of length n without property t, and $\mathcal{B}$ consists of all such records with property t. One then determines a set S that separates B from A, and uses that set to guess whether a given $\{0, \pm 1\}$ vector r of length n is in $\mathcal{A}$ or $\mathcal{B}$. That is, we guess r to be in $\mathcal{B}$ if at least one $s \in S$ is nested in r, and to be in $\mathcal{A}$ otherwise.

Of course, the classification of r based on S is correct if r is in A or B, but otherwise need not be correct. Specifically, we may guess a record of $\mathcal{A} - A$ to be in $\mathcal{B}$, and a record of $\mathcal{B} - B$ to be in $\mathcal{A}$. Let us call an error of the first kind a *type $\mathcal{A}$ error*, and one of the second kind a *type $\mathcal{B}$ error*.

The utility of S depends on which type of error is made how many times. In some settings, an error of one of the two types may be annoying, but may not be nearly as objectionable as an error of the other type. For example, a non-invasive diagnostic system for cancer that claims a case to be benign when a malignancy is present has failed badly. On the other hand, prediction of a malignancy for an actually benign case triggers additional tests, and thus is annoying but not nearly as objectionable as an error of the first type.

We can influence the extent of type $\mathcal{A}$ errors versus type $\mathcal{B}$ errors by an appropriate choice of the objective function $\sum_{i=1}^{n} [c_{p_i}(p_i) + c_{q_i}(q_i)]$ of the MINSAT problem (11). In connection with that problem, we have seen that a certain choice leads to a separating vector s'' with min support, and that another choice produces an s'' with max support. Specifically, the first choice defines the cost functions $c_{p_i}(p_i)$ and $c_{q_i}(q_i)$ to have value 1 (resp. 0) if the argument if *True* (resp. *False*). The second choice consists of the opposite rule. When each s'' determined for S has min (resp. max) support, we say that S itself has *min* (resp. *max*) *support*.

If we use a single vector s'' to classify a vector r, then we guess r to be in $\mathcal{B}$ if s'' is nested in r. The latter condition tends to become less stringent when the number of nonzero entries in s'' is reduced. Hence, we heuristically guess that a solution vector s'' with min support tends to avoid type $\mathcal{B}$ errors. Conversely, an s'' with max support tends to avoid type $\mathcal{A}$ errors. We apply this heuristic argument to the separating set S produced under one of the two choices of objective functions for (11), and thus expect that a set S with min (resp. max) support tends to avoid type $\mathcal{B}$ (resp. $\mathcal{A}$) errors. Computational results for various logic data sets have proved that heuristic argument to be valid. Section 9 includes details.

The above control of errors is rather simple-minded since it does not allow the user to specify the level of accuracy with which vectors are to be classified. The subsequent sections introduce a much more elaborate control scheme that relies on several votes and that supports error control. We begin with a discussion of the construction of separations that are used for the votes.

7.   SEPARATIONS FOR VOTING PROCESS

The basic idea is superficially similar to, but ultimately quite different from, the notion of the stacked generalization originally described in [Wolpert, 1992], (see also [Breiman, 1996a, 1996b]). In that setting, one constructs several classifiers from given training data. When an additional record is to be evaluated, one applies each one of the classifiers, computes a consensus of the results, and classifies the record accordingly. Here, we construct the classifiers as follows.

We select an integer $d \geq 5$ and partition A into d nonempty subsets A^1, $A^2, \ldots, A^d$ of essentially equal cardinality. We justify the bound $d \geq 5$ in Section 8. We use $d = 10$ in the implemented system, which is called *Lsquare*

(Learning Logic). The assignment of the records of A to the subsets A^1, A^2, ..., A^d is done randomly. But if A itself was selected randomly from $\mathcal{A}$, it suffices that we assign records sequentially to the subsets.

Let m be the smallest integer that is larger than $d/2$; thus, $m = \lfloor d/2 \rfloor + 1$. For the moment, view A^1, A^2, ..., A^d as a circular list. We use indices in agreement with that convention. In particular, A^{i+j} denotes the j-th successor of A^i. For $i = 1, 2, \ldots, d$, we take the union of A^i and of the $(m-1)$ subsequent A^j and call that union A_i; that is, $A_i = \bigcup_{j=i}^{i+m-1} A^j$. Thus, we obtain A_1, A_2, ..., A_d. Applying the analogous process to B, we obtain via B^1, B^2, ..., B^d the sets B_1, B_2, ..., B_d, where $B_i = \bigcup_{j=i}^{i+m-1} B^j$. The derivation of A_1, A_2, ..., A_d and B_1, B_2, ..., B_d from A and B is the type of process employed in stratified cross-validation; for example, see the book by [Efron, 1993]. However, we use $m = \lfloor d/2 \rfloor + 1$ instead of $m = d - 1$ of the cross-validation case. As we shall see in the next section, the different choice of m is crucial for the estimation of the probability distributions. For each (A_i, B_i), we compute four *separating sets* of $\{0, \pm 1\}$ vectors using the basic scheme described in Section 3. We denote the four sets by S_i^1, S_i^2, S_i^3, and S_i^4. When S_i^l declares a record r to be in $\mathcal{A}$ (resp. $\mathcal{B}$), we say that S_i^l outputs a *vote* of 1 (resp. -1). Since i ranges from 1 to d, the entire collection of separating sets produces a total of $4 \cdot d$ votes. We add them up to the *vote-total*, which thus is even and ranges from $-4 \cdot d$ to $4 \cdot d$.

The vote-totals for the records of $\mathcal{A} - A$ (resp. $\mathcal{B} - B$) may be considered as samples of a random variable $Z_{\mathcal{A}}$ (resp. $Z_{\mathcal{B}}$). We want to estimate the probability distributions of $Z_{\mathcal{A}}$ and $Z_{\mathcal{B}}$ since such estimates allow prediction of the accuracy and reliability of the method. The next section shows how these distributions, as well as probabilities related to classification errors, can be estimated without use of any record beyond those of A and B.

8.   PROBABILITY DISTRIBUTION OF VOTE-TOTAL

We present the results of this section in such a way that they may be used in other data mining tools. Accordingly, for $i = 1, 2, \ldots, d$, we define C_i to be any classification method that for any record r outputs the sum of $e \geq 1$ votes as *vote-count*. Let C be the collection of C_1, C_2, ..., C_d. The sum of the vote-counts of the C_i is the *vote-total* produced by C. Since that vote-total essentially decides the classification, we permit a minor abuse of notation and let the just defined C also denote the classification method. Since each C_i produces e votes, the vote-total of C ranges from $-d \cdot e$ to $d \cdot e$ and is always odd or always even. The vote-totals of C for the records of $\mathcal{A} - A$ (resp. $\mathcal{B} - B$) are samples of the random variable $Z_{\mathcal{A}}$ (resp. $Z_{\mathcal{B}}$). Due to the symmetry, it suffices that we treat the case of $Z_{\mathcal{A}}$.

Here, C_i essentially consists of the four separating sets S_i^1, S_i^2, S_i^3, and S_i^4, and the vote-count is the sum of the four votes of those sets. Thus $e = 4$. Since we have $d = 10$, the vote-total ranges from $-10 \cdot 4 = -40$ to $10 \cdot 4 = 40$ and is always even.

We need the notion of unseen records for any member C_i of C. That is, if a record k of $\mathcal{A}$ is not used in the training of C_i, then it is *unseen* for C_i.

The computation of the estimated probability distribution for Z_A is sufficiently complicated that we have broken up the description into several steps, sometimes with substeps.

First, we estimate the mean and variance of Z_A. For this, we view the vote-counts of C_i on the records of $\mathcal{A}$ unseen for C_i as samples of a random variable X_i. Estimation of the mean of Z_A is then straightforward. The estimation of the variance of Z_A relies on several substeps where covariance results are obtained for the X_i.

Second, we define random variables Y_i, each of which is the sum of several X_i, and estimate probability distributions for the Y_i.

Third, we define a random variable Y to be the average of the Y_i. From the estimated probability distributions of the Y_i, we estimate the probability distribution of Y using a certain hypothesis. Computational results included in Section 4 lend strong experimental support to that hypothesis.

Fourth, we derive from the estimated probability distribution for Y an estimated probability distribution for Z_A.

Due to the symmetry, the same approach produces an estimated probability distribution for Z_B. Suppose both estimated distributions have been computed. Standard techniques produce estimated probabilities related to classification errors. For completeness, we include the relevant formulas in a fifth step, where we also discuss an example case.

We begin with the first step, where the mean and variance of Z_A are estimated.

8.1 Mean and Variance for Z_A

We denote the vote-count of C_i for one of its unseen records k by $x_{i,k}$. Let X_i be the random variable representing the vote-count of C_i for records of $\mathcal{A}$ that are unseen for C_i.

Mean and Variance for X_i

Since the proper subset A_i of A was used in the training of C_i, the records k of $\overline{A}_i = A - A_i$ are precisely the unseen records of A for C_i, and the corresponding vote-counts $x_{i,k}$ are sample values for X_i that may be used to estimate via standard formulas the mean and variance of X_i as

$$\hat{\mu}_{X_i} = [1/|\overline{A}_i|] \sum_{k \in \overline{A}_i} x_{i,k} \tag{17}$$

$$\hat{\sigma}^2_{X_i} = [1/(|\overline{A}_i| - 1)] \sum_{k \in \overline{A}_i} [x_{i,k} - \hat{\mu}_{X_i}]^2 \tag{18}$$

respectively.

Mean for Z_A

Since Z_A is the vote-total of C and thus is the sum of the vote-counts of the C_i, we have

$$Z_A = \sum_{i=1}^{d} X_i \qquad (19)$$

Hence, the mean value for Z_A is estimated by

$$\hat{\mu}_{Z_A} = \sum_{i=1}^{d} \hat{\mu}_{X_i} \qquad (20)$$

covariance Matrix for the X_i

The variance of Z_A is the sum of the entries of the covariance matrix for X_1, $X_2, \ldots, X_d$. We estimate the entries of that matrix as follows. For the diagonal entries of that matrix, which are the variances, we already have the estimates from (18). To estimate the other entries of the matrix, we note that, for $i \neq j$, the set $\overline{A}_{ij} = \overline{A}_i \cap \overline{A}_j$ is the set of records that are unseen for both C_i and C_j. We proceed depending on whether $\overline{A}_{ij}$ is nonempty. The details for the two subcases are as follows.

Subcase 1: $\overline{A}_{ij}$ nonempty

We estimate the covariance of X_i and X_j as

$$\hat{\sigma}_{X_i X_j} = [1/|\overline{A}_{ij}|] \sum_{k \in \overline{A}_{ij}} [x_{i,k} - \hat{\mu}_{X_i}][x_{j,k} - \hat{\mu}_{X_j}] \qquad (21)$$

We address a minor point concerning the denominator $|\overline{A}_{ij}|$ of (21). Except for that denominator, (21) is the standard formula for unbiased estimation of the covariance. The denominator should be $|\overline{A}_{ij}| - 1$ if $\hat{\mu}_{X_i}$ and $\hat{\mu}_{X_j}$ were computed using just the records of $\overline{A}_{ij}$. But here we estimate $\hat{\mu}_{X_i}$ and $\hat{\mu}_{X_j}$ using the sets $\overline{A}_i$ and $\overline{A}_j$, respectively, which properly contain $\overline{A}_{ij}$. We are not aware of results covering that situation, and have chosen the denominator $|\overline{A}_{ij}|$, which seems more appropriate than $|\overline{A}_{ij}| - 1$. At any rate, the cardinalities of $\overline{A}_{ij}$ occurring in practical applications are usually large enough that the two choices produce very similar estimates.

Subcase 2: $\overline{A}_{ij}$ empty

Compared with the number of covariance values that are computed under Subcase 1, the number of values to be estimated here is not large unless d is small. Indeed, it is easily checked that the ratio of the number of covariance values estimated via (21) divided by the total number of covariance values is $2(d - m - 1)/(d - 1)$, which, for example, is 2/3 for $d = 10$, and which rapidly approaches 1 as d increases. On the other hand, that ratio is 0 for $d = 4$ and 1/2 for $d = 5$, which justifies the condition $d \geq 5$ introduced in Section 7.

One can expect that X_i and X_j with empty $\overline{A}_{ij}$ are highly and positively correlated if the training subsets A_i and A_j from which C_i and C_j were produced have a relatively large intersection $A_i \cap A_j$. Based on that observation, we estimate the remaining covariance values via a linear function of the form $a \cdot |A_i \cap A_j| + b$. We use ridge regression [Hoerl and Kennard, 1970a, 1970b] and the $\hat{\sigma}_{X_i X_j}$ values computed via (21) to determine a and b. As just observed, increasing values of $|A_i \cap A_j|$, which reflect a larger common subset of training data for C_i and C_j, should produce a larger covariance estimate. Accordingly, we would want the coefficient a of the linear function to be nonnegative. If ridge regression produces such a coefficient a, then for each empty $\overline{A}_{ij}$ we use the cited linear function to estimate the covariance of X_i and X_j. If the coefficient a produced by ridge regression is negative, as we have observed occasionally, then the linear function is not appropriate. In that case, we force a to be 0. This effectively means that we average all $\hat{\sigma}_{X_i X_j}$ values obtained via (21) to obtain the estimated covariance for all X_i and X_j with empty $\overline{A}_{ij}$.

We are ready to estimate the variance of Z_A.

Variance of Z_A

At this point, we have estimates of the variances $\hat{\sigma}^2_{X_i}$ and the covariances $\hat{\sigma}_{X_i X_j}$ that make up the covariance matrix of $X_1, X_2, \ldots, X_d$. The sum of these entries is an estimate of the variance $\hat{\sigma}^2_{Z_A}$ of Z_A. That is,

$$\hat{\sigma}^2_{Z_A} = \sum_{i=1}^{d} \hat{\sigma}^2_{X_i} + 2 \cdot \sum_{i<j} \hat{\sigma}_{X_i X_j} \tag{22}$$

We turn to the second step, where we define random variables Y_i and estimate their distributions.

8.2 Random Variables Y_i

When d is not small, say when $d \geq 10$, then one may be tempted to guess that Z_A, which is the sum of the d random variables $X_1, X_2, \ldots, X_d$, has a distribution that can be approximated by the normal distribution. But examination of a few test examples quickly dispels that notion. So we discard that untenable assumption and obtain a reasonable approximation via some other sample distributions, as follows.

In Section 7, we viewed $A^1, A^2, \ldots, A^d$ as a circular list. We now do this for $\overline{A}_1, \overline{A}_2, \ldots, \overline{A}_d$, for $C_1, C_2, \ldots, C_d$, and for $X_1, X_2, \ldots, X_d$ as well. As before, we use indices in agreement with this definition. In particular, A^{i-1} is the immediate predecessor of A^i, and X_{i+j} is the j-th successor of X_i. For $i = 1, 2, \ldots, d$, define Y_i to be the sum of random variable X_i and the next $(d - m - 1)$ random variables X_j. We use $\tilde{C}_i$ to denote the method that to a given record applies C_i and the next $(d - m - 1)$ members C_j and that outputs the sum of the vote-counts so obtained. We call that output the *vote-sum* of $\tilde{C}_i$. We define a record to be *unseen* for $\tilde{C}_i$ if it is unseen for C_i and the next

$(d - m - 1)$ members C_j. Evidently, the vote-sums of $\tilde{C}_i$ on unseen data are samples of Y_i that may be used to estimate the distribution of Y_i.

We know that, for each j, $\overline{A}_j$ contains the records of A that are unseen for C_j. Hence, the intersection of $\overline{A}_i$ and the next $(d - m - 1)$ $\overline{A}_j$ contains the records of A that are unseen for $\tilde{C}_i$. It is easily checked that A^{i-1} is that intersection. Hence, the vote-sums of $\tilde{C}_i$ for the records of A^{i-1} may be used to estimated the distribution of Y_i.

We are ready for the third step, where we estimate the distribution of the average Y of the Y_i.

8.3   Distribution for Y

Since Y is the average of the Y_i, we have

$$
\begin{aligned}
Y &= [1/d]\sum_{i=1}^{d} Y_i \\
  &= [1/d]\sum_{i=1}^{d}(X_i + X_{i+1} \ +\ldots+\ X_{i+d-m-1}) \\
  &= [(d - m)/d]\sum_{i=1}^{d} X_i \\
  &= [(d - m)/d]\cdot Z_A
\end{aligned}
\tag{23}
$$

Hence, we effectively have an estimate of the distribution of Z_A once we have an estimate for the distribution of Y.

Since no record of A is unseen for all C_i, we cannot compute samples of Y directly from the records of A and estimate the distribution of Y from these samples. But there is an intuitive argument that supports estimation of that distribution from estimated distributions of the Y_i, as follows. First, for any $k \neq l$, X_k and X_l are likely to be positively correlated since C_k and C_l, which were trained on partially identical training data, presumably are similarly voting classifiers. Second, each Y_i is the sum of $(d-m)$ X_k, and several pairs Y_i and Y_j contain common X_k. These facts support the conjecture that any two Y_i and Y_j are positively correlated and have similar distributions. Accordingly, one is justified to guess that a reasonable estimate of the distribution of Y can be obtained by averaging the estimated distributions for the Y_i. In Section 4, we report empirical evidence that provides strong support for this guess.

We proceed to estimate the distribution for Y using the just described approach. Since the records of A unseen for $\tilde{C}_i$ constitute the set A^{i-1}, each one of the sets $A^1, A^2, \ldots, A^d$ may be used to obtain samples for a different Y_i. Furthermore, the sets $A^1, A^2, \ldots, A^d$ are essentially of equal cardinality. This implies that we may estimate the distribution of Y as an average of the distributions of the Y_i by simply taking each record of A, applying the unique $\tilde{C}_i$ for which that record is unseen to obtain a vote-sum, and finally view the vote-sums so found as samples of Y. Accordingly, we compute from these samples by standard formulas an estimated mean $\hat{\mu}_Y$, an estimated variance $\hat{\sigma}_Y$, and an estimated probability density function $\hat{h}(y)$ for Y.

We come to the fourth step, where the distribution of Z_A is estimated.

8.4   Distribution for Z_A

We could use the relationship $Y = [(d - m)/d] \cdot Z_A$ of (23) to convert the estimated density function for Y to one for Z_A, but shall not do so. Instead, we derive from the estimated density function for Y an estimated density function for Z_A that has as mean and variance the estimated values $\hat{\mu}_{Z_A}$ and $\hat{\sigma}^2_{Z_A}$ of (20) and (22). One might argue that the two possible ways of estimating a distribution for Z_A should produce the same outcome. But this need not be the case since the variance estimate of (22) is partially based on estimation via a linear function and thus need not match the variance of Z_A computed directly from the estimated variance of Y. This has been confirmed by test calculations. We should note, however, that these tests also showed that the difference between the two variance estimates for Z_A was at most moderate.

The derivation of the estimated distribution for Z_A is therefore done as follows. We take each value y of Y for which we have a positive estimated probability density value $\hat{h}(y)$ and transform it to a value z using

$$z = (y - \hat{\mu}_Y)(\hat{\sigma}_{Z_A}/\hat{\sigma}_Y) + \hat{\mu}_{Z_A} \qquad (24)$$

We round the z of (24) to the nearest integer for which Z_A may have a positive probability density and assign $\hat{h}(y)$ as the estimated probability density value to z. It may happen that several probability density values of Y are assigned to the same z value. In particular, this is possible for the largest or smallest possible value z that Z_A may take on with positive probability. For each such case, the $\hat{h}(y)$ values assigned to the same z are added together. Note that the rounding of z values causes the resulting probability density function to have mean and variance not exactly equal to $\hat{\mu}_{Z_A}$ and $\hat{\sigma}^2_{Z_A}$ of (20) and (22). In tests, the differences were small enough to be of no concern.

At this point, we have obtained an estimated probability density function $\hat{f}_A()$ for Z_A. By letting B play the role of A in the above process, we also obtain an estimated probability density function $\hat{f}_B()$ for Z_B.

The next, fifth, step provides standard formulas that derive from $\hat{f}_A()$ and $\hat{f}_B()$ estimated probabilities for classification errors.

8.5   Probabilities of Classification Errors

For the discussion below, define an *A-record* (resp. *B-record*) to be a record in $\mathcal{A}$ (resp. $\mathcal{B}$). Furthermore, Z is random variable of the vote-total of records in $\mathcal{A} \cup \mathcal{B}$. In the definition and use of probabilities, we always use odd integer values as lower or upper bounds on Z. Indeed, as we assume that the vote-total is always even, the probability of Z being odd is 0, and any lower or upper bound can always be expressed as a strict inequality $Z > z$ or $Z < z$ with odd-valued z. We use the following notation for the estimated distribution functions and power functions.

$$\begin{aligned}
\hat{F}_A(z) &= \sum_{x<z} \hat{f}_A(x) \\
\hat{F}_B(z) &= \sum_{x<z} \hat{f}_B(x) \\
\hat{G}_A(z) &= \sum_{x>z} \hat{f}_A(x) \\
\hat{G}_B(z) &= \sum_{x>z} \hat{f}_B(x)
\end{aligned} \tag{25}$$

Let $\hat{p}_A$ and $\hat{p}_B$ be estimates of the prior probabilities that a record is in A or B. That is,

$$\begin{aligned}
\hat{p}_A &\cong P[A \text{ record}] \\
\hat{p}_B &\cong P[B \text{ record}]
\end{aligned} \tag{26}$$

Then by Bayes' theorem,

$$\begin{aligned}
P[A \text{ record} \mid Z < z] &\cong \hat{p}_A \cdot \hat{F}_A(z)/[\hat{p}_A \cdot \hat{F}_A(z) + \hat{p}_B \cdot \hat{F}_B(z)] \\
P[B \text{ record} \mid Z > z] &\cong \hat{p}_B \cdot \hat{G}_B(z)/[\hat{p}_A \cdot \hat{G}_A(z) + \hat{p}_B \cdot \hat{G}_B(z)]
\end{aligned} \tag{27}$$

Suppose we select a value z and classify any record as follows. If the vote-total is greater than z, we declare the record to be in A. If it is less than z, we declare the record to be in B. Then the probability of a type A error given that $Z > z$ is 0, and the probability of that error given $Z < z$ is as follows.

$$P[\text{type } A \text{ error} \mid Z < z] = P[A \text{ record} \mid Z < z] \tag{28}$$

On the other hand, the probability of a type B error given that $Z < z$ is 0, and the probability of that error given $Z > z$ is as follows.

$$P[\text{type } B \text{ error} \mid Z > z] = P[B \text{ record} \mid Z > z] \tag{29}$$

Hence, the formulas of (27) allow us to estimate the probabilities of such errors. Moreover, the same scheme can be used to choose the value of z in an optimal way with respect to the estimated probability of the two types of error and to the specific requirements of an application.

As an example, consider the hepatocellular carcinoma data described in [Di Giacomo et al., 2001]. Each record represents a patient and contains 56 $\{0, \pm 1\}$ entries representing various symptoms and test results. The original training data set A contains 64 records of patients with the disease, while B contains 64 records of patients free of the disease. One record of A is nested in a number of records of B. Removal of that record from A results in two training data sets where no record of one set is nested in a record of the other set, as required for consistency.

The estimated probability distribution $\hat{F}_A()$ and power function $\hat{G}_B()$ of Table 1 are part of the output of Lsquare for this case.

Suppose we classify a record as being in A if the vote-total exceeds 9. Then using the line of Table 1 for $z = 9$, we have

$$\begin{aligned}
P[Z < z \mid A \text{ record}] &\cong \hat{F}_A(9) = 0.1095 \\
P[Z > z \mid B \text{ record}] &\cong \hat{G}_B(9) = 0.0266
\end{aligned} \tag{30}$$

Table 1. Estimated $\hat{F}_A(z)$ and $\hat{G}_B(z)$.

z	$\hat{F}_A(z)$	$\hat{G}_B(z)$	z	$\hat{F}_A(z)$	$\hat{G}_B(z)$
-41	0.0000	1.0000	1	0.0762	0.0359
-39	0.0000	0.8031	3	0.0952	0.0313
-37	0.0000	0.6937	5	0.0952	0.0313
-35	0.0000	0.5938	7	0.0952	0.0313
-33	0.0000	0.4938	9	0.1095	0.0266
-31	0.0000	0.4313	11	0.1286	0.0203
-29	0.0000	0.3812	13	0.1476	0.0141
-27	0.0000	0.3359	15	0.1667	0.0078
-25	0.0000	0.3047	17	0.1857	0.0016
-23	0.0000	0.2734	19	0.2048	0.0000
-21	0.0000	0.2375	21	0.2238	0.0000
-19	0.0000	0.2000	23	0.2460	0.0000
-17	0.0016	0.1641	25	0.2778	0.0000
-15	0.0079	0.1328	27	0.3095	0.0000
-13	0.0143	0.1016	29	0.3603	0.0000
-11	0.0206	0.0797	31	0.4175	0.0000
-9	0.0270	0.0609	33	0.4651	0.0000
-7	0.0317	0.0469	35	0.4841	0.0000
-5	0.0317	0.0469	37	0.5032	0.0000
-3	0.0317	0.0469	39	0.6556	0.0000
-1	0.0508	0.0422	41	1.0000	0.0000

Suppose a family doctor or general practitioner in a routine examination determines that a patient possibly has hepatocellular carcinoma and refers the patient to a clinic for expert diagnosis. Let the probability of the clinic making a positive diagnosis of carcinoma be about 5% for such a referral. Thus, we have the estimated prior probabilities

$$
\begin{aligned}
\hat{p}_A &= 0.05 \\
\hat{p}_B &= 1 - \hat{p}_A = 0.95
\end{aligned}
\tag{31}
$$

If $z = 9$ is used to classify each patient, then the above formulas allow us to estimate probabilities of diagnostic errors as follows.

$$
\begin{aligned}
P[\text{type } A \text{ error} \mid Z < 9] &= P[A \text{ record} \mid Z < 9] \\
&\cong 0.0059 \\
P[\text{type } B \text{ error} \mid Z > 9] &= P[B \text{ record} \mid Z > 9] \\
&\cong 0.3625
\end{aligned}
\tag{32}
$$

We used $z = 9$ just for example calculations and are not suggesting that this value actually be employed for diagnostic decision making. Indeed, let x (resp. y) be the the largest (resp. smallest) value of z for which $P[A \text{ record} \mid Z < z]$

(resp. $P[\mathcal{B}$ record $\mid Z > z]$) is estimated to be 0. By (27), x (resp. y) is the largest (resp. smallest) z for which $\hat{F}_A(z) = 0$ (resp. $\hat{G}_A(z) = 0$). From Table 1, $x = -19$ and $y = 19$. Suppose that the record of a patient is to be evaluated, and that the vote-total z_p has been computed. If $z_p < x$ (resp. $z_p > y$), then the disease is estimated to be absent (resp. present) with probability 1, and treatment is not needed (resp. should be initiated). If $x < z_p < y$, $P[$type $\mathcal{A}$ error $\mid Z < z_p]$ and $P[$type $\mathcal{B}$ error $\mid Z > z_p]$ are estimated by (27) and (28) and may be used to select the course of action. The estimates of the probabilities $P[$type $\mathcal{A}$ error $\mid Z < z_p]$ and $P[$type $\mathcal{B}$ error $\mid Z > z_p]$ allow the physician and patient to assess the situation rationally and to arrive at appropriate decisions that account for the attendant risks and benefits.

8.6   Summary of Algorithm

We summarize the entire scheme.

> *Program CONSTRUCT VOTING SYSTEM:*

1. From A and B, construct 10 subsets pairs (A_i, B_i). For each pair (A_i, B_i), compute with Program FIND SEPARATING SET the 4 separating sets S_i^l.

2. Declare each of the 40 separating sets S_i^l to be a rule for producing a ± 1 vote for the evaluation of records. Define the vote-total to be the sum of these votes.

3. Compute the probability distributions. They are used to certify the reliability of classifications made with the vote-total.

The next section presents computational results.

9.   COMPUTATIONAL RESULTS

We have tested the accuracy of the estimated distribution functions using the six well-known data sets Australian Credit Card, Breast Cancer, Congressional Voting, Heart Disease, Diabetes, and Boston Housing, which may be obtained from the UCI Machine Learning Repository [1].

The logic-based approach requires the records of $\mathcal{A}$ and $\mathcal{B}$ of each data set to contain $\{0, \pm 1\}$ entries only. We call these $\{0, \pm 1\}$ entries *logic entries* to differentiate them from other types of entries such as Boolean, integer, nominal, or rational. A nominal entry is a member of a finite set of descriptive terms. The interpretation associated with the logic entries $+1$, and -1 does not matter, while 0 is reserved for "Do not know value." For example, one might associate $+1$ with *True* or *Yes* and -1 with *False* or *No*. Some entries of the six data sets are not in the $\{0, \pm 1\}$ form and require transformations. We summarize

---
[1] http://www.ics.uci.edu/~mlearn/MLRepository.html

that step in the following subsections when we cover the results for each data set. But first we use the data sets to provide empirical justification for the estimation of the distribution of Y in Section 8, where that distribution is estimated to be the average of the estimated distributions for $Y_1, Y_2, \ldots, Y_d$.

For each of the six data sets $\mathcal{A}$ and $\mathcal{B}$, we randomly select as A and B half the data and construct a family $\mathcal{C}$. To establish validity of the estimating procedure for the distribution of $Z = Z_{\mathcal{A}}$ or $Z = Z_{\mathcal{B}}$ via estimated distributions of the Y_i, we apply $\mathcal{C}$ to $\mathcal{A} - A$ or $\mathcal{B} - B$, respectively, to get estimated distributions for Z and for the Y_i. We emphasize that we apply $\mathcal{C}$ to $\mathcal{A} - A$ or $\mathcal{B} - B$ and not to any subsets of A or B. The reason is that we want to establish the validity of guessing the distribution of Z from those of the Y_i and thus want to eliminate any variability not related to that comparison. For the same reason, we estimate the mean $\hat{\mu}_Z$ and variance $\hat{\sigma}_Z^2$ of Z from the just determined distribution.

We average the estimated distributions for the Y_i to obtain an estimated distribution for Y. Let $\hat{\mu}_Y$ and $\hat{\sigma}_Y^2$ be the mean and variance of the latter distribution. We transform the estimated distribution for Y using equation (24) and the rounding process described in Section 8. We denote by Z' the random variable represented by the resulting distribution. Finally, we compare the distribution of Z' with the estimated distribution of Z. A close match would empirically justify the approximation of the distribution of Z via those of the Y_i.

For each pair of A and B derived from the six data sets, we get two cases of Z and Z'. Hence, we have a total of twelve pairs Z and Z'. In each case, the distribution of Z' turned out to be virtually identical to the estimated distribution of Z. In Figure 1 we show graphs of the distributions for the pairs obtained from the Australian Credit Card data set.

Figure 1. Distributions for $Z = Z_{\mathcal{A}}$ (left), $Z = Z_{\mathcal{B}}$ (right), and related Z'.

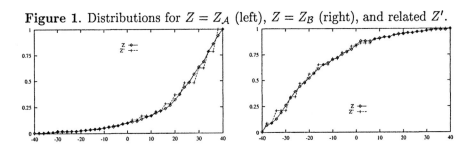

These results empirically justify the estimation of the distribution of Y by the average of the estimated distributions for $Y_1, Y_2, \ldots, Y_d$.

We are ready to discuss the computational results obtained for $\mathcal{A}$ and $\mathcal{B}$ of each data set. We obtain from $\mathcal{A}$ and $\mathcal{B}$ randomly selected subsets A and B, each containing 50% of the respective source set. We apply Lsquare to A and B, obtain the family $\mathcal{C}$ of classification methods, and compute the estimated functions $\hat{F}_A()$ and $\hat{G}_B(z)$ of (25). Then we apply $\mathcal{C}$ to $\mathcal{A} - A$ and $\mathcal{B} - B$ to verify the accuracy. From $\hat{F}_A(z)$ and $\hat{G}_B(z)$, the functions of (27) can be estimated. The latter estimates have good accuracy if this is so for $\hat{F}_A(z)$ and $\hat{G}_B(z)$.

In the drawings below, the curves plotted with diamonds give the estimated values $\hat{F}_A(z)$ and $\hat{G}_B(z)$ produced by Lsquare, while the curves plotted with crosses provide the values computed produced by $\mathcal{C}$ using the verification sets $\mathcal{A} - A$ and $\mathcal{B} - B$. Close agreement of the two curves means that the estimates are quite accurate and that the estimated functions are useful.

9.1   Breast Cancer Diagnosis

[Mangasarian et al., 1990] (see also [Mangasarian and Wolberg, 1990], and [Mangasarian et al., 1995]) provide breast cancer data for 699 patients. We view the data as rational data where each record corresponds to a patient. A record has 9 entries that are produced by some tests. The possible values for each entry are 1, 2,..., 10. Of the 699 records, 16 have missing entries. The outcome of each record may be viewed as the value of a Boolean variable t that indicates whether the case is benign or malignant. We convert the rational data to logic data and obtain $\{0, \pm 1\}$ logic records representing a patient with 45 entries.

In Figure 2 are the results. Evidently, the agreement between the estimated and verified curves is very good.

Figure 2. Estimated and verified F_A(left) and G_B (right) for Breast Cancer.

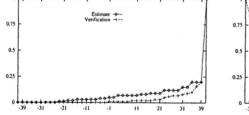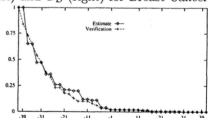

A predecessor paper [Felici and Truemper, 2002] compares other methods with a version of Lsquare that differs slightly from the present one and does not have the statistical prediction process. The comparison is based on 10 randomly selected 50% training subsets of the given data set. For the prediction, a record with positive (resp. negative) vote-total is claimed to be in $\mathcal{A}$ (resp. $\mathcal{B}$). A vote-total of 0 is predicted consistently to be in $\mathcal{A}$ or $\mathcal{B}$, based on a prior random selection of either $\mathcal{A}$ or $\mathcal{B}$. Below, we include these results with each case. For the Breast Cancer Data, the best prior prediction accuracy for 50% training sets reported in [Boros et al., 1996] is 96.9%. That accuracy is achieved for a reduced data set where all records containing missing data have been deleted. Lsquare has 97.1% accuracy without deletion of any records.

9.2   Australian Credit Card

The data were collected by R. Quinlan (see [Quinlan, 1993]). They represent 690 MasterCard applicants of which 307 are declared as positive and 383 as negative. The data contain 37 records with missing entries. Each record consists of 15 attributes, of which 4 are Boolean, 5 nominal, and 6 rational. For prior computational results, see [Carter and Catlett, 1987], and [Boros et al., 1996].

The representation of the 15 attributes requires a total of 67 logic variables. With this transformation, $\mathcal{A}$ and $\mathcal{B}$ had one record in common. We have removed that record from $\mathcal{A}$.

The graphs in Figure 3 show the results. Evidently, there is very good agreement between the curves.

Figure 3. Estimated and verified $F_{\mathcal{A}}$(left) and $G_{\mathcal{B}}$ (right) for Australian Credit Card.

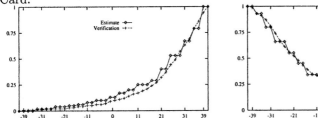

[Boros et al., 1996] show that the best prior recognition rate is 85.4% for training sets of size 50%. Lsquare has 86.0% accuracy.

9.3   Congressional Voting

The problem concerns the prediction of party affiliation from 435 voting records of 267 Democrats and 168 Republicans. The data were collected by J. Schlimmer. Each record contains 16 entries of the form "for", "against", and "did not vote". For prior computational results, see [Holte, 1993] and [Boros et al., 1996].

In the logic data, we represent "for" by 1, "against" by -1, and "did not vote" by 0. We define $\mathcal{A}$ (resp. $\mathcal{B}$) to be the set of records of the Republicans (resp. Democrats).

In Figure 4 are the results. The agreement among the curves is excellent.

The best prior result in [Boros et al, 1996] for 50% training sets has 96.2% accuracy, achieved after removal of 6 records with missing entries. Lsquare has 95.8% accuracy without removal of any records.

9.4   Diabetes Diagnosis

This problem concerns the diagnosis of diabetes based on observations for 768 patients, of which 268 had signs of diabetes, while 500 did not. The data were

Figure 4. Estimated and verified F_A(left) and G_B (right) for Congressional Voting.

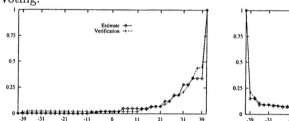

collected by V. Sigillito. There are 8 attributes, of which 2 have discrete values, and 6 are rational. For prior computational results, see [Smith et al., 1988], [Murthy at al., 1994], and [Boros et al., 1996].

The transformations adopted produce a total of 55 logic variables. With these transformations, A and B had one record in common. We have removed one such record from A to achieve consistency.

Results are reported in Figure 5. The agreement among the curves is very good.

Figure 5. Estimated and verified F_A(left) and G_B (right) for Diabetes.

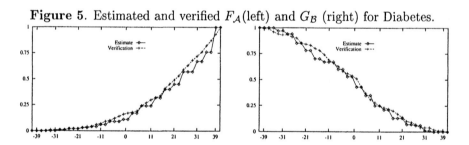

The best prior rate for 50% training sets according to [Boros et al., 1996] is 71.9%. Lsquare has 73.3%.

9.5   Heart Disease Diagnosis

Observations for 303 patients are given, of which 165 are healthy, while 139 have some heart disease. Of the 303 records, 6 have some missing entries. Each record provides 13 attributes, of which 3 are Boolean, 4 nominal, and 6 rational. For prior computational results, see [Gennari et al., 1989], [Shavlik et al., 1991], [Holte, 1993], and [Boros et al., 1996].

We transform the records to logic data and obtain a total of 50 logic variables. We collect in A (resp. B) the logic records corresponding to the healthy patients (resp. the patients with heart disease).

The computational results are given In Figure 6. The agreement among the curves is good.

Figure 6. Estimated and verified F_A(left) and G_B (right) for Heart Disease.

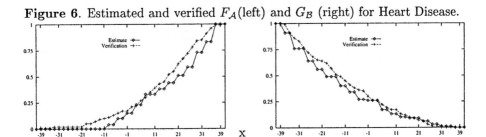

The best result for 50% training sets cited in [Boros et al., 1996] is a recognition rate of 82.3%. Lsquare has 80.7%.

9.6   Boston Housing

The data set is taken from [Harrison and Rubinfeld, 1978]; see also [Quinlan, 1993]. The data consist of 506 records concerning housing values in the Boston area. Each record is composed of 13 attributes, of which 12 have rational values, while one is Boolean. The median value of the owner-occupied houses is used as a threshold to split the entire set of records into two sets. For prior computational results, see [Boros et al., 1996].

After the transformations, the total number of logic variables is 109. It turns out that the sets A and B so defined from the original two data sets have two records in common. We delete these records from A to achieve consistency.

In Figure 7 are the results. The agreement among the curves is good.

Figure 7. Estimated and verified F_A(left) and G_B (right) for Boston Housing.

The best prior result reported by [Boros et al, 1996] for 50% training sets is 84.0% accuracy, compared with 83.5% by Lsquare.

10.   CONCLUSIONS

The computational results show that the estimated probability distributions have good to excellent accuracy, and that the overall accuracy matches the best prior results. These results are achieved without use of any additional data beyond those employed for the training. Moreover, the results are produced without any tuning or other adjustment or manual intervention. A potentially useful fact is that the estimating formulas derived in Section 8 are sufficiently general so that they may be employed in other data mining systems. Suppose such a system already produces votes or results that can be converted to votes. Given training data A and B, one only needs to apply the system to the pairs composed of A_i and B_i and to proceed as described in Section 8, to obtain estimated distribution functions and related error probabilities.

Acknowledgments

The authors wish to acknowledge Giovanni Rinaldi for advice and support during the research work. Partial financial support for this research was given by the Office of Naval Research under grant N000145-93-1-0096.

REFERENCES

Bennett, K. P., Mangasarian, O. L. 1992. Robust linear programming discrimination of two linearly inseparable sets. in: *Optimization Methods and Software I*, Gordon & Breach Science Publishers, pp. 23-34.

Bhargava, H. K. 1999. Data Mining by Decomposition: Adaptive Search for Hypothesis Generation. *INFORMS Journal on Computing* 3 239-247.

Boros, E., Hammer, P. L., Ibaraki, T., Kogan, A., Mayoraz, E., and Muchnik, I. 1996. An Implementation of Logical Analysis of Data. *RUTCOR Research Report* 29-96, Rutgers University, NJ, July 1996.

Boros, E., Ibaraki, T., and Makino, K. 1999. Logical Analysis of Binary Data with Missing Bits. *Artificial Intelligence* 107 219–263.

Bradley, P. S., Fayyad, U. M., and Mangasarian, O. L. 1999. Mathematical Programming for Data Mining: Formulations and Challenges. *INFORMS Journal on Computing* 3 217-238.

Breiman, L. 1996a. Stacked Regressions. *Machine Learning*, 24. 49-64.

Breiman, L. 1996b. Bias, Variance, and Arcing Classifiers. Technical Report 460, Statistics Department, University of California, Berkeley.

Breiman, L., Friedman, J. H., Olshen, R. A., and Stone, C. J. 1984. *Classification and Regression Trees*. Wadsworth International, 1984.

Carter, C., Catlett, J. 1987. Assessing Credit Card Applications Using Machine Learning. *IEEE Expert* Fall 1987 pp. 71-79.

Chandru, V., Hooker, J. N. 1999. *Optimization Methods for Logical Inference*. John Wiley and Sons, New York, 1999.

Cohen, W. W. 1995. Pac-learning non-recursive Prolog clauses. *Artificial Intelligence* 79 1-38.

Crama, Y., Hammer, P. L., and Ibaraki, T. 1988. Cause-Effect Relationships and Partially Defined Boolean Functions. *Annals of Operations Research* 16 299-325.

Domany, E., van Hemmen, J. L., and Schulten, K. (eds.) 1991. *Models of Neural Networks.* Springer-Verlag, Berlin, 1991.

Felici, G. 1995. *Il Problema di Riconoscimento Automatico: Proprietà ed Algoritmi di Soluzione.* Tesi di Dottorato, Biblioteca Nazionale di Roma, Italy, 1995.

Felici, G., Truemper, K. 2002. A MINSAT approach for learning in logic domains. *INFORMS Journal on Computing* **14** 20-36 .

Freed, N., Glover, F. 1981. Simple but Powerful Goal Programming Models for Discriminant Problems. *European Journal of Operational Research***7** 44-60.

Freed, N., Glover, F. 1986. Evaluating Alternative Linear Programming Models to Solve the Two-Group Discriminant Problem. *Decision Sciences* **17** 151-162.

Garey, M. R., Johnson, D. S. 1979. *Computers and Intractability: A Guide to the Theory of NP-Completeness.* Freeman, San Francisco, 1979.

Gennari, J. H., Langley, P., and Fisher, D.1989 Models of Incremental Concept Formation. *Artificial Intelligence* **40** 11-61.

Di Giacomo, P., Felici, G., Maceratini, R., and Truemper, K. 2001. Application of a new logic domain method for the diagnosis of hepatocellular carcinoma. Proceedings of *Tenth World Congress on Health and Medical Informatics (medinfo2001)*, London, UK pp. 434-438.

Golea, M. 1995. Average Case Analysis of a Learning Algorithm for μ-DNF Expressions. in: *Computational Learning Theory*, Proceedings of the Second European Conference EuroCOLT '95 (Paul Vitányi, eds.), Barcelona, Spain, Springer-Verlag 1995 pp. 342-356.

Harrison, D., Rubinfeld, D. L. 1978. Hedonic prices and the demand of clean air. *Journal of Environment Economics and Management* **5** 111-143.

Hertz, J., Krogh, A., and Palmer, R. G. 1991. *Introduction to the Theory of Neural Computation.* Addison Wesley, 1991.

Hoerl, A. E. Kennard, R. W.. 1970a. Ridge regression: Biased estimation for nonorthogonal problems. *Technometrics* **12** 55-67

Hoerl, A. E. Kennard, R. W.. 1970b. Ridge regression: Applications to nonorthogonal problems. *Technometrics* **12** 69-82

Holte, R. C. 1993. Very Simple Classification Rules Perform Well on Most Commonly Used Datasets. *Machine Learning* **11** 63-91.

Kamath, A. P., Karmarkar, N. K., Ramakrishnan, K. J., and Resende, M. G. C. 1992. A Continuous Approach to Inductive Inference. *Mathematical Programming* **57** 215-238.

Leibniz System 2000. Version 5.0. Leibniz, Plano, Texas, http://leibnizsystem.com.

Makino, K., Yano, K., and Ibaraki, T. 1997. Positive and Horn Decomposability of Partially Defined Boolean Functions. *Discrete Applied Mathematics* **74** 251-274.

Mangasarian, O. L. 1993. Mathematical programming in Neural Networks. *ORSA Journal on Computing* **5** 349-360.

Mangasarian, O. L., Setiono, R., and Wolberg, W. H. 1990. Pattern Recognition via Linear Programming: Theory and Application to Medical Diagnosis. in: *Large-scale numerical optimization*, (Thomas F. Coleman and Yuying Li, eds.), SIAM Publications, Philadelphia pp. 22-30.

Mangasarian, O. L., Wolberg, W. H. 1990. Cancer Diagnosis via Linear Programming. *SIAM News* **23** pp. 1-18.

Mangasarian, O. L., Street, W. N., and Wolberg, W. H. 1995. Breast Cancer Diagnosis and Prognosis via Linear Programming. *Operations Research* **43** 570-577.

Muggleton, S. 1999. Inductive Logic Programming: Issues, Results and the Challenge of Learning Languages in Logic. *Artificial Intelligence* **114** 289-296.

Murthy, S. K., Kasif, S., and Salzberg, S. 1994. A System for Induction of Oblique Decision Trees. *Journal of Artificial Intelligence Research* **2** 1-32.

Nelson, M. M., Illingworth, W. T. 1990. *A Practical Guide to Neural Nets.* Addison-Wesley, Reading, MA, 1990.

Quinlan, R. 1993. Combining instance-based and model-based learning. in: *Proceedings of the Tenth International Conference on Machine Learning*, University of Massachusetts, Amherst, Morgan Kaufmann, 1993, pp. 236-243.

Shavlik, J. W., Mooney, R. J., and Towell, G. G. 1991. Symbolic and Neural Learning Algorithms: An Experimental Comparison. *Machine Learning* **6** 111-143.

Smith, J. W., Evelhart, J. E., Dickinson, W. C., Knowler, W. C., and Johannes, R. S. 1988. Using the ADAP Learning Algorithm to Forecast the Onset of Diabetes Mellitus. in: *Proceedings of the 12th Annual Symposium on Computer Applications in Medical Care* (R. A. Greenes, ed.), IEEE Computer Society Press, 1988, pp. 261-265.

Thrun, S. B., Bala, J., Bloedorn, E., Bratko, I., Cestnik, B., Cheng, J., De Jong, K., Džeroski, S., Fahlman, S. E., Fisher, D. H., Hamann, R., Kaufmann, K., Keller, S., Kononenko, I., Kreuziger, J., Michalski, R. S., Mitchell, T., Pachowics, P., Reich, Y., Vafaie, H., Van de Welde, W., Wenzel, W., Wnek, J., and Zhang, J. 1991. The MONK's Problems - A Performance Comparison of Different Learning Algorithms. Technical Report CS-CMU-91-197, Carnegie Mellon University, December 1991.

Triantaphyllou, E., Soyster, A. L., and Kumara, S. R. T. 1994. Generating Logical Expressions From Positive and Negative Examples via a Branch-and-Bound Approach. *Computers and Operations Research* **21** 185-197.

Triantaphyllou, E., Soyster, A. L. 1996. On the Minimum Number of Logical Clauses Inferred from Examples. *Computers and Operations Research* **21** 783-799.

Truemper, K. 1998. *Effective Logic Computation.* Wiley-Interscience, New York, 1998.

Valiant, L. G. 1985. Learning Disjunctions and Conjunctions. in: *Proceedings of the 9th IJCAI*, August 1985, 550-556.

Wolpert, D. H. 1992. Stacked Generalization. *Neural Networks* 5 241-259.

AUTHORS' BIOGRAPHICAL STATEMENTS

Dr. **Giovanni Felici** graduated in Statistics at the University of Rome "La Sapienza". He received his M.Sc. in Operations Research and Operations Management at the University of Lancaster, UK, in 1990, and his Ph.D. in Operations Research at the University of Rome La Sapienza in 1995. He is presently a permanent researcher in IASI, the Istituto di Analisi dei Sistemi ed Informatica of the Italian National Research Council (CNR), where he started his research activity in 1994 working on research projects in Logic Programming and Mathematical Optimization. His current research activity is mainly devoted to the application of Optimization Techniques to Data Mining problems, with particular focus on Integer Programming algorithms for Learning in Logic and Expert Systems.

Dr. **Fu-Shing Sun** is currently an assistant professor in Computer Science Department at Ball State University. He received his Ph.D. degree from University of Texas at Dallas in Computer Science in 1998. His research interest includes data mining and communication networks.

Dr. **Klaus Truemper** is Professor of Computer Science at the University of Texas, Dallas. Dr. Truemper received his doctorate in Operations Research from Case Western Reserve University in 1973. In 1988, he received the prestigious Senior Distinguished U.S. Scientist Award from the Alexander von Humboldt Foundation (Germany). Dr. Truemper's work includes the books Matroid Decomposition and Effective Logic Computation, and the Leibniz System software.

Chapter 6 [1]

FEATURE SELECTION FOR DATA MINING

Vanda de Angelis*, Giovanni Felici**, Gabriella Mancinelli*

* *Dipartimento di Statistica Probabilità e Statistiche Applicate*

Università di Roma "La Sapienza"
Piazzale A. Moro 5, 00185 Rome, Italy

** *Istituto di Analisi dei Sistemi ed Informatica "A. Ruberti"*

Consiglio Nazionale delle Ricerche
Viale Manzoni 30, 00185 Rome, Italy
Email: felici@iasi.cnr.it

Abstract:
Feature Selection methods in Data Mining and Data Analysis problems aim at selecting a subset of the variables, or features, that describe the data in order to obtain a more essential and compact representation of the available information. The selected subset has to be small in size and must retain the information that is most useful for the specific application. The role of Feature Selection is particularly important when computationally expensive Data Mining tools are used, or when the data collection process is difficult or costly. Feature Selection problems are typically solved in the literature using search techniques, where the evaluation of a specific subset is accomplished by a proper function (filter methods) or directly by the performance of a Data Mining tool (wrapper methods). In this work we show how the Feature Selection problem can be formulated as a subgraph selection problem derived from the lightest k-subgraph problem, and solved as an Integer Program. The proposed formulation is very flexible, as additional conditions on the solution can be added in the formulation. Although optimal solutions for such problems are difficult to find in the worst case, a large number of test instances have been solved efficiently by commercial tools. Finally, an application to a database on urban mobility is presented, where the proposed method is integrated in the Data Mining tool named Lsquare and is compared with other approaches.

Keywords: Feature Selection, Data Mining, Integer Programming.

---

[1] Triantaphyllou, E. and G. Felici (Eds.), **Data Mining and Knowledge Discovery Approaches based on Rule Induction Techniques**, Massive Computing Series, Springer, Heidelberg, Germany, pp. 227-252, 2006.

1. INTRODUCTION

The abundance of large bodies of structured and semi structured information is a direct effect of the many ways that are now available to collect data. Nevertheless, it is common opinion that the rate of growth of the information available is not matched by the development of methods that properly use this information.

For this reason, the field of Data Mining (DM) has seen rising interest both in the scientific community and in the market, and several methods are being developed to try and extract high quality information hidden in data.

Typical problems tackled by Data Mining are a) the identification of association rules, that is, rules that express particular combinations of factors that are present in the data with high frequency or probability; and b) classification, where one is given "objects" belonging to different classes and is to find a rule able to tell elements of one class from elements of another class.

When dealing with large data sets, it is often the case that the information available is somehow redundant for the scopes of the DM application; many mining tools deal with this issue by trying to provide classification or association rules that are as compact as possible. The reduction of the original feature set to a smaller one preserving the relevant information while discarding the redundant one is referred to as *feature selection* (FS). It is appropriate here to point out that with *feature* we intend the original attributes or variables associated with each record of the data set rather than some particular transformation of such attributes.

In many cases FS can be looked at as an independent task in the DM process, that pre-processes the data before they are treated by a DM method, that often may fail or have significant computational problems in treating directly data set with a large number of features.

The main benefits in using FS in DM may thus be outlined as follows:

- reduction in the amount of information needed to train a DM algorithm;

- better quality of the rules learned from data;

- easier acquisition and storage of the information related to a smaller number of "useful" features;

- reduced cost for acquiring the information (often FS aims at defining a good subset of the available features by minimizing a cost function derived from the effective economical cost of acquiring that feature in the real world).

A very extensive treatment of the use of FS in DM applications is given by [Liu and Motoda, 2000]. These authors provide a complete overview of the methods developed since the 70s, confronting the results of several applications and providing suggestions on how to orient the choice of the proper method for each problem.

In this chapter we consider the main approaches to FS, and then propose a method which is based on a well known subgraph selection problem.

The chapter is organized as follows. In Section 2 we present the main methods and results currenlty available in the literature, founding our analysis on the well established distinction between *Filter Methods* and *Wrapper Methods*. Section 3 considers the linkage between the FS problems and the lightest k-subgraph selection problem, and addresses some computational complexity issues related to this problem. Then, in Section 4, the mathematical programming formulation adopted to model a FS problem is presented, taking into account some of the possible variants that may be required for a correct use of the model in the applications. Computational experience and results obtained on real data are reported in Section 5. Finally, Section 6 proposes some conclusions.

2. THE MANY ROUTES TO FEATURE SELECTION

Feature Selection is a non trivial task. Its main difficulty is the fact that its goal is to select a subset of a larger set that has some desiderable properties, where such properties strongly depend on the whole subset and is thus not always appropriate to measure them by means of simple or low order functions in the elements. Moreover, the number of candidate subsets is exponential in the size of the initial set. Many successful methods thus propose heuristic approaches, typically greedy, where the final subset is not guaranteed to be the best possible one, but is verified, by some proper method, to function "well". On the other hand, optimal approaches, that guarantee the minimization of some quality function, need some approximation in the evaluation function to become tractable.

In order to give a general overview of the methods avaiable, we refer to the work of [Langley, 1994], according to whom a FS method is based on four main steps, as follows:

1. generation procedure;

2. evaluation function;

3. stopping criterion;

4. validation procedure.

The **generation procedure** is in charge of generating the subsets of features to be evaluated. From the computational standpoint, the number of possible subsets from a set of N features is 2^N. It is therefore very crucial to generate good subsets by trying to avoid the exploration of all the search space, using heuristic strategies, that at each step select a new feature amongst the available ones to be added to the existing set, or random strategy, where a given number of subsets is generated at random, and the one with the best evaluation value is chosen. The generation starts with the empty set, and then adds a new feature at each iteration (*forward strategy*). Alternatively, it may start from the complete set of features removing one at each step (*backward strategy*) . Finally, some methods propose to start from a randomly generated subset to which forward or backward strategy is applied.

The **evaluation function** is used to measure the quality of a subset. Such value is then confronted with the best available value obtained, and the latter is updated if appropriate. More specifically, the evaluation function measures the classification power of a single feature or of a subset of the features. An interesting classification is given by [Dash and Liu, 1997], who propose four classes based on the type of evaluation functions:

- *distance* measures: given 2 classes C_1 and C_2, feature X is preferred to Y if $P(C_1|X) - P(C_2|X) > P(C_1|Y) - P(C_2|Y)$, that is, if X induces a larger increase in the class conditional probabilities with respect to Y;

- *information* measures, that tend to indicate the quantity of information retained by a given feature. For example, feature X is preferred to feature Y if the improvement in the entropy function obtained by adding X is larger that the one obtained by adding Y;

- *dependance* or *correlation* measures: they indicate the capability of a subset of features to predict the value of other features. In this setting, X is preferred to Y if its correlation with the class to be predicted is larger. These measures may also indicate redundancies in the features, based on the cross-correlation between the features themselves;

- *consistency* measures: their purpose is to evaluate the capacity of the selected feature to separate the objects in different classes. For example, a particular feature may be considered uninteresting if two elements of the data set have the same value for that feature but belong to different classes.

The **stopping criterion** is needed to avoid time consuming exhaustive search of the solution space without a significant improvement in the evaluation function. The search may be stopped if a given number of attributes has been reached, or when the improvement obtained by the new subset is not relevant.

Finally, the **evaluation procedure** measures the quality of the selected subset. This is typically accomplished by running the DM algorithm by using only the selected features on additional data.

According to the type of evaluation function adopted, FS methods are divided into two main groups: *filter methods* and *wrapper methods*. In the former, the evaluation function is independent from the DM algorithm that is to be applied. In the latter, the DM algorithm is, to a certain extent, the essence of the evaluation function: each candidate subset is tested by using the DM algorithm and then evaluated on the basis of its performances.

In Figure 1 below the general design of a filter and a wrapper method is depicted, where the DM algorithm is represented by a generic Classifier. The opinion that wrapper methods can provide better results in term of final accuracy is widely shared in the scientific community. However, these methods are extremely expensive from the computational standpoint, and also suffer from the limitations of having their acccuracy limited to the classification or the DM algorithm used.

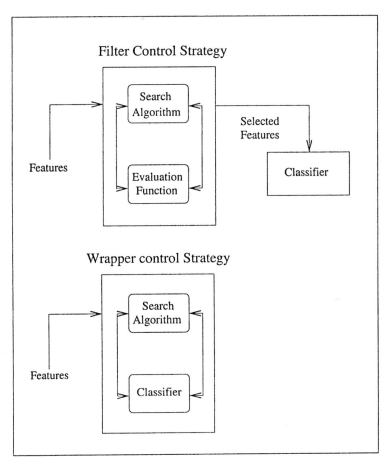

Figure 1. Wrappers and Filters.

On the other hand, the filter approach appears to be more general, and indeed faster, although it presents several weak points, amongst which are:

- several methods are not designed to deal appopriately with noisy data;

- they often leave the choice amongst a number of "good" subsets to the user;

- in most methods the user is asked to specify the dimension of the final set of features, or to define a threshold value of some sort that drives the stopping condition of the algorithm;

- some methods pose some constraints on the format of the data (e.g., they may require all data to be in binary format), introducing potential noise and furtherly increasing the number of features to start from.

Nevertheless, the contained computational complexity of filter methods turns out to be very important in the application of DM techniques to large datasets, where the dimensions involved forbid the application of certain sophisticated classification techniques which use the complete set of features. In such cases, wrapper methods could not be applied in the first place. In order to strengthen these considerdations, we provide below some additional insight into the two classes of methods and also some examples.

2.1   Filter methods

Filter methods are characteterized by the use of an evaluation function that is based on the general properties of the data to be analyzed. As anticipated, they are typically faster than wrapper methods and are thus more indicated on very large data sets. Below, we list some of the filter methods proposed in the literature, according to the nature of the evaluation function adopted.

Methods based on consistency. The main idea behind this class of methods is searching for the smallest subset of the available features that is as consistent as possible. In [Almuallim and Dietterich, 1991] propose FOCUS, a method conceived for Boolean domains. The method searches the solution space until the feature subset is such that each combination of feature values belongs to one and only one class. Starting from the selected subset, the learning task is then performed using decision trees. The main drawback of this approach, as pointed out by [Caruana and Freitag, 1994], is the explosion of the dimension of the search space when the number of original features increases. They also propose some variants of the original algorithm to speed up the search procedure. One of them, based on entropy, is skecthed below.

Given a subset of features S, the training data is divided into a number of groups, each of them having the same values for the features in S. Assuming that p_i and n_i represent the number of positive and negative examples in the $i - th$ group respectively, N is the dimension of the training set, the formula:

$$E(S) = - \sum_{i=0}^{2^{|S|}-1} \frac{p_i + n_i}{N} \left[\frac{p_i}{p_i + n_i} \log_2 \frac{p_i}{p_i + n_i} + \frac{n_i}{p_i + n_i} \log_2 \frac{n_i}{p_i + n_i} \right] \quad (1)$$

is used to avaluate all candidate features that may be added to the current subset and then select the one that shows the lowest value of $E(S)$.

A similar approach has been exploited by [Liu and Setiono, 1996] with the LVF algorithm, where they measure inconsistency through the following formula:

$$I(S) = \sum_{g=1}^{G_s} \frac{n_g - f_g}{n}, \quad (2)$$

where G_s is the number of different groups of objects defined by the features in S, n_g is the number of objects in group g, f_g is the number of objects in group g that belong to the most frequent class, and n is the total number of objects in the training set.

The LVF algorithm then proceeds with the following steps:

- the best subset B is filled with all the original features, and $I(B)$ is then computed;

- a random subset S of the features is chosen;

- if the cardinality of S is less than or equal to the cardinality of B, then $I(S)$ is computed;

- if $I(S) \leq I(B)$, then $B \leftarrow S$, and iterate.

This method can have good behavior in the presence of noisy data, and may be efficient in practice. It may although be misled by features that take on a large number of different values in the training set; in these cases such a feature would provide a high contribution to the consistency measure, but would not be particularly effective for generalization. Similar techniques have been investigated also by [Schlimmer, 1993] and [Oliveira and Vincitelli, 1992].

Methods based on Information Theory. This class of filter methods uses a measure of the information conveyed by a subset to direct the search of the final features. Good examples of such methods are the Minimum Description Length Method (MDLM) [Sheinvald et al., 1992] and the probabilistic approach by [Koller and Sahami, 1997], that we briefly describe below.

The main idea in [Koller and Sahami, 1997] is that a good subset of the features should present a class probability distribution as close as possible to the distribution obtained with the original set of features. More formally, let C be the set of classes, V the set of the features, X is a subset of V, $v = (v_1,...,v_n)$ the values taken on by the features V, and v_x the projection of v on X. Then, FS should aim at finding a subset S such that $Pr(C|X = v_x)$ is as close as possible to $Pr(C|V = v)$.

The proposed algorithm starts with all the features and applies backward elimination. At each step, it removes the feature that minimizes the distance between the original and the new class probability distribution. Such distance is measured by means of *cross-entropy* , defined as follows:

$$D(Pr(C|V_i = v_i, V_j = v_j), Pr(C|V_j = v_j)) =$$
$$\sum_{c \in C} p(c|V_i = v_i, V_j = v_j) \log_2 \frac{p(c|V_i = v_i, V_j = v_j)}{p(c|V_j = v_j)}. \quad (3)$$

Features are then removed iteretively until the desired number of features is reached. Given the nature of the formulas involved, the method must operate on binary features, and thus may require additional transformations of the data.

Methods based on Correlation. The FS process for classification problems is strongly related to the correlation among the features and to the correlation of the features with the class attribute, as in [Gennari et al., 1989]. Thus, a feature is useful if it is highly correlated with the class attribute. In this case, it will have a good chance of correctly predicting its value. Conversely, a feature will be redundant if its value can be predicted from the values of other features, that is, if it is highly correlated with other features. Such considerations lead to the claim that a good subset of features is composed of those features that are strongly correlated with the class attribute and very poorly correlated amongst themselves. One example of such methods is the Correlation-based Feature Selector method (CFS), proposed in [Hall, 2000], where features are selected on the basis of the correlation amogst nominal attributes.

Combinational Approaches to FS. In [Charikar et al., 2000] it is analyzed and discuss the following combinatorial problem: given a set S, select a subset K such that a number of properties $\Pi_i, i = 1, \ldots n$ held by S are mantained in K. According to the nature of the problem, the dimension of K is to be maximized or minimized. They consider such problem a fundamental model for FS, and state two main variants:

1. subspace selection: S does not satisfy some Π; identify the largest subset $K \in S$ such that $S_{|K}$ (S projected onto K) satisfies all Π;

2. dimension reduction: S satisfies all Π; identify the smallest subset K such that $S_{|K}$ satisfies all Π.

Such setting appears to be very interesting from the formal point of view, and is inspiring the features selection method later proposed in this chapter.

2.2   Wrappers methods

The strategy adopted by wrapper methods is based on the use of an induction algorithm that, while performing the DM task of interest, implicitly provides an evaluation of the set of features that have been submitted to the algorithm. Such a strategy may easily provide better final results when it is compared with filter methods; nevertheless, its efficacy is strongly related to the DM algorithm used. Such algorithm may be invoked a very large number of times, and the overall computational time required could be excessive. Several techniques have been considered to reduce the computational complexity of Wrappers, some of them will be referred and outlined below.

Wrappers based on decision trees. The majority of the methods in this class are based on the classic induction algorithms ID3, C4.5 and ID4.5 for decision trees, originally introduced by [Quinlan, 1993]. Amongst the most interesting contributions are [John et al., 1994, Cherkauer and Shavlik, 1996, Langley and Sage, 1994, Vafaie and De Jong, 1995, Caruana and Freitag, 1994].

[John et al., 1994] were the first to assess the validity of Wrapper methods for FS problems. They consider that features can be relevant in the *strong sense*, when the class probability distribution obtained with all features changes when the feature is removed; and in the *weak sense*, when the class probability distribution obtained with a given subset of the features changes when the feature is removed from that subset. All attributes that are not strongly or weakly relevant may be removed from the feature set without damage. The class probability distribution for a given subset is evaluated with a full-blown call to the decision tree algorithm.

[Cherkauer and Shavlik, 1996] made use of a genetic algorithm to guide the search for the best subset while using decision trees. Their SET-gen algorithm is based on the fitness function below:

$$Fitness(X) = \left(\frac{3}{4}\right) A + [1 - \left(\frac{S+F}{2}\right)] \tag{4}$$

where X is a subset of the features, A is the accuracy obtained with cross-validation after the application of C4.5, S is the average dimension of the trees produced by C4.5, and F is the cardinality of X. Formula (4) directs the search towards those feature subsets for which the computed trees are small in size but show high accuracy on the available data.

[Langley and Sage, 1994] investigated the role of *nearest neighbour* algorithms in determining non-relevant features. They showed, with large experimental evidence, that the dimension of the training data needed for good classification increases exponentially with the number of non-relevant features. The algorithm proposed by these authors proved able to remove most of redundant features and to speed up the training process of standard C4.5 when tested on simulated data.

Context-based Wrappers methods. In classification problems it is frequently the case that some of the features are relevent to discrimination only for some portion of the training data, while they may be non-relevant elsewhere. Another possible cause of poor quality on the classification results arises when some features are relevant only if they are combined with particualar values of other features, and non-relevant otherwise. All these cases are, up to a certain extent, dealt with when Wrapper methods are used in a backward elimination scheme, as the elimination of useful features may be avoided when the accuracy in the validation decreases. Some methods that attempt to exploit these considerations are the RC algorithm, introduced by [Domingos, 1997], the method proposed by [Moore and Hill, 1992] and the one by [Skalak, 1994]. In order to provide insight into this class of methods, we sketch below the main steps of the RC algorithm:

1. the algorithm is initialized by running a classification algorithm on all the features, and its accuracy is estimated via cross-validation;

2. an element of the training set is chosen, and its nearest neighbor of the same class is identified; then, all features where the two elements differ are removed;

3. a classification algorithm is run with the reduced set of features, and its accuracy estimated via cross-validation;

4. if the accuracy has not decreased with respect to the previous feature set, the element is accepted, otherwise it is restored in its pristine state and flagged not to be chosen in the next iterations;

5. if all elements are flagged, stop. Otherwise, go to step 1.

Experiments conducted on simulated data have shown no particular contribution of *context sensitive* approaches, in particual when the majority of the features are either relevant or non relevant. Moreover, when the number of features is limited, or the data is noisy, standard wrapper methods tend to perform better in identifying non-relevant features. It must also be pointed out that these approaches iterate on the number of pairs of elements in the training data, and that the number of iterations is thus bound by a quadratic function on the dimension of the training set.

Wrappers methods for Bayesian Classifiers. The important role of FS has not been overlooked by the experts in Bayesian classification. In particular, [Pazzani, 1995] introduced two alternative methods that use a Bayesian Classifier in a Wrapper scheme; the first based on a forward strategy and the second on a backward strategy. In the first case, features are added to the (initially empty) current set based on the performances of the classification algorithm. When a good feature is found, additional artificial features are also created by combining the new feature with the ones already in the current set. The second algorithm inverts this scheme, by eliminating non-relevant features and substituting pairs of old features with single artificial features obtained as the union of the two features in the pair. Experiments reported show that both techniques improve the performance of the standard Bayesian classifier.

Other Wrapper Methods. As already mentioned, one of the main drawbacks of wrapper methods is their computational cost. Several methods have been proposed with the specific objective of containing this cost.

[Moore and Lee, 1994] designed a strategy where different feature subsets race against each other, their performance being computed using leave-one-out cross validation. If, based on this validation, a subset is considered unlikely to lead to new subsets better than the best current one, then the evaluation of that subset is terminated; moreover, if two subsets are very similar to each other (in terms of the features they contain) one of them is terminated as well, and cancelled from the race. This racing scheme is embedded in forward selection; the algorithm stops when then set of racing subsets is made of only one subset.

Another interesting contribution is the one by [Kohavi and John, 1996], who introduced the notion of *compound operators*, with the aim of improving the computational efficiency of the selection strategy. First, all possible local changes (insertion or elimination of features) are consider as operators. Then, each operator is applied to the current set and the result is evaluated. The two operators that provided the best accuracy are now combined into a new operator, that is applied to the training set. The modified set of operators will then be considered in the next iteration, combining the two best current operators into a new one. The authors claim that the use of compound operators results in a much faster identification of strongly relevant features. Experimental evidence based on ID3, C4.5 and naive Bayes classifiers showed that compound operators are effective with backward selection strategies, while their effect when combined with forward selection strategies appears to be negligible.

3.   FEATURE SELECTION AS A SUBGRAPH SELECTION PROBLEM

Subgraph selection problems have been studied under different angles in the graph theoretical and mathematical programming community, and have been used in many contextes to model real life problems. Here we overview the different models of such type, the computational problems associated, and sketch the main ideas related to the application of such models to FS.

We start by introducing some general notation and few definitions. Let $G = (V, E)$ be a graph, defined by the set of vertices V and the set of edges E. Given $V' \subseteq V$, then $G' = (V', E')$ is the *subgraph induced by* V' *on* G if $E' = (v_i, v_j) : v_i \in V', v_j \in V', (v_i, v_j) \in E$. We define $d_G = 2|E|/|V|$ is the *density* of G, and also say that G is *complete* if and only if, for each pair of vertices $u, v \in V$, there exists $e \in E$ connecting them. One of the possible formulations of a subgraph selection problem is the following:

> Given a graph $G = (V, E)$ and weights $w_{ij} = w_{ji}$ on the edges $(i, j) \in E$, the lightest k-subgraph problem is solved by determining a subset $S \subseteq V$ with dimension k such that the sum of the weights associated to the edges of the subgraph induced by S on G is mimimum.

When unit weights are associated to the edges, the lightest k-subgraph problem amounts to the selection of the subgraph of dimension k with the minimum number of edges, namely, the sparsest k-subgraph problem. By switching the sense of the objective functions of the two problems above, it is then easy to obtain the heaviest k-subgraph and densest k-subgraph problems. Equivalently, heaviest k-subgraph and densest k-subgraph can be obtained from the lightest k-subgraph and the sparsest k-subgraph, respectively, with a trivial transformation of the objective function coefficients.

We model a generic FS problem by starting from one of the lightest k-subgraphs on the complete graph $G = (V, E)$ where the set V is indexed by the original features, and the weight of edge (v_i, v_j) is proportional to the degree of association (correlation, concordance, distance) between features i and j. Some additional conditions need to be added to this model to make it interesting for the purpose of FS, as it will be described in Section 4. First, we consider the main computational complexity issues related to this class of problems.

Feige and Seltser ([Feige and Seltser, 1997, Feige et al., 2001]) propose a reduction of the densest k-subgraph to the *Clique* problem, that in turn has been shown to belong to the NP-complete class in [Garey and Johnson, 1979]. Moreover, the same authors show with additional arguments that the densest k-subgraph problem is in the NP-complete class even for bipartite graphs with the node degree bounded by 3. For these reasons, they have also analyzed efficient approximation schemes for the densent k-subgraph problem, and, under the condition that G contains a clique on k nodes, provide an approximation algorithm that, for each $0 < \varepsilon < 1$ determines a subgraph on k verteces with at least $(1 - \varepsilon)\binom{k}{2}$ edges with computational complexity equal to $n^{O((1+\log \frac{n}{k})/\varepsilon)}$.

The authors of [Charikar et al., 2000], in the framework of combinatorial feature selection, are interested in the solution of a *max distinct points* problem that reduces to he problem of the densest k-subgraph. They also provide evidence that an α-approximated algorithm for the *max distinct points* problem results in a 2α-approximated algorithm for the densest k-subgraph problem, and that an α-approximated algorithm for the *min-l distinct dimension* problem gives an $\alpha(\alpha + 1)$-approximated algorithm for the *densest subgraph* problem. On the other hand, the greedy algorithm with backward selection has been shown to provide an approximation ratio of $O(k/n)$ for any k by [Asahiro et al., 1996]. [ye and Zhang, 1999] studied the case of the heaviest k-subgraph problem where $k = n/2$ and produces an algorithm with worst case approximation equal to 0.519 when n is large.

The same case has been considered by [Goemans, 1996] with a randomized technique that produces an approximation ratio of 0.25. In general, all approximated ratios obtained for this class of problems are constant in k and linear in n.

4.   BASIC IP FORMULATION AND VARIANTS

We start by describing the plain Integer Programming formulation for the ligthest k-subgraph problem. Let $N = \{1, ..., n\}$ be the set of nodes, and k the cardinality of the set to be selected. We define the binary variable x_i, $i \in N$

such that

$$
x_i = \begin{cases} 1, & \text{if node } i \text{ is chosen} \\ 0, & \text{otherwise.} \end{cases}
$$

Then, let y_{ij} be a binary variable associated to the edge connecting nodes i and j, with the following meaning:

$$
y_{ij} = \begin{cases} 1, & \text{if } (i,j) \text{ is in the subgraph induced by the selected nodes} \\ 0, & \text{otherwise.} \end{cases}
$$

Finally, each edge (i,j) is associated with a cost c_{ij}.

The constraints needed to represent the problem are then:

$$
\sum_{i=1}^{n} x_i = k, \tag{5}
$$

where it is required thast exaclty k nodes are chosen, and:

$$
y_{ij} \geq x_i + x_j - 1, \qquad \forall i, j \in N \tag{6}
$$

that link coherently the value of the y-variables to to the values of the x-variables. Then, by also considering the objective function (linear in y_{ij}) and the binary constraints, the complete formulation is as follows:

$$
\min \sum_{i=1}^{n} \sum_{j=1}^{n} c_{ij} y_{ij}
$$

$$
\text{s.t.}
$$

$$
\sum_{i=1}^{n} x_i \quad = \quad k, k \in Z^+
$$

$$
y_{ij} \quad \geq \quad x_i + x_j - 1, \qquad \forall i, j \in N
$$

$$
x_i \in (0,1), \quad i \in N
$$

$$
y_{ij} \in (0,1), \quad i, j \in N
$$

As already anticipated, the model above can be used for FS by associating each node with one of the original features and each edge with a similarity measure between the two features connected by that edge. The standard lightest k-subgraph would then represent the subset of k features with the mimumum total cross-correlation. Such characteristic is indeed desirable, as discussed in Section 2. Nevertheless, it is not sufficient to guarantee a good quality of the selected subset for the DM task. Two main aspects are not treated in a satisfactory way, and precisely: the number of node to be selected, and the modeling of the linkage among the features and the class value. Below we discuss some variants to address such issues.

Feature Selection Model 1. Some additional constraints must be activated to take into account the quality of each feature with respect to its ability to *explain* the class variable. If we assume h to be an additional feature representing the class variable, y_{ih} to represent the similarity measure of feature i with the class variable, and λ a properly calibrated threshold, then constraint (7) below

$$\sum_{i=1}^{n} c_{ih} y_{ih} \geq \lambda, \tag{7}$$

enforces the selection of a subset of features that are likely to perform better in the DM application. Another appropriate modification is to relax the constraint on the number of features to be selected. We do so by the introduction of the additional constraint:

$$\sum_{i=1}^{n} x_i \geq k, \tag{8}$$

The standard lighest k-subgraph model with the modifications proposed here will be referred to as FSM1.

Feature Selection Model 2. The introduction of the additional constraints of FSM1 may lead to the undesirable case of solutions with too large feature subsets. It is thus appropriate to also provide an upper bound on the dimension of the set. Such modification may contribute to the stabilization of the solutions for particular combinations of the parameters k and λ. The new model is as follows:

$$\min \sum_{i=1}^{n} \sum_{j=i+1}^{n} c_{ij} y_{ij}$$

$$\begin{aligned}
\text{s.t.} \\
\sum_{i=1}^{n} x_i &\geq & k_1, k_1 \in Z^+ \\
\sum_{i=1}^{n} x_i &\leq & k_2, k_2 \in Z^+, k_1 \leq k_2 \\
\sum_{i=1}^{n} c_{ih} y_{ih} &\geq & \lambda \\
y_{ij} &\geq & x_i + x_j - 1, & \forall i, j \in N, i < j \\
x_i &\in & (0, 1), & i \in N \\
y_{ij} &\in & (0, 1), & i, j \in N
\end{aligned} \tag{9}$$

This is model FSM2.

Feature Selection Model 3. Both FSM1 and FSM2 may be misled in the identification of a good feature subset. For example, consider a subset for which $\sum_{i=1}^{n} c_{ih}y_{ih} \geq \lambda$, with a certain value of the objective function, say z^*. Such subset will be preferred to subsets with objective function $z' = z^* + \epsilon$ but a much larger value of $\sum_{i=1}^{n} c_{ih}y_{ih}$. In other words, subsets with better explanatory power may be discarded for neglibigle gain in the cross-similarity amongst the features. The modification below has been designed with the intention of overcoming this problem, bringing the measure of the explanatory power of the subset directly in the new objective function:

$$\min \sum_{i=1}^{n} \sum_{j=1}^{n} c_{ij}y_{ij} - \gamma \sum_{i=1}^{n} c_{ih}y_{ih},$$

where γ is the weight to be given to the new component with respect to the total cross-similarity. As the magnitude of the two terms is measured on the same scale, the tuning of γ must take into account that the number of terms in the positive component of the objective function increases quadratically with the number of the selected features, while the negative component increases only linearly. With the modified objective function the constraints added in model FSM1 and FSM2 must obviously be dropped. The model, reproduced below, will be referred to as FSM3.

$$\min \sum_{i=1}^{n} \sum_{j=1}^{n} c_{ij}y_{ij} - \gamma \sum_{i=1}^{n} c_{ih}y_{ih}$$

$$\text{s.t.}$$

$$\sum_{i=1}^{n} x_i \geq k_1, k_1 \in Z^+$$

$$\sum_{i=1}^{n} x_i \leq k_2, k_2 \in Z^+, k_1 \leq k_2 \qquad (10)$$

$$y_{ij} \geq x_i + x_j - 1, \qquad \forall i,j \in N$$

$$x_i \in (0,1), \quad i \in N$$

$$y_{ij} \in (0,1), \quad i,j \in N$$

The application and the discussion of the computational experience with the above models will be the topic of the next section.

5.   COMPUTATIONAL EXPERIENCE

In this section we consider some experiments conducted with FS approach described in the previous section. First, we run a set of experiments by using randomly generated data, in order to test specifically the behavior of the

Table 1. Functions used to compute the target variable.

Type	Function	Name
Logic	$(X_1 \wedge X_2) \vee (X_3 \wedge \neg X_5) \vee (X_9 \wedge X_{11})$	A
Logic	$(X_1 \wedge X_3) \vee (X_4 \wedge \neg X_5 \wedge X_8) \vee$ $\vee (X_{10} \wedge X_{13} \wedge \neg X_{15}) \vee (X_{16} \wedge X_{18} \wedge \neg X_{20})$	B
Math.	$10X_1 + 35X_7 - 18X_3$	C
Math.	$5 + 10X_1 + 35X_7 - 18X_3 + \text{rand}(100)/100 * 50$	D
Math.	$5 + X_1 * X_2$	E
Math.	$5 + X_3/X_4$, if $X_4 \neq 0$ $5 + X_3/100$, if $X_4 = 0$	F

method in particularly interesting situations. Second, we have applied the proposed FS method to a database derived from a large survey on urban mobility conducted in Italy in 2002.

5.1   Test on Generated Data

The experiments consider data sets composed by a set of randomly generated features. Different target function have been obtained with particular logic or mathematical functions on the generated features. The training data was generated using independent uniform distributions for each of the features considered. The target functions were constructed ad hoc, and are described in Table 1 above. In the following they will be referred to also as *classification functions*. The mathematical classification functions were constructed with the specific objective of representing different possible situations, some of which particularly simple (fucntion C) and some other with different degrees of complexity (D, E, F). Logic functions (A,B) were intended to represent propositional formulas thay would be difficult to learn in a real application.

We thus consider our method to be successful if it is able to select, with some degree of approximation due to the incompleteness of the knowledge contained in the training sample, the subset of features that effectively are the argument of the function that computes the target variable.

As far as feature dissimilarity is concerned, we adopt standard correlation for the cases where the features are quantitative, and standard concordance index for logic data. The tables that follow report some of the results obtained. Extensive computations have been conducted to assess the performances of the proposed three different models (i.e., FSM1, FSM2, and FSM3). These experiments provided solid evidence that FSM3 outperforms the other two, is not computationally more demanding and does not require excessive tuning for the objective function parameters. We omit such results here for brevity and confine to model FSM3. All experiments were run using the IP solver CPLEX version 7.2 on a 2.0 GHz Pentium-4 processor with 512 Mb RAM running Debian Linux 3.0.

The first column of each table contains the name of the experiments, which is defined by 4 parameters (as in Table 2): the type of objective function, the number of elements in the training set, the number of original features, and finally a letter associated to the particular seed used to start up the random generator for that experiment. In the second column, named "model", other configuration parameters are defined: the mathematical model adopted (3 for FSM3), the upper and lower bound on the number of features to be selected, and the weight assigned to the second term of the objective function. Then, the dimensions of the associated IP are reported: number of rows (R), number of columns (C), and the number of non-zero elements (NZ). Some parameters related to the solution process follow, namely, solution time in seconds (S), number of nodes in the branch-and-bound tree (N) and optimality gap (Gap), which is equal to 0% when the optimal solution is found. Finally, we use a synthetic index to assess, *ex post* the quality of a subset, based on the proportion of the selected features that are also argument of the classification function:

$$Q(S) = \frac{n(S, C)}{min(n(S), n(C))} * 100, \qquad (11)$$

where $n(S, C)$ is the number of features selected that are also in the classification fucntion; $n(S)$ is the number of features selected, and $n(C)$ the number of features in the classification function. Such quality measure is reported in the last column of the tables.

According to this scheme, in Table 2 the behavior of the solution is considered when the dimension of the trainings sample and the weight γ vary for classification function A. Table 3 considers the same type of experiment for different initial random seeds. Table 4 considers problems with larger training data and feature sets.

Table 2. Results for increasing values of γ for classification function A.

EXP	Model	IP Dimensions			Solution			Quality
		R	C	NZ	S	N	Gap	
A.200.30.a	3.7.7.1	356	385	1095	0.17	51	0.00%	57.14%
A.400.30.a	3.7.7.1	342	371	1053	0.13	24	0.00%	85.71
A.600.30a	3.7.7.1	332	361	1023	0.01	0	0.00%	85.71%
A.600.30.a	3.7.7.1,50	332	361	1023	0.00	0	0.00%	100%
A.600.30.a	3.7.7.2	332	361	1023	0.00	0	0.00%	100%
A.800.30.a	3.7.7.1	330	359	1017	0.12	2	0.00%	100%

Table 5 reports some of the results obtained for the other classification functions described in Table 1.

Another set of tests have been conducted to verify the effectivess of this approach to exclude correlated features. We have thus introduced some constraints in the data generation procedure, imposing:

- for classification function A: $X_2 = X_3$;

- for classification function C: $X_3 = X_7$.

Table 3. Results for different random seeds for classification function A.

EXP	Model	IP Dimensions			Solution			Quality
		R	C	NZ	S	N	Gap	
A.500.30.a	3.7.7.2	358	387	1101	0.00	0	0.00%	85.71%
A.500.30.b	3.7.7.2	356	385	1095	0.13	9	0.00%	100%
A.500.30.c	3.7.7.2	372	401	1143	0.08	2	0.00%	100%
A.500.30.d	3.7.7.2	373	402	1146	0.02	0	0.00%	100%
A.500.30.e	3.7.7.2	357	386	1098	0.16	18	0.00%	100%

Table 4. Results for larger instances for classification function A.

EXP	Model	IP Dimensions			Solution			Quality
		R	C	NZ	S	N	Gap	
A.1000.50.a	3.7.7.1	890	939	2717	0.42	8	0.00%	85.71%
A.1000.50.a	3.7.7.2	890	939	2717	0.41	8	0.00%	85.71%
A.2000.50.a	3.7.7.1	772	821	2363	0.38	3	0.00%	85.71%
A.2000.50.b	3.7.7.1	759	808	2324	0.22	5	0.00%	85.71%
A.2000.50.c	3.7.7.1	758	807	2321	0.00	0	0.00%	85.71%
A.2000.50.a	3.7.7.2	772	821	2363	0.02	0	0.00%	100%
A.2000.50.b	3.7.7.2	759	808	2324	0.11	3	0.00%	100%
A.2000.50.c	3.7.7.2	758	807	2321	0.01	0	0.00%	100%

Table 5. Results for classification functions B, C and D.

EXP	Model	IP Dimensions			Solution			Quality
		R	C	NZ	S	N	Gap	
B.1000.30.a	3.11.11.2	321	350	990	0.23	10	0.00%	90.90%
B.1000.30.b	3.11.11.2	312	341	963	0.18	2	0.00%	90.90%
B.1000.30.a	3.11.11.3	321	350	990	0.01	0	0.00%	100%
B.1000.30.b	3.11.11.3	312	341	963	0.01	0	0.00%	90.90%
B.1000.30.c	3.11.11.3	329	358	1014	0.02	0	0.00%	90.90%
B.1000.30.d	3.11.11.3	328	357	1011	0.08	2	0.00%	90.90%
B.1000.30.e	3.11.11.3	314	343	969	0.02	0	0.00%	100%
C.600.30.a	1.3.1,50	436	465	1335	0.01	0	0.00%	100%
C.2000.50.a	3.3.3.1	743	792	2276	0.01	0	0.00%	100%
C.2000.50.b	3.3.3.1	814	863	2489	0.02	0	0.00%	100%
C.2000.50.c	3.3.3.1	803	852	2456	0.00	0	0.00%	100%
C.2000.50.d	3.3.3.1	801	850	2450	0.00	0	0.00%	100%
D.2000.50.a	3.3.3.1	743	792	2276	0.00	0	0.00%	100%
D.2000.50.b	3.3.3.1	809	858	2474	0.01	0	0.00%	100%
D.2000.50.c	3.3.3.1	813	862	2486	0.01	0	0.00%	100%
D.2000.50.d	3.3.3.1	789	838	2414	0.02	0	0.00%	100%
D.2000.50.e	3.3.3.1	814	863	2489	0.01	0	0.00%	100%

Next we verify if the solutions provided, beside expressing good overall quality, do not select the two identical variables in the same subset. This is exactly what happened in the experiments reported in Table 6.

Table 6. Performances with duplicated features on classification function A.

EXP	Model	IP Dimensions			Solution			Quality
		R	C	NZ	S	N	Gap	
A.500.30.a	3.7.7.2	425	455	1303	0.11	2	0.00%	83.33%
A.2000.50.a	3.7.7.1	1050	1100	3198	0.03	0	0.00%	83.33%
A.2000.50.b	3.7.7.1	1079	1129	3285	0.92	13	0.00%	100%
A.2000.50.c	3.7.7.1	1070	1120	3258	0.03	0	0.00%	83.33%
A.2000.50.d	3.7.7.1	1074	1124	3270	0.05	0	0.00%	83.33%
A.2000.50.e	3.7.7.1	1093	1143	3327	0.01	0	0.00%	100%
A.2000.50.a	3.7.7.2	1050	1100	3198	0.00	0	0.00%	100%
A.2000.50.b	3.7.7.2	1079	1129	3285	0.02	0	0.00%	100%
A.2000.50.c	3.7.7.2	1070	1120	3258	0.02	0	0.00%	100%
A.2000.50.d	3.7.7.2	1074	1124	3270	0.02	0	0.00%	100%
A.2000.50.e	3.7.7.2	1093	1143	3327	0.01	0	0.00%	100%
C.2000.50.a	3.3.3.1	1226	1275	3725	0.02	0	0.00%	100%
A.5000.50.a	3.7.7.1	1226	1275	3725	0.06	0	0.00%	100%
A.5000.50.b	3.7.7.1	1059	1109	3225	0.09	0	0.00%	83.33%
A.5000.50.c	3.7.7.1	1050	1100	3198	0.03	0	0.00%	83.33%
A.5000.50.d	3.7.7.1	1087	1137	3309	0.01	0	0.00%	100%
A.5000.50.e	3.7.7.1	1051	1101	3201	0.07	0	0.00%	100%
A.5000.50.f	3.7.7.1	1065	1115	3243	0.06	0	0.00%	100%

Another relevant aspect that needs investigation is the behavior of the solution algorithm. As previously stated, in the worst possible case the problem may not be easy to solve according to its combinatorial structure; however, the efforts for solving practical cases with reasonable dimensions must be evaluated.

In Table 7 are synthetized some of the results for FSM3 for classification function A when then number of features is increased. Similar results can be found in Table 8 for classification functions D, E, and F.

Table 7. Times for different size instances and parameters for function A.

EXP	Model	IP Dim.		Solution		Quality
		R	C	S	Gap	
A.5000.50.a	3.5.15.1	1226	1275	0.02	0.00%	85.71%
A.5000.100.a	3.5.15.1	4951	5050	0.71	0.0%	85.71%
A.5000.200.a	3.5.15.1	19901	20100	14.87	0.00%	85.71%
A.5000.500.a	3.5.15.1	124751	125250	267.18	0.00%	71.43%
A.5000.1000.a	3.5.15.1	499501	500500	2103.83	0.00%	85.71%
A.5000.1000.a	3.45.55.1	363221	364221	739.64*	121.46%	85.71%
A.5000.1000.a	3.90.110.1	363221	364221	1978.34*	107.72%	85.71%

Table 8. Times for instances and parameters for functions D, E, F.

EXP	Model	IP Dimensions			Solution			Quality
		R	C	NZ	S	N	Gap	
D.2000.50.a	3.3.10.1	743	792	2276	0.02	0	0.00%	100%
D.2000.50.b	3.3.10.1	809	858	2474	0.02	0	0.00%	100%
D.2000.50.c	3.3.10.1	813	862	2486	0.02	0	0.00%	100%
D.2000.50.d	3.3.10.1	789	838	2414	0.03	0	0.00%	100%
D.2000.50.e	3.3.10.1	814	863	2489	0.00	0	0.00%	100%
E.2000.50.a	3.2.10.1	1051	1100	3249	0.07	1	0.00%	100%
E.2000.50.b	3.2.10.1	1051	1100	3249	0.06	2	0.00%	100%
E.2000.50.c	3.2.10.1	1064	1113	3288	0.08	3	0.00%	100%
E.2000.50.d	3.2.10.1	1042	1091	3222	0.07	2	0.00%	100%
E.2000.50.e	3.2.10.1	1066	1115	3294	0.05	0	0.00%	100%
F.2000.50.a	3.2.10.1	1051	1100	3249	0.31	4	0.00%	100%
F.2000.50.b	3.2.10.1	1056	1105	3264	0.06	1	0.00%	100%
F.2000.50.c	3.2.10.1	1034	1083	3198	0.37	6	0.00%	100%
F.2000.50.d	3.2.10.1	1030	1079	3186	0.31	7	0.00%	100%
F.2000.50.e	3.2.10.1	1059	1108	3273	0.34	4	0.00%	100%

The experiments described allow to draw some conclusions, that, although may not be extended with complete confidence to other settings, appear to be quite general.

- The solution time are contained; in very few cases they exceeded 90 seconds. Such behavior is to be accounted both to the power of the latest commercial solvers and to the effect of the constraints added to the standard lightest k-subgraph;

- The results are stable with respect to different samples;

- The subsets obtained are, in most cases, correct; in more than 60% of the experiments conducted the quality index is equal to 100%, while only in one case is below 85%;

- The quality of the subsets is affected by the dimension of the training data. When this set is small compared to the number of features, the information available may not be sufficient to identify the currect subset. Such behavior may be also affected by the sampling procedure;

- The quality of the subsets is affected by the value of the objective function parameter γ; higher values of this parameter push the model to find solutions that are more correlated with the target variable.

5.2   An Application

We have considered the database of the $14,003$ questionnaires of the quarterly survey on Italian urban mobility conducted by ISFORT in year 2002

[Alleva et al., 2002] and kindly made available by the Department of Geo-
economical, Linguistic, Historical Studies for Regional Analysis of the University of Rome "La Sapienza". The variables that describe each questionnaire
(a record of the database) are both of qualitative and quantitative nature, and
are 59 in total. The objective of this application is to identify explanatory
models that use Boolean logic data to express the relation that links the type
of urban mobility with the other variables. In particular, the FS method has
been applied as a pre-processor for the Logic Data Miner *Lsquare*, described
in [Felici and Truemper, 2002], and also in Chapter 5 of this book. For this
purpose, the original data set has been transformed by stardard binarization
techniques to obey the input format for such method. We have then adopted
model FSM3 as defined in the previous sections.

The similarity measure between features (or variables) is then measured by
concordance; from the complete set of binary variables available, we remove
those that have a value of concordance with the target variables not significantly
different from zero. We thus derive a graph with 76 nodes, and apply the
described optimization model with different parameters. The most interesting
results are summarized in Tables 9 and 10, for different values of the bounds
imposed on the dimension of the feature subset.

Table 9. Logic variables selected by FSM3-B with $k_1=5$, $k_2=20$ and $\gamma=2.00$.

Obj.Function: -1.9740	Time: 22.24 sec.	
Node	Description	Similarity with target
1	sex(female)	0.237
5	age(36-50)	0.242
10	number_of_vehicles(0-1)	0.250
22	marital_status(not married)	0.210
60	activity(others)	0.603

Table 10. Logic variables selected by FSM3-B with $k_1=10$, $k_2=20$ and $\gamma=2.00$.

F.O: 1.1620	Time: 168.83 sec.	
Node	Description	Similarity with target
1	sex(female)	0.237
5	age(36-50)	0.242
7	family_dimension(3-4)	0.150
10	number_of_vehicles(0-1)	0.250
22	marital_status(not married)	0.210
25	education(diploma)	0.234
28	professional_status(employed)	0.603
51	position_in_profession(others)	0.603
61	family_income(0-5)	0.155

The selected features have been used to project the training data on a smaller
dimension logic space, and we have then applied *Lsquare*. The system was able

to determine separation formulas for the target variable *type of daily mobility* = {*regular, irregular*} from subsets of 500 records sampled from the available data, obtaining, on average, a percentage of correct recognition on the remaining data of approximately 75%. These results were compared with those obtained with Discriminant Analysis and Classification Trees. They show several points of interest, as reported in [Felici and Arezzo, 2003]: while their precision level is comparable, if not better, to the one of the other two methods, the formulas obtained are more compact with respect to the decision trees, are obtained with smaller training sets, and use, on average, smaller subsets of the original features.

6.   CONCLUSIONS

In this chapter we have considered the main issues related to feature selection for data mining problems. Such issues arise when the data to be analyzed presents a large number of features, and one is to select a small subsetof them in order to efficiently perform the mining process. We have considered different methods based on search procedures, that are divided into two main categories: the filter methods and the wrapper methods. We have then modeled the problem as an optimization problem, defining an objective function and constraints that, altoghter, express an integer programming problem. Such problem is straight-forwardly related to a well studied NP-complete problem, the lightest k-subgraph problem, known to be a computationally challenging problem. We have then presented the results of some experiments run to test the proposed model and discussed the results obtained, both in term of computational efficiency and solution quality. The results show that the method is effective and stable, and can provide a flexible tool to determine good subsets of features for data mining applications.

REFERENCES

[Alleva et al., 2002] G. Alleva, F. D. Falorsi, S. Falorsi. Modelli interpretativi e previsivi della domanda di trasporto locale. *Rapporto finale di ricerca - 28 febbraio 2002 ISFORT.*

[Almuallim and Dietterich, 1991] H. Almuallim and T. G. Dietterich. Learning with many irrelevant features. In *Proceedings of the 9th National Conference on Artificial Intelligence.* MIT Press, Cambridge, Mass., 1991.

[Asahiro et al., 1996] Y. Asahiro, K. Iwama, H. Tamaki, T. Tokuyama. Greedily finding a dense subgraph. *Proceedings of the 5th Scandinavian Workshop on Algorithm Theory (SWAT).* Lecture Notes in Computer Science, 1097, p. 136-148, Springer-Verlag,Reykjavik, Iceland, 1996.

[Charikar et al., 2000] M. Charikar, V. Guruswami, R. Kumar, S. Rajagopalan and A. Sahai. Combinatorial Feature Selection Problems. In *Proceedings of FOCS 2000.*

[Caruana and Freitag, 1994] R. Caruana and D. Freitag. Greedy attribute selection. In *Machine Learning: Proceedings of the 11th International Conference.* Morgan Kaufmann, New Brunswick, New Jersey, 1994.

[Cherkauer and Shavlik, 1996] K.J.Cherkauer and J.W.Shavlik. Growing simpler decision trees to facilitate knowledge discovery. In *Proceedings of the Second International Conference on Knowledge Discovery and Data Mining.* AAAI Press, Portland, Oregon, 1996.

[Dash and Liu, 1997] M. Dash and H. Liu. Feature Selection for Classification. *Intelligent Data Analysis,* I(3), 1997.

[Domingos, 1997] P.Domingos. Context-sensitive feature selection for lazy learners. *Artificial Intelligence Review,* (11):227-253, 1997.

[Feige and Seltser, 1997] U. Feige and M. Seltser. On the densest k-subgraph problem. Technical Report CS97-16, *Weizmann Institute of Science.*

[Feige et al., 2001] U. Feige, G. Kortsarz, and D. Peleg. The Dense k-Subgraph Problem. *Algoritmica,* 2001.

[Felici and Arezzo, 2003] G. Felici and M. F. Arezzo. Tecniche avanzate di Data Mining applicate all'analisi della mobilità individuale, *www.ing.unipi.it/input2003.*

[Felici and Truemper, 2002] G. Felici and K. Truemper. A Minsat Approach for Learning in Logic Domains, *INFORMS Journal of Computing,* Vol. 14, No. 1, 20-36, 2002.

[Garey and Johnson, 1979] M. R. Garey and D. S. Johnson. *Computers and Intractability.* Freeman, 1979.

[Gennari et al., 1989] J. H. Gennari, P. Langley, and D. Fisher. Models of incremental concept formation. *Artificial Intelligence* 40, :11-61, 1989.

[Goemans, 1996] M. X. Goemans. *Mathematical programming and approximation algorithms*, Lezione su Approximate Solution of Hard Combinatorial Problems, Summer School, Udine 1996.

[Goemans and Williamson, 1995] M. X. Goemans and D. P. Williamson. *Improved approximation algorithms for Maximum Cut and Satisfiability Problems Using Semidefinite Programming*. Journal of ACM, VOl 42, p. 1115-1145, 1995.

[Hall, 2000] M. A. Hall. Correlation-based Feature Selection for Machine Learning. In *Proceedings of the 17th International Conference on Machine Learning*, Stanford University, C.A. Morgan Kaufmann Publishers, 2000.

[John et al., 1994] G. H. John, R. Kohavi, and P. Pfleger. Irrelevant features and the subset selection problem. In *Machine Learning: Proceedings of the 11th International Conference*. Morgan Kaufmann, 1994.

[Kohavi and John, 1996] R. Kohavi and G. John. Wrappers for feature subset selection. *Artificial Intelligence, special issue on relevance*, 97(1-2):273-324, 1996.

[Koller and Sahami, 1997] D. Koller and M. Sahami. Hierachically classifying documents using very few words. In *Machine learning: Proceedings of the 14th International Conference*, 1997.

[Langley, 1994] P. Langley. Selection of relevant features in machine learning. In *Proceedings of the AAAI Fall Symposium on Relevance*. AAAI Press, 1994.

[Langley and Sage, 1994] P. Langley and S. Sage. Scaling to domains with irrelevant features. In R. Greiner, editor, *Computational Learning Theory an Natural Learning Systems*, volume 4. MIT Press, 1994.

[Liu and Motoda, 2000] H. Liu and H. Motoda. *Feature Selection for knowledge discovery and data mining*. Kluwer Academic Publishers, 2000.

[Liu and Setiono, 1996] H. Liu and R. Setiono. A probabilistic approach to feature selection: A filter solution. In *Machine learning: Proceedings of the 13th International Conference on Machine Learning*. Morgan Kaufmann, 1996.

[Sheinvald et al., 1992] J. Sheinvald, B. Dom and W. Niblack. Unsupervised image segmentation using the minimum description length principle. In *Proceedings of the 10th International Conference on Pattern Recognition*, 1992.

[Oliveira and Vincitelli, 1992] A. L. Oliveira and A. S. Vincetelli. Constructive induction using a non-greedy strategy for feature selection. In *Proceedings of the 9th International Conference on Machine Learning*, 355-360, Morgan Kaufmann, Aberdeen, Scotland, 1992.

[Moore and Lee, 1994] A. W. Moore and M. S. Lee. Efficient algorithms for minimizing cross validation error. In *Machine learning: Proceedings of the 11th International Conference*. Morgan Kaufmann, 1994.

[Moore and Hill, 1992] A. W. Moore, D. J. Hill and M. P. Johnson. *Computational Learning Theory and Natural Learning Systems*, Volume 3. MIT Press, 1992.

[Pazzani, 1995] M. Pazzani. Searching for dependencies in Bayesian classifiers. In *Proceedings of the 5th International Workshop on AI and Statistics*, 1995.

[Quinlan, 1993] J. R. Quinlan. *C4.5: Programs for Machine Learning*. Morgan Kaufmann, San Mateo, CA, 1993.

[Schlimmer, 1993] J. C. Schlimmer. Efficiently inducing determinations: A complete and systematic search algorithm that uses optimal pruning. In *Proceedings of the 10th International Conference on Machine Learning*, pp. 284-290, Amherst, MA: Morgan Kaufmann (1993).

[Skalak, 1994] D. B. Skalak. Prototype and feature selection by sampling and random mutation hill climbing algorithms. In *Machine Learning: Proceedings of the 11th International Conference*. Morgan Kaufmann, 1994.

[Vafaie and De Jong, 1995] H. Vafaie and K. De Jong. Genetic algorithms as a tool for restructuring feature space representations. In *Proceedings of the International Conference on Tools with A.I.* IEEE Computer Society Press, 1995.

[ye and Zhang, 1999] Y. Ye and J. Zhang. Approximation of Dense-$\frac{n}{2}$-Subgraph and the Complement of Min-Bisection, Working Paper, Department of Management Sciences, The University of Iowa (1999).

AUTHORS' BIOGRAPHICAL STATEMENTS

Vanda de Angelis is an Associate Professor at the faculty of Statistics of the Univerity "La Sapienza" In Rome since 1985, where she teaches courses on Operations Research. She is an active member ot the European Working Group in OR applied to Health Services, and has been involved in several international projects. Her main research interests relate with the application of optimization techniques to a wide range of problems, amongst which are health services planning and transportation problems.

Giovanni Felici graduated in Statistics at the University of Rome "La Sapienza". He received his M.Sc. in Operations Research and Operations Management at the University of Lancaster, UK, in 1990, and his Ph.D. in Operations Research at the University of Rome "La Sapienza" in 1995. He is presently a permanent researcher in IASI, the Istituto di Analisi dei Sistemi ed Informatica of the Italian National Research Council (CNR), where he started his research activity in 1994 working on research projects in logic programming and mathematical optimization. His current research activity is mainly devoted to the application of optimization techniques to data mining problems, with particular focus on integer programming algorithms for learning in logic and expert systems.

Gabriella Mancinelli received her degree in Statistics from the University of Rome "La Sapienza" in 2003. She is currently consultant at Unicab, a data analysis company based in Rome.

Chapter 7 [1]

TRANSFORMATION OF RATIONAL DATA AND SET DATA TO LOGIC DATA

Stephen Bartnikowski*, Matthias Granberry*, Jonathan Mugan*,
and Klaus Truemper*

* *Department of Computer Science*

University of Texas at Dallas
Richardson, TX 75083-0688, U.S.A.
Email: truemper@utdallas.edu

Abstract: Frequently one wants to extend the use of a classification method that in principle requires records with *True/False* values, such as decision trees and logic formula constructors, so that records can be processed that contain rational number and/or nominal values. A nominal value is an element or subset of a given finite set. In such cases, the rational numbers or nominal values must first be transformed to *True/False* values before the method may be applied. This chapter describes methods for the transformation. For nominal entries, the transformation depends on the size of the given finite set and on whether elements or subsets of that set occur. In particular, the scheme for subsets first transforms the entries to rational data. The transformation of rational numbers to *True/False* values uses a technique called Cutpoint that determines abrupt changes of classification cases. The methods of this chapter are rather new and have been found to be effective and reliable in preliminary tests.

Keywords: Data Transformation, Rational/Set/Logic Data, Cut Detection, Learning Logic Formulas, Data Classification.

---

[1] Triantaphillou, E. and G. Felici (Eds.), **Data Mining and Knowledge Discovery Approaches based on Rule Induction Techniques**, Massive Computing Series, Springer, Heidelberg, Germany, pp. 253-278, 2006.

1.   INTRODUCTION

One often desires to apply classification methods that in principle require records with *True/False* values, such as decision trees and logic formula constructors, to records that besides *True/False* values contain rational numbers and/or *nominal* values. An entry of the latter kind is an element or subset of some finite set. To differentiate among the cases, we call *True/False* entries *logic data*, rational number entries *rational data*, and nominal entries *set data*.

In such situations, all rational and set data must first be converted to logic data. This chapter covers several methods for that transformation. The methods are such that the transformed data allow complete classification when logic formulas are constructed. Though the discussion of the transformation methods exclusively assumes that context, the reader should have little difficulty to adapt the methods to other classification schemes such as decision trees.

We focus here on the case where the records of two training classes A and B have been randomly selected from two populations $\mathcal{A}$ and $\mathcal{B}$, respectively. The logic formulas are to be derived from the records of A and B and later are to be applied to records of $\mathcal{A} - A$ and $\mathcal{B} - B$.

For the purpose of a simplified discussion in this section, we assume for the moment that the records have no missing entries. That restriction is removed in the next section. Thus, all transformation methods of this chapter handle records with missing entries.

1.1   Transformation of Set Data

For nominal data, the transformation depends on the size of the underlying finite set and on whether the entries are elements or subsets of that set. When the given set is small and element entries are to be transformed, then the approach is simple and well known. One associates with each element a logic variable and encodes presence of an element by *True/False* values in the obvious way. When the given set is large or when subset entries must be transformed, different schemes are used. In the particular case of subsets, the entries are first converted to rational numbers, which are then transformed to *True/False* values using the scheme sketched next.

1.2   Transformation of Rational Data

For rational data, the conversion to logic data may be accomplished by the following, well-known approach. One defines for a given attribute $k \geq 1$ breakpoints and encodes each rational number of the attribute by k *True/False* values where the jth value is *True* if the rational number is greater than the jth breakpoint, and is *False* otherwise. The selection of the k breakpoints requires care if the logic formulas are to classify the records of $\mathcal{A} - A$ and $\mathcal{B} - B$ with good accuracy.

A number of techniques for the selection of the breakpoints have been proposed. Subsections 1.4–1.6 give a review. Suffice it to say here that the most effective methods to-date are based on the notion of entropy. In these methods, the breakpoints are so selected that the rational numbers of a given attribute can be most compactly classified by a decision tree as coming from A or B. Here, we describe a method called *Cutpoint* that is based on a different goal. Recall that the records of the sets A and B are presumed to be random samples of the populations $\mathcal{A}$ and $\mathcal{B}$. Taking a different viewpoint, we may view each record of $\mathcal{A} - A$ and $\mathcal{B} - B$ to be a random variation of some record of A or B, respectively. The goal of the selected breakpoints is then that these random variations largely leave the *True/False* values induced by the selected breakpoints unchanged.

Cutpoint aims for the stated goal by selecting breakpoints called *markers* that correspond to certain abrupt changes in classification patterns, as follows. First, for a given attribute, the rational numbers are sorted. Second, each value is labeled as A or B depending on whether the value comes from a record of A or B, respectively. For the sake of a simplified discussion, we ignore for the moment the case where a rational number occurs in both a record of A and a record of B. Third, each entry with label A (resp. B) is assigned a *class value* of 1 (resp. 0). Fourth, Gaussian convolution is applied to the sequence of class values, and the midpoint between two adjacent entries where the smoothed class values change by the largest amount, is declared to be a marker.

For example, if the original sorted sequence, with class membership in parentheses, is ..., $10.5(A)$, $11.7(A)$, $15.0(A)$, $16.7(A)$, $19.5(B)$, $15.2(B)$, $24.1(B)$, $30.8(B)$, ..., then the sequence of class values is ..., 1, 1, 1, 1, 0, 0, 0, 0, ... Note the abrupt transition of the subsequence of 1s to the subsequence of 0s. When a Gaussian convolution with small standard deviation σ is performed on the sequence of class values, a sequence of smoothed values results that exhibits a relatively large change at the point where the original sequence changes from 1s to 0s. If this is the largest change for the entire sequence of smoothed class values, then the original entries $16.7(A)$ and $19.5(B)$, which correspond to that change, produce a marker with value $(16.7 + 19.5)/2 = 18.2$.

Evidently, a large change of the smoothed class values corresponds in the original sorted sequence of entries to a subsequence of rational numbers mostly from A followed by a subsequence of numbers mostly from B, or *vice versa*. We call such a situation an *abrupt pattern change*. Thus, markers correspond to abrupt pattern changes.

We differentiate between two types of abrupt pattern changes. We assume, reasonably, that an abrupt change produced by all records of the populations $\mathcal{A}$ and $\mathcal{B}$ signals an important change of behavior and thus should be used to define a *True/False* value. The records of the subsets A and B may exhibit portions of such pattern changes. We say that these pattern changes of the records of A and B are of the *first kind*. The records of A and B may also have additional abrupt pattern changes that do not correspond to abrupt pattern changes in the records of the populations $\mathcal{A}$ and $\mathcal{B}$. This is particularly so if A and B are comparatively small subsets of the populations $\mathcal{A}$ and $\mathcal{B}$, as is typically the case. We say that the latter pattern changes are of the *second kind*.

There is another way to view the two kinds of pattern changes. Suppose we replace records r of $A \bigcup B$ by records $\tilde{r}$ of $(\mathcal{A}-A) \bigcup (\mathcal{B}-B)$, respectively, where $\tilde{r}$ is similar to r. Then abrupt pattern changes of the first (resp. second) kind produced by the records r likely (resp. unlikely) are abrupt pattern changes produced by the records $\tilde{r}$.

There is a third interpretation. Suppose we extract from the sorted sequence of numerical values just the A and B labels. For example, the above sequence ..., $10.5(A)$, $11.7(A)$, $15.0(A)$, $16.7(A)$, $19.5(B)$, $15.2(B)$, $24.1(B)$, $30.8(B)$, ... becomes ..., A, A, A, A, B, B, B, B, ... We call this a *label sequence*. Then for an abrupt pattern change of the first (resp. second) kind, the random substitution of records r by records $\tilde{r}$ is unlikely (resp. likely) to change the label sequence.

Cutpoint relies on the third interpretation in an attempt to distinguish between the two kinds of pattern changes, as follows. The method estimates the probability that A or B is selected in label sequences of abrupt pattern changes of the second kind, by assuming $p = |A|/(|A| + |B|)$ (resp. $q = |B|/(|A| + |B|)$) to be the probability for the label A (resp. B) to occur. Then the standard deviation of the Gaussian convolution process is so selected that the following is assured. Suppose there is at least one abrupt pattern change that according to the probabilities p and q has low probability and thus is estimated to be of the first kind. Then the largest change of the smoothed class values and the associated marker tends to correspond to one such abrupt pattern change. Informally, one may say that the standard deviation σ is so selected that marker positions corresponding to abrupt pattern changes of the first kind are favored.

Cutpoint has been added to a version of the Lsquare method [Felici and Truemper, 2002]; see also [Truemper, 2004] and Chapter 5 "Learning Logic Formulas and Related Error Distributions." The method computes DNF (disjunctive normal form) logic formulas from logic training data. Cutpoint initially determines one marker for each attribute of the original data as described above. Let the transformation of A and B via these markers produce sets A' and B'. If A' and B' cannot be separated by logic formulas, then Cutpoint recursively determines additional markers. The Cutpoint/Lsquare combination is so designed that it does not require user specification of parameters or rules except for a limit on the maximum number of markers for any attribute. To-date, that maximum has been fixed to 6 in all tests, and that limit likely is appropriate in general.

1.3   Computational Results

The methodology described in this chapter is rather new, and to-date we have only preliminary computational results. First, in several application projects such as credit rating, video image analysis, and word sense disambiguation we have found the transformations to be effective and reliable. Second, in tests on four standard datasets, Cutpoint/Lsquare usually achieved somewhat higher accuracy than combinations of entropy-based methods and Lsquare. For these tests, the classes A and B were randomly selected from populations $\mathcal{A}$ and $\mathcal{B}$, and the testing was done on records of $\mathcal{A} - A$ and $\mathcal{B} - B$. Also, the classification accuracy usually declined more slowly when the size of the training sets A and B was reduced.

In the remainder of this section, we review prior work on the transformation of rational data to logic data. Though work has been done for rule extraction from set data—see, for example, [Hand *et al.*, 2001]— there has been little work on the conversion to logic data. Indeed, as far as we know, just the trivial case has been treated where the entries are elements of a small set. For completeness, we cover that case here, too, but then focus on the two additional cases where the entries are elements of a large set or are subsets of a set.

Prior work on the conversion of rational data to logic data typically uses the word *discretization*. Since we also treat the conversion of set data, which by the assumption of finiteness of the underlying set are discrete already, we use terms such as *transformation* or *conversion* instead of the term discretization. An exception is the subsequent review of prior work, where the term discretization has generally been employed.

1.4   Entropy-Based Approaches

The concept of entropy, as used in information theory, measures the purity of an arbitrary collection of examples [Mitchell, 1997]. Suppose we have two classes of data, labeled N and P. Let n be the number of N instances, and define p to be the number of P instances. An estimate of the probability that class P occurs in the set is $p/(p+n)$, while an estimate of the probability that class N occurs is $n/(p+n)$. Entropy is then estimated as

$$entropy(p,n) = -\frac{p}{p+n}\log_2\frac{p}{p+n} - \frac{n}{p+n}\log_2\frac{n}{p+n} \qquad (1)$$

Another value, called *gain*, indicates the value of separating the data records on a particular attribute. Let V be an attribute with two possible values. Define p_1 (resp. n_1) to be the number of P (resp. N) records that contain one of the two values. Similarly, let p_2 (resp. n_2) be the number of P (resp. N) records that contain the second value. Then

$$gain = entropy(p,n) - [\frac{p_1+n_1}{p+n}entropy(p_1,n_1) + \frac{p_2+n_2}{p+n}entropy(p_2,n_2)] \quad (2)$$

In generating decision trees, for example, the attribute with the highest gain value is used to split the tree at each level.

The simplest approach to transforming rational data to logic data is as follows. Assume that each record has a rational attribute, V. The records are first sorted according to V, yielding rational values $v_1, v_2, \ldots, v_k$. Thus, for each pair of values, v_i and v_{i+1}, the average of the two can be computed, indicating a potential marker to separate the P records from the N records. For each possible marker, the associated gain can be computed. The highest gain indicates the best marker that separates the two classes of data [Quinlan, 1986].

The entropy-based method has been further developed to separate rational data into more than just two classes. In [Fayyad and Irani, 1992, 1993], a recursive heuristic for that task is described. The multi-interval technique first chooses a marker giving minimal entropy. It then recursively uses a principle called the Minimum Description Length Principle (MDLP) to determine whether additional markers should be introduced.

Another concept, called *minimum splits*, is introduced in [Wang and Goh, 1997]. Minimum splits minimize the overall impurity of the separated intervals with respect to a predefined threshold. Although, theoretically, any impurity measurement could be used, entropy is commonly chosen. Since many minimum splits can be candidates, the optimal split is discovered by searching the minimum splits space. The candidate split with the smallest product of entropy and number of intervals is elected to be the optimal split.

Entropy-based methods compete well with other data transformation techniques. In [Dougherty *et al.*, 1995], it is shown not only that discretization prior to execution of Naive Bayes decision algorithms can significantly increase learning performance, but also that recursive minimal entropy partitioning performs best when compared with other discretization methods such as equal width interval binning and Holte's 1R algorithm [Holte, 1993]. More comparisons involving entropy-based methods can be found in [Kohavi and Sahami, 1996], which demonstrates situations in which entropy-based MDLP methods slightly outperform error-minimization methods. The error-minimization methods used in the comparison can be found in [Maass, 1994] and [Auer *et al.*, 1995]. For information regarding the performance of entropy-based methods for learning classification rules, see [An and Cercone, 1999].

1.5   Bottom-Up Methods

Bottom-up methods initially partition the data set, then recombine similar adjacent partitions. The basic method is introduced in [Srikant and Agrawal, 1996]. Major problems are low speed and bloating of the produced rule set. To offset long execution times, the number of intervals must be reduced. Uninteresting excess rules may be pruned using an interest measure. Data clustering has been used [Miller and Yang, 1997] to generate more meaningful rules. Yet another approach to merging related intervals is used in the so-called contrast set miner [Bay and Pazzani, 1999]. The use of one such machine, called STUCCO, is illustrated in [Bay, 2000].

1.6   Other Approaches

Bayes' Law has also been utilized to discretize real-valued data into intervals. [Wu, 1996] demonstrates one such method. In it, curves are constructed based upon the Bayesian probability of a particular attribute's value in the data set. Markers are placed where leading curves differ on two sides.

A number of investigations have focused on simultaneous analysis of attributes during the transformation process. [Dougherty *et al.*, 1995] coin the term *dynamic* to refer to methods that conduct a search through the space of possible k values for all features simultaneously. For an example method, see [Gama *et al.*, 1998].

Relatedly, publications tend to use the term *multivariate* with different interpretations. [Kwedlo and Krętowski, 1999] refer to a multivariate analysis as one that simultaneously searches for threshold values for continuous-valued attributes. They use such an analysis with an evolutionary algorithm geared for decision rule induction. [Bay, 2000], however, declares that a multivariate test of differences takes as input instances drawn from two probability distributions and determines if the distributions are equivalent. This analysis maintains the integrity of any hidden patterns in the data.

[Boros *et al.*, 1997] explore several optimization approaches for the selection of breakpoints. In each case, all attributes of the records of the training sets A and B are considered simultaneously. For example, minimization of the total number of breakpoints is considered. The reference provides polynomial solution algorithms for some of the optimization problems and establishes other problems to be $\mathcal{N P}$-hard.

2.   DEFINITIONS

We need a few definitions for the discussions of the methods of this chapter.

2.1   Unknown Values

At times, the records of A and B may be incomplete. Following [Truemper, 2004], we consider two values signaling that entries are unknown. They are *Absent* and *Unavailable*. The value *Absent* means that the value is unknown but could be obtained, while *Unavailable* means that the value cannot be obtained. Of course, there are in-between cases. For example, a diagnostic value could be obtained in principle but is not determined since the required test would endanger the life of the patient. Here, we force such in-between cases to be classified as *Absent* or *Unavailable*. For the cited diagnostic case, the choice *Unavailable* would be appropriate.

Another way to view *Absent* and *Unavailable* is as follows. *Absent* means that the value is unknown, and that this fact is, in some sense, independent from the case represented by the given record. On the other hand, *Unavailable* tells that the reason why the value is not known is directly connected with the case of the record. Thus, *Unavailable* implicitly is information about the case of the record, while *Absent* is not. This way of differentiating between *Absent* and *Unavailable* implies how irrelevant values are handled. That is, if a value is declared to be *irrelevant* or *inapplicable*, then this fact is directly connected with the case of the record and thus is encoded by the value *Unavailable*.

In prior work, the treatment of unknown values typically does not depend on whether the unknown value could be obtained. For example, the average value of the attribute is often used for missing values [Mitchell, 1997]. As another example, database methods such as SQL use NULL to represent unknown entries [Ramakrishnan and Gehrke, 2003]. In applications, we have found the distinction between *Absent* and *Unavailable* to be useful. For example, a physician may declare that it is unnecessary that a certain diagnostic value be obtained. In that case, we call the value *irrelevant* and encode it by assigning the value *Unavailable*. Conversely, if a diagnostic value is deemed potentially useful but is not yet attained, we assign the value *Absent*.

It is convenient that we expand the definition of the three data types so that *Absent* and *Unavailable* are allowed. Thus, *logic data* have each entry equal to *True, False, Absent*, or *Unavailable*; *rational data* have each entry equal to a rational number, *Absent*, or *Unavailable*; and *set data* have each entry equal to an element of a finite set, a subset of a finite set, *Absent*, or *Unavailable*.

2.2   Records

A *record* contains any mixture of logic data, rational data, and set data. There are two sets A and B of records. Each record of the sets has the same number of entries. For each fixed j, the jth entries of all records are of the same data type. We want to transform records of A and B to records containing just logic data, with the objective that logic formulas determined by any appropriate method can classify the records correctly as coming from A or B.

2.3   Populations

Typically, the sets A and B come from populations $\mathcal{A}$ and $\mathcal{B}$, respectively, and we want the transformations and logic formulas derived from A and B to classify the remaining records of $\mathcal{A} - A$ and $\mathcal{B} - B$ with high accuracy.

There is a multipopulation version where several populations and sets are given. Say, population $\mathcal{A}_1, \mathcal{A}_2, \ldots, \mathcal{A}_m$ containing sets $A_1, A_2, \ldots, A_m$, respectively, are given. One desires to classify the records by logic formulas. This problem can be reduced to one two-population case or to m two-population cases where in the ith case A_i and $\mathcal{A}_i$ play the role of A and $\mathcal{A}$ and where $\bigcup_{k \neq i} A_k$ and $\bigcup_{k \neq i} \mathcal{A}_k$ play the role of B and $\mathcal{B}$. [Truemper, 2004] includes details for the situation where Lsquare is used.

2.4   DNF Formulas

A *literal* is the occurrence of a possibly negated variable in a logic formula. A *disjunctive normal form* (DNF) formula is a disjunction of conjunctions of literals. For example, $(x_1 \wedge \neg x_2) \vee (x_2 \wedge x_3) \vee (x_1 \wedge \neg x_3)$ is a DNF formula. The evaluation of DNF formulas requires the following adjustments when the values *Absent* and *Unavailable* occur. Let D be the DNF formula $D = D_1 \vee D_2 \vee \cdots \vee D_k$, where the D_j are the DNF clauses. For example, we may have $D_j = x \wedge y \wedge \neg z$, where x, y and $\neg z$ are the literals of logic variables x, y, and z.

The DNF clause D_j evaluates to *True* if the variable of each literal has been assigned a *True/False* value so that the literal evaluates to *True*. For example, $D_j = x \wedge y \wedge \neg z$ evaluates to *True* if $x = y = True$ and $z = False$. The clause D_j evaluates to *False* if, for at least one variable occurring in D_j, the variable has a *True/False* value so that the corresponding literal evaluates to *False*, or if the variable has the value *Unavailable*. For example, $x = False$ or $x = Unavailable$ cause $D_j = x \wedge y \wedge \neg z$ to evaluate to *False*. If one of the above cases does not apply, then D_j has the value *Undecided*. Thus, the *Undecided* case occurs if the following three conditions hold: (1) Each variable of D_j has *True*, *False*, or *Absent* as values; (2) there is at least one *Absent* case; and (3) all literals for the *True/False* cases evaluate to *True*. For example, $D_j = x \wedge y \wedge \neg z$ evaluates to *Undecided* if $x = Absent$, $y = True$, and $z = False$.

The DNF formula $D = D_1 \vee D_2 \vee \cdots \vee D_k$ evaluates to *True* if at least one D_j has value *True*, to *False* if all D_j have value *False*, and to *Undecided* otherwise. Thus in the *Undecided* case, each D_j has value *False* or *Undecided*, and there is at least one *Undecided* case.

As an aside, prior rules on the treatment of unknown values effectively treat them as *Absent*. For example, the above evaluation of DNF formulas for *Absent* values is consistent with the evaluation of logic formulas of SQL for NULL values [Ramakrishnan and Gehrke, 2003].

2.5   Clash Condition

We assume that the desired classifying formulas are to be in DNF, and that two such formulas must exist, where one of them evaluates to *True* on the records derived from A and to *False* on the records derived from B, and where the second formula achieves the opposite *True/False* values. We call these formulas *separating*. Note that the outcome *Undecided* is not allowed. That value may occur, however, when a DNF formula evaluates records of $(A{-}A) \cup (B{-}B)$. Effectively, a formula then votes for membership in A or B, or declares the case to be open. We associate with the vote for A and B a numerical value of 1 or -1, resp., and assign to the *Undecided* case the value 0. This rule is useful when sets of formulas are applied, since then the vote total expresses the strength of belief that a record is in A or B.

There is a simple necessary and sufficient condition for the existence of the separating formulas. We call it the *clash condition*. For the description of the condition, we assume for the moment that the records of A and B contain just logic data. We say that an A record and a B record *clash* if the A record has a *True/False* entry for which the corresponding entry of the B record has the opposite *True/False* value or *Unavailable*, and if the B record has a *True/False* entry for which the corresponding entry of the A record has the opposite *True/False* value or *Unavailable*.

For example, let each record of $A \cup B$ have three entries x_1, x_2, and x_3, and suppose that an A record is ($x_1 = $ *True*, $x_2 = $ *Unavailable*, $x_3 = $ *False*) and that a B record is ($x_1 = $ *False*, $x_2 = $ *True*, $x_3 = $ *False*). Then the entry $x_1 = $ *True* of the A record differs from $x_1 = $ *False* of the B record, and thus the two records clash. On the other hand, take the same A record, but let the B record be ($x_1 = $ *True*, $x_2 = $ *Unavailable*, $x_3 = $ *Unavailable*). Then there is no *True/False* value in the B record for which the A record has the opposite *True/False* value or *Unavailable*, and thus the two records do not clash.

Define the *clash condition* to be satisfied by sets A and B containing only logic data if every record of A clashes with every record of B. The following theorem links the existence of separating DNF formulas and the clash condition. We omit the straightforward proof.

Theorem 2.1. *Let sets A and B contain just logic data. Then two separating DNF formulas exist if and only if the clash condition is satisfied.*

3.   OVERVIEW OF TRANSFORMATION PROCESS

Let sets A and B of records be given. In the general case, the records contain a mixture of logic data, rational data, and set data. We accomplish the transformation to records having only logic data in two main steps. First, we convert the set data to logic data and/or to rational data. This step is covered in Section 4. Second, we convert in the resulting records the rational data to logic data. This step is described in Sections 5–7.

4.   SET DATA TO LOGIC DATA

In this section, we describe the transformation of set data to logic data or rational data. The conversion is carried out separately for each index j for which the jth entries of A and B are set data. Thus, for such j, there is a finite set W such that all jth entries different from *Absent* or *Unavailable* are elements or subsets of W. We do not allow a mixture of elements and subsets, so either all entries in jth position and different from *Absent* or *Unavailable* are elements, or all such entries are subsets. The transformation to logic data depends on which of the two cases is at hand.

4.1   Case of Element Entries

Suppose the set W has m element, say $W = \{w_1, w_2, \ldots, w_m\}$. Thus, each entry in jth position that is different from *Absent* and *Unavailable* is some $w_i \in W$.

If m is small, say $m \leq 5$, we use a well-known approach. We introduce $k = m$ logic variables $x_1, x_2, \ldots, x_k$ and encode occurrence of entry w_i by

$$x_l = \begin{cases} True & \text{if } i = l \\ False & \text{otherwise} \end{cases} \qquad (3)$$

For example, let $W = \{w_1, w_2, w_3\}$. Then $k = m = 3$, and w_1 is encoded by $x_1 = \textit{True}$, $x_2 = \textit{False}$, $x_3 = \textit{False}$, w_2 is encoded by $x_1 = \textit{False}$, $x_2 = \textit{True}$, $x_3 = \textit{False}$, and w_3 is encoded by $x_1 = \textit{False}$, $x_2 = \textit{False}$, $x_3 = \textit{True}$.

If m is large, we select an integer $f \geq 1$ and derive from W two sets W_A and W_B where W_A (resp. W_B) contains the $w_i \in W$ that occur at least f times as jth entry in records of A (resp. B) and never as jth entry in records of B (resp. A). We use a single logic variable x and encode w_i by

$$x = \begin{cases} \textit{True} & \text{if } w_i \in W_A \\ \textit{False} & \text{if } w_i \in W_B \\ \textit{Unavailable} & \text{otherwise} \end{cases} \tag{4}$$

Note that this encoding introduces the value *Unavailable*.

For example, let $W = \{w_1, w_2, \ldots, w_{50}\}$ and $f = 5$. Suppose w_4, w_5, w_{10} are the $w_i \in W$ that occur at least five times as jth entry in records of A and that never occur as jth entry in records of B. Thus, $W_A = \{w_4, w_5, w_{10}\}$. Assume that, similarly, $W_B = \{w_7, w_9, w_{17}, w_{35}\}$. We encode three example cases w_5, w_{17}, and w_{31} using these sets. The entry w_5 is in W_A, so it is represented by $x = \textit{True}$. The entry w_{17} is in W_B and is encoded by $x = \textit{False}$. The entry w_{31} is not in W_A or W_B, and is encoded by $x = \textit{Unavailable}$.

An alternative method for the case of large m combines the ideas of the above two schemes. We define a small integer $k \geq 1$ and collect in a set W' the k elements of W that occur most frequently as jth entry in the records of $A \cup B$. Suppose $W' = \{w_1, w_2, \ldots, w_k\}$. Let $W'' = W - W'$. If $w_i \in W'$, we represent w_i by *True/False* values of variables $x_1, x_2, \ldots, x_k$ as described above for small m. We also assign the value *Unavailable* to an additional variable x_{k+1}. If $w_i \in W''$, we define $x_1 = x_2 = \cdots = x_k = \textit{Unavailable}$ and assign a *True/False/Unavailable* value to x_{k+1} according to the above method for large m. The set W and variable x used there are W'' and x_{k+1} here.

For example, let $W = \{w_1, w_2, \ldots, w_{50}\}$ and $k = 3$. Suppose the k most frequently occurring entries in jth position are w_1, w_2, w_3. Then $W' = \{w_1, w_2, w_3\}$ and $W'' = W - W' = \{w_4, w_5, \ldots, w_{50}\}$. We show the encoding for example cases $w_2 \in W'$ and $w_8 \in W''$. Using the above scheme for small m, the encoding for $w_2 \in W'$ is $x_1 = \textit{False}$, $x_2 = \textit{True}$, $x_3 = \textit{False}$. We add to that encoding $x_{k+1} = x_4 = \textit{Unavailable}$. For the encoding of $w_8 \in W''$, suppose that the above method for large m determines from W'' the sets $W_A = \{w_4, w_5, w_8\}$ and $W_B = \{w_7, w_9, w_{17}, w_{35}\}$. Then $w_8 \in W''$ is encoded by $x_4 = \textit{True}$ plus $x_1 = x_2 = x_3 = \textit{Unavailable}$.

Another transformation appears to be interesting, provided the elements of W can be interpreted as approximate descriptions of values on a numerical scale. In such a situation, we sort the elements w_i of W so that the corresponding implied values are in increasing order. Let the order be $w_1, w_2, \ldots, w_m$. Then we replace each jth entry w_i by an integer $y_i = i$.

For example, suppose the speed of a car is characterized by the elements of the set $w = \{\textit{slow, medium, fast}\}$. We let $w_1 = \textit{slow}$, $w_2 = \textit{medium}$, $w_3 = \textit{fast}$ and encode w_i by $y_i = i$. Thus, *slow, medium, fast* are replaced by 1, 2, 3, respectively.

Once all the jth entries w_i have been transformed to the integer entries y_i, we replace those rational data y_i by logic data as described in Sections 5–7.

In the above methods, each $w_i \in W$ is replaced by $l \geq 1$ *True/False/Unavailable* values $x_1, x_2, \ldots, x_l$ or by an integer y_i. Now suppose that a jth entry is not some $w_i \in W$ but is *Absent* or *Unavailable*. Then we assign to all variables introduced for the jth entry, that is, to the x_l or y_i, that value.

4.2   Case of Set Entries

Suppose subsets $V_1, V_2, \ldots, V_m$ of a set W may occur as jth entry. We could define $\tilde{W} = \{V_1, V_2, \ldots, V_m\}$ and use one of the methods of the preceding subsection to encode each V_i. That approach ignores possible relationships among the V_i and thus may be unsatisfactory. For example if $W = \{red, green, blue\}$ and $V_1 = \{red, blue\}$, $V_2 = \{red, green\}$, and $V_3 = \{blue, green\}$, then V_1 and V_2 have the element red in common, while V_2 and V_3 have the element $green$ in common. The following method recognizes such relationships and uses them for the encoding.

Define W_A (resp. W_B) to be the union of the V_i occurring as jth entry in records of A (resp. B) and never in records of B (resp. A). We define a *strength of membership* value $s(V_i)$ by

$$s(V_i) = \frac{|V_i \cap W_A| - |V_i \cap W_B|}{|V_i \cap (W_A \cup W_B)|} \tag{5}$$

Since $|V_i \cap W_A|$ and $|V_i \cap W_B|$ cannot be larger than $|V_i \cap (W_A \cup W_B)|$, we have $-1 \leq s(V_i) \leq 1$. In the records of A and B, we replace each V_i occurring as jth entry by the rational value $s(V_i)$. If instead of a set V_i we have *Absent* or *Unavailable* as jth entry, we leave that entry unchanged.

For example, let $W_A = \{w_1, w_2, \ldots, w_{10}\}$ and $W_B = \{w_{11}, w_{12}, \ldots, w_{30}\}$. If the jth entry of a record is $V_i = \{w_2, w_7, w_{10}, w_{14}, w_{36}, w_{54}\}$, then $V_i \cap W_A = \{w_2, w_7, w_{10}\}$, $V_i \cap W_B = \{w_{14}\}$, and $V_i \cap (W_A \cup W_B) = \{w_2, w_7, w_{10}, w_{14}\}$. Thus, $s(V_i) = (|V_i \cap W_A| - |V_i \cap W_B|)/|V_i \cap (W_A \cup W_B)| = (3 - 1)/4 = 0.5$.

Once all jth entries V_i have been transformed to rational entries $s(V_i)$, we replace those rational data by logic data. Sections 5–7 cover that transformation for the general case.

5.   RATIONAL DATA TO LOGIC DATA

We summarize algorithm Cutpoint, which carries out the conversion of rational data to logic data. Let J be the set of indices j for which the jth entries of the given records contain rational data.

Initially, we analyze the jth entries of each $j \in J$ in isolation and replace such entries by logic data. Specifically, we select one marker and encode each rational jth entry by one *True/False* value defined via the marker. Let A' and B' be the two sets of records with *True/False* values obtained that way from the records of the original training sets A and B, respectively. If A' and B' satisfy the clash condition of Section 2.5, then they can be separated, and we stop. Otherwise, we begin a recursive process where in each pass an index j is selected and one additional marker is defined for that index. We refine the logic data for the jth entries accordingly and check if the latter data allow full separation. If this is so, the process stops, and the desired transformation has been accomplished. Otherwise, we begin another pass. The next two sections describe Cutpoint in detail. First, we cover the selection of the initial markers.

6.   INITIAL MARKERS

Since the initial markers are determined for each $j \in J$ in isolation, we only need to describe the process for a fixed $j \in J$. For that index j, we denote the rational numbers in jth position, sorted in increasing order, by $z_1 \leq z_2 \leq \cdots \leq z_N$. For the moment, we ignore all *Absent* and *Unavailable* values that may occur in the jth position.

6.1   Class Values

We associate with each z_i a *class value* v_i that depends on whether z_i is equal to any other z_h, and whether z_i is in a record of set A or B. Specifically, if z_i is unique and thus not equal to any other z_h, then v_i is 1 (resp. 0) if the record with z_i as jth entry is in A (resp. B). If z_i is not unique, let H be the set of indices h for which $z_h = z_i$. Note that $i \in H$. Let H_A (resp. H_B) be the subset of the $h \in H$ for which z_h is the jth entry of a record in set A (resp. B). If $h \in H_A$ (resp. $h \in H_B$), we say that z_h produces a *local class value* equal to 1 (resp. 0). The class value v_i is then the average of the local class values for the z_h with $h \in H$. Thus, $v_i = [1 \cdot |H_A| + 0 \cdot |H_B|]/|H|$ or, compactly,

$$v_i = |H_A|/|H| \tag{6}$$

The formula also covers the case of unique z_i, since then $H = \{i\}$ and either $H_A = \{i\}$ or $H_A = \emptyset$ depending on whether the record with z_i as jth entry is in A or B, respectively.

For example, suppose $z_1 = 2$, $z_2 = 5$, and $z_5 = 10$ occur in records of set A, and $z_3 = 7$ and $z_4 = 10$ occur in records of set B. Since z_1 and z_2 are unique and occur in records of set A, we have $v_1 = v_2 = 1$. Similarly, uniqueness of z_3 and occurrence in a B record produce $v_3 = 0$. The values z_4 and z_5 are equal and exactly one of them, z_5, occurs in a record of set A. Thus for both z_4 and z_5, we have $H = \{4, 5\}$ and $H_A = \{5\}$, and by (6), $v_4 = v_5 = |H_A|/|H| = 0.5$.

Recall that a marker corresponds to an abrupt change of classification pattern. In terms of class values, a marker is a value c where many if not all z_i close to c and satisfying $z_i < c$ have high class values, while most if not all z_i close to c and satisfying $z_i > c$ have low class values, or *vice versa*. We identify markers following a smoothing of the class values by Gaussian convolution, a much used tool. For example, it is employed in computer vision for the detection of edges in digitized images; see [Forsyth and Ponce, 2003].

6.2   Smoothed Class Values

Gaussian convolution uses the normal distribution with mean equal to 0 for smoothing of data. For completeness, we include the relevant formulas. For mean 0 and standard deviation $\sigma \geq 0$, the probability density function of the normal distribution is

$$f(y) = \frac{1}{\sigma\sqrt{2\pi}}e^{-y^2/(2\sigma^2)}, \quad 0 < y < \infty \tag{7}$$

In our case, we always choose σ to be a positive integer. We cover the selection in a moment.

For any integer g and the selected σ, let β_g denote the probability that the random variable defined by $f(y)$ falls into the open interval $(g - 0.5, g + 0.5)$. Since g is the midpoint of the open unit interval $(g - 0.5, g + 0.5)$, we have

$$\beta_g = \int_{g-0.5}^{g+0.5} f(y)\,dy \cong f(g) \tag{8}$$

The smoothing process uses the β_g values to derive, from the class values v_i, smoothed values v_i' by the formula

$$v_i' = \sum_{g=-\infty}^{\infty} \beta_g \cdot v_{i+g}, \quad 1 \leq i \leq N \tag{9}$$

The formula relies on the convention that each v_{i+g} without defined value, that is, with $i + g < 1$ or $i + g > N$, is declared to be 0. For the values of σ of interest and for $|g| \geq 2\sigma + 1$, the β_g are sufficiently small that they can be ignored. That fact and the relation $\beta_g = \beta_{-g}$, for all g, allow us to simplify (9) for each actual computation to

$$v_i' = \beta_0 \cdot v_i + \sum_{g=1}^{2\sigma} \beta_g \cdot (v_{i+g} + v_{i-g}), \quad 1 \leq i \leq N \tag{10}$$

The assumption of $v_i = 0$ outside the known values $v_1, v_2, \ldots, v_N$ results in biased or, rather, unusable values v_i' values for $1 \leq i \leq 2\sigma$ and $N - 2\sigma + 1 \leq i \leq N$. As a consequence, we ignore these values and declare the remaining v_i' values *usable*.

6.3   Selection of Standard Deviation

We select the standard deviation σ via an analysis of classification patterns. Suppose we produce sequences made up of the letters A and B. We construct a given sequence by randomly selecting one letter at a time, choosing the letter A with probability p and the letter B with probability $q = 1 - p$. In the construction of a sequence, we begin with the sequence AB. For given $k \geq 1$ and $l \geq 1$, we adjoin $k - 1$ As in front of AB and $l - 1$ Bs behind AB. At this point, we have k As followed by l Bs. Finally, we add a B in front and an A at the end. What is the probability that such a sequence S is constructed from AB when we randomly select letters and add them first in front and then at the end, until a sequence of the described form is achieved? Since the initial sequence AB is given, the probability is

$$P[S] = p^k q^l \tag{11}$$

For $m \geq 1$, consider the event E_m where the above process constructs any S for which $k \geq m$ or $l \geq m$. We add up the appropriate probabilities of (11) to get the probability α_m that E_m occurs. Using the fact that the sum of the probabilities of all possible cases is 1, that is,

$$\sum_{\substack{k \geq 1 \\ l \geq 1}} p^k q^l = 1 \tag{12}$$

we compute α_m as

$$
\begin{aligned}
\alpha_m &= \sum_{\substack{k \geq m \\ l \geq 1}} p^k q^l + \sum_{\substack{k \geq 1 \\ l \geq m}} p^k q^l - \sum_{\substack{k \geq m \\ l \geq m}} p^k q^l \\
&= p^{m-1} \sum_{\substack{k \geq 1 \\ l \geq 1}} p^k q^l + q^{m-1} \sum_{\substack{k \geq 1 \\ l \geq 1}} p^k q^l - (pq)^{m-1} \sum_{\substack{k \geq 1 \\ l \geq 1}} p^k q^l \\
&= p^{m-1} + q^{m-1} - (pq)^{m-1} \tag{13}
\end{aligned}
$$

Define the *length* of S to be the number of As and Bs minus 2, which is $k + l$. Effectively, we do not count the initial B of S and the final A of S. The expected length L of S is

$$
\begin{aligned}
L &= \sum_{\substack{k \geq 1 \\ l \geq 1}} (k + l) p^k q^l \\
&= \sum_{k \geq 1} k p^k \sum_{l \geq 1} q^l + \sum_{k \geq 1} p^k \sum_{l \geq 1} l q^l \\
&= \frac{p}{(1-p)^2} \cdot \frac{q}{1-q} + \frac{p}{1-p} \cdot \frac{q}{(1-q)^2} \\
&= \frac{1}{pq} \tag{14}
\end{aligned}
$$

Suppose we have a sequence T of N randomly selected As and Bs. What is the expected number of the above sequences S occurring in T? For our purposes, a sufficiently precise estimate is

$$N/L = Npq \tag{15}$$

Of the expected number of sequences S occurring in T, the fraction of sequences that qualify for being sequences of event E_m is approximately equal to

α_m. Thus, a reasonable estimate of the expected number of sequences of E_m occurring in T, which we denote by $K(N, m)$, is

$$K(N,m) = (N/L)\alpha_m = Npq\left[p^{m-1} + p^{m-1} - (pq)^{m-1}\right] \qquad (16)$$

Each S occurring in T is a potential case for a marker that corresponds to the point where k As transition to l Bs. We do not want markers to result from sequences S that likely can be produced by randomness. Thus, we avoid considering sequences S of any event E_m for which the expected value $K(N, m)$ is greater than or equal to 1. Since $K(N, m)$ decreases as m increases, there either is a largest value $m^* \geq 1$ for which $K(N, m^*) \geq 1$, or $K(N, 1) \leq 1$. In the latter case, we define $m^* = 1$.

We select the standard deviation σ of the Gaussian convolution so that sequences of E_m with $m \leq m^*$ likely do not produce a marker if there is a sequence S' with length greater than m^*.

By the above arguments, the latter sequence S' is unlikely to have been produced by randomness, and thus is likely due to a particular behavior of the values of the attribute under consideration. In terms of the discussion in the introduction, we estimate that we have an abrupt pattern change of the first kind.

We achieve this desired effect by selecting $\sigma = m^*$. Indeed, that choice produces significant probabilities β_g for g, $m < g \leq 2m$, and these probabilities tend to smooth out the classification values v_i associated with the As and Bs of randomly produced sequences S of E_{m^*}.

When N is not large, certain boundary effects should be addressed. We describe the adjustment and then justify it. Instead of demanding that $K(N, m^*) \geq 1$, we ignore the first and last m^* As and Bs of the sequence T, and demand that $K(N - 2m^*, m^*) \geq 1$. Using (16), m^* is thus the largest value m satisfying

$$K(N - 2m, m) = (N - 2m)pq\left[p^{m-1} + p^{m-1} - (pq)^{m-1}\right] \geq 1 \qquad (17)$$

unless we have, for $m = 1$, $K(N - 2m, m) < 1$. In the latter case we select $m^* = 1$. We motivate the adjustment as follows. When Gaussian convolution is performed with $\sigma = m^*$, the first smoothed class value is computed using the values v_i of the $4\sigma + 1$ As and Bs at the beginning of T. Denote that subsequence by T'. If the central $2\sigma + 1$ As and Bs of T' contain an S of some E_m with $m \leq m^*$, then the class values of the As and Bs of any such S tend to be smoothed out. Thus, S is unlikely to result in a marker if a subsequence S' with length greater than m^* exists.

In the implementation of the algorithm, we modify the rule for m^* slightly, by selecting m^* to be the integer for which $K(N - 2m, m)$ of (17) is closest to 1. This choice avoids the case where $K(N - 2m^*, m^*)$ is greater than 1 while $K(N - 2(m^* - 1), m^* - 1)$ is less than but also very close to 1. In such a case, $m^* - 1$ should be the preferred value of σ. The rule also covers the case where $K(N - 2m, m) < 1$ for $m = 1$.

We establish the probability p and compute m^* via (17) as follows. We take p to be the fraction of the number of training records of class A divided by the total number of training records, and we find m^* by dichotomous search.

We note that, due to the symmetry of the formula $K(N - m, m)$, the choice of m^* implicitly also considers subsequences in which the roles of A and B are reversed. Table 1 shows σ as a function of N, for $\sigma \leq 10$ and $p = q = 0.5$.

Table 1. σ as function of N for $\sigma \leq 10$ and $p = q = 0.5$

N	σ
0–7	1
8–11	2
12–15	3
16–31	4
32–54	5
55–99	6
100–186	7
187–359	8
360–702	9
703–1387	10

There is an exceptional case where the selected σ must be reduced. As we argue shortly—see the discussion following (19)—we do not consider a marker between z_i and z_{i-1} if $v_i = v_{i-1}$. Thus, no marker can be placed if no i satisfies $2\sigma + 2 \leq i \leq N - 2\sigma$ and $v_i \neq v_{i-1}$. If that case occurs, several corrective actions are possible. We have found that reduction of σ to 1 is a good choice. If for the reduced σ there still is no index i satisfying $2\sigma + 2 \leq i \leq N - 2\sigma$ and $v_i \neq v_{i-1}$, then we declare that no intervals should be created for the jth entry; as a consequence, we delete the jth entry from all records of A and B. Otherwise, we proceed with the reduced $\sigma = 1$.

For example, if $N = 37$, $\sigma = 6$, and $v_{13} = 1$, $v_{14} = v_{15} = \cdots v_{30} = 0$, $v_{31} = 1$, then no i satisfies $2\sigma + 2 = 14 \leq i \leq N - 2\sigma = 25$ and $v_i \neq v_{i-1}$. Thus, σ should be reduced to 1. For that value, both $i = 14$ and $i = 31$, and possibly other values of i, satisfy $2\sigma + 2 = 4 \leq i \leq N - 2\sigma = 35$ and $v_i \neq v_{i-1}$. Thus, $\sigma = 1$ should be used. On the other hand, let $N = 37$ and $\sigma = 6$ as before, but suppose $v_1 = 1$, $v_2 = v_3 = \cdots = v_{35} = 0$, $v_{36} = 1$, $v_{37} = 0$. For $\sigma = 6$, no i satisfies $2\sigma + 2 = 14 \leq i \leq N - 2\sigma = 25$. Reduction of σ to 1 produces the same negative conclusion. Thus, no intervals should be created for the jth entries, and we delete these entries from all records of A and B.

6.4   Definition of Markers

Suppose we have selected σ as described above and have computed the smoothed class values v_i'. As we move along the sequence of usable values v_i', the absolute difference δ_i between adjacent v'_{i-1} and v'_i,

$$\delta_i = |v'_i - v'_{i-1}| \tag{18}$$

measures the abruptness with which class values change. We call δ_i a *difference value*. The largest such value, say δ_{i^*}, produces a marker c between z_{i^*-1} and z_{i^*}. That is,

$$c = (z_{i^*-1} + z_{i^*})/2 \tag{19}$$

The selection rule for c requires a small adjustment due to a quirk that may be introduced by the convolution process. It is possible that, for the selected c, the corresponding original class values v_{i^*-1} and v_{i^*} are equal. In case all z_i are distinct, the values z_{i^*-1} and z_{i^*} separated by c come both either from A records or from B records. If several z_i are equal, more complex interpretations are possible. However, all of them reflect unattractive cases.

To rule out all such situations, we restrict the selection of the difference values δ_{i^*} by considering δ_i values only if $v_i \neq v_{i-1}$. Thus,

$$\delta_{i^*} = \max_i \{\delta_i \mid v_i \text{ and } v_{i-1} \text{ usable}, \ v_i \neq v_{i-1}\} \tag{20}$$

If the maximum is attained by several i^*, we pick one closest to $N/2$, breaking any secondary tie by a random choice.

For example, if $\sigma = 6$ and $N = 60$, then the v'_i with index i satisfying $2\sigma + 1 = 13 \leq i \leq N - 2\sigma = 48$ are usable. Suppose these values are $v'_{13} = 0.3214$, $v'_{14} = 0.3594$, $v'_{15} = 0.4042$, $v'_{16} = 0.4439$, $v'_{17} = 0.4760$, $v'_{18} = 0.4986,\ldots$, $v'_{45} = 0.4740$, $v'_{46} = 0.4410$, $v'_{47} = 0.4007$, and $v'_{48} = 0.3612$. For these values, formula (18) produces $\delta_{14} = 0.0380$, $\delta_{15} = 0.0448$, $\delta_{16} = 0.0397$, $\delta_{17} = 0.0321$, $\delta_{18} = 0.0226,\ldots$, $\delta_{46} = 0.0330$, $\delta_{47} = 0.0403$, and $\delta_{48} = 0.0395$. Suppose the largest δ_i for which $v_i \neq v_{i-1}$, is unique and is $\delta_{15} = 0.0448$. Thus, $i^* = 15$. If $z_{i^*} = z_{15} = 7$ and $z_{i^*-1} = z_{14} = 5$, the marker c is defined by $c = (z_{i^*-1} + z_{i^*})/2 = (5 + 7)/2 = 6$.

The next scheme summarizes the computation producing the initial marker c. The scheme also outputs the standard deviation σ of the convolution process since that information is needed later in another application of the algorithm.

Algorithm INITIAL MARKER

Input: Rational numbers $z_1 \leq z_2 \leq \cdots \leq z_N$ of the jth attribute of the records of A and B.

Output: Either: Marker c for the jth attribute, standard deviation σ of the convolution process, and the difference value δ_i^* associated with the marker. Or: "Marker cannot be determined."

Procedure:

1. (Check if N is too small or if $\sigma = 1$ cannot produce a marker.) If $N \leq 6$ or if, for $\sigma = 1$, there is no index i satisfying $2\sigma + 2 \leq i \leq N - 2\sigma$ and $v_i \neq v_{i-1}$, then output "Marker cannot be determined," and stop. (In that case, one should delete the jth entries from all records of A and B.)

2. (Compute class values.) For $i = 1, 2, \ldots, N$, define $H^i = \{h \mid z_h = z_i\}$, $H_A^i = \{h \in H \mid z_h$ is taken from an A record$\}$, and compute the class value $v_i = |H_A^i|/|H^i|$.

3. (Define p, q, and σ.) Define $p = |A|/(|A| + |B|)$ and $q = 1 - p$. Let m^* be the value of $m \geq 1$ for which $K(N - 2m, m)$ is closest to 1. Let $\sigma = m^*$. If there is no index i satisfying $2\sigma + 2 \leq i \leq N - 2\sigma$ and $v_i \neq v_{i-1}$, lower σ to 1.

4. (Compute smoothed class values.) For $i = 1, 2, \ldots, N$, use the class values v_i, the standard deviation σ, and the β_g values of (8) to compute the smoothed class values $v_i' = \beta_0 \cdot v_i + \sum_{i=1}^{2\sigma} \beta_g (v_{i+g} + v_{i-g})$.

5. (Select marker.) For $i = 2\sigma + 2, 2\sigma + 3, \ldots, N - 2\sigma$, let $\delta_i = |v_i' - v_{i-1}'|$. Select i^* so that $\delta_{i^*} = \max_i \{\delta_i \mid v_i \neq v_{i-1}\}$. If i^* is not unique, select an i^* closest to $N/2$ and break any secondary tie by random choice. Define the marker c by $c = (z_{i^*-1} + z_{i^*})/2$. Output the marker c, the standard deviation σ, and the difference value δ_i^*.

6.5 Evaluation of Markers

For each $j \in J$, we carry out Algorithm INITIAL MARKER and thus get either a marker, say c_j, or conclude that a marker cannot be obtained. In the latter case, attribute j is deleted from all records of A and B. To the reduced sets, which we again denote by A and B, we apply the transformations implied by the markers, and get sets A' and B'. If A' and B' satisfy the clash condition, the sets can be separated by logic formulas and thus the desired transformation has been found. Otherwise, at least one record of A' and one record of B' do not clash. In that case, we compute one additional marker for some $j \in J$; details are given in the next section. When we get the additional marker, we proceed recursively as described above. That is, we derive from A and B sets A' and B', test if the clash condition is satisfied, and so on. The process stops either when A' and B' satisfy the clash condition, or when an additional marker cannot be determined. In the implementation of the method, we also stop introducing additional markers for a $j \in J$ when the number of markers reaches a specified maximum. In tests to-date, that limit has been set to 6, and this limit likely is appropriate in general.

Regardless of the cause of termination, we output the collection of markers on hand as well as the final A' and B'. If the latter sets do not satisfy the clash condition, we also output the warning message "A and B cannot be fully separated."

7. ADDITIONAL MARKERS

This section describes how an additional marker is determined.

7.1   Critical Interval

The markers on hand define intervals of the rational line for each index $j \in J$, and these markers produce a transformation of A and B to A' and B'. Define such an interval to be *critical* if a properly chosen subdivision can lead to a transformation of A and B to, say, A'' and B'' such that A'' and B'' have more clashing pairs of records than A' and B'. Clearly, each critical interval is associated with a particular attribute $j \in J$, and all critical intervals are readily determined via the nonclashing pairs of records of A' and B'. We omit the obvious process. For each critical interval, we compute an additional marker using a method virtually identical to Algorithm INITIAL MARKER. Specifically, the input sets A and B of the algorithm are now the subsets $\bar{A} \subseteq A$ and $\bar{B} \subseteq B$ of records for which the values of the associated attribute $j \in J$ falls into the critical interval.

The algorithm either outputs a marker together with the associated standard deviation σ and the difference value δ_{i^*}, or it declares that a marker cannot be found. In the latter case, we do not delete any attribute values from A and B, but instead record that the interval cannot be refined, and thus exclude it from further consideration.

When all critical intervals have been processed, two cases are possible. Either we have at least one additional marker, or no additional markers could be determined. In the latter case, the transformation process outputs A', B', the markers on hand, and the warning message "A and B cannot be fully separated," and then stops.

If at least one additional marker has been determined, we select one of them and proceed recursively as described above. The selection of the marker is based on a measure that considers the attractiveness of pattern change at the point of the marker and on the number of nonclashing pairs of records of A' and B' that determine the interval to be critical. The latter number is called the *relevance count*. We first discuss the attractiveness of the pattern change.

7.2   Attractiveness of Pattern Change

The attractiveness of a pattern change is based on a lower bound ε on the difference values δ_i of (18) for certain label subsequences. Each such subsequence has, for some $n \geq 1$ yet to be specified, $k \geq n + 1$ As followed by $l \geq n + 1$ Bs, and δ_i is the difference value produced by the last A and the first B of the sequence. We establish a lower bound ε for δ_i.

Theorem 7.1. *Let a label sequence be given for which the original rational numbers z_i are all distinct. For some $n \geq 1$, let a label subsequence have $k \geq n + 1$ As followed by $l \geq n + 1$ Bs. Then $\varepsilon = \beta_0 - 2\beta_{n+1}$ is a lower bound for δ_i of (18).*

Proof: Since $\delta_i \geq 0$, the claim is trivial if $\beta_0 - 2\beta_{n+1} \leq 0$. Hence we suppose that $\beta_0 > 2\beta_{n+1}$. Using the formula (10) for v_i' in the definition of δ_i of (18), we have

$$
\begin{aligned}
\delta_i &= \left| \left[\beta_0 v_i + \sum_{g=1}^{\infty} \beta_g \left(v_{i+g} + v_{i-g} \right) \right] - \left[\beta_0 v_{i-1} + \sum_{g=1}^{\infty} \beta_g \left(v_{i+g-1} + v_{i-g-1} \right) \right] \right| \\
&= \left| \sum_{g=0}^{\infty} \left(\beta_g - \beta_{g+1} \right) \left(v_{i+g} - v_{i-g-1} \right) \right| \qquad (21)
\end{aligned}
$$

Consider δ_i produced by the last A and first B of the label sequence. Due to the $k \geq n+1$ As (resp. $l \geq n+1$ Bs) in the label subsequence, we have $v_{i-1} = v_{i-2} = \cdots = v_{i-n-1} = 1$ (resp. $v_i = v_i + 1 = \cdots = v_{i+n} = 0$). We use these class values in (21) and simplify to get

$$
\delta_i = \left| \beta_{n+1} - \beta_0 + \sum_{g=n+1}^{\infty} \left(\beta_g - \beta_{g+1} \right) \left(v_{i+g} - v_{i-g-1} \right) \right| \qquad (22)
$$

Since $\beta_0 > 2\beta_{n+1}$ and, for all $g \geq 0$, $\beta_g \geq \beta_{g+1}$, the right hand side of (22) is minimum if, for all $g \geq n+1$, we have $v_{i+g} = 1$ and $v_{i-g-1} = 0$. For that case, δ_i becomes $\delta_i = |2\beta_{n+1} - \beta_0| = \beta_0 - 2\beta_{n+1} = \varepsilon$.   □

If n is sufficiently large, then the label subsequence of Theorem 7.1 is quite unlikely to be a random occurrence. Thus, if the label subsequence does occur, we estimate that it corresponds to an abrupt pattern change of the first kind. Indeed, the discussion of Section 6 states that, as n grows beyond σ, the above conclusion tends to become valid. For example, $n = \lfloor 1.5\sigma \rfloor$ is large enough for the desired conclusion, and we choose this value of n to compute the lower bound ε. Thus,

$$
\varepsilon = \beta_0 - 2\beta_{\lfloor 1.5\sigma \rfloor + 1} \qquad (23)
$$

Let c be a marker, and define δ_{i^*} to be the change of smoothed class values corresponding to the marker c. To measure how likely the marker c corresponds to a pattern change of the first kind, we compare δ_{i^*} with ε. Specifically, if the ratio

$$
\delta_{i^*}/\varepsilon = \delta_{i^*}/(\beta_0 - 2\beta_{\lfloor 1.5\sigma \rfloor + 1}) \qquad (24)
$$

is near or above 1, then we estimate that we likely have a pattern change of the first kind. Thus, the ratio δ_{i^*}/ε measures the attractiveness of the marker. We say that the marker c has *attractiveness* δ_{i^*}/ε.

7.3   Selection Of Marker

For each critical interval for which we have determined an additional marker, define the *potential* of the marker to be the product of the relevance count of the interval and the attractiveness of the marker. Letting γ and R denote the potential and relevance count, respectively, we have, for each marker, the potential γ as

$$
\gamma = R\delta_{i^*}/\varepsilon = R\delta_{i^*}/(\beta_0 - 2\beta_{\lfloor 1.5\sigma \rfloor + 1}) \qquad (25)
$$

We select the marker with highest potential, add that marker to the list of markers on hand, and proceed recursively as described earlier.

For example, suppose we have two critical intervals. For the first interval, we have $\sigma = 6$, $N = 58$, $\delta_{i^*} = 0.037$, and $R = 12$. For $\sigma = 6$, we have $\varepsilon = \beta_0 - 2\beta_{\lfloor 1.5\sigma \rfloor + 1} = 0.035$, and the potential is $\gamma = R\delta_{i^*}/\varepsilon = 12(0.037/0.035) = 12.7$. If the second critical interval has a smaller potential, then we refine the first interval. Suppose that for the first interval we have $z_{i^*} = 17$ and $z_{i^*-1} = 14$. Then the new marker is $p = (z_{i^*-1} + z_{i^*})/2 = (14 + 17)/2 = 15.5$.

We summarize the selection process.

Algorithm ADDITIONAL MARKER
Input: List of critical intervals.
Output: Either: "No critical interval can be refined." or: Additional marker for one critical interval.
Procedure:

1. For each critical interval, do Algorithm INITIAL MARKER where the input sets are the subsets $\overline{A} \subseteq A$ and $\overline{B} \subseteq B$ of records for which the value of the associated attribute $j \in J$ falls into the critical interval. If the algorithm declares that no marker can be determined, remove the interval from the list of candidates.

2. If the list of critical intervals is empty, output "No critical interval can be refined," and stop.

3. For each critical interval, use the value δ_{i^*} and σ determined in Step 1 and the relevance count R to compute the potential $\gamma = R\delta_{i^*}/(\beta_0 - 2\beta_{\lfloor 1.5\sigma \rfloor + 1})$.

4. Select the critical interval with maximum potential. In case of a tie, favor the interval with larger number of z_i values, and break any secondary tie randomly. Using i^* of the associated δ_{i^*}, output the marker $p = (z_{i^*-1} + z_{i^*})/2$ for the selected interval, and stop.

8.   COMPUTATIONAL RESULTS

So far, the transformation methods have been used in several projects in areas such as credit rating, video image analysis, and word sense disambiguation. In these projects, the methods have proved to be effective and reliable. Results will be reported in separate papers.

We also have conducted some experiments where the Cutpoint/Lsquare combination and two Entropy/Lsquare combinations have been applied to four standard data sets. In the Entropy/Lsquare combinations, we used either entropy plus the recursive refinement method of Cutpoint or the minimum description length principle of [Fayyad and Irani; 1992, 1993] as methods to determine the markers. Compared with either one of the Entropy/Lsquare

Table 2. Performance of Cutpoint vs. Entropy

Dataset	Cutpoint	Entropy	Entropy (MDLP)
Heart	78.43	77.13	78.82
Australian	84.68	84.44	84.27
Hepatitis	81.54	82.31	80.51
Horse Colic	85.29	83.82	83.82

combinations, Cutpoint/Lsquare had modestly better performance in three of the four cases. Table 2 shows the results.

The datasets were taken from the UC Irvine repository of machine learning databases. For each of the Cleveland heart, Australian credit card, and the Hepatitis datasets, five iterations of 50% training and 50% testing were tested and averaged to give the results shown in Table 2. For the Horse Colic data, the results are for the training and testing file as given in the database. Missing entries were declared to have the value *Unavailable*.

Similar conclusions are obtained when the training sets are reduced. That is, in almost all cases, Cutpoint/Lsquare is more accurate than the two Entropy/Lsquare combinations.

At this time, we have no test results about the use of Cutpoint as a preprocessing tool for other classification methods such as decision trees, neural nets, or support vector machines.

9. SUMMARY

The transformations of set data and rational data to logic data detailed in this chapter are computationally fast and easy to implement and use. No manual effort is needed beyond decisions concerning the transformation of set data, where several transformation approaches are available.

When the transformations of this chapter are combined with the Lsquare method, a complete system for the extraction of logic formulas is at hand that does not require tuning or other adjustment or manual intervention.

ACKNOWLEDGEMENT

This research was supported in part by the Technical Support Working Group (TSWG) under contract N41756-03-C-4045.

REFERENCES

An, A. and Cercone, N. 1999. Discretization of Continuous Attributes for Learning Classification Rules. in: *Proceedings of the Third Pacific-Asia Conference on Methodologies for Knowledge Discovery and Data Mining,* pp. 509-514.

Auer, P., Holte, R. C., and Maass, W. 1995. Theory and Applications of Agnostic PAC-Learning with Small Decision Trees. in: *Proceedings of the Eighth European Conference on Machine Learning,* pp. 21-29.

Bay, S. D. and Pazzani, M. J. 1999. Detecting Change in Categorical Data: Mining Contrast Sets. in: *Proceedings of the Fifth* ACM SIGKDD *International Conference on Knowledge Discovery and Data Mining,* pp. 302-306.

Bay, S. D. 2000. Multivariate Discretization of Continuous Variables for Set Mining. in: *Proceedings of the Sixth* ACM SIGKDD *International Conference on Knowledge Discovery and Data Mining,* pp. 315-319.

Boros, E., Hammer, P. L., Ibaraki, T., and Kogan, A. 1997. A Logical Analysis of Numerical Data. *Mathematical Programming* 79, pp. 163-190.

Dougherty, J., Kohavi, R., and Sahami, M. 1995. Supervised and Unsupervised Discretization of Continuous Features. in: *Machine Learning: Proceedings of the Twelfth International Conference,* pp. 194-202.

Fayyad, U. M. and Irani, K. B. 1992. On the Handling of Continuous-Valued Attributes in Decision Tree Generation. in: *Machine Learning* 8, pp. 87-102.

Fayyad, U. M. and Irani, K. B. 1993. Multi-Interval Discretization of Continuous-Valued Attributes for Classification Learning. in: *Proceedings of the Thirteenth International Joint Conference on Artificial Intelligence,* Morgan Kaufmann, pp. 1022-1027.

Felici, G. and Truemper, K. 2002. A MINSAT approach for learning in logic domains. *INFORMS Journal on Computing* 14 20-36.

Forsyth, D. A. and Ponce, J. 2003. *Computer Vision: A Modern Approach.* Prentice Hall, Englewood Cliffs, New Jersey.

Gama, J., Torgo, L., and Soares, C. 1998. Dynamic Discretization of Continuous Attributes. in: *Proceedings of the Sixth Ibero-American Conference on Artificial Intelligence,* pp. 160-169.

Hand, D., Mannila, H., and Smyth, P. 2001. *Principles of Data Mining.* MIT Press, Cambridge, Massachusetts.

Holte, R. C. 1993. Very Simple Classification Rules Perform Well on Most Commonly Used Datasets. in: *Machine Learning* 11, pp. 63-91.

Kohavi, R. and Sahami, M. 1996. Error-Based and Entropy-Based Discretization of Continuous Features. in: *Proceedings of the Second International Conference on Knowledge Discovery and Data Mining,* pp. 114-119.

Kwedlo, W. and Krętowski, M. 1999. An Evolutionary Algorithm Using Multivariate Discretization for Decision Rule Induction. in: *Proceedings of the*

European Conference on Principles of Data Mining and Knowledge Discovery, pp. 392-397.

Maass, W. 1994. Efficient Agnostic PAC-Learning with Simple Hypotheses. in: *Proceedings of the Seventh Annual* ACM *Conference on Computerized Learning Theory*, pp. 67-75.

Miller, R. J. and Yang, Y. 1997. Association Rules over Interval Data. in: *Proceedings of the* ACM SIGMOD *International Conference on Management of Data*, pp. 452-461.

Mitchell, T. 1997. *Machine Learning.* McGraw Hill, Boston, Massachusetts.

Quinlan, J. R. 1986. Induction of Decision Trees. in: *Machine Learning 1*, pp. 81-106.

Srikant, R. and Agrawal, R. 1996. Mining Quantitative Association Rules in Large Relational Tables. in: *Proceedings of the* ACM SIGMOD *International Conference on Management of Data*, pp. 1-12.

Truemper, K. 2004. *Design of Logic-based Intelligent Systems.* Wiley, New York.

Wang, K. and Goh, H. C. 1997. Minimum Splits Based Discretization for Continuous Features. in: *Proceedings of the Fifteenth International Joint Conference on Artificial Intelligence*, pp. 942-951.

Wu, X. 1996. A Bayesian Discretizer for Real-Valued Attributes. in: *The Computer Journal 39*, pp. 688-691.

AUTHORS' BIOGRAPHICAL STATEMENTS

Stephen Bartnikowski is currently a graduate student in the Department of Computer Science of the University of Texas at Dallas, where he also received his BS. His research interests include intelligent systems and computer vision.

Matthias Granberry is currently a graduate student in the Department of Computer Science of the University of Texas at Dallas, where he also received his BS. His research interests include machine learning and natural language processing.

Jonathan Mugan is currently a graduate student in the Department of Computer Science of the University of Texas at Dallas. He received his MBA and his BA from Texas A&M University. His research interests include machine learning, data mining, and computer vision.

Dr. **Klaus Truemper** is Professor of Computer Science at the University of Texas, Dallas. Dr. Truemper received his doctorate in Operations Research from Case Western Reserve University in 1973. In 1988, he received the prestigious Senior Distinguished U.S. Scientist Award from the Alexander von Humboldt Foundation (Germany). Dr. Truemper's work includes the books Matroid Decomposition and Effective Logic Computation, and the Leibniz System software.

Chapter 8 [1]

DATA FARMING: CONCEPTS AND METHODS

Andrew Kusiak
Intelligent Systems Laboratory
Mechanical and Industrial Engineering
2139 Seamans Center
The University of Iowa
Iowa City, Iowa 52242 - 1527
Email: andrew-kusiak@uiowa.edu
Web: http://www.icaen.uiowa.edu/~ankusiak

Abstract: A typical data mining project uses data collected for various purposes, ranging from routinely gathered data, to process improvement projects, and to data required for archival purposes. In some cases, the set of considered features might be large (a wide data set) and sufficient for extraction of knowledge. In other cases the data set might be narrow and insufficient to extract meaningful knowledge or the data may not even exist.

Mining wide data sets has received attention in the literature, and many models and algorithms for feature selection have been developed for wide data sets.

Determining features for which data should be collected in the absence of an existing data set or when a data set is partially available has not been sufficiently addressed in the literature. Yet, this issue is of paramount importance as the interest in data mining is growing. The methods and process for the definition of the most appropriate features for data collection, data transformation, data quality assessment, and data analysis are referred to as data farming. This chapter outlines the elements of a data farming discipline.

Key Words: Data Farming, Data Mining, Feature Definition, Feature Functions, New Features.

---

[1] Triantaphyllou, E. and G. Felici (Eds.), **Data Mining and Knowledge Discovery Approaches Based on Rule Induction Techniques**, Massive Computing Series, Springer, Heidelberg, Germany, pp. 279-304, 2006.

1. INTRODUCTION

Data farming is concerned with methods and processes used to define the most appropriate features for data collection, data transformation, data quality assessment, and data analysis. The experience indicates that the magnitude of a data farming effort often outweighs the data mining task, especially in an industrial setting. This might be due to the fact that the industrial data is often collected for reasons other than decision-making. This data may involve a wide range of attributes (features) that go beyond traditional models. The lack of analysis tools, the limited awareness of data mining and data farming tools, and the cost reduction initiatives have contributed to scaling down some data collection efforts. Data farming mitigates this "loss" of information by enhancing the data on hand and determining the most relevant data that need to be collected.

Many data mining projects are based on data sets collected for various purposes, ranging from routinely collected data to process improvement projects and data required for archival purposes. In some cases, the set of considered features might be large (a wide data set) and sufficient for extraction of knowledge. In other cases the data set might be narrow and insufficient to extract meaningful knowledge, or the data may not even exist.

The mining of wide data sets has received the most attention in the literature. Numerous feature selection models and algorithms have been developed for such data sets. The feature selection methods can be divided into two classes:

- Open-loop methods. These methods are also called filter, preset bias, and front-end methods [Cios, *et al.,* 1998]. Features are selected based on between-class reparability criteria, e.g., covariance defined for different classes [Duda and Hart ,1973] and [Fukunaga, 1990]
- Closed-loop methods. These methods are also referred to as wrapper, performance bias, and classifier feedback methods [John, *et al.,* 1994]. Features are selected based on the performance criteria, e.g., classification accuracy.

Examples of methods for feature selection include the principle component analysis [Duda and Hart, 1973] and a branch-and-bound algorithm [Fukunaga, 1990]. The feature selection problem is computationally complex as the total number of subsets for a set with n features is 2^n, and the number of subsets with m features is $n!/(n - m)!m!$ [Cios, *et al.,* 1998].

Determining the most appropriate features for which data should be collected in the absence of a data set or its partial availability (a narrow set) has not been sufficiently addressed in the literature. Yet, this issue is of paramount importance as the interest in data mining is growing. Feature selection and data farming cover the opposite ends of the data spectrum. The former deals with a redundant number of features and the latter begins with a potentially empty set of features that gradually leads to a set of features satisfying the selected performance criteria. Feature extraction supports a push approach to data mining as the selected features determine the quality of the extracted knowledge. On the other hand, data farming pulls the data necessary for knowledge extraction.

One of the goals of data farming is to define metrics capturing the quality of the data in terms of the performance criteria, e.g., the prediction accuracy. Some of these metrics are listed next.

Section 2 of this chapter outlines elements of data farming methods. The data farming process is discussed in Section 3. The case study of Section 4 illustrates the benefits of data farming. Conclusions are drawn in Section 5.

2. DATA FARMING METHODS

The most important criteria of data farming are to obtain data that:
- Maximize performance measures (e.g., prediction accuracy, knowledge utility), and
- Minimize the data collection cost.

The two criteria directly translate into cost savings and other tangible or non-tangible benefits.

The basic methods of data farming are categorized as follows:
- Feature evaluation
- Data transformation
- Knowledge transformation
- Outcome definition
- Feature definition

Each of these data farming methods is discussed next.

2.1   Feature Evaluation

The appropriateness of data sets for knowledge extraction can be directly evaluated by the following metrics:
- Upper and lower approximation measures (defined in [Pawlak, 1991]).
- Classification quality [Pawlak, 1991].
- Entropy measure [Quinlan, 1986].
- Gini index [Breiman, *et al.,* 1984].
- Correlation, distribution type, and so on.
- Other metrics such as percentage of missing values, data error, discretization parameters, and so on.

Cross-validation [Stone, 1974] is a widely used indirect method for feature evaluation. However, this method is computationally expensive, as it requires multiple uses of learning and decision-making algorithms [Vafaie and De Jong, 1998].

The feature evaluation metrics are of interest to data farming as they assess the quality of the data set without knowledge extraction, which is computationally complex. An ideal direct feature evaluation method should be able to determine whether a given data set will satisfy the required classification accuracy or any other performance measure without the repetitive knowledge extraction process.

2.2   Data Transformation

Data sets can be mined in their raw collected form or they can be transformed. The following transformation methods can be used:
- Filling in missing values
- Discretization
- Feature content modification (generalization, specialization)
- Feature transformation
- Data evolution

The data engineering methods are illustrated next. The first three data engineering methods have received some coverage in the data mining literature.

2.2.1   Filling in Missing Values

Examples of methods and algorithms for filling in missing values include:
- The removal of examples with missing values.

- The most common value method. The missing values are replaced with the most frequent values.
- The data set decomposition method. The data set is partitioned into subsets without missing values that are in turn used for mining [Ragel and Cremilleux, 1998], [Kusiak, 2000].

Other methods for handling missing values are surveyed in [Han and Kamber, 2001].

2.2.2 Discretization

The most widely referenced discretization methods (also referred to as binning methods) are as follows:

- Equal width interval. The range of observed values is divided into k intervals of equal size. This method is vulnerable to outliers that may dramatically skew the value range, e.g., accidental typo of one value may significantly change the range.
- Equal frequency interval. The continuous values are grouped into k intervals with each interval containing m/k (possibly duplicated) adjacent values, where m is the number of examples. This method may lead to the inclusion of the same values in adjacent intervals. Both methods, the latter and the former fall into the category of unsupervised discretization methods as they do not consider decision values [Dugherty, *et al.,* 1995].
- Clustering. The intervals are created by clustering the examples [Tou and Gonzalez, 1974].
- Recursive minimal entropy. The intervals are established by considering the class information entropy [Carlett, 1991], [Fayyad and Irani, 1993].
- Recursive minimal Gini index. Similar to the entropy, the Gini index characterizes the impurity of an arbitrary collection of examples [Breiman, *et al.,* 1984].
- Recursive minimal deviance: The deviance measure aims at selecting the best binary split [Venables and Ripley, 1998].

Other discretization methods are discussed in [Cios, *et al.,* 1998] and [Han and Kamber, 2001].

2.2.3 Feature Content Modification

The feature content modification method is illustrated with the data set in Figure 1, which is representative of numerous data sets considered in medical and industrial applications.

Example 1

Consider the data set with five features and the decision shown in Figure 1.

Number	Index	Color	Material	Time	Temperature	Decision
1	TN-01	Blue	C-O-01	12	289.5	Good
2	NM-02	Red	C-R-30	78	333	Bad
3	NM-05	Orange	C-R-12	123	228	Bad
4	TN-04	Orange	C-O-02	15	321.7	Good
5	TN-14	Red	C-O-03	45	423	Good
6	NM-03	Red	C-R-11	77	630	Bad

Figure 1. A Data Set with Five Features.

A set of decision rules extracted from the data set in Figure 1 is shown in Figure 2.

```
Rule 1. IF (Index = TN-01) THEN (Quality = Good);
[1, 33.33%, 100.00%][1]
Rule 2. IF (Index = TN-04) THEN (Quality = Good);
[1, 33.33%, 100.00%][4]
Rule 3. IF (Index = TN-14) THEN (Quality = Good);
[1, 33.33%, 100.00%][5]
Rule 4. IF (Index = NM-02) THEN (Quality = Bad);
[1, 33.33%, 100.00%][2]
Rule 5. IF (Index = NM-05) THEN (Quality = Bad);
[1, 33.33%, 100.00%][3]
Rule 6. IF (Index = NM-03) THEN (Quality = Bad);
[1, 33.33%, 100.00%][6]
```

Figure 2. Rule Set Obtained from the Data Set in Figure 1.

The decision rules in Figure 2 are presented in the following format:

IF (Condition) THEN (Outcome); [Rule support, Relative rule strength, Confidence] [Objects represented by the rule].

The metrics characterizing each rule are defined next:

- *Rule support* is the number of all objects in the data set that share the property described by the conditions of the rule;
- *Rule strength* is the number of all objects in the data set that have the property described by the conditions and the action of the rule;
- *Relative rule strength* is the ratio of the rule strength and the number of all objects in a given class;
- *Confidence* is the ratio of the rule strength and the rule support.

The support of each rule in Figure 2 is only 1. These rules can be easily generalized by modifying the content of the feature "Index" in Figure 1 from TN-xx to TN and NM-xx to NM (see Figure 3).

Number	Index	Color	Material	Time	Temperature	Decision
1	TN	Blue	C-O-01	12	289.5	Good
2	NM	Red	C-R-30	78	333	Bad
3	NM	Orange	C-R-12	123	228	Bad
4	TN	Orange	C-O-02	15	321.7	Good
5	TN	Red	C-O-03	45	423	Good
6	NM	Red	C-R-11	77	630	Bad

Figure 3. Modified Data Set with Five Features.

The rules in Figure 4 have been extracted from the modified data set in Figure 3.

Rule 1:
IF (Index = TN) THEN (Quality = Good);
                [3, 100.00%, 100.00%][1, 4, 5]
Rule 2:
IF (Index = NM) THEN (Quality = Bad);
                [3, 100.00%, 100.00%][2, 3, 6]

Figure 4. Two Rules Generated from Data Set of Figure 3.

The feature generalization method is of interest to mining temporal data sets as the value of generalized features tend to be time invariant. The one-out-of n ($n = 5$) cross-validation scheme has been applied to the data sets in Figures 1 and 3. The results of cross-validation are presented in Figure 5.

As it is visible in Figures 5(c) and (d) the average classification accuracy for the data set in Figure 1 is 0% while for the modified data set of Figure 3 is 100%.

2.2.4   Feature Transformation

Constructive induction is a process of describing objects for improved classification [Wnek and Michalski, 1994] and [Bloedorn and Michalski, 1998]. New features are built from the existing ones, and some features (attributes) of objects are modified or deleted. It should be noted that the deletion of features is related to the feature selection problem [Yang and Honavar, 1998].

In this chapter, the data transformation aspect of constructive induction will be emphasized in order to improve usability, transparency, and the decision-making accuracy of the extracted rules.

While traditional data mining concentrates on establishing associations among feature values, temporal data farming is to determine the nature of feature behavior in time. In some cases, the temporal behavior of a singular feature might be difficult to capture and may not be appropriate for making predictions. Rather than concentrating on individual features, the data mining approach presented in this chapter advocates capturing relationships among feature functions.

(a)

	Good	Bad	None
Good	0	2	1
Bad	2	0	1

(b)

	Good	Bad	None
Good	3	0	0
Bad	0	3	0

Figure 5 (Part 1).   Cross-validation results: (a) Confusion Matrix for the Data Set in Figure 1, (b) Confusion Matrix for the Modified Data Set of Figure 3.

(c)	Correct	Incorrect	None
Good	0%	66.67%	33.33%
Bad	0%	66.67%	33.33%
Average	0%	66.67%	33.33%

(d)	Correct	Incorrect	None
Good	100%	0%	0%
Bad	100%	0%	0%
Average	100%	0%	0%

Figure 5 (Part 2).   Cross-validation Results: (c) Classification Accuracy for the Data Set in Figure 1, (d) Classification Accuracy for the Data Set of Figure 3.

Most data mining algorithms establish associations among individual feature values. The approach proposed in this chapter captures relationships among features in the form of feature functions. Examples of feature functions include [Kusiak, 2001]:

- Logic expression of features F_i, F_j, ..., F_n, where the <logic operator> = {AND, OR, NOT, EXOR}. Note that an ordered set of features linked by the AND operator becomes a sequence, e.g., the expression F2 AND F9 AND F4 is denoted as the sequence F2_F9_F4.

- Arithmetic expression of features F_i, F_j, ..., F_n, where the <arithmetic operator> = {+, -, /, ×, $\sqrt{}$, ^{n}, | }, e.g., F3 - 4.5×F8, |F3 - 4.2×F8|, $(.7 \times F2^3 - F4)/(2.1 \times F5^2 + .2 \times F8)$. Note that the inequality relation $F_i \geq F_j$ is equivalent to the ratio $F_i/F_j \geq 1$.

A rule involving two feature functions, a sequence 5_7_2 (a set of features F2_F4_F9), and an inequality relation is shown next.

IF (F2_F4_F9 = 5_7_2) AND (F3 < F7) THEN (D = Hot)

The feature transformation method is illustrated using Example 2. In this example the term classification quality will be used. *Classification quality* of a feature is a measure used in rough set theory to expresses the degree of association between the feature values and the outcome. It can be loosely defined as the number of objects with non-conflicting values to the total number of object in the data set. For a formal definition of the classification quality the reader may refer to [Pawlak, 1991].

Example 2

Consider the "as-is" data set in Figure 6.

No.	F1	F2	F3	F4	D
1	0	1	0	2	0
2	1	1	0	2	2
3	0	0	0	0	0
4	0	1	1	1	1
5	0	0	1	3	0

Figure 6. A Data Set with Four Features.

The classification quality (CQ) of each feature in Figure 6 is as follows: $CQ(F1) = 1/5 = .2$, $CQ(F2) = 2/5 = .4$, $CQ(F3) = 0/5 = 0$, $CQ(F4) = 3/5 = 0.6$.

The data set in Figure 6 has been transformed in the data set of Figure 7, where two features F2, F4 have been replaced with the feature sequence F2_F4 denoted for short as F2_4.

No.	F1	F2_4	F3	D
1	0	1_2	0	0
2	1	1_2	0	2
3	0	0_1	0	0
4	0	1_0	1	1
5	0	0_3	1	0

Figure 7. Transformed Data Set of Figure 6.

The classification quality of the feature sequence F2_4 has the value $CQ(F2\_4) = .6$, which is higher than the individual features F2 and F4. The one-out-of n ($n = 5$) cross-validation scheme has been applied to the rules generated from the data sets in Figures 6 and 7. The cross-validation results of the original data set (Figure 6) and the transformed dataset (Figure 7) are presented in Figure 8. The average classification accuracy has increased from 20% for the rules extracted from the data set in Figure 6 to 60% for the transformed data in Figure 7.

(a)

	Correct	Incorrect	None
Average	20%	60%	0%

(b)

	Correct	Incorrect	None
Average	60%	40%	0%

Figure 8.   Cross Validation Results: (a) Average Classification Accuracy for the Data Set in Figure 6, (b) Average Classification Accuracy for the Transformed Data Set of Figure 7.

Example 2 illustrates one of many feature transformation methods involving sequences (sets) of features. The need for more elaborate feature transformations discussed earlier in this section leads to the evolutionary computation methods. Both, the feature transformation method and the previously discussed feature content modification method can be applied simultaneously. Moreover, numerous data farming methods can be combined for the same application.

2.2.5   Data Evolution

In a typical data mining process the knowledge is extracted from the historical data. The values of each feature can be described with various statistics, e.g., the probability density function as symbolically illustrated in Figure 9. The relationships between the features (columns F1 - F4) themselves and the decision D can be also characterized by appropriate metrics, e.g., a correlation coefficient.

Rather than extracting knowledge from the original data a derived data set could be used. The latter data set could be created by using the statistical and other properties of the original data set. Changing the parameter values of these measures would evolve the source data and the extracted knowledge.

2.3   Knowledge Transformation

Structuring knowledge may result in the discovery of patterns useful in understanding the knowledge content and may lead to its generalization. The need for knowledge structuring is supported by the notion of cognitive maps and mental models discussed in [Caroll and Olson, 1987] and [Wickens, *et al.,* 1998]. Structured decision rules are easier to evaluate by a user.

As an alternative to evolving the source data, the knowledge extracted from such data could be evolved.

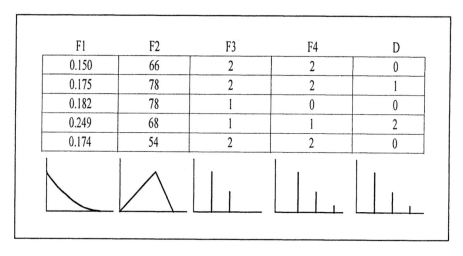

F1	F2	F3	F4	D
0.150	66	2	2	0
0.175	78	2	2	1
0.182	78	1	0	0
0.249	68	1	1	2
0.174	54	2	2	0

Figure 9. Data Set and the Corresponding Statistical Distributions.

One of the main reasons for extracting knowledge from data sets is decision-making – an area that has not received sufficient attention in the literature in the context of data mining. Most decision-making algorithms are rather simplistic and are usually based on partial or full matching schemes [Kusiak, *et al.,* 2000]. Many users have difficulty accepting decision rules that are non-intuitive and algorithms making decisions based on non-transparent matching. Here we address a gap in the presentation of knowledge for effective decision-making.

The rule-structuring concept illustrated in Example 3 generates knowledge in a form that meets user expectations.

Example 3

Consider the eight rules R1 – R8 represented as the rule-feature matrix in Figure 10.

F1_F6_F7	F2	F3	F4	F5	D	Rule	Algorithm
B_C_D	a				Low	R1	A1
C_F		<4			Medium	R8	A1
			>2		Medium	R5	A1
			(2, 9]		Medium	R2	A2
		(2, 6]		=<8	High	R3	A2
			<2	(2, 5]	Low	R7	A3
E_F_G	b				Low	R4	A3
		>=2		[1, 3]	High	R6	A3

Figure 10.   Rule-Feature Matrix with Eight Rules.

Three different learning algorithms A1 – A3 were used to extract the eight decision rules R1 – R8 from a data set. To simplify our considerations the information pertinent to each rule such as support, classification quality, and so on has not been included. The first row (beside the header) in Figure 10 reads as follows: IF (F1_ F6_ F7 = B_ C_ D) AND (F2 = a) THEN (D = Low). The last entry of this row indicates that this rule has been derived with algorithm A1.

Though the rule set in Figure 10 is small, its analysis is not simple. Transforming the matrix in Figure 10 into the structured matrix in Figure 11 significantly improves interpretation and understanding of this rule set. Solving the model (1) – (5), presented later in this section, for the data in Figure 10 has resulted in the matrix of Figure 11. Two rules, R7 and R8, have been removed from the structured matrix as they are dissimilar to the rules R1 through R6.

F3	F5	F2	F1_F6_F7	F4	D	Rule	Algorithm
(2, 6]	=<8				High	R3	A2
>=2	[1, 3]				High	R6	A3
		a	B_C_D		Low	R1	A1
		b	E_F_G		Low	R4	A3
				>2	Medium	R2	A2
				(2, 9]	Medium	R5	A1

Figure 11.   Structured Rule-Feature Matrix.

The contents of the matrix in Figure 11 are structured and they allow drawing numerous conclusions, for example:

- The decisions D = High, Medium, and Low are totally separated by features, i.e., decision D = High is made based on values of two features F3 and F5 that do not appear in the other two decisions.
- The rules R3 and R6 are good candidates for the following generalization IF (F3 ≥ 2) AND (F5 ≤ 8) THEN (D = High).
- The decision D = Low can be reached in alternative ways, using the feature values F2 = a, or F1_F6_F7 = B_C_D, or F2 = b, or F1_F6_F7 = E_F_G.
- Rule R2 is more general than rule R5.

Example 3 illustrates only a few of the users' requirements that can be incorporated in the rule-structuring algorithm, such as:

- Classification accuracy. The knowledge included in the structured matrix is cross validated and tested to ensure the required level of classification accuracy.
- Matrix structure. To help the user better understand the rule-feature matrix, different structures may be considered, e.g., a block-diagonal (see Figure 11), a block-diagonal matrix with overlapping features, the block-diagonal matrix with overlapping rules, a triangular (for dependency analysis among rules), an L-shape matrix, a T-shape matrix, etc.
- Differentiation of decisions on features. This occurs when each decision value is associated with an independent subset of features.
- Differentiation of decisions on feature values. This occurs when any two decision values are discernable on a unique subset of feature values.
- Inclusion of user preferences. To increase confidence in the rules, a user may wish to have her/his feature preferences included in the selected rules, to exclude some features, to establish a lower bound on the number of features, and so on.
- Contrasting positive rules against negative ones.

The learning classifier systems (e.g., [Wilson, 1995] and [Kovacs, 2001]) and other learning concepts such as decision tree and decision rule algorithms are perceived as different. The former is based on concepts from evolutionary biology and the latter draws from information theory and mathematical logic. It appears that the two classes of algorithms share more commonality than indicated in the current literature. This unifying view results from the fact that the "machine learning school" assumes that the learning data set remains static. Filling in missing data, discretization, and feature content modification are the only three methods of data transformation. The two data transformation methods of data engineering discussed in this chapter (i.e., feature transformation and data evolution) involve the evolutionary computation concepts. For example, a typical learning algorithm produces a decision rule as follows:

```
IF (F3 = 7) AND (F5 ∈ [7.1, 12.4]) AND (F6 = 4)
THEN (D = No)
```

Each term in the above rule is concerned with a single feature.

The data and knowledge transformation concepts advocated in this chapter lead to richer decision rules that may contain relationships between feature functions, in particular the feature sequence Seq illustrated by the following rule:

```
IF (F3 < F4) AND (F5/F8 ≥ 3) AND (Seq = f7_f9_f11) THEN
(D = No)
```

The computational experience presented in [Cattral, *et al.*, 2001] indicates that the classification accuracy of the decision rules involving relationships between features exceeds those of the traditional decision rules.

To generate these robust and high quality results, the learning algorithms may remain essentially unchanged or in some cases require only minor modifications.

A user is interested in viewing the context of the knowledge used for decision-making from different perspectives, even if a decision is reached autonomously. The variability among knowledge viewing preferences grows with the number of users. Potential knowledge visualization patterns include a decision table, a decision rule, a decision tree, a graph, a bar chart, a pie chart, and a data cube that can be expressed with a Voronoi diagram, a Gabriel graph, Delaunay's approach, a relative neighborhood graph, a minimum spanning tree [Preparata and Shamos, 1985]. Note that one pattern, e.g., a decision tree, can be transformed into another pattern, e.g., a decision table. The decision table provides a multitude of knowledge visualization patterns (views) such as:

- Rule – feature view (see Figure 11).
- Rule – feature function view.
- Object – feature view.
- Cluster of objects – feature view.
- Cluster of objects – group of features view.
- Rule – rule view.
- Chain of rules view (for multistage decision processes).

- Rule performance metric (e.g., rule strength, confidence, discrimination) view.

The rules themselves can be illustrated graphically. One possible representation of a cluster of two rules is shown in Figure 12.

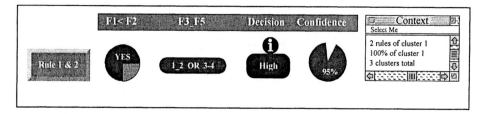

Figure 12.   Visual Representation of a Cluster of Two Rules.

The above views call for knowledge structuring to be accomplished by solving various models. One of such models, the generalized p–median model, is illustrated next [Kusiak, 2002].

Define:
n   =   the total number of decision rules
m   =   the number of features (used to compute the distance d_{ij})
l =   the number of rule categories
F_k =   the set of decision rules from source k, k $= 1,..., l$, where $|\cup_k F_k| = n$
p   =   the minimum number of rule clusters
q_k =   the minimum number of rules to be selected for rule category k
d_{ij} =   the distance between rules i and j
c_j =   the performance index of rule j
α, β =   constants used in the objective function
x_{ij} =   1, if rules i and j are selected, otherwise $x_{ij} = 0$
x_j =   1, if rules j is selected, otherwise $x_j = 0$

The objective of the generalized p–median model is to minimize the total weighted distance between the rules and the rule performance index. The two constants α and β are used as the weights.

Min $\alpha \sum_i \sum_j d_{ij} x_{ij} + \beta \sum_j c_j x_{jj}$ (1)

s.t. $\sum_{i \in F_k} \sum_j x_{ij} \geq q_k$ for all $k = 1,..., l;$ $j = 1,..., n$ (2)

          $\sum_j x_{ij} \geq p$ for all $j = 1,..., n$ (3)

          $x_{ij} \leq x_{jj}$ for all $i = 1,..., n ;$ $j = 1,..., n$ (4)

          $x_{ij} = 0, 1$ for all $i = 1,..., n ;$ $j = 1,..., n$ (5)

Constraint (2) ensures that for each rule category at least q_k rules are selected. Constraint (3) imposes a lower bound on the number of rule clusters. Constraint (4) ensures that a pair of rules, i and j, can be selected only when the corresponding cluster is formed. Constraint (5) imposes the integrality of the decision variable.

The input to the p–median model is a set of rules of different categories. For example, a rule category can be based on the learning algorithm type, decision type, rule type (positive, negative, etc.), feature transformation method, and so on.

Solving the generalized p–median model for the data in Figure 10 has resulted in the structured matrix in Figure 11. The p–median model has been solved with the LINDO software [LINDO, 2003].

2.4   Outcome Definition

Some outcomes may be either not defined or assigned in error, e.g., misclassified by one or two classes. For unsupervised learning (not defined outcomes), clustering methods can be applied to define and validate the outcome values. For cases with the outcomes assigned in error, unsupervised and supervised learning may be warranted. An outcome definition method is illustrated in Example 4.

Example 4

Consider the data in Figure 13 with five features (e.g., maximum torque, temperature, and number of hours and corresponding rules (Figure 14) derived using a rough set algorithm.

No.	F1	F2	F3	F4	F5	D
1	0	0	1	0	2	0
2	2	1	1	0	2	1
3	0	0	0	0	1	0
4	1	0	1	1	0	1
5	0	0	0	1	3	0

Figure 13. A Data Set with Five Features.

Rule 1:
IF (F1 = 0) THEN (D = 0);
                    [3, 100.00%, 100.00%][1, 3, 5]
Rule 2:
IF (F1 ∈ {1, 2}) THEN (D = 1);
                    [2, 100.00%, 100.00%][2, 4]

Figure 14. Rules from the Data Set of Figure 13.

Assume that some values of the outcome D in Figure 13 were assigned in error, e.g., the fault type was improperly coded. The analysis of the data in Figure 13 and other background information has lead to changing the value of the decision for object 2 from D = 1 to D = 2. The rules extracted from the data set with the modified outcome are shown in Figure 15.

Rule 3:
IF (F1 = 0) THEN (D = 0);   [3, 100.00%, 100.00%][1, 3, 5]
Rule 4:
IF (F1 = 1) THEN (D = 1);   [1, 100.00%, 100.00%][4]
Rule 5:
IF (F1 = 2) THEN (D = 2);   [1, 100.00%, 100.00%][2]

Figure 15. Rules Extracted from the Transformed Data Set of Figure 13.

The one-out-*n* (*n* = 5 objects) cross-validation scheme was applied to the data set in Figure 13 and its transformed form.   The results of cross-validation are shown in Figure 16.

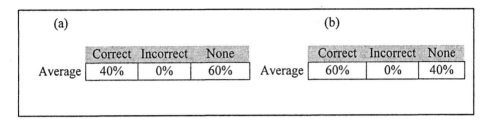

Figure 16.   Cross Validation Results: (a) Average Classification Accuracy for the Modified Data Set in Figure 13; (b) Average Classification Accuracy of the Data Set with Modified Outcome.

Figure 16, parts (a) and (b), shows that the data set with modified outcome provided better classification accuracy than the source data set of Figure 13.

2.5   Feature Definition

The previously discussed data farming methods enhance the data and knowledge of an existing set of features. The feature definition approach is concerned with the definition of new features for which the data must be collected.   In this setting, the maximization of the performance of the extracted knowledge and the minimization of the data collection cost are extremely important.

Methods of defining candidate features include:
- Parameters and variables of equations
- Object and environment descriptions
- Design of experiments

The ultimate goal of data farming is to extract useful knowledge that represents associations among features and decisions. Science offers expressions (e.g., reliability formula) that might be helpful in the definition of new features. In some cases it may be useful to map the associations as a methodology, e.g., the process methodology presented in [Kruchten *et al.* 2000].

The newly defined features should allow for building strong associations with the outcome. The data mining experience with numerous data sets indicates that the most promising feature types include:

- Chemistry based features (e.g., calcium content)
- Biology based features (e.g., genetics)
- Time and frequency (e.g., number of years in use, number of tasks performed)
- Control parameters (e.g., temperature)

3.   THE DATA FARMING PROCESS

Data mining applications call for the definition of appropriate features and data collection at minimal cost. The data farming process includes the following steps:

Step 1. Setting a data farming goal.
Step 2. Definition of candidate features and dependency analysis (discussed later in this section).
Step 3. Selection and application of suitable data farming methods.
Step 4. Data mining process.
Step 5. Evaluation of the data farming goal.

These steps can be implemented sequentially or in parallel.

Step 2 above has not been discussed thus far. It involves determining a candidate set of features and the identification of the dependencies between them. These features may be targeted for data collection. Dependencies among features, though not absolutely essential in data farming, may be important for understanding the data set. Some of the methods for feature dependency analysis are discussed in the following paragraphs.

Numerous methods and tools have been developed for the analysis of systems. The primary methods that can be used for feature dependency recording and analysis are as follows:

- Feature map. For example, a graph showing relationships between features that may take different forms, e.g., a fish bone diagram used in statistics and a link analysis graph [Barry and Linoff, 1997].
- Structure breakdown methods for a problem, a process, or a product. For example, a diagram visualizing hierarchical representation of the studied phenomenon (a problem, a process, or a product).

- Process models. Numerous process models and tools developed in the context of process engineering can be used to analyze dependencies among features (see [Kusiak, 1999] for review of process modeling tools and methods).
- Semantic networks. Though primarily used to represent knowledge, semantic networks can be applied to represent concepts, including the relationships between features.

In addition to the above tools, methodologies and software used to model information systems or processes can be used to analyze dependencies among features, e.g., Yourdon, Gane-Sarson, Express-G, and Rumbaugh diagrams.

The dependency among features can be analyzed in two modes:
- Forward mode (feature – decision direction)
- Reverse mode (decision – feature direction)

Most often the two modes are combined while analyzing features.

The type of data farming method used depends on the purpose of data mining. The main purposes of data mining are as follows:
- Gaining insights into the problem studied
- Learning
- Decision-making with the discovered knowledge

While the first purpose may be accomplished with a rather small data set, the last two call for sufficiently wide and long data sets that are typically obtained at a higher cost.

4.   A CASE STUDY

Some of the data farming concepts discussed in this chapter have been applied to an equipment diagnosis application.   A database with the maintenance records in excess of 1 GB was available for analysis. The data collected on more than 300 features was distributed over 26 different Microsoft Access tables. The number of objects in each table varied from twenty to about 100,000. The goal of the study was to predict the duration MAINT_TIME of a service action performed on different types of equipment. The analysis of the data with dependency diagrams has revealed that most features were irrelevant to the study as the data was collected over many years to meet operational requirements imposed over time.

For the purpose of prediction of MAINT_TIME a data set with 644 objects was extracted by merging three data tables with maintenance related features. The length of the shortest data set dictated the number of objects. Some objects were missing most feature values and therefore the number of objects was reduced to 599 and 17 features (15 categorical and integer, and two continuous) and the decision MAINT_TIME which was continuous. The data set was discretized with three intervals resulting in the following classes (1, 2, and 3) for the decision MAINT_TIME:

MAINT_TIME: (< 0.25) ~ 1, [0.25, 0.35) ~ 2, [>0.35) ~ 3,

where (<0.25) ~ 0 means that the maintenance time of less than .25 [hour] was labeled as category 0, the maintenance time in the interval [0.25, 0.35) was labeled as category 1, and the maintenance time greater than 0.35 [hour] was labeled as category 2.

Different learning algorithms have been applied to extract rules and the number of rules was generally large. A rough set algorithm [Pawlak, 1982; and 1991] produced some of the most interesting rules (102 exact and 19 approximate rules).

The $k = 10$ fold validation with the rough set algorithm has produced the results in Figure 17, which are encouraging considering the nature of the data considered in this study.

	Correct	Incorrect	None
Average	68.45%	31.38%	0.17%

Figure 17.   Average Classification Accuracy for the 599-Object Data Set.

Further analysis of the 599-object data set has revealed that some maintenance actions involved multiple elementary actions. The results in Figure 17 include both types of actions. The MAINT_TIME for multiple maintenance actions in the 599-object data set were aggregated thus resulting in 525 objects.

The 525-object data set was discretized with the previously used scheme and produced the cross validation results in Figure 18. These results are not substantially different from the results in Figure 17.

	Correct	Incorrect	None
Average	69.19%	30.61%	0.19%

Figure 18. Average Classification Accuracy for the 525-Object Data Set.

Creating sequences of two variables at a time produced some of the most interesting results. Two such results are illustrated in Figure 19 for the following MAINT_TIME discretization scheme:

MAINT_TIME: (<0.25) ~ 0, [0.25, 4.75) ~ 1, [>4.75) ~ 2

	Correct	Incorrect	None
Average	79.52%	20.48%	0.00%

Figure 19. Average Classification Accuracy for the 525-Object Data Set with the Feature Sequence.

Please also notice that the results in Figure 19 indicate that the average classification accuracy is much better than that of Figure 18.

The main goal of this case study was to prove that the maintenance data collected during regular operations contained some useful patterns that could be used to predict values of parameters, including the maintenance time. Some of the data farming methods applied in this study enhanced the value of this data set. Extensions of the classification quality measure and some statistical metrics will be used to define more relevant features for which the data should be collected.

5.   CONCLUSIONS

The purpose of knowledge discovery is to gain insights into the problem studied, or using the discovered knowledge for decision-making. These objectives can be realized, if proper data is collected. The appropriateness of data and the data collection cost are the goals of data farming that, among others, offers tools for the definition of appropriate features for which the data is to be collected at an acceptable cost. The data farming methods presented in this chapter are intended to enhance the data collection process, add value to the collected data, and define new features for which the data should be collected. The data farming concepts presented in this chapter were illustrated with numerical examples and a case study.

REFERENCES

Barry, M.J.A. and G. Linoff (1997), *Data Mining Techniques: For Marketing, Sales, and Customer Support*, John Wiley, New York.

Bloedorn, E. and R.S. Michalski (1998), Data-driven constructive induction, *IEEE Intelligent Systems*, Vol. 13, No. 2, pp. 30-37.

Breiman, L., J.H. Friedman, R.A. Olshen, and P.J. Stone (1984), *Classification and Regression Trees*, Wadworth International Group, Belmont, CA.

Carlett, J. (1991), Megainduction: Machine Learning on Very Large Databases, Ph.D. Thesis, Department of Computer Science, University of Sydney, Australia.

Caroll, J.M. and J. Olson (1987), *Mental Models in Human-Computer Interaction: Research Issues About the User of Software Knows*, National Academy Press, Washington, DC.

Cattral, R., F. Oppacher, and D. Deugo (2001), Supervised and unsupervised data mining with an evolutionary algorithm, *Proceedings of the 2001 Congress on Evolutionary Computation*, IEEE Press, Piscataway, NJ, pp. 767-776.

Cios, K., W. Pedrycz, and R. Swiniarski (1998), *Data Mining: Methods for Knowledge Discovery*, Kluwer, Boston, MA.

Dugherty, D., R. Kohavi, and M. Sahami (1995), Supervised and unsupervised discretization of continuous features, *Proceedings of the 12th International Machine Learning Conference*, pp. 194-202.

Duda, R.O. and P.E. Hart (1973), *Pattern Recognition and Scene Analysis*, John Wiley, New York.

Fayyad, U.M. and K.B. Irani (1993), Multi-interval discretization of continuously-valued attributes for classification learning, *Proceedings of the 13th International Joint Conference on Artificial Intelligence*, pp. 1022-1027.

Fukunaga, K. (1990), *Introduction to Statistical Pattern Analysis*, Academic Press, San Diego, CA.

Han, J. and M. Kamber (2001), *Data Mining: Concepts and Techniques*, Morgan Kaufmann, San Diego, CA.

John, G., R. Kohavi, and K. Pfleger (1994), Irrelevant features and the subset selection problem, *Proceedings of the 11th International Conference on Machine Learning, ICLM'94*, Morgan Kaufmann, San Diego, CA, pp. 121-127.

Kruchten, P. (2000), *The Rational Unified Process: An Introduction*, Addison-Wesley, New York, 2000.

Kovacs, T. (2001), What should a classifier system learn, *Proceedings of the 2001 Congress on Evolutionary Computation*, IEEE Press, Piscataway, NJ, pp. 775-782.

Kusiak, A. (1999), *Engineering Design: Products, Processes, and Systems*, Academic Press, San Diego, CA.

Kusiak, A. (2000), Decomposition in data mining: an industrial case study, *IEEE Transactions on Electronics Packaging Manufacturing*, Vol. 23, No. 4, pp. 345-353.

Kusiak, A., J.A. Kern, K.H. Kernstine, and T.L. Tseng (2000), Autonomous decision-making: A data mining approach, *IEEE Transactions on Information Technology in Biomedicine*, Vol. 4, No. 4, pp. 274-284.

Kusiak, A. (2001), Feature transformation methods in data mining, *IEEE Transactions on Electronics Packaging Manufacturing*, Vol. 24, No. 3, 2001, pp. 214-221.

Kusiak, A. (2002), A Data Mining Approach for Generation of Control Signatures, *ASME Transactions: Journal of Manufacturing Science and Engineering*, Vol. 124, No. 4, pp. 923-926.

LINDO (2003), http://www.lindo.com (Accessed June 5, 2003).

Pawlak Z. (1982), Rough sets, *International Journal of Information and Computer Science*, Vol. 11, No. 5, pp. 341-356.

Pawlak, Z. (1991), *Rough Sets: Theoretical Aspects of Reasoning About Data*, Kluwer, Boston, MA.

Preparata, F.P. and Shamos, M.I. (1985), *Pattern Recognition and Scene Analysis*, Springer-Verlag, New York.

Quinlan, J.R. (1986), Induction of decision trees, *Machine Learning*, Vol. 1, No 1, pp. 81-106.

Ragel, A. and B. Cremilleux (1998), Treatment of missing values for association rules, *Proceedings of the Second Pacific Asia Conference, PAKDD '98*, Melbourne, Australia.

Stone, M. (1974), Cross-validatory choice and assessment of statistical predictions, *Journal of the Royal Statistical Society*, Vol. 36, pp.111-147.

Slowinski, R. (1993), Rough set learning of preferential attitude in multi-criteria decision making, in Komorowski, J. and Ras, Z. (Eds), *Methodologies for Intelligent Systems*, Springer-Verlag, Berlin, Germany, pp. 642-651.

Tou, J.T. and R.C. Gonzalez (1974), *Pattern Recognition Principles*, Addison Wesley, New York.

Vafaie, H. and K. De Jong (1998), Feature space transformation using genetic algorithms, *IEEE Intelligent Systems*, Vol. 13, No. 2, pp. 57-65.

Venables, W.N. and B.D. Ripley (1998), *Modern Statistics with S-PLUS*, Springer-Verlag, New York.

Wickens, G., S.E. Gordon, and Y. Liu (1998), *An Introduction to Human Factors Engineering*, Harper Collins, New York.

Wilson, S.W. (1995), Classifier fitness based on accuracy, *Evolutionary Computation*, Vol. 3, No. 2, pp. 149-175.

Wnek, J. and R.S. Michalski (1994), Hypothesis-driven constructive induction in AQ17-HCI: A method and experiments, *Machine Learning*, Vol. 14, No, 2, pp. 139-168.

Yang, J. and V. Honavar (1998), Feature subset selection using a genetic algorithm, *IEEE Intelligent Systems*, Vol. 13, No. 2, pp. 44-49.

AUTHOR'S BIOGRAPHICAL STATEMENT

Dr. Andrew Kusiak is a Professor of Mechanical and Industrial Engineering at the University of Iowa, Iowa City. He is interested in applications of data mining, computational intelligence, and optimization in engineering and medicine. He has authored and edited books and handbooks and published papers in journals sponsored by societies, such as AAAI, ASME, IEEE, IIE, ESOR, IFIP, IFAC, INFORMS, ISPE, and SME. He speaks frequently at international meetings, conducts professional seminars, and consults for industrial corporations. He has served on editorial boards of over twenty journals and as editor of book series. Dr. Kusiak is the Editor-in-Chief of the *Journal of Intelligent Manufacturing*.

Chapter 9 [1]

RULE INDUCTION THROUGH DISCRETE SUPPORT VECTOR DECISION TREES

Carlotta Orsenigo and Carlo Vercellis [2]
Politecnico di Milano
P.za Leonardo da Vinci 32, I20133 Milano, Italy
Email: carlotta.orsenigo@polimi.it, carlo.vercellis@polimi.it
Web: http://www.dep.polimi.it/eng/comunita/cl.php?id=70

Abstract: We present a rule induction method based on decision trees for classification and prediction problems. Our approach to tree construction relies on a discrete variant of support vector machines, in which the error is expressed by the number of misclassified instances, in place of the misclassification distance considered by traditional SVMs, and an additional term is included to reduce the complexity of the generated rule. This leads to the formulation of a mixed integer programming problem, whose approximate solution is obtained via a sequential LP-based algorithm. The decision tree is then built by means of a multivariate split derived at each node from the approximate solution of the discrete SVM. Computational tests on well-known benchmark datasets indicate that our classifier achieves a superior trade-off between accuracy and complexity of the induced rules, outperforming other competing approaches.

Key Words: Classification, Decision Trees, Support Vector Machines, Rule Induction.

---

[1] Triantaphyllou, E. and G. Felici (Eds.), **Data Mining and Knowledge Discovery Approaches Based on Rule Induction Techniques**, Massive Computing Series, Springer, Heidelberg, Germany, pp. 305-326, 2006.

[2] Corresponding Author.

1.   INTRODUCTION

The ability to extract general rules from a set of observed data is a fundamental requirement of knowledge acquisition. For this reason, rule induction algorithms have been widely adopted to solve classification and prediction tasks in machine learning and data mining applications in such diversified fields as marketing, credit approval and medical diagnosis. For example, suppose we are investigating the behavior of the customers of an insurance company to understand which features determine their loyalty. Hence, we know for each customer a binary *target class* indicating whether the customer has remained loyal or has switched to a competitor. Furthermore, we are given the values of a number of *attributes*, such as age, income, number of owned cars, for each customer in our database. We are then required to learn from the available data and to predict with the maximum accuracy the unknown class for new customers in the future. The logical structure of this example can be easily generalized. In classification problems a dataset is given, composed by a set of *instances* whose associated *class* is already known. It is asked to learn from the existing data, discovering hidden patterns useful to predict the *class* of new unseen instances. Although this prediction process could derive from a black-box approach, in most applications of data mining it is also required the classification rules generated be simple, modular, intuitive, intelligible and easy to understand by decision makers and domain experts.

Decision trees have been widely recognized as one of the most effective techniques for rule induction in classification problems, particularly when dealing with business oriented applications, such as those arising in the frame of customer relationship management. Indeed, it has been empirically observed that for most classification problems decision trees easily lead to discrimination rules which can be well understood by marketing managers, without a relevant loss in accuracy with respect to alternative classification approaches, such as neural networks or statistical discriminant analysis. The reader is referred to (Murthy, 1998), (Safavin and Landgrebe, 1991) for comprehensive surveys on classification trees. Most authors focused on myopic univariate splits, based on information theoretic concepts, for deriving the ramifications at each node of a decision tree, as in CART (Breiman, et al., 1984) or C4.5 (Quinlan, 1993); more sophisticated approaches based on a multivariate split at each node have been recently proposed, aimed at achieving an overall better accuracy. Again, refer to (Murthy, 1998) for a review of the most significant contributions in this field.

In this chapter we propose a rule induction method based on decision trees for binary classification problems. The optimization problem formulated at each node of the tree to derive a multivariate linear split is a *minimum features discrete support vector machine* (FDVM). By this term we refer to a variant of discrete support vector machines (DSVM), a family of optimization models in which the classification error is expressed by the count of misclassified instances, denoted as misclassification *rate*, in place of the misclassification *distance* considered by traditional SVM approaches. From the solution to model FDVM, obtained at each node of the tree, we derive a linear combination of the attributes, representing the *best* hyperplane which separates the instances belonging to the node. The first contribution within the DSVM framework has been proposed in (Orsenigo and Vercellis, 2004), where the generation of an optimal separating hyperplane is based on the simultaneous maximization of the accuracy and the generalization capability of the classifier, by solving a mixed integer problem (MIP) via a tabu search heuristic. An extension of this model has been provided in (Orsenigo and Vercellis, 2003), where a third term into the objective function is introduced, in order to reduce the number of active attributes utilized for discrimination, and a new approximate algorithm based on the iterative solution of a finite sequence of linear programming problems is developed to solve the resulting MIP model.

The methodology described in this chapter significantly extends previous mathematical programming approaches to multivariate splits for the construction of classification trees, due to differences in the objective function and in the solution technique. The minimization of the misclassification rate has been considered previously in the literature. From one side, some papers (Mangasarian, 1994, 1996; Chunhui Chen and Mangasarian, 1996; La Torre and Vercellis, 2003) focused on the misclassification rate alone, not in conjunction with the generalization capability, and transformed the discrete problem into a nonlinear optimization model by means of appropriate smoothing techniques. On the other hand, some MIP models were formulated (Koehler and Erenguc, 1990; Lam, et al., 1996), but again without including generalization concepts into the objective function. Furthermore, several linear and quadratic programming models to build classification trees were proposed (Mangasarian, et al., 1990; Mangasarian 1993; Bennett and Mangasarian 1992, 1994), but they were confined to the minimization of the misclassification distance. More recently, Bennett et al. (2000) considered the combined inclusion into the objective function of both generalization and misclassification distance; however, they did not consider the misclassification rate, which leads to remarkable improvements in both classification accuracy and complexity of the generated rules, as the computational experiences discussed in section 6 seem to show.

To obtain an empirical validation of the proposed algorithm, we have tested it on several well-known datasets used in the literature for benchmarking alternative classifiers. The comparison with other classification approaches, particularly those based on decision trees, shows that our classifier is able to generate trees that are more accurate, capable of good generalization and characterized by simple rules, where rule complexity is evaluated by counting both the number of leaves of the resulting decision trees and the number of active attributes utilized for discrimination. In particular, we show that even when our algorithm is forced to build trees with only one rule and two leaves, yet it still achieves the highest accuracy among all competing techniques. Furthermore, the empirical evidence indicates also that the inclusion of the term accounting for the generalization capability into the objective function brings an advantage over the approach in which only the misclassification rate is minimized. Finally, trees generated by means of the misclassification rate are significantly more accurate than their counterparts obtained by taking into the objective function the misclassification distance.

2.   LINEAR SUPPORT VECTOR MACHINES

In classification we are required to extract rules for discriminating between distinct pattern sets. A classification problem can be formally stated as follows. Given m points $(x_i, y_i), i \in M = \{1, 2, \ldots m\}$, in the $(n+1)$-dimensional real space $\mathbf{R}^{n+1}$, where $x_i = (x_{i1}, x_{i2}, \ldots x_{in})$ is a n-dimensional vector and y_i a scalar, we are required to determine a discriminant function f_α from $\mathbf{R}^n$ into the real line $\mathbf{R}$, such that $f_\alpha(x_i) = y_i, i \in M$. Here α is a vector of adjustable parameters by which the discriminant function is labeled. Each point can be interpreted as an instance, the coordinates of the vector x_i as the values of the attributes, and the target y_i as the class to which the instance belongs. It is further assumed that the m points are independently drawn from some common unknown probability distribution $P(x, y)$. The attention in this chapter is confined to the two-class classification problem, in which the target y_i can assume only two different values, labeled by $\{-1, +1\}$; that is, $y_i \in \{-1, +1\}$. Let also A and B denote the two sets of points represented by the vectors x_i in the space $\mathbf{R}^n$ and corresponding respectively to the classes $y_i = -1$ and $y_i = +1$. If the two point sets A and B are linearly separable at least a discriminating hyperplane $f_\alpha(x) = wx - b$ exists separating the points in A from those in B, i.e.

$$wx_i - b > 0, \quad x_i \in A, \quad \text{and} \quad wx_i - b < 0, \quad x_i \in B. \tag{1}$$

In this case, arising whenever the convex hulls of the point sets A and B do not intersect, the coefficients $w \in \mathbf{R}^n$ and $b \in \mathbf{R}$ can be determined from the solution of a linear programming problem, as in (Mangasarian, 1965). If the point sets A and B are not linearly separable, more complex classification algorithms have to be designed, such as decision trees, neural networks and support vector machines. All these approaches are aimed at deriving a discriminant function which minimizes some measure of violation for inequalities (1). In order to assess the accuracy of a classification method, and to identify the best classifier among alternative competing techniques, the point set $A \cup B$ is usually partitioned into two disjoint subsets, termed respectively as the *training* and the *validation* set. For a given classifier, the discriminant function is then computed using only instances from the training set, and then applied to predict the class of each instance in the validation set, in order to estimate the accuracy of the classifier against unseen data.

In this section we summarize the basics of linear *support vector machines* (SVM), an effective approach to classification based upon the structural risk minimization (SRM) principle formulated by Vapnik (1995, 1998). The SRM principle, described below, formally establishes that a good classifier trained on a given dataset should minimize a weighted sum of the empirical classification error and the generalization error, in order to achieve a high discrimination capability on unseen data. The SVM approach approximates the misclassification error with the sum of the slacks of the training points from the canonical supporting hyperplanes, as described below, albeit in a classification problem the error should be evaluated by a discrete function counting the number of misclassified instances. However, the continuous proxy of the error has the computational advantage of avoiding the overwhelming complexity of mixed integer programming models, permitting to apply efficient techniques of linear programming (LP).

The *actual risk* associated to a discriminant function f_α is defined as the expectation of the test error for the given trained machine f_α

$$R(\alpha) = \int \frac{1}{2} | y - f_\alpha(x) | \, dP(x, y). \tag{2}$$

The mean error rate evaluated over the training set is called instead *empirical risk*, and is defined as

$$R_{emp}(\alpha) = \frac{1}{2m} \sum_{i=1}^{m} | y_i - f_\alpha(x_i) |. \tag{3}$$

The expression $\frac{1}{2} | y_i - f_\alpha(x_i) |$ is called *loss*, and can assume only the values 0 and 1 in binary classification problems, so that $m R_{emp}(\alpha)$ counts the number of misclassified points. Let h be an assigned nonnegative integer parameter, called the Vapnik-Chervonenkis (VC) dimension. It can be shown that the VC dimension h for the class of linear discriminating functions, represented by the hyperplanes in $\mathbf{R}^n$, equals $n+1$. Given a desired probability level $1-\eta$, $0 \leq \eta \leq 1$, the following fundamental bound was shown to hold (Vapnik, 1995):

$$R(\alpha) \leq \sqrt{\left(\frac{h(\log(2m/h)+1)-\log(\eta/4)}{m} \right)} + R_{emp}(\alpha). \tag{4}$$

According to the SRM principle, in order to reduce the expected error $R(\alpha)$, at least in a probabilistic sense, we are led to minimize the right hand-side in (4), called *risk bound*. The first term in this bound is called *VC confidence*, and expresses a measure of the generalization capacity of the discriminant function.

For the particular case of linear discriminating functions, the minimization of the VC confidence is related to the maximization of the *margin of separation*, defined as the distance between the pairs of the parallel canonical supporting hyperplanes $wx - b - 1 = 0$ and $wx - b + 1 = 0$. The margin of separation, whose geometric interpretation is provided in Figure 1 for two linearly inseparable point sets, is given by:

$$\frac{2}{\|w\|_2}, \quad \text{where} \quad \|w\|_2 = \sqrt{\sum_{j \in N} w_j^2} \quad \text{denotes the 2-norm } (N = \{1, 2, \ldots n\}). \tag{5}$$

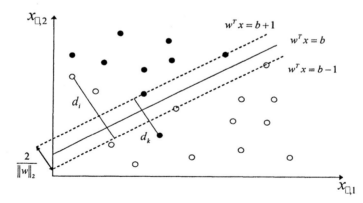

Figure 1. Margin Maximization for Linearly non Separable Sets.

The problem of determining the best separating hyperplane is formulated as follows in the SVM framework. For each instance of the dataset define a nonnegative variable $d_i, i \in M$, representing the slack between the point x_i and the canonical supporting hyperplane corresponding to its class. Notice that the slack can be geometrically interpreted as the distance along the vertical axis between the point itself and the canonical hyperplane, as shown in Figure 1. It is clear that $d_i \geq 1$ whenever point i is misclassified. One can therefore determine the optimal hyperplane by solving the following quadratic programming model, where $\beta \in [0,1]$ is a parameter available to users in order to control the trade-off between the misclassification error and the generalization capability of the classifier:

$$\min_{w,b,d} \quad \frac{\beta}{2}\|w\|_2^2 + (1-\beta)\sum_{i \in M} d_i \qquad \text{(QSVM)}$$

$$\text{s.to} \quad y_i(wx_i - b) \geq 1 - d_i, \quad i \in M \qquad (6)$$

$$d_i \geq 0, i \in M.$$

The two addends in the objective function of model QSVM correspond to the two terms in the right hand side of (4). We have already seen that the reciprocal of the margin of separation translates the VC confidence, whereas the second term is introduced in the SVM context as a continuous proxy of the discrete empirical error. Thus, what is actually minimized in QSVM is a weighted sum of the reciprocal of the margin and a concept of misclassification distance, which only approximately measures the empirical error, actually represented by the misclassification rate.

Notice that problem QSVM can be reformulated as a linear programming model if the 2-norm is replaced by the 1-norm $\|w\|_1 = \sum_{j \in N} |w_j|$, introducing at the same time the upper bounding variables $u_j, j \in N$, to obtain

$$\min_{w,b,d,u} \quad \frac{\beta}{2}\sum_{j \in N} u_j + (1-\beta)\sum_{i \in M} d_i \qquad \text{(LSVM)}$$

$$\text{s.to} \quad y_i(wx_i - b) \geq 1 - d_i, \quad i \in M \qquad (7)$$

$$-u_j \leq w_j \leq u_j, \quad j \in N \qquad (8)$$

$$d_i \geq 0, i \in M, \ u_j \geq 0, j \in N.$$

3.   DISCRETE SUPPORT VECTOR MACHINES WITH MINIMUM FEATURES

In this section we propose a mathematical programming model for deriving a linear discriminant function. This technique will be applied to obtain a multivariate split at each node of a decision tree, as described in section 5, using a sequential LP-based heuristic developed in section 4. Our model is based on a discrete version of linear support vector machines. Model LSVM in section 2 attains the benefits of a linear programming formulation: very fast computation of the optimal solution, and hence a high degree of scalability towards large scale classification problems. However, as already noticed for its predecessor QSVM, problem LSVM evaluates the empirical error using the slack variables $d_i, i \in M$, instead of the misclassification rate. This latter is given by the count of misclassified points, and appears to be the most appropriate measure of inaccuracy, as the definition of the empirical risk in (3) suggests.

We therefore propose a discrete variant of model LSVM, in which the misclassification rate is used in the objective function in place of the second term; subsequently, a third term is introduced to reduce the number of attributes that actively contribute to the definition of the optimal separating hyperplane. In order to count the number of misclassified points, define the binary variables

$$\theta_i = \begin{cases} 0 & \text{if } x_i \text{ is correctly classified} \\ 1 & \text{if } x_i \text{ is misclassified} \end{cases}$$

and let $c_i, i \in M$, denote the misclassification cost associated to instance i. The proper setting of the cost parameters c_i will be discussed in section 6. Let also Q be a sufficiently large constant value. We can now formulate the following optimization problem, aimed at minimizing a weighted sum of the reciprocal of the margin and the misclassification rate, and indicated as *linear discrete support vector machine*:

$$\min_{w,b,\theta,u} \quad \frac{\beta}{2} \sum_{j \in N} u_j + (1 - \beta) \sum_{i \in M} c_i \theta_i \qquad \text{(LDVM)}$$

$$\text{s.to} \quad y_i(wx_i - b) \geq 1 - Q\theta_i, \quad i \in M \qquad (9)$$

$$-u_j \leq w_j \leq u_j, \quad j \in N \qquad (10)$$

$$\theta_i \in \{0,1\} \quad i \in M, \ u_j \geq 0, \quad j \in N.$$

Model LDVM does not consider the number of attributes that directly contribute, with nonzero coefficient, to the discriminating hyperplane generated. In order to take into account the complexity of the rule model LDVM can be extended as follows. Define the binary variables

$$\tau_j = \begin{cases} 0 & \text{if } w_j = 0 \\ 1 & \text{if } w_j \neq 0 \end{cases} \quad j \in N,$$

and let $p_j, j \in N$, denote the penalty cost for using attribute j. Let also R be a sufficiently large constant value and $\beta_1, \beta_2, \beta_3$ the parameters to control the trade-off among the objective function terms. The following *minimum features discrete support vector machine* model can therefore be formulated:

$$\min_{w,b,\theta,u,\tau} \quad \frac{\beta_1}{2} \sum_{j \in N} u_j + \beta_2 \sum_{i \in M} c_i \theta_i + \beta_3 \sum_{j \in N} p_j \tau_j \qquad \text{(FDVM)}$$

$$\text{s.to} \quad y_i (wx_i - b) \geq 1 - Q\theta_i, \quad i \in M \qquad (11)$$

$$-u_j \leq w_j \leq u_j, \quad j \in N \qquad (12)$$

$$u_j \leq R\tau_j, \quad j \in N \qquad (13)$$

$$\theta_i \in \{0,1\} \quad i \in M, \quad u_j \geq 0, \quad \tau_j \in \{0,1\} \quad j \in N.$$

Models LDVM and FDVM are linear mixed integer programming problems, which are notoriously much more difficult to solve to optimality than the continuous linear programming model LSVM. However, the increase in solution complexity is balanced by a more accurate representation of the misclassification error. In the next section we will propose an efficient sequential LP-based heuristic for obtaining suboptimal solutions to problems LDVM and FDVM.

Many authors who proposed mathematical programming models for discrimination have devoted some efforts to preventing trivial solutions with $w = 0$, corresponding to degenerate separating hyperplanes. Often, this issue determined the inclusion into the proposed models of special purpose constraints, in quadratic or linear form (Koehler and Erenguc, 1990; Bennett and Mangasarian, 1992). However, we believe that what is thought to be a trivial solution $w = 0$ actually represents an acceptable optimal solution to the classification concept, when no better discrimination can be achieved: a solution with $w = 0$ corresponds to labeling all instances with the same class, and arises when any separating hyperplane (with $w \neq 0$) causes the objective function in LDVM and FDVM to increase.

4. A SEQUENTIAL LP-BASED HEURISTIC FOR PROBLEMS LDVM AND FDVM

In order to generate a feasible suboptimal solution to models LDVM and FDVM we apply a finite sequence of linear programs. Since model LDVM can be derived from FDVM by simply letting $\beta_3 = 0$ and removing the set of constraints (13), the following heuristic can be applied to both problems. The sequence starts by considering the LP relaxation of problem FDVM, denoted as FDVMLP$_0$. Each subsequent linear program FDVMLP$_{t+1}$ is obtained from its predecessor FDVMLP$_t$ by fixing to zero the relaxed binary variable with the smallest fractional value in the optimal solution to FDVMLP$_t$. More formally, let t be the iteration index in the sequence of linear programs, and let Z_t^1, Z_t^2 be the set of indices of the vectors of binary variables ϑ, τ respectively, fixed to zero up to iteration t. Define the t-th LP problem in the sequence as follows:

$$\min_{w,b,\theta,u,\tau} \quad \frac{\beta_1}{2}\sum_{j \in N} u_j + \beta_2 \sum_{i \in M} c_i \theta_i + \beta_3 \sum_{j \in N} p_j \tau_j \qquad \text{(FDVMLP}_t\text{)}$$

$$\text{s.to} \quad y_i(wx_i - b) \geq 1 - Q\theta_i, \quad i \in M \qquad (14)$$

$$-u_j \leq w_j \leq u_j, \quad j \in N \qquad (15)$$

$$u_j \leq R\tau_j, \quad j \in N \qquad (16)$$

$$0 \leq \theta_i \leq 1, i \in M, \; \theta_i = 0, i \in Z_t^1, \; 0 \leq \tau_j \leq 1, \tau_j = 0, j \in Z_t^2$$

$$u_j \geq 0, j \in N.$$

Assume first that FDVMLP$_t$ is feasible, and let $(w^{LP}, b^{LP}, \theta^{LP}, u^{LP}, \tau^{LP})$ be any of its optimal solutions. If this optimal solution is integer feasible, then it is feasible and suboptimal for problem FDVM as well. In this case the procedure is stopped, and the solution generated at iteration t is retained as an approximation to the optimal solution of problem FDVM. Otherwise, suppose that at least one component of the vectors θ^{LP}, τ^{LP} is not integer. Hence, let K^1, K^2 be the set of indices such that the corresponding variables θ_i^{LP}, τ_j^{LP} are basic and fractional: $K^1 = \{i, 1 \leq i \leq m : 0 < \theta_i^{LP} < 1\}$,

$K^2 = \{j, 1 \leq j \leq n : 0 < \tau_j^{LP} < 1\}$. Let also s^1, s^2 be the indices of the variables in K^1, K^2 assuming the smallest values: $s^1 = \arg\min\{\theta_i^{LP}, i \in K^1\}$, $s^2 = \arg\min\{\tau_j^{LP}, j \in K^2\}$. Possible ties in the definition of s^1, s^2 are arbitrarily broken. We then distinguish two cases: if $\theta_{s^1}^{LP} \leq \tau_{s^2}^{LP}$, we impose that the variable $\theta_{s^1}^{LP}$ be fixed to zero in the subsequent LP problem FDVMLP$_{t+1}$, and update the set Z_t^1 according to $Z_{t+1}^1 = Z_t^1 \cup \{s^1\}$, whereas $Z_{t+1}^2 = Z_t^2$; otherwise, if $\theta_{s^1}^{LP} > \tau_{s^2}^{LP}$, variable $\tau_{s^2}^{LP}$ is fixed to zero in problem FDVMLP$_{t+1}$, updating $Z_{t+1}^2 = Z_t^2 \cup \{s^2\}$, $Z_{t+1}^1 = Z_t^1$. Finally, if problem FDVMLP$_t$ is unfeasible, we go back to the previous LP problem FDVMLP$_{t-1}$, and redefine FDVMLP$_t$ by fixing to one all fractional variables. This involves the substitution of the conditions $\theta_i = 0, i \in Z_t^1$, $\tau_j = 0, j \in Z_t^2$ with the conditions $\theta_i = 0, i \in Z_{t-1}^1$, $\tau_j = 0, j \in Z_{t-1}^2$, $\theta_i = 1, i \in K^1$, $\tau_j = 1, j \in K^2$. It is clear that problem FDVMLP$_t$ redefined in this way admits of a feasible solution, and also that any of its optimal solutions is integer. In this case, we therefore reach an alternative stopping rule for the sequential procedure, and the solution found for FDVMLP$_t$ is retained as an approximation to the optimal solution of FDVM.

To show that the proposed iterative procedure is finite, simply observe that at each iteration one new variable is fixed to zero, and therefore no more than $m+n$ iterations can take place. The actual number of iterations is much lower in practice, since fixing one of the variables θ^{LP} to zero at the generic iteration t has the consequence of implicitly fixing to either zero or one a number of other variables. There is an intuitive explanation to this behavior: fixing variable θ_{s^1} to zero implies that the separating hyperplane must correctly classify the corresponding instance. However, if the point corresponding to θ_{s^1} is correctly classified, it usually happens that some other points are also necessarily well classified whereas some others have to be misclassified. In our computational experiences we observed that the actual number of iterations performed rarely exceeds one tenth of the total number of instances in the training set.

Sequential LP-based algorithm SLP

1. Set the iteration counter $t = 0$, consider the LP relaxation of problem FDVM, denoted as FDVMLP$_0$, and empty the sets of indices of the variables fixed to zero, $Z_t^1 = \{0\}, Z_t^2 = \{0\}$. Let $(w^1, b^1, \theta^1, u^1, \tau^1)$ indicate the approximation to the optimal solution of problem FDVM.

2. Solve problem FDVMLP$_t$. If it is not feasible go to step 3; otherwise, if any of its optimal solutions $(w^{LP}, b^{LP}, \theta^{LP}, u^{LP}, \tau^{LP})$ is integer feasible, then set $(w^1, b^1, \theta^1, u^1, \tau^1) = (w^{LP}, b^{LP}, \theta^{LP}, u^{LP}, \tau^{LP})$ and stop. Otherwise, if one of the components of vectors θ^{LP}, τ^{LP} is not

integer, set $s^1 = \arg\min\{\theta_i^{LP}, i \in K^1\}$ and $s^2 = \arg\min\{\tau_j^{LP}, j \in K^2\}$ where $K^1 = \{i, 1 \le i \le m : 0 < \theta_i^{LP} < 1\}$, $K^2 = \{j, 1 \le j \le n : 0 < \tau_j^{LP} < 1\}$. If $\theta_{s^1}^{LP} \le \tau_{s^2}^{LP}$, fix $\theta_{s^1}^{LP} = 0$ and update the collections Z_t^1, Z_t^2 according to $Z_{t+1}^1 = Z_t^1 \cup \{s^1\}, Z_{t+1}^2 = Z_t^2$; otherwise, set $\tau_{s^2}^{LP} = 0$ and $Z_{t+1}^2 = Z_t^2 \cup \{s^2\}, Z_{t+1}^1 = Z_t^1$. Then, set $t = t + 1$ and repeat step 2.

3.   Modify the formulation of problem FDVMLP_t by imposing the conditions $\theta_i = 0, i \in Z_{t-1}^1$, $\tau_j = 0, j \in Z_{t-1}^2$, $\theta_i = 1, i \in K^1$, $\tau_j = 1, j \in K^2$. Return to step 2.

5.   BUILDING A MINIMUM FEATURES DISCRETE SUPPORT VECTOR DECISION TREE

Rule induction by means of decision trees is relatively simple, readable and fast. Unlike many statistical alternative approaches, tree generation does not rely on critical assumptions about distribution and independence of the attribute values, leading to an overall robustness of the learning process.

Top-down induction of decision trees (TDIDT) (Quinlan, 1993) represents a general framework in which a partitioning of the instances is recursively applied for the construction of classification trees. Starting from the root node, that includes all the instances, the points of the training set are repeatedly subdivided at each node, by deriving appropriate splitting rules. The growth of the tree is stopped when no admissible splits can be applied to the tree leaves. At the end, the discriminant function is obtained by applying a simple majority voting scheme: a leaf is labeled as $\{-1\}$ if most of its points belong to A, and is labeled as $\{1\}$ when most of its points belong to B. When the class of new instances has to be predicted, the tree is traversed from the root to the appropriate leaf by applying the splitting rule at each

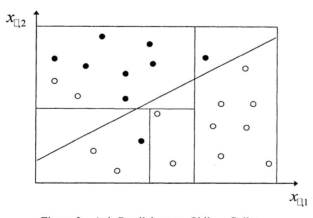

Figure 2.   Axis Parallel versus Oblique Splits.

node along the path, and the new instance is classified according to the label of the leaf reached by this way.

The most significant difference among specific algorithms fitting into the outlined framework is due to the way splits are derived at each node. Early approaches to tree induction have confined themselves to single-attribute splits, in which the attribute and its threshold value are selected for the split in a way to minimize some information theoretic measure of "confusion" among the partitions determined by the split itself. For instance, Quinlan's (1993) well-known C4.5 algorithm picks up the attribute k, and its threshold value b, maximizing the information gain determined by the subsequent split. This means that the rule for splitting instances at the given node becomes $x_{ik} > b$ or $x_{ik} < b$, with the tie $x_{ik} = b$ arbitrarily broken. However, the accuracy achieved by these simple univariate classifiers, also termed *axis-parallel* due to their geometric interpretation in the point space $\mathbf{R}^n$, is not always satisfactory. This led to consider more general multivariate splits, in the form of linear combinations of the attributes, i.e. in the form $wx_i \geq b$. These approaches, that in many cases are based upon mathematical programming models (Mangasarian, et al., 1990; Mangasarian, 1993; Bennett and Mangasarian, 1992; 1994), have been called *oblique trees* (Murthy, et al., 1994), or *perceptron trees* (Bennett, et al., 2000), according to different authors.

A graphical representation of decision rules produced by TDIDT classifiers is given in Figure 2 for the two-dimensional space. The regions for classification determined by the leaves in axis-parallel approaches correspond to hyperrectangles in the space $\mathbf{R}^n$. If instead oblique splits are allowed, by means of linear combinations of attributes, a single powerful separating hyperplane like the one in Figure 2 may achieve a higher accuracy with much less effort, growing trees with fewer leaves and generating simpler rules. Actually, axis-parallel splits try to approximate nonorthogonal nonlinear patterns with a sequence of hyperrectangles, so that classification easily becomes a complex task, with a large number of cumbersome rules and presumably an even larger error on unseen test data. On the other side, it has been argued that axis-parallel rules may be easier to accept by the user, due to their simple structure in the form $x_{ik} > b$ or $x_{ik} < b$. Oblique rules, on the contrary, may involve powerful but complex linear combinations of attributes. To partially overcome this objection, we have introduced in model FDVM the binary variables $\tau_j, j \in N$, to keep the number of active attributes utilized in the linear combination low.

Below we outline the scheme of the proposed *minimum features discrete support vector decision tree* classifier, denoted as $FDSDT_{SLP}$, based on optimal multivariate splits:

Algorithm FDSDT$_{SLP}$

1. Include all instances of the training dataset into the root node, and put it into the list L of pending nodes.
2. If the list L is empty or the maximum number of iterations is reached, then stop. Otherwise, select any node from L, remove it from L, and set it as the current node J.
3. Determine the optimal separating hyperplane by solving the mixed integer problem FDVM. Dichotomize the instances I belonging to the current node J according to the side of the hyperplane they belong. Specifically, let

$$I_1 = \{x_i, i \in I : wx_i - b \geq 0\}, \quad \text{and} \quad I_2 = \{x_i, i \in I : wx_i - b < 0\},$$

   be the sets of instances falling respectively above or below the given hyperplane. If one of the two sets I_1 and I_2 is empty, then J is a leaf of the tree, and it is labeled on the basis of majority voting. Otherwise, derive from J two child nodes J_1 and J_2 including respectively the sets of instances I_1 and I_2.
4. For each child node $J_h, h = 1, 2$, perform the following: if the percentage of instances in I_h belonging to the same class falls above a given threshold, or if the number of points contained in I_h is below a predefined minimum value, then the child node J_h is a leaf of the tree, and it is labeled according to majority voting. Otherwise, the child node J_h is appended to the list L. Repeat from step 2.

As noticed above, the solution of problem FDVM at each node of the tree keeps the number of attributes utilized for the splitting rule low. This is due to the role of variables $\tau_j, j \in N$. However, it may happen that at each node a different set of attributes is chosen, with the undesirable effect that a large number of attributes are selected for some split along the whole tree. To address this issue we dynamically update the penalty costs $p_j, j \in N$, at each child node by increasing the penalty of those attributes that were not selected for the split at the father node. In general, the best results were achieved by applying a percentage increase of the penalty factors ranging between 50% and 100%.

To determine an optimal separating hyperplane, different classifiers can be derived by introducing variants into the above procedure FDSDT$_{SLP}$, either by solving different models at step 3 or by adopting alternative solution methods. In this chapter we consider two additional algorithms, denoted respectively as LDSDT$_{SLP}$ and LSDT$_{LP}$: in the first case, model LDVM is considered at step 3 in place of model FDVM and solved by the sequential LP-based heuristic; in the second case, model LSVM is solved at step 3 by standard linear programming. This latter approach is equivalent to framing a traditional linear SVM within the TDIDT algorithm, using the misclassification distance instead of the misclassification rate in the objective function.

6. DISCUSSION AND VALIDATION OF THE PROPOSED CLASSIFIER

To validate the proposed classifier FDSDT$_{SLP}$ we have compared it with four well-known classification techniques based on decision trees, in terms of accuracy as well as simplicity of the induced rules. Specifically, the complexity of the derived rules is evaluated by the number of leaves of the classification trees generated and the number of active attribute utilized for discrimination along the whole tree. The methods were selected since they represent a broad range of classification approaches, including the univariate algorithm C4.5 (Quinlan, 1993), the multivariate algorithm OC1 (Murthy, et al., 1994), its variant MOC2 based on margin maximization (Bennett, et al., 2000) and the version of Quest (Loh and Shih, 1997) employing linear splits; furthermore, these methods generally appear rather accurate, as pointed out by a recent benchmark of thirty-three classification algorithms (Lim, et al., 2000).

In Table 1 and Table 2 respectively we compare the accuracy of algorithm FDSDT$_{SLP}$ with the four alternative classifiers indicated above and with four of its possible variants: LDSDT$_{SLP}$ and LSDT$_{LP}$, already described in section 5; FDSDT$_{SLP}^2$, derived from FDSDT$_{SLP}$ by imposing that only one split with two leaves be generated, leading therefore to a perceptron classifier; FDSDT$_{SLP}^{\beta_1=0}$, obtained from FDSDT$_{SLP}$ by dropping the margin of separation from the objective function of model FDVM, letting $\beta_1 = 0$. Whereas the accuracy of method FDSDT$_{SLP}$ and its four variants has been directly computed using our implementation, the remaining results from Table 1 are derived from the literature.

The classifiers were tested on six publicly benchmark datasets, available from the UCI Machine Learning Repository of the University of California at Irvine (http://www.ics.uci.edu/~mlearn/). The datasets used were: Cleveland Heart Disease (Heart), Wisconsin Breast Cancer (Cancer), Johns Hopkins University Ionosphere (Ionosphere), Pima Indians Diabetes (Diabetes), Bupa Liver Disorders (Liver), and 1984 United States Congressional Voting Records (House). Notice that the original Pima Indians Diabetes dataset was filtered, to remove the noisy attribute "serum insulin", together with some records containing several missing values. The actual size and the number of attributes of each dataset are then given in Tables 1 and 2. To measure the learning ability of the alternative classifiers, for each dataset we applied ten-fold cross-validation (Kohavi, 1995); the average testing set accuracy across the ten partitions of each dataset is reported in Tables 1 and 2. In particular, for the datasets marked with (°) we used the same ten-fold partition as in (Lim, et al., 2000). Our tests were conducted on Intel Pentium 4 2400 and AMD 2600 CPUs, under Windows 2000 OS.

In applying method FDSDT$_{SLP}$ and its four variants we have performed a scaling of the numeric values in the datasets, so that the resulting coefficients varied in the range $[-1,+1]$. This was done to avoid numeric ill-conditioning and singularities in the formulation of problems FDVM, LDVM and LSVM. Furthermore, we have noticed that a great benefit in accuracy is achieved when the cost of misclassification $c_i, i \in M$, appearing in the formulation of models FDVM, LDVM and LSVM, is taken equal to the percentage of instances of the opposite class. That is, if the class of instance i is $y_i = -1$, take its cost equal to the percentage of instances of class $\{+1\}$, and vice versa. The threshold percentage of instances of one class for a node to be considered as a leaf at step 4 of procedure FDSDT$_{SLP}$ and its variants ranges in our tests between 60% and 99%. At the same time, the threshold for the number of instances belonging to a node ranges between 5 and 10.

Table 1. Accuracy Results – Comparison among *FDSDT$_{SLP}$* and Alternative Classifiers.

Dataset	Points x Attributes	Accuracy results (%) – Computational times (sec, min)				
		Method				
		FDSDT$_{SLP}$	C4.5	OC1	MOC2	Quest
Heart°	270 x 13	**87.2** 0.8s	80.4 4s	77.8 4.2m	77.8 --	84.8 1.2m
Cancer°	699 x 9	**98.8** 0.5s	95.7 4s	95.9 13.3m	95.9 --	96.9 1.5m
Ionosphere	351 x 34	**97.1** 1.6s	93.7 3s	89.5 --	--	--
Diabetes°	532 x 7	**84.7** 1.3s	75.8 8s	75.3 17.2m	72.5 --	77.7 2.3m
Liver°	345 x 6	**79.1** 0.8s	70.8 6s	72.1 8.3	70.2 --	69.4 1.4m
House	435 x 16	**97.5** 0.7s	95.2 2s	94.2 4.2m	--	96.4 1.5m

The accuracy results presented in Table 1 show that algorithm $FDSDT_{SLP}$ outperforms the competing classification techniques on all datasets considered for these tests. For the most difficult classification datasets, such as those denoted as Diabetes, Liver and Heart, the improvement in accuracy achieved by classifier $FDSDT_{SLP}$ is noteworthy large, driving the empirical conclusion that our approach appears particularly suited to discover hidden patterns in hard classification problems. The results presented in Table 2 point out a number of other interesting issues. First, the comparison with algorithm $FDSDT_{SLP}^{\beta_1=0}$ shows that the inclusion of the margin of separation into the objective function of model FDVM leads to a notably greater accuracy with respect to the approach in which only the misclassification rate is minimized. Therefore, the margin plays a crucial role in increasing the generalization capability of the classifier. Moreover, the comparison with algorithm $LSDT_{LP}$ indicates that trees generated by means of the misclassification rate are significantly more accurate than their counterparts obtained using traditional support vector machines, in which the misclassification distance is considered as a continuous proxy for the empirical risk. Furthermore, since classifier $FDSDT_{SLP}$ achieves a higher accuracy than its variant $LDSDT_{SLP}$ we may conclude that the inclusion of the third term in model FDVM with respect to model LDVM leads to a better generalization capability on test data. Finally, albeit the superimposed simplicity of the trees it can generate, algorithm $FDSDT_{SLP}^2$ achieves a quite excellent score: on all tests its prediction accuracy is greater or equal than the accuracy of competing approaches. We also notice that the computing time required by algorithm $FDSDT_{SLP}$ and its variants is quite low.

In Table 3 we turn our attention to rule complexity. For each classifier and for each problem we provide the number of leaves of the resulting trees and the number of active attributes selected along the tree for discrimination, averaged over the ten-fold datasets. The results presented allow to conclude that algorithm $FDSDT_{SLP}^2$ attains an ideal trade-off between accuracy and complexity, since in front of the high accuracy performances displayed in Tables 1 and 2 it grows the simplest trees by construction. The number of active attributes is also kept reasonably low, below half the total number of available attributes for almost all datasets. As an alternative which might be preferable in some cases, $FDSDT_{SLP}$ achieves the best accuracy, at the expense of a slight increase in the number of leaves.

To further demonstrate that the rules derived by our classifier $FDSDT_{SLP}$ are intrinsically powerful in discrimination, we performed the following exercise. We selected the two datasets that appeared most difficult for the classification task, i.e. Diabetes and Liver. From Table 1 one can see that the average improvement in accuracy achieved by $FDSDT_{SLP}$ over the axis-parallel classifier C4.5 equals 8.9% and 8.3%, respectively. Then, for each of the partitions generated by the ten-fold cross validation, we derived a new variable as a linear combination of the original dataset variables, by using as coefficients the same coefficients found by algorithm FDSDT$_{SLP}$ for the optimal separating hyperplane at the root node. For each dataset this new variable was then added to the original ones and fed into the C4.5 classifier, to see if an improvement in accuracy could be obtained by this way. Interestingly, we found that the accuracy on the dataset Diabetes, again averaged over the ten-fold cross partitions, raised from 75.8% to 79.9%, whereas for Liver the increase was from 70.8% to 74.1%. From these results one is tempted to further speculate on the apparent strength exhibited by oblique splits over axis-parallel splits. It is also worth to mention that we conducted a similar exercise using the principal component analysis (PCA) technique for generating the new derived variables. The increase in accuracy obtained by including these new set of variables in the input to C4.5 was not so relevant as for the optimal separating hyperplanes derived from our approach.

Table 2. Accuracy Results – Comparison among $FDSDT_{SLP}$ and its Variants.

Dataset	Points x Attributes	Accuracy results (%) – Computational times (sec, min)				
		Method				
		FDSDT$_{SLP}$	FDSDT$_{SLP}^2$	FDSDT$_{SLP}^{\beta_1=0}$	LDSDT$_{SLP}$	LSDT$_{LP}$
Heart°	270 x 13	**87.2** 0.8s	84.8 0.6s	82.2 0.8s	86.7 0.7s	84.8 0.4s
Cancer°	699 x 9	**98.8** 0.5s	97.6 0.4s	97.3 0.5s	97.8 0.5s	97.6 0.3s
Ionosphere	351 x 34	**97.1** 1.6s	93.8 1.1s	88.0 1.6s	94.0 1.5s	92.0 1.2s
Diabetes°	532 x 7	**84.7** 1.3s	80.6 1.1s	76.6 1.3s	83.9 1.3s	77.9 1s
Liver°	345 x 6	**79.1** 0.8s	75.8 0.4s	69.9 0.8s	78.3 0.8s	69.3 0.5s
House	435 x 16	**97.5** 0.7s	96.4 0.6s	90.1 0.7s	96.5 0.7s	96.5 0.5s

7.   CONCLUSIONS

A rule induction method for binary classification problems based on decision trees has been proposed in this chapter. At each node of the tree, a multivariate linear split is obtained as an optimal separating hyperplane by solving a mixed integer programming problem, whose formulation derives from a new discrete version of support vector machines (FDVM). The way of representing the misclassification error determines the difference between SVM and FDVM: in our approach the inaccuracy measure is based on the discrete count of misclassified instances, whereas in traditional SVMs the misclassification distance is considered, as a continuous proxy of the discrete error. Although misclassification distance has clear computational advantages, permitting to apply fast techniques of linear programming, we have shown that the complexity of the MIP problem formulated at each node in our classifier can be efficiently tackled by a sequential LP-based heuristic. Computational comparisons performed on well-known benchmark datasets indicate that our classifier achieves a trade-off between accuracy and the complexity of the derived rules considerably superior with respect to other competing methods.

Future extensions will be concerned with multi-category classification problems. In particular, discrete support vector machines models will be framed within one-against-all and pairwise decomposition schemes, to derive multiclass discrimination algorithms. Furthermore, a probabilistic version of the FDVM classifier will be developed.

Table 3. Rule Complexity – Comparison among Alternative Classifiers.

Dataset	Points x Attributes	Number of leaves – Number of active attributes						
		Method						
		$FDSDT_{SLP}$	$FDSDT^2_{SLP}$	$LSDT_{SLP}$	C4.5	OC1	MOC2	Quest
Heart°	270 x 13	6.2 8	2 5	3.2 13	23 --	3 --	2.1 --	2 --
Cancer°	699 x 9	5 5	2 3	2.7 9	11 --	5 --	2.9 --	2 --
Ionosphere	351 x 34	11.9 17	2 10	3.1 33	12 --	6 --	-- --	-- --
Diabetes°	532 x 7	13.9 6	2 4	5.3 7	18 --	5 --	11.4 --	2 --
Liver°	345 x 6	18.6 5	2 4	5.1 6	26 --	5 --	7.4 --	4 --
House	435 x 16	2.4 8	2 6	2.3 15	6 --	2 --	-- --	2 --

REFERENCES

K. Bennett and O.L. Mangasarian, "Robust linear programming discrimination of two linearly inseparable sets", *Optimization Methods and Software*, Vol. 1, pp. 23-34, 1992.

K. Bennett and O.L. Mangasarian, "Multicategory discrimination via linear programming", *Optimization Methods and Software*, Vol. 3, pp. 29-39, 1994.

K. Bennett, N. Cristianini, J. Shawe-Taylor and D. Wu, "Enlarging the margins in perceptron decision trees", *Machine Learning*, Vol. 41, pp. 295-313, 2000.

L. Breiman, J. H. Friedman, R. A. Olshen, C. J. Stone, *Classification and regression trees*, Wadsworh International Group, Belmont, CA, USA, 1984.

Chunhui Chen and O. L. Mangasarian,. "Hybrid misclassification minimization", Advances *in Computational Mathematics*, Vol. 5, pp. 127-136, 1996.

G.J. Koehler and S. Erenguc, "Minimizing misclassifications in linear discriminant analysis", *Decision Science*, Vol. 21, pp. 63-85, 1990.

R. Kohavi, "A study of cross-validation and bootstrapping for accuracy estimation and model selection", *Proceedings of the 14th International Joint Conference on Artificial Intelligence*, Morgan Kaufmann, San Francisco, CA, USA, pp. 338-345, 1995.

K.F. Lam, E.U. Choo and J.W. Moy, "Minimizing deviations from the group mean: a new linear programming approach for the two-group classification problem", *European Journal of Operational Research*, Vol. 88, pp. 358-367, 1996.

D. La Torre and C. Vercellis, " $C^{1,1}$ approximations of generalized support vector machines", *Journal of Concrete and Applicable Mathematics*, Vol. 1, pp. 125-134, 2003.

T.S. Lim, W.Y. Loh and Y.S. Shih, "A comparison of prediction accuracy, complexity, and training time of thirty-three old and new classification algorithms", *Machine Learning*, Vol. 40, pp. 203-229, 2000.

W.Y. Loh and Y.S. Shih, "Split selection methods for classification trees", *Statistica Sinica*, Vol. 7, pp. 815-840, 1997.

O.L. Mangasarian, "Linear and nonlinear separation of patterns by linear programming", *Operations Research*, Vol. 13, pp. 444-452, 1965.

O.L. Mangasarian, "Mathematical programming in neural networks", *ORSA J. on Computing*, Vol. 5, pp. 349–360, 1993.

O.L. Mangasarian, "Misclassification minimization", *Journal of Global Optimization*, Vol. 5, pp. 309-323, 1994.

O.L. Mangasarian, "Machine learning via polyhedral concave minimization", In H. Fischer et al. eds., *Applied mathematics and parallel computing*, Physica-Verlag, Heidelberg, Germany, pp. 175-188, 1996.

O.L. Mangasarian, R. Setiono and W. Wolberg, "Pattern recognition via linear programming: theory and application to medical diagnosis", In T.F. Coleman and Y. Li eds., *Large-scale numerical optimization*, SIAM, 1990.

S.K. Murthy, "Automatic construction of decision trees from data: A multi-disciplinary survey", *Data Mining and Knowledge Discovery*, Vol. 2, pp. 345-389, 1998.

S.K. Murthy, S. Kasif and S. Salzberg, "A system for induction of oblique decision trees", *Journal of Artificial Intelligence Research*, Vol. 2, pp. 1-32, 1994.

C. Orsenigo and C. Vercellis, "Multivariate classification trees based on minimum features discrete support vector machines", *IMA Journal of Management Mathematics*, Vol. 14, pp. 221-234, 2003.

C. Orsenigo and C. Vercellis, "Discrete support vector decision trees via tabu-search", *Journal of Computational Statistics and Data Analysis*, 2004, to appear.

J.R. Quinlan, *C4.5: Programs for machine learning*, Morgan Kaufmann, San Mateo, CA, USA, 1993.

S.R. Safavin and D. Landgrebe, "A survey of decision tree classifier methodology," *IEEE Trans. on Systems, Man and Cybernetics*, Vol. 21, pp. 660–674, 1991.

V. Vapnik, *The nature of statistical learning theory*, Springer-Verlag, New York, NY, USA, 1995.

V. Vapnik, *Statistical learning theory*, Wiley, New York, NY, USA, 1998.

AUTHORS' BIOGRAPHICAL STATEMENTS

Dr. Carlotta Orsenigo is a Research Assistant at Politecnico di Milano, where she teaches courses in Operations Research and Business Intelligence. She graduated in Management and Production Engineering at Politecnico di Milano in 2003. Her current research interests include optimization models and algorithms for data mining and knowledge discovery, such as support vector machines and classification trees. She is author of papers which appeared in international journals such as *IMA Journal of Management Mathematics* and *Computational Statistics and Data Analysis*.

Dr. Carlo Vercellis is a Full Professor at Politecnico di Milano, where he teaches courses in Operations Research and Business Intelligence. He is also director of the Business Intelligence Laboratory (LabInt). Previously, after his graduation in Mathematics in 1978 at the Università degli Studi di Milano, he has been with the National Research Council (CNR), the Bocconi University, the Università degli Studi di Milano. He has coordinated national and international research programs funded by EEC, CNR and MURST. His current research interests include mathematical models for data mining and machine learning, such as support vector machines and classification trees; applications of these methods to customer relationship management; optimization models and methods, in particular with applications to supply chain management. In the past he was involved in research on decision support systems, forecasting models, marketing models, project management, design and analysis of algorithms for combinatorial optimization. He is author of several papers, mostly appeared in sound international journals, among which the *European Journal of Operational Research, Annals of Operations Research, Mathematical Programming, International Journal of Production Economics, Discrete Applied Mathematics, Annals of Discrete Mathematics, Optimization, Production Planning and Control, Operations Research Letters, Transportation Science, International Journal of Production Research, IMA Journal of Management Mathematics, Computational Statistics and Data Analysis, Journal of Concrete and Applicable Mathematics*.

Chapter 10 [1]

MULTI-ATTRIBUTE DECISION TREES AND DECISION RULES

Jun-Youl Lee and Sigurdur Olafsson [2]
Iowa State University
2019 Black Engineering, Ames, IA 50010
Email: olafsson@iastate.edu
Web: http://www.public.iastate.edu/~olafsson

Abstract: Among the numerous learning tasks that fall within the field of knowledge discovery in databases, classification may be the most common. Furthermore, top-down induction of decision trees is one of the most popular techniques for inducing such classification models. Most of the research in decision tree induction has focused on single attribute trees, but in this chapter we review multi-attribute decision trees induction and discuss how such methods can improve both the accuracy and simplicity of the decision trees. As an example of this approach we consider the recently proposed second order decision tree induction (SODI) algorithm, which uses conjunctive and disjunctive combinations of two attributes for improved decision tree induction in nominal databases. We show via numerical examples that in many cases this generates more accurate classification models and easier to interpret decision trees and rules.

Key Words: Decision Trees, Decision Rules, Multi-Attribute Splits.

---

[1] Triantaphyllou, E. and G. Felici (Eds.), **Data Mining and Knowledge Discovery Approaches Based on Rule Induction Techniques**, Massive Computing Series, Springer, Heidelberg, Germany, pp. 327-358, 2006.

[2] Corresponding Author

1.   INTRODUCTION

Data mining and knowledge discovery in databases has recently received a great deal of interest from both academia and industry. Research in the field is rapidly evolving and draws on numerous disciplines, including statistics, data warehousing, visualization, machine learning, decision support systems, and optimization (Fayyad, et al., 1996; 1998; Witten and Frank, 1999). The increased attention to this field may be partially attributed to the explosion of large and relatively inexpensively databases that can be accessed from almost anywhere. In particular, with the widespread use of databases and the tremendous growth of their sizes, individuals and organizations are faced with the problem of making intelligent use of large amounts of data.

Knowledge discovery in databases may be defined as the automated or semi-automated process of discovering meaningful and useful information in large databases (Fayyad, et al., 1996; 1998). Within this larger process, the term data mining is often used to describe the particular step that involves the use of algorithms to extract patterns from the data, but there are many other steps in the process that are also important. This includes data preparation, data selection, data cleaning, incorporating appropriate prior knowledge, and interpretation and deployment of the data mining results (Fayyad, et al., 1996). The data mining step itself may take various forms depending on the type of patterns to be extracted from the data. The most common types are: classification, where the objective is to induce a model that can accurately predict the value of a given class attribute based on the remaining attributes; clustering, where the objective is to identify natural groups or clusters of data instances; and association rule discovery, where the objective is to identify meaningful correlations in the database. This chapter focuses on the first of those, namely classification.

There are two types of methods that can be used to induce classification models from data: black box methods, where the logic of the model is effectively incomprehensible, and transparent box methods, where the construction reveals some structural patterns (Witten and Frank, 1999). Many black-box methods, such as artificial neural networks, have been found to be very effective in terms of making accurate predictions, but they have the serious drawback of not providing any additional insight into why the prediction is made. On the other hand, from a transparent method such as top-down induction of decision trees, it is possible to infer exactly how a particular prediction is made. As one of the most popular data mining methods, decision tree induction has received a great deal of attention, but most research into decision tree induction has focused on inducing decision trees that use one attribute at a time (Witten and Frank, 1999; Quinlan, 1986; 1993; Quinlan and Rivest, 1989; Breiman et al., 1984). Although a few researchers have considered multi-attribute decision making for numerical attributes only (Benett and Mangasarian, 1994; Brodley and Utgoff, 1995; Heath, Kasif, and Salzberg, 1993), very little research has been done to date related to the disjunctive descriptions or logic combinations of multiple nominal attributes (Murphy and Pazzani, 1991).

In this chapter, we focus on decision tree induction and in particular on second-order decision trees for nominal attributes. We discuss a new algorithm called Second Order Decision tree Induction (SODI) proposed by Lee and Olafsson (2003), and compare this new algorithm to three other methods: the classic ID3 decision tree algorithm, the popular C4.5 decision tree algorithm, and the PART decision rule induction algorithm of Frank and Witten (1998). Our results demonstrate that while the hypothesis description for each decision node becomes more complex in SODI, the size of the decision tree tends to be less than the more conventional decision trees. This implies that the SODI decision tree generates fewer decision rules and in many cases these decision rules have more intuitive appeal. Furthermore, the accuracy of the SODI generated trees and rules compares very favorably to the other methods.

2.   DECISION TREE INDUCTION

Many classification techniques have been proposed by the statistics and machine learning communities, including decision trees, artificial neural networks, and statistical methods. Probably the best-known and most widely used method is the induction of decision trees (Quinlan, 1986; Breiman et al., 1984). A decision tree is a top-down tree structure consisting of internal nodes, leaf nodes, and branches. Each internal node represents a decision on a data attribute or a function of data attributes, and each outgoing branch corresponds to a possible outcome. The internal nodes are usually referred to as decision nodes or split nodes. Each leaf node represents a class. In order to classify an unlabeled data sample (a record in the database), the classifier tests the attribute values of the sample against the decision tree. A path is traced from the root to a leaf node, which holds the class predication for that sample. Decision trees can easily be converted into IF-THEN decision rules.

A great deal of both theoretical and empirical research has been devoted to top-down induction of decision trees, and how to make the process and final results accurate, reliable, efficient, and valuable. One of the key issues is the order in which attributes are selected to be used in the decision or split nodes. This selection affects the performance of the tree in almost every way, including its accuracy, size, and interpretability.

2.1   Attribute Evaluation Rules

The basic idea of all decision tree induction algorithms is to select the attributes used for splitting the data in decreasing order of importance. However, measuring what makes an attribute important is far from trivial and many methods have been proposed in the literature. One framework that is useful in thinking about these methods is the taxonomy proposed by Ben-Bassat (1987). According to this taxonomy, attribute evaluation rules are divided into three categories:

– Rules based on information theory.
– Rules based on distance measures.
– Rules based on dependence measures.

Information theory based rules are derived from Shannon's entropy concept (Shannon, 1948), and several algorithms use this approach for decision tree construction. The basic idea of most of these methods is to maximize the global mutual information. In other words, at each node an attribute should be selected that contributes to the largest gain in average mutual information of the whole tree (Sethi and Sarvarayudu, 1982; Talmon, 1986). Tree construction that locally reduces the entropy as much as possible, which can also be thought of as maximizing information gain, has been explored in several of the diverse fields that contribute to the data mining literature, including pattern recognition (Casey and Nagy, 1984), machine learning (Quinlan, 1986), and sequential fault diagnosis (Varshney, Hartmann, and De Faria, 1982). Other work drawing on the entropy concept includes the G-statistic, an information theoretic measure that approximates the distribution for tree construction (Van De Merckt, 1993), and the combination of geometric distance with information gain for attribute evaluation, which is particularly effective for numeric attribute spaces. As information theory based measures are used in the algorithms to be introduced later in this chapter, such measures are discussed further in Section 2.2.

Other measures focus on the distance between the probability distributions of the class, and in particular take the attribute evaluation criteria as separability or the divergence between classes. Perhaps the most widely used measure in this category is the Gini diversity index. Similarly to the entropy concept, this popular approach has been used for decision tree construction in numerous fields, including statistics (Breiman, et al., 1984), pattern recognition (Gelfand, Ravishankar, and Delp, 1991), and sequential fault diagnosis (Pattipati and Alexandridis, 1990). However, it has been suggested that the Gini index has some difficulty when there are a relatively large number of classes (Breiman et al., 1984; Murphy, Kasif, and Salzberg, 1994), and that it overemphasizes equal sized branches and purity of these branches (Taylor and Silveramn, 1993). Thus, as for other measures it has certain biases and may not be appropriate for all situations.

The final category in the Ben-Basset taxonomy includes rules that measure the statistical dependence between two random variables. This can be taken as a separate category, but it is possible to interpret all dependence-based measures as belonging to one of the other two categories (Ben-Bassat, 1987).

Although the Ben-Basset taxonomy covers a large class of attribute selection criteria and includes the most commonly used measures, there are also some attribute selection criteria that do not clearly belong to any one of the categories, and in particular many combination measures have been proposed that cut across the categories. For example, by combining mutual information and a distance measure, a criterion has been suggested that first measures the gain in average mutual information due to a new split and then quantifies the probability that this gain is due to chance (Talmon, 1986).

Another category of measures that has been used for decision tree construction uses the activity of an attribute (Miyakawa, 1989). The activity of an attribute is defined in this context as the testing cost of the attribute multiplied by the a priori probability that it will be tested. For example, the well-known Minimum Description Length (MDL) principle (Risannen, 1989) has been used to select attributes for splits and for pruning decision trees (Quinlan and Rivest, 1989). This is particularly significant as it has been noted that criteria such as the information gain and the Gini index are concave and thus are not able to assure an improvement after split, which implies that there is no natural way of assessing where to stop splitting a node (Kalkanis, 1993). This is where the MDL can prove particularly useful.

The simplest of all attribute selection criteria is to base the selection directly on the number of misclassified instances. Following this line of thought, two measures, the max minority and sum minority have been suggested, respectively denoting the maximum and the sum of the number of misclassified points on either side of a binary split (Heath, Kasif, and Salzberg, 1993). An important theoretical property of the max minority is that the depth of the tree constructed using this measure is at worst logarithmic in the number of training instances.

From this brief survey it should be clear that many measures have been suggested for defining split nodes in decision trees. Furthermore, each of those has certain strengths but also biases and weaknesses. Several studies have been conducted to compare the various criteria for selecting split attributes but conclusive recommendations cannot be drawn regarding the best attribute selection method for an arbitrary problem. For example, an experiment comparing eleven attribute evaluation criteria concluded that the attribute rankings induced by various rules are very similar (Baker and Jain, 1976). In this study several attribute evaluation criteria, including entropy (Shannon, 1948) and divergence measures (Murthy, Kasif, and Salzberg, 1994; Pattipati and Alexandridis, 1990; Gelfand, Ravishankar, and Delp, 1991), are compared using simulated data on a sequential, multi-class classification problem (Ben-Bassat, 1978). The conclusions are that no attribute selection rule is consistently superior to the others, and that no specific strategy for alternating different rules seems to be significantly more effective.

2.2   Entropy-Based Algorithms

As noted above, several decision tree algorithms incorporate information theory based measures for attribute selection. The earliest of those is the ID3 algorithm (Quinlan, 1986), an inductive algorithm that constructs a decision tree consistent with a set of data instances as follows. The tree is constructed in a recursive top-down manner. At each step in the tree's construction, the algorithm works on the instances associated with a node in the partial tree. If the instances at the node all have the same class value for the attribute to be predicted, the node is made into a leaf node. Otherwise, a set of tests is evaluated to determine which test best partitions the instances down each branch. The metric used to evaluate the partition made by a particular test is the information gain. Once a test is selected for a node, the cases are partitioned down each branch, and the algorithm is recursively called on the instances at the end of each branch. The algorithm terminates once all branches have been terminated in a leaf node. The ID3 algorithm has been widely used and studied in the past but has some very well known weaknesses that limit its applicability. For example, in the form described here the algorithm can only deal with nominal attributes and since the splitting is not terminated until each branch becomes a leaf node, it is prone to reflect the training data too closely, that is to overfit the data, and thus may result in a decision tree that does not generalize well to new data.

Several researchers have also pointed out that the information gain is biased towards attributes with a large number of possible values. Quinlan suggested the gain ratio as a remedy for this bias of the information gain, and this is the attribute selection method used by the C4.5 algorithm (Quinlan, 1993; Quinlan and Rivest, 1989). Màntaras (1991) argued that the gain ratio approach had its own set of problems, and suggested using an information theory-based distance between partitions for tree construction.

He formally proved that his measure is not biased towards multiple-valued attributes. However, White and Liu (1994) present experiments to conclude that information gain, gain ratio and Màntaras' measure are worse than a measure based on the chi-square distribution in terms of their bias towards multiple-valued attributes. A hypergeometric distribution has been proposed as a means to avoid this bias (Martin, 1995). Kononenko (1995) also pointed out that Minimum Description Length (MDL) based attribute evaluation criteria have the least bias towards multi-valued attributes.

2.3 Other Issues in Decision Tree Induction

The selection of attributes for the decision nodes is probably the dominant issue in decision tree construction, but there are several other issues of great importance. For example, in general one of the potential weaknesses of decision tree induction is the variance of its construction, a problem that is particularly acute when there are few instances and many attributes (Dieterich and Kong, 1995). The source of the variance can be the random selection of training and testing instances, having numerous equally good attributes at each node, the cross-validation process, and other reasons. To address this issue, a few authors have suggested that a collection of decision trees might be used instead of just one, which presumably reduces the variance in classification performance (Kwok and Carter, 1990; Buntine, 1992). This approach involves building multiple trees, for example using randomness (Heath, Kasif, and Salzberg, 1993) or by using different subsets of attributes for each tree (Shlien, 1990; 1992), and then combining the results. The combination can for example be done by using simple voting procedures ((Heath, Kasif, and Salzberg, 1993) or by using statistical methods for combining evidence (Shlien, 1990; 1992).

Related to this idea is also the decision forest, which consists of all the decision trees that can be induced from a training data set generated from a series of experiments. In analyzing this decision forest, Murphy and Pazzani (1994) present a relationship between the size of a decision tree consistent with some training data and accuracy of the tree on test data. They show empirically that smaller decision trees are more recommendable for simpler problem domains. However, the average accuracy of smaller consistent decision trees is less than that of slightly larger trees for many real problems (Pazzani et al., 1994). This implies that a slightly larger decision tree can be recommended for more complex problems even thought its reliability may be slightly less than smaller decision trees.

Another idea is the fulfringe constructive induction algorithm, which belongs to a family of constructive induction algorithms that identify patterns near the fringes of the decision tree and uses them to build new attributes (Oliveria and Vincentelli, 1993). Learning from interpretations has also received increased interest in recent years, and an example of this is the HYDRA algorithm that automatically learns concept descriptions consisting of rules with relational and attribute-value conditions (Ali and Pazzani, 1995; Blockeel and De Raedt, 1998). In order to reduce the prediction errors, this approach builds more complex decision nodes than a single attribute-value approach. However, it only builds them after the construction of a decision tree. An additional relatively recent approach is the Top-down Induction of Logical Decision Trees (TILDE) that uses the concept of 'first-order logic', which is defined as simple logical combinations of attribute-value descriptions (Bioch, Van der Meer, and Potharst, 1997). TILDE employs logical queries and first-order upgrades of existing attribute-value descriptions, rather than just using simple attribute-value tests in the nodes of a decision tree.

3.   MULTI-ATTRIBUTE DECISION TREES

From the last section it is clear that a great deal of research has been devoted to how attributes should be selected for split nodes in decision trees. However, this has mainly focused on determining which single attribute to select, and one of the potential weaknesses of most traditional decision tree algorithms is that there is no accounting for interactions between attributes. When attributes are used one at a time for the split nodes any resulting decision rules can only combine them in a conjunctive manner. All other potential interactions between attributes are not taken into account, which may lead to large trees with very deep branches and multiple replicated subtrees. Such trees are difficult to interpret and may therefore loose a key advantage that is inherent in transparent decision tree models, namely simplicity and interpretability. Multi-attribute trees offer a way in which this difficulty can be overcome, and several researchers have recently considered this type of decision trees.

3.1   Accounting for Interactions between Attributes

As opposed to traditional decision trees, multi-attribute decision trees can use splits that contain more than one attribute at each internal node. Recently, a number of methods for constructing decision trees with multi-attribute tests have been suggested. Murphy and Pazzani (1991) showed a conceptual approach of the constructive induction of multi-attribute decision trees that have better performance than single attribute trees. They introduced the *m*-of-*n* concepts that are also known as Boolean threshold functions. The '*m*-of-*n* concepts' means all possible logical combinations of *m* attributes among *n* total attributes. They developed the GS algorithm (*m*-of-*n* concept construction) to compare multi-attribute decision trees to conventional ones. However, the drawback is that the problem of generating all possible combinations of multi-attribute decision-making descriptions is NP-complete and no adequate pruning method was suggested.

Most of the existing work on multi-attribute splits considers linear trees (Brodley and Utgoff, 1995; Murthy, Kasif, and Salzberg, 1994). These are trees that have tests based on a linear combination of the attributes at some internal nodes. The problem of finding an optimal linear split with respect to any of the attribute evaluation measures is more difficult than that of finding the optimal single attribute split. In fact, finding optimal linear splits is known to be intractable for some attribute evaluation rules. Thus, heuristic methods are required for finding good, partially sub-optimal, linear splits. Multi-attribute decision trees are often more accurate and smaller than single attribute trees. However, a linear combination of attributes at each split node is not always easy to interpret and understanding how many such linear combinations interact in a decision tree can be very complex. Thus, the use of linear combinations of the attributes may result in trees that are hard to interpret, again loosing the inherent advantage of transparency. To address this issue, some research on combinations of at most two attributes has been done, and it has been shown that such bi-attribute decision trees can often take advantage of both single attribute and multi-attribute trees (Bioch, Van der Meer, and Potharst, 1997). However, this work focused on classification with numerical attributes only.

3.2   Second Order Decision Tree Induction

To illustrate the advantages of multi-attribute decision trees, we consider the recently proposed Second-Order Decision-tree Induction (SODI) algorithm. More details regarding SODI, including the proofs of the theorems included here for completeness, can be found in Lee and Olafsson (2003). SODI generates a top-down decision tree with the consideration of the second-order decision-making of nominal attributes, and uses the information gain-ratio suggested by Quinlan (1993) as measure of the quality of attributes or combination of attributes. The intuitive motivation behind SODI is the desire to take advantage of multi-attribute splits to obtain smaller and higher accuracy decision trees, while at the same time limiting the possible combinations to at most two attributes so that the result decision trees can be easily interpreted.

To motivate the SODI algorithm mathematically some terminology needs to be introduced. We let Y be a random variable, with density $p(Y)$, that represents the class attribute, and $A_1, A_2, ..., A_N$ represents the other (decision) attributes. The values of these attributes are denoted with the corresponding lower case letter, e.g. $a_{i1}, a_{i2}, ..., a_{in_i}$ are the values of attribute A_i. We let N_{ij} denote the subset of instances at the jth internal node or end-leaf of the ith tree, where $i=1,2,...,n$, and $j=1,2,...k$. We let $P(N_{ij})$ denote the empirical probability of instances that are discovered at the jth node of the ith tree, that is,

$$P(N_{ij}) = \frac{|N_{ij}|}{\sum_j |N_{ij}|}.$$

We let $H(Y)$ denote the entropy of classes without any attribute information, that is,

$$H(Y) = -\sum_{y \in \{Y\}} p(y) \cdot \log_2 p(y),$$

and similarly, $H_{A_i}(Y)$ is the average entropy of classes when the attribute A_i is known, and $H_{A_i A_j}(Y)$ is the average entropy of classes when both A_i and A_j are known. The information gain of the tree that branches at an attribute A_i is denoted with $G(A_i)$, that is,

$$G(A_i) = H(Y) - H_{A_i}(Y).$$

We let $S(A_i)$ denote the split entropy of a tree T that is branched by an attribute, A_i, that is,

$$S(A_i) = -\sum_{a_i = a_{i1}}^{a_{in_i}} p(A_i = a_i \mid T) \cdot \log_2 p(A_i = a_i \mid T).$$

Finally, $G_R(A_i)$ denotes the information gain ratio of a tree due to A_i, that is, $G_R(A_i) = G(A_i) / S(A_i)$. Consistent with the above notation, we let $H(A_i, A_j)$, $G(A_i, A_j)$, $S(A_i, A_j)$, $G_R(A_i, A_j)$ denote the entropy, information gain, split entropy, and gain ratio, respectively, of a tree due to both A_i and A_j. Furthermore, we define the mutual information of the two attributes as

$$M(A_i, A_j) = H(A_i) + H(A_j) - H(A_i, A_j).$$

As mentioned above, entropy related measures such as these are commonly used in decision tree induction. The ID3 algorithm aims at quickly reducing entropy by selecting at each split node the attribute that has the highest information gain. Other algorithms, such as the C4.5 algorithm that selects the attribute with the highest gain ratio, work in a similar fashion. The basic motivation behind the SODI algorithm is that such entropy reduction can be better achieved by sometimes using two attributes simultaneously in the decision node. In particular, the information gain of knowing two attributes is larger than or equal to the sum of the information gain of knowing each attribute independently, and the equality holds if and only if the attributes are independent. Thus, any two dependent attributes could reduce entropy faster if used together, either conjunctively or disjunctively, in a split node. This is formalized in the following theorem.

THEOREM 1:

a) *The average information entropy when two attributes are known is less than or equal to the entropy of knowing either one of the attributes:*

$$H_{A_i A_j}(Y) \leq \min\{H_{A_i}(Y), H_{A_j}(Y)\}.$$

b) *The information gain of knowing two attributes is larger than or equal to the gain of knowing each of the thee attributes separately:*

$$\max\{G(A_i), G(A_j)\} \leq G(A_i, A_j).$$

c) *The information gain of knowing two attributes can be calculated using the following relation:*

$$G(A_i, A_j) = G(A_i) + G(A_j \mid A_i) \leq G(A_i) + G(A_j).$$

d) *Independent attributes can be characterized in terms of the following relationship between their joint information gain and split entropy. Two attributes A_i and A_j are independent if and only if $G(A_i, A_j) = G(A_i) + G(A_j)$ and $S(A_i, A_j) = S(A_i) + S(A_j)$.*

e) *If the mutual information of knowing two attributes is zero, then the gain ratio of the two attributes is less than or equal to the larger of the two individual gain ratios:*

$$M(Y \mid A_i, Y \mid A_j) = 0 \Rightarrow G_R(A_i, A_j) \leq \max\{G_R(A_i), G_R(A_j)\}.$$

Proof: See Lee and Olafsson (2003).

Theorem 1(a) implies that any pair of two attributes has less uncertainty than any of individual attributes. Similarly, Theorem 1(b) proves the information gain of a bi-attribute split is always larger than any of single attribute split. It also provides a lower bound on the information of a bi-attribute split. On the other hand, Theorem 1(c) provides an upper bound on the information of bi-attribute splits, and thus provides a weak condition for eliminating unnecessary pair-combinations among all attributes. Specifically, suppose that there exist two smallest information gains from any single attribute. From these two attributes the joint information gain can be computed. If the sum of single information gains of a pair of other two attributes is larger than the joint information gain, then the computation of this joint information gain of that pair is not necessary. Theorem 1(d) shows the characteristics of a pair of independent attributes with respect to their information gain and split entropy. If $M(Y|A_i, Y|A_j) = 0$, the classification is independent on these two attributes. Theorem 1(e) shows that the information gain-ratio of two independent attributes is always less than that of any individual attribute. From this result the following corollary can be concluded.

COROLLARY 1:

If all attributes affect the class attribute independently, the single attribute or first-order decision tree has the greatest gain ratio.

Proof: See Lee and Olafsson (2003).

On the other hand, a second-order decision tree is possibly better than any single attribute decision tree if some attributes are correlated. Indeed, there exists an optimal decision tree with multi-attribute decision nodes, which is optimal in the sense that it has the greatest gain ratio among all possible decision trees. However, it is NP-complete to find an optimal solution by searching all possible combinations (Heath, Kasif, and Salzberg, 1993). Therefore, a second-order decision tree induction algorithm may be considered a heuristic approach to quickly obtain a good solution for the classification.

Suppose A_i is a node in the nth depth of a first-order decision tree, and A_j is the only child node of A_i. If these consequent attributes are correlated to the classification, the number of branches of the joint condition, A_i and A_j, is less than the product of individual branches of these two attributes. By aggregating two correlated attributes the split entropy can be reduced even if the information gain remains the same. Therefore, the following corollary gives us a stronger motivation for the SODI algorithm.

COROLLARY 2:

If the class attribute is simultaneously correlated to a consequent attribute from a first-order decision tree, then there is a second-order decision tree that has better gain ratio than any other first-order decision tree.

Proof: See Lee and Olafsson (2003).

3.3   The SODI Algorithm

The new SODI algorithm does not only employ conjunctive expressions ('AND'), but also disjunctive expressions ('OR') to aggregate similar results from training instances. Furthermore, SODI adopts a new logical concept of 'OTHERWISE', which forces the aggregation of all trivial instances that are not included in any other logical conditions. The motivation for this is that it is important to aggregate trivial attributes that have very little information gain by the current split rules, so that the next split node may be introduced to obtain higher information gain.

More flexible logical description than 'AND' logic can reduce the number of decision rules or branches, resulting in simpler and easier to interpret decision trees, and fewer decision rules generated from the tree. To see this, note that the decision boundaries of conventional single attribute methods are orthogonal to each attribute, and intuitively it is clear that this requires more branches to approximate the ideal decision boundaries if only orthogonal approximations can be used. In other words, adopting a pair of attributes can be a better approximation to describing nonlinear classification than conventional single attribute methods. This also motivates the fact that SODI is able to improve the classification accuracy over single attribute decision trees.

To state a detailed description of the SODI algorithm, a few more terms and mathematical notations are required. We let T_i denote the decision sub-tree of the ith evolution, and L_{ij} be the jth internal node or end-leaf of the ith evolution of trees $i=1,2,...,n$, $j=1,2,...k$. Consistent with our prior notation, $G(L_{nk})$ is the information gain of an end-leaf (L_{nk}) from a tree (T_n), that is,

$$G(L_{nk}) = -\sum_{c \in Y} P(Y = c \mid L_{nk}) \log_2 P(Y = c \mid L_{nk}),$$

and $G(T_n)$ is the average information gain of the decision tree T_n, that is,

$$G(T_n) = \sum_{k=1}^{n_m} G(L_{nk}) P(L_{nk}).$$

Similarly, $S(T_n)$ is the split entropy of the decision tree T_n, that is,

$$S(T_n) = -\sum_{k=1}^{n_m} P(L_{nk}) \log_2 P(L_{nk}),$$

and $G_R(T_n)$ is the gain ratio of the tree, that is, $G_R(T_n) = G(T_n) / S(T_n)$.

The information gain of constructive decision trees is recursively computed using the relation:

$$G(T_n) = \sum_{a_k \in A_p} G(T_{n+1}) p(T_{n+1})$$
$$T_{n+1} = T(N_{nk} | A_p = a_k), \text{ for } n = 0, 1, 2, ...,$$

where T_0 is the whole tree with the root, N_0 = the whole set of training instances, and $p(T_{n+1})$ is the empirical probability that instances among N_{nk} belong to the sub-tree T_{n+1}. Furthermore,

$$A_p = \underset{A \notin T_n}{\arg \max} \left\{ \frac{G(N_{nk} | A)}{S(N_{nk} | A)} \right\},$$

and

$$G\left(N_{nk} | A_p\right) = \sum G(N_{nk} | A_p = a_k) \cdot p(N_{nk} | A_p = a_k),$$
$$S\left(N_{nk} | A_p\right) = -\sum p(N_{nk} | A_p = a_k) \cdot \log_2 p(N_{nk} | A_p = a_k),$$

where $T(N_{nk} | A_p=a_k)$ is a sub-tree of T_n branched at $A_p=a_k$, and $(N_{nk} | A_p=a_k)$ is the subset of instances with the value of $A_p=a_k$ among N_{nk}. The probability $p(N_{nk} | A_p=a_k)$ can be computed empirically as follows:

$$p\left(N_k | A_p = a_k\right) = \frac{\left|\left(N_{nk} | A_p = a_k\right)\right|}{\left|N_{nk}\right|}.$$

There are two primary components to define SODI. The first is the selection of an attribute or a pair of attributes for splitting, and the second is the pruning process that eliminates and combines branches while the tree is being constructed (that is, pre-pruning or forward pruning). We start by describing how attributes are selected and then discuss the pruning process.

Figure 1 shows the pseudo code for the main function of the SODI algorithm. As in any decision tree algorithm, the key issue is to select the order in which to use the attributes in the split nodes. To this end, SODI first constructs a list of attributes sorted according to their information gain. To find the best pair, the algorithm starts by considering the first two attributes from the list. If the gain ratio of the pair is higher than any of single attribute, the value becomes a lower bound for the gain ratio of all remaining pairs. The expected upper bound of the information gain ratio of a pair is the sum of the information gains of these two attributes divided by the maximum split information between those attributes. If it is lower than the current lower bound, this pair of attributes can be skipped. This process continues through the list of attributes until the best pair of attributes has been identified. In the worst-case scenario, $n(n-1)/2$ information gain ratio calculations are required to traverse the entire list. In practice, however, many candidate pairs can be eliminated by the bound of the best gain ratio, and finding the best pair is thus likely to take much fewer iterations.

```
Function SODI(R,S,DC)
    R: a set of attributes={A₁,A₂,…,Aₙ};
    S: a set of training instances;
    C: a default class value;
Begin
If S is empty, return NULL;
    Let C be the dominant class index;
    If Pr(C)=Pr(DC), then C:=DC, else DC:=C;
    If H(R)<α, return a single node with class C;
    Sort by Gain Ratio: Gᵣ(A₁)> Gᵣ(A₂)>…> Gᵣ(Aₙ);
    (Aᵢ,Aⱼ):=Find_Best_Pair(A₁,A₂,…,Aₙ);
    Let dj:=description of decision-making.
    Let Sj:=subset of S corresponding to dj.
    If Gᵣ(A₁)> Gᵣ(Aᵢ,Aⱼ)
        {(dj,Sj)|j=1..m}:=SODI_Rules(S,A₁);
        Let T be a tree with the root labeled A₁;
        Rnew:=R-{A₁};
    Else
        {(dj,Sj)|j=1..m}:=SODI_Rules(S,Aᵢ,Aⱼ);
        Let T be a tree with the root labeled (Aᵢ,Aⱼ);
        Rnew:=R-{Aᵢ,Aⱼ};
    End If
    For j=1 to m
        Add an arc labeled dj to T;
        Branch T from the arc with SODI(Rnew,C,DC);
    End For
    return T;
End.
```

Figure 1. The SODI Decision Tree Construction Algorithm.

In SODI, branches or decision arcs are aggregated while a decision tree is constructed using a set of rules that we call the second-order logic descriptions (see Figure 2). These rules can be thought of as a pre-pruning process. The first three rules attempt to reduce the size of the tree by combining branches or decision arcs where there is no or little information gain in keeping all the branches. These three rules should be applied in order and if the first rule is satisfied there is no need to check the last two, and so forth. The fourth and final rule deals with small branches with little information gain and combines all such trivial branches into a single "OTHERWISE" branch. The details of the four pre-pruning rules are as follows:

Rule 1. Start by eliminating all arcs or branches where there is no or little reduction in entropy. Specifically, aggregate all decision arcs where the entropy after splitting relative to the entropy before splitting is less than some pre-specified constant $\alpha > 0$, that is,

$$H(N_{nk} \mid T_n)/H(T_n) < \alpha .$$

Note that here N_{nk} is the subset of instances obtained by the kth branch from T_n. Also note that the larger the constant α, the more aggressive the pruning is, and vice versa. The default value of α in our implementation of SODI is set to $\alpha = 0.25$, which from numerical experience appears to give good performance.

The extreme case of this rule is $H(N_{nk} \mid T_n) = 0$, which means the instances in this subset have the same class and the decision node becomes a leaf node. This rule generalizes this concept to merging branches with almost pure classification.

Rule 2. If there are no more instances that satisfy Rule 1, then a majority dominance rule will be considered. Let $p(c_n \mid N_{nk})$ be the proportion of instances with class c_n in the N_{nk}. If for some subsets of instances a given class c_n is more prevalent than all the others combined, that is, if $p(c_n \mid N_{nk}) > \sum_{m \neq n} p(c_m \mid N_{nk})$, then these subsets can be merged.

Rule 3. If Rule 1 and Rule 2 do not apply, but the proportion of a class is significantly larger than any other classes (by some discrimination parameter, β), these subsets are still merged. The default value of $\beta = 0.2$ is used in our implementation of SODI.

Rule 4. The final rule combines small subsets that have negligible information gain. In particular, any subset of small size (as determined by some constant ϵ) with gain ratio smaller than α can be considered trivial and an overfitting problem may occur if such branches are included in the decision tree. Thus, all such branches are aggregated in an "OTHERWISE" branch, which could be split further in the next iteration using different attributes. We use the default value of $\varepsilon = 3$ in our SODI implementation.

```
Global Parameters:
    α: Approximation level (default:0.25);
    β: Discrimination level (default:0.2);
    ε: Minimum attractive number of instances (default: 3);

Function SODI_Rules(S,A,B)
    S: a set of training instances;
    A,B: decision attributes such that G_R(A)>G_R(B);
Begin
    If B is empty
        Let {d_k=(a_k)|a_k∈A} be the mutual decision;
        Let S_k be the subset of S corresponding to d_k.
    Else
        Let {d_k=(a_i,b_j)|k=(i,j),a_i∈A,b_j∈B} be the mutual decision;
        Let S_k be the subset of S corresponding to d_k.
    Endif
    Let S_p be the group of {S_k};
    Let d_p be the condition of attributes,(A,B), corresponding to S_p;
    For each class C_i:
    p:=1; d_p:=FALSE; S_p:=∅;
    For rule_no = 1 to 3
        Repeat
            Find S_k such that it satisfies the Rule(rule_no)
            S_p := S_p ∪ S_k; d_p := d_p OR d_k;
        Until Rule(rule_no) cannot satisfy all remained S_k;
        {(dj,Sj)|j=1..k} := Refine_Logics(S_p,d_p); p:=p+k;
    End For
    End For
    For all ungrouped subsets,
        If (sizeOf(S_k)>ε) or (sizeOf(S_k)<=ε and G(S_k)/H(S)>α)
            p:=p+1; d_p=(a_i,b_j) OR a_k; S_p=S_k;
        Endif
    End For
    p:=p+1; d_p:='OTHERWISE';
    Aggregate all ungrouped subsets {S_k} to S_p;
    return {(dj,Sj)|j=1..p};
End;
```

Figure 2. The SODI Rules for Pre-Pruning.

4.   AN ILLUSTRATIVE EXAMPLE

In this section, we illustrate the SODI algorithm described in Section 3.3 through a very simple classification problem with a class attribute Y that can take two values $Y \in \{X, O\}$, and four additional decision attributes A_1, A_2, A_3, and A_4 that can take values 1, 2, and 3. There are 25 instances in the training data set and those are shown in Table 1.

Table 1. A Simple Classification Problem.

A_1	A_2	A_3	A_4	Y
1	1	1	1	X
1	1	1	2	O
1	1	2	1	O
1	1	2	2	X
1	1	3	2	X
1	2	1	1	O
1	2	1	2	O
1	2	3	2	X
2	1	1	1	O
2	1	1	2	O
2	1	2	1	O
2	2	1	1	O
2	2	1	2	O
2	2	2	1	O
2	2	2	2	O
3	1	1	2	X
3	1	2	1	X
3	1	2	2	O
3	1	3	1	X
3	1	3	2	X
3	2	2	1	X
3	2	2	2	X
3	2	3	1	X
3	1	1	1	O
3	2	3	2	X

The global SODI parameters are set as $\alpha = 0.05$, $\beta = 0.10$, and $\varepsilon = 3$. Figure 3(a) and 3(b) shows the results of ID3 and SODI, respectively; and both algorithms classify all of the training instances correctly (no training error). The tree size for ID3 is 22, the number of decision rules is 13, and the split entropy is 2.9778. On the other hand, the tree size for SODI is 11, the number of decision rules is 8, and the split entropy is 2.6970. (Thus in this example, SODI results in a much smaller decision tree and fewer decision rules).

To understand how SODI achieves the reduction in tree size through the use of bi-attribute split nodes and a pre-pruning process, we consider the construction of the tree more closely. Start by noting that the information gain ratios of A_1, A_2, A_3, and A_4 are 0.2486, 0.0015, 0.2274, and 0.0107, respectively. Therefore, A_1 and A_3 are the first two attributes on the ordered list of all attributes and are considered first.

Representing the two highest gain ratio attributes, the pair (A_1, A_3) is a candidate attribute pair for the first split node. The information gain of (A_1, A_3) is 0.5792, and its split entropy is 2.2774. Its gain ratio is thus 0.2543, which is bigger than 0.2486, the gain ratio of A_1, and the current lower bound of gain ratios for the first split is therefore taken as 0.2543. The next candidate is (A_1, A_4). The approximate upper bound of the gain ratio of (A_1, A_4) can be computed as follows:

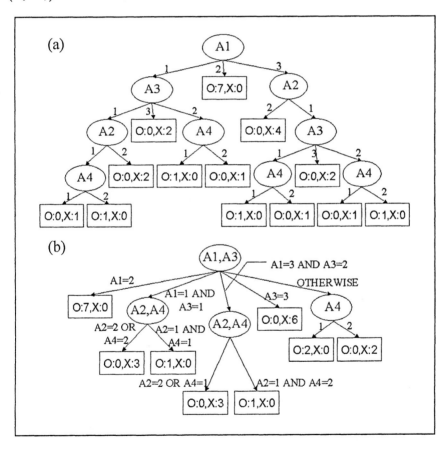

Figure 3. Decision Trees Built by (a) ID3, and (b) SODI.

$$G_R\left(A_1,A_4\right)=\frac{G\left(A_1,A_4\right)}{S\left(A_1,A_4\right)}\leq\frac{G\left(A_1\right)+G\left(A_4\right)}{\max\left\{S\left(A_1\right),S\left(A_4\right)\right\}}.$$

$$=\frac{0.2486+0.0107}{1.5690}=0.1693$$

This is less than the current lower bound and the candidate $\left(A_1,A_4\right)$ is thus rejected. Furthermore, similar calculations show that the upper bounds of gain ratios from any other combinations are all less than the current lower bound. Therefore, the first decision node is selected to be $\left(A_1,A_3\right)$.

Now that the split node has been selected, the next step is to consider all its possible values:

$$\left(A_1,A_3\right)=\left(1,1\right)\quad\left(A_1,A_3\right)=\left(2,1\right)\quad\left(A_1,A_3\right)=\left(3,1\right),$$
$$\left(A_1,A_3\right)=\left(1,2\right)\quad\left(A_1,A_3\right)=\left(2,2\right)\quad\left(A_1,A_3\right)=\left(3,2\right),$$
$$\left(A_1,A_3\right)=\left(1,3\right)\quad\left(A_1,A_3\right)=\left(2,3\right)\quad\left(A_1,A_3\right)=\left(3,3\right).$$

At first glance this might indicate nine branches, but the pre-pruning rules must also be applied. First, let's consider the three cases where $A_1=2$. From Table 1 we observe that there is no instance where both $A_1=2$ and $A_3=3$. Furthermore, for the other two potential branches with $A_1=2$ both have all instances classified as $Y=O$. Therefore, $\left(A_1=2\text{ AND }A_3=1\right)$ and $\left(A_1=2\text{ AND }A_3=2\right)$ have zero entropy and can be combined by Rule 1. Thus, the three branches can be simplified to $A_1=2$ as shown in Figure 3(b). Secondly, the decision arc $A_3=3$ from the decision node $\left(A_1,A_3\right)$ is aggregated from $\left(A_1=1\text{ AND }A_3=3\right)$ and $\left(A_1=3\text{ AND }A_3=3\right)$ for the same reason. Thirdly, the sets of instances corresponding to $\left(A_1=1\text{ AND }A_3=2\right)$ and $\left(A_1=3\text{ AND }A_3=1\right)$ are both determined to be small as they have only two instances each, which is less than the threshold of $\varepsilon=3$. They also have zero information gain and are thus combined in an "OTHERWISE" condition according to Rule 4, which aggregates all small subsets of trivial unclassified instances. Thus, the nine potential branches become five branches as pre-pruning is applied.

From this example it is clear that the reason why the SODI decision tree is appealing is two-fold: First, the use of bi-attribute splits allows for modeling of interactions between attributes. For example, 13 of the 25 instances are completely classified by the value of A_1 ($A_1=2$) or A_3 ($A_3=3$), but the remaining 12 instances require considering interactions. Second, the disjunctive and "OTHERWISE" logic allows for simplification of the tree. For example, two branches are combined into an

"OTHERWISE" branch at the top level, which is then classified perfectly by A_4 at the next level. Also, for both of the split nodes involving A_2 and A_4 as a bi-attribute split, the use of a disjunctive OR branch allows us to combine what would otherwise be four branches into two. Thus, the combination of bi-attribute splits and extended logic descriptions makes for a simpler, easier to interpret, and potentially more useful tree.

5. NUMERICAL ANALYSIS

The simple example in Section 4 provides some intuition into why the SODI algorithm may perform well when compared to the ID3 algorithm and shows how it classifies the same dataset using a much simpler decision tree and fewer rules. In this section we present extensive numerical results that compare SODI with C4.5 and PART along two dimensions: the improvement in simplicity and the improvement in accuracy. The C4.5 algorithm is chosen for comparison because just like SODI it uses the gain ratio to select attributes (see Section 2.2), and the PART algorithm is chosen because it infers rules by repeatedly generating partial C4.5 decision trees.

We analyzed eight classification problems that are widely used in the data mining literature (see e.g., Witten and Frank, 1999):

1. Fitting contact lenses (5 attributes, 3 classes, 24 instances)
2. Balance scale weight and distance (4 attributes, 3 classes, 625 instances)
3. Breast cancer (9 attributes, 2 classes, 286 instances)
4. Chess end-game (36 attributes, 2 classes, 3196 instances)
5. 1984 United States Congressional voting (17 attributes, 2 classes, 435 instances)
6. Lymphography domain (17 attributes, 4 classes, 148 instances)
7. Mushroom records (22 attributes, 2 classes, 8124 instances)
8. Zoo classification (17 attributes, 7 classes, 101 instances)

We are interested in two quality measures for each of the classification methods: accuracy and simplicity. The prediction error of each method is estimated by randomly dividing the data set into a training dataset (2/3 of data) and a test dataset (1/3 of data). The simplicity is measured by the number of classification rules, or leaf nodes in the decision tree, generated by the model.

The reduction in the estimated error rate of the three more advanced models relative to the ID3 decision tree is shown in Figure 4. All of the methods achieve considerable reduction in error rate except for the 'Mushroom' databases, where all four methods have estimated error rate of zero, and PART for the 'Chess End-Game' database, where the estimated error rate of PART is actually worse that the estimated error rate of ID3.

Furthermore, the error rate of SODI is very competitive. Only for the 'Contact Lenses' database is the error rate of SODI worse than both of the other methods, and for four of the databases ('Balance Scale', 'Breast Cancer', 'Chess End-Game', and 'Lymphography') it is strictly better than both. In comparison, the C4.5 decision tree is strictly better than both for only the '1984 USA Voting' database, and the estimated accuracy of the PART decision rules is never strictly better than both of the other models. We conclude that the accuracy of SODI compares very favorably to the two other methods, which have both been found to be useful in data mining practice.

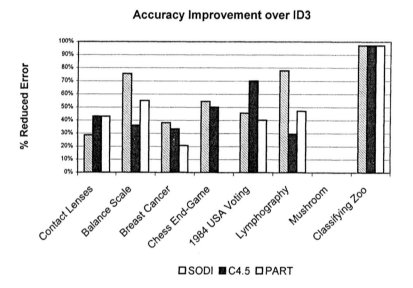

Figure 4. Improvement of Accuracy over ID3 for SODI, C4.5, and PART.

The simplicity of the tree types of models, as measured by the number of decision rules (leaves in the decision trees), relative to the number of ID3 generated rules is shown in Figure 5. All of the methods achieve an improvement for each of the eight test problems. However, although SODI has impressive improvements over ID3 for all the test problems, it does not compare quite as favorably as before relative to C4.5 and PART, as its improvement is less than the two other algorithms for four of the test problems ('Contact Lenses', 'Breast Cancer', '1984 USA Voting', and 'Lymphography'). It should be noted that for two of these problems ('Breast Cancer' and 'Lymphography'), SODI had better accuracy than either of the other methods, so at least to some extend there is a tradeoff between simplicity and accuracy. However, there is also simply a difference in the applicability of the methods to individual problems. For example, both C4.5 and PART perform better than SODI on both measures for the 'Contact Lenses' database and C4.5 performs better on both for the '1984 USA Voting' database. Vice versa, SODI is for example clearly better than both for the 'Balance Scale' database and clearly better than PART for the 'Chess End-Game' database. We conclude that while SODI performs competitively in terms of the simplicity of the decision tree, the lack of post-pruning rules may result in slightly larger trees than those generated by C4.5 and PART.

To further compare the three techniques, the actual models induced for the lymphography data (test problem 6) are shown in the Appendix of this chapter, along with the confusion matrices that illustrate what types of error are made by each model.

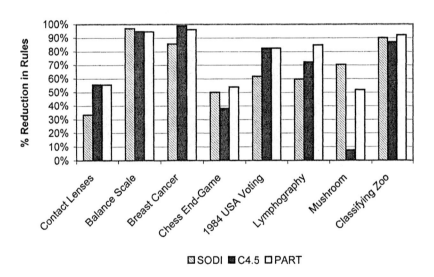

Figure 5. Reduction in the Number of Decision Rules over ID3 for SODI, C4.5, and PART.

6. CONCLUSIONS

As no single classification method can be shown to be superior to all others, it is very common in data mining practice that multiple classification methods must be tried. Each application has its own characteristics and no algorithm performs best for all situations. Thus, many useful decision tree algorithms have been proposed in the literature but most of those use single attribute splits. In this chapter we have argued for the value of using multi-attribute splits and also presented the SODI algorithm that takes advantage of second-order information or bi-attribute splits. We believe that this approach is an important addition to the available classification algorithms.

We compared SODI to ID3, C4.5, and PART using numerical experiments on well-known test problems and concluded that SODI performs quite well. Taking ID3 as a benchmark, we evaluated the improvements of the three more advanced algorithms along two dimensions: accuracy and simplicity. All the algorithms improve on ID3 on both of these quality measures, and SODI compares favorably relative to both C4.5 and PART. For some problems we observed a tradeoff between simplicity and accuracy, but for others one approach clearly outperformed the others on both measures. Thus, our numerical results support the claim that the relative performance of each of these methods is application dependent and for a given problem it is recommended to try multiple approaches. However, these results also clearly illustrate that there is a clear advantage to multi-attribute decision tree construction.

Although SODI has been demonstrated to be a viable alternative for decision tree induction, considerable work remains to be done with respect to its development. In particular, although the pre-pruning rules appear to work effectively, the trees generated by SODI tend to be slightly larger than the models generated by both C4.5 and PART. Thus, we are investigating post-pruning processes for SODI. Also, SODI has only been developed for nominal attributes and we are currently investigating how to use support vector machines (SVM) to extend SODI to numeric and mixed attribute problems.

APPENDIX: DETAILED MODEL COMPARISON

In order to further compare the three main methods discussed in this chapter (SODI, C4.5, and PART), this appendix presents the actual models for the lymphography problem. The performance of the algorithms on this problem was reported in Section 3.5. To compare how the different models make classification error, the confusion matrices for this problem are also shown. Recall from Section 3.5 that for this problem, the SODI decision tree is more complicated than the C4.5 tree and the PART decision rules, but the estimated accuracy of the SODI model is much better.

The lymphography data set has 9 attributes that are Boolean valued (yes/no): *block_of_affere, bl_of_lymph_c, bl_of_lymph_s, by_pass, extravasates, regeneratio_of, early_uptake_in, dislocation_of, exclusion_of_no.* There are 9 others nominal attributes: *lymphatics* ∈ {normal, arched, deformed, displaced}, *changes_in_lym* ∈ {bean, oval, round}, *defect_in_node* ∈ {no, lacunar, lac_margin, lac_central}, *changes_in_node* ∈ {no, lacunar, lac_margin, lac_central}, *changes_in_stru* ∈ {no, grainy, drop_like, coarse, diluted, reticular, stripped, faint}, *special_forms* ∈ {no, chalices, vesicles}, *lym_nodes_dimin* ∈ {1, 2, 3}, *lym_nodes_enlar* ∈ {1, 2, 3, 4}, *no_of_nodes_in* ∈ {1, 2, 3, 4, 5, 6, 7, 8}. The class attribute is nominal and takes one of five values: normal, metastases, malign_lymph, and fibrosis.

C4.5 DECISION TREE

```
lym_nodes_dimin = 1
|  changes_in_node = no
|  |  defect_in_node = no: normal (3.0/1.0)
|  |  defect_in_node = lacunar: malign_lymph (2.0)
|  |  defect_in_node = lac_margin: normal (0.0)
|  |  defect_in_node = lac_central: normal (0.0)
|  changes_in_node = lacunar
|  |  exclusion_of_no = no: metastases (10.0/1.0)
|  |  exclusion_of_no = yes
|  |  |  special_forms = no: metastases (3.0/1.0)
|  |  |  special_forms = chalices
|  |  |  |  changes_in_lym = bean: malign_lymph (0.0)
|  |  |  |  changes_in_lym = oval: malign_lymph (3.0)
|  |  |  |  changes_in_lym = round: metastases (2.0)
|  |  |  special_forms = vesicles: malign_lymph (19.0/1.0)
|  changes_in_node = lac_margin
|  |  block_of_affere = no
|  |  |  extravasates = no
|  |  |  |  lymphatics = normal: metastases (0.0)
|  |  |  |  lymphatics = arched
|  |  |  |  |  early_uptake_in = no: metastases (5.0/1.0)
|  |  |  |  |  early_uptake_in = yes: malign_lymph (4.0/1.0)
|  |  |  |  lymphatics = deformed: metastases (5.0)
|  |  |  |  lymphatics = displaced: malign_lymph (1.0)
|  |  |  extravasates = yes: malign_lymph (4.0)
|  |  block_of_affere = yes: metastases (56.0/3.0)
|  changes_in_node = lac_central: malign_lymph (25.0/2.0)
lym_nodes_dimin = 2: metastases (3.0/2.0)
lym_nodes_dimin = 3: fibrosis (3.0)
```

PART DECISION RULES

1. lym_nodes_dimin = 1 AND changes_in_node = lac_margin AND block_of_affere = yes: metastases (56.0/3.0)
2. lym_nodes_dimin = 1 AND exclusion_of_no = yes AND early_uptake_in = yes AND special_forms = vesicles: malign_lymph (42.0/2.0)
3. regeneratio_of = no AND changes_in_lym = round: metastases (11.0/1.0)
4. regeneratio_of = no AND defect_in_node = lacunar AND changes_in_node = lacunar AND exclusion_of_no = no: metastases (7.0/1.0)
5. regeneratio_of = yes: fibrosis (5.0/1.0)
6. exclusion_of_no = no AND special_forms = vesicles: malign_lymph (3.0)
7. exclusion_of_no = yes AND no_of_nodes_in = 2: malign_lymph (9.0/1.0)
8. exclusion_of_no = yes AND special_forms = no: metastases (6.0)
9. lymphatics = arched: metastases (3.0/1.0)
10. lymphatics = deformed: malign_lymph (3.0)
11. : normal (3.0/1.0)

SODI DECISION TREE

```
lym_nodes_dimin = 1
|   changes_in_node = lac_central: malign_lymph (23)/ metastases (2)
|   changes_in_node = lac_margin
|   |   (block_of_affere, extravasates) = (no, no)
|   |   |   lymphatics = arched
|   |   |   |   (changes_in_lym, defect_in_node)
|   |   |   |   = {(oval, lac_margin), (round, lacunar)}: malign_lymph (4)
|   |   |   |   (changes_in_lym, defect_in_node)
|   |   |   |   = {(oval, lac_central), (oval, lacunar), (round, lac_margin)}: metastases (5)
|   |   |   |   (changes_in_lym, defect_in_node) = OTHERWISE: N/D (Not Defined)
|   |   |   lymphatics = deformed: metastases (5)
|   |   |   lymphatics = displaced: malign_lymph (1)
|   |   |   lymphatics = normal: N/D (Not Defined)
|   |   (block_of_affere, extravasates) = {(no, yes), (yes, no)} : malign_lymph (25)
|   |   (block_of_affere, extravasates) = (yes, yes)
|   |   |   early_uptake_in = no: metastases (14)
|   |   |   early_uptake_in = yes
|   |   |   |   bl_of_lymph_c = yes: metastases (8)
|   |   |   |   bl_of_lymph_c = no
|   |   |   |   |   no_of_nodes_in = {1, 2}: metastases (8)
|   |   |   |   |   no_of_nodes_in = {3, 4}
|   |   |   |   |   |   changes_in_stru = {grainy}: metastases (2)
|   |   |   |   |   |   changes_in_stru = {diluted, stripped, faint}: malign_lymph (3)
|   |   |   |   |   |   changes_in_stru = OTHERWISE: N/D (Not Defined)
|   |   |   |   |   no_of_nodes_in = OTHERWISE: N/D (Not Defined)
|   changes_in_node = lacunar
|   |   exclusion_of_no = no: metastases (9) / malign_lymph (1)
|   |   exclusion_of_no = yes
|   |   |   special_forms = chalices
|   |   |   |   changes_in_lym = oval: malign_lymph (3)
|   |   |   |   changes_in_lym = round: metastases (2)
|   |   |   |   changes_in_lym = OTHERWISE: N/D (Not Defined)
|   |   |   special_forms = no
```

```
|  |  |  |  dislocation_of = no: malign_lymph (1)
|  |  |  |  dislocation_of = yes: metastases (2)
|  |  |  special_forms = vesicles: malign_lymph (18) / metastases (1)
|  changes_in_node = no
|  |  dislocation_of = yes
|  |  |  early_uptake_in = yes: malign_lymph (2)
|  |  |  early_uptake_in = no: metastases (1)
|  |  dislocation_of = no: normal (2)
lym_nodes_dimin = 2
|  (regeneratio_of, early_uptake_in) = (yes, yes): N/D (Not Defined)
|  (regeneratio_of, early_uptake_in) = (yes, no): fibrosis (1)
|  (regeneratio_of, early_uptake_in) = (no, yes): malign_lymph (1)
|  (regeneratio_of, early_uptake_in) = (no, no): metastases (1)
lym_nodes_dimin = 3: fibrosis (3)
```

The detailed accuracy of the three models as estimated by 10-fold cross validation is shown in the following confusion matrices:

C4.5 DECISION TREE

Estimated prediction accuracy 76.5%

Classified As

		Normal	metastases	malign_lymph	fibrosis
Actual Class	Normal	0	1	1	0
	Metastases	1	69	11	0
	malign_lymph	1	14	46	0
	Fibrosis	1	1	2	1

SODI DECISION TREE

Estimated prediction accuracy 92.6%

Classified As

		Normal	metastases	malign_lymph	fibrosis
Actual Class	Normal	2	0	0	0
	Metastases	0	75	5	1
	malign_lymph	0	4	57	0
	Fibrosis	0	1	0	3

PART DECISION RULES

Estimated prediction accuracy 88.3%

		Classified As			
		Normal	metastases	malign_lymph	fibrosis
Actual Class	Normal	0	1	1	0
	Metastases	0	71	9	1
	malign_lymph	0	10	51	0
	fibrosis	0	0	0	4

REFERENCES

M. Ali and M. Pazzani, "HYDRA: A nose-tolerant relational concept learning algorithm," *International Joint Conference on Artificial Intelligence*, Chambery, France, 1995.

M. Ali and M. Pazzani, "Reducing the small disjuncts problems by learning probabilistic concept descriptions," *Computational Learning Theory and Natural Learning Systems*, Vol. 3, pp.183-199, 1995.

E. Baker and A. K. Jain, "On feature ordering in practice and some finite sample effects," *Proceedings of the 3rd International Joint Conference on Pattern Recognition*, pp. 45-49, San Diego, CA, USA, 1976.

M. Ben-Bassat, "Use of distance measures, information measures and error bounds on feature evaluation," *Classification, Pattern Recognition and Reduction of Dimensionality*, In K. P. R. Krishnaiah and L. N. Kanal, editors, *Vol. 2 of Handbook of Statistics*, North-Holland Publishing Company, Amsterdam, The Netherlands, pp. 773-791, 1987.

M. Ben-Bassat, "Myopic policies in sequential classification," *IEEE Transactions on Computing*, Vol. 27, No, 2, pp. 170-174, 1978.

K. P. Bennett and O. L. Mangasarian, "Multicategory Discrimination via Linear Programming," *Optimization Methods and Software*, Vol. 3, pp. 29-39, 1994.

J. C. Bioch, O. Van der Meer, and R. Potharst, "Bivariate Decision Trees", in J. Komorowski, J. Zytkow, eds. *Principles of Data Mining and Knowledge Discovery, Lecture Notes in Artificial Intelligence 1263*, Springer Verlag, 1997, New York, NY, USA, pp. 232-243.L.

H. Blockeel and L. De Raedt, "Top-down induction of first order logical decision trees," *Artificial Intelligence*, Vol. 101, pp.285-297, 1998.

L. Breiman, J. H. Friedman, R. A. Olshen, C. J. Stone, *Classification and regression trees*, Wadsworh International Group, Belmont, CA, USA, 1984.

C. E. Brodley and P. E. Utgoff, "Multivariate Decision Trees," *Machine Learning*, Vol. 19, pp. 45-77, 1995.

W. Buntine, "Learning classification trees," *Statistics and Computing*, Vol. 2, pp. 63-73, 1992.

R. G. Casey and G. Nagy, "Decision tree design using a probabilistic model," *IEEE Transactions on Information Theory*, IT-30, No. 1, pp. 93-99, 1984.

T. G. Dietterich and E. B. Kong, "Machine learning bias, statistical bias and statistical variance of decision tree algorithms," *Machine Learning: Proceedings of the 12th International Conference*, Tahoe City, CA, USA, 1995.

L. De Màntaras, "Technical note: A distance-based attribute selection measure for decision tree induction," *Machine Learning*, Vol. 6, No. 1, pp.81-92, 1991.

U. M. Fayyad, G. Piatetsky-Shapiro, P. Smyth, and R. Uthurusamy. *Advances in Knowledge Discovery and Data Mining*, MIT Press, Cambridge, MA, USA, 1996.

U. M. Fayyad, J. E. Laird, K. B. Irani, *The Fifth International Conference on Machine Learning, AI Magazine* Vol. 10, No. 2, pp. 79-84, 1989.

E. Frank and I. H. Witten, "Generating accurate rule sets without global optimization," *Machine Learning: Proceedings of the 15th International Conference* edited by J. Shavlik, Morgan Kaufmann, San Francisco, CA, USA, 1998.

S. B. Gelfand, C. S. Ravishankar, and E. J. Delp, "An iterative growing and pruning algorithm for classification tree design," *IEEE Transaction on Pattern Analysis and Machine Intelligence*, Vol. 13, No. 2, pp. 163-174, 1991.

M. Golea and M. Marchand, "A growth algorithm for neural network decision trees," *EuroPhysics Letters*, Vol. 12, No. 3, pp.205-210, 1990.

D. Heath, S. Kasif, and S. Salzberg, "Learning oblique decision trees," *IJCAI-93: Proceedings of the 13th International Joint Conference On Artificial Intelligence*, Vol. II, Chambery, France, 1993, Morgan Kaufmann, Vol. 160, pp. 1002-1007.

D. Heath, S. Kasif, and S. Salzberg, "k-DT: A multi-tree learning method," *Proceedings of the 2nd International Workshop on Multistrategy Learning*, Harpers Ferry, WV, 1993. George Mason University, pp. 138-149.

G. Kalkanis, "The application of confidence interval error analysis to the design of decision tree classifiers," *Pattern Recognition Letters*, Vol. 14, No. 5, pp. 355-361, 1993.

I. Kononenko, "On biases in estimating multi-valued attributes," in C. Mellishpages, ed, *IJCAI-95: Proceedings of the 14th International Joint Conference on Artificial Intelligence*, Montreal, Canada, August 1995, Morgan Kaufmann, San Francisco, CA, USA, pp. 1034-1040.

S. W. Kwok, and C. Carter, "Multiple decision trees," *Uncertainty in Artificial Intelligence*, Elsevier Science, Amsterdam, Vol. 4, pp. 327-335, 1990.

J. Lee, S. Olafsson, "SODI: A new approach of second order decision tree induction," Working Paper, *Department of Industrial and Manufacturing Systems Engineering*, Iowa State University, Ames, IA, USA, 2002.

J. K. Martin, "An exact probability metric for decision tree splitting and stopping," *AI&Stats-95: the 5th International Workshop on Artificial Intelligence and Statistics*, Ft. Lauderdale, FL, 1995. *Society for AI and Statistics*, pp. 379-385.

J. Mingers, "Expert systems: rule induction with statistical data," *Journal of the Operational Research Society*, Vol. 38, No. 1, pp. 39-47, 1987.

M. Miyakawa, "Criteria for selecting a variable in the construction of efficient decision trees," *IEEE Transactions on Computers*, Vol. 38, No. 1, pp. 130-141, 1989.

P. M. Murphy and M. Pazzani, "ID2-of-3: Constructive induction of M-of-N concepts for discriminators in decision trees," *Proceedings of the 8th International Workshop of Machine Learning*, 1991.

P. M. Murphy and M. Pazzani, "Exploring the decision forest: An empirical investigation of Occam's Razor in decision tree induction," *Journal of Artificial Intelligence Research*, Vol. 1., pp.257-275, 1994.

S. K. Murthy, S. Kasif, and S. Salzberg, "A system for induction of oblique decision trees" *Journal of Artificial Intelligence Research*, Vol. 2, pp.1-33, 1994.

A. L. Oliveria and A. S. Vincentelli, "Learning complex Boolean functions: Algorithms and applications," *Advances in Neural Information Processing Systems 6*, Morgan Kaufmann, San Francisco, CA, USA, 1993

K. R. Pattipati and M. G. Alexandridis, "Application of heuristic search and information theory to sequential fault diagnosis," *IEEE Transactions on Systems, Man and Cybernetics*, Vol. 20, No. 4, pp. 872-887, 1990.

M. Pazzani, P. Murphy, K. Ali, and D. Schulenburg, "Trading off coverage for accuracy in forecasts: Applications to clinical data analysis," *AAAI Symposium on AI in Medicine*, Stanford, CA, USA, pp. 106-110, 1994.

J. R. Quinlan, "Induction of decision trees," *Machine Learning*, Vol. 1, pp. 81-106, 1986.

J. R. Quinlan, *C4.5: Programs for machine learning*, Vol. 29, pp. 5-44, Morgan Kaufmann, 1993.

J. R. Quinlan and R. L. Rivest, "Inferring decision trees using the minimum description length principle. Information and Computation," Vol. 80, No. 3, pp. 227-248, 1989.

J. Risannen, *Stochastic Complexity in Statistica Enquiry*, World Scientific, Teaneck, N.J, USA, 1989.

I. K. Sethi and G. P. R. Sarvarayudu, "Hierarchical classifier design using mutual information," *IEEE Transactions on Pattern Analysis and Machine Intelligence*, PAMI-4, No. 4, pp. 441-445, 1982.

C.E. Shannon, "A Mathematical Theory of Communication", *Bell System Technical Journal*, Vol. 27, pp. 379-423, pp. 623-656, 1948.

S. Shlien, "Multiple binary decision tree classifiers," *Pattern Recognition*, Vol. 23, No. 7, pp.757-763, 1990.

S. Shlien, "Nonparametric classification using matched binary decision trees," *Pattern Recognition Letters*, Vol. 13, No. 2, pp. 83-88, 1992.

J. L. Talmon, "A multiclass nonparametric partitioning algorithm," *Pattern Recognition Letters*, Vol. 4, pp. 31-38, 1986.

P. C. Taylor and B. W. Silverman, "Block diagrams and splitting criteria for classification trees," *Statistics and Computing*, Vol. 3, No. 4, pp. 147-161, 1993.

T. Van De Merckt, "Decision trees in numerical attribute spaces," In IJCAI-93: Proceedings of the 13th International Joint Conference on Artificial Intelligence, Vol. 2, Chambery, France, September 1993, Morgan Kaufmann, pp. 1016-1021.

P. K. Varshney, C. R. P. Hartmann, and J. M. De Faria Jr., "Applications of information theory to sequential fault diagnosis," *IEEE Transactions on Computers*, Vol. 31, No. 2, pp.164-170, 1982.

P. White and W. Z. Liu, "Technical note: Bias in information-based measures in decision tree induction," *Machine Learning*, Vol. 15, No. 3, pp. 321-329, 1994.

H. Witten and E. Frank, *Data mining: practical machine learning tools and techniques with Java implementations*. Morgan Kaufmann, San Francisco, CA, USA, 1999.

AUTHORS' BIOGRAPHICAL STATEMENTS

Mr. Jun-Youl Lee is a Ph.D. candidate in the Industrial and Manufacturing Systems Engineering Department at Iowa State University. He holds a BS and MS from Korea University and a MS in Electrical Engineering from Iowa State University. His research interests include neural networks, support vector machines, and decision tree induction.

Dr. Sigurdur Olafsson is an Assistant Professor in the Industrial and Manufacturing Systems Engineering Department at Iowa State University, where he has been on the faculty since 1998. He received his BS in Mathematics from the University of Iceland in 1994, and his MS and Ph.D. in Industrial Engineering from the University of Wisconsin – Madison in 1996 and 1998, respectively. His research interests in knowledge discovery include optimization-based approaches to data mining and data mining of production planning and scheduling data.

Chapter 11 [1]

KNOWLEDGE ACQUISITION AND UNCERTAINTY IN FAULT DIAGNOSIS: A ROUGH SETS PERSPECTIVE

Lian-Yin Zhai[*], Li-Pheng Khoo[*], and Sai-Cheong Fok[**]

[*] *School of Mechanical and Production Engineering, Nanyang Technological University, 50 Nanyang Avenue, Singapore 639798*
Email: mlyzhai@ntu.edu.sg, mlpkhoo@ntu.edu.sg
Web: http://www.ntu.edu.sg/mpe/Admin/Divisions/mechatronics&design/staff.asp

[**] *Faculty of Engineering & Surveying, University of Southern Queensland, Toowoomba, Qld 4350, Australia*
Email: foksai@usq.edu.au
Web: http://www.usq.edu.au/users/foksai/

Abstract: The ability to acquire knowledge from empirical data or the environment is an important requirement in better understanding many natural and artificial organisms. This ability relies heavily on the quality of the raw information available about the target system. In reality, these raw information/data may contain uncertainty and fuzziness, that is, it may be imprecise or incomplete. A number of techniques, such as the Dempster-Shafer theory of belief functions and fuzzy set theory, have been developed to handle knowledge acquisition in environments that exhibit uncertainty and fuzziness. However, the advent of the rough set theory in the early 80's provides a novel and promising way of dealing with vagueness and uncertainty. This chapter will address the issue systematically by covering a broad area including knowledge acquisition / extraction, uncertainty in general, and techniques for handling uncertainty. The basic notions of rough set theory as well as some recent applications are also included. Two simple case studies related to fault diagnosis in manufacturing systems are used to illustrate the concepts presented in this chapter.

Key Words: Rough Sets, Rule Induction, Knowledge Acquisition, Fuzzy Reasoning, Fault Diagnosis.

---

[1] Triantaphyllou, E. and G. Felici (Eds.), **Data Mining and Knowledge Discovery Approaches Based on Rule Induction Techniques**, Massive Computing Series, Springer, Heidelberg, Germany, pp. 359-394, 2006.

1.   INTRODUCTION

The ability of acquiring decision rules from empirical data or the environment is an important requirement for both natural and artificial organisms. For example, in an intelligent system, decision rules can be extracted by performing inductive learning (Wong *et al.*, 1986). Many techniques such as decision tree learning (Quinlan, 1986b), neural network learning (Fausett, 1994), and genetic algorithm-based learning (Goldberg, 1989), have been developed to carry out such a task. With the rapid advent of IT technology, it has often been said that we live in the 'information age'. This verdict is best manifested by the immense creation, availability, and use of enormous volumes of data (Triantaphyllou *et al.*, 2002). As a result, the ability to automatically and efficiently extract knowledge from the huge amount of raw data has become an important research area. In reality, the raw data gleaned from a specific environment may contain uncertainty, that is, the data may be imprecise or incomplete. Imprecise data refer to information that is fuzzy or even conflicting. For example, the opinions about the performance of a machine as assessed by two engineers can be different. This will introduce inconsistency in the knowledge concerning the performance of the machine. On the other hand, incomplete data refer to missing data in the data records and may be caused by the unavailability of equipment or oversight of operators. This imprecise and incomplete nature of raw data is obviously the greatest obstacle to the task of rule extraction.

Over the past decades, many theories and techniques have been developed to deal with uncertainty in rule induction, for example, fuzzy set theory (Zadeh, 1965) and the Dempster-Shafer theory of belief functions (Shafer, 1976; 1982). Rough set theory, which was introduced by Pawlak (1982) in the early 80's, provides a novel and powerful way of dealing with vagueness and uncertainty. It focuses on the discovery of patterns in imprecise data and can be used as a basis to perform formal reasoning, machine learning and rule discovery. In less than two decades, rough set theory has rapidly established itself in many real-life applications such as medical diagnosis, control algorithm acquisition and process control, and information retrieval (Pawlak, 1992; 1994a; 1994b). The main advantages of rough set theory are as follows:

- It does not need any preliminary or additional information about data;
- It is easy to handle mathematically;
- Its algorithms are relatively simple.

Furthermore, rough set theory is more justified for situations in which the set of experimental data is too small to employ standard statistical methods

(Pawlak, 1991); it demonstrates great advantages when dealing with inconsistent information (Khoo et al., 1999).

This chapter will review the various techniques used to deal with uncertainty, including a brief outline of fuzzy set theory and Dempster-Shafer theory of belief functions. The basic notions of rough set theory as well as some recent applications of rough sets are also included. Two simple case studies related to fault diagnosis of manufacturing systems are used to illustrate the concepts presented.

2.   AN OVERVIEW OF KNOWLEDGE DISCOVERY AND UNCERTAINTY

Human beings acquire knowledge through learning, which is also true in intelligent systems. Since its advent, knowledge discovery has been of growing interest to researchers in intelligent reasoning, statistics and, especially, in machine learning.

2.1   Knowledge Acquisition and Machine Learning

Automated knowledge acquisition and machine learning are two important areas in intelligent systems. Knowledge acquisition focuses on improving and partially automating the acquisition of knowledge from human experts by knowledge engineers. Machine learning research concentrates on developing autonomous algorithms for the acquisition of knowledge from data and improving the organization of the obtained knowledge (Tecuci and Kodratoff, 1995). However, as machine learning moves into more complex domains, and knowledge acquisition attempts to automate the acquisition process even more, the two fields increasingly find themselves addressing common issues with different approaches and become more and more complementary in many applications.

2.1.1   Knowledge Representation

Knowledge representation is a common issue concerned by both machine learning and knowledge acquisition techniques. Basically, knowledge representation must take a form where its structure becomes meaningful and easy to be manipulated by a computer. Many schemes have been proposed to represent knowledge. The more popular ones are rule-based representation, frame-based representation, multiple context-based representation, model-based representation, and blackboard representation. The first two schemes are widely used for representing knowledge in many intelligent systems. Rule-based (If-Then rules) representation, in particular, is the most popular.

The main advantages of employing rule-based representation in intelligent systems are as follows (Morik, 1989):

- Rules are relatively easy to construct;
- It enables rapid prototyping, and tests can begin with just a few rules;
- It is a natural way to summarize human knowledge.

2.1.2   Knowledge Acquisition

Knowledge acquisition is an integral process in the development of intelligent systems. As the process of acquiring knowledge is labor intensive, it has also been identified as a bottleneck in building intelligent systems. Knowledge acquisition techniques can be broadly classified into two categories, namely the manual method and the computer-based method (Figure 1).

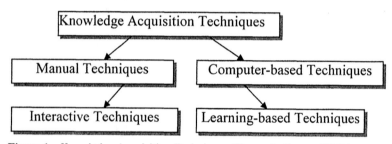

Figure 1. Knowledge Acquisition Techniques (Grzymala-Busse, 1991b).

Briefly stated, the manual method involves interview, knowledge gathering and elicitation session with domain experts. The computer-based method, on the other hand, attempts to automate the process of acquiring knowledge (Mrozek, 1992). It can be implemented using the interactive technique (semi-automated) or a learning-based technique (automated). There is a continuing and growing research interest in these areas.

2.1.3   Machine Learning and Automated Knowledge Extraction

Machine learning plays a critical role in automated knowledge acquisition. It is the study of computational methods to automate the process of knowledge acquisition using the information (training data) gleaned from a process or domain experts. It aims at replacing the much time-consuming human activity in acquiring knowledge with automated techniques that can possibly improve the accuracy or the efficiency of the process by discovering and exploiting regularities in a training data set.

The empirical learning approach might be the most popular method among those methods developed to perform machine learning. The empirical learning method comprises four different modes of learning namely, rote learning, learning by being told, learning by analogy and inductive learning (Figure 2). Inductive learning can be further classified into learning from examples and learning from observations. Between the two, learning from examples, also known as concept acquisition, which uses a set of 'positive' and a set of 'negative' training examples to induce a set of high-level concept descriptions, has been investigated by many researchers. It appears to be the most practical and is widely used in many intelligent systems. Using such a technique, knowledge in the form of rules and decision trees that is easy for human to comprehend, can be induced from training examples. Besides, the rules obtained may be incorporated into the knowledge base of a rule-based intelligent system and subsequently, used for reasoning.

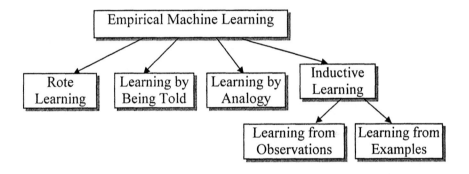

Figure 2. Machine Learning Taxonomy.

On the other hand, knowledge extraction, which can be considered as a sub-field or an application area of machine learning, is primarily concerned with finding and extracting useful knowledge from a depository of raw data which may be incomplete, imprecise and noisy (Ziarko, 1994a). In other words, knowledge extraction attempts to search for hidden regularities in a training data set. These hidden regularities form the basis for making decisions. Knowledge extraction tools are able to find the trends and generate rules to explain these regularities. Prediction can also be made based on the rules generated. Figure 3 presents the main processes involved in knowledge extraction. In this sense, machine learning methods can be viewed as a useful tool to implement the knowledge extraction tasks. Essentially, the differences between the two are more historical than scientific.

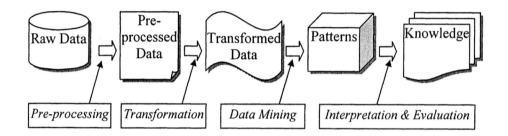

Figure 3. Processes for Knowledge Extraction.

2.1.4 Inductive Learning Techniques for Automated Knowledge Extraction

One important step in applying a machine learning technique is to decide an effective representation scheme for both the training data and the knowledge to be learned. Using attributes to describe training data or characterize the results is one of the most widely used methods. In this case, knowledge is expressed in the form of rules generated from a set of training data by a learning algorithm. The quality of the rules and hence the knowledge discovered is very much dependent upon the algorithm used. In other words, central to the problem of knowledge extraction is the technique or method used to generate such rules.

There have been many inductive learning techniques emerged in recent years to automate the process of knowledge acquisition. Quinlan (1990) grouped these techniques into two broad categories, namely the covering technique and the divide-and-conquer technique. For the covering technique, the so-called AQ (Algorithm Quasi-optimal) family approaches and their derivatives (Michalski *et al.*, 1983; Pham and Dimov, 1997) are available. However, the AQ family approaches have not been widely used mainly because of their complexity. On the contrary, the divide-and-conquer technique has received considerable attention by most researchers (Quinlan, 1986b; Fournier and Crémilleux, 2002; Triantaphyllou, 2003), and the most representative algorithm should be the ID3 system developed by Quinlan (1986b). ID3 attempts to learn decision trees from labeled training examples. The algorithm learns decision trees by constructing them top-down. The general idea behind the decision tree approach is to recursively separate data into sub-classes using the Concept Learner Systems (CLS) algorithm proposed by Hunt (Quinlan, 1986b). Briefly, the procedure of the algorithm is as follows:

1. Select a random subset (called a window) of the training examples;
2. Use the CLS algorithm to build a decision tree that correctly classifies all the training examples in the current window;
3. Scan all the training instances serially to find exceptions to the current rules;
4. Form a new window by combining some of the training examples from the current window with some of the exceptions obtained in Step 3;
5. Repeat Steps 2 through 4 until there is no exception to the rule set.

It is known that computationally it is impractical to find the smallest decision tree for a given training data set. ID3 uses a procedure that tends to build smaller trees by ordering or ranking the attributes: attributes that discriminate best are selected for evaluation first. This implies that each node should be associated with the attribute that is the most informative among the attributes not yet considered in the path from the root. This enables the algorithm to produce a smaller decision tree that can correctly classify all of the training examples. In other words, preference (inductive) bias is used to find a small tree consistent with the training examples.

In ID3, nodes are selected according to the entropy or information content of associated object attributes. The application of entropy provides a rational and effective means to construct decision trees. Besides, the algorithm has some other advantages:

- The results are comprehensible;
- The classification can be done quite fast;
- The technology involved is mature.

On the other hand, there are also some problems with the ID3 algorithm. The ID3-like algorithms (Quinlan, 1986b; Mingers, 1989), during the process of inducing decision trees as well as refining the induced decision trees, implicitly assume that enough information is available in the data to decide exactly how each object should be classified. This implies that there is a single correct label for any given combination of attribute values describing objects in the training set. Such an assumption has limited the capability of ID3-like algorithms in dealing with uncertainty in the training data set. The drawbacks include:

- The decision trees produced may not be very general. Some of the decision rules represented by them may contain unnecessary or irrelevant conditions;
- The algorithm has to break up a larger set of training examples into subsets during the 'windowing' process. Such a process does not always yield the same decision;
- The algorithm is very sensitive to noise. As previously mentioned, it cannot deal with uncertainty.

Since the advent of ID3, many researchers have attempted to improve this algorithm and have produced new ones called ID4 and ID5. A comparison of the three ID-series of algorithms can be found in the work by Utgoff (Pham and Dimov, 1997). Quinlan (1992) had also improved the algorithm under the name of C4.5 and C5.0 (http://www.rulequest.com/).

2.2   Uncertainties in Fault Diagnosis

Uncertainty occurs in many real-life problems. It may be caused by the information used for problem solving being unavailable, incomplete, imprecise, unreliable, contradictory, and changing. Human beings are equipped with the ability to apply qualitative reasoning techniques to deal with it. In the case of a computerized system, uncertainty is frequently managed by using quantitative approaches that are computationally intensive. For example, a binary or crisp system that processes '*TRUE* or *FALSE*', or '*YES* or *NO*' type of decisions, is likely to arrive at a conclusion or a solution faster than one that needs to handle uncertainty.

Managing uncertainty is a big challenge to knowledge-processing systems. ID3, for example, failed when subjected to inconsistent inputs (Khoo *et al.*, 1999; Khoo and Zhai, 2001a). Uncertainty management and related topics such as plausible reasoning are always active research areas. In some problem domains, uncertainty can possibly be neglected, though at the risk of compromising the performance of a decision support system. However, in most cases, the management of uncertainty becomes necessary because of critical system requirements or more complete rules are needed. In these cases, eliminating inconsistent or incomplete information when extracting knowledge from an information system may introduce inaccurate or even false results, especially when the available source information is limited. In general, the nature of uncertainty comes from the following three sources: inconsistent data, incomplete data, and noisy data.

2.2.1   Inconsistent Data

In general, an *object* (or *observation*) can be described or characterized in a universe using the *values* attained by a set of *attributes* (*attribute-value* pairs). The category that an object (observation) belongs to is defined as a *class* (*concept*). Hence, a concept may be viewed as a set of objects with the same decision values. When the description of all the objects with respect to a particular concept (class) is complete and precise enough, it is possible to describe the concept unambiguously. Inconclusive (*conflicting* or *inconsistent*) data in a training data set are objects having the same description but belonging to different concepts (Uthurusamy *et al.*, 1991).

For example, Patients 1 and 2 in Table 1 are in a conflicting situation. They have the same attribute-value pairs, but belong to two different concepts (classes). Concepts in an inconsistent information table cannot be precisely defined. By incorporating the confidence level when classifying the objects, these concepts can be reasonably described or approximated. Many methods were proposed to deal with the approximation of a concept. Fuzzy set theory, for example, characterizes a concept approximately by a membership grade, which ranges from 0 to 1. Another approach is to use rough set theory that provides the lower and upper approximations of a concept. Details of fuzzy sets and rough sets are presented in Sections 2.3.4 and 3.1, respectively.

Table 1. Information Table with Inconsistent Data (Pawlak *et al.*, 1995).

Patient	Attributes			Decision
	Headache	Muscle Pain	Temperature	Flu
1	*yes*	*yes*	*High*	*no*
2	*yes*	*yes*	*High*	*yes*
3	yes	yes	Very high	yes
4	no	yes	Normal	no
5	no	No	High	no
6	no	Yes	Very high	yes

2.2.2 Incomplete Data

In practice, information about a manufacturing system is usually organized and collected around the needs of organizational activities. At times, some of the information may not be recorded, be mistakenly erased, or be forgotten. This may result in imprecise and incomplete data being collected and thus hamper the rule discovery task. In an information system, such unknown attribute-value pairs are called null or missing values. Table 2 shows an information table with some null attribute values (denoted as '?'). This phenomenon is fairly common in the domain of learning from examples.

Table 2. Information Table with Missing Data (Grzymann-Busse, 1991a).

Object	Attributes			Decision
	Feel	Cuddliness	Material	Attitude
1	soft	Smooth	plastic	negative
2	*hard*	*?*	*plastic*	*positive*
3	soft	Furry	wool	neutral
4	*?*	*smooth*	*plastic*	*negative*
5	*hard*	*fuzzy*	*?*	*positive*
⋮	⋮	⋮	⋮	⋮
n	soft	Fuzzy	wool	positive

Recent years have seen a lot of efforts made to address the null-attribute problem [Luba and Lasocki, 1994; Grzymala-Busse, 1991a; Thiesson, 1995]. Normally when a data set contains missing attribute values, either the corresponding observations are discarded or an attempt is made to replace the unknown values with the most likely ones. Quinlan (1986b) employed this approach in his inductive decision tree algorithm. In a separate work, Quinlan (1989) suggested to construct rules that predict the value of the missing attributes, based on the values of other attributes in the set of training examples, and the classification information. These values can then be used to '*fill in*' the missing attribute values and the resulting data set could then be used for classification

Grzymala-Busse (1991a) cited the drawbacks of the above approaches adopted by Quinlan. In his work, a given information table with unknown attribute values has been transformed into a new and possibly inconsistent information table, in which every attribute value is known. The unknown value of an attribute is replaced with all possible values attainable by that attribute. In order words, the so-called missing value problem has been transformed into one that concerns learning from inconsistent examples.

In a similar manner, Barbara *et al.* (1992) treated missing attribute values as uninteresting values and associated them with probability measures. On the other hand, Thiesson (1995) solved the missing value problem using the so-called EM algorithm. Basically, the EM algorithm assumes that the missing values happen at random. The importance of this method lies in its underlying message, that is, even when the data are complete, it is often useful to treat the data as a missing value problem for computational purposes (Elder-IV and Pregibon, 1995). Felici and Truemper (2002) proposed a learning system for logic domains that models the learning problem via minimum cost satisfiability problems and deals with incomplete data and missing values using ternary variables (i.e., logic variables that can assume the values True / False / Unknown).

2.2.3   Noisy Data

Non-systematic errors, which can occur during data entry or collection of data, are usually referred to as *noise*. Erroneous data pose a significant problem in real-world data mining or knowledge discovery work. This problem has been extensively investigated for a variety of inductive decision trees (Quinlan, 1986a).

If a training data set is corrupted with noise, the diagnostic system should be able to identify and deal with it. The presence of noise in the training data set may affect the accuracy of the generated diagnostic rules. An attempt should therefore be made to eliminate or manage noise that affects the classification of the objects in the training data set. Quinlan (1986a) performed a series of experiments to investigate the effect of noise on classifying training examples from the testing data set. The results indicate that for some systems, adding substantial noise to the training data may produce a lower level of misclassification of unseen examples in testing data. It is also interesting to note that the rules gleaned from the corrupted training data set perform better in classifying noisy testing data than those obtained from noise-free training data set. Chan and Wong (1991) used statistical techniques to analyze the effect of noise. Their approach involved estimating the class conditional density in the presence of noise, comparing it with the true class density and then determining a classifier whose level of confidence is appropriately set.

2.3   Traditional Techniques for Handling Uncertainty

Many techniques have been proposed to deal with uncertainty and vagueness in the past decades. In this section, some typical approaches widely used for handling uncertainty are reviewed, including MYCIN's model of certainty factors, Bayesian probability theory, the Dempster-Shafer theory of belief functions, and fuzzy set theory.

2.3.1   MYCIN's Model of Certainty Factors

The model of certainty factors was proposed and implemented in MYCIN, a medical diagnostic expert system (Shortliffe and Buchanan, 1975), as a basis for the system to deal with uncertainty. A certainty factor is a relatively simple and ad-hoc concept for handling uncertainty. It was developed in an attempt to model more closely the reasoning process adopted by medical practitioners in diagnosing patients. In traditional probabilistic theory, the sum of the confidence for a hypothesis and the confidence against that hypothesis must add to 1. However, it is often the case that an expert may agree that his/her confidence in a particular conclusion is 0.7, but may not be prepared to say that his/her confidence in not achieving the conclusion is 0.3. He/she may think that it is 0. More specifically, the certainty measure can be defined as follows.

> For a *proposition*, A, a number called *certainty measure* $(C(A))$ is associated. $C(A) = 1$ if A is known to be true, $C(A) = -1$ if A is known to be false, and $C(A) = 0$ if nothing is known about A.

Thus, every rule can be associated with a number from the interval [-1, 1]. This number is known as the *certainty factor* (*CF*). The rules can then be expressed as follows (where $1 \geq x \geq -1$):

If *A* Then *B* with *CF* = *x*.

The certainty factor concept is simple to use and implement. It is intuitive in some domains such as manufacturing diagnosis. In addition, it is ad-hoc and has no strong mathematical basis or foundation. However, the application of combining the function for obtaining the measure of belief and disbelief can lead to erroneous results if the two observations are related. Lack of sound supporting theory for certainty factors is considered as a disadvantage. Certainty factors, with some modifications, may be interpreted by probability theory. However, pieces of evidence must be conditionally independent. The hypothesis and its negation, and the inference network must have a tree structure. However, all these assumptions are seldom satisfied in the real world (Newton *et al.*, 1987).

2.3.2   Bayesian Probability Theory

Among all the numerical approaches to deal with uncertainty, probability theory is one of the oldest. Although probability theory is viewed as an inadequate model for managing uncertainty in intelligent systems, many researchers still think that it is the best tool (Rao, 1984). Some intelligent systems such as PROSPECTOR and AL/X, used Bayes' rule as the tool to handle uncertainty (Grzymala-Busse, 1991b).

The probability theory based method for handling uncertainty adopts *probability* as a measure of subjective belief. It uses the Bayes' Theorem for uncertain evidence. The probability of a hypothesis *H*, *P[H]*, is a real number between 0 and 1, which represents a measure of belief in that hypothesis. The conditional probability *P[H/E]*, is the probability of Hypothesis *H* in the light of Evidence *E*. The degree of belief in a hypothesis is subject to change when new evidence becomes available. For a given hypothesis, H_k, there is a prior probability, $P[H_k]$, that H_k could be true. Given some evidence, *E*, the belief is altered to produce a posterior probability, $P[H_k|E]$, for the hypothesis H_k. Using Bayes' Theorem, $P[H_k|E]$ can be computed from $P[H_k]$. However, Bayes' Theorem cannot be directly used when the evidence itself is doubtful. The uncertain evidence, *E'*, can be expressed as the evidence *E* with probability *P[E|E']*, or as its complement E^c with probability $P[E^c |E']$. With some assumptions, the formula for uncertain evidence can be obtained.

The Bayesian probability theory has a well-established and sound mathematical basis; however, its applicability is limited by the requirement of knowing the prior probabilities. Furthermore, the assumption of conditional independence may introduce errors. Another limitation of this method is that any alteration made to an event will require recalculation of all probabilities to preserve coherence and consistency.

2.3.3   The Dempster-Shafer Theory of Belief Functions

The Dempster-Shafer theory of belief functions also known as the evidence theory, is an extension of the classical theory of probability. It originated from Dempster's work on multi-valued mapping (Dempster, 1967) and was later reformulated by Shafer (1976; 1982). In his original work, Dempster related belief functions to the so-called *upper and lower probabilities*, which provide a very general framework for modeling uncertainty. The theory uses a number between 0 and 1 to indicate the *degree of belief or evidence* for a proposition. Reasoning is then carried out using the rule of combination of the degrees of belief.

A sample space in the Dempster-Shafer theory is called a *frame of discernment (F)*, and a *belief function (BEL)* is a function on the power set of F with certain properties. *BEL(A)* measures the degree of belief in Event A. Unlike probability functions in the Bayesian approach, belief functions are not additive in general, that is $BEL(A) + BEL(B) \neq BEL(A \cup B)$ when $A \cap B = \varnothing$. The 'non-additive' nature also captures the fact that a person's degree of belief in an event A does not necessarily give the information on his belief in $\neg A$ (i.e., negation of A).

One of the basic strategies of the Dempster-Shafer theory is to decompose a set of evidence into two or more unrelated sets of evidence, make probability judgments separately on these sets of evidence, and then combine these judgments by the Dempster's Rule. In addition, the Dempster-Shafer theory provides a way to discount one's belief, which is convenient to express doubts about the evidence.

The Dempster-Shafer theory of belief functions is very flexible and can be applied to a given situation in different ways. The theory is appealing because it is a natural mathematical generalization of the classical probability theory. It captures the fact that beliefs are generally non-additive. Furthermore, the Dempster-Shafer theory is not as demanding as probability theory: for example, it does not need prior probabilities or conditional probabilities. It permits the sum of the belief for a proposition and the belief for its negation to be smaller than one. However, the computational complexity of the Dempster's rule of combination is enormous, and some suggestions have been given to remove this obstacle (Shafer and Logan, 1987). Critics of the theory argue that it is inadequate for empirical data (Lemmer, 1986) or that in some cases the Dempster's rule of combination should not be applied at all (Zadeh, 1986), for example, when there are considerable disagreements among the evidence. Moreover, the numerical stability of the theory has not been analyzed in great detail. In some cases, a small variation in the basic probability assignments can produce a large variation in the results (Dubois and Prade, 1985).

2.3.4   The Fuzzy Sets Theory

The fuzzy sets theory is based on the generalization of set theory and was formalized by Zadeh (1965). It has been developed so extensively that currently an entire spectrum of fuzzy theories has evolved. Fuzzy set theory was introduced to represent uncertainty, especially the type of uncertainty that arises from imprecision and ambiguity, in the sense of vagueness rather than incomplete information. A fuzzy set is a class of objects characterized by a *membership function* which assigns to each object a grade of membership which is a number in the interval [0, 1] (Kaufmann, 1988). The basic notions of a crisp set such as union, intersection, complement, etc., can be extended to fuzzy sets.

Each element, x, of a *fuzzy subset, A*, on a *universe of discourse U* can be characterized by the value (μ_A) of a function known as *membership function*. A fuzzy subset A has no sharp boundary. The value, $\mu_A(u)$, for $u \in U$, is a number in the real interval [0,1] and is called the *grade of membership* of u. Therefore, a fuzzy set is characterized by the membership function μ_A: $U \rightarrow [0,1]$. In other words, the membership function, $\mu_A(x)$, expresses the grade of membership of each element, x_i, in the fuzzy subset, A. For example, '$\mu_A(x_i) = 0$' denotes no membership, and '$\mu_A(x_i) = 1$' represents full membership, while $\mu_A(x_i)$ with a value between 0 and 1 denotes partial membership. An ordinary (crisp) set is the special case of a fuzzy set with either $\mu_A(u) = 1$ or $\mu_A(u) = 0$. Some definitions and operations of fuzzy set theory are as follows:

Two fuzzy subsets A and B are equal (denoted by $A = B$), if and only if for all $u \in U$ we have $\mu_A(u) = \mu_B(u)$.

An empty set, $\varnothing$, is defined as follows:
For all $u \in U$, we have $\mu_\varnothing(u) = 0$.
For the universe, U, $\mu_U(u) = 1$, for any $u \in U$.

The union and intersection of two fuzzy subsets, A and B, are defined as follows:
$\mu_{A \cup B}(x) = \text{Max}(\mu_A(x), \mu_B(x))$, and $\mu_{A \cap B}(x) = \text{Min}(\mu_A(x), \mu_B(x))$, for every $x \in U$.

The complement $-A$ of a fuzzy set A is defined by the membership function:
$\mu_{-A}(x) = 1 - \mu_A(x)$, for every $x \in A$.

Fuzzy set theory is controversial. On one hand, it is an extremely popular area of research. The idea of fuzzy sets seems appealing because it allows imprecise linguistic terms such as 'large', 'very small', and 'more or less equal' to be represented and manipulated in a well-defined mathematical way. Traditional logic is extended to incorporate uncertainties by the introduction of fuzzy implication (*IF A THEN B ELSE C*) and fuzzy quantifiers such as 'some', 'most', and 'not many'. Many successful real-life systems based on fuzzy set theory have been implemented (Bandemer and Gottwald, 1995; Zimmermann, 1996). Moreover, possibility theory, which is based on fuzzy set theory, is the most popular approach used to handle uncertainty in intelligent systems. Some new applications of fuzzy set theory in intelligent systems can be found in the work by di Nola *et al.*, (1989). On the other hand, there is also opposition to fuzzy set theory in the intelligent system community. In a mild form of criticism, fuzzy set theory is prohibited from describing uncertainty at all and instead, it is assumed to be able to deal with ambiguity in describing events (Pearl, 1988). In a stronger form of criticism (Cheeseman, 1986), the fundamental rules of fuzzy set theory are seen as false. Some other problems of fuzzy set theory are associated with assigning values for a membership function. Moreover, membership functions are context sensitive (Lee *et al.*, 1987).

2.3.5   Comparison of Traditional Approaches for Handling Uncertainty

Newton *et al.* (1987) presented a comparison among the four approaches based on six aspects, namely the theoretical background, the complexity of computation, the model set-up, the model execution, the complexity of theory, and the ease of application. It provides the basic guidelines for the selection of an appropriate technique to solve problems associated with uncertainty (Table 3).

Table 3. A Comparison of the Four Approaches (Newton *et al.*, 1987).

	MYCIN's Model	Bayesian Probability	Dempster-Shafer Theory	Fuzzy Set Theory
Theoretical Background	Weak	Strong	Strong	Moderate
Computational Complexity	Low	Low	Moderate	Moderate
Model Set-up	Low	Moderate	Moderate	Moderate
Model Execution	Low	Low	Moderate	Moderate
Complexity of Theory	Low	Low	Moderate	Moderate
Ease of Application	Easy	Easy	Difficult	Easy

2.4   The Rough Sets Approach

2.4.1   Introductory Remarks

The rough sets theory was proposed by Pawlak (1982) as a novel and powerful mathematical tool for reasoning about imprecision, vagueness and uncertainty. It overlaps, to some extent, with many other theories dealing with uncertainty and vagueness, especially with the Dempster-Shafer theory of belief functions (Slowinski and Stefanowski, 1992) and the fuzzy set theory (Wygralak, 1989; Dubois and Prade, 1990; 1992). Nevertheless, rough set theory can be viewed on its own right, as an independent, complementary, and not competing discipline (Pawlak, 1991). The main difference between rough sets and the Dempster-Shafer theory is that the latter uses belief functions as the main tool, while the rough set theory makes use of a set of lower and upper approximations. The relationship between rough sets and fuzzy sets are rather complicated and is discussed in Section 2.4.2. Furthermore, some relationships exist between rough sets theory and statistics (Krusinska *et al.*, 1990), Boolean reasoning methods (Skowron and Rauszer, 1992), and decision analysis (Pawlak, 1994b).

The philosophy of rough sets theory is based on the idea of classification. The ability to classify is a fundamental feature of any living organism, a robot or an agent, which, in order to behave rationally in the external world, must constantly classify concrete or abstract objects such as entities, events, processes, and signals. In order to do so, one has to ignore minor differences between objects, thus forming classes of objects that are not noticeably different. These indiscernible classes can be viewed as *elementary concepts* used by an agent to build up its knowledge about reality. Consider, for example, the task of monitoring and diagnosing a group of machine tools in a workshop. Normally a domain expert will check a set of data such as the operating temperature, noise level, and the overall vibration level, to evaluate the condition of each one of the machines. All the machines having the same symptoms are *discernible (similar)* in view of the available information can be classified in blocks, which can be understood as *elementary granules (atoms)* of knowledge about machines (or conditions of machines). These granules are called *elementary sets* or *concepts*, and can be considered as elementary building blocks of knowledge about these machines. Elementary concepts can be combined into compound concepts that are uniquely defined in terms of elementary concepts. Any union of elementary sets is called a *crisp (or precise) set*. However, the granularity of knowledge results in situations in which some notions cannot be expressed precisely within the available knowledge and can be defined only approximately. Such sets are referred to *as rough* (*vague, imprecise*).

In rough set theory, for every set X, it is possible to associate it with two crisp sets known as *the lower* and *the upper approximation* of X. Thus, each vague concept is replaced by a pair of precise concepts. The lower approximation of a concept consists of all the objects that *surely* belong to the concept, whereas the upper approximation of a concept consists of all the objects that *possibly* belong to the concept. For example, the concept of odd (even) number is precise, because for every number it can be decided whether it is odd (even) or not. However, based on visual inspection, the concept of the good working condition of a machine is vague unless it is thoroughly examined. Between the lower and upper approximations of a concept is a *boundary region* of the concept. It consists of all the objects that cannot be classified with certainty under the concept or its complement employing the available knowledge. The greater the boundary region, the more vague is the concept. As a special case, if the boundary region of a concept is empty, the concept is precise. In other words, approximations are the basic and most important tools (operators) in the rough-set philosophy to deal with uncertainty and vagueness.

2.4.2   Rough Sets and Fuzzy Sets

The similarity of the terms 'rough set' and 'fuzzy set' tends to create a misunderstanding. More specifically, a fuzzy set is a class with a blurred boundary whereas a rough set is a crisp set that is *coarsely* defined. There is a close connection, however, between the concept of a rough set and that of a fuzzy graph (Pawlak, 1985). A fuzzy graph is a disjunction of granules that collectively approximate to a function or a relation, with a granule being a clump of points that are drawn together by the indiscernibility, similarity or functionality. In the case of rough sets, the granules are equivalence classes that are the elements of a partition. When the concept of equivalence is generalized to that of similarity, as was done in some of the recent extensions of the rough set theory, the concept of a rough set and that of a fuzzy graph become very close in meaning.

Although there is this point of contact between the theories of rough sets and fuzzy sets, these two theories evolved in different directions and are largely complementary rather than competitive. However, the recent extensions of rough set theory in which the focus moves away from indiscernibility – a crisp concept – to similarity, which is a fuzzy concept, bring the two theories closer together (Dubois and Prade, 1992). What is more fundamental is that both theories address, each in its own way, the basic issues of information granulation, with the rough set theory focused on crisp information granulation and the fuzzy set theory focused on fuzzy information granulation. What is true of both theories is that information granulation plays a central role in most of their applications.

Thus, the theories of rough sets and fuzzy sets are distinct and a complementary generalization of set theory. They are two independent approaches to handle imperfect knowledge. There have been extensive studies on the relationship between rough sets and fuzzy sets (Pawlak, 1985; Wygralak 1989; Chanas and Kuchta, 1992; Lin, 1994). Many proposals have been made for the combination of rough sets and fuzzy sets, which lead to the introduction of the notions of fuzzy rough sets and rough fuzzy sets (Dubois and Prade, 1990; 1992; Nanda and Majumdar, 1992).

2.4.3 Development of Rough Sets Theory

Since the origination of rough set theory in the early 80's, within less than two decades it has turned out that the theory is of substantial importance to intelligent systems and cognitive sciences. In particular, to intelligent systems, decision support systems, machine learning, knowledge acquisition, pattern recognition, decision tables and inductive reasoning (Slowinski R., 1992; Ziarko, 1994b; Lin, 1995; Lin and Cercone, 1997). It has a wide spread of applications, which include medicine, pharmacology, industry, engineering, control, social sciences and earth sciences (Slowinski R., 1992). Several computer systems based on rough sets were implemented on personal computers and workstations such as LERS (Grzymala-Busse, 1992), ROUGHDAS and ROUGH-CLASS (Slowinski and Stefanowski, 1992), and INFER (Wong and Ziarko, 1987). By now, rough set theory has been mainly used for vague data analysis. Machine learning is another important area where rough sets can be applied.

In general, the basic problems in data analysis that can be tackled using a rough set approach are as follows.

- Characterization of a set of objects in terms of attribute values;
- Finding the dependencies (total or partial) between attributes;
- Reduction of superfluous attributes (data);
- Finding the most significant attributes;
- Generation of decision rules.

Rough set theory offers simple algorithms to handle the above domains and allows straightforward interpretation of the results.

2.4.4 Strengths of Rough Sets Theory and Its Applications in Fault Diagnosis

Over the years, much work has been done enabling rough set theory to handle imprecise information analysis problems (Slowinski and Stefanowski, 1989). Compared with other techniques dealing with uncertainty and vagueness, rough set theory has its unique advantages and thus reveals its robust abilities in solving such problems (Pawlak, 1996; 1997). Generally, the most outstanding advantage of rough set theory is that it does not require:

- Any preliminary or additional information about data such as the probability distribution in statistics;
- The basic probability assignment in the Dempster-Shafer theory, or the grade of membership or the value of possibility in the fuzzy set theory (Pawlak *et al.*, 1995).

Another advantage of rough set theory is that it is more suitable when the data set is too small to employ statistical methods, as mentioned earlier. Mathematically, there are two other advantages of using rough sets as a tool to deal with information analysis. First, the theory provides a collection of mathematical techniques to deal, with full mathematical rigor, with data classification problems, particularly when the data are noisy, incomplete or imprecise. Second, the rough set theory includes a formal model of knowledge defined as a family of indiscernibility relations so that the knowledge has a clearly defined mathematical sense, and can be analyzed and manipulated using mathematical techniques (Ziarko, 1994b).

Rough set theory can also be applied to fault diagnosis. A diagnostic system is basically a classification system that is trained to classify a given record (Pawlak, 1984). The intelligence of a trained system may be materialized in the form of weights (neural networks and statistical methods) or a set of rules (rule-based and fuzzy rule-based systems). The rough set approach was initially employed to solve some diagnostic problems by Nowicki *et al.* (1992), where the data analyzed were not suitable for statistical methods as the size of the sample was rather small and the traditional methods failed to produce any conclusive result. Many researchers have also employed rough set theory for medical data analysis and medical diagnosis (Slowinski K., 1992). Nowicki *et al.* (1992) demonstrated the possibility of using rough sets to solve the following problems:

- Evaluating the usefulness of a fault symptom to the condition of a system;
- Pruning a set of fault symptoms to arrive at a subset of relevant fault symptoms for the evaluation of the condition of a system;
- Classifying the condition of a system.

3.   **ROUGH SETS THEORY IN CLASSIFICATION AND RULE INDUCTION UNDER UNCERTAINTY**

3.1   Basic Notions of Rough Sets Theory

The approximation space and the lower and upper approximations of a set form two important notions of rough set theory. The approximation space of a rough set is the classification of the domain of interest into disjoint categories (Pawlak, 1991). Such a classification refers to the ability to characterize all the classes in a domain. The upper and lower approximations represent the classes of indiscernible objects that possess sharp descriptions on concepts but with no sharp boundary.

3.1.1   The Information System

In general, the data to be analyzed using rough set theory comprise a set of *objects* whose properties can be described by multi-valued *attributes*. The data that describe the objects can be represented by a structure called the *information system* (S). An information system can be viewed as an information table with its rows and columns corresponding to objects and attributes, respectively (Table 4).

Table 4. A Typical Information System.

Object	Attributes		Decision
(U)	q_1	q_2	(d)
x_1	1	0	0
x_2	1	1	1
x_3	1	2	1
x_4	0	0	0
x_5	0	1	0
x_6	0	2	1
x_7	0	1	1
x_8	0	2	0
x_9	1	0	0
x_{10}	0	0	0

Thus, an information system (S) with 4 tuples can be represented as follows:

$$S = \langle\, U, Q, V, \rho\,\rangle,$$

where U is the *universe* which consists of a finite set of objects,

Q is a finite set of attributes,

V_q is a domain of the attribute q,

$V = \bigcup_{q \in Q} V_q$, and

$\rho: U \times Q \rightarrow V$ is the information function
such that $\rho(x, q) \in V_q$ for every $q \in Q$ and $x \in U$ and any pair (q, v),

$q \in Q, v \in V_q$ is called a *descriptor* in S.

Table 4 shows a typical information system used for rough set analysis with the $x_i (i = 1, 2, ...10)$ representing the objects of the set, U, to be classified; the $q_i (i = 1, 2)$ denoting the *condition attributes*; and d representing the *decision attribute*. As a result, the $q_i (i = 1, 2)$ and d form the set of attributes, Q.

3.1.2   Approximations

Indiscernibility is one of the most important concepts in rough set theory. It is caused by imprecise information about the observed objects. The *indiscernibility relation* (R) is an equivalence relation on the set U and can be defined in the following manner:

If $x, y \in U, P \in Q$, then it is said that x and y are *indiscernible* by the set of attributes P in S, that is,

$x \hat{P} y$ iff $\rho(x, q) = \rho(y, q)$ for every $q \in P$.

An *approximation space* can be defined by an ordered pair (U, R). Equivalent classes of relation $\hat{P}$ are known as *P-elementary sets* in S. Any finite union of P-elementary sets is called a *P-definable* set in S. Q-elementary sets are termed *atoms* in S. *Concepts* can be represented by the *decision-elementary* sets.

For example, in the information system depicted in Table 4, the $\{q_1\}$-elementary sets, atoms and concepts are expressed as follows:

$\{q_1\}$- elementary sets:

$E_1 = \{x_1, x_2, x_3, x_9\}$, $E_2 = \{x_4, x_5, x_6, x_7, x_8, x_{10}\}$

Atoms:

$A_1 = \{x_1, x_9\}, \quad A_2 = \{x_2\}, \quad A_3 = \{x_3\}, \quad A_4 = \{x_4, x_{10}\}$,

$A_5 = \{x_5\}, \quad A_6 = \{x_6\}, \quad A_7 = \{x_7\}, \quad A_8 = \{x_8\}$

Concepts:

$C_1 = \{x_1, x_4, x_5, x_8, x_9, x_{10}\} \quad \Rightarrow \quad$ Class = 0 $(d = 0)$,

$C_2 = \{x_2, x_3, x_6, x_7\} \qquad\quad \Rightarrow \quad$ Class = 1 $(d = 1)$.

Obviously x_5 and x_7 in Table 4 are indiscernible by the condition attributes q_1 and q_2 as they have different decision attributes (ds). This shows that there exists a *conflict* (or *inconsistency*) between x_5 and x_7. Similarly, another conflict also exists between objects x_6 and x_8.

Rough set theory offers a means to deal with this inconsistency. For a concept, called C, the greatest definable set contained in the concept is called the *lower approximation* of C (denoted as $\underline{R}(C)$). This greatest definable set represents the set of objects in U which can be *certainly* classified as belonging to concept C by the set of attributes, R, such that

$$\underline{R}(C) = \bigcup \{Y \in U \,/\, R : Y \subseteq C\}.$$

The least definable set containing concept C is called the *upper approximation* of C (denoted as $\overline{R}(C)$). This least definable set represents the set of objects in U which can be *possibly* classified as belonging to concept C by the set of attributes, R, such that

$$\overline{R}(C) = \bigcup \{Y \in U \,/\, R : Y \cap C \neq \varnothing\},$$

where U/R represents the set of all atoms in the approximation space (U, R).

Elements belonging only to the upper approximation compose the *boundary region* (BN_R) or the *doubtful area*. Mathematically, a boundary region can be expressed as:

$$BN_R(C) = \overline{R}(C) - \underline{R}(C),$$ i.e., all elements from $\overline{R}(C)$ that are not in $\underline{R}(C)$.

A boundary region represents the set of objects that cannot be certainly classified as belonging to concept C by the set of attributes R. Such a concept, C, is called a *rough set*. In other words, rough sets are sets having non-empty boundary regions. Based on rough set theory, the approximations of concepts C_1 and C_2 can be easily obtained. For example, the lower approximation of concept C_1 is given by: $\underline{R}(C_1) = \{x_1, x_4, x_9, x_{10}\}$; while its upper approximation can be expressed as:

$$\overline{R}(C_1) = \{x_1, x_4, x_5, x_6, x_7, x_8, x_9, x_{10}\}.$$

Thus, the boundary region of concept C_1 is given by:

$$BN_R(C_1) = \overline{R}(C_1) - \underline{R}(C_1) = \{x_5, x_6, x_7, x_8\}.$$

For concept C_2, the approximations can be similarly obtained as follows:

$$\underline{R}(C_2) = \{x_2, x_3\}; \qquad \overline{R}(C_2) = \{x_2, x_3, x_5, x_6, x_7, x_8\}; \text{ and}$$

$$BN_R(C_2) = \overline{R}(C_2) - \underline{R}(C_2) = \{x_5, x_6, x_7, x_8\} = BN_R(C_1).$$

An intuitive description to the basic notions of rough sets for this illustrative example is depicted in Figure 4.

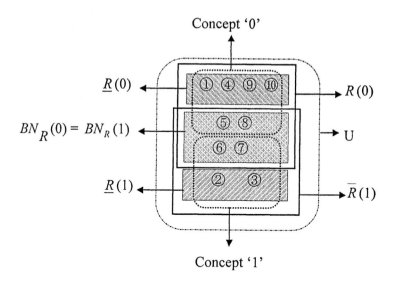

Figure 4.   Basic Notions of Rough Set Theory for Illustrative Example.

3.2   Rough Sets and Inductive Learning

3.2.1   Inductive Learning, Rough Sets and the RClass

As already mentioned, Quinlan's ID3 was once the most successful decision tree based inductive learning system before superseded by its later versions. The ID3 algorithm develops a decision tree from training data by constructing it top-down. The general idea behind decision tree learning is to recursively split data into sub-populations. Such an approach can also be seen in the Concept Learner Systems (CLS) algorithm that was developed by Hunt (Quinlan, 1986b). One great advantage of ID3 is that the algorithm used is simple but effective. The ID3 algorithm first orders or ranks the attributes that discriminate best and then evaluates them in that order. This enables ID3 to produce a smaller decision tree that can correctly classify the given training data. ID3 employs the principle of information gain to choose the best attribute to construct the decision tree recursively. However, ID3 requires the training data to be perfect and consistent and cannot handle incomplete, inconsistent or imprecise training data. Nevertheless, ID3 has later influenced many other inductive learning systems and was modified by many researchers under the name of ID4 and ID5 (Pham and Aksoy, 1995; Pham and Dimov, 1997). C4.5 (Quinlan, 1992) and later C5 (http://www.rulerequest.com), are commercial software packages developed based on ID3.

Grzymala-Busse (1992) proposed a system called LERS for inductive learning based on rough set theory, aiming at handling inconsistencies in training data. However, as observed by the author, LERS becomes not so practical when the size of the input data is very large. This is largely due to the computational complexity of its algorithm. Furthermore, the rules induced by LERS are more complicated and difficult to understand. Attempts to make comparisons between the ID3-family of algorithms and rough set based inductive learning algorithms can be found in the work by Wong et al. (1986) and Grzymala-Busse D. M. and Grzymala-Busse J. W. (1995).

Different from LERS, the prototype system described in this chapter, called the RClass, integrates rough set theory with an ID3-like learning algorithm. The ID3's algorithm was modified by incorporating rough set principles to handle the inconsistency in the training data.

3.2.2   Framework of the RClass

The framework of the RClass is depicted in Figure 5. It comprises three main modules: a consistency analyzer, a rough classifier and an induction engine. The consistency analyzer analyses the training data and performs two tasks:

- Elimination of redundant data items;
- Identification of conflicting training data.

The rough classifier has two approximators, namely the upper approximator and the lower approximator. The rough classifier is employed to treat inconsistent training data. Using the approximators, the lower and upper approximations of a concept (C) can be respectively derived. As already explained in Section 3.1.2, the lower approximation of C contains the greatest definable set that can be certainly classified as belonging to C, that is, the *certain training data set*. Similarly, the upper approximation of C is the least definable set that can be possibly classified as belonging to C, that is, the *possible training data set*.

The induction engine module has an ID3-like learning algorithm based on the minimum-entropy principle. The concept of entropy is used to measure how informative an attribute is. For clarity, the basic notions of information entropy used in this work are explained as follows.

In information theory, if there are n messages, then it needs $\log_2(n)$ bits to identify each message (Gray, 1990). As a special case, if there are n equally probable messages, then the probability p of each of the messages is $1/n$. Thus, the information conveyed by a message is $- \log_2(1/n)$ bits. It is apparent that the more probable a message is, the less information it conveys. In general, given a probability distribution, $P = (p_1, p_2, ..., p_n)$, the information conveyed by the distribution is called the *Entropy* of P and is denoted as:

$$-\{p_1 \log(p_1) + p_2 \log(p_2) + ... + p_n \log(p_n)\}.$$

The basic principles mentioned above can be applied to classification problems. It is assumed that a set of n objects can be classified into two classes namely *positive* and *negative*. Let h_i represent the fraction of objects that belong to class C_i. The minimum information needed to classify the set of objects is then given by:

$$H_c = -\sum\{h_i \log_2(h_i)\}.$$

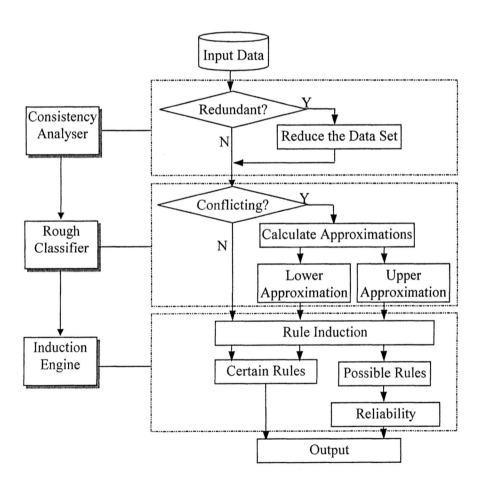

Figure 5.   Framework of the RClass System.

In the next step, a specific attribute is used to break the set of objects into subsets. Suppose that an attribute, A_j, which can take k different values, a_{j1}, a_{j2}, ..., a_{jk}, can be used to separate the set into subsets. Then the information needed to classify the subset of objects with attribute value a_{jk} is given by

$$H_{jk} = \sum \{-(c_{ijk} / n_{jk}) \times \log_2 (c_{ijk} / n_{jk})\},$$

where c_{ijk} is the number of objects that belong to class C_i and whose attribute A_j has value a_{jk}, and n_{jk} is the total number of objects having value a_{jk}.

The greater the value of H_{jk} is, the more information it takes to break the sub-groups down to their component levels.

The average information of H_j is defined as:

$$E(H_j) = \sum \{(n_{jk} / n) \times H_{jk}\},$$

where n is the total number of objects.

Then the *gain* G_j of attribute A_j is given by: $G_j = H_c - E(H_j)$.

The value of G_j shows how informative the corresponding attribute is. The algorithm chooses the attribute with the largest gain value to construct the branches of the decision tree at each level. Such an approach can ensure a smaller decision tree to be built without loss of accuracy.

In the induction engine module, a routine is designed to read the decision tree constructed and output the result in form of production rules. Compared to a decision tree, decision rules are more user friendly and easier to understand. Another task of this routine is to calculate the confidence level of each possible rule. The calculation can be mathematically expressed as:

Confidence level =

$$\frac{Number\ of\ examples\ correctly\ classified\ by\ the\ rule}{Number\ of\ examples\ with\ same\ condition\ attribute\text{-}value\ pairs} \times 100\%$$

Details of the calculation will be illustrated in the example validated below.

3.3   Validation and Discussion

The efficient use of critical machines or equipment in a manufacturing system requires reliable knowledge about their current operating condition. This knowledge is often used as a basis for machine condition monitoring and diagnosis (Mitchell, 1981). Traditionally, diagnosis is carried out by practicing engineers who have accumulated vast knowledge or experience about a manufacturing system. In general, when a manufacturing system or a machine deviates from its nominal operating condition, it is considered to exhibit symptoms of malfunction, that is, there are rules to follow. These rules can possibly be induced from the empirical data gathered from the process.

3.3.1   Example 1: Machine Condition Monitoring

It is assumed here that an engineer is tasked to monitor the condition of a reciprocating machine. Preliminary observations show that the condition of the machine (normal or faulty) is related to its cooling water temperature (attribute *Temperature*) and machine vibration (attribute *Vibration*). A set of observations are assumed to have been recorded as shown in Table 5.

Table 5. Machine Condition and Its Parameters.

Observation	Attributes		Decision
	Temperature	Vibration	State
1	High	Low	Normal
2	High	High	Faulty
3	High	very high	Faulty
4	Normal	Low	Normal
5	Normal	High	Normal
6	Normal	very high	Faulty
7	Normal	High	Faulty
8	Normal	very high	Normal
9	High	Low	Normal
10	Normal	Low	Normal

In order to process the information in Table 5, the *linguistic descriptions* of the conditions (both attributes and decision) need to be transformed into real values (Table 6). This is done by using the following conversion scheme: normal, low $\Rightarrow$ 0; high, faulty $\Rightarrow$ 1; very high $\Rightarrow$ 2.

Table 6. Machine Condition after Transformation.

Observation	Attributes		Decision
	Temperature	Vibration	State
1	1	0	0
2	1	1	1
3	1	2	1
4	0	0	0
5	0	1	0
6	0	2	1
7	0	1	1
8	0	2	0
9	1	0	0
10	0	0	0

Clearly, observations 6 and 8 contradict each other. Using the RClass system, two sets of rules, the *certain rules* and the *possible rules*, can be induced (Table 7).

As already mentioned, the values recorded in the parentheses following each *possible rule* represent the confidence level (reliability) of the rule. For example, for the first possible rule in Table 7, IF (Temperature < high) THEN State = normal, there are in total 6 examples in Table 5 that have the condition-attribute pair 'Temperature < high', i.e., examples 4, 5, 6, 7, 8, and 10, but only examples 4, 5, 8, and 10 can be correctly classified by the rule. Therefore the confidence level of this possible rule should be 4/6, namely 66.7%.

Table 7. Rules Induced by ID3 and the RClass System.

ID3	No solution. System hung. However, by removing the inconsistent incidents, ID3 is able to produce rules identical to the certain rules induced by the RClass system.

RClass	Certain Rules:
	 IF (Vibration < high) THEN State = normal;
	 IF (Temperature >= high) & (Vibration >= high) THEN State = faulty;
	 Possible Rules:
	 IF (Temperature < high) THEN State = normal; (66.7%)
	 IF (Vibration >= high) THEN State = faulty; (66.7%)

3.3.2   Example 2: A Chemical Process

It is assumed that the product quality of a chemical process (Rojas-Guzman, 1993) is dependent upon three parameters (attributes), namely *atomization quality, injector tip quality* and *plugging*. Nine observations were recorded and are summarized in Table 8.

Table 8. Process Quality and Its Parameters.

Observation	Attributes			Decision
	Atomization	Injector Tip	Plugging	Quality
1	Poor	Not broken	moderate	normal
2	poor	broken	none	normal
3	Normal	Not broken	severe	normal
4	Poor	broken	severe	abnormal
5	Poor	broken	moderate	abnormal
6	normal	broken	severe	abnormal
7	Poor	broken	none	abnormal
8	normal	broken	none	normal
9	Poor	broken	moderate	abnormal

Similarly, Table 8 can be transformed into Table 9 for ease of processing.

Table 9. Process Quality (after Transformations).

Observation	Attributes			Decision
	Atomization	Injector Tip	Plugging	Quality
1	1	0	1	0
2	1	1	0	0
3	0	0	2	0
4	1	1	2	1
5	1	1	1	1
6	0	1	2	1
7	1	1	0	1
8	0	1	0	0
9	1	1	1	1

Notes: Plugging: none$\Rightarrow$0, moderate$\Rightarrow$1, severe$\Rightarrow$2; Injector Tip: not broken$\Rightarrow$0; broken$\Rightarrow$1; Atomization: normal$\Rightarrow$0, poor$\Rightarrow$1; Quality: normal$\Rightarrow$0, abnormal$\Rightarrow$1.

Observations 2 and 7 contradict each other. Based on rough set theory discussed in Section 3.1, the concepts and approximations can be represented as follows and rules induced are summarized in Table 10.

Concepts:

$C_1 = \{e_1, e_2, e_3, e_8\}$ $\Rightarrow$ Class = 0 (process quality = normal);
$C_2 = \{e_4, e_5, e_6, e_7, e_9\}$ $\Rightarrow$ Class = 1 (process quality = abnormal).

Approximations:

$\underline{R}(C_1) = \{e_1, e_3, e_8\}$; $\overline{R}(C_1) = \{e_1, e_2, e_3, e_7, e_8\}$;
$\underline{R}(C_2) = \{e_4, e_5, e_6, e_9\}$; $\overline{R}(C_2) = \{e_2, e_4, e_5, e_6, e_7, e_9\}$;
$BN_R(C_1) = BN_R(C_2) = \{e_2, e_7\}$.

Where the e_i s denote the observation numbers shown in Table 8.

Table 10. Rules Induced by ID3 and the RClass System for the Second Illustrative Example.

ID3	No solution. System hung. By removing the inconsistent incidents, ID3 can produce rules identical to the certain rules induced by the RClass system.

RClass	Certain Rules:
	 IF (Injector Tip=broken)&(Plugging>=moderate) THEN Quality=abnormal;
	 IF (Injector Tip=not broken) THEN Quality=normal;
	 IF (Atomization=normal)&(Plugging<=moderate) THEN Quality=normal;
	 Possible Rules:
	 IF (Atomization=poor)&(Injector Tip=broken) THEN Quality=abnormal; (80%)
	 IF (Plugging>=moderate) THEN Process Quality=abnormal; (66.7%)
	 IF (Atomization=normal) THEN Process Quality=normal; (66.7%)
	 IF (Plugging=none) THEN Process Quality=normal; (66.7%)

4.   CONCLUSIONS

Rule induction from training examples seems to be the most practical way of knowledge discovery and data mining. However, such a task is often forced to deal with uncertainty. Rough set theory provides a new and powerful mathematical notion to deal with this issue. The prototype system developed in this chapter, RClass, successfully integrated the advantages of both rough set theory and an inductive learning algorithm to yield a new approach for rule induction under uncertainty, especially inconsistent information. Two sets of rules, *certain* rules and *possible* rules, can be induced by the RClass system from the training data set containing conflicting information. The two simple examples presented in this chapter are for the purpose of illustrating the basic idea of the proposed approach. When dealing with more complicated cases, effectiveness and computational complexity of the induction process should be taken into consideration and some modifications should be done to improve the system.

Compared with other competing methods presented in Table 3, rough set theory shows its advantages in rule induction when dealing with uncertainties, especially inconsistent information. It has sound theoretical background and low computational complexity. Setting up and execution of the model (information system) is easy as the theory itself is very simple. Rough set theory can be easily applied in many areas and the last decade has seen its development in data mining and knowledge discovery. However, like the advent of any other new theory or technology, there are still some issues facing the research on rough set theory. For example, the discretization of continuous-valued attributes (Khoo and Zhai, 2001b), the treatment of missing values in the information table (Khoo and Zhai, 2001c), and so on, are issues that need to be addressed immediately. Despite these challenges, rough set methodology is believed to be going to shine in application areas such as system control, decision support, and pattern classification, while it may also impact the design and operations of future computing devices.

REFERENCES

Barbara, D., Garcia-Molina, H., and Porter, D., "The management of probabilistic data", *IEEE Trans. on Knowledge and Data Engineering*, Vol. 4, No. 5, pp. 487-502, 1992.

Chan, K. C. C. and Wong, A. K. C., "A statistical technique for extracting classificatory knowledge from database", in G. Piatetsky-Shapiro, W. J. Frawley, eds, *Knowledge Discovery in Database*, 1991, Cambridge, MA, U.S.A.: AAAI/MIT, pp. 107-123.

Chanas, S. and Kuchta, D., "Further remarks on the relation between rough sets and fuzzy sets", *Fuzzy Sets and Systems*, 47, pp. 391-394, 1992.

Cheeseman, P., "Probabilistic vs. fuzzy reasoning", in L. N. Kanal, J. F. Lemmer, eds, *Uncertainty in Artificial Intelligence*, 1986. Amsterdam: North Holland Press, pp. 85-102.

Dempster, A. P., "Upper and lower probabilities induced by a multivariate mapping", *Annals of Mathematical Statistics*, 38, pp. 325-339, 1967.

Dubois, D. and Prade, H. "Combination and propagation of uncertainty with belief functions", in *Proceedings of the 9th International Joint Conference on Artificial Intelligence*, 1985, Los Angeles, CA, U.S.A., pp. 18-23.

Dubois, D. and Prade, H., "Putting rough sets and fuzzy sets together", in R. Slowinski, ed, *Intelligent Decision Support - Handbook of Applications and Advances of the Rough Sets Theory*, 1992. Dordrecht: Kluwer Academic Publishers. pp. 203-231.

Dubois, D. and Prade, H., "Rough fuzzy sets and fuzzy rough sets", *International Journal of General Systems*, 17, pp. 191-209, 1990.

Elder-IV, J. F. and Pregibon, "DA statistical perspective on KDD", in U. Fayyad, R. Utnurusamy, eds, *The 1st Int. Conf. on Knowledge Discovery and Data Mining*, 1995. Montreal, Quebec, Canada, pp. 87-93.

Fausett, L. V., *Fundamentals of Neural Networks: Architectures, Algorithms, and Applications*. Englewood Cliffs, NJ, U.S.A.: Prentice-Hall. 1994.

Felici G. and Truemper K., "A MINSAT approach for learning in logic domains", *INFORMS Journal on Computing*, 14, pp. 20-36, 2000.

Fournier, D. and Crémilleux, "A quality index for decision tree pruning", *Knowledge-Based Systems*, Vol. 15, No. 1-2, pp. 37-43, 2002.

Goldberg, D. E.. *Genetic Algorithms in Search, Optimisation and Machine Learning*, Reading, Mass., U.S.A.: Addison-Wesley. 1989.

Gray, R. M., *Entropy and Information Theory*. New York, U.S.A.: Springer-Verlag. 1990.

Grzymala-Busse, D. M. and Grzymala-Busse, J. W., "The usefulness of a machine learning approach to knowledge acquisition", *Computational Intelligence*, Vol. 11, No. 2, pp. 268-279. 1995.

Grzymala-Busse, J. W. and Wang Chien Pei, B., "Classification and rule induction based on rough sets", in *1996 IEEE International Conference on Fuzzy Systems*, 1996. Vol. 2, pp. 744-747. Piscataway, NJ, U.S.A..

Grzymala-Busse, J. W., "LERS - A system for learning from examples based on rough sets", in R. Slowinski, ed, *Intelligent Decision Support - Handbook of Applications and Advances of the Rough Sets Theory*, 1992. Dordrecht: Kluwer Academic Publishers. pp. 3-18.

Grzymala-Busse, J. W., "On the unknown attribute values in learning from examples", in Z. W. Ras, M. Zemankova, eds, *Methodologies for Intelligent Systems*, 1991a, New York, U.S.A.: Springer-Verlag. pp. 368-377.

Grzymala-Busse, J. W., ed, *Managing Uncertainty in Expert Systems*, 1991b, Boston, MA, U.S.A: Kluwer Academic Publishers.

H. Bandemer and S. Gottwald, eds, *Fuzzy Sets, Fuzzy Logic, Fuzzy Methods with Applications*. Chichester, New York, U.S.A.: Wiley J. 1995.

Kaufmann, A. ed, *Fuzzy Mathematical Models in Engineering and Management Science*, New York, U.S.A.: North-Holland Press. 1988.

Khoo L.P. and Zhai L.Y., "A rough set approach to the treatment of continuous-valued attributes in multi-concept classification for mechanical diagnosis", *Artificial Intelligence for Engineering Design, Analysis and Manufacturing (AIEDAM)*, Vol. 15, No. 3, pp.211-221. 2001b.

Khoo L.P. and Zhai L.Y., "Multi-concept classification of diagnostic knowledge to manufacturing systems: analysis of incomplete data with continuous-valued attributes", *International Journal of Production Research*, Vol. 39, No. 17, pp.3941-3957. 2001c.

Khoo L.P. and Zhai L.Y., "RClass*: a prototype rough-set and genetic algorithms enhanced multi-concept classification system for manufacturing diagnosis", in J. Wang, A. Kusiak eds, *Computational Intelligence in Manufacturing Handbook*, CRC Press LLC, Boca Raton, FL, U.S.A., pp. 19-1 to 19-20. 2001a.

Khoo, L. P., Tor, S. B., and Zhai, L. Y., "A rough-set based approach for classification and rule induction", *International Journal of Advanced Manufacturing*, 15, pp. 438-444. 1999.

Krusinska, E., Slowinski, R., and Stefanowski, J., "Discriminate versus rough sets approach to vague data analysis", *Journal of Applied Statistics and Data Analysis*, Vol. 8, No. 2, pp.43-56. 1990.

Lee, N. S., Grize, Y. L., and Dehnad, K., "Quantitative models for reasoning under uncertainty in knowledge-based expert systems", *International Journal of Intelligent Systems*, 2, pp. 15-38. 1987.

Lemmer, J. F., "Confidence factors, empiricism and the Dempster-Shafer theory of evidence", in L. N. Kanal, J. F. Lemmer, eds, *Uncertainty in Artificial Intelligence*, pp. 117-125. New York, U.S.A.: North-Holland Press. 1986.

Lin, T. Y. and Cercone, N. eds, *Rough Sets and Data Mining - Analysis for Imprecise Data*. Boston, Mass, U.S.A.: Kluwer Academic Publishers. 1997.

Lin, T. Y. ed, *Proceedings of the 3rd International Workshop on Rough Sets and Soft Computing*. San Jose, CA, U.S.A.. 1995.

Lin, T. Y., "Fuzzy reasoning and rough sets", in W. Ziarko, ed, *Rough Sets, Fuzzy Sets and Knowledge Discovery - Proceedings of the Int. Workshop on Rough Sets and Knowledge Discovery*, pp. 343-348. London: Spring-Verlag. 1994.

Luba, T. and Lasocki, R., "On unknown attribute values in functional dependencies", in *Proceedings of the 2nd Int. Workshop on Rough Sets and Soft Computing*, pp. 490-497. San Jose, CA, U.S.A.. 1994.

Michalski, R., Garbonell, J. G., and Mitchell, T. M., *Machine Learning: An Artificial Intelligence Approach*, Vol. 2. Los Altos, CA, U.S.A.: Morgan Kaufmann Publishers. 1983.

Mingers, J., "An empirical comparison of selection measures for decision tree induction", *Machine Learning*, 3, pp. 319-342. 1989.

Mitchell, J. S., *An Introduction to Machinery Analysis and Monitoring*. Tulsa, Oklahoma, U.S.A.: PannWell Books Company. 1981.

Morik, K., ed, *Knowledge Representation and Organization in Machine Learning*. New York, U.S.A.: Springer-Verlag. 1989.

Mrozek, A., "Rough sets in computer implementation of rule-based control of industrial process", in R. Slowinski, ed, *Intelligent Decision Support - Handbook of Applications and Advances of the Rough Sets Theory*, pp. 19-32. Dordrecht: Kluwer Academic Publishers. 1992.

Nanda, S. and Majumdar, S., "Fuzzy rough sets", *Fuzzy Sets and Systems*, 45, pp. 157-160. 1992.

Newton, S. L., Yves, L. G., and Khosrow, D., "Quantitative models for reasoning under uncertainty in knowledge-based expert systems", *International Journal of Intelligent Systems*, 2, pp. 15-38. 1987.

Nowicki, R., Slowinscki, R., and Stefanoski, J., "Analysis of diagnostic symptoms in vibroacoustic diagnostics by means of rough sets theory", in R. Slowinski, ed, *Intelligent Decision Support - Handbook of Applications and Advances of the Rough Sets Theory*, pp. 33-48. Dordrecht: Kluwer Academic Publishers. 1992.

Pawlak, Z., "Hard and soft sets", in W. Ziarko, ed, Rough Sets, *Fuzzy Sets and Knowledge Discovery - Proceedings of the Int. Workshop on Rough Sets and Knowledge Discovery*, pp. 130-135. London: Spring-Verlag. 1994a.

Pawlak, Z., "Rough classification", *International Journal of Man-Machine Studies*, 20, pp. 469-483. 1984.

Pawlak, Z., "Rough set approach to multi-attribute decision analysis", *European Journal of Operational Research*, Vol. 72, No. 3, pp. 443-459. 1994b.

Pawlak, Z., "Rough set: A new approach to vagueness", in L. A. Zadeh, J. Kacprzyk, eds, *Fuzzy Logic for the Management of Uncertainty*, pp. 105-108. New York, U.S.A.: John Wiley and Sons. 1992.

Pawlak, Z., "Rough sets and fuzzy sets", *Fuzzy Sets and Systems*, 17, pp. 99-102. 1985.

Pawlak, Z., "Rough sets", in T. Y. Lin, N. Gercone, eds, *Rough Sets and Data Mining - Analysis for Imprecise Data*,   pp. 3-7. Boston, Mass, U.S.A.: Kluwer Academic Publishers. 1997.

Pawlak, Z., "Rough sets", *International Journal of Computer and Information Sciences*, Vol. 11, No. 5, pp. 341-356. 1982.

Pawlak, Z., "Why rough sets", in *1996 IEEE International Conference on Fuzzy Systems*: Vol. 2, pp. 738-743. Piscataway, NJ, U.S.A. 1996.

Pawlak, Z., Grzymala-Busse, J., Slowinski, R., and Ziarko, W., "Rough sets", *Communications of the ACM*, Vol. 38, No. 11, pp. 89-95. 1995.

Pawlak, Z., *Rough Sets - Theoretical Aspects of Reasoning about Data*. Dordrecht: Kluwer Academic Publishers. 1991.

Pearl, J., *Probabilistic Reasoning in Intelligent Systems: Networks of Plausible Inference*. San Mateo, CA., U.S.A.: Morgan Kaufmann Publishers. 1988.

Pham, D. T. and Aksoy, M. S., "A new algorithm for inductive learning", *Journal of Systems Engineering*, 5, pp. 115-122. 1995.

Pham, D. T. and Dimov, S. S., "An efficient algorithm for automatic knowledge acquisition", *Pattern Recognition*, Vol. 30, No. 7, pp. 1137-1143. 1997.

Quinlan, J. R., "Induction of decision trees", *Machine Learning*, 1, pp.81-106. 1986b.

Quinlan, J. R., "Learning logical definitions from relations", *Machine Learning*, 5, pp. 239-266. 1990.

Quinlan, J. R., "The effect of noise on concept learning", in R. Michalski, J. Carbonell, T. Mitchell, eds, *Machine Learning: An Artificial Intelligent Approach*: Vol. 2, pp. 149-166. San Mateo, CA, U.S.A.: Morgan Kauffman Publishers. 1986a.

Quinlan, J. R., "Unknown attribute values in induction", in A. M. Segre, ed, *Proceedings of the 6th Int. Machine Learning Workshop*, pp. 164-168. San Mateo, CA, U.S.A.: Morgan Kaufmann Publishers. 1989.

Quinlan, J. R., *C4.5: Programs for Machine Learning*. San Mateo, CA, U.S.A.: Morgan Kaufmann Publishers. 1992.

Rao, M. M., *Probability Theory with Applications*. New York, U.S.A.: Academic Press. 1984.

Rojas-Guzman, C., "Comparison of belief networks and rule-based expert systems for fault diagnosis of chemical processes", *Engineering Application of Artificial Intelligence*, Vol. 6, No. 3, pp. 191-202. 1993.

Shafer, G. and Logan, R., "Implementing Dempster's rule for hierarchical evidence", *Artificial Intelligence*, 33, pp. 248-271. 1987.

Shafer, G., "Belief functions and parametric models", *Journal of Royal Statistical Society*, 44, pp. 322-352. 1982.

Shafer, G., *A Mathematical Theory of Evidence*. Princeton, NJ, U.S.A.: Princeton Univ. Press. 1976.

Shortliffe, H. and Buchanan, B. G., "A model of inexact reasoning in medicine", *Mathematical Biosciences*, 23, pp. 351-379. 1975.

Skowron, A. and Rauszer, C., "The discernibility matrices and functions in information systems", in R. Slowinski, ed, *Intelligent Decision Support - Handbook of Applications and Advances of the Rough Sets Theory*, pp. 331-362. Dordrecht: Kluwer Academic Publishers. 1992.

Slowinski, K., "Rough classification of HSV patients", in R. Slowinski, ed, *Intelligent Decision Support - Handbook of Applications and Advances of the Rough Sets Theory*, pp. 77-94. Dordrecht: Kluwer Academic Publishers. 1992.

Slowinski, R. and Stefanowski, J., "Rough classification in incomplete information systems", *Mathematical & Computer Modeling*. Vol. 12, No. 10/11, pp. 1347-1357. 1989.

Slowinski, R. and Stefanowski, J., "ROUGHDAS and ROUGH-CLASS software implementation of the rough sets approach", in R. Slowinski, ed, *Intelligent Decision Support - Handbook of Applications and Advances of the Rough Sets Theory*, pp. 445-456. Dordrecht: Kluwer Academic Publishers. 1992.

Slowinski, R. ed, *Intelligent Decision Support – Handbook of Applications and Advances of the Rough Sets Theory*. Dordrecht: Kluwer Academic Publishers. 1992.

Tecuci, G. and Kodratoff, Y. eds, *Machine Learning and Knowledge Acquisition: Integrated Approaches*. London: Academic Press. 1995.

Thiesson, B., "Accelerated qualification of Bayesian network with incomplete data", in U. Fayyad, R. Uthurusamy, eds, *The 1st International Conference on Knowledge Discovery and Data Mining*, pp. 306-311. Montreal, Quebec, Canada. 1995.

Triantaphyllou, E., "The OCAT (One Clause At a Time) approach to data mining and knowledge discovery", in E. Triantaphyllou, G. Felici, eds, *Data Mining and Knowledge Discovery Approaches Based on Rule Induction Techniques*. Kluwer Academic Publishers. 2003.

Triantaphyllou, E., Liao, T. W., and Iyengar, S. S., "A focused issue on data mining and knowledge discovery in industrial engineering", *Computers and Industrial Engineering*, Vol. 43, No. 4, pp. 657-659. 2002.

Uthurusamy, R., Fayyad, U., and Spangler, S., "Learning useful rules from inconclusive data", in G. Piatetsky-Shapiro, W. J. Frawley, eds, *Knowledge Discovery in Database*, pp. 83-96. Cambridge, MA, U.S.A.: AAAI/MIT. 1991.

Wong, S. K. M. and Ziarko, W., "INFER - an adaptive decision support system based on the probabilistic approximate classification", in *The 6th International Workshop on Expert Systems and Their Applications*, Vol. 1, pp. 713-726. Avignon, France. 1987.

Wong, S. K. M., Ziarko, W., and Li, Y. R., "Comparison of rough-set and statistical methods in inductive learning", *International Journal of Man-Machine Studies*, 24, pp.53-72. 1986.

Wygralak, W., "Rough sets and fuzzy sets - some remarks on interrelations", *Fuzzy Sets and Systems*, 29, pp. 241-243. 1989.

Zadeh, L. A., "Fuzzy sets", *Information and Control*, 8, pp. 338-353. 1965.

Zadeh, L. A., "Is probability theory sufficient for dealing with uncertainty in AI: A negative view", in L. N. Kanal, J. F. Lemmer, eds, *Uncertainty in Artificial Intelligence*, pp. 103-116. New York, U.S.A.: North Holland Press. 1986.

Ziarko, W. ed, *Rough Sets, Fuzzy Sets and Knowledge Discovery - Proceedings of the Int. Workshop on Rough Sets and Knowledge Discovery*. London: Spring -Verlag. 1994b.

Ziarko, W., "Rough sets and knowledge discovery: an overview", in W. Ziarko, ed, *Rough Sets, Fuzzy Sets and Knowledge Discovery - Proceedings of the Int. Workshop on Rough Sets and Knowledge Discovery*, pp. 11-15. London: Spring-Verlag. 1994a.

Zimmermann, H. J., *Fuzzy Set Theory: And Its Applications* (3rd ed). Boston, MA, U.S.A.: Kluwer Academic Publishers. 1996.

AUTHORS' BIOGRAPHICAL STATEMENTS

Mr. Lian-Yin Zhai earned his B.Eng. degree from Xi'an Jiaotong University and M.Eng. degree from the Nanyang Technological University. He is currently a Research Associate at the School of Mechanical and Production Engineering, Nanyang Technological University, Singapore. His research interests include intelligent systems, modeling and simulation, biomedical engineering and applications, and design optimisation.

Dr. Li-Pheng Khoo is a Professor in the School of Mechanical and Production Engineering, Nanyang Technological University, Singapore. He graduated from the University of Tokyo in 1978 and earned his MSc in Industrial Engineering from the National University of Singapore and his PhD from the University of Wales in the UK. His research interests include AI and its applications, systems diagnosis, CIM, DFMA. He is currently a member of the ASME and JSME.

Dr. Sai-Cheong Fok is an Associate Professor in the Faculty of Engineering and Surveying, the University of Southern Queensland. He earned his B.A.Sc. from the University of Ottawa and the PhD from Monash University. His research interests include smart manufacturing, virtual reality, and mechatronics applications in bio-engineering.

Chapter 12 [1]

DISCOVERING KNOWLEDGE NUGGETS WITH A GENETIC ALGORITHM

Edgar Noda
School of Electrical & Comp. Eng.(FEEC)
State University of Campinas (UNICAMP)
Campinas –SP, Brazil
E-mail: edgar@dt.fee.unicamp.br

Alex A. Freitas [2]
Computing Laboratory, University of Kent
Canterbury, Kent, CT2 7NF, UK.
Email: A.A.Freitas@kent.ac.uk
Web: http://www.cs.kent.ac.uk/people/staff/aaf

Abstract: Measuring the quality of a prediction rule is a difficult task, which can involve several criteria. The majority of the rule induction literature focuses on discovering accurate, comprehensible rules. In this chapter we also take these two criteria into account, but we go beyond them in the sense that we aim at discovering rules that are interesting (surprising) for the user. Hence, the search for rules is guided by a rule-evaluation function that considers both the degree of predictive accuracy and the degree of interestingness of candidate rules. The search is performed by two versions of a genetic algorithm (GA) specifically designed to the discovery of interesting rules - or "knowledge nuggets." The algorithm addresses the dependence modeling task (sometimes called "generalized rule induction"), where different rules can predict different goal attributes. This task can be regarded as a generalization of the very well known classification task, where all rules predict the same goal attribute. This chapter also compares the results of the two versions of the GA with the results of a simpler, greedy rule induction algorithm to discover interesting rules.

Key Words: Genetic Algorithms, Rule Interestingness, Prediction, Dependence Modeling.

---

[1] Triantaphyllou, E. and G. Felici (Eds.), **Data Mining and Knowledge Discovery Approaches Based on Rule Induction Techniques**, Massive Computing Series, Springer, Heidelberg, Germany, pp. 395-432, 2006.

[2] Corresponding Author

1.   INTRODUCTION

There are several kinds of data mining tasks that can be addressed by data mining algorithms. Some of the most well-known and investigated tasks include classification, clustering, and discovery of association rules [Fayyad, et al., 1996].

The classification task consists of predicting the class of an example out of a predefined set of classes, given the values of predictor attributes for that example [Hand, 1997]. The classes to be predicted can be considered values of a goal attribute, so that the objective is to predict the value of the goal attribute for an example based on the values of the other attributes (the predictor attributes) for that example. We emphasize that classification is a predictive task. The challenge is to predict the class of new, unknown-class examples, by using a classification model that was trained with known-class examples.

This Chapter addresses a kind of generalization of the classification task, called dependence modeling, where there are several goal attributes to be predicted, rather than just one goal attribute. In this context, we addresses the discovery of prediction rules of the form:

> *IF* some conditions on the values of predicting attributes are verified
> *THEN* predict a value for some goal attribute.

In our approach for dependence modeling the user specifies a small set of potential goal attributes, which she/he is interested in predicting. Although we allow more than one goal attribute, each prediction rule has a single goal attribute in its consequent (THEN part). However, different rules can have different goal attributes in their consequent.

Note that the dependence modeling task is very different from the well-known task of discovery of association rules. For instance, in the latter the task is completely symmetric with respect to the attributes, i.e., any attribute can occur either in the antecedent or in the consequent of the rule. In contrast, in the above-described dependence modeling task, just a few user-selected attributes can occur either in the antecedent or in the consequent of the rule. All the other, non-goal attributes can occur only in the rule antecedent. In addition, and even more important, the discovery of association rules do not involve prediction, whereas the concept of prediction is essential in the above-described dependence modeling task. For a more comprehensive discussion about the differences between the task of association-rule discovery and tasks involving prediction, such as classification and dependence modeling, the reader is referred to [Freitas, 2000].

In principle, the prediction rules discovered by a data mining algorithm should satisfy three properties, namely: predictive accuracy, comprehensibility and interestingness [Freitas, 2002a]. Among these three properties, overall predictive accuracy seems to be the most emphasized in the literature. In any data mining task involving prediction, which includes the dependence modeling task addressed in this Chapter, discovered knowledge should have high predictive accuracy.

Discovered knowledge should also be comprehensible to the user. Assuming that the output of the data mining algorithm will be used to support a decision ultimately made by a human being, knowledge comprehensibility is an important requirement [Spiegelhalter, et al., 1994]. Knowledge represented as high-level rules, as in the above-mentioned IF-THEN format, has the advantage of being closely related to natural language. Therefore, the output of rule discovery algorithms tends to be more comprehensible than the output of other kinds of algorithms, such as neural networks and various statistical algorithms. This is the case particularly when the number of discovered rules and the number of conditions per rule is relatively small.

Discovered knowledge should also be interesting to the user. Among the three above-mentioned desirable properties of discovered knowledge, interestingness seems to be the most difficult one to be quantified and to be achieved. By "interesting" we mean that discovered knowledge should be novel or surprising to the user. We emphasize that the notion of interestingness goes beyond the notions of predictive accuracy and comprehensibility. Discovered knowledge may be highly accurate and comprehensible, but it is uninteresting if it states the obvious or some pattern that was previously-known by the user. A very simple, classical example shows the point. Suppose one has a medical database containing data about a hospital's patients. A data mining algorithm could discover the following rule from such a database: IF (patient is pregnant) THEN (patient is female). This rule has a very high predictive accuracy and it is very comprehensible. However, it is uninteresting, since it states an obvious, previously-known pattern.

In this Chapter we focus on the issue of interestingness of discovered prediction rules, but we are also interested in the predictive accuracy and the comprehensibility of the rules. In essence, our approach consists of developing data mining algorithms designed to discover a few rules that are both interesting (according to a given interestingness measure) and accurate. Both these criteria are directly taken into account by a function used to evaluate the quality of the candidate rules produced by the algorithm. The issue of comprehensibility is addressed in a more indirect manner. Instead of incorporating a comprehensibility measure in the rule evaluation function (which is already quite complex due to the need for measuring both predictive accuracy and interestingness), we follow the approach of designating, as the output of the algorithms, a small set of rules. We can think of the discovered rules as valuable "knowledge nuggets" extracted from the data.

It should be noted that, in general, there is a trade-off between predictive accuracy and interestingness. It is not so difficult to "discover" accurate knowledge if the algorithm is allowed to discover previously-known patterns, as the above example involving pregnancy and gender shows. On the other hand, the discovery of truly interesting knowledge often requires some sacrifice in either the predictive accuracy or the generality of the discovered rules.

As a real-world example of how the discovery of truly interesting knowledge may require some sacrifice in predictive accuracy (as estimated by the algorithm), we can quote the following result of a case study reported by [Wong & Leung, 2000; p. 166] concerning rules for scoliosis classification:

"...the system found rules with confidence factors around 40% to 60% [a relatively low accuracy]. Nevertheless, the rules ... show something different in comparison with the rules suggested by the clinicians. ... After discussion with the domain expert, it is agreed that the existing rules are not defined clearly enough, and our rules are more accurate than theirs. Our rules provide hints to the clinicians to re-formulate their concepts."

Despite the above successful example of relatively low predictive accuracy but high degree of interestingness, in many cases there is a danger of reducing too much predictive accuracy without necessarily discovering highly interesting knowledge. Hence, it seems that a safer approach to discover interesting knowledge consists of sacrificing a discovered rule set's generality (rather than predictive accuracy) in order to increase its interestingness. This is the approach followed in this Chapter. The basic idea is that, instead of trying to discover rules predicting goal attribute values for all examples, one focuses on discovering a few interesting rules (the "knowledge nuggets"), each of them possibly covering a few examples. This kind of rule has a good potential to represent knowledge that is not only accurate but also interesting (novel, surprising), because it focuses on exceptions, rather than very general relationships. In general users are already familiar with general relationships in the underlying application domain, and rules covering few examples, representing more specific relationships in the data, are more likely to be previously-unknown by the user.

The term small disjuncts is used in the literature to refer to rules covering a few examples [Holte, et al., 1989], [Weiss, 1995], [Weiss, 1998], [Weiss & Hirsh, 2000], [Carvalho & Freitas, 2000], [Carvalho & Freitas, 2002]. The potential of small disjuncts to represent interesting knowledge has also been pointed out by other authors, such as [Provost & Aronis, 1996]:

"... small disjuncts are often of most interest to scientists and business analysts, since they are precisely the rules that were unknown previously; analysts usually know the common cases. "

It should be noted, however, that in the majority of the literature on small disjuncts the rule discovery algorithm uses an evaluation function which is based on predictive accuracy only. Whether or not a discovered rule is interesting is manually determined by the analyst, by looking at each of the discovered rules. In this Chapter we prefer to use the term "knowledge nuggets" rather than the term "small disjuncts" to reflect the fact that our rule discovery algorithms use an evaluation function based on both predictive accuracy and a measure of rule interestingness.

The remainder of this Chapter is organized as follows. Section 2 reviews the motivation for genetic algorithm-based rule discovery. Sections 3 and 4 describe two versions of a genetic algorithm and a greedy rule induction algorithm, respectively, for discovering knowledge nuggets. Section 5 presents computational results comparing these two kinds of algorithm in four public domain, real-world data sets. Finally, section 6 concludes the Chapter.

2.   THE MOTIVATION FOR GENETIC ALGORITHM-BASED RULE DISCOVERY

This section is divided into three parts. Subsection 2.1 presents an overview of Genetic Algorithms, in order to make this Chapter self-contained. Subsection 2.2 reviews the basic idea of greedy rule induction algorithms and discusses its associated drawback of not coping well with attribute interactions. This subsection paves the way for the discussion presented in subsection 2.3, where it is argued that in general Genetic Algorithms tend to cope better with attribute interactions than greedy rule induction algorithms.

2.1   An Overview of Genetic Algorithms (GAs)

Genetic Algorithms (GAs) are perhaps the most well known class of algorithms belonging to the broad paradigm of evolutionary computation [Back, et al., 2000]. A GA is essentially a search algorithm inspired by the principle of natural selection. The basic idea is to evolve a population of individuals (also called "chromosomes"), where each individual represents a candidate solution to a given problem. Each individual is evaluated by a fitness function, which measures the quality of its corresponding solution. At each generation (iteration) the fittest (the best) individuals of the current population survive and produce offspring resembling them, so that the population gradually contains fitter and fitter individuals – i.e., better and better candidate solutions to the underlying problem. In GAs the population of individuals usually evolves via a selection method, which selects the best individuals to reproduce, and via genetic operators such as crossover and mutation, which produce new offspring out of the selected individuals [Michalewicz, 1996], [Mitchell, 1996], [Goldberg, 1989]. At a high level of abstraction, a GA can be described by the pseudocode shown in Figure 1.

```
create (usually at random) an initial population of individuals;
compute the fitness (a quality measure) of each individual;
REPEAT
    select individuals based on fitness;
    apply genetic operators to selected individuals, creating offspring;
    compute fitness of each offspring individual;
    update the current population;
UNTIL (stopping criterion)
```

Figure 1. Pseudocode for a Genetic Algorithm at a High Level of Abstraction.

The central step of the REPEAT-UNTIL loop of the algorithm in Figure 1 is the selection of individuals based on fitness. In general the better the fitness of an individual (i.e., the better the quality of its candidate solution) the higher the probability of an individual being selected. Among the several selection methods available in the literature, here we mention just one, namely tournament selection [Blickle, 2000], since this is the one used in our GA – to be described in section 3. Tournament selection can be considered a simple and effective selection method. For a more comprehensive discussion of selection methods the reader is referred to [Back, et al., 2000]. In tournament selection the GA randomly chooses k individuals from the current population, where k is the tournament size, a user-specified parameter. Then the k individuals "play a tournament", whose winner is the individual with the best fitness among the k individuals playing the tournament.

Once individuals are selected, the next step of the algorithm in Figure 1 is to apply genetic operators to the selected individuals (parents), in order to produce new individuals (offspring) that, hopefully, will inherit good genetic material from their parents. This step will be discussed below. Then the fitness of each of the new individuals is computed, and another iteration of the REPEAT-UNTIL loop is started. This process is repeated until a given stopping criterion is satisfied. Typical stopping criteria are a fixed number of iterations (generations) or the generation of an individual representing a very good solution. The solution returned to the user is the best individual produced by the GA.

Recall that an individual corresponds to a candidate solution to a given problem. In GAs an individual is usually a linear string of "symbols", often called "genes". A gene can be any kind of symbol, depending on the kind of candidate solution being represented. For instance, in GAs for prediction-rule discovery (such as our GA described in section 3) a gene can be a condition (an attribute-value pair) of a rule antecedent.

In general the main genetic operator of GAs is the crossover operator. It essentially consists of swapping genes between (usually two) individuals [Goldberg, 1989]. Figure 2 illustrates a well-known kind of crossover, called uniform crossover [Syswerda, 1989]. In this kind of crossover, in addition to the user-specified probability for applying crossover to a pair of individuals, there is another probability for swapping each gene's value in the genome of two individuals. (This second probability is often implicitly assumed to be 0.5 in the literature.) Whatever the value of this second probability, the main point is that it is the same for each gene in the genome, so that each gene has the same probability of having its value swapped, independent of the gene's position in the genome.

In order to illustrate the action of uniform crossover, Figure 2(a) shows two individuals, called the parents, before crossover. Suppose that the second and fifth genes (marked with a box in the figure) are randomly chosen to have their values swapped. As a result, uniform crossover produces the new individuals (offspring) shown in Figure 2(b).

In addition to crossover, it is also common to use some kind of mutation. In essence mutation replaces the value of a gene with a new randomly-generated value (among the values that are valid for the gene in question). Note that mutation can yield gene values that are not present in the current population, unlike crossover, which swaps existing gene values between individuals. Therefore, mutation helps to increase population diversity.

X1	X2	X3 X4	X5		X1	Y2	X3 X4	Y5
Y1	Y2	Y3 Y4	Y5		Y1	X2	Y3 Y4	X5

(a) Before crossover   (b) After crossover

Figure 2. An Example of Uniform Crossover in Genetic Algorithms.

Both crossover and mutation are stochastic operators, applied with user-defined probabilities. In GAs the probability of mutation is usually much lower than that of crossover. This is at least in part due to the use of the biological metaphor, since in nature mutations tend to be harmful much more often than they are beneficial.

For a comprehensive review of GAs in general the reader is referred to [Michalewicz, 1996], [Mitchell, 1996], [Goldberg, 1989]. For a comprehensive review of GAs applied to data mining the reader is referred to [Freitas, 2002a].

2.2   Greedy Rule Induction

There are many kinds of rule induction algorithm. However, the majority of them use a greedy rule induction procedure, whose basic idea is described in the pseudocode of Figure 3. This procedure starts with a rule containing an empty set of conditions, and it incrementally constructs a rule by adding one-condition-at-a-time to the rule until a given stopping criterion is satisfied. This procedure is greedy because it constructs a candidate solution (a candidate rule) in a sequence of steps and at each step the best possible local choice is made – i.e., the "best" rule condition is added to the current rule.

```
Rule = φ;
DO /* specialize the rule */
        add the "best" condition to the rule;
UNTIL (stopping criterion)
```

Figure 3. The Basic Idea of a Greedy Rule Induction Procedure.

Note that the pseudocode in Figure 3 shows the top-down version of a greedy rule induction procedure. Of course, there is a dual bottom-up version, which starts with a full set of conditions and incrementally constructs a rule by deleting one-condition-at-a-time. It should also be noted that, although the pseudocode in Figure 3 refers to the construction of a rule, most decision tree induction algorithms use the same basic idea of greedy search. The difference is that, instead of adding one-condition-at-a-time to the current rule, greedy decision tree induction algorithms add one-attribute-at-a-time to the current decision tree.

This greedy rule (or tree) induction procedure tries to find a global optimum in the search space by a series of local optimizations. However, there is no guarantee that a series of local optimizations will lead the search to the global optimum. In particular, the greedy search performed by most rule induction algorithms makes them quite sensitive to attribute interaction problems [Freitas, 2001].

As a very simple example of the fact that greedy rule induction procedures do not cope well with attribute interaction, consider the eXclusive OR (XOR) problem, shown in Figure 4. The value of the XOR function is true if and only if exactly one of two attributes A_1 and A_2 take on the value true. Hence, knowing the value of a single attribute, either A_1 or A_2, is useless for determining the value of the XOR function. Unfortunately, any greedy procedure that tries to evaluate the predictive power of attributes A_1 and A_2 separately, one-attribute-at-a-time, will conclude that these two attributes are irrelevant for determining the value of the XOR function. This conclusion is wrong, because A_1 and A_2 are entirely relevant for determining the value of the XOR function. The caveat is that we have to evaluate the predictive power of A_1 and A_2 together, considering the interaction between these two attributes.

A_1	A_2	XOR
false	False	False
false	True	True
true	False	True
true	True	False

Figure 4. Attribute Interaction in a XOR (eXclusive OR) Function.

In passing, we note that the XOR problem is in reality a particular case of parity problems, where the target function returns true if and only if an odd number of predictor attributes is true. The complexity of attribute interaction in parity problems increases very fast with the number of predictor attributes, which makes this kind of problem very difficult for greedy rule induction algorithms, as shown, e.g., by [Schaffer, 1993].

2.3   The Global Search of Genetic Algorithms (GAs)

In general, GAs tend to cope better with attribute interaction problems than greedy rule induction algorithms [Dhar, et al., 2000], [Papagelis & Kalles, 2001], [Freitas, 2001], [Freitas, 2002a], [Freitas, 2002b]. This has to do with the fact that, in contrast to the local search performed by greedy rule induction algorithms, GAs performs a global search. This is due to several factors, as follows.

First of all, GAs work with a population of candidate rules (individuals), rather than working with a single candidate rule at a time. At a given moment during the search, a population of individuals is concurrently exploring different parts of the search space. Second, the fitness function evaluates an individual (a complete candidate rule) as a whole, which is in contrast with the fact that greedy rule induction algorithms evaluate only a partial rule when they are considering the insertion of a new condition into a rule. Third, the crossover operator, which is the major genetic operator used to create new individuals out of the current individuals, modifies individuals on a several-genes (conditions)-at-a-time basis, rather than on a single-gene (condition)-at-a-time basis. Finally, GAs use stochastic search operators, which contributes to make them more robust and less sensitive to noise.

3.   GA-NUGGETS

This section presents our genetic algorithm (GA) designed for dependence modeling, called GA-Nuggets. We have developed two versions of GA-Nuggets, whose main differences are as follows. The first version, described in subsection 3.1, maintains a single, centralized population of individuals where different individuals can represent rules predicting different goal attributes. The second version, described in subsection 3.2, maintains a distributed population, consisting of several subpopulations, each of them evolving in an independent manner (although from time to time some individuals can migrate from one subpopulation to another). In this version, each subpopulation is associated with a different goal attribute to be predicted, so that in each subpopulation all individuals represent rules predicting the same goal attribute. These differences, as well as other aspects of the two versions, are described in the next two subsections.

3.1   Single-Population GA-Nuggets

This subsection describes the main characteristics of the single-population GA-Nuggets [Noda, et al., 1999], more precisely, its individual representation, fitness function, selection method and genetic operators.

3.1.1   Individual Representation

Each individual represents a candidate prediction rule of the form: IF *Ant* THEN *Cons*, where *Ant* is the rule antecedent and *Cons* is the rule consequent. *Ant* consists of a conjunction of conditions, where each condition is an attribute-value pair of the form $A_i = V_{ij}$, where A_i is the *i-th* attribute and V_{ij} is the *j-th* value of the domain of A_i. The current version of the system handles only categorical attributes. Hence, continuous attributes are discretized in a preprocessing step. *Cons* consists of a single attribute value pair of the form $G_k = V_{kl}$, where G_k is the *k-th* goal attribute and V_{kl} is the *l-th* value of the domain of G_k. The user selects, among all attributes available in the data being mined, a set of goal attributes whose prediction is considered interesting or useful. The other attributes are used only as predictor attributes, and can occur only in a rule antecedent.

Of course, when a goal attribute occurs in the consequent of a rule it cannot occur in its antecedent. However, if a goal attribute does not occur in the consequent of a rule, it can occur in the antecedent of that rule - in this case that goal attribute would be acting as a predictor attribute, in the context of that rule. In other words, only a goal attribute specified by the user can occur in a rule consequent, but a rule antecedent can contain predictor attributes and/or goal attributes, as long the antecedent's goal attribute(s) do not occur in the rule consequent.

An individual is encoded as a fixed-length string containing z genes, where z is the number of attributes (considering both predictor and goal attributes), as shown in Figure 5. The *i-th* gene, $i = 1,..., z$, represents the value that the *i-th* attribute takes on in the corresponding rule antecedent, if the attribute occurs in that rule's antecedent. Only a subset of the attribute values encoded in the genome will be decoded into attribute values occurring in the rule antecedent. In order to implement this we use the flag "-1" to indicate that a given attribute value is not decoded into a rule antecedent's condition. More precisely, the *i-th* gene can take on either the value "-1" or one of the values belonging to the domain of the *i-th* attribute. The gene is decoded into a rule antecedent's condition if and only if the gene value is different from "-1". Therefore, although the genome length is fixed, its decoding mechanism effectively represents a variable-length rule antecedent.

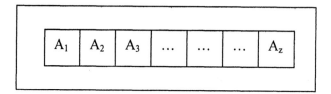

Figure 5. Individual Representation.

Once the rule antecedent is formed, the algorithm chooses the best consequent for each rule in such a way that maximizes the fitness of an individual (candidate rule). In effect, this approach gives the algorithm some knowledge of the data mining task being solved. A similar approach has been used by some GAs designed for discovering classification rules – see e.g. [Green & Smith, 1993].

This approach also has the benefit of being, in a certain sense, an efficient way of implementing a genetic search for rules, as follows. For each new rule antecedent produced by the GA – as a result of the creation of the initial population or the application of any genetic operator – the system performs a single scan of the training set in order to compute the fitness that the individual would have for each goal attribute value, and then chooses the goal attribute value maximizing the fitness of the individual. Hence, for a given rule antecedent, with a single scan of the training set the system is actually evaluating several different candidate rules (one different rule for each different goal attribute value being considered) and choosing the best one. This is an efficient use of a genetic search, because the bottleneck of fitness evaluation – viz., scanning the training set – is performed just once in order to evaluate multiple candidate rules.

3.1.2   Fitness Function

The fitness function consists of two parts. The first one measures the degree of interestingness of the rule, while the second measures its predictive accuracy. The degree of interestingness of a rule, in turn, consists of two terms. One of them refers to the antecedent of the rule and the other to the consequent.

The degree of interestingness of the rule antecedent is calculated by an information-theoretical measure, which is a normalized version of the measure proposed by [Freitas, 1998]. Initially, as a preprocessing step, the algorithm calculates the information gain of each attribute (*InfoGain*) [Cover

& Thomas, 1991]. Then, the degree of interestingness of the rule antecedent (*AntInt*) is given by:

$$AntInt = 1 - \left| \frac{\sum_{i=1}^{n} InfoGain(A_i)/n}{\log_2\left(\left| dom(G_k)\right|\right)} \right|, \qquad (1)$$

where n is the number of attributes occurring in the rule antecedent and $|dom(G_k)|$ is the domain cardinality (i.e. the number of possible values) of the goal attribute G_k occurring in the consequent. The log term is included in formula (1) to normalize the value of *AntInt*, so that this measure takes on a value between *0* and *1*. The *InfoGain* is given by:

$$InfoGain(A_i) = Info(G_k) - Info(G_k|A_i), \qquad (2)$$

where

$$Info(G_k) = -\sum_{i=1}^{mk} \left(Pr\left(V_{kl}\right) \log_2\left(Pr\left(V_{kl}\right)\right)\right), \qquad (3)$$

and

$$Info(G_k|A_i) = \sum_{i=1}^{n_i} \left(Pr\left(V_{ij}\right) \left(-\sum_{j=1}^{mk} Pr\left(V_{kl}\,|\,V_{ij}\right) \log_2\left(Pr\left(V_{kl}\,|\,V_{ij}\right)\right)\right)\right), \qquad (4)$$

where m_k is the number of possible values of the goal attribute G_k, n_i is the number of possible values of the attribute A_i, $Pr(X)$ denotes the probability of X and $Pr(X|Y)$ denotes the conditional probability of X given Y.

The *AntInt* measure can be justified as follows [Freitas, 1998]. In general, if a given predictor attribute A_i has a high information gain with respect to a given goal attribute G_k, this leads us to believe that A_i is a good predictor of the value of G_k, when A_i is considered individually – i.e., ignoring its interaction with other predictor attributes. (Note that in formulas (2), (3) and (4) – as well as in the vast majority of rule induction algorithms using an evaluation function based on information theory – the computation of the information gain of a predictor attribute is independent from the computation of the information gain of other predictor attributes.)

However, from a rule interestingness point of view, as discussed in the Introduction, it is likely that the user already knows what are the best predictors (individual attributes) for its application domain, and rules containing these attributes would tend to have a low degree of interestingness for the user.

On the other hand, the user would tend to be more surprised if she/he saw a rule antecedent containing attributes with low information gain. The user probably considered these attributes as irrelevant, and they are kind of irrelevant for prediction when considered individually, one at a time. However, attribute interactions can render an individually irrelevant attribute into a relevant one, and this phenomenon is intuitively associated with rule interestingness.

Therefore, all other things (such as the predictive accuracy) being equal, it can be argued that rules whose antecedent contain attributes with low information gain are more interesting (surprising) than rules whose antecedent contain attributes with high information gain.

The computation of the rule consequent's degree of interestingness is based on the idea that the prediction of a rare goal attribute value tends to be more interesting to the user than the prediction of a very common goal attribute value [Freitas, 1999]. In other words, the larger the relative frequency (in the training set) of the value being predicted by the consequent, the less interesting it tends to be. Conversely, the rarer a value of a goal attribute, the more interesting a rule predicting it tends to be. For instance, all other things being equal, a rule predicting a rare disease is much more interesting than a rule predicting a healthy condition, when 99% of the patients are healthy. More precisely, the formula for measuring the degree of interestingness of the rule consequent (*ConsInt*) is:

$$ConsInt = \left(1 - \Pr\!\left(G_{kl}\right)\right)^{1/\beta} \qquad (5)$$

where $\Pr(G_{kl})$ is the prior probability (relative frequency) of the goal attribute value G_{kl}, and β is a user-specified parameter. The value of β was set to 2 in our experiments, since this value – resulting in an exponent of $\frac{1}{2}$ in formula (5) – was empirically determined as a good value to reduce the influence of the rule consequent interestingness in the value of the fitness function. In any case, we make no claim that this value is an optimal value for this parameter.

To illustrate the use of formulas (1)–(5), consider the following very simple example, involving a goal attribute G_k called *Credit*, indicating whether the *Credit* of a customer is *good* or *bad*, and a predictor attribute A_i called *Income*, indicating whether the *Income* of a customer is *low*, *medium* or *high*. Suppose that the current candidate rule is: IF (*Income* = *low*) THEN (*Credit* = *bad*). Suppose also that we have the following probabilities for the two goal attribute values: Pr(*Credit=good*) = 0.4, Pr(*Credit =bad*) = 0.6; and the following conditional probabilities for the goal attribute values given the predictor attribute values:

- Pr(*Credit* = *good* | *Income* = *low*) = 0,
- Pr(*Credit* = *bad* | *Income* = *low*) = 1,
- Pr(*Credit* = *good* | *Income* = *medium*) = 0.4,
- Pr(*Credit* = *bad* | *Income* = *medium*) = 0.6,
- Pr(*Credit* = *good* | *Income*= *high*) = 1,
- Pr(*Credit* = *bad* | *Income*=*high*) = 0.

Then we have *Info*(*Credit*) = 0.97 (using formula (3)), *Info*(*Credit**Income*) = 0.485 (using formula (4)), and *InfoGain*(*Credit**Income*) = 0.485 (using formula (2)). Finally, using formula (1) we would have *AntInt* = 1 – (0.485 / 1) = 0.515. This reflects the fact that the rule antecedent is not very interesting, since there is an obvious correlation (probably previously-known by the user) between *Income* = *low* and *Credit* = *bad*. The degree of interestingness of the rule consequent would be computed by formula (5) as *ConsInt* = $(1 - 0.6)^{1/2}$ = 0.63. Again, this rule consequent does not have a high degree of interestingness, reflecting the fact that the predicted goal attribute value is relatively common in the data set (occurring in 60% of the examples). Note that a rule predicting *Credit* = *good* would have a somewhat higher *ConsInt*, namely 0.77, since the value *good* is somewhat less common in the data set (occurring in 40% of the examples).

The second part of the fitness function measures the predictive accuracy (*PredAcc*) of the rule, and it is given by:

$$PredAcc = \frac{|A \& C| - 1/2}{|A|} \qquad (6)$$

where |*A&C*| is the number of examples that satisfy both the rule antecedent and the rule consequent, and |*A*| is the number of examples that satisfy only the rule antecedent. The term ½ is subtracted in the numerator of formula (6) to penalize rules covering few training examples – see [Quinlan, 1987].

Finally, the fitness function is:

$$\text{Fitness} = \frac{w_1 \left(AntInt + ConsInt \right)/2 + w_2 \, PredAcc}{w1 + w2}, \qquad (7)$$

where w_1 and w_2 are user-defined weights. In a real-world scenario the values of w_1 and w_2 should be chosen by the user, in order to incorporate into the algorithm the preferences of the user. In our scientific experiments there is no direct "user". Hence, we performed the role of the user, and we have chosen the weight values of w_1 = 1 and w_2 = 2 according to our own evaluation about the relative importance of interestingness and predictive accuracy. Although interestingness is certainly important, in general there is little point in discovering an interesting rule if its estimated accuracy is low, i.e., a good predictive accuracy is a basic requirement of any prediction rule. This justifies the choice of a w_2 value larger than the w_1 value. Note also that formula (7) returns a value normalized in the range [0...1], since the three terms *AntInt*, *ConsInt*, and *PredAcc* are normalized.

3.1.3   Selection Method and Genetic Operators

GA-Nuggets uses a well-known tournament selection method with tournament size 2 – see section 2.1 –and it uses uniform crossover extended with a "repair" procedure. As mentioned in section 2.1, in uniform crossover there is a probability for applying crossover to a pair of individuals and another probability for swapping each gene (attribute)'s value in the genome (rule antecedent) of two individuals. After this crossover is done, the algorithm analyses if any invalid individual was created. If so, a repair procedure is performed to produce valid-genotype individuals. The rates used in our experiments were 0.7 for the crossover operator and 0.5 for attribute value swapping. The mutation operator randomly transforms the value of an attribute into another value belonging to the domain of that attribute. The mutation rate used in our experiments was 0.05. We made no attempt to optimize these settings, as they represent relatively common settings in the literature.

In addition to crossover and mutation, there are two operators, called condition-insertion and condition-removal operators, which control the size of the rules being evolved by randomly inserting/removing a condition into/from a rule antecedent. The probability of applying each of these operators depends on the current number of attributes in the rule antecedent. The larger the number of conditions in the current rule antecedent, the smaller the probability of applying the condition-insertion operator. In particular, this operator is not applied if the rule antecedent has the maximum number of conditions (as specified by the user). Conversely, the larger the number of conditions in the current rule antecedent, the larger the probability of applying the condition-removal operator. This operator is not applied if the rule antecedent has just one condition.

The condition-insertion and condition-removal operators are implemented by replacing the "-1" flag with a value V_{ij} and by replacing the value V_{ij} with the "-1" flag in a gene, respectively. In order to illustrate the application of these operators, Figure 6(a) shows an individual's genome with five genes representing a rule antecedent with three conditions, since only three of the five genes have a value V_{ij} different from the flag "-1". Figure 6(b) shows the result of applying the condition-insertion operator into the individual of Figure 6(a), by replacing the "-1" flag with a value V_{ij} in the third gene, so that the number of rule conditions is increased to four. Figure 6(c) shows the result of applying the condition-removal operator into the individual of Figure 6(a), by replacing the value V_{ij} with the "-1" flag in the fourth gene, so that the number of rule conditions is reduced to two.

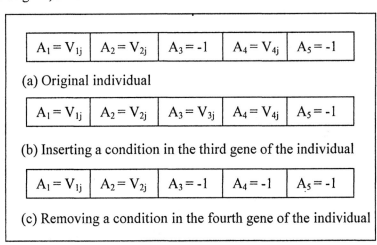

| $A_1 = V_{1j}$ | $A_2 = V_{2j}$ | $A_3 = -1$ | $A_4 = V_{4j}$ | $A_5 = -1$ |

(a) Original individual

| $A_1 = V_{1j}$ | $A_2 = V_{2j}$ | $A_3 = V_{3j}$ | $A_4 = V_{4j}$ | $A_5 = -1$ |

(b) Inserting a condition in the third gene of the individual

| $A_1 = V_{1j}$ | $A_2 = V_{2j}$ | $A_3 = -1$ | $A_4 = -1$ | $A_5 = -1$ |

(c) Removing a condition in the fourth gene of the individual

Figure 6. Examples of Condition Insertion/Removal Operations.

3.2   Distributed-Population GA-Nuggets

This subsection describes the main characteristics of the distributed-population GA-Nuggets [Noda, et al., 2002], more precisely, its individual representation, distributed population issues, fitness function, selection method and genetic operators.

3.2.1   Individual Representation

As mentioned before, the distributed population of GA-Nuggets consists of several subpopulations, each of them evolving independently from the others (except for some occasional migrations of individuals between subpopulations). Each subpopulation is associated with a different goal attribute to be predicted, so that in each subpopulation all individuals represent rules predicting the same goal attribute.

As a result, the individual representation of the distributed-population version of GA-Nuggets is similar to the individual representation of the single-population version of GA-Nuggets, described in subsection 3.1. The only difference is that the goal attribute is fixed for all individuals of the same subpopulation – only the predicted value of the goal attribute can vary between individuals in the same subpopulation. The goal attribute value predicted by each individual (rule) is chosen by the same deterministic procedure used to choose the rule consequent of single-population GA-Nuggets, namely, by choosing the goal attribute value that maximizes the fitness of the individual.

3.2.2   Distributed Population

The entire population is divided into p subpopulations, where p is the number of goal attributes. In each subpopulation all individuals are associated with the same goal attribute. As mentioned before, each consequent consists of a single goal attribute-value pair of the form $G_k = V_{kl}$, where G_k is the *k-th* goal attribute and V_{kl} is the *l-th* value of the domain of G_k. For instance, suppose there are two goal attributes, G_1 and G_2, with G_1 having the domain $\{V_{11}, V_{12}\}$ and G_2 having the domain $\{V_{21}, V_{22}, V_{23}\}$. In this case there would be two subpopulations. The first subpopulation would contain some individuals predicting $G_1 = V_{11}$ and some individuals predicting $G_1 = V_{12}$; whereas the second subpopulation would contain some individuals predicting $G_2 = V_{21}$, some individuals predicting $G_2 = V_{22}$, and some individuals predicting $G_2 = V_{23}$. (Recall that the value V_{ij} predicted by an individual of the *i-th* subpopulation is chosen as the value that maximizes the fitness of the individual, as mentioned in the previous subsection.)

One advantage of this distributed population approach, with a fixed goal attribute for each subpopulation, is to reduce (on average) the number of crossovers performed between individuals predicting different rules consequents. Since crossover is restricted to individuals of the same subpopulation, one makes sure that crossover swaps genetic material of two parents which represent candidate rules predicting the same goal attribute. Note that this is not the case with single-population GA-Nuggets, where crossover can swap genetic material between parents representing rules predicting different goal attributes.

Note that this idea of distributing goal attributes across multiple subpopulations could be taken further, by associating with each subpopulation a single goal attribute-value pair (a specific rule consequent) to be predicted, rather than a goal attribute, as in the current version. This would further restrict crossover, so that in this case crossover would always swap genetic material between two parents representing rules predicting the same goal attribute value, avoiding the problem of crossover between two individuals predicting different values for the same goal attribute which occurs in the current version of distributed-population GA-Nuggets. However, this alternative approach would have one disadvantage related to a smaller search efficiency. More precisely, it would not have the benefit of, in a single scan of the training set, considering different goal attribute values to be associated with the individual and then choosing, as the value predicted by the individual (rule), the value that maximizes the fitness of the individual.

As usual in distributed-population GAs, GA-Nuggets has a migration procedure where, from time to time, an individual of a subpopulation is copied into another subpopulation. In the case of GA-Nuggets, we have developed a migration procedure tailored for our prediction-rule discovery task, as follows.

The subpopulations evolve in a synchronous manner, so that in each subpopulation the i-th generation is started only after the $(i - 1)$-th generation has been completed in all subpopulations, for $i = 2,...,g$, where g is the number of generations (which is the same for all subpopulations).

Migration takes place every m generations, where m is a user-specified parameter. Each population sends individuals to all the other subpopulations. More precisely, in each subpopulation S_i, $i = 1,...,p$ (recall that p is the number of subpopulations), the migration procedure chooses $(p - 1)$ individuals to be migrated. Each of those $p - 1$ migrating individuals will be sent to a distinct subpopulation. Only a copy of the individual is sent, i.e. the original individual remains in its subpopulation.

The choice of the individuals to be migrated is driven by the fitness function, taking into account the fact that different subpopulations are associated with different goal attributes. In each subpopulation S_i the migration procedure knows, for each individual, not only the actual value of its fitness in that subpopulation (associated with the i-th goal attribute), which is called its *home* fitness, but also what would be the value of the fitness of that individual if it were placed in another subpopulation S_j, $j \neq i$, predicting a value of the j-th goal attribute. We call this the *foreign* fitness of the individual in the j-th subpopulation.

It is important to note that the computation of the foreign fitness of an individual in each of the other subpopulations S_j, $j \neq i$, is computationally cheap, for the following reason. In order to compute the actual fitness of an individual in its home subpopulation, the system has to scan the entire training set and, for each training example, to determine whether or not the example satisfies all conditions of the rule antecedent associated with the individual. The set of examples satisfying the rule antecedent is called the coverage of the rule. The actual fitness of the individual in its home subpopulation involves a measure of the predictive accuracy of its associated rule, and this measure depends on the frequency distribution of the goal attribute values in the rule's coverage. Once the coverage of a rule has been computed, that same coverage is also used to compute the foreign fitness of the individual in the other subpopulations, by computing the frequency distribution of the values of the other goal attributes associated with the other subpopulations. In other words, both the individual's home fitness and its foreign fitness in each of the other subpopulations can be computed in a single scan of the training set, which is required for the computation of the individual's home fitness, anyway. (In an efficient implementation, both the home fitness value and all the foreign fitness values of an individual can be computed along with the computation of its rule's coverage, by incrementing appropriate frequency counters right after a training example is found to belong to the rule's coverage. This efficient implementation is used in our system.)

Once all the foreign fitness values of each individual of every subpopulation have been computed, the migration procedure is finally ready to choose the $(p-1)$ individuals to be migrated from each subpopulation. Each subpopulation S_i, $i = 1,...,p$, sends to the j-th subpopulation, $j = 1,...,p$ and $j \neq i$, the individual that has the maximum foreign fitness value for the j-th subpopulation.

As a result of this process, each subpopulation S_i, $i = 1,...,p$, receives $p - 1$ individuals, each of them coming from a different subpopulation S_j, $j = 1,...,p$ and $j \neq i$. Among these $p - 1$ individuals, only one is accepted by subpopulation S_i. The accepted individual is the one with the largest fitness value. (At this point the distinction between foreign fitness and home fitness is irrelevant. Once a copy of an individual is sent from subpopulation S_i to subpopulation S_j by the migration procedure, the corresponding foreign fitness of that copy is immediately considered as its actual fitness in subpopulation S_j.) This is equivalent to a tournament selection among the incoming individuals. Only the tournament winner is accepted, and the other $p - 2$ incoming individuals are discarded. The selected individual replaces the worst-fitness individual in the subpopulation S_i.

3.2.3   Fitness Function

The fitness function of distributed-population GA-Nuggets is the same as the fitness function of single-population GA-Nuggets (see subsection 3.1.2). Therefore, the fitness function of distributed-population GA-Nuggets is given by formula (7), which is in turn computed by formulas (1) through (6).

3.2.4   Selection Method and Genetic Operators

In the distributed-population version of GA-Nuggets the application of the selection method and genetic operators is independently performed in each of the subpopulations. Each subpopulation uses the same selection method and genetic operators (described in subsection 3.1.3), which are applied only to the local individuals in that subpopulation.

4.   A GREEDY RULE INDUCTION ALGORITHM FOR DEPENDENCE MODELING

Dependence modeling is a data mining task far less investigated than classification in the rule induction literature. As a result, there are relatively few rule induction algorithms for dependence modeling, such as ITRULE [Smyth & Gooodman, 1991]. However, a direct comparison between GA-Nuggets and IT-RULE or another rule induction algorithm for dependence modeling would not be very fair, for the following reasons.

First, in general rule induction algorithms use an evaluation function different from the one used by GA-Nuggets. More precisely, the vast majority of rule induction algorithms use an evaluation function designed for estimating the predictive accuracy of a rule, whereas GA-Nuggets' evaluation function (the fitness function) was designed for estimating both the predictive accuracy and the degree of interestingness of a rule. One of the goals of our experiments is to compare the global search strategy of a GA with the local search strategy of a greedy rule induction algorithm, by using the same evaluation function and the same model for the two kinds of algorithm.

Second, there is also a subtle difference in the model of GA-Nuggets and the model of most rule induction algorithms. GA-Nuggets' output consists of a set of rules where each rule predicts a different goal attribute value. This restriction is not usually incorporated into rule induction algorithms for dependence modeling, where different discovered rules can predict the same goal attribute value and some goal attribute may be missing in the discovered rule set.

Hence, we decided to develop a greedy rule induction algorithm with exactly the same model and the same evaluation function as GA-Nuggets. Fixing these characteristics, we can effectively evaluate the differences in performance associated with the differences between the global search typically performed by a GA and the local search typically performed by a greedy rule induction algorithm.

The developed rule induction algorithm performs a greedy search by selecting rule conditions one-at-a-time (see section 2.2). In order for this algorithm to discover the same number of rules as GA-Nuggets (so that their comparison is as fair as possible) we run it once for every possible goal-attribute value to be predicted. More precisely, the greedy algorithm works as follows.

The rule consequent is fixed with the goal-attribute value corresponding to the current run of the algorithm. The algorithm starts with an empty rule antecedent (i.e., with 0 conditions), which covers all the training examples. Then it iteratively adds to the current rule antecedent the rule condition (attribute-value pair) which leads to the largest value of the evaluation function for the extended rule antecedent. This iterative procedure is repeated until no new rule condition can improve the value of the evaluation function or there are no more attributes to be chosen to compose the rule antecedent. Note that each attribute can be chosen only once to compose a rule condition for a given rule antecedent, since the occurrence of two or more conditions with the same attribute in the same rule antecedent would correspond to an invalid rule antecedent – e.g., "IF *sex* = *male* AND *sex* = *female*...".

5.   COMPUTATIONAL RESULTS

This section reports the results of computational experiments with some public domain data sets. Subsection 5.1 describes the data sets used in the experiment, whereas subsection 5.2 reports the computational results with respect to both predictive accuracy and interestingness. Subsection 5.3 summarizes the results and discussions of this section.

5.1   The Data Sets Used in the Experiments

The data sets used to evaluate the previously-described algorithms were obtained from the UCI repository of machine learning databases (http://www.ics.uci.edu/AI/Machine-Learning.html). The data sets used are Zoo, Car Evaluation, Auto Imports and Nursery. They are normally used for evaluating algorithms performing the classification task. In the absence of a specific benchmark data set for the dependence modeling task, these data sets were chosen because they seem to contain more than one potential goal attribute. The main characteristics of these four data sets are as follows:
- The Zoo data set contains 101 instances and 18 attributes. Each instance corresponds to an animal. In the preprocessing phase the attribute containing the name of the animal was removed, since

this attribute has no generalization power. The attributes in the Zoo data set are all categorical. The attribute names are as follows: *hair, feathers, eggs, milk, predator, toothed, domestic, backbone, fins, legs, tail, catsize, airborne, aquatic, breathes, venomous* and *type*. Except *type* and *legs*, the attributes are Boolean. In our experiments the set of potential goal attributes used was *predator, domestic* and *type*. *Predator* and *domestic* are Boolean attributes, whereas the type attribute can take on seven different values.

- The Car Evaluation data set contains 1728 instances and 6 attributes. All attributes are categorical and there are no missing values. The attribute names are *buying, maint, doors, persons, lug_boot, safety* and *car acceptability*. The attributes *buying* and *car acceptability*, with 4 values each, were used as potential goal attributes.

- The Auto Imports data set contains 205 instances and 26 categorical attributes. The attribute *normalized-losses* and 12 instances were removed because of missing values. This simplifies the computation of the probabilities involved in formulas (3) and (4) – subsection 3.1.2 – and makes sure that the information gain of all attributes is computed with respect to the same number of examples. Attributes *symboling, body-style* and *price*, with 7, 5, and 3 values, were chosen as goals.

- The Nursery data set contains 12960 instances and 9 attributes. The attributes are all categorical. The attribute names are as follows: *parents, health, form, children, finance, housing, social, has_nurs* and *recommendation*. In our experiments, the attributes used as potential goal attributes *were finance, social* and *health*, with 2, 3 and 5 values, respectively.

5.2   Results and Discussion

The target of this work is the dependence modeling task which, as mentioned before, is a generalization of the classification task where different rules can predict different attributes. In both tasks the evaluation of the discovered rules must take into account their predictive accuracy on a separate test set. The difference is as follows. In classification we usually aim at discovering a rule set that can classify any test instance that appears in the future. Hence it makes sense to compute an accuracy rate or related measure over all instances in the test set.

In dependence modeling, in the sense addressed in this Chapter, we do not aim to classify the whole test set. Rather, the goal is to discover a few interesting rules to be shown to a user (see Introduction). We can think of the discovered rules as the most valuable "knowledge nuggets" extracted from the data. These knowledge nuggets are valuable even if they do not cover the whole test set. In other words, the value of the discovered rules depends on their predictive accuracy on the part of the test set covered by those rules, but not on the test set as a whole. After all, there are several goal attributes, and we do not expect that the discovered rules can predict the value of all goal attributes for all instances in the test set. In fact, we could mine such a large rule set by running one classification algorithm for each goal attribute, but we would get too many rules, and the task being solved would be simply "multiple classification". In contrast, in the dependence modeling task addressed in this Chapter we aim at discovering a much smaller set of interesting rules.

Hence, it does not make much sense to evaluate the performance of the discovered rule set as a whole in test set, and the discovered rules are better evaluated on a rule-by-rule basis. Within this spirit, for each data set (Zoo, Car Evaluation, Auto Imports, and Nursery), the experiment consisted of using 10-fold cross-validation to evaluate the quality of the rules discovered by three algorithms, namely: single-population GA-Nuggets (section 3.1), distributed-population GA-Nuggets (section 3.2), and the greedy rule induction algorithm (section 4). Hereafter these algorithms will be denoted by GA-Nuggets, Distributed GA-Nuggets and the greedy algorithm, for short. The 10-fold cross-validation procedure works as follows. First, the data set is divided into 10 mutually exclusive and exhaustive partitions. Then each of the three algorithms is run 10 times. Each time a different partition is used as the test set and the other 9 partitions are merged and used as the training set. The results (in the test set) of the 10 runs are then averaged for each algorithm.

In order to make the comparison between GA-Nuggets and Distributed GA-Nuggets as fair as possible, both GAs use the same total population size, as follows. For each data set, each GA is allocated 30 individuals for each goal attribute value to be predicted. For instance, in the case of the Nursery data set, there are three goal attributes, with 2, 3 and 5 values, so that in total there are 10 goal attribute values to be predicted. Therefore, GA-Nuggets uses a single population with 300 individuals, whereas Distributed GA-Nuggets uses three subpopulations having 60, 90 and 150 individuals, respectively (with total size of 300). Both GAs are run for 100 generations. The parameter m of Distributed GA-Nuggets was set to 10, so that migration happens every 10 generations. We make no claim that these parameter settings are optimal. Actually, so far we have made no attempt to optimize these parameters. Such a parameter optimization might be tried in the future, but for now it is worth noting that even with the current non-optimized parameters the GAs are already obtaining good results, as will be seen later.

5.2.1   Predictive Accuracy

In this subsection we compare the predictive accuracy of the three above-mentioned algorithms in all the four data sets. The results are reported in Tables 1 through 4. In each of these tables, each row represents the results for a given rule consequent – i.e., a combination of a goal attribute and one of its values, as indicated in the first two columns. The remainder of each table is divided into three parts. Each part contains the results for one of the three algorithms, and it consists of two columns. The first one reports the coverage (Cov.) of the rules discovered by that algorithm. The coverage of a rule is the number of examples (in the test set) covered by the rule – i.e., the number of examples satisfying all the conditions of the rule antecedent. The second column reports the accuracy rate (in the test set) of the rules discovered by that algorithm. The coverage of the rules is shown for completeness, but the main performance measure analyzed in this section is the accuracy rate.

In the columns reporting the accuracy rate of each algorithm, the numbers after the "±" are standard deviations. In order to compare the three algorithms, we have considered the greedy algorithm as a "baseline", since it is the simplest of the three algorithms. Hence, for each of the two GAs, the table cells where the GA's accuracy rate is significantly better (or worse) than the greedy algorithm's accuracy rate are indicated by the symbol "(+)" (or "(-)"). The accuracy rate of a GA was considered significantly better than the accuracy rate of the greedy algorithm if and only if the corresponding accuracy rate intervals (taking into account the standard deviations) do not overlap. Let us now analyze the results of Tables 1 to 4.

- In Table 1 (Zoo data set) both GAs obtained rules with significantly higher accuracy rate than the rules obtained by the greedy algorithm in four cases. GA-Nuggets obtained rules with significantly lower accuracy rate than the rules obtained by the greedy algorithm in just one case, whereas Distributed GA-Nuggets did not obtain rules with significantly lower accuracy rate than the rules obtained by the greedy algorithm in any case.

- In Table 2 (Car Evaluation data set) GA-Nuggets and Distributed GA-Nuggets obtained rules with significantly higher accuracy rate than the rules obtained by the greedy algorithm in two cases and three cases, respectively. There was no case where the GAs obtained rules with significantly lower accuracy rate than the rules obtained by the greedy algorithm.

Table 1. Accuracy Rate (%) in the Zoo Data Set.

Goal	Attrib. Value	Greedy algorithm		GA-Nuggets		Distributed GA-Nuggets	
		Cov	Accuracy	Cov	Accuracy	Cov	Accuracy
Predator	False	1.8	43.2 ± 12.9	4.4	50.5 ± 8.9	3.2	48.0 ± 8.2
	True	1.6	48.0 ± 15.2	2.8	75.0 ± 11.2 (+)	2.4	84.0 ± 11.1 (+)
Domestic	False	4.4	88.3 ± 4.8	5.2	97.1 ± 5.2	6.2	90.5 ± 4.4
	True	0.4	0.0 ± 0.0	0.8	0.0 ± 0.0	0.8	0.0 ± 0.0
Type	1	17.6	0.0 ± 0.0	6.4	100.0 ± 0.0 (+)	6.4	100.0 ± 0.0 (+)
	2	6.6	100.0 ± 0.0	3.6	100.0 ± 0.0	3.6	100.0 ± 0.0
	3	3.6	100.0 ± 0.0	0.2	0.0 ± 0.0 (-)	1.1	95.0 ± 13.8
	4	0.4	0.0 ± 0.0	2.2	100.0 ± 0.0 (+)	2.2	100.0 ± 0.0 (+)
	5	2.2	100.0 ± 0.0	0.5	100.0 ± 0.0	0.8	100.0 ± 0.0
	6	0.4	20.0 ± 13.7	1.1	90.0 ± 10.0 (+)	1.1	90.0 ± 10.0 (+)
	7	0.7	60.0 ± 16.3	2.0	83.3 ± 10.2	2.0	85.0 ± 11.0

Table 2. Accuracy Rate (%) in the Car Evaluation Data Set.

Goal	Attrib. Value	Greedy algorithm		GA-Nuggets		Distributed GA-Nuggets	
		Cov	Accuracy	Cov	Accuracy	Cov	Accuracy
Buying	V-high	1.2	60.0 ± 16.3	1.2	60.0 ± 16.3	1.0	50.0 ± 16.7
	High	2.0	0.0 ± 0.0	2.5	4.5 ± 3.0 (+)	2.2	7.5 ± 3.8 (+)
	Med	1.7	0.0 ± 0.0	2.5	2.5 ± 2.5	2.3	5.0 ± 3.3 (+)
	Low	2.3	80.0 ± 13.3	2.3	100.0 ± 0.0 (+)	2.0	100.0 ± 0.0 (+)
Accept.	Unacc	12.6	100.0 ± 0.0	10.4	100.0 ± 0.0	10.4	100.0 ± 0.0
	Acc	0.0	0.0 ± 0.0	0.1	0.0 ± 0.0	0.0	0.0 ± 0.0
	Good	0.0	0.0 ± 0.0	0.0	0.0 ± 0.0	0.1	0.0 ± 0.0
	V-good	0.0	0.0 ± 0.0	0.0	0.0 ± 0.0	0.1	0.0 ± 0.0

- In Table 3 (Auto Imports data set) both GAs obtained rules with significantly higher accuracy rate than the rules obtained by the greedy algorithm in seven cases. GA-Nuggets and Distributed GA-Nuggets obtained rules with significantly lower accuracy rate than the rules obtained by the greedy algorithm in two cases and one case, respectively.

Table 3. Accuracy Rate (%) in the Auto Imports Data Set.

Goal	Attrib. Value	Greedy algorithm		GA-Nuggets		Distributed GA-Nuggets	
		Cov	Accuracy	Cov	Accuracy	Cov	Accuracy
Simb.	-3	0.0	0.0 ± 0.0	0.0	0.0 ± 0.0	0.0	0.0 ± 0.0
	-2	1.2	20.0 ± 13.3	0.0	0.0 ± 0.0 (-)	0.8	0.0 ± 0.0 (-)
	-1	0.0	0.0 ± 0.0	1.2	55.0 ± 13.8 (+)	1.6	63.3 ± 14.4 (+)
	0	2.0	85.0 ± 7.6	2.2	96.0 ± 2.7 (+)	2.0	98.0 ± 2.0 (+)
	1	1.4	80.0 ± 13.3	1.7	70.0 ± 15.3	2.3	70.0 ± 10.2
	2	0.0	0.0 ± 0.0	1.2	63.3 ± 14.4 (+)	1.3	90.0 ± 10.0 (+)
	3	0.6	20.0 ± 13.3	1.2	70.0 ± 15.3 (+)	1.9	70.0 ± 12.6 (+)
Body	Hardtop	0.2	0.0 ± 0.0	0.6	0.0 ± 0.0	0.4	0.0 ± 0.0
	Wagon	0.4	10.0 ± 6.7	0.6	0.0 ± 0.0 (-)	1.6	13.3 ± 5.4
	Sedan	0.1	10.0 ± 10.0	0.6	60.0 ± 16.3 (+)	2.1	82.5 ± 9.9 (+)
	Hatch	1.3	30.0 ± 15.3	2.6	76.7 ± 6.7 (+)	2.8	71.7 ± 5.4 (+)
	Convert.	0.6	20.0 ± 13.3	0.6	40.0 ± 16.3	1.0	25.0 ± 8.3
Price	Low	10.4	100.0 ± 0.0	11.4	100.0 ± 0.0	13.4	100.0 ± 0.0
	Average	2.6	77.5 ± 6.9	3.2	90.0 ± 4.1 (+)	3.7	81.7 ± 9.7
	High	0.5	50.0 ± 16.7	1.4	72.5 ± 12.6	1.3	90.0 ± 10.0 (+)

- In Table 4 (Nursery data set) GA-Nuggets and Distributed GA-Nuggets obtained rules with significantly higher accuracy rate than the rules obtained by the greedy algorithm in three cases and two cases, respectively. There was no case where the GAs obtained rules with significantly lower accuracy rate than the rules obtained by the greedy algorithm.

Table 4. Accuracy Rate (%) in the Nursery Data Set.

Goal	Attrib. Value	Greedy algorithm		GA-Nuggets		Distributed GA-Nuggets	
		Cov	Accuracy	Cov	Accuracy	Cov	Accuracy
Finance	Conv	0.6	22.2 ± 13.1	2.2	80.0 ± 13.3 (+)	3.4	100.0 ± 0.0 (+)
	Inconv	4.1	100.0 ± 0.0	3.4	100.0 ± 0.0	3.9	100.0 ± 0.0
Social	Non-prob	3.2	0.0 ± 0.0	3.2	1.11 ± 1.1	2.2	0.0 ± 0.0
	Slightly Prob	3.4	0.0 ± 0.0	27.7	6.4 ± 4.3 (+)	2.0	0.0 ± 0.0
	Problem	6.0	100.0 ± 0.0	4.4	100.0 ± 0.0	10.2	100.0 ± 0.0
Health	Recomm	0.0	0.0 ± 0.0	0.0	0.0 ± 0.0	0.0	0.0 ± 0.0
	Priority	0.1	0.0 ± 0.0	291.6	0.0 ± 0.0	0.2	0.0 ± 0.0
	Not Recomm	0.0	0.0 ± 0.0	54.5	12.8 ± 9.8 (+)	15.8	41.8 ± 14.4 (+)
	Spec Priority	4.8	100.0 ± 0.0	4.6	100.0 ± 0.0	10.0	100.0 ± 0.0
	Very Recomm	14.4	100.0 ± 0.0	10.8	100.0 ± 0.0	8.6	100.0 ± 0.0

Overall, considering the results in the four data sets, both GA-Nuggets and Distributed GA-Nuggets obtained better results than the greedy algorithm, with respect to predictive accuracy. (These results will be summarized in subsection 5.2.3.) The three algorithms obtained rules with a low coverage, in general. As explained in the Introduction, this can be considered part of the price to pay for obtaining rules that are both accurate and interesting. From the perspective of an algorithm searching for knowledge nuggets, predictive accuracy and interestingness are considered more important than coverage.

5.2.2 Degree of Interestingness

In this subsection we compare the degree of interestingness of the rules discovered by the three algorithms in all the four data sets. The results are reported in Tables 5 through 8. Similarly to the previous subsection, in each of these tables each row represents the results for a given rule consequent –

i.e., a combination of a goal attribute and one of its values, as indicated in the first two columns. The third column of these tables reports the value of the degree of interestingness of the rule consequent (as measured by formula (5)). Note that this value is independent of the algorithm, since all algorithms discover rules with the same rule consequents. On the other hand, the degree of interestingness of the rule antecedent depends on the algorithm, since different algorithms discover rules with different rule antecedents. Hence, the fourth, fifth and sixth columns of Tables 5 through 8 report the degree of interestingness of the rule antecedent (as measured by formula (1)) for the greedy algorithm, GA-Nuggets and Distributed GA-Nuggets, respectively.

Again, similarly to the previous subsection, the greedy algorithm was considered as a baseline algorithm, the numbers after the "±" symbol in the last three columns are standard deviations, and the table cells where the degree of interestingness of the rule antecedents discovered by the GA is significantly better (worse) than the greedy algorithm's ones are indicated by the symbol "(+)" ("(-)"). Let us now analyze the results of Tables 5 to 8.

- In Table 5 (Zoo data set) the degree of interestingness of the rule antecedent discovered by GA-Nuggets was significantly better than the greedy algorithm's one in three cases, whereas the opposite was true in four cases. The degree of interestingness of the rule antecedent discovered by Distributed GA-Nuggets was significantly better than the greedy algorithm's one in two cases, whereas the opposite was also true in two cases.
- In Table 6 (Car Evaluation data set) the degree of interestingness of the rule antecedent discovered by GA-Nuggets was significantly better than the greedy algorithm's one in three cases, whereas the opposite was true in two cases. Distributed GA-Nuggets had a better performance. The degree of interestingness of the rule antecedent discovered by Distributed GA-Nuggets was significantly better than the greedy algorithm's one in four cases, whereas the opposite was true in just one case.
- In Table 7 (Auto Imports data set) the degree of interestingness of the rule antecedent discovered by GA-Nuggets was significantly better than the greedy algorithm's one in just one case, whereas the opposite was true in six cases. Distributed GA-Nuggets had a considerably better performance. The degree of interestingness of the rule antecedent discovered by Distributed GA-Nuggets was significantly better than the greedy algorithm's one in five cases, whereas the opposite was true in three cases.

Table 5. Rule Interestingness (%) in the Zoo Data Set.

Goal	Attrib. Value	Cons. Inst.	Antecedent Interestingness		
			Greedy	GA-Nuggets	Distrib. GA-Nuggets
Predator	False	74.4	96.1 ± 0.9	97.5 ± 0.4 (+)	95.9 ± 1.0
	True	66.8	97.2 ± 0.6	94.9 ± 0.5 (-)	96.4 ± 0.4
Domestic	False	35.7	95.7 ± 0.4	96.3 ± 0.5	96.9 ± 0.6 (+)
	True	93.3	97.9 ± 0.2	96.9 ± 0.7 (-)	97.9 ± 0.4
Type	1	77.1	99.1 ± 0.0	94.7 ± 0.2 (-)	94.6 ± 0.1 (-)
	2	89.0	94.1 ± 0.1	93.9 ± 0.3	93.9 ± 0.3
	3	97.5	93.8 ± 0.3	93.2 ± 0.6	92.3 ± 0.2 (-)
	4	94.3	95.1 ± 0.3	93.4 ± 0.2 (-)	94.7 ± 0.3
	5	97.9	93.6 ± 0.2	94.3 ± 0.4	94.0 ± 0.3
	6	95.9	92.9 ± 0.3	93.4 ± 0.3 (+)	92.4 ± 0.4
	7	94.9	93.5 ± 0.2	95.3 ± 0.1 (+)	95.1 ± 0.2 (+)

Table 6. Rule Interestingness (%) in the Car Evaluation Data Set.

Goal	Attrib. Value	Cons. Inst.	Antecedent Interestingness		
			Greedy	GA-Nuggets	Distrib. GA-Nuggets
Buying	V-high	86.6	99.3 ± 0.0	99.4 ± 0.0 (+)	99.4 ± 0.0 (+)
	High	86.6	99.3 ± 0.0	99.4 ± 0.0 (+)	99.4 ± 0.0 (+)
	Med	86.6	99.4 ± 0.0	99.3 ± 0.0 (-)	99.4 ± 0.0
	Low	86.6	98.8 ± 0.0	98.8 ± 0.0	99.0 ± 0.0 (+)
Accept.	Unacc	54.7	93.2 ± 0.0	96.5 ± 0.0 (+)	96.4 ± 0.0 (+)
	Acc	88.3	94.3 ± 0.0	93.2 ± 0.0 (-)	93.3 ± 0.0 (-)
	Good	97.9	94.3 ± 0.0	94.3 ± 0.0	94.3 ± 0.0
	V-good	98.1	94.3 ± 0.0	94.3 ± 0.0	94.3 ± 0.0

- In Table 8 (Nursery data set) the degree of interestingness of the rule antecedent discovered by GA-Nuggets was significantly better than the greedy algorithm's one in three cases, whereas the opposite was true in two cases. Again, Distributed GA-Nuggets had a considerably better performance. The degree of interestingness of the rule antecedent discovered by Distributed GA-Nuggets was significantly better than the greedy algorithm's one in six cases, whereas the opposite was not true in any case.

Table 7. Rule Interestingness (%) in the Auto Imports Data Set.

Goal	Attrib. Value	Cons. Inst.	Antecedent Interestingness		
			Greedy	GA-Nuggets	Distrib. GA-Nuggets
Simb.	-3	100.0	100.0 ± 0.0	99.3 ± 0.1 (-)	100.0 ± 0.0
	-2	99.2	97.7 ± 0.1	98.3 ± 0.1 (+)	99.0 ± 0.3 (+)
	-1	94.1	97.5 ± 0.1	97.7 ± 0.1	97.8 ± 0.1 (+)
	0	82.1	97.8 ± 0.1	97.7 ± 0.2	97.5 ± 0.1 (-)
	1	85.8	98.0 ± 0.0	97.8 ± 0.2	97.9 ± 0.1
	2	91.6	98.8 ± 0.1	97.4 ± 0.2 (-)	98.1 ± 0.1 (-)
	3	93.8	98.9 ± 0.2	98.1 ± 0.1 (-)	98.7 ± 0.1
Body	Hardtop	97.9	97.8 ± 0.8	97.5 ± 0.3	98.3 ± 0.4
	Wagon	93.6	97.9 ± 0.1	97.6 ± 0.2	98.1 ± 0.3
	Sedan	72.3	98.1 ± 0.1	96.5 ± 0.5 (-)	97.8 ± 0.5
	Hatch	82.1	98.0 ± 0.3	97.1 ± 0.3 (-)	97.5 ± 0.1 (-)
	Convert.	98.4	98.5 ± 0.2	98.1 ± 0.2	98.6 ± 0.1
Price	Low	64.8	94.6 ± 0.2	94.2 ± 0.5	96.8 ± 0.1 (+)
	Average	80.8	93.9 ± 0.3	92.9 ± 0.9	95.1 ± 0.3 (+)
	High	96.3	95.0 ± 0.5	90.8 ± 0.4 (-)	96.1 ± 0.2 (+)

Table 8. Rule Interestingness (%) in the Nursery Data Set.

Goal	Attrib. Value	Cons. Inst.	Antecedent Interestingness (%)		
			Greedy	GA-Nuggets	Distrib. GA-Nuggets
Finance	Conv.	71.1	99.9 ± 0.0	99.8 ± 0.0 (-)	99.9 ± 0.0
	Inconv.	70.3	99.8 ± 0.0	99.8 ± 0.0	99.9 ± 0.0 (+)
Social	Non-prob	81.7	99.8 ± 0.0	99.7 ± 0.0 (-)	99.9 ± 0.0 (+)
	Slightly prob	81.6	99.8 ± 0.0	99.8 ± 0.0	99.9 ± 0.0 (+)
	Problem.	81.6	99.7 ± 0.0	99.7 ± 0.0	99.8 ± 0.0 (+)
Health	Recomm.	81.7	94.9 ± 0.0	94.9 ± 0.0	94.9 ± 0.0
	Priority	99.9	95.8 ± 0.0	99.7 ± 0.0 (+)	99.9 ± 0.0 (+)
	Not recomm.	98.7	94.6 ± 0.0	96.3 ± 0.7 (+)	94.6 ± 0.4
	Spec priority	81.9	93.7 ± 0.0	93.5 ± 0.3	93.4 ± 0.3
	Very recomm.	82.9	92.6 ± 0.0	94.1 ± 0.3 (+)	94.3 ± 0.3 (+)

Overall, considering the results in the four data sets, the greedy algorithm obtained better results than GA-Nuggets. More precisely, in three data sets (Zoo, Car Evaluation and Nursery) the two algorithms had a similar level of performance, but the greedy algorithm obtained considerably better results than GA-Nuggets in the Auto Imports data set. On the other hand, overall Distributed GA-Nuggets obtained better results than the greedy algorithm. In particular, the performance of the former was considerably better than the latter particularly in the Nursery data set.

5.2.3   Summary of the Results

Table 9 contains a summary of the results presented in subsections 5.2.1 and 5.2.2. Again, the greedy algorithm was considered as a baseline algorithm. Hence, Table 9 summarizes how many times the results of each GA was significantly better or worse than the result of the greedy algorithm, with respect to both accuracy rate (in the test set) and degree of interestingness of the antecedents of the discovered rules.

More precisely, the results for each of the two GAs are reported in two columns, titled "Accuracy" and "Interestingness". For each of the two GAs, each cell of the Accuracy column reports three numbers following the format of the formula $X - Y = Z$, where X (Y) is the number of cases where the accuracy rate of the GA was significantly better (worse) than the accuracy rate of the greedy algorithm, for the corresponding data set indicated by the first column. Hence, the values of X and Y are the number of occurrences of the symbols "+" and "-" in the corresponding Tables 1 through 4. The value of Z can be thought of as the "overall score" of the GA. The larger the value of this score, the better the results of the GA by comparison with the results of the greedy algorithm, with respect to predictive accuracy. The values of the cells of the Interestingness columns have an analogous meaning, summarizing the number of times that the result of each GA was significantly better than the results of the greedy algorithm, i.e., the number of occurrences of the symbols "+" and "-" in the corresponding Tables 5 through 8. The last row of Table 9 contains the total score of each GA over the four data sets, for each performance criterion.

Note that reporting the average value of the predictive accuracy or degree of interestingness over the four data sets would not be very meaningful, since each data set represents a completely different problem for a data mining algorithm. By contrast, the total score reported in the last row of Table 9, based on the number of significantly better (worse) results obtained by each GA, is more meaningful.

As shown in Table 9, both GA-Nuggets and Distributed GA-Nuggets obtained large positive values in their total scores of Accuracy (13 and 15, respectively), indicating that overall the two GAs considerably outperformed the greedy algorithm in these four data sets, with respect to predictive accuracy.

Table 9. Summary of the Results.

Data set	GA-Nuggets		Distributed GA-Nuggets	
	Accuracy	Interestingness	Accuracy	Interestingness
Zoo	4 - 1 = 3	3 - 4 = -1	4 - 0 = 4	2 - 2 = 0
Car Evaluation	2 - 0 = 2	3 - 2 = 1	3 - 0 = 3	4 - 1 = 3
Auto Imports	7 - 2 = 5	1 - 6 = -5	7 - 1 = 6	5 - 3 = 2
Nursery	3 - 0 = 3	3 - 2 = 1	2 - 0 = 2	6 - 0 = 6
Totals	16 - 3 = 13	10 - 14 = -4	16 - 1 = 15	17 - 6 = 11

With respect to the degree of interestingness of the discovered rules, GA-Nuggets obtained a negative total score of –4, indicating that the greedy algorithm outperformed GA-Nuggets with respect to interestingness. The explanation for this relatively bad result of GA-Nuggets is as follows. First of all, note that this result was mainly determined by a single data set, namely the Auto Imports data set. Note also that in this data set the greedy algorithm obtained in general a low predictive accuracy, i.e., it sacrificed too much predictive accuracy in order to increase the degree of interestingness. Indeed, GA-Nuggets clearly outperformed the greedy algorithm in the Auto Imports data set with respect to accuracy, as can be seen in Table 9. In the other three data sets GA-Nuggets and the greedy algorithm have a similar performance with respect to rule interestingness. Distributed GA-Nuggets obtained a large positive score of 11, indicating that it significantly outperformed the greedy algorithm with respect to the degree of interestingness of the discovered rules.

Finally, a comment about computational time is appropriate here. Both versions of GA-Nuggets are about two orders or magnitude slower than the greedy algorithm. This is a well-known disadvantage of GAs. However, there are two mitigating factors. First, predictive data mining is typically an off-line task, and it is well-known that in general the time spent with running a data mining algorithm is a small fraction (less than 20%) of the total time spent with the entire knowledge discovery process [Michalski & Kaufman, 1998]. Data preparation is usually the most time consuming phase of this process. Hence, in many applications, even if a data mining algorithm is run for several hours or several days, this can be considered an acceptable processing time, at least in the sense that it is not the bottleneck of the knowledge discovery process. In addition, if necessary the time taken by one run of GA-Nuggets can be considerably reduced by using parallel processing techniques, since in general GAs can be easily parallelized in an effective way [Freitas & Lavington, 1998]. Hence, the increase in computational time associated with GAs is a small price to pay for the overall increase in both predictive and interestingness, as obtained particularly by the distributed version of GA-Nuggets.

6.   CONCLUSIONS

We have presented three algorithms for discovering "knowledge nuggets" – rules that have both a good predictive accuracy and a good degree of interestingness. The algorithms were developed for discovering prediction rules in the dependence modeling task of data mining. This task can be regarded as a generalization of the very well-known classification task. In classification there is a single goal attribute to be predicted, whereas in dependence modeling there are several goal attributes to be predicted.

We believe that the three main characteristics of the research described in this Chapter are: (a) to address the dependence modeling task, which, despite its importance, has been little explored in the literature on prediction-rule discovery; (b) the focus on the discovery of "knowledge nuggets", which can also be considered a relatively little explored area in the literature on prediction-rule discovery, particularly in the context of the dependence modeling task; and (c) performing controlled-experiments comparing two paradigms of algorithms for prediction-rule discovery, namely genetic algorithms and greedy rule induction algorithms, as explained in the following.

Two of the three algorithms presented in this Chapter are actually two different versions of a genetic algorithm (GA). One of these versions uses a single population of individuals (candidate rules), whereas the other version uses a distributed population of individuals. With the exception of this major difference, the other characteristics of the GA were kept the same, as much as possible, in the two versions, in order to allow us to compare the two versions in a manner as fair as possible.

The third algorithm is a greedy rule induction algorithm. It was designed to discover rules expressed in the same knowledge representation used by the GA and to evaluate candidate rules by using the same rule-quality measure used by the GA. This has allowed us to compare the performance of the two versions of the GA with the performance of the greedy rule induction algorithm in a fair way as well.

This comparison was performed across four public-domain, real-world data sets. The computational experiments measured both the predictive accuracy (accuracy rate in the test set) and the degree of interestingness of the rules discovered by the three algorithms.

As discussed in subsection 5.2.3, overall the computational results indicate that both versions of the GA considerably outperformed the greedy rule induction algorithm in those four data sets, with respect to predictive accuracy. With respect to the degree of interestingness of the discovered rules, the single-population version of the GA obtained results somewhat worse than the results of the greedy algorithm, whereas the distributed-population version of the GA obtained results considerably better than the greedy algorithm.

One direction for future research consists of developing a new version of the distributed-population GA where each subpopulation is associated with a goal attribute value, rather than with a goal attribute as in the current distributed version. It is interesting to compare the performance of this future version with the performance of the current distributed version, in order to empirically determine the cost-effectiveness of these approaches, considering their pros and cons discussed in subsection 3.2.2. It would also be useful to extend the computational experiments reported in this Chapter to other data sets, to further validate the reported results.

REFERENCES

[Back, et al., 2000] T. Back, D.B. Fogel and Z. Michalewicz (Eds) Evolutionary Computation 1: Basic Algorithms and Operators. Institute of Physics Publishing, Bristol. 2000.

[Blickle, 2000] T. Blickle. Tournament selection. In: Back T, Fogel DB and Michalewicz T. (Eds) Evolutionary Computation 1: Basic Algorithms and Operators, pp 181-186. Institute of Physics Publishing, Bristol. 2000.

[Carvalho & Freitas, 2000] D.R. Carvalho and A.A. Freitas. A genetic algorithm-based solution for the problem of small disjuncts. Principles of Data Mining and Knowledge Discovery (Proc. 4th European Conf., PKDD-2000. Lyon, France). Lecture Notes in Artificial Intelligence 1910, 345-352. Springer-Verlag, 2000.

[Carvalho & Freitas, 2002] D.R. Carvalho and A.A. Freitas. A genetic algorithm with sequential niching for discovering small disjunct rules. Proc. Genetic and Evolutionary Computation Conf. (GECCO-2002), pp. 1035-1042. Morgan Kaufmann, 2002.

[Cover & Thomas, 1991] T.M. Cover and J.A. Thomas. Elements of Information Theory. John Wiley &Sons, 1991.

[Dhar, et al., 2000] V. Dhar, D. Chou and F. Provost. Discovering interesting patterns for investment decision making with GLOWER – a genetic learner overlaid with entropy reduction. Data Mining and Knowledge Discovery Journal, 4 (4), 251-280. Oct. 2000.

[Fayyad, et al., 1996] U.M. Fayyad, G. Piatetsky-Shapiro and P. Smyth. From data mining to knowledge discovery: an overview. In: U.M. Fayyad, G. Piatetsky-Shapiro, P. Smyth and R. Uthurusamy (Eds.) Advances in Knowledge Discovery and Data Mining, 1-34. AAAI/MIT Press, 1996.

[Freitas, 1998] A.A. Freitas. On objective measures of rule surprisingness. Principles of Data Mining and Knowledge Discovery (Proceedings of the 2nd European Symp., PKDD'98) – Lecture Notes in Artificial Intelligence 1510, 1-9. Springer-Verlag, 1998.

[Freitas, 1999] A.A. Freitas. A genetic algorithm for generalized rule induction. In: R. Roy et al. Advances in Soft Computing - Engineering Design and Manufacturing. (Proceedings of the WSC3, 3rd on-line world conf., hosted on the internet, 1998), 340-353. Springer-Verlag, 1999.

[Freitas, 2000] A.A. Freitas. Understanding the crucial differences between classification and discovery of association rules - a position paper. ACM SIGKDD Explorations, 2(1), 65-69. ACM, 2000.

[Freitas, 2001] A.A. Freitas. Understanding the crucial role of attribute interaction in data mining. Artificial Intelligence Review, 16(3), Nov. 2001, pp. 177-199.

[Freitas, 2002a] A.A. Freitas. Data Mining and Knowledge Discovery with Evolutionary Algorithms. Berlin: Springer-Verlag, 2002.

[Freitas, 2002b] A.A. Freitas. Evolutionary Computation. In: J. Zytkow and W. Klosgen. (Eds.) Handbook of Data Mining and Knowledge Discovery, pp. 698-706. Oxford: Oxford University Press, 2002.

[Freitas & Lavington, 1998] A.A. Freitas and S.H. Lavington. Mining Very Large Databases with Parallel Processing. Kluwer, 1998.

[Goldberg, 1989] D.E. Goldberg. Genetic Algorithms in Search, Optimization and Machine Learning. Addison-Wesley, Reading, MA. 1989.

[Greene & Smith, 1993] D.P. Greene, and S.F. Smith. Competition-based induction of decision models from examples. Machine Learning 13, 229-257. 1993.

[Hand, 1997] D.J. Hand. Construction and Assessment of Classification Rules. John Wiley&Sons, 1997.

[Holte, et al., 1989] R.C. Holte, L.E. Acker, and B.W. Porter. Concept Learning and the Problem of Small Disjuncts, Proc. IJCAI – 89, 813-818. 1989.

[Michalewicz, 1996] Z. Michalewicz Z. Genetic Algorithms + Data Structures = Evolution Programs. 3rd Ed. Springer-Verlag, Berlin. 1996.

[Michalski & Kaufman, 1998] R.S. Michalski and K.A. Kaufman. Data Mining and Knowledge Discovery: A Review of Issues and Multistrategy Approach. In: Michalski, R.S., Bratko, I. and Kubat, M. (Eds.), Machine Learning and Data Mining: Methods and Applications, pp. 71-112. London: John Wiley & Sons. 1998.

[Mitchell, 1996] M. Mitchell. An Introduction to Genetic Algorithms. MIT Press, 1996.

[Noda, et al., 1999] E. Noda, A.A. Freitas, and H.S. Lopes. Discovering interesting prediction rules with a genetic algorithm. Proc. of the Congress on Evolutionary Computation (CEC-99), pp. 1322-1329. IEEE Press, 1999

[Noda, et al., 2002] E. Noda, A.A. Freitas and A. Yamakami. A distributed-population genetic algorithm for discovering interesting prediction rules. 7th Online World Conference on Soft Computing (WSC7). Held on the Internet, Sep. 2002.

[Papagelis & Kalles, 2001] A. Papagelis and D. Kalles. Breeding decision trees using evolutionary techniques. Proc. 18th Int. Conf. on Machine Learning (ICML-2001), 393-400. San Mateo, CA: Morgan Kaufmann, 2001.

[Provost & Aronis, 1996] F.J. Provost and J.M. Aronis. Scaling up inductive learning with massive parallelism. Machine Learning 23(1), April 1996, pp. 33-46.

[Quinlan, 1987] J.R. Quinlan. Generating production rules from decision trees. Proc. of the Tenth Int. Joint Conf. on Artificial Intelligence (IJCAI-87), 304-307. San Francisco: Morgan Kaufmann, 1987.

[Schaffer, 1993] C. Schaffer. Overfitting avoidance as bias. Machine Learning 10, 1993, 153-178.

[Smyth & Goodman, 1991] P. Smyth and R.M. Goodman. Rule induction by using information theory. In G. Piatetsky-Shapiro and W.J. Frawley (Eds.) Knowledge Discovery in Databases, 159-176. Menlo Park, CA: AAAI Press, 1991.

[Spiegelhalter, et al., 1994] D.J. Spiegelhalter, D. Michie and C.C. Taylor. Machine Learning, Neural and Statistical Classification. New York: Ellis Horwood, 1994.

[Syswerda, 1989] G. Syswerda. Uniform Crossover in genetic Algorithms. Proc. 3rd Int. Conf. on Genetic Algorithms (ICGA-89), 2 – 9. 1989.

[Weiss, 1995] G.M. Weiss. Learning with Rare Cases and Small Disjuncts, Proc. 12th International Conference on Machine Learning (ICML-95), 558-565. 1995.

[Weiss, 1998] G.M. Weiss. The Problem with Noise and Small Disjuncts, Proc. Int. Conf. Machine Learning (ICML – 98), 1998, 574-578.

[Weiss & Hirsh, 2000] G.M. Weiss and H. Hirsh. A Quantitative Study of Small Disjuncts, Proc. of Seventeenth National Conference on Artificial Intelligence. Austin, Texas, 665-670. 2000.

[Wong & Leung, 2000] M.L. Wong and K.S. Leung. Data mining using grammar-based genetic programming and applications. Kluwer, 2000.

AUTHORS' BIOGRAPHICAL STATEMENTS

Mr. Edgar Noda received the B.Sc. degree in Computer Science from the Federal University of Parana - UFPR, Brazil, in 1998; the M.Sc. degree in Electrical Engineering and Industrial Informatics from the Federal Technological Center of Parana – CEFET-PR, Brazil, in 2000; and is currently a Ph.D. student at the School of Electrical and Computing Engineering at the State University of Campinas – UNICAMP, Brazil. Throughout his academic formation, he has always shown a special interest in the field of computational intelligence. In this area he has published works on intelligent tutoring systems, neural networks navigation, and genetic algorithms applied to data mining. Currently, his main research interests concentrate on data mining with evolutionary algorithms and prediction-rule interestingness measures.

Dr. Alex A. Freitas received the B.Sc. degree in Computer Science from the "Faculdade de tecnologia de Sao Paulo", Brazil, in 1989; the M.Sc. degree in Computer Science from the "Universidade Federal de Sao Carlos", Brazil, in 1993; and the Ph.D. degree in Computer Science from the University of Essex, UK, in 1997. He was a visiting lecturer at the "Centro Federal de Educacao Tecnologica", in Curitiba, Brazil, from 1997 to 1998; and a lecturer at the "Pontificia Universidade Catolica", also in Curitiba, Brazil, from 1999 to 2002. Since 2002 he is a lecturer at the University of Kent, in Canterbury, UK. His publications include two books on data mining and more than 70 refereed research papers published in journals, books, conferences or workshops. He has organized two international workshops on data mining with evolutionary algorithms, and delivered tutorials on this theme in several international conferences. He is a member of the Editorial Board of the Intelligent Data Analysis - an international journal, and a guest co-editor of a special section of the IEEE Trans. on Evolutionary Computation journal on Data Mining and Knowledge Discovery with Evolutionary Algorithms. He has also coordinated a research cluster in Swarm Intelligence involving more than 15 institutions in the UK, from July/2003 to Dec./2003. At present his main research interests are data mining, bioinspired algorithms, and bioinformatics.

Chapter 13 [1]

DIVERSITY MECHANISMS IN PITT-STYLE EVOLUTIONARY CLASSIFIER SYSTEMS

Michael Kirley[*], Hussein A. Abbass[2][**] and Robert (Bob) I. McKay[***]

* Department of Computer Science and Software Engineering
University of Melbourn, Australia
Email: mkirley@unimelb.edu.au

** Artificial Life and Adaptive Robotics Lab, School of Information Technology and Electrical Engineering, University of New South Wales@ADFA, Canberra, ACT 2600, Australia
Email: h.abbass@optusnet.com.au
Web: http://www.itee.adfa.edu.au/~abbass

*** School of Information Technology and Electrical Engineering, University of New South Wales@ADFA, Canberra, ACT 2600, Australia
Email: rim@cs.adfa.edu.au
Web: http://www.itee.adfa.edu.au/~rim

Abstract: In this chapter we investigate the application of diversity-preserving mechanisms in Pitt-style evolutionary classifier systems. Specifically, we analyze the effects of implicit fitness sharing, spatially distributed subpopulations, and combinations of the two, using a range of standard knowledge discovery tasks. The proposed models are compared based on (a) their ability to promote and/or maintain diversity across the evolving population; (b) the ability of the algorithm to evolve rule sets, which accurately classify data; and (c) the relative ease of parallel implementation of the models. Conclusions are drawn regarding the suitability of the approaches in both sequential and parallel environments.

Key Words: Classifier Systems, Diversity, Genetic Algorithms, Rule Discovery, Data Mining.

---

[1] Triantaphyllou, E. and G. Felici (Eds.), **Data Mining and Knowledge Discovery Approaches Based on Rule Induction Techniques**, Massive Computing Series, Springer, Heidelberg, Germany, pp. 433-457, 2006.

[2] Corresponding Author

1.   INTRODUCTION

The information age thrives and evolves on knowledge. Knowledge is derived from information gleaned from a wide variety of reservoirs of data (databases). Not only does the data itself directly contribute to information and knowledge, but also the trends, patterns and regularities existing in the data files. Consequently, the ability to automatically discover knowledge from databases, that is, extract useful information from the data and the associated properties of the data, is both an attractive and challenging task.

Rule discovery is one of the most important data mining tasks. In this chapter we focus on a specific subset of rule discovery – *rules for classification*. In a classification task, the goal is to use previously observed data to construct a model, which is able to predict the categorical or nominal value (the class) of a dependent variable given the values of the independent variables. In this context, we want the discovered model to have a high predictive accuracy. The process of building this model is undertaken by presenting a sample (training set) of instances, formed by the independent variables and the corresponding dependent variable, to the classification algorithm. Typically, an algorithm searches for a model which can accurately map the values of the independent variables to their corresponding value of the dependent variables. When the algorithm finds a suitable model, the training phase terminates and the model is tested using some unseen data (test set) to examine its performance (generalization) beyond the training set.

A classification model can take different representations. We may distinguish between two broad categories of classification models: inner and outer models. In inner models, each class is clustered into groups, where each group is defined by some prototype such as its mean or median. When a new instance is presented to the classifier, the distance between the instance and each prototype is measured. The instance is then given the class of the closest prototype to it. In outer classification, the objective is to approximate the boundaries of each class. This approximation can be undertaken using a neural network, a linear programming model, a decision graph, a classification tree, or a set of classification rules.

A number of studies have been undertaken in the literature for modeling classification as an optimization problem (Bradley, Fayyad, & Mangasarian, 1999) including discriminant analysis for classification, which uses an unconstrained optimization technique for error minimization (Ragsdale, 2001). Neural networks and nonlinear optimization methods may be more accurate than other models; however they are often difficult to understand.

Often there is a trade-off between the accuracy and the comprehensibility of a set of classification rules. Nevertheless, in many real life problems, classification rules are the preferred choice for a decision-maker keen to understand the model.

Traditionally, rule discovery has been based on deterministic approaches such as decision tree learning. Evolutionary classifier systems (Holland, 1998) belong to an alternative class of techniques, which have proven to be competitive with other machine learning techniques (Abbass, Sarker, & Newton, 2002). Evolutionary classifier systems are idealized computational versions of neo-Darwinian evolution; they gain reinforcement from the environment based on an evolving set of condition-action rules. A population of individuals (or solutions), each of which represents a specific set of parameters, is placed under a selective regime that favours the survival and reproduction of the "best" individuals. A simulated natural selection process builds on past innovations, adopting those genetic changes that provide improved fitness. In this way, an endless process of change replaces one solution with another, with each solution somewhat better suited to the environment than were its immediate predecessors. The primary motivation for applying simulated evolutionary processes to data mining tasks is their robustness and adaptability as search methods, performing a global search in the space of candidate solutions (that is, rule sets or some other form of knowledge representation).

Evolutionary classifier systems for rule discovery can be divided into two broad approaches, based on how rules are encoded in the population of individuals (See section 3 for further discussion):

- the *Michigan approach* – each individual encodes a single prediction rule,
- the *Pittsburgh approach* – each individual encodes a set of prediction rules.

There are a number of identifiable shortcomings in each of the models, such as limitations of the attribute encoding chosen, or high sensitivity to parameter values (Holland et al., 2000). The so called "credit-assignment problem", that is, determining the way in which a classifier is rewarded for its performance is common to both models (Riolo, 1987; Smith, 1994). In classification tasks, we usually evaluate the quality of the rule set as a whole, rather than the quality of a single rule. Therefore, the Pittsburgh model seems a more natural choice for rule induction, and as such will be the model investigated in this chapter.

When using evolutionary classifier systems, the objective is to evolve individuals (rules or rule sets) with high predictive accuracy. Ideally, the population should maintain diversity to sample the search space effectively. In addition, a related objective is to maximize the coverage of the data, that is, the percentages of data classified by each rule. Unfortunately, evolutionary classifier systems suffer from the same fate as evolutionary algorithms in the optimization domain – the problem of premature convergence and loss of genetic diversity. To date, however, diversity has been investigated more widely in the evolutionary optimization domain, and very few studies have investigated diversity in evolutionary data mining. Recently, in related fields such as machine learning, there has been increasing emphasis on diversity mechanisms, to ensure that the individual solutions are well separated and do not simply replicate each other (Burke, Gustafson, & Kendall, 2002).

In evolutionary systems techniques for maintaining and/or promoting diversity fall naturally into two classes: mechanisms which subdivide the population into separately evolving populations with limited interactions (non-correlation mechanisms); and mechanisms which in some way alter the local fitness landscape to encourage a wider spread of individuals over the landscape (anti-correlation mechanisms). In this chapter, we investigate the efficacy of alternative diversity mechanisms in *Pitt-style* (Pittsburgh approach) evolutionary classifiers. Our underlying hypothesis is that non-correlation and anti-correlation mechanisms will improve the quality of solutions found in Pitt-style classifier systems.

The remainder of this chapter is organized as follows: In Section 2 a brief introduction to genetic algorithms is presented. In Section 3 the Michigan and Pitt models are described in more detail. Background material relating to diversity mechanisms in evolutionary computation follows in Section 4. In Section 5 we expand our discussion of diversity mechanism to incorporate classifiers systems. Section 6 describes our evolutionary classifiers, the experimental set up and the results obtained. Section 7 discusses the results and examines the relationship and interaction between diversity and solution quality. This chapter concludes with the implications of the findings and future research directions.

2.   BACKGROUND – GENETIC ALGORITHMS

Evolutionary computation and algorithms (Goldberg, 1989; Holland, 1998; Mitchell, 1996) embrace a range of approaches, inspired by natural selection, to optimize the parameters of a system in order to satisfy certain performance criteria. They have been applied successfully to many problems in diverse fields including social systems, optimisation, planning and scheduling, pattern recognition, data mining, and design (Abbass et al., 2002; Gen & Chang, 2000; Mitchell, 1996).

Genetic Algorithms (GAs) (Goldberg, 1989; Holland, 1998; Mitchell, 1996) are perhaps the best known evolutionary algorithms for finding good solutions to many search and optimisation problems. GAs can be considered a "generate-and-test" metaheuristic, based on the foundations of natural selection and genetic recombination. The major advantage GAs have over other stochastic, iterative methods is that they work with a population of individuals (potential solutions to the problem) rather than adapting a single solution. The basic outline of a simple GA is described in Figure 1.

```
begin
        t = 0
        initialize P(t)
        evaluate P(t)
        while( not termination condition ) do
                t = t + 1
                select P(t) from P(t-1)
                alter P(t)
                evaluate P(t)
        end do
end
```

Figure 1.   Outline of a Simple Genetic Algorithm. Here P(t) denotes the population of solutions at time t. Other terms have their intuitive meaning.

In GAs specifying the fitness function and encoding scheme are essential aspects of problem definition. For a given problem, there will be many different ways to construct the search space, and some of the resultant search spaces will be easier to search than others (Mitchell, 1996). Traditionally, GAs have used binary encoding for all kinds of problems. In binary encoding, each chromosome is a vector of zeroes and ones, with each bit representing a gene. Alternative binary encoding schemes, such as Gray encoding, (which preserves the adjacency relation of the genes with respect to the Hamming distance[1] - a measure of similarity between binary strings), have also been used with success.

Almost any space can form the genotype space, as long as it supports appropriate crossover and mutation operators (see next section). It is well

---

[1]   The Hamming distance between two binary vectors is the number of corresponding elements in the two vectors with different values.

known that the choice of proper representation is crucial for the success of evolutionary algorithms. Recently there has been a trend toward using a higher-level of representation, more related to the problem domain. However, there is still no consensus about the properties of high-quality representations, and exactly how representations affect the performance of evolutionary algorithms.

There is abundant literature on a wide range of variants of crossover and mutation, and their relative importance. In the classical GA view, crossover is the fundamental operator and mutation only plays an ancillary role. The encoding of individuals dictates the format of the genetic operators that are used. For binary representations, n point crossover is typically used. The operator is performed with a probability p_{cross}. If the operator is not performed, one of the parents is returned as the offspring. Another common implementation is uniform crossover. Here, the bits of the parents are swapped with a given probability p_{cross}, position by position. In GAs, a mutation usually refers to a change in a gene's value – for instance, in binary encoding a gene with value 1 may be mutated to value 0. Typically, this bitwise inversion mutation is implemented with probability p_{mut} (often the reciprocal of the string length).

It is clear that different operators play different roles at different stages of the evolutionary process. Within the evolutionary computation community there is often debate about how often each operator should be used, what mutation rate should be used, and which crossover style should be chosen. Although there are standard rates and implementations, for many problems empirical trials are required to determine the most effective combination.

For both natural and artificial systems, the fitness value of an individual (solution) measures how well the individual has adapted to the current environmental conditions. Individuals that do well (i.e. have higher fitness values) have a greater probability of passing their genetic information on to the next generation. The fitness value can be calculated by any method that gives a good estimate of the quality of the solution. Typically, the fitness value allocated to a solution is the value of the objective function (phenotype) based on the decoded genotype.

The identification of the GA population itself is not as simple as it first seems. At the simplest level, there is the question of how one population is created from another. GAs have a selection mechanism to identify the fittest individuals of the current population to serve as parents of the next generation. The selection mechanism can take many forms, but it always ensures that the best individuals have a higher probability to reproduce and breed to form the new generation. Mechanisms can be deterministic or stochastic; threshold, linear or non-linear functions; and based on rank, actual fitness values, or more complicated features (Goldberg, 1989).

There are a range of different algorithms for population update. The most common scheme in GAs is the generational approach, where the new population is created from the old one. This scheme is often referred to as the $\mu = \lambda$ update scheme, where μ is the current population and λ is the children composing the new population generated via the selection-recombination process). At the other extreme, a steady state GA typically replaces only a small number of the most poorly performing individuals (i.e., $\lambda = 1$ or 2) in the current population. Other GAs employ variants of the generational approach where $\lambda < \mu$. Alternatively, offspring and parents can be combined into the one pool ($\mu + \lambda$) and the fittest μ individuals are selected to form the next generation.

Given the stochastic nature of GAs, it is possible that individuals with very high fitness values disappear from the population forever. To combat this problem, elitist models may be used. An elitist model maintains the best individuals from one generation to the next. Elitism is not itself a selection mechanism, but rather it is an optional feature of many selection methods. Elitism is simply the guarantee that the fittest individuals found to date will remain within the evolving population.

3.   EVOLUTIONARY CLASSIFIER SYSTEMS

3.1   The Michigan Style Classifier System

Perhaps the best-known evolutionary data mining techniques are Learning Classifier Systems (Holland et al., 2000; Lanzi & Riolo, 2000). In these, a GA creates a production system that searches for many classifiers at the same time, rather than maintaining a single 'best' classification structure. Each individual in the evolving population is represented by a fixed-length string, and corresponds to a partial concept description (or single rule). The target concept is represented by a whole set of individuals in the population. It is only through cooperation with the other rules in the population that the problem is solved. Here, the objective is to discover a set of rules, rather than a single rule.

This model is a hierarchical adaptive system in which schemata (building blocks) are combined (by the recombination operator) to make classifiers, and the classifiers are combined (by a choice mechanism) to make firing sequences. Adaptation in the lower levels of the hierarchy is achieved by a GA. Adaptation in the higher levels is achieved by a local reward scheme based on an explicit credit assignment method, traditionally a bucket brigade

(Riolo, 1987), though Q-learning and other methods are possible. A variant called XCS (Wilson, 1995) differs from the traditional Michigan style classifiers systems in two main respects:

- the definition of fitness, which is based on the accuracy of the payoff prediction rather than on the prediction itself;
- the application of the GA to the environmental niches defined by the action sets.

3.2   The Pittsburgh Style Classifier System

In the Pitt-style classifier system (DeJong, 1988; Smith, 1980) the issue of credit assignment is side-stepped to some extent, by explicitly requiring the evaluation of entire rule sets. In this model, each individual is represented by a variable-length string, and corresponds to a whole target concept. Here, the GA acts on a population of concatenated rules. This approach leads to syntactically-longer individuals, which tends to make fitness evaluation computationally expensive. However, it directly takes into account rule interaction when computing the fitness function of an individual. The recombination process has the effect of allowing migration of classifiers between concatenated rule sets.

There is an on-going debate in the evolutionary computation community about the relative merits of the evolutionary classifier models. In this chapter, we are primarily interested in investigating the relative merits of alternative diversity mechanisms in evolutionary classifier systems. Many of the techniques examined are more amenable to the Pitt-style system. Consequently, the Michigan model will not be discussed further.

4.   DIVERSITY MECHANISMS IN EVOLUTIONARY ALGORITHMS

In evolutionary algorithms, genetic diversification is akin to an experimental approach – testing a range of alternatives along the way. An individual's ability to thrive depends on its own genetic composition as well as the genetic composition of the other individuals present. The purpose of the selection mechanism is to reward individuals that perform well; that is, individuals with higher fitness. The right selection pressure is critical in:

- ensuring sufficient progress towards the target;
- preserving genetic diversity such that the algorithm is able to escape from local optima.

Selection pressures directly affect the level of heterogeneity in the evolving population. Unfortunately, a common problem associated with evolutionary algorithms is that the evolving population may converge prematurely to a "suboptimal solution" if selection pressure is too intense. Consequently, one of the major challenges when applying evolutionary algorithms is the preservation of genetic diversity.

A wide range of mechanisms to preserve diversity, and delay convergence, has been proposed in the literature. The approaches fall into two main classes:

- mechanisms based on fitness evaluation;
- mechanisms that constrain reproduction.

One important difference between them lies in the degree of diversity promotion. The fitness evaluation mechanisms typically reward diversity; that is, they promote anti-correlation in the object population. Mechanisms which constrain reproduction, on the other hand simply permit diversity by limiting the effect of the fitness pressure towards uniformity; that is, they promote non-correlation in the object population.

In the following sections, we will review the more common techniques in detail. This discussion will provide a suitable framework for developing diversity mechanisms appropriate for Pitt-style classifiers in the later sections of this chapter.

4.1   Niching

Niching in evolutionary algorithms is inspired by the natural phenomena of speciation and specialisation in natural ecosystems. Niching modifies the way fitness is distributed, so that solutions are rewarded both for being fit relative to the problem solved, and also for being distinct from other solutions. Consider multi-modal optimisation problems. Here, the aim is to find all of the optima, or to find all optima that are above some threshold value, or to find a certain number of local optima. For such problems, it is necessary to prevent the best individuals in the population from replacing all copies of competing rivals. Niching techniques can be used to help meet this goal. Niching induces restorative pressure (Horn, 1997), to balance the convergence pressure of selection.

4.2   Fitness Sharing

Fitness sharing, and variants thereof, modifies the search landscape by reducing the payoff in densely populated regions. Here, the fitness value of an individual is scaled by some measure of similarity among individuals.

Explicit fitness sharing uses the distance metric d_{ij} between two individuals i and j; the distance is used to calculate how much reward has to be shared between i and j, with nearer individuals sharing more (and hence suffering greater reduction in their fitness). Usually, the similarity measure is based on either:

- *genotypic* properties - generally the Hamming distance for binary strings or

- *phenotypic* properties - usually linked to real parameters of the search space.

Deb and Goldberg (Deb & Goldberg, 1989) suggest that sharing based on phenotypic properties may give slightly better results than sharing with genotypic similarity. Typically, the shared fitness f_i' of an individual i with fitness f_i is defined as:

$$f_i' = \frac{f_i}{m_i},$$

where m_i is the niche count which measures the approximate number of individuals with whom fitness f_i is shared. It is usually calculated by summing up a sharing function over all members of the population:

$$m_i = \sum_{j=1}^{N} sh(d_{ij}),$$

where N is the population size and d_{ij} the distance between individuals i and j. The sharing function sh returns one if the elements are identical, zero if their distance exceeds the threshold of dissimilarity, and an intermediate value otherwise.

Fitness sharing is highly effective in many cases, but nevertheless suffers from a number of difficulties:

- Defining the sharing function sh requires *a priori* knowledge;

- The scheme is computationally expensive;

- Reducing the fitness at fitness peaks may make it difficult for fitness sharing to find an exact optimum, as a deceptive fitness landscape is introduced.

The last problem is usually handled by the use of fitness scaling (Darwen & Yao, 1995), using a formula such as:

$$f_i' = \frac{f_i^{\beta}}{m_i},$$

where β determines the level of dominance - or the amount of genetic drift within the population. However choosing β appropriately is not simple: high values are likely to cause premature convergence, while low values leave the problem of deceptive fitness landscapes.

Implicit Fitness Sharing

Smith, Forrest, and Perlson (1992) introduced *implicit fitness sharing* to address problems associated with explicitly stating the value of the sharing function. The underlying assumption, that fitness is calculated as a sum of rewards for particular instances, is particularly suitable for learning problems such as those considered here:

$$f_{raw}(i) = \sum_{c \in cases} reward(i(c)).$$

In implicit fitness sharing, the reward is divided amongst all population individuals giving the same prediction for a given instance:

$$f_{share}(i) = \sum_{c \in cases} \frac{reward\ (i(c))}{\sum_{i':i'(c)=i(c)} reward\ (i'(c))}.$$

When rewards are computed with this approach, there is no need to calculate the distance between the individuals.

4.3   Crowding

Another very common diversity mechanism is *crowding* (DeJong, 1975). In crowding, a large number of recombination pairs are generated at random from the population, without regard to fitness. These pairs are then subjected to a form of selection where each of the children competes against one of its parents in order to enter the new population. An alternative is to choose certain individuals as dominant individuals and, each generation, clear out all solutions that do not fall within a certain (phenotypic) radius of the individual according to some domain-specific metric. Mahfoud's (Mahfoud, 1995) deterministic crowding – where offspring replace their most similar parent if they have a better fitness value – has performed better than the original crowding scheme on a variety of problems. Unfortunately, a problem with this technique is that the "similarity" measure is typically problem dependent and computationally expensive, because each individual has to be compared with all other individuals in the population.

4.4   Isolated Populations

The benefit of isolating subpopulations has long been known (Cohoon, Hegde, Martin, & Richards, 1987; Manderick & Spiessens, 1989; Tanese, 1989). Once subpopulations are isolated, they may genetically diverge due either to random drift, or to differences in the selective pressures of their separate environments. This approach encapsulates the genetic dynamics of populations evolving in space, offering ways to improve the performance of evolutionary algorithms through niching.

The stochastic nature of the algorithms potentially permits different solutions being identified. However, there is no guarantee that different subpopulations will converge on different optima. If migration is allowed, the influx of good solutions may lead to all subpopulations converging to the same solution.

The Fine-grained Model

In fine-grained parallel GAs (or cellular GAs), individuals are usually placed on a large toroidal two-dimensional grid, one individual per grid location (Manderick & Spiessens, 1989; Mühlenbein, Gorges-Schleuter, & Krämer, 1988; Whitley, 1994). Fitness evaluation is done simultaneously for all individuals. Selection and reproduction take place within a local neighbourhood (deme). The spatial structure of the population provides a mechanism for restricting mating to a local neighbourhood. A mate from the local neighbourhood is typically chosen either by proportional or linear ranking selection. One of the offsprings is randomly chosen to replace the parent in the current grid location.

In (Kirley, 2002), a novel fine-grained parallel genetic algorithm with flexible population sizes was introduced. Here, the introduction of a "disturbance-colonization" cycle provided a mechanism for maintaining flexible subpopulation sizes and self-adaptive controls on migration, and consequently population diversity. Unfortunately, the synchronisation constraints embedded in fine-grained models limits their application in parallel systems. Serial implementations are possible, but they are computationally expensive.

The Course-grained Model

Coarse-grained parallel GAs (also known as distributed or "island" models) rely on spatial separation of the evolving populations (Belding, 1995; Cantú-Paz, 2000; Cohoon et al., 1987; Tanese, 1989). This approach divides the entire evolutionary system into separate subpopulations, which evolve separately on different processors, with small numbers of individuals being migrated asynchronously between populations. The segregation into separate populations can permit the survival of genetic structures which would be removed by selective pressure from a single large population, helping to avoid premature convergence.

The subpopulations can be arranged in various topologies – chain (circle), grid (toroidal) or hypercube. Perhaps the most common topology is where migration takes place between nearest neighbour subpopulations – the stepping stone model (See also Figure 2). In the majority of cases, migration is synchronous, occurring at predetermined constant intervals. However, migration can also be asynchronous, with communication between demes taking place only after some events have occurred. The parameters of course-grained models (topology, population size, migration rate, migration policy) have received close attention (Cantú-Paz, 2001), and the benefits and limitations are well known in the optimisation domain.

The loose synchronisation between subpopulations in coarse-grained models particularly suits them for distributed memory parallel architectures (MIMD), and for workstation clusters with limited communication bandwidth. Compared with fine-grained approaches, coarse-grained parallelism imposes low communication requirements.

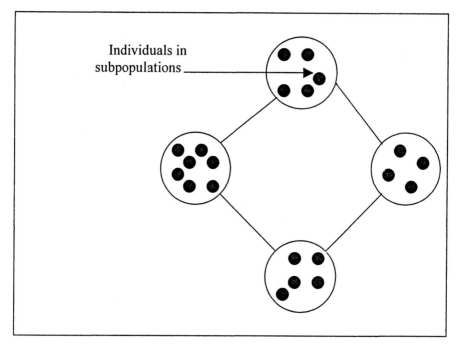

Figure 2.   The Island Model. Each subpopulation evolves independently. Selected individuals are migrated from one subpopulation to another subpopulation in the neighborhood of the first.

5.   CLASSIFIER DIVERSITY

The previous section discussed a range of techniques commonly used to foster diversity in evolutionary computation. Typically, some measure of diversity is used to quantify the variety in the population, or to measure the differences between individuals, and then to modify the selection pressure. Alternatively, a spatially distributed population structure may be used to slow the rate of convergence. In the case of evolutionary classifier systems, it is not at all obvious which technique (or combination of techniques) is the most appropriate. Classifier evolution requires the generation of "rule sets" that can accurately predict target attributes, rather than convergence to a single global optimum.

An important related issue is *generalization*. Over-fitting occurs when the induced model reflects idiosyncrasies of the particular data set, which do not generalize reliably for predictions involving new data. Ensembles of classifiers, with mechanisms to combine their decisions, form an important approach to reducing over-fitting. Theoretical and experimental results have clearly shown that classifier combinations are effective only when the individual classifiers are "accurate" and "diverse", that is, if they exhibit low error rates and make different errors (Hansen & Salamon, 1990; Kuncheva, Whitaker, Shipp, & Duin, 2000; Sharkey, 1999; Tumer & Ghosh, 1999). Several mechanisms to differentiate members of an ensemble have been proposed. The most common approach is to train members on different subsets of the training data. This can be done systematically by *bootstrapping* (sampling with replacement) different training sets from the training data. Such an approach has been applied with great success in learning systems such as artificial neural networks (NNs) (Hansen & Salamon, 1990) or decision trees (Breiman, 1996; Quinlan, 1993).

Negative correlation learning provides an alternative approach, which has proven to be a competitive training method for artificial neural networks and genetic programming (McKay & Abbass, 2001). The idea of negative correlation learning is to encourage different individual networks to learn different parts or aspects of the training data, so that the ensemble can better learn the entire training data. Here, the individual networks are trained simultaneously, rather than independently or sequentially. This provides an opportunity for the individual networks to interact with each other and to specialize. This technique incorporates a measure of diversity into the error function of networks, so that each network increases not only its accuracy, but also its diversity from other network errors. It is widely recognized that negative correlation should be considered when designing ensembles of NN classifiers, and many such designs have been proposed – predominantly altering the individual training set to build the classifiers.

When we talk of diversity in machine learning and evolutionary computation we are really talking about heterogeneity between the elements which make up the system. In rule discovery, diversity is obviously an important issue. However, as alluded to in the introduction, rule comprehensibility is also an important factor. In genetic programming, the issue of code "bloat" – that is, the rate of growth of the tree structures – has received considerable attention (Burke et al., 2002). The growth in the size of the rule set in Pitt-style classifier systems has also received attention. The most common technique used to address this problem has been to introduce a parsimony pressure into the fitness function so that the fitness of larger individuals is decreased (Basset & Jong, 2000; Mansilla, Mekaoche, & Garrell, 1999; Garell, Golobardes, Mansilla, & Llora, 1999). In this approach, when the number of rules encapsulated by an individual exceeds a certain maximum, its fitness is decreased abruptly.

The difficulty lies in setting the threshold to an appropriate value. It has been observed that shorter rule sets tend to have more generalization capabilities (Mansilla, Mekaoche, & Garrell; Nordin & Banzhaf, 1995).

Llora and co-workers (Llora & Garrell, 2001) have extended the genetic programming work of Bleuler and colleagues (Bleuler, Brack, Thiele, & Zitzler, 2001) into the learning system domain. They introduced a multi-objective technique where two objectives, accuracy and compactness of the individual, provided the selection pressures. Here, the first objective corresponds with "how good is the solution" and the second objective with generalized pressure toward compact solutions.

6.   EXPERIMENTS

The primary objective of this study was to investigate the performance and utility of alternative mechanisms for promoting and maintaining diversity in Pitt-style classifier systems. To our knowledge, there has not been a study that has systematically analysed implicit fitness sharing and course-grained parallel models using a Pitt-style classifier system.

Theoretical and experimental studies in evolutionary computation suggest that anti-correlation mechanisms will exhibit slower convergence, and consequently greater resistance to premature convergence to local minima, than non-correlation mechanisms (Liu & Yao, 1999). In this study, we test this hypothesis and examine what impact the diversity level has on the ability of the Pitt-style classifier to evolve accurate rule sets.

6.1   Architecture of the Model

The system is based on the Pitt model for classifier systems. In this model, each individual in the evolving population represents a candidate complete solution to the classification problem. Each individual consists of a set of rules, each of which specifies the classification to be recorded when its antecedents are satisfied. The Pitt model is relatively simple and comprehensible, and hence its behavior is relatively straightforward to analyze. The downside is the computational cost, arising from the need to train a full classifier system for each fitness evaluation.

There have been several proposals of genetic operators designed specifically for rule discovery (Freitas, 2002). We have tested five different enhanced crossover operators – cloning, rule deletion, rule split, rule generalization, rule specialization – as well as conventional crossover operators. Empirical studies using the data sets below indicate that the *selectdrop*, a uni-sexual crossover which operates on a single parent by selecting a condition and dropping it, was the most effective one. Consequently, the results reported in section 6.4 have used this operator.

Diversity is a difficult concept to measure in the Pitt model. The Hamming distance between two rule sets can be very misleading, because two rule sets may be the same but with different Hamming distances. For example, assume five rules per a rule set. Assume two rule sets x_1 and x_2. Now, let us assume that there are three rules with coverage 0 in x_1 and x_2; these three rules are the first of the five in x_1 and the last in x_2. The other two rules in each are the same. The Hamming distance will give a misleading value if used to measure the distance between x_1 and x_2. Therefore, our diversity measure starts by re-ordering the rules within a rule set before applying the Hamming distance measure. This is a computationally very expensive process. Diversity is measured as the total of the minimum Hamming distances between each chromosome and the rest of the population.

6.2   Data Sets

We have used five standard data sets taken from the UCI Repository of Machine Learning (Merz & Murphy, 1998): the Wisconsin Diagnostic Breast Cancer, Diabetes, Hepatitis, Liver, and Tic Tac Toe data sets.

6.3   Treatments

Four alternative diversity promotion/maintenance mechanisms were compared in this study.
1. No diversity mechanisms;
2. fitness sharing;
3. island model; and
4. a combined treatment with both fitness sharing and the island model.

In the island model, four separate populations were maintained. In the combined treatment, fitness sharing was carried out within each island, potentially combining some of the key advantages of the island model (intrinsically parallel) and fitness sharing (increased diversity pressure).

6.4   Model Parameters

Each treatment was evaluated using 10 fold cross-validation; the data set was divided into training and test data sets (90% training, 10% test). Class distribution was maintained in each subset. Each subset was run 50 times. A 100% crossover probability and 10% mutation probability were adopted. The population size was set to 200. When the island model was used, each island contained 50 individuals. The Roulette Wheel Selection method was used.

7.   RESULTS

In Tables 1 to 4, we present the results obtained on the five data sets. Diversity preserving mechanisms do not seem to play a significant role in improving the performance of the Pitt-style classifier. It is also interesting to note that implicit fitness sharing resulted in degradation in performance. A closer examination of Tables 1-4, columns labeled "Training Coverage" and "Test Coverage", reveals that a significant decrease in coverage occurred with fitness sharing. This resulted in a corresponding downgrade in accuracy. Note that *coverage* here is the percentage of the data that at least one base classifier can classify correctly. Cases not covered by the rule set are classified using the default rule (majority class). Therefore, we may encounter zero coverage with a considerable accuracy level because of the default class.

Table 1. Results for the five data sets – percentage and standard deviations for accuracy, coverage and diversity from the stratified ten-fold cross-validation runs using island model and fitness sharing.

	Training Accuracy	Training Coverage	Test Accuracy	Test Coverage	Population Diversity
Breast Cancer	0.74±0.04	0.09±0.04	0.73±0.07	0.07±0.03	196.23±5.07
Diabetes	0.65±0	0±0	0.65±0	0±0	635.20±17.84
Hepatitis	0.87±0.02	0.03±0.01	0.86±0.09	0.01±0.04	518.22±27.16
Liver	0.59±0.01	0.01±0.01	0.58±0.03	0.01±0.02	486.14±16.55
Tic Tac Toe	0.46±0.04	0.16±0.05	0.48±0.07	0.15±0.08	51.43±1.05

Table 2. Results for the five data sets – percentage and standard deviations for accuracy, coverage and diversity from the stratified ten-fold cross-validation runs using island model without fitness sharing.

	Training Accuracy	Training Coverage	Test Accuracy	Test Coverage	Population Diversity
Breast Cancer	0.90±0.01	0.37±0.05	0.86±0.04	0.37±0.08	197.10±4.02
Diabetes	0.66±0.02	0.04±0.04	0.67±0.01	0.03±0.04	747.40±111.04
Hepatitis	0.88±0.02	0.05±0.01	0.83±0.05	0.06±0.08	520.17±64.57
Liver	0.62±0.02	0.13±0.09	0.61±0.06	0.17±0.14	484.07±22.72
Tic Tac Toe	0.69±0.12	0.74±0.22	0.70±0.09	0.73±0.23	53.82±6.24

Table 3. Results for the five data sets – percentage and standard deviations for accuracy, coverage and diversity from the stratified ten-fold cross-validation runs using fitness sharing without island model.

	Training Accuracy	Training Coverage	Test Accuracy	Test Coverage	Population Diversity
Breast Cancer	0.74±0.03	0.10±0.02	0.74±0.05	0.10±0.05	201.52±5.66
Diabetes	0.67±0.01	0.03±0.02	0.68±0.03	0.04±0.03	664.90±35.05
Hepatitis	0.88±0.02	0.04±0.01	0.84±0.07	0.03±0.05	504.77±5.95
Liver	0.59±0	0.01±0.00	0.59±0.04	0.01±0.02	485.42±14.49
Tic Tac Toe	0.51±0.08	0.23±0.23	0.50±0.08	0.24±0.23	52.34±1.67

Table 4. Results for the five data sets – percentage and standard deviations for accuracy, coverage and diversity from the stratified ten-fold cross-validation runs without fitness sharing or island model.

	Training Accuracy	Training Coverage	Test Error	Test Accuracy	Population Diversity
Breast Cancer	0.89±0.02	0.40±0.04	0.88±0.04	0.41±0.07	201.74±6.03
Diabetes	0.67±0.01	0.04±0.02	0.66±0.01	0.03±0.02	751.48±107.25
Hepatitis	0.88±0.01	0.05±0.01	0.83±0.05	0.06±0.08	525.26±60.21
Liver	0.62±0.03	0.10±0.08	0.60±0.05	0.14±0.11	474.05±7.02
Tic Tac Toe	0.72±0.01	0.82±0.07	0.70±0.04	0.82±0.08	52.98±6.97

Interestingly, the diversity value recorded does not change significantly when using diversity maintaining/promotion mechanisms. Fitness sharing does not appear to improve the performance of the algorithm for the given data sets. This can be attributed to the high diversity pressure imposed by this method on the rule set. This diversity pressure simply forces the rules to specialize, and therefore a decrease in coverage may be experienced. In contrast, the use of spatially distributed subpopulations resulted in an improved performance in some cases although the difference is not significant.

8.   CONCLUSIONS

In evolutionary optimization, diversity is usually a crucial factor in obtaining the global optimum for the problem in hand. In data mining, obtaining the global optimum on the training set is mostly seen as over-fitting the data. The model that yields the best accuracy on the training set may not be the ideal model for test set. Consequently, we may question whether evolutionary optimization and evolutionary data mining share the same objectives.

In this chapter, our objective was to examine the relative efficacy of alternative diversity promotion / maintenance mechanisms using Pitt-style evolutionary classifier systems. A motivating factor behind this work was the belief that diversity in the evolving population would help to evolve individuals (rules or rule sets) with high predictive accuracy. We have presented a comparative study between two diversity preserving mechanisms – implicit fitness sharing, and island parallel models – and a combination of the two. A systematic analysis of the models using five benchmark data sets suggests that there are no performance advantages – accuracy of the rule sets and coverage – when diversity enhancing mechanisms are used; and moreover, the more effective the diversity mechanisms used, the worse the results. This result is somewhat surprising.

Diversity mechanisms have proven highly effective in GA research (Deb & Goldberg, 1989). Classifier systems differ from GA in not having a fixed size genotype, but diversity mechanisms have also been shown to enhance performance in a range of variable sized representations, such as genetic programming and neural networks (e.g. (McKay & Abbass, 2001)). It should be noted that a relatively large population size and mutation rate were used in the experiments. In this case, the model parameters may help to maintain a certain diversity level. In addition, the level of noise inherited in a learning problem adds stochasticity to the fitness landscape. Nevertheless, diversity did not seem to be a crucial factor when evolving rules for the five data sets that we used in this chapter. One plausible explanation is that the naïve application of diversity mechanisms to Pitt-style classifier systems is imposing diversity at the wrong level. In Pitt-style classifiers, each individual effectively comprises a committee, so that internal diversity within each individual is perhaps as important as population diversity; imposing a diversity measure on the population may act to increase the diversity between individuals in the population, at the cost of internal diversity within individuals.

It is interesting to note that the results obtaining using the island model were better that the results obtained using implicit fitness sharing for some of the data sets. This raises the important question of implementation details and parallelism. The island model is inherently parallel, and the computational cost of the model is usually less than simply running the algorithm on a single population. This is an advantage, not only in terms of the accuracy as evident in this chapter, but also of the generalization ability of the model. In their standard forms, anti-correlation mechanisms are poorly amenable to parallel implementation, as the calculation of population-wide properties imposes unacceptable synchronization requirements. In future research, we will investigate alternative techniques for combining anti-correlation and non-correlation methods in evolutionary classifier systems.

Classification rules have no causal semantics. They represent correlations in data, and correlation is not necessarily causation. When mining a real life database, we sometimes have initial domain knowledge which we need to bias or initialize the rule miner with. Domain knowledge can help to bias the miner with some causal semantics that otherwise are difficult to incorporate in classification. Knowledge initialization for inducing rules in an evolutionary environment is still an open area of research.

REFERENCES

Abbass, H. A., Sarker, R., & Newton, C. (Eds.). (2002). *Data Mining: A Heuristic Approach.* Hershey, PA: IGP publishing.

Basset, J. K., & Jong, K. A. D. (2000). *Evolving Behaviours for Cooperating Agents.* Paper presented at the Twelfth International Symposium on Methodologies for Intelligent Systems, Lecture Notes in Artificial Intelligence 1932, Berlin, Springer.

Belding, T. C. (1995). *The Distributed Genetic Algorithm Revisited.* Paper presented at the Sixth International Conference on Genetic Algorithms.

Bleuler, S., Brack, M., Thiele, L., & Zitzler, E. (2001). *Multiobjective genetic programming: Reducing blot using SPEA2.* Paper presented at the IEEE 2001 Congress on Evolutionary Computation.

Bradley, P. S., Fayyad, U. M., & Mangasarian, O. L. (1999). Mathematical Programming for Data Mining: Formulations and Challenges. *INFORMS Journal on Computing, 11,* 217-238.

Breiman, L. (1996). Stacked Regressions. *Machine Learning, 24,* 49-64.

Burke, E., Gustafson, S., & Kendall, G. (2002). *A Survey and Analysis of Diversity Measures in Genetic Programming.* In W. B. Langdon et al. (eds) GECCO 2002: Proceedings of the Genetic and Evolutionary Computation Conference. Morgan Kaufmann Publishers. pp 716-723

Cantú-Paz, E. (2000). *Efficient Parallel Genetic Algorithms*: Kluwer Academic Publishers.

Cantú-Paz, E. (2001). Migration Policies, Selection Pressure, and Parallel Evolutionary Algorithms. *Journal of Heuristics, 7*(3), 311-334.

Cohoon, J. P., Hegde, S. U., Martin, W. N., & Richards, D. (1987). *Punctuated Equilibria: a Parallel Genetic Algorithm.* Paper presented at the Second International Conference on Genetic Algorithm.

Darwen, P., & Yao, X. (1995). *A dilemma for fitness sharing with a scaling function.* Paper presented at the IEEE Conference on Evolutionary Computation.

Deb, K. and Goldberg, D.E. (1989). *An investigation of niche and species formation in genetic function optimisation.* In J.D. Schaffer (ed.) Proceedings of the Third International Conference on Genetic Algorithms. pp 42-50.

DeJong, K. (1975). *An analysis of the behavior of a class of genetic adaptive systems.* Unpublished PhD, University of Michigan.

DeJong, K. (1988). Learning with Genetic Algorithms: An Overview. *Machine Learning, 3*(2), 121-138.

Freitas, A. A. (2003). A survey of evolutionary algorithms for data mining and knowledge discovery. In A. Ghosh & S. Tsutsui. (Eds.), Advances in Evolutionary Computation: Springer-Verlag. (pre-print, unformatted version available at http://www.ppgia.pucpr.br/~alex/papers.html)

Garell, J. M., Golobardes, E., Mansilla E.B., & Llora, X. (1999). Automatic Diagnosis with Genetic Algorithms and Case-Based Reasoning. *Artificial Intelligence in Engineering, 13,* 367-372.

Gen, M., & Chang, R. (2000). *Genetic Algorithms and Engineering Applications.* New York, N.Y., USA: John Wiley & Sons.

Goldberg, D. (1989). *Genetic algorithms: in search optimization and machine learning*: New York, N.Y., Addison Wesley.

Hansen, L., & Salamon, P. (1990). Neural Network Ensembles. *IEEE Transactions on Pattern Analysis and Machine Intelligence, 12,* 993-1001.

Holland, J. (1998). *Adaptation in natural and artificial systems*: MIT press.

Holland, J., Booker, L. B., Colombetti, M., Dorigo, M., Goldberg, D., Forrest, S., Riolo, R. L., Smith, R. E., Lanzi, P. L., Stolzmann, W., & Wilson, S. W. (2000). What is a Learning Classifier System? In P. Lanzi & W. Stolzmann & S. Wilson (Eds.), *Learning Classifier Systems, From Foundations to Applications* (Vol. LNAI 1813, pp. 3-32): Springer-Verlag.

Horn, J. (1997). *The nature of niching: Genetic Algorithms and the evolution of optimal, cooperative populations* (PhD): University of Illinois at Urbana-Champaign.

Kirley, M. (2002). A Cellular Genetic Algorithm with Disturbances: Optimisation Using Dynamic Spatial Interactions. *Journal of Heuristics, 8*(3), 321-242.

Kuncheva, L. I., Whitaker, C. A., Shipp, C. A., & Duin, R. P. W. (2000, 3-8 September). *Is independence good for combining classifiers?* Paper presented at the 15th International Conference on Pattern Recognition, Barcelona, Spain.

Lanzi, P. L., & Riolo, R. L. (2000). A Roadmap to the Last Decade of Learning Classifier System Research. In P. Lanzi & W. Stolzmann & S. Wilson (Eds.), *Learning Classifier Systems, From Foundations to Applications* (Vol. LNAI 1813, pp. 33-62): Springer-Verlag.

Liu, Y., & Yao, X. (1999). Simultaneously training of negatively correlated neural networks in an ensemble. *IEEE Trans. Syst. Man. Cybern. B., 296*, 716-725.

Llora, X., & Garrell, J. M. (2001). *Knowledge-Independent Data Mining With Fine-Grained Evolutionary Algorithms.* Paper presented at the Genetic and Evolutionary Computation Conference, pp 461-468, Morgan Kaufmann.

Mahfoud, S. (1995). *A comparison of parallel and sequential niching methods.* Paper presented at the Sixth International Conference on Genetic Algorithms.

Manderick, B., & Spiessens, P. (1989). *Fine-Grained Parallel Genetic Algorithms.* Paper presented at the Third International Conference on Genetic Algorithms.

Mansilla, E.B., Mekaouche, A Guiu, J. M. G. (1999). *A Study of a Genetic Classifier System Based on the Pittsburgh Approach on a Medical Domain* In I. F. Imam et al. (eds). Multiple Approaches to Intelligent Systems. 12th International Conference on Industrial and Engineering Applications of Artificial Intelligence and Expert Systems IEA/AIE-99. Lecture Notes in Computer Science. Vol. 1611, pp. 175-184

McKay, R. I., & Abbass, H. A. (2001). Anti-correlation: A Diversity Promoting Mechanisms in Ensemble Learning. *The Australian Journal of Intelligent Information Processing Systems, 7*(3/4), 139-149.

Merz, C. J., & Murphy, P. M. (1998). *UCI repository for Machine Learning Data Base.* Irvine CA., University of California. Department of Information and Computer Science. Retrieved, from the World Wide Web:
http://www.ics.uci.edu/~mlearn/MLRepository.html

Mitchell, M. (1996). *An Introduction to Genetic Algorithms*: MIT Press.

Mühlenbein, H., Gorges-Schleuter, M., & Krämer, O. (1988). Evolutionary algorithms in combinatorial optimization. *Parallel Computing, 7*, 65-88.

Nordin, P., & Banzhaf, W. (1995). *Complexity Compression and Evolution.* Paper presented at the Sixth International Conference.

Quinlan, R. (1993). *C4.5: Programs for Machine Learning*: Morgan Kaufmann.

Ragsdale, C. T. (2001). *Spreadsheet Modeling and Decision Analysis.* USA: South-Western College Publishing.

Riolo, R. L. (1987). *Bucket Brigade Performance: I. Long Sequences of Classifiers.* Paper presented at the Second International Conference on Genetic Algorithms (ICGA87), Cambridge, MA.

Scott, D. W. (1992). *Mutivariate Density Estimation.* New York: John Wiley and Sons.

Sharkey, A. J. C. (1999). Multi-Net Systems, *Combining Artificial Neural Nets Ensemble and Modular Multi-Net Systems* (pp. 1-27): Springer.

Smith, R. E. (1994). Memory Exploitation in Learning Classifier Systems. *Evolutionary Computation, 2*(3), 199-220.

Smith, R. E., Forrest, S., & Perlson, A. S. (1992). Searching for diverse cooperative populations with genetic algorithms. *Evolutionary Computation, 12*, 127-149.

Smith, S. F. (1980). *A learning system based on genetic adaptive algorithms.* Unpublished PhD, University of Pittsburgh, Pittsburgh, PA, U.S.A.

Tanese, R. (1989). *Distributed genetic algorithms.* Paper presented at the third International Conference on Genetic Algorithms.

Tumer, K., & Ghosh, J. (1999). Linear and order statistics combiners for pattern classification, *Combining Artificial Neural Nets Ensemble and Modular Multi-Net Systems* (pp. 127-157). Berlin: Springer.

Whitley, D. (1994). A genetic algorithm tutorial. *Statistics and Computing, 4*, 65–85.

Wilson, S. W. (1995). Classifier Fitness Based on Accuracy. *Evolutionary Computation, 32*, 149-175.

AUTHORS' BIOGRAPHICAL STATEMENTS

Dr. Michael Kirley is currently a Lecturer in the Department of Computer Science and Software Engineering, University of Melbourne. Previously, he was a Lecturer in the School of Environmental and Information Sciences, Charles Sturt University. Michael's qualifications include a BEd (Mathematics) and PhD (Information Systems). His research interests include complex systems science, multi-agent systems, and the theory and application of evolutionary computation. In particular, Michael's work has examined the implications of connectivity and diversity mechanisms within a natural computation framework. He has published several papers on related topics.

Dr. Hussein A. Abbass is a Senior Lecturer at the School of Information Technology and Electrical Engineering, University of New South Wales at ADFA, Canberra, Australia, where he leads the artificial life and adaptive robotics lab. Dr. Abbass holds six academic degrees and has 14 years experience in industry and academia. His research focus is on traditional and evolutionary multiobjective optimization and machine learning techniques for multi-agent systems and robotics. He served as a guest editor for a number of books and journals. Dr. Abbass is the chair of the Task Force on Artificial Life and Complex Adaptive Systems by IEEE Neural Network Society EC committee. He has chaired a number of conferences and is on the program committee of several conferences such as CEC, GECCO, and ALife.

Dr. Robert I. (Bob) McKay graduated with a PhD in Mathematical Logic from Bristol University (UK) in 1976. Since 1985 he has been an academic in the University of New South Wales at ADFA, researching logic-based artificial intelligence, applications of AI in ecological modeling, and more recently, genetic programming and evolutionary computation.

Chapter 14 [1]

FUZZY LOGIC IN DISCOVERING ASSOCIATION RULES: AN OVERVIEW [2]

Guoqing Chen and Qiang Wei
School of Economics and Management
Tsinghua University, Beijing 100084, China
Email: chengq@em.tsinghua.edu.cn

Etienne E. Kerre
Department of Applied Mathematics and Computer Sciences
University of Gent, Krilgslaan 281/S9, 9000 Gent, Belgium
Email: eekerre@gent.edu.be

Abstract: Associations reflect relationships among items in databases, and have been widely studied in the fields of knowledge discovery and data mining. Recent years have witnessed many efforts on discovering fuzzy associations, aimed at coping with fuzziness in knowledge representation and decision support processes. This chapter focuses on associations of three kinds: association rules, functional dependencies and pattern associations. Accordingly, it overviews major fuzzy logic extensions. Primary attention is paid (1) to fuzzy association rules in dealing with partitioning quantitative data domains, crisp taxonomic belongings, and linguistically modified rules, (2) to various fuzzy mining measures from different perspectives such as interestingness, statistics and logic implication, (3) to fuzzy/partially satisfied functional dependencies for handling data closeness and noise tolerance, and (4) to time-series data patterns that are associated with partial degrees.

Key Words: Data Mining, Association Rules, Functional Dependency, Pattern Association, Fuzzy Logic.

---

[1] Triantaphyllou, E. and G. Felici (Eds.), **Data Mining and Knowledge Discovery Approaches Based on Rule Induction Techniques**, Massive Computing Series, Springer, Heidelberg, Germany, pp. 459-493, 2006.

[2] Partly supported by China's National Natural Science Foundation (79925001/70231010), and the Bilateral Scientific & Technological Cooperation Programmes between China and Flanders/Czech.

1.   INTRODUCTION

Data mining is regarded as a non-trivial process of identifying valid, novel, potentially useful, and ultimately understandable knowledge in large scale databases (Fayyad & Piatesky-Shapiro et al., 1996). Many research attempts and applications concentrate on clustering, classification, association, regression, summarization, change and deviation detection, etc., in order to discover knowledge that is of interest and of different forms to support decision makers. Of particular interest in this chapter is the discovery of associations that reflect relationships among items in databases. Generally speaking, associations may be categorized into several kinds, such as association rules, functional dependencies, and pattern associations, each one expressing specific semantics in linking data items together.

1.1   Notions of Associations

Usually, associations of a typical kind are association rules (*AR*), which have also been extensively investigated in the field. An example of an association rule is "Apples & Bananas $\Rightarrow$ Pork, with degree of support = 20% and degree of confidence = 80%" meaning that "20% of all the customers bought Apples, Bananas and Pork simultaneously, and 80% of the customers who bought Apples and Bananas also tended to buy Pork". If both the degree of support (*Dsupport*) and the degree of confidence (*Dconfidence*) of a rule are large enough, then the rule could be regarded as a valid rule (or interchangeably referred to as a qualified rule, otherwise indicated where necessary). In general, an association rule $X\Rightarrow Y$ expresses the semantics that "occurrence of X is associated with occurrence of Y", where X and Y are collections of data items. Such association rules are also called Boolean association rules, as the association concerned is the correspondence of the states, each being a binary value *1* or *0* (e.g., X occurs or X does not occur). Since Agrawal et al. introduced the notion of (Boolean) association rules in 1993 (Agrawal & Imielinski et al., 1993), mining of association rules has attracted many research efforts along with a large number of *AR* applications in various fields, such as finance, stock market, aerography, marketing, medicine, manufacturing, e-business, etc (Fayyad & Piatesky-Shapiro et al., 1996; Brin & Motwani et al., 1997; Delgado & Sánchez et al., 2001)

Furthermore, the approach proposed by Agrawal & Srikant et al. (1994) to discovering association rules is considered as a basic mining approach with their Apriori algorithm being deemed as a typical mining algorithm. Two directions of research have then been emerged (Chen & Wei, et al., 1999):

1) One is to improve the efficiency of the mining process as discussed in (Houtsma & Swarmi, 1993; Fayyad & Uthurusamy, 1994; Mannila & Toivonen, 1994; Savasere & Omiecinski et al., 1995; Agrawal & Mannila, 1996; Rastogi & Shim, 1998). Moreover, some methods also construct their algorithms upon sampling operations (Yilmaz & Triantaphyllou et al., 2003) In addition to the above serial algorithms, some parallel and distributed algorithms are also presented (Mueller, 1995; Agrawal & Shafer 1996).

2) The other direction is to extend the semantics and expressions of rules from a number of perspectives. For example, Srikant & Agrawal (1995) presented a method to discover generalized association rules (GAR), by which more abstract rules could be derived. Srikant & Agrawal (1996) extended Boolean association rule mining for quantitative association rule mining using partitioning for quantitative data domains. Some other studies focused on mining association rules with constraints and contexts (Fukuda & Morimoto et al, 1996; Han & Fu, 1995; Klemettinen & Mannila et al., 1994; Srikant & Vu et al., 1997; Wei & Chen, 2000) Instead of the previous *Dsupport* and *Dconfidence* measures, some other interestingness measures, based on statistics and information theory, have also been proposed aimed at making the discovered rules more understandable and simpler (Tseng, 2001; Maimon & Kandel et al., 2001). Chen & Wei et al. (2002) introduced simple association rules (SAR) and related rule derivation notions, based on which the set of other qualified association rules could be obtained without scanning the transaction dataset.

In addition to association rules, functional dependencies (FD) are another kind of associations of interest. Functional dependency is an important notion in relational databases and has been widely discussed as integrity constraints and semantic knowledge for database modeling (Codd, 1970; Chen, 1998). Generally speaking, a functional dependency $X \rightarrow Y$ states that values of Y are uniquely determined by values of X, where X and Y are collections of data items (attributes). Notably, for the sake of clarity and notational convention, $\rightarrow$ is used for functional dependency, while $\Rightarrow$ for association rule throughout the chapter. An example of an FD is "equal student numbers lead to equal student ages (Student # determines Student Age)". Classically, functional dependencies could be assumed or constructed logically, based on which relation schemas are designed. On the other hand, in the context of data mining as a type of reverse engineering, the discovery of functional dependencies has received considerable attention (Castellanos & Saltor, 1993; Bell & Brockhausen, 1995; Huhtala & Karkkainen, 1998a, 1998b; Liao & Wang et al., 1999; Savnik & Flach, 2000; Bosc & Pivert et al., 2001; Wei & Chen et al., 2002). The basic idea behind is that numerous database applications over decades have generated and maintained a huge amount of data stored in distributed environments and with diversified structures. Many functional dependencies might not originally be known or thought of being important, or have been hidden over time, but may be useful and interesting as integrity constraints and semantic knowledge.

Finally, pattern associations are a third kind of associations. Consider time-series patterns that are commonly encountered in real applications in the form of, for example, production, sales, economics, and stock data (Chen & Wei et al., 2001) Discovering the relationships among time-series data is of particular interest since the time-series patterns reflect the evolution of changes in data values with sequential factors such as time. A time series pattern is a series of values of an attribute over time, denoted as $S(s_1, s_2, ..., s_m)$, where s_t ($t = 1, 2, ..., m$) is the value of attribute S at time point t. Usually, time series patterns are associated with each other in various ways. For instance, pattern similarity is a case of pattern association. Patterns S and S' may be regarded similar to each other based upon similarity measures or matching criteria. An example of such a case is "Firm A's IT expenditure pattern is similar to Firm B's IT expenditure pattern" in the context of IT organizational learning/diffusion. Another case of pattern association is pattern movement. Patterns S and S' may be regarded associated in change directions. An example of such a case is "Firm A's stock price increase is associated with Firm B's stock price decrease" in the context of stock price movement. Apparently, discovering such pattern associations can be useful.

However, it will be shown in later sections that in many situations discovering the above-mentioned associations involves uncertainty and imprecision, particularly fuzziness. The necessity of applying fuzzy logic in data mining is twofold: one is that fuzziness is inherent in many problems of knowledge representation and discovery, and the other is that high-level managers or complex decision processes often deal with generalized concepts and linguistic expressions, which are generally fuzzy in nature.

1.2   Fuzziness in Association Mining

Treatment of uncertainty is considered as one of the key issues in data mining (Fayyad & Uthurusamy, 1994; Kruse & Nanck et al., 2001; Mitra & Pal et al., 2001; Rifqi & Monties, 2001). For instance, in finding the "truth" of rule $X{\Rightarrow}Y$ with massive datasets, relative frequencies are used to estimate the corresponding probabilities. More concretely, the *Dsupport* value of an association rule $X{\Rightarrow}Y$ could be regarded as the estimation of probability $\Pr(XY)$, while the *Dconfidence* value of $X{\Rightarrow}Y$ as the estimation of conditional probability $\Pr(Y|X)$ (Aumann & Lindell, 1999) In this way, one may find out the knowledge that $X{\Rightarrow}Y$ holds in a statistically significant fashion.

On the other hand, a different type of uncertainty is fuzziness in concept. A typical example of fuzziness is to define "large numbers" in the domain of real numbers. In association rule mining, for instance, rules like "If the customers are at ages in the interval [*20, 30*], then they tend to buy electronics at prices in the interval [$*5000*, $*10000*]", and "Young customers tend to buy Expensive electronics" may all be meaningful depending on different situations. However, while the former is more specific and the latter is more general in semantic expressions, the former has a so-called "boundary problem" that, for example, a customer aged *31* with a purchase of $*15000* may not be identified/discovered. By contrast, the latter is more flexible and could reflect this customer's buying behavior. Notably, here "young customers" and "expensive electronics" are linguistic terms that are fuzzy in nature.

Furthermore, as data items may be categorized in classes upon specific properties, which can be represented in hierarchies or taxonomies in terms of subclass and super-class (e.g., apple, fruit, food, etc.), data mining may refer to data items at different levels of taxonomies. For instance, Generalized Association Rules (Srikant & Agrawal, 1995) deals with the relationships across taxonomic nodes of higher levels, reflecting more general semantics, such as "Fruit $\Rightarrow$ Meat" instead of "Apple $\Rightarrow$ Beef". However, there are situations where a subclass belongs to its super-class at a partial degree in $[0, 1]$, resulting in fuzzy taxonomies. For example, Tomato may be regarded to belong to both Fruit and Vegetable with membership degrees at *0.7* and *0.6*, respectively. Moreover, fuzziness may prevail in many other association cases in which imprecision, matching, similarity, implication, partial truth or the like is present.

Fuzzy logic plays an important role in dealing with fuzziness and therefore fuzzy data mining. Fuzzy logic, or interchangeably referred to as fuzzy set theory, had its inception by Lofti Zadeh (1965). A fuzzy set is a generalization of an ordinary set. Formally, let U be the universe of discourse (domain), a fuzzy set F on U is characterized by a membership function $\mu_F: U \rightarrow [0, 1]$, which associates each element u of U with a number $\mu_F(u)$ representing the grade of membership of u in F. The expression $\mu_F(u) = 0$ means non-membership, $\mu_F(u) = 1$ means full membership, and $\mu_F(u)$ in $(0, 1)$ means partial membership.

For example, a fuzzy set *"Young"* for *Age* on U_{Age} (domain of *Age*) may be defined by the following membership function: $\mu_{Young}: U_{Age} \rightarrow [0, 1]$, where U_{Age} is the set of positive numbers. Then for any $a \in U_{Age}$,

$$\mu_{young}(a) = \begin{cases} 1 & 0 < a \le 25 \\ \dfrac{40-a}{15} & 25 < a \le 40 \\ 0 & 40 < a \end{cases}.$$

If U is discrete, a fuzzy set can be denoted as $F = \{\mu_F(u)/u \mid u \in U\}$.

Another important notion in fuzzy logic is that of linguistic variables (e.g., *Age*), which take linguistic terms as their values (e.g., *Young, Old, Middle-aged*). Usually, a linguistic variable can be modeled using fuzzy sets and it can be further modified with linguistic hedges. Linguistic hedges, such as "*very*", "*more-or-less*", "*sort-of*", are not themselves modeled by fuzzy sets as primary terms are, but rather are modeled as operators acting on the fuzzy sets representing the primary terms. Consider a hedge operator H_λ, which can be used to deal with a number of linguistic hedges. Let $F(U)$ be the class of all fuzzy sets on domain U, and H_λ be a hedge operator with $\lambda \in [0, \infty)$. Then H_λ is a mapping from $F(U)$ to $F(U)$ such that $\forall A \in F(U)$ (Chen, 1998):

$$H_\lambda(A) = A^\lambda \in F(U) \ or \ \forall a \in U, \ \mu_{H_\lambda(A)}(a) = [\mu_A(a)]^\lambda \in [0,1].$$

When $\lambda > 1$, H_λ reduces the membership degrees for the elements of the fuzzy set being modified, which is called a concentration operator. When $\lambda < 1$, H_λ increases the membership degrees for the elements of the fuzzy set being modified, which is called a dilation operator. For example, $H_{1/2}$ is referred to as a concentration operator for hedge "sort-of" semantically. Given a linguistic hedge h = sort-of and a fuzzy term (item) w = "Fruit" = {1/Apple, 0.7/Tomato, 1/Banana}, then hw = sort-of Fruit = {1/Apple, 0.84/Tomato, 1/Banana}. In addition, given a fuzzy item w = "Young", hw = "*very* Young" could be constructed along with membership function $\mu_{very-young}(a)$ as follows:

$$\mu_{very-young}(a) = \begin{cases} 1 & 0 < a \le 25 \\ (\dfrac{40-a}{15})^2 & 25 < a \le 40 \\ 0 & 40 < a \end{cases}.$$

As will be seen in later sections, many other concepts and techniques of fuzzy logic are relevant to discovering associations, and will be referred to in certain detail. More detailed discussions of these concepts and techniques can be found in (Zadeh, 1965; Kerre, 1993; Chen, 1998; De Cock & Kerre, 2002).

1.3   Main Streams of Discovering Associations with Fuzzy Logic

As indicated already, existing efforts on fuzzy logic extensions can be distinguished into three main streams, namely, fuzzy association rules (*FAR*), fuzzy/partial satisfied functional dependencies (*FFD/FD$_d$*), and fuzzy logic in pattern associations (*FPA*). While the other two streams (*FFD/FD$_d$* and *FPA*) are attracting more and more attention (Huhtala & Karkkainen et al., 1998a, 1998b; Chen & Wei et al., 2001; Wei & Chen et al., 2002; Wang & Shen et al., 2002), the stream of fuzzy association rules (*FAR*) has accounted for most of the existing efforts and is continuously attracting considerable attention by researchers and practitioners. The *FAR* research and applications center around issues of partitioning quantitative data domains, fuzzy taxonomies, *FAR* with linguistic hedges, fuzziness-related interestingness measures, and degree of fuzzy implication, e.g., Lee & Hyung (1997), Kuok & Fu et al. (1998), Cai & Fu et al. (1998), Wei & Chen et al. (1999, 2000), Hong & Kuo (1999a, 1999b), Gyenesei (2000a, 2000b, 2001), Shu & Tsang et al. (2000), Dubois & Hullermeier et al. (2001), Ishibuchi & Nakashima et al., (2001), Hullermeier (2001a, 2001b), Bosc & Pivert (2001); Chen & Wei (2002).

The chapter is organized as follows. Sections 2 and 3 will concentrate on two main directions of fuzzy logic extension in association rules mining: one is to discover fuzzy quantitative association rules, and the other is to discover fuzzy association rules with fuzzy taxonomies. In section 4, some other fuzzy extensions and considerations on fuzzy association rules will be introduced, such as fuzzy logic in interestingness measures, fuzzy extensions of Dsupport/Dconfidence measures, weighted fuzzy association rules, etc. More specifically, section 5 will discuss fuzzy association rules in a more logic-oriented perspective, namely, fuzzy implication based association rules. Additionally, section 6 will deal with the problem of mining functional dependencies with uncertainties, including fuzzy functional dependencies and functional dependencies with degrees. Finally in section 7, the third type of associations, i.e., pattern associations, will be discussed in terms of pattern matching and similarities.

2.   FUZZY LOGIC IN QUANTITATIVE ASSOCIATION RULES

This section starts with Boolean association rules, followed by efforts on crisp partitioning for quantitative association rules. Then, fuzzy extensions in dealing with quantitative association rules will be discussed.

2.1   Boolean Association Rules

Originally, association rules often dealt with binary databases, in which values of each attribute are *0*'s or *1*'s, and are usually referred to as Boolean association rules (or simply, association rules, otherwise indicated where necessary). A binary database D can exist for its own or can be converted from a transaction dataset T. A symbolic example of T and D is provided as shown in Table 1. Concretely, I_1, I_2, I_3, and I_4 can be, for instance, products sold in a supermarket with five transactions.

Table 1. Example of a Transaction Dataset T and a Binary Database D.

(a)

T			
ID1	I_1	I_3	
ID2	I_2		
ID3	I_1	I_3	I_4
ID4	I_2	I_3	
ID5	I_3	I_4	

(b)

D	I_1	I_2	I_3	I_4
ID1	1	0	1	0
ID2	0	1	0	0
ID3	1	0	1	1
ID4	0	1	1	0
ID5	0	0	1	1

Let $I = \{I_1, I_2, ..., I_m\}$ be a set of attributes (also called items), D be a relational database of n tuples (or records) with respect to schema $R(I)$, in which each tuple d is represented as a binary vector with $d[I_k] \in \{0, 1\}$ ($k = 1, 2, ..., m$), and X be a subset of I (also referred to as an itemset), then d is called to support X if for all items J in X, $d[J] = 1$. An association rule is of the form: $X \Rightarrow Y$, where X and Y are two disjoint itemsets of I, i.e., $X, Y \subset I$ and $X \cap Y = \varnothing$. The degree of support for itemset X is defined as follows: $Dsupport(X) = \|X\|/|D|$ (Agrawal & Imielinski et al., 1993; Agrawal & Srikant, 1994; Agrawal & Mannila et al., 1996). As an example in Table 1, $Dsupport(I_1) = 2/5$, and $Dsupport(I_3) = 4/5$.

Furthermore, the degree of support and degree of confidence for rule $X \Rightarrow Y$ are defined as: $Dsupport(X \Rightarrow Y) = \|X \cup Y\|/|D|$, and $Dconfidence(X \Rightarrow Y) = \|X \cup Y\|/\|X\|$, respectively, where $\|X\|$ is the number of tuples in D that support X, $\|X \cup Y\|$ is the number of tuples in D that support X and Y, and $|D|$ is the number of tuples in D. Given a threshold α for minimal support and a threshold β for minimal confidence, $X \Rightarrow Y$ is called a valid association rule if $Dsupport(X \Rightarrow Y) \geq \alpha$ and $Dconfidence(X \Rightarrow Y) \geq \beta$. Statistically, $Dsupport$ could be regarded as the significance of a rule supported by a dataset, while $Dconfidence$ could be regarded as the certainty of a rule. For example, in Table 1, $Dsupport(I_3 \Rightarrow I_1) = 2/5$ and $Dconfidence(I_3 \Rightarrow I_1) = 2/4$. A typical algorithm for discovering such association rules based on binary databases is the well-known Apriori algorithm proposed in (Agrawal & Imielinski et al., 1993; Agrawal & Srikant, 1994; Agrawal & Mannila et al., 1996).

2.2   Quantitative Association Rules

Though Boolean association rules are meaningful in real-world applications, there are many other situations where data items concerned are usually categorical or quantitative. Examples of such items are Month, Age, Income, Quantity of Product, and so on. Without loss of generality, we consider here only quantitative items. Apparently, association rules linking quantitative items are meaningful as well, giving rise to so-called quantitative association rules. Usually, quantitative items are represented in a database as attributes whose values are elements of continuous domains such as Real Number Domain $\mathcal{R}$ Such a database is exemplified as D in Table 2.

Table 2. Database D with Continuous Domains.

D	Age	Income
ID1	30	8890
ID2	25	12500
ID3	19	79000
ID4	47	1500
ID5	68	5000

It can easily be seen that the typical Apriori algorithm is incapable of dealing directly with such databases for quantitative association rules. Therefore, Srikant & Agrawal (1996) proposed an approach that is composed of two steps: (1) transforming D into a binary database D' by partitioning continuous domains, and (2) applying the Apriori algorithm on D'. For example, if attribute Age takes values from (0, 100], then one could partition (0, 100] into three intervals such as (0, 30], (30, 60], and (60, 100], resulting in three new attributes, namely, Age(0,30], Age(30,60], and Age(60,100], respectively. Likewise, if one partitions the domain of Income into (0, 5000], (5000, 15000], (15000, ∞), then three new attributes related to Income are Income(0, 5000], Income(5000, 15000], Income(15000, ∞). As a result, D' becomes a binary database with 7 attributes as shown in Table 3.

Table 3. Database D' Transformed from D by Partitioning Domains.

D'	Age (0, 30]	Age (30, 60]	Age (60, 100]	Income (0, 5000)	Income (5000, 15000]	Income (15000, ∞)
ID1	1	0	0	0	1	0
ID2	1	0	0	0	1	0
ID3	1	0	0	0	0	1
ID4	0	1	0	1	0	0
ID5	0	0	1	1	0	0

Differently from Boolean AR that represents semantics "Occurrence of X is associated with Occurrence of Y", quantitative AR represents semantics "Quantity of X is associated with Quantity of Y".

More formally, for $I = \{I_1, I_2, ..., I_m\}$ and D with d being a tuple of D and $d[I_k]$ belonging to a continuous domain ($1 \leq k \leq m$), suppose that each I_k is partitioned into p_k intervals ($p_k \geq 1$). Then D' is with respect to schema $R(I')$ where $I' = \{ I_1^1, ..., I_1^{p_1}, ..., I_k^1, ..., I_k^{p_k}, ..., I_m^1, ..., I_m^{p_m} \}$. For any tuple d' in D' and I'_k in I', if $d[I_k]$ in D belongs to interval p_k, we have $d'[I'_k] = 1$, otherwise $d'[I'_k] = 0$.

Apparently, the way of partitioning domains affects the mining outcomes. Several efforts have been made for improvement. Instead of equal intervals, average partitioning (Srikant & Agrawal, 1996) and clustering

(Mazlack, 2000) have been proposed, attempting at reaching certain balance between information loss and granularity. However, "sharp boundary" remains a problem, which may under-emphasize or over-emphasize the elements near the boundaries of intervals in the mining process (Gyenesei, 2000a), and may therefore lead to an inaccurate representation of semantics. This gives rise to a need for fuzzy logic extensions due to the fact that "sharp boundary" is of a typical fuzziness nature.

2.3   Fuzzy Extensions of Quantitative Association Rules

Fuzzy sets defined on the domains are used to deal with the "sharp boundary" problem in partitioning (Fu et al., 1998; Wu, 1999; Mazlack, 2000; Chien & Lin et al., 2001; Gyenesei, 2001), such sets are usually expressed in forms of labels or linguistic terms. For example, for attribute *Age*, some fuzzy sets may be defined on its domain U_{Age} such as *Young*, *Middle* and *Old*. In this way, such new attributes (e.g., *Young-Age*, *Middle-Age* and *Old-Age* in place of *Age*) will be used to constitute a new database *D"* with partial belongings of original attribute values (in *D*) to each of the new attributes (in *D"*). Table 4 illustrates an example of *D"* (in part) obtained from *D* of Table 2, given fuzzy sets *Young(Y)*, *Middle(M)* and *Old(O)* as characterized by membership functions shown in Figure 1.

Table 4. Database *D"* (in part) with Fuzzy Items.

D"	Young-Age	Middle-Age	Old-Age	... ...
ID1	0.8	0.7	0.2	......
ID2	0.9	0	0.1	......
ID3	1	0	0	......
ID4	0.4	1	0.6	......
ID5	0	0	1	......

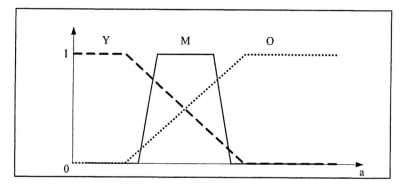

Figure 1. Fuzzy Sets Young(Y), Middle(M) and Old(O)
with Y(20, 65), M(25, 32, 53, 60), O(20, 65).

Generally, for original $I = \{I_1, I_2, \ldots, I_m\}$ and D, each I_k ($1 \leq k \leq m$) can be associated with q_k fuzzy sets defined on the domain of I_k, and usually labeled as q_k new attributes. That is, the new database D'' is with respect to schema $R(I'')$ where $I'' = \{I_1^1, \ldots, I_1^{q_1}, \ldots, I_k^1, \ldots, I_k^{q_k}, \ldots, I_m^1, \ldots, I_m^{q_m}\}$. For any d'' in D'' and I''_k in I'', $d''[I''_k]$ is the degree that $d[I_k]$ in D belongs to I''_k in D'', i.e., $d''[I''_k] = \mu_{I''k}(d[I_k]) \in [0, 1]$ where $\mu_{I''k}$ is the membership function of I''_k. In other words, d'' supports I''_k with a (partial) degree in $[0,1]$.

Several attempts have been made in defining fuzzy sets on continuous domains. For instance, fuzzy clustering methods are used such as fuzzy c-mean based clustering (Chien & Lin et al., 2001), goodness index based clustering (Gyenesei, 2000a), CLARANS clustering (Fu et al, 1998; Gyenesei, 2000a), self-organized learning based clustering (Shu & Tsang, et al., 2000), and other methods (Liu, 1998; Roychowdhury & Pedrycz, 2001), as well as the method used by Kovalerchuk, Triantaphyllou et al. (1997). Many clustering methods are sensitive on the initiative values, so the clustering process may usually run several times on adjusted initiatives in order to select the mostly appropriate results. However, the expert's evaluation is highly recommended after the process.

With the above extended database D'', conventional notions of degrees of support and of confidence need to be extended as well. Though a few measures have been proposed, they are in a similar spirit that $\Sigma count$ operator is used for fuzzy cardinality (Concretely, for example, given a fuzzy set A on U, i.e., A = $\{ \mu_i/u_i \mid u_i \in U, 1 \leq i \leq n \}$, $\Sigma count_{ui \in U}(A) = \Sigma_{1 \leq i \leq n}(\mu_i)$). A more detailed treatment is represented in section 3.2. Subsequently, with these extended measures incorporated, several mining algorithms have been proposed as extensions of the conventional one, such as the method by Lee & Hyung (1997), the FTDA method by Kuok & Fu et al. (1998), the algorithm by Hong & Kuo (1999a, 1999b), the fuzzy extensions by Gyenesei (2000a, 2001), the SQL-based fuzzy extended method by Shu & Tsang et al. (2001), and the work by Chan & Au (2001).

3.   FUZZY ASSOCIATION RULES WITH FUZZY TAXONOMIES

This section will discuss fuzzy extensions on association rules, particularly on fuzzy association rules with fuzzy taxonomies as well as with linguistic hedges. The motivation was to represent and discover knowledge with more general semantics and natural language expressions.

3.1   Generalized Association Rules

Srikant & Agrawal (1995) presented a method to discover the so-called generalized association rules based on concept taxonomies as the ones shown in Figure 2 (a).

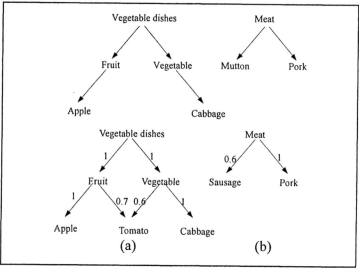

Figure 2.   Exact Taxonomies and Fuzzy Taxonomies.

The algorithm in (Srikant & Agrawal, 1995) allows the discovery of generalized association rules that represent the relationships between original items, as well as between items at all levels of related taxonomies, e.g., "*Fruit⇒Meat*", which is more general and have more potential to be discovered. Formally, generalized association rules could be illustrated as follows.

For original $I = \{I_1, I_2, ..., I_m\}$ and database D with respect to schema $R(I)$, $\forall d \in D$, $d[I_k]$ belongs to $\{0, 1\}$, $k = 1, 2, ..., m$. Given a collection G of taxonomies, in which all leaf items belong to I, then adding all the interior items (nodes) of G into I will result in a new set of items I_G. Subsequently, a new database D_G with respect to $R(I_G)$ can be derived, in which each tuple d' in D_G is also a binary vector. For any $J \in I_G$, if J is also in I, then $d'[J] = d[J]$. If $J \in I_G - I$, then (i) $d'[J] = 1$ if there exists any descendant J' of J that $d[J'] = 1$; and (ii) $d'[J] = 0$ otherwise. Likewise, let X be a subset of I_G (also referred to as an itemset), then a tuple d' is called to support X if for any item J in X, $d'[J] = 1$. Thus, mining generalized association rules in D on $R(I)$ with taxonomies G becomes equivalent as discovering Boolean association rules in D_G on $R(I_G)$.

As an example, Table 5 shows a database D_G with respect to scheme $R(Apple, Fruit, Cabbage, Vegetable, Vegetable-dishes, Mutton, Pork, Meat)$ in accordance with G in Figure 2(a). Notably, D_G degenerates to D when projecting **R**(*Apple, Fruit, Cabbage, Vegetable, Vegetable-dishes, Mutton, Pork, Meat*) on (*Apple, Cabbage, Mutton, Pork*).

Table 5. Example of Extended Database D_G in Accordance with G in Figure 2(a).

D_G	Apple	Fruit	Cabbage	Vegetable	Vegetable-dishes	Mutton	Pork	Meat
ID1	1	1	0	0	1	1	0	1
ID2	0	0	1	1	1	0	0	0
ID3	1	1	0	0	1	1	1	1

3.2   Generalized Association Rules with Fuzzy Taxonomies

In 1999, Wei & Chen extended generalized association rules with fuzzy taxonomies, by which partial belongings could be incorporated. For example, given fuzzy taxonomies in Figure 2(b), Tomato not only belongs to *Fruit* with degree 0.7, but also belongs to *Vegetable* with degree 0.6, which may be semantically meaningful.

Generally, given fuzzy taxonomies G^f as exemplified in Figure 2(b), the degree that any node y belongs to its ancestor x can be obtained as follows (Chen & Wei, 1999, 2002; Wei & Chen, 1999):

$$\mu_{xy} = \underset{\forall l:x \to y}{\oplus} (\underset{\forall e \, on \, l}{\otimes} \mu_{le})$$

where $l: x \to y$ is one of the accesses (paths) of attributes x and y, e *on* l is one of the edges on access l, μ_{le} is the degree on the edge e on l If there is no access between x and y, then $\mu_{xy} = 0$. Notably, what specific forms of the operators to use for $\oplus$ and $\otimes$ depends on the context of the problems at hand. Possible operators include **max** for $\oplus$ and **min** for $\otimes$. Then based on all the μ_{xy} derived between any two nodes, an interior item in G^f could be represented as a fuzzy set, each element of which is a leaf item with its membership degree to the interior item. For example, *Fruit* = {1/*Apple*, 0.7/*Tomato*}, *Vegetable dishes* = {1/*Apple*, 0.7/*Tomato*, 1/*Cabbage*} in Figure 2(b).

Then, with original *I*, *D*, and given G^f, the newly obtained set of items I_{Gf} is in the same form as I_G discussed in section 3.1, except for the fact that any interior item in I_{Gf} is generally a fuzzy set, not an ordinary super-class. Moreover, it is worth mentioning that an interior item in I_{Gf} is different from an item in *I"* of section 2.3 for fuzzy quantitative association rules. The former is a fuzzy set in terms of leaf items of taxonomies, while the latter is a fuzzy set on a continuous domain.

Correspondingly, the extended database D_{Gf} can be derived from D on $R(I)$ such that $\forall t \in D_{Gf}$, $\forall J \in I_{Gf}$, $t[J] = \max_{\forall L \in l}(\mu_{JL})$. An example of D_{Gf} in accordance with Figure 2(b) and Table 5 is tabulated in Table 6.

Table 6. Example of Extended Database D_{Gf} in Accordance with G_f in Figure 2(b).

D_{Gf}	Apple	Fruit	Tomato	Cabbage	Vegetable	Vegetable-dishes	Sausage	Pork	Meat
ID1	1	1	1	0	0.6	1	1	0	0.6
ID2	0	0.7	1	1	1	1	0	0	0
ID3	1	1	0	0	0	1	1	1	1

In addition, let X be a fuzzy itemset in I_{Gf}, then a tuple t in D_{Gf} is called to support X with a certain degree $t[X] = \bigwedge_{J \in X} t[J]$, where $\wedge$ is an operator representing "and". Furthermore, a fuzzy association rule is of the form: $X \Rightarrow Y$, where X and Y are fuzzy itemsets. The degree of support for X is extended as follows (Chen & Wei, 2002):

$$Dsupport(X) = \|X\|/|D_{Gf}| = \frac{\sum count_{t \in D_{Gf}}(\bigwedge_{J \in X} t[J])}{|D_{Gf}|} = \frac{\sum count_{t \in D_{Gf}}(t[X])}{|D_{Gf}|},$$

where $|D_{Gf}|$ is the number of all tuples in D_{Gf}, and $\|X\|$ is $\sum count$ values of tuples in D_{Gf} supporting X, also called fuzzy cardinality of X (Chen & Wei, 2002). In real applications, the $\prod$ (product) and min operators are often used for $\wedge$. For instance, in (Chen & Wei, 2002) the min operator is used, while in (Kuok & Fu, 1999; Gyenesei, 200a), the $\prod$ (product) operator is used, depending on different contexts. Moreover, the $Dsupport$ and $Dconfidence$ for rule $X \Rightarrow Y$ are defined as follows:

$$Dsupport(X \Rightarrow Y) = Dsupport(X \cup Y) = \frac{\sum count_{t \in D_{Gf}}(t[X] \wedge t[Y])}{|D_{Gf}|},$$

$$Dconfidence(X \Rightarrow Y) = Dsupport(X \Rightarrow Y) / Dsupport(X) = Dsupport(X \cup Y) / Dsupport(X).$$

Accordingly, these extended measures have been incorporated into the extended algorithm so as to discover generalized association rules with fuzzy taxonomies (Chen & Wei, 2002).

3.3   Fuzzy Association Rules with Linguistic Hedges

In this section, we will consider the work on linguistic hedges used to modify fuzzy association rules, aimed at generalizing and enriching knowledge representation semantically. A recent effort has been made as described in (Wei & Chen et al., 2000; Chen & Wei et al., 2002) where Chen & Wei et al present an approach to incorporate linguistic hedges on existing fuzzy taxonomies. The basic idea is that, if in the fuzzy taxonomies G^f an interior node could be expressed as a fuzzy set on its child-nodes, then the interior node could also be modified in forms of hedges with the same child nodes. Then after applying all the proper hedges in a given linguistic pool H onto the items in G^f, new fuzzy taxonomies G^{fH} with all modified items could be derived, as shown in Figure 3. In so doing, the problem of mining linguistic association rules with hedges pool H on fuzzy taxonomies G^f could be transferred to the problem of mining fuzzy association rules on the new taxonomic structures G^{fH}.

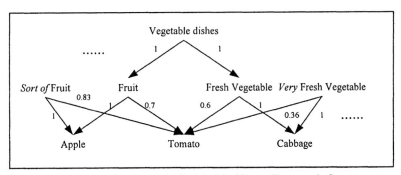

Figure 3. Part of a Linguistically Modified Fuzzy Taxonomic Structure.

Note that, though the approach to integrating linguistic hedges proposed in (Chen & Wei, 2002) focuses on fuzzy generalized association rules, clearly it could also be easily applied to fuzzy quantitative association rules. In general, let $I^f = \{I_1, I_2, ..., I_m\}$ be a set of fuzzy items, each with a membership function f_k ($k = 1, 2, ..., m$), and D^f be a database with scheme $R(I^f)$ and a pool of hedges H (where assuming that H contains a certain hedge h (e.g., "same") with $\lambda = 1$ such that for any primary linguistic term $hw = w$). After applying H on I^f, then I^H could be derived as follows: $I^H = \{hJ \mid hJ$ is a linguistic item modified by h on J with membership function $(f_J)^\lambda$, $h \in H$, and $J \in I^f\}$. It can be seen that all the original items and the modified items are contained in I^H. Moreover, not every h in H can be applied onto J in I^f. This is due to the semantic constraints of linguistic terms. For example, given $I^f = \{Young, Fruit\}$, $H = \{(Same, 1), (Very, 2), (Sort-of, 1/2)\}$, then $I^H = \{Young, Very Young, Sort-of Young, Fruit, Sort-of Fruit\}$. Further, let D^H be the extended database on schema $R(I^H)$, in which each tuple t is represented as a vector with $t[hJ] = [f_J(t)]^\lambda$. After filtering with thresholds α and β given by experts or decision-makers, the discovered rules could look like "*Expensive Electronics* $\Rightarrow$ *Very Cool Jeans*", etc. Generally speaking, this extension of knowledge representation of fuzzy association rules could be represented as rules in forms of $H_X X \Rightarrow H_Y Y$, where X and Y are fuzzy sets and H_X and H_Y are linguistic hedges onto X and Y, respectively.

Accordingly, Chen et al. (1999) proposed an extended Apriori-based mining algorithm to discover fuzzy association rules with linguistic terms. Further, they introduced a method to integrate linguistic hedges (Wei & Chen et al., 2000; Chen & Wei, 2002). Since an itemset containing two fuzzy items resulting from the same original item is usually considered meaningless (e.g., an itemset containing *Young-Age* and *Old-Age*), this may be integrated in the mining process as an optimization strategy (Wei & Chen et al., 2000). Their method shows that the computational complexity is linear with the number of transactions and polynomial to the number of items, which is similar to the non-fuzzy association rule mining. Synthetic experiments revealed that the system consumption of fuzzy association rule mining is stably a bit higher than that of a classical method, but at the same level of computational complexity due to the computations in calculating fuzzy degrees.

4.   OTHER FUZZY EXTENSIONS AND CONSIDERATIONS

In this section, some other fuzzy extensions and considerations will be discussed, such as fuzzy extensions on interestingness measures, other fuzzy extensions on Dsupport/Dconfidence and weighted fuzzy association rules, etc.

4.1   Fuzzy Logic in Interestingness Measures

Though in general degrees of support and confidence (*Dsupport* and *Dconfidence*) could be viewed as measures of interestingness of particular kinds, many existing studies on interestingness have centered around measures used to filter the association rules discovered based upon *Dsupport* and *Dconfidence*. In other words, interestingness measures usually deal with issues of semantic concerns for valid association rules obtained upon *Dsupport* or *Dconfidence*. These measures reflect interestingness in different perspectives such as Laplace (Clark & Boswell, 1991), p-s measure (Piatesky-Shapiro, 1991), lift (IBM, 1996), intense of implication (Suzuki & Kodratoff, 1998), improvement (Roberto & Bayardo et al., 1999), gain (Fukuda & Morimoto, 1996), R-interest (Srikant & Agrawal, 1995), item constraint (Srikant & Vu, 1997), etc. and may also be incorporated with domain knowledge in relation to application contexts.

Similarly, in fuzzy association rule mining, some of the interestingness measures are worth being considered and therefore extended. An attempt is made with *R-interest* (also called *interesting degree*), based on the notion of conditional probability in the context of fuzzy taxonomic structure (Wei & Chen, 1999). For example, consider the taxonomies as shown in Figure 2(b), and suppose that there are 100 transactions containing *Fruit* and 50 transactions containing *Tomato* in the database. Since *Tomato* belongs to *Fruit* at 0.7, then for a discovered rule *Fruit* $\Rightarrow$ *Pork* (*Dsupport* = 20%, *Dconfidence* = 80%), it could be expected readily that *Tomato* $\Rightarrow$ *Pork* has *Dsupport* of 7% (0.2×(50/100)×0.7) and 80% *Dconfidence*. If such a rule (*Tomato* $\Rightarrow$ *Pork* at 7% and 80%) is really generated from the database in the mining process, it can be considered redundant since it does not convey any additional information and is less general than the first rule (*Fruit* $\Rightarrow$ *Pork*).

Generally, the interesting degree for rule $X \Rightarrow Y$ is defined as:

$$Interest(X \Rightarrow Y) = \frac{Dsupport(X \cup Y)}{Dsupport(X)} - \frac{Dsupport(Y)}{|D|}.$$

The measure can be seen as an estimation of $\Pr(Y|X) - \Pr(Y)$, which is the increase in probability of Y caused by the occurrence of X (Hullermeier, 2001b). With fuzzy taxonomic structures, it can be extended for fuzzy association rule mining. Briefly speaking, given a threshold R, a rule of interest will be the rule whose *Dsupport* is more than R times or less than $1/R$ times of the expected *Dsupport* (or whose *Dconfidence* is more than R times or less than $1/R$ times of the expected *Dconfidence*). Further, Graff & Kosters et al. (2001) calculate the expected *Dsupport* for $X \Rightarrow Y$ upon $X^\wedge \Rightarrow Y$ ($X^\wedge$ is a super-class of X) as follows:

$$Dsupport_{E(X^\wedge \Rightarrow Y)}(X \Rightarrow Y) = Dsupport(X^\wedge \Rightarrow Y) \times \frac{Dsupport(X)}{Dsupport(X^\wedge)},$$

and then compare this number with the real *Dsupport*($X \Rightarrow Y$) in terms of given R to decide whether $X \Rightarrow Y$ is redundant or not against $X^\wedge \Rightarrow Y$.

Moreover, Chen & Wei et al. (1999) have dealt with *R-interest* in a more general fashion. Consider a rule $X \Rightarrow Y$, where $X = \{x_1, x_2, ..., x_p\}$ and $Y = \{y_1, y_2, ..., y_q\}$. $X^\wedge$ and $Y^\wedge$ are called the ancestors of X and Y respectively, if $X^\wedge = \{x^\wedge_1, x^\wedge_2, ..., x^\wedge_p\}$ where $x^\wedge_i$ is an ancestor of or identical to x_i, $1 \leq j \leq p$, and $Y^\wedge = \{y^\wedge_1, y^\wedge_2, ..., y^\wedge_q\}$, where $y^\wedge_j$ is an ancestor of or identical to y_j, $1 \leq j \leq q$. Then the rules $X^\wedge \Rightarrow Y$, $X^\wedge \Rightarrow Y^\wedge$ and $X \Rightarrow Y^\wedge$ are called the ancestors of the rule $X \Rightarrow Y$. Let $Dsupport_{E(X^\wedge \Rightarrow Y^\wedge)}(X \Rightarrow Y)$ denote the "expected" value of the

Dsupport of $X \Rightarrow Y$ on $X^\wedge \Rightarrow Y^\wedge$ and *Dconfidence*$_{E(X^\wedge \Rightarrow Y^\wedge)}(X \Rightarrow Y)$ denote the "expected" value of *Dconfidence* of $X \Rightarrow Y$ on $X^\wedge \Rightarrow Y^\wedge$, then with fuzzy taxonomic structures, we have:

$$Dsupport_{E(X^\wedge \Rightarrow Y^\wedge)}(X \Rightarrow Y) = \frac{Dsupport(\{x_1\}) \times ... \times Dsupport(\{x_p\})}{Dsupport(\{x^\wedge_1\}) \times ... \times Dsupport(\{x^\wedge_p\})} \times$$

$$\frac{Dsupport(\{y_1\}) \times ... \times Dsupport(\{y_q\})}{Dsupport(\{y^\wedge_1\}) \times ... \times Dsupport(\{y^\wedge_q\})} \times Dsupport(X^\wedge \Rightarrow Y^\wedge),$$

and

$$Dconfidence_{E(X^\wedge \Rightarrow Y^\wedge)}(X \Rightarrow Y) =$$

$$\frac{Dsupport(\{y_1\}) \times ... \times Dsupport(\{y_q\})}{Dsupport(\{y^\wedge_1\}) \times ... \times Dsupport(\{y^\wedge_q\})} \times Dconfidence(X^\wedge \Rightarrow Y^\wedge).$$

Then with threshold R, the extended measures may be used to filter out redundant rules.

4.2   Fuzzy Extensions of Dsupport / Dconfidence

In recent years, some methods differing from the fuzzy extensions of *Dsupport* and *Dconfidence* discussed in section 3.2 have also been proposed. In 1997, Lee & Hyung (1997) used a threshold ω for each item I as a filtering criterion. That is, given a threshold $\omega \in [0, 1]$, $t[I]$ is replaced by $t'[I]$, where $t'[I] = 1$ if $t'[I] \geq \omega$, $t'[I] = 0$ otherwise. In doing so, the extended fuzzy database D' (e.g., D'' and D_{Gf} as shown in Tables 4 and 6) becomes an ω-cut binary database, based on which the non-fuzzy mining approach can be applied. Further, Kuok & Fu et al. (1998) proposed that $t'[I] = t[I]$ if $t[I] \geq \omega$, $t'[I] = 0$ otherwise, maintaining a new fuzzy database. The purpose is to handle those items of tuples with too low membership degrees that contribute no votes to *Dsupport*. However, these attempts need to consider a trade-off, as the number of such thresholds (ω's) (which are mostly qualitative in nature) would itself be a problem of concern if the number becomes large.

In addition, Hullermeier (2001b) has recently defined *Dsupport*($X \Rightarrow Y$) by using min for $\wedge$ in $\wedge(t[X], t[Y])$ in a similar form to that of the notion described in section 3.2. However, it can generally be regarded as a special case of that notion. Another extension is by Shragai & Scgreider (2001), who introduced three measures for a fuzzy *AR*: *Dsupport*, *Dstrength* and *Dconfidence*. While *Dsupport* is defined similarly, frequency *Number*(X) is used to count the occurrence of fuzzy itemset X, with which *Dstrength* and *Dconfidence* are defined:

$Dstrength(X) = Dsupport(X) / Number(X),$

$Dstrength(X{\Rightarrow}Y) = Dstrength(X{\cup}Y) = Dsupport(X{\cup}Y) / Number(X{\cup}Y),$

$Dconfidence(X{\Rightarrow}Y) = Number(X{\cup}Y) / Number(X).$

The value of *Dstrength* of a rule represents the mean level of agreement (the support intersection) between the items in the itemset concerned, and the value of *Dconfidence* of a rule reflects the part of the relevant database that fulfils the rule. Thus the distinction between the small number of occurrences with high agreement and the large number of occurrences with bad agreement could be discovered to some extent. Furthermore, the corresponding mining method can be developed upon these measures, which is also an Apriori-type extension.

Recently, Gyenesei & Teuhola (2001) discussed a series of measures to replace *Dconfidence* (which are still based on *Dsupport*), namely, Fuzzy Covariance Measure, Fuzzy Correlation Measure, Fuzzy I-Measure, Fuzzy Unconditional Entropy (UE) Measure, Fuzzy Conditional Entropy (CE) Measure, and Fuzzy J-Measure. The first three measures stem from statistics theory, while the last three are based on information theory, especially on entropy. More in-depth investigations are expected to emerge in the light of theoretical properties and algorithmic concerns.

Another attempt to mention is the work by Au & Chan (1997, 1998), who proposed a certainty measure, called adjusted difference. The notion of adjusted difference is defined as:

$$adjusted\_diff(X,Y) = \frac{st\_diff(X,Y)}{\sqrt{max\_est(X,Y)}},$$

where st_diff(X, Y) is the standardized difference between X and Y, and max_est(X, Y) is the maximum likelihood estimation of variance of standardized difference between X and Y.

If $|adjusted\_diff(X, Y)| > 1.96$ (the 95% of the normal distribution), $X{\Rightarrow}Y$ is considered valid. An adjusted difference based method for fuzzy *AR*, called F-APACS, is proposed, which could distinguish positive associations if $adjusted\_diff(X, Y) > 1.96$ (or negative associations if $adjusted\_diff(X, Y) < -1.96$). Subsequently, such valid rules may be further evaluated using a measure, called weight of evidence, defined as:

$$Weight\_of\_Evidence(X \Rightarrow Y) = \log\frac{Dconfidence(X \Rightarrow Y)}{Dsupport(X \Rightarrow Y)},$$

which provides a measure of the difference in the gain of information.

4.3   Weighted Fuzzy Association Rules

Sometimes, one may think of users paying more attention to certain attributes than to others. For example, a CFO (Chief Financial Officer) of a company may be more interested in "Return on Equity" than "Number of Employees", while a manager of human resources may have just the opposite interest. Therefore, if weights could be assigned to items in advance, then the rules associating more heavily weighted items will receive more attention. As a result, those rules will have more chances to come to front, and the mining efficiency could also improve due to the fact that fewer frequent itemsets (i.e., the itemsets whose degrees of support are greater than or equal to threshold α) will be involved in the mining process.

Similarly, in fuzzy association rule mining, weights could also be applied to distinguish the importance of different items. Some approaches by Cai & Fu et al. (1998), Gyenesei (2000b), Shu & Tsang et al. (2000) etc. have already been proposed, which are thought of to be basically similar. For instance, for $I' = \{I_1, I_2, ..., I_m\}$ and D' on $R(I')$, each I_k ($k = 1, 2, ..., m$) is assigned a certain weight w_k, $0 \le w_k \le 1$. Thus, the extended support (in number) for X is defined as follows:

$$W\_Support(X) = [\wedge_{x \in X}(w_x)] \times Dsupport(X),$$

where the $\wedge$ operator is used to account for the total weight of X, say Σ is used in (Cai & Fu et al., 1998), and $\prod$ is used in (Shu & Tsang et al., 2000). Based on $W\_Support(X)$, $W\_Support(X \Rightarrow Y)$ and $W\_Dconfidence(X \Rightarrow Y)$ can be defined as:

$$W\_Support(X \Rightarrow Y) = W\_Support(X \cup Y),$$

$$W\_Dconfidence(X \Rightarrow Y) = W\_Support(X \Rightarrow Y) / W\_Support(X) = W\_Support(X \cup Y) / W\_Support(X).$$

Further, when considering degrees of support (rather than support in number), $W\_Dsupport$ can be further defined. For the Σ operator, the arithmetic mean may be applied (Cai & Fu et al., 1998), while for the $\prod$ operator, geometric mean may be applied (Shu & Tsang et al., 2000), which are described below, respectively:

$$W\_Dsupport_n(X) = \frac{1}{|X|}[\sum_{x \in X}(w_x)] \times Dsupport(X),$$

$$W\_Dsupport_n(X) = [\prod_{x \in X}(w_x)]^{\frac{1}{|X|}} \times Dsupport(X).$$

A concern with these measures is that the Apriori-based mining methods could not be applied directly, because the property that $W\_Dsupport(V) \leq W\_Dsupport(U)$ for $U \subseteq V$ will not hold in general. In this regard, when the $\prod$ is used, Gyenesei (2000b) introduced a notion of the so-called z-potential frequent subset, i.e., X is a z-potential frequent subset if:

$$[\prod\nolimits_{x \in X}(w_x) \times \prod\nolimits_{y \in Y}(w_y)]^{1/z} \times Dsupport(X) \geq \text{min-support},$$

where z is the difference between $|X|$ and the maximum possible size of the frequent itemset, and Y $(Y \neq X)$ is the remaining itemset with maximum weights. Thus, a mining algorithm could be developed with certain optimization strategies applied to the itemsets generation.

When the Σ operator is used, Cai & Fu et al. (1998) introduced another notion called the maximum possible weight for a k-itemset (i.e., the itemset with k items) that contains X as follows:

$$W(X) = \sum\nolimits_{x \in X}(w_x) + \sum\nolimits_{\substack{x_i \in I-X \\ i=1 \text{ to } k-|X|}}(w_{x_i}).$$

Based on this, the minimum support needed for a frequent k-itemset which contains X is given by $B(Y) = k \times \dfrac{\text{min} - \text{support}}{W(X)}$, which is called the k-bound of itemset X. In this way, the optimized mining algorithm of itemsets generation could be achieved to certain extent.

Differently from the above *W-Dsupport* and *W_Dconfidence*, Shu & Tsang et al. (2000) have proposed the following notions:

$$W\_Dsupport(X) = \frac{\sum \text{count}_{t \in D}[\prod\nolimits_{x \in X}(w_x \times \mu_{xt})]}{|D|},$$

$$W\_Dsupport(X \Rightarrow Y) = \frac{\sum \text{count}_{t \in D}\{[\prod\nolimits_{x \in X}(w_x \times \mu_{xt})] \wedge [\prod\nolimits_{y \in Y}(w_y \times \mu_{yt})]\}}{|D|},$$

$$W\_Dconfidence(X \Rightarrow Y) = W\_Dsupport(X \Rightarrow Y) / W\_Dsupport(X).$$

The corresponding mining algorithm is then of Apriori-type with certain optimization properties.

However, there may exist two issues of weighted fuzzy association rules (*WFAR*), which are worthy to mention. One is related to the nature of data mining, and therefore limiting the applicability of *WFAR* Since data mining deals with hidden knowledge and assumes little about the data beforehand, there may be some items (data attributes) whose usefulness and importance is unclear until being discovered. That is, an uneven treatment of items (such as weights) may result in overlooking certain items and therefore the associations that are potentially important and useful. The other issue is related to the determination of the weights. Like many thresholds that are qualitative and heuristic involving human judgment, weights are of similar nature. In the case of many attributes (i.e., many weights) and highly sensitive weight settings, the measures and then the discovery outcomes can be too unstable or strongly dependent on the settings, which may not be desirable.

5.   FUZZY IMPLICATION BASED ASSOCIATION RULES

As indicated previously, traditionally a rule of $X \Rightarrow Y$ is referred to as an association between X and Y and it is modeled by conditional probability (e.g., *Dconfidence*) for X-to-Y. In further investigating X-to-Y relationships, a more logic-oriented view may be taken so as to reflect, to certain extent, implication from X to Y. Still in terms of association rules and in fuzzy contexts, a few efforts have been made to consider partial degrees that X implies Y. For instance, in (Chen & Wei et al., 1999; Dubois & Hullermeier et al., 2001; Hullermeier, 2001a), fuzzy implication is introduced to represent the degree that a tuple supports X-to-Y. Specifically, Chen & Wei et al. (1999) presented a new notion of *Dsupport*$(X \Rightarrow Y)$ based on fuzzy implication as follows:

$$Dsupport_t(X \Rightarrow Y) = Truth\_value(Dsupport_t(X) \Rightarrow Dsupport_t(Y)) = FIO(Dsupport_t(X), Dsupport_t(Y)),$$

$$Dsupport(X \Rightarrow Y) = \frac{\sum count_{t \in D}[Dsupport_t(X \Rightarrow Y)]}{|D|}.$$

Here, *FIO* stands for fuzzy implication operator, which is a mapping from $[0, 1] \times [0, 1]$ to $[0, 1]$ (Chen, 1998), whose specific forms need to be determined according to concrete situations at hand. Since *FIO* is generally not symmetric, $X \Rightarrow Y$ and $Y \Rightarrow X$ could be distinguished. Notably, if the *min* operator is used instead of the *FIO*, fuzzy implication based association rules are degenerated to conventional fuzzy association rules.

Furthermore, in order to avoid the situation that *Dsupport*$_t(X)$ is too small (or even equal to 0) where semantically $X \Rightarrow Y$ can hardly be regarded as being supported by such a tuple t, *Dsupport*$_t(X \Rightarrow Y)$ has been defined as follows:

$$Dsupport_t(X \Rightarrow Y) = \wedge(Dsupport_t(X), FIO(Dsupport_t(X), Dsupport_t(Y)),$$

in generally with $\wedge$, and in particular with the *min* operator (Chen & Wei, 1999). Note that Dubois & Hullermeier et al. (2001) and Hullermeier (2001) used the $\prod$ operator for $\wedge$.

Based on the Dsupport measure, the Dconfidence measure could also be extended in a fuzzy implication context. For instance, Chen & Wei et al. (1999) introduced the following extension:

$$Dconfidence(X \Rightarrow Y) = \frac{\sum count_{t \in D}[Dsupport_t(X \Rightarrow Y)]}{\sum count_{t \in D}[Dsupport_t(X)]}.$$

Similar attempts are found in Dubois & Hullermeier et al. (2001), Hullermeier (2001). Further, in (Hullermeier, 2001) another possibility is to relate $Dsupport(X \Rightarrow Y)$ to $Dsupport(X \Rightarrow \neg Y)$. In this case rule $X \Rightarrow Y$ should be supported much better than rule $X \Rightarrow \neg Y$:

$$Dconfidence(X \Rightarrow Y) = \frac{\sum count_{t \in D}[Dsupport_t(X \Rightarrow Y)]}{\sum count_{t \in D}[Dsupport_t(X \Rightarrow \neg Y)]}.$$

Hullermeier (2001) further considers to represent an implication-based fuzzy rule $X \Rightarrow Y$ as a convex combination:

$$Dsupport(X \Rightarrow Y) = \sum_{X \Rightarrow_m Y \in G} p_m \times Truth\_value(Dsupport(X) \Rightarrow_m Dsupport(Y))$$

$$= \sum_{X \Rightarrow_m Y \in G} p_m \times FIO_m(Dsupport(X), Dsupport(Y)),$$

where G is a class of (modified) pure gradual rules and p_m's are weights that might be interpreted as probability degrees. FIO_m is the modified Rescher-Gaines implication operator with $FIO_m(a, b) = a \Rightarrow_m b = 1$, if $m(a) \le b$ and 0 otherwise, where m is a mapping $[0, 1] \rightarrow [0, 1]$. Based on the definition, a fuzzy association rule $X \Rightarrow Y$ can be regarded as an implication-based (gradual) fuzzy rule, and can be seen as a convex combination of simple or pure gradual association rules, each of which in turn corresponds to a collection $X_\lambda \Rightarrow Y_{m(\lambda)}$ ($\lambda \in L$, where L is an underlying finite scale of membership degrees and A_λ is the λ-cut of A) of ordinary association rules.

Recently, Chen & Yan et al. (2002) introduced a notion called degree of implication (denoted as $Dimp$) to evaluate the strength of association rules from a more logic-oriented viewpoint. That is, $Dimp$ is used to reflect the logic relationship between X and Y as follows:

$$Dimp_t(X \Rightarrow Y) = FIO(Dsupp_t(X), Dsupp_t(Y)), Dimp(X \Rightarrow Y)$$

$$= \frac{\sum_{t \in D} Dimp_t(X \Rightarrow Y)}{|D|}.$$

An association rule satisfying *Dsupport* and *Dimp* is denoted as *ARsi* For *Dimp*, a proper selection of *FIO* and t-norm combinations could help avoid database scanning, and therefore improve the efficiency of rule generation. In doing so, certain properties are proven so as to form rule derivation and pruning strategies. Moreover, desirable properties of simple association rules (*SAR*) are incorporated in optimizing the mining process (Chen & Wei, et al., 2002).

6.   MINING FUNCTIONAL DEPENDENCIES WITH UNCERTAINTIES

In this section, another type of association, namely, functional dependency, will be discussed in a viewpoint of data mining as well as uncertainties. Two aspects of consideration are fuzzy functional dependencies and functional dependencies with degrees.

6.1   Mining Fuzzy Functional Dependencies

A functional dependency (*FD*) is considered as a piece of semantic knowledge in terms of integrity constraints, and also an important notion in database modeling. Classically, for attribute collections X and Y in a relational schema of database D, a *FD*, $X \rightarrow Y$, represents "*equal Y* values are dependent on *equal X* values". More concretely,

$X \rightarrow Y \Leftrightarrow$ for any two tuples t and t' in D, if $t[X] = t'[X]$ then $t[Y] = t'[Y]$.

This section focuses on two types of efforts in discovering fuzzy functional dependencies (*FFD*), and discovering functional dependencies with partial degrees (*FD_d*), respectively.

First, fuzzy functional dependencies (*FFD*) are extensions of classical *FD*, aimed at dealing with fuzziness in databases and reflecting the semantics that *close* values of a collection of attributes are dependent on *close* values of a collection of different attributes. During the past couple of decades, considerable attention has been attracted to fuzzy databases and *FFD*. Please refer to a recent overview by Chen (1999) for more details. It is worthwhile to notice that various *FFD* extensions are related to their corresponding frameworks of data representation (i.e., fuzzy database models). Generally, fuzzy functional dependencies have different forms, depending on the different aspects of integrating fuzzy logic in classical functional dependencies.

Somewhat differently from the ways that are of a typical data mining nature, Cubero et al. (1995, 1999) presented a method of data summarization through fuzzy functional dependencies in both crisp and fuzzy databases, in which projection operations are applied to reduce the amount of data in databases without loss of information.

Recently, Wang & Shen et al (2002) presented a method to discover fuzzy functional dependencies in similarity-based relational databases with an incremental strategy, which has an advantage in dealing with non-static databases. Thus fuzzy functional dependency mining could tolerate noises which exist mostly in real databases. Generally speaking, the discovered fuzzy functional dependencies expressed the semantics that "similar Xs infer to similar Ys" to some extent. Moreover, Yang & Singhal (2001) attempted to present a framework of linking fuzzy functional dependencies and fuzzy association rules in a closer manner. Generally, functional dependencies and association rules are both associations between data, but in different forms. More attempts in this direction are expected to emerge in the near future. In the next subsection we will discuss the other type of efforts on data mining to discover FD_d.

6.2   Mining Functional Dependencies with Degrees

In massive databases where noisy or incomplete/imprecise information exists, classical FD may be too restrictive to hold, since the correspondence of equal X-Y values must be 100% satisfied, by definition. However, it may be meaningful to take into account partial satisfaction of FD, being capable of tolerating the noisy or incomplete/imprecise information at certain degrees.

Huhtala et al. (1998a, 1998b) have explored a notion called approximate dependency so as to represent functional dependency that "almost holds". For example, *Gender* is approximately determined by *First Name*, taking consideration of nulls, errors or exceptions. Though this approximation can be modeled with fuzzy logic in the light of *FFD*, they concentrated on *FD* in terms of error rates. In particular, the following is true:

$$\text{error}(X \rightarrow Y) = \frac{\min\{|S| \mid S \subseteq D \text{ and } X \rightarrow Y \text{ holds in } (D-S)\}}{|D|},$$

which has a natural interpretation as the fraction of transactions with exceptions or errors affecting the dependency. Given an error threshold $\varepsilon \in [0, 1]$, we say that $X \rightarrow Y$ is a valid approximate (functional) dependency if and only if $\text{error}(X \rightarrow Y) \leq \varepsilon$. Thus the task of mining an approximate dependency could be done by means of mining classical functional dependencies with an efficient algorithm, called *TANE*, proposed in (Huhtala & Karkkainen et al. 1998a).

Recently, Wei & Chen et al. (2002) presented the notion of functional dependency with degree of satisfaction, which is another measure for degree of satisfaction that a functional dependency holds in D. For a classical database D in schema $R(I)$ where $I = (I_1, I_2, ..., I_m)$, and X, Y are collections of attributes (items) in I, then Y is called to functionally depend on X for a tuple pair (t, t') of D, denoted as $_{(t,t')}(X \rightarrow Y)$, if $t[X] = t'[X]$ then $t[Y] = t'[Y]$. Let $TRUTH_{(t, t')}(X \rightarrow Y)$ denote the truth value that $_{(t, t')}(X \rightarrow Y)$ holds. Apparently, $TRUTH_{(t, t')}(X \rightarrow Y) \in \{0, 1\}$, which is consistent with truth values of classical logic. In other words, (t, t') satisfies $X \rightarrow Y$ if $TRUTH_{(t,t')}(X \rightarrow Y) = 1$, and (t, t') dissatisfies $X \rightarrow Y$ if $TRUTH_{(t, t')}(X \rightarrow Y) = 0$. Consequently, the degree that D satisfies $X \rightarrow Y$, denoted as $\mu_D(X \rightarrow Y)$, is $TRUTH_D(X \rightarrow Y)$:

$$TRUTH_D(X \rightarrow Y) = \frac{\sum_{\substack{\forall t,t' \in D \\ t \neq t'}} TRUTH_{(t,t')}(X \rightarrow Y)}{|P_D|},$$

where $|P_D|$ is the number of pairs of tuples in D. Clearly, $|P_D| = n(n-1)/2$. Thus, a functional dependency with degree of satisfaction (FD_d) is of a form: $X \rightarrow Y$ at $\mu_D(X \rightarrow Y) \in [0, 1]$. It can be easily seen that FD is a special case of FD_d. Furthermore, several desirable properties of FD_d have been obtained, some of which can be incorporated into the extended mining algorithm as computational optimization strategies.

7.   FUZZY LOGIC IN PATTERN ASSOCIATIONS

Discovering relationships among time-series data is of particular interest since time-series patterns reflect the evolution of changes in attribute values (values of variables) with sequential factors such as time, and have often been encountered in real applications in forms of, say, sales, production, economics, and stock data. There may exist many types of relationships among time series data and therefore the methods used to study the relationships can be different (Agrawal & Srikant, 1995; Srikant & Agrawal, 1996; Berndt & Clifford, 1996; Ketterlin, 1997; Das et al., 1998; Gavrilov & Anguelov et al., 2000; Last & Klein, 2001). Unlike the relationships studied by traditional approaches such as time series analysis and econometrics, the relationship represented by the similarities of time series patterns was the focal point of the efforts (Agrawal & Srikant, 1995; Srikant & Agrawal, 1996; Berndt & Clifford, 1996). In other words, the value evolution of each time-series variable is viewed as a pattern over time, and the similarity between any two such patterns is measured by pattern matching.

Before discussing pattern similarities, a different attempt is worth mentioning, which deals with pattern association in terms of association rules. A straightforward approach is to use periodic segments and then transfer the time series dataset into the conventional binary database (Lu & Han et al., 1998). This is in a similar spirit to domain partitioning in discovering quantitative *AR*, as discussed in previous sections, such that conventional association rules mining methods can be applied.

In this section, instead, we will briefly discuss the approaches to discovering pattern associations according to similarities of time series data. Two major issues are involved in dealing with similar time-series patterns. One is the measurement for pair-wise similarities. The problems related to this issue center around how to define the difference between any two patterns, say, in terms of "distance" and how to match the series in points of time. The other issue is the grouping of the similar patterns, in which fuzzy relations and clustering may play an important role. Usually, static similarities relationship are studied, which could be obtained by computing the "distance" pair-wisely in a fixed matching fashion as shown in Figure 4. In this case, the matching scheme for curves *a* and *b* cannot be applied to the matching between curves *b* and *c*; and vice versa. Thus, any pair of curves *a*, *b* and *c* reflects a certain matching scenario, which is static schematically.

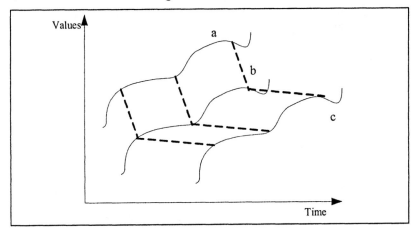

Figure 4.   Static Matching Schemes.

Furthermore, the way to discover the similarities among the curves could be improved by matching the patterns dynamically. This can be done by using the *Dynamic Time Warping (DTW)* method, a method used in speech recognition (Berndt & Clifford, 1996). Chen & Wei et al. (2001) presented a method based on *DTW* to discover pattern associations.

Given two series $S(s_1, s_2, \ldots, s_m)$ and $T(t_1, t_2, \ldots, t_n)$, S and T can be matched point to point, where (i, j) represents that s_i matches t_j, which is called a matching pair. The matching distance of s_i and t_j is defined as: $\delta(i, j) = |s_i - t_j|$ or $\delta(i, j) = (s_i - t_j)^2$. Then, s_i min-matches t_j, if in $s_1, s_2, \ldots, s_i$ and $t_1, t_2, \ldots, t_j$, the sum of matched distances of all the matching pairs (denoted as $r(i, j)$) is minimal. Formally,

$$r(i, j) = \min \sum_{k=1}^{p} \delta(i_k, j_k),$$

where $i_k = 1, ..., i, j_k = 1, ..., j, p = max(i, j)$. Since S and T are time series, so pairs should be matched continuously, which means $0 \le i_k - i_{k-1} \le 1$, $0 \le j_k - j_{k-1} \le 1$. Thus, S matching T means that S_n min-matches T_m. Therefore the distance between S and T is:

$$DTW(S, T) = r(n, m) = \min \sum_{k=1}^{p} \delta(i_k, j_k),$$

where $i_k = 1, ..., n, j_k = 1, ..., m, p = max(n, m)$, $0 \le i_k - i_{k-1} \le 1$, $0 \le j_k - j_{k-1} \le 1$. Furthermore, based on the notion of dynamic optimization, one may have:

$$r(i, j) = \delta(i, j) + min(r(i-1, j), r(i, j-1), r(i-1, j-1)).$$

Thus, with the *DTW* method, any two time-series patterns are matched dynamically in distance. There are a number of techniques to convert "distance" into "closeness", which is then normalized on [0, 1]. Furthermore, with fuzzy clustering methods based on the relationship set, whose elements are the closeness degrees, a complete graph could be derived.

Finally, it is worthwhile to indicate that, though at the inception stage, discovering pattern associations is deemed a promising area of theoretical and practical explorations and many attempts are expected to emerge, in that fuzzy logic will play an important role.

8.   CONCLUSIONS

This chapter has aimed at providing readers with a state-of-the-art overview on discovering fuzzy associations. Discussions have centered around fuzzy association rules in dealing with partitioning quantitative data domains; crisp taxonomic belongings and linguistically modified rules; various fuzzy mining measures from different perspectives such as interestingness, statistics and logic implication; fuzzy/partially satisfied functional dependencies for handling data closeness and noise tolerance; and time-series data patterns that are similar with partial degrees.

Fuzzy association mining has been regarded as a promising area for both researchers and practitioners, due to its advantage in expressing natural language and coping with uncertainty of knowledge. In addition to theoretical explorations, some applications and pilot systems have been developed or used. Examples include fuzzy *AR* for medical cases (Delgado & Sánchez et al., 2001), fuzzy *AR* for web access (Wong & Shiu et al., 2001), fuzzy associations for dynamic financial forecasting with *FAPACS* (Romahi & Shen, 2001), and fuzzy *AR* in intrusion detection (Luo et al., 1999, 2000), etc.

Future research in the field may emerge from various perspectives by broadening and deepening explorations of the issues discussed in this chapter. While a remarkable number of theoretical investigations including knowledge representation, uncertainty models, properties, computational complexity and algorithmic improvement are expected to appear continuously in forthcoming years, an increasingly rich variety of applications and implementations will be motivated. More concretely, fuzzy association rules may still be one of the focal points of research interest, where partitioning or clustering for continuously valued data, as well as semantic summarization, linguistic modification and logic implication for rule expressiveness, will attract considerable attention. In addition, interestingness and related measures will be another track of efforts. Major focus may be on the incorporation of measure-related properties into the mining process so as to improve the algorithmic efficiency and rule usefulness, which may further be coupled with domain knowledge and real contexts. Moreover, increasing attempts will be witnessed at discovering uncertainty-related data dependencies. Particularly, FFD and FD_d will be further explored to address issues of semantic expression (notions, extension operators, properties, etc.) and optimization strategies (massive data nature and corresponding mining algorithms). Finally, discovering pattern associations is considered a promising area of future research. Time-series data and sequence behaviors are expected to be of primary interest. A characteristic of the efforts is the multi-disciplinary nature in that various techniques and theories may combine, including fuzzy logic (e.g., in matching, similarity, clustering, etc.).

It is worth mentioning, as far as fuzzy extension and knowledge discovery is concerned, that fuzzy logic may be applied when fuzziness appears in the problem at hand (whereas other kinds of uncertainty may require to apply different approaches, e.g., probability theory for randomness), and that data mining techniques and conventional methods sometimes are supplements, rather than substitutes, for each other (e.g., pattern associations vs. time-series analysis and econometrics).

REFERENCES

Agrawal, R.; Imielinski, T.; Swarmi, A., 1993. Mining Association Rules between Sets of Items in Large Databases, In Proceedings of the ACM-SIGMOD 1993 International Conference on Management of Data, Washington D. C., US.A., pp. 207-216.

Agrawal, R.; Mannila, H.; Srikant, R.; Toivonen, H.; Verkamo, A. I., 1996. *Fast Discovery of Association Rules* in Advances in Knowledge Discovery and Data Mining, AAAI Press/The MIT Press, Boston, MA, U.S.A.

Agrawal, R.; Shafer, J.C., 1996. Parallel Mining of Association Rules, in IEEE TRANSACTIONS ON KNOWLEDGE AND DATA ENGINEERING, Vol. 8, No. 6.

Agrawal, R.; Srikant, R., 1995. Mining Sequential Patterns, In *Proc. 1995 Int. Conf. Data Engineering*, pp. 3-14. Taipei, Taiwan.

Srikant, R.; Agrawal, 1996. Mining Sequential Patterns: Generalizations and Performance Improvements, in PROC. OF THE FIFTH INT'L CONFERENCE ON EXTENDING DATABASE TECHNOLOGY (EDBT), Avignon, France.

Agrawal, R.; Srikant, S., 1994. Fast Algorithms for Mining Association Rules, In Proceedings of the 20th Conference on VLDB, Santiago, Chile.

Au W. H., Chan, K C. C., 1997. FARM: A Data Mining System for Discovering Fuzzy Association Rules, in Proc.of the 6th International Conference on Information and Knowledge Management, Las Vegas, Nevada, U.S.A., pp. 209-215.

Au, W. H.; Chan, K C. C., 1998. An Effective Algorithm for Discovering Fuzzy Rules in Relational Databases, Proceedings of the 7th IEEE International Conference on Fuzzy Systems, pp.1314--1319.

Aumann, Y.; Lindell, Y., 1999. A statistical theory for quantitative association rules. In Knowledge Discovery and Data Mining, pp. 261-270.

Bell, S.; Brockhausen, P., 1995. *Discovery of Data Dependencies in Relational Databases*, University of Dortmund, German, Computer Science Department, LS-8 Report 14.

Berndt, D. J.; Clifford, J., 1996. Finding Patterns in Time Series: A Dynamic Programming Approach, in *Advances in Knowledge Discovery and Data Mining*, AAAI/MIT Press, MA, U.S.A., pp. 1-37.

Bosc, P.; Pivert, O., 2001. On some Fuzzy Extensions of Association Rules, in Proceeding of IFSA/NAFIPS2001 Congress, Vancouver BA, Canada, pp. 1104-1109.

Brin, S.; Motwani, R.; Ullman, J.; and Tsur, S. 1997, *Dynamic Itemset Counting and Implication Rules for Market Basket Data*, in Proc. of the 1997 ACM-SIGMOD Int'l conf on the Management of Data, May 13-15, Tucson, Arizona, U.S.A., pp.255-264.

Cai, C. H.; Fu, A. W.; Cheng, C. H.; Kwong; W. W., 1998. Mining association rules with weighted items. In Proceedings of 1998 Intl. Database Engineering and Applications Symposium (IDEAS'98), pages 68--77, Cardiff, Wales, UK.

Castellanos, M.; Saltor, F., 1993. Extraction of Data Dependencies. European-Japanese conferences on Information Modelling and Knowledge Bases, Budapest, Hungary, May 31 - June 3. pp. 401-421.

Chan, K.C.C.; Au, W. H., 2001. Mining Fuzzy Association Rules in a Database Containing Relational and Transactional Data, in A. Kandel, M. Last, and H. Bunke (Eds.), Data Mining and Computational Intelligence, Heidelberg, Germany; New York, NY, U.S.A.: Physica-Verlag, pp. 95-114.

Chen G. Q., 1999. Data models for representing and manipulating linguistic and imprecise information, in Zadeh L. A. and Kacprzyk J. (eds.), Computing with Words in Intelligent/Information Systems. Physica-Verlag (Springer-Verlag Group, Germany).

Chen G. Q.; Wei, Q.; Kerre, E. E., 1999. *Fuzzy Data Mining: Discovery of Fuzzy Generalized Association Rules*, in Recent Research Issues on Management of Fuzziness in Databases, in the Physica-Verlag series "Studies in Fuzziness and Soft Computing", Springer-Verlag, NY, U.S.A.

Chen, G. Q.; Yan, P.; Kerre, E. E., 2002. Mining Fuzzy Implication-Based Association Rules in Quantitative Databases, Proceedings of FLINS2002, Belgium.

Chen, G. Q., 1998. Fuzzy Logic in Data Modeling: semantics, constraints and database design, Kluwer Academic Publishers, Boston, MA, U.S.A.

Chen, G Q.; Wei, Q; Liu, D.; Wets, G.., 2002. Simple Association Rules (SAR) and the SAR-Based Rule Discovery, Journal of Computer & Industrial Engineering 43 (2002), 721-733.

Chen, G. Q.; Wei, Q, 2002. Fuzzy Association Rules and the Extended Mining Algorithms, Information Sciences, 147, pp. 201-228.

Chen, G. Q.; Wei, Q.; Zhang, H., 2001. Discovering Similar Time-Series Patterns with Fuzzy Clustering and DTW Methods, IFSA/NAFIPS2001, Vancouver, BA, Canada.

Chien, B. C.; Lin, Z. L.; Hong, T. P., 2001. An Efficient Clustering Algorithm for Mining Fuzzy Quantitative Association Rules, in Proceedings of the 9th International Fuzzy Systems Association World Congress, July 25-28, Vancouver, Canada, pp. 1306-1311.

Clark, P.; Boswell, P., 1991. Rule Induction with CN2: some recent improvements. In Machine Learning: Proc. of the Fifth European Conference, 151-163.

Codd EF, 1970. A Relational Model for Large Shared Data Banks. Communications of the ACM, 13(6): 377-387.

Cubero, J. C. et al, 1999. Data Summarization in Relational Databases through Fuzzy Dependencies, Information Sciences, Vol. 121 (3-4), pp.233-270.

Cubero, J.C.; Medina, J. M.; Pons, O.; Vila, M.A., 1995. *Rules discovery in fuzzy relational databases* In Conference of the North American Fuzzy Information Processing Society, NAFIPS'95. Maryland (USA). IEEE Computer Society Press, pp. 414-419.

De Cock, M., Kerre, E. E., 2002. A Context-Based Approach to Linguistic Hedges, International Journal of Applied Mathematics and Computer Science, Vol. 12(3), pp. 371 – 382.

Delgado, M.; Sánchez, D.; Martín-Bautista, M., J.; Vila, M. A., 2001. Mining Association Rules with Improved Semantics in Medical Databases. Artificial Intelligence in Medicine 21, pp. 241-245.

Dubois, D.; Hullermeier, E.; Prade, H., 2001. Toward the Representation of Implication-Based Fuzzy Rules in Terms of Crisp Rules, in Proceedings of IFSA/NAFIPS2001, Vancouver, BA, Canada.

Fayyad U.; Uthurusamy, R., 1994. *Efficient Algorithms for Discovering Association Rules*, AAAI Workshop on Knowledge Discovery in Databases,181-192, Seattle, Washington, DC, USA.

Fayyad, U.; Piatesky-Shapiro, G..; Smyth, P., 1996. *From Data Mining to Knowledge Discovery: An Overview*, in Advances in Knowledge Discovery and Data Mining, U, Fayyad, G. Piatesky-Shapiro, P. Smyth, R. Uthurusamy, Eds. Cambridge, MA: AAAI Press/The MIT Press, U.S.A., pp. 1-30.

Fu, A et al., 1998. Finding fuzzy sets for the mining of fuzzy association rules for numerical attributes, in Proceedings of 1st Intl. Symposium on Intelligent Data Engineering and Learning (IDEAL'98), pages 263--268.

Fukuda, T.; Morimoto, Y.; Morishita, S., 1996. *Data Mining Using Two-Dimensional Optimized Association Rules: Scheme, Algorithms, and Visualization*, in Proc. of the 1996 ACM-SIGMOD Int'l Conf. on the Management of Data, pp. 12-13.

Das, G.; Lin, K.-I.; Mannila, H.; Renganathan, G.; & Smyth, P., 1998. *Rule discovery from time series*. In Proceedings of the 3rd International Conference on Knowledge Discovery and Data Mining. August 14-17, 1997, Newport Beach, CA, U.S.A.

Gavrilov, M.; Anguelov, D.; Indyk, P.; Motwani, R., 2000. Mining the Stock Market: Cluster Discovery, in *Proc. Sixth ACM SIGKDD Int. Conf. Knowledge Discovery & Data Mining*.

Graff, J. M.; Kosters, W. A.; Witteman, J. J. W., 2001. Interesting Fuzzy Association Rules in Quantitative Databases, Lecture Notes in Computer Science, Vol. 2168, pp. 140--151.

Gyenesei, A., 2000a. *A fuzzy approach for mining quantitative association rules*, TUCS technical reports 336, University of Turku, Department of Computer Science, Lemminkisenkatu 14, Finland.

Gyenesei, A., 2000b. *Mining Weighted Association Rules for Fuzzy Quantitative Items* In Proceedings of PKDD Conference, September 13-16, 2000, Lyon, France. pp. 416-423.

Gyenesei, A., 2001. Fuzzy Partitioning of Quantitative Attribute Domains by a Cluster Goodness Index, http://citeseer.nj.nec.com/440030.html.

Gyenesei, A.; Teuhola, J., 2001. Interestingness Measures for Fuzzy Association Rules, PKDD 2001: Freiburg, Germany, pp. 152-164.

Han, J.; Fu, Y., 1995. *Discovery of Multiple-level Association Rules from Large Databases*, Proceedings of the 21st International Conference on Very Large Databases, Zurich, Switzerland.

Hong, T. P.; Kuo, C. S.; Chi, S. C., 1999a. A fuzzy data mining algorithm for quantitative values, The Third International Conference on Knowledge-Based Intelligent Information Engineering Systems, pp. 480-483.

Hong, T. P.; Kuo, C. S.; Chi, S. C., 1999b. Mining association rules from quantitative data, Intelligent Data Analysis, Vol. 3, No. 5, pp. 363-376.

Houtsma, M.; Swarmi, A., 1993. *Set Oriented Mining of Association Rules*, Technical Report RJ 9567, IBM Almaden Research Center, 650 Harry Road, San Jose, CA 95120. U.S.A.

Huhtala, Y.; Karkkainen, J.; Paokka, P.; Toivonen, H., 1998a. TANE: An Efficient Algorithm for Discovering Functional and Approximate Dependencies. It can be found at URL: http://citeseer.nj.nec.com/huhtala99tane.html.

Huhtala, Y.; Karkkainen, J.; Porkka, P.; & Toivonen, H., 1998b. *Efficient Discovery of Functional and Approximate Dependencies Using Partitions* Proc. 14th Int. Conf. on Data Engineering, IEEE Computer Society Press.

Hullermeier, E., 2001a. Implication-Based Fuzzy Association Rules, ECML/PKDD 2001, Freiburg, Germany.

Hullermeier, E., 2001b. Fuzzy Association Rules: Semantics Issues and Quality Measures, http://citeseer.nj.nec.com/.

Ishibuchi, H.; Nakashima, T.; Yamamoto, T., 2001. Fuzzy Association Rules for Handling Continuous Attributes, Proc. of 2001 IEEE International Symposium on Industrial Electronics, June 2001, Pusan, Korea, pp.118-121.

Kerre, E. E., 1993. Introduction to Basic Principles of Fuzzy Set Theory and Some of Its Applications. 2nd edition. Gent, Belgium: Communication & Cognition.

Ketterlin, A., 1997. Clustering Sequences of Complex Objects, in Proceedings of *PKDD97*, Trondheim, Norway, June 24-27 1997.LNAI 1263. Springer, NY, U.S.A.

Klemettinen, M.; Mannila, H.; Ronkainen, P.; Toivonen, H.; Verkamo, A. I., 1994. *Finding Interesting Rules from Large Sets of Discovered Association Rules*, Proceedings of Third International Conference on Information and Knowledge Management.

Kovalerchuk, B., E. Triantaphyllou, J.F. Ruiz, and J. Clayton, 1997. Fuzzy Logic in Computer-Aided Breast Cancer Diagnosis: Analysis of Lobulation, Artificial Intelligence in Medicine, No. 11, pp. 75-85.

Kruse, R.; Nanck, D.; Borgelt, C., 2001. Data Mining with Fuzzy Methods: Status and Perspectives, http://citeseer.nj.nec.com/245408.html .

Kuok, C. M.; Fu, A.; Wong, M H., 1998. *Mining Fuzzy Association Rules in Databases*, SIGMOD Record, pp. 41-46, Vol. 27, No. 1.

Last, M.; Klein, Y,; Kandel, A., 2001. Knowledge Discovery in Time Series Databases, *IEEE Transactions on Systems, Man, and Cybernetics-Part B: Cybernetics*, 1083-4419, IEEE.

Lee, J. H.; Hyung, L. K., 1997. An Extension of Association Rules using Fuzzy Sets, Seventh IFSA World Congress, Prague, pp. 399-402.

Liao, S. Y.; Wang, H. Q.; Liu, W. Y., 1999. Functional Dependencies with Null Values, Fuzzy Values, and Crisp Values, IEEE Transactions on Fuzzy Systems, Vol. 7, No. 1, pp. 97-103.

Liu, B.; 1998. Integrating Classification and Association Rule Mining, in Proceedings of KDD98, http://citeseer.nj.nec.com/liu98integrating.html.

Lu, H.; Han, J.; Feng, L., 1998. Stock Movement and N-dimensional Inter-transaction Association Rules, in *Proc. 1998 SIGMOD Workshop on Research Issues on Data Mining and Knowledge Discovery (DMKD'98)*, pp. 12:1-12:7, Seattle, Washington.

Luo, J. X., 1999. Integrating Fuzzy Logic with Data Mining Methods for Intrusion Detection, Thesis of Master Degree of Science in the Department of Computer Science, Mississippi State University.

Luo, J. X.; Bridges, S. M., 2000. *Mining fuzzy association rules and fuzzy frequency episodes for intrusion detection.* International Journal of Intelligent Systems (IJIS), 15(8): 687-703.

Maimon, O.; Kandel, A.; Last, M., 2001. Information-Theoretic Fuzzy Approach to Knowledge-Discovery in Databases, Advances in Soft Computing - Engineering Design and Manufacturing, R. Roy, T. Furuhashi and P.K. Chawdhry (Eds.), Springer-Verlag, London, pp. 315-326, 1999.

Mannila, H.; Toivonen, H.; Verkamo, A. I., 1994. *Efficient Algorithms for Discovering Association Rules,* AAAI Workshop on Knowledge Discovery in Databases, pp. 181-192, Seattle, Washington.

Mazlack, L. J., 2000. Approximate Clustering in Association Rules, *19th International Conference of the North American Fuzzy Information Processing Society - NAFIPS 2000,* Atlanta, pp. 256-260.

Mitra, S.; Pal, S. K.; Mitra, P., 2001. *Data Mining in Soft Computing Framework: A Survey,* http://citeseer.nj.nec.com/mitra01data.html.

Mueller, A., 1995. *Fast sequential and parallel algorithms for association rule mining: A comparison* Technical Report CS-TR-3515, Dept. of Computer Science, Univ. of Maryland, College Park, MD, U.S.A.

Piatesky-Shapiro G., 1991. Discovery, Analysis, and Presentation of Strong Rules. In Chapter 13 of Knowledge Discovery in Databases, AAAI/MIT Press.

Rastogi, R.; Shim, K., 1998. Mining Optimized Association Rules with Categorical and Numerical Attributes, In Proc. of the 14th Int'l Conf. on Data Engineering, pages 503-512.

Rifqi, M.; Monties, S., 2001. Fuzzy Prototypes for Fuzzy Data Mining, http://citeseer.nj.nec.com/44393.html.

Roberto, J., Bayardo, Jr., Agrawal, R., Gunopulos, D., 1999. Constraint-Based Rule Mining in Large, Dense Databases, In Proc. of the 15th Int'l Conf. on Data Engineering, 188-197.

Romahi, Y; Shen, Q., 2001. Dynamic Financial Forecasting with Automatically Induced Fuzzy Associations, http://citeseer.nj.nec.com/284097.html.

Roychowdhury, S.; Pedrycz, W., 2001. Linguistic Association Rules, In Proceedings of IFSA/NAFIPS2001 Congress, pp. 645-650, Vancouver BA, Canada.

Savasere, E.; Omiecinski, S.; Navathe, 1995. *An Efficient Algorithm for Mining Association Rules in Large Databases,* Proceedings of the VLDB Conference, Zurich, Switzerland.

Savnik, I.; Flach, P. A., 2000. Discovery of Multi-valued Dependencies from Relations, report00135, http://citeseer.nj.nec.com/savnik00discovery.html.

Shragai, A.; Scgreider, M., 2001. Discovering Quantitative Association Rules in Database, http://citeseer.nj.nec.com/.

Shu, J. Y.; Tsang, E. C. C.; Daniel; Yeung, S., 2001. Query Fuzzy Association Rules in Relational Database, Proceedings of IFSA/NAFIPS 2001, Vancouver, BA, Canada.

Shu, J.; Tsang, E.; Yeung, D. S.; Shi, D., 2000. Mining fuzzy association rules with weighted items, In: Proc. IEEE Int'l Conf. on System, Man and Cybernetics (SMC2000), Nashville, Tennessee.

Srikant, R.; Agrawal, R., 1995. *Mining Generalized Association Rules,* in Proc. of the 21st Int'l Conference on Very Large Databases, Zurich, Switzerland.

Srikant, R.; Agrawal, R., 1996. *Mining Quantitative Association Rules in Large Relational Tables,* SIGMOD'96 6/96 Montreal, Canada.

Srikant, R.; Vu, Q.; Agrawal, R., 1997. *Mining Association Rules with Item Constraints,* in Proc. of the 3rd Int'l Conference on Knowledge Discovery in Databases and Data Mining, Newport Beach, California, USA.

Suzuki, E., Kodratoff, Y., 1998. Discovery of Surprising Exception Rules Based on Intensity of Implication. In Proceedings of PKDD-98.

Tseng, S. M., 2001. Mining Association Rules with Interestingness Constraints in Large Databases, International Journal of Fuzzy Systems, Vol. 3, No. 2, June.

Wang, S. L.; Shen, J. W.; Hong, T. P., 2003. Incremental discovery of functional dependencies based on partitions, Intelligent Data Analysis (in revision).

Wei, Q.; Chen, G. Q., 1999. *Mining Generalized Association Rules with Fuzzy Taxonomic Structures*, in 18th Int'l Conf. of NAFIPS, New York, NY, USA, 477-481.

Wei, Q.; Chen, G. Q, 2000. Association Rules with Opposite Items in Large Categorical Database, FQAS2000. Warsaw, Poland.

Wei, Q.; Chen, G.. Q.; Kerre, E. E., 2002. Mining Functional Dependencies with Degrees of Satisfaction in Databases, in Proceedings of Joint Conference on Information Sciences, Durham, NC, USA.

Wei, Q.; Chen, G. Q.; Wets, G.., 2000. Modifying Fuzzy Association Rules with Linguistic Hedges, in 19th Int'l Conf. Of NAFIPS, Atlanta, GA, U.S.A.

Wong, C.; Shiu, C.; Pal, S., 2001. Mining Fuzzy Association Rules for Web Access Case Adoption, http://citeseer.nj.nec.com/

Yang Y. P.; Singhal, M., 2001. Fuzzy Functional Dependencies and Fuzzy Association Rules, http://citeseer.nj.nec.com/.

Yilmaz, E., Triantaphyllou, E., Chen, J., & Liao, T. W., 2003. A heuristic for mining association rules in polynomial time, Mathematical and Computer Modelling, No 37, pp. 219-233.

Zadeh, L., 1965. Fuzzy Sets, *Information and Control*, pp. 338-358, Vol. 8.

AUTHORS' BIOGRAPHICAL STATEMENTS

Dr. Guoqing Chen received his Ph.D. from the Catholic University of Leuven (KUL), Belgium, in 1992. Currently he is a Professor at the School of Economics and Management, Tsinghua University, Beijing China. Professor Chen has over 80 publications worldwide in many journals, books, and conference proceedings, including two books (on fuzzy data modeling and soft computing) published by Kluwer Academic Publishers, Boston, in 1998 and 1999 respectively. His areas of interest include data mining, databases, fuzzy logic, and IT management.

Dr. Qiang Wei received his PhD in Management Science from Tsinghua University, Beijing China, in 2003 and currently he is an assistant professor at Tsinghua's School of Economics and Management. Dr. Wei's major research interests are information systems, fuzzy logic, and data mining. He has many publications including in international journals such as *Information Sciences* and *Computers and Industrial Engineering*.

Dr. Etienne E. Kerre received his Ph.D. from Gent University (RUG), Belgium, in 1970, and since then a professor at RUG's Department of Applied Mathematics and Computer Science. He has published more than 160 papers in international journals and conference proceedings, including a book (on the Basic Principles of Fuzzy Set Theory and some of its Applications) published in 1991. He has been chair and member of many international conferences and journals. His areas of interest include fuzzy mathematics, information retrieval and databases, knowledge systems and discovery.

Chapter 15 [1]

MINING HUMAN INTERPRETABLE KNOWLEDGE WITH FUZZY MODELING METHODS: AN OVERVIEW

T. Warren Liao
Industrial & Manufacturing Systems Engineering Department
3128 CEBA Building
Louisiana State University, Baton Rouge, LA 70803
Web: http://www.imse.lsu.edu/liao
Email: ieliao@lsu.edu

Abstract: This chapter focuses on one particular class of data mining methodologies that expresses the mined knowledge in the form of fuzzy If-Then rules or fuzzy decision trees that can be easily understood by a human. Past studies on generating fuzzy If-Then rules (mostly from exemplar crisp data and a few from exemplar fuzzy data) are grouped into six major categories: grid partitioning, fuzzy clustering, genetic algorithms, neural networks, hybrid methods, and others. The representative method in each category is detailed. The latest improvements and advancements in each category are also reviewed. Similarly, past studies on generating fuzzy decision trees (from exemplar nominal and/or numeric data as well as from exemplar fuzzy data) are surveyed. The essence of each method is presented. Moreover, we discuss selected studies that address most of the necessary conditions for a fuzzy model to be interpretable and highlight areas for future studies. To give an idea of where fuzzy modeling methods have been applied, major application areas are also summarized.

Key Words: Data mining, Fuzzy modeling, Fuzzy clustering, Genetic algorithms, Neural networks, Fuzzy-neural networks, Fuzzy If-Then rules, Fuzzy decision trees.

---

[1] Triantaphyllou, E. and G. Felici (Eds.), **Data Mining and Knowledge Discovery Approaches Based on Rule Induction Techniques**, Massive Computing Series, Springer, Heidelberg, Germany, pp. 495-550, 2006.

1.   BACKGROUND

Zadeh [1965] proposed the idea of fuzzy sets and subsequently introduced this very idea into systems theory [1973]. A new class of systems called fuzzy systems was thus created. Since then, based on Zadeh's ideas successful applications of fuzzy sets and systems have been reported in many areas. Other than their effectiveness in problem solving, the attractiveness of fuzzy sets and systems lies mainly in their ability to capture human thinking and understanding.

The issues of modeling, control, and optimization are important to any system concept, and fuzzy systems are no exception. The modeling issue must be addressed first because a good system model is essential to successful system control and optimization. The importance of fuzzy system modeling is well recognized by the research communities, evidenced by the high activity in this area. Entering "fuzzy models" as the keyword, the Science Citation Index (SCI) database generates close to 15,000 records. Research in this area has been and still is very active.

Fuzzy modeling efforts were largely started by researchers in fuzzy control where fuzzy sets and fuzzy logic found early success. Since then, continuous developments were made and never ceased. The bulk of fuzzy models comprise a set of If-Then rules. Roughly speaking, there are two major categories of such fuzzy model forms: *linguistic models* based on collections of If-Then rules with vague predicates and operated on Mamdani-like fuzzy reasoning [Mamdani and Assilian, 1975] and *TSK models* based on the Takagi-Sugeno-Kang (TSK) method of reasoning [Takagi and Sugeno, 1985; Sugeno and Kang, 1986]. A rule of a MISO (multi-input and single output) linguistic system model has the following form: If $(x_1$ is $A_{1j})$ and $(x_2$ is $A_{2j})$ and ... and $(x_n$ is $A_{nj})$ Then y is B_k, where x_i is the i-th input $(i = 1, ..., n)$; A_{ij} is the j-th linguistic term defined on x_i and B_k is the k-th linguistic term defined on the output y. For classification problems, B_k is simply a constant and is treated as a fuzzy singleton. A rule of a TSK model can be described as If $(x_1$ is $A_{1j})$ and $(x_2$ is $A_{2j})$ and ... and $(x_n$ is $A_{nj})$ Then $y = f(x_i)$, in which the mapping function, f, could be linear, nonlinear, or simply a constant. Among the two, linguistic models are better suited for the discovery of human understandable knowledge from real world data. Therefore, this study will focus only on fuzzy linguistic models. It should be noted that there are other special forms of fuzzy rules and generation methods. For example, Kim [1997] presented an algorithmic method to generate rules taking the form "If ..., else if ..., else if ..., end if." Such rules resemble a decision tree in which the branch points indicate the divided search route. Special fuzzy models such as this one are outside the scope of this review.

Two major aspects in the identification of a fuzzy model are structural identification and parameter identification. The number of variables, the number and shape of fuzzy terms of each variable, and the number of rules constituting the model determine the structure of a fuzzy model. In a fuzzy model, the parameters are those associated with the membership functions of the fuzzy terms. Guillaume [2001] recently performed an interpretability-oriented review of three families of automatic rule generation methods (i.e., grid partitioning, clustering, and hybrid methods) and two structural optimization issues (i.e., variable selection and rule reduction). In that, he defined three necessary conditions for a set of fuzzy rules to be interpretable as follows:

1) The fuzzy partition must be readable, in the sense that the fuzzy sets can be interpreted as linguistic labels.
2) The set of rules must be as small as possible.
3) The rules should allow for the definition of the if-part by using a subset of independent variables rather than the full set.

Pedrycz [1998] envisioned an important synergy between fuzzy models and methods of knowledge discovery, especially where data mining leads to a multivariable model in the form of $y = f(x_1, x_2, ..., x_n)$ and this model needs to be easily comprehensible and fully interpretable. Following this thinking, this chapter intends to give an overview of those fuzzy modeling methods that produce human understandable knowledge, in the form of either fuzzy If-Then rules or fuzzy decision trees, from data. As mentioned above, the TSK models successfully used in control but not as comprehensible are excluded here. To prevent the loss of interpretability, the number of rules or the size of a tree should not be too large. Therefore, studies to control or reduce the size of a rule base and a tree are also of interest. This review differs from Guillanume's [2001] in several aspects. First, the scope of this review is wider in the sense that not only rule generation and structural optimization, but also parameter identification and tuning are considered. In addition, many papers not covered by Guillanume are reviewed here. Secondly, other than fuzzy If-Then rules, fuzzy decision trees are also included. As a result of this enlarged scope, we propose to add one more necessary condition below to make it four for a set of fuzzy rules to be interpretable.

The fuzzy partitions for each variable should not be too many (to the point that is difficult to comprehend) and commonly shared by all rules. To minimize performance degradation, the fuzzy partitions and the associated parameters should be data-driven and optimized using some algorithm.

This review will examine the following fuzzy modeling issues:

1) Number of variables;
2) Number of fuzzy terms per variable;
3) Subset of variables per rule;

4) Rule weight;
5) Number of rules (initial/selection);
6) Shape of fuzzy terms;
7) Parameters of fuzzy terms (initial/tuned).

The first six are structural identification issues, while the last one is related to parametric identification and tuning. Most papers addressed part of the above-mentioned issues in various ways. For better identify their differences, a summary table is also provided. Due to the plenteous works in this area, it is nearly impossible not to let out a few of them. Our apologies go to all authors contributing to this field of research that have been unintentionally missed.

The next section briefly summarizes the basic concepts used in nearly all fuzzy modeling methods. Section 3 surveys those methods developed for the generation of fuzzy If-Then rules. Section 4 is devoted to those methods developed for the generation of fuzzy decision trees. Section 5 summarizes the applications that have been selected for fuzzy modeling. The discussion is given in Section 6, followed by the conclusions.

2.   BASIC CONCEPTS

Two fundamental issues that every fuzzy modeling method must address are how to represent the fuzzy concepts in the appropriate level of granularity, and how to use the fuzzy model to derive a conclusion. According to the fuzzy set theory, the fuzzy concepts are represented as membership functions. The decisions to be made include what function form, how many, and what parameter values to use. Commonly used membership function forms are triangular, trapezoidal, Gaussian, sigmoidal, and B-spline for real-valued variables, and singletons for discrete-valued variables.

Most fuzzy modeling studies assumed that all variables have the same form and the form was often arbitrarily chosen. One exception is the work of Shi *et al.* [1999]. They allowed the algorithm to select any one of the six pre-selected types of membership functions for each variable appearing in a rule. The number of membership functions used determines the granularity of fuzzy partitions. The simplest and naive approach is to arbitrarily pick a number and assume that all the membership functions are uniformly distributed in the universe of discourse of each variable. A more sophisticated approach is to fix a different number of membership functions for each variable and allow the parameters to be tuned by some methods such as genetic algorithms, gradient descent, and fuzzy clustering based on the training data. Liao [2001] proposed generalized π functions for fitting the membership functions defined by fuzzy c-medians. The most sophisticated approach is to allow the algorithm to determine the optimal number of membership functions for each variable and to tune the associated parameters as well. While most studies define membership functions for each variable separately, it should be pointed out that some studies define n-dimensional membership functions for the entire input product space instead. Such a treatment is desirable if the interdependency between variables cannot be ignored and/or the system dimension is high. The problem is that it is difficult to interpret n-dimensional membership functions, especially when n is large. We are not aware of any fuzzy decision tree that uses n-dimensional membership functions. Such use might require the aggregation of features leading to the reduction of tree size.

One common task that every fuzzy modeling method has to perform is to check the performance of the fuzzy model generated during the construction process. To this end, every method must employ a fuzzy inference method in order to derive the solution for a test datum. In the following we describe the basic components of a fuzzy inference method.

A. *Pattern matching* – This step matches a membership function in a rule (or a tree) with the input value of an unknown vector for which an output is to be determined. If the input value is crisp, this step is also called fuzzification. If the input value is fuzzy, this operation is performed based on some concept to compute the similarity between the two fuzzy sets being compared. The result is a crisp value called the matching degree. The input and membership functions could be one-dimensional or n-dimensional, depending upon what type of rules are induced in the first place.

B. *Aggregation of matching degrees* – This step combines the matching degrees of all variables appearing in the if-part of a rule (or all the branch nodes leading to a leaf in a tree) together. It is unnecessary if n-dimensional fuzzy sets are defined. This operation can be accomplished by any t-norm operator such as the "product" operator or the "minimum" operator.

C. *Implication operation* – This step computes the result of a rule (or a leaf) by linking its if-part (or all branch nodes leading to the leaf) with the then-part (or the leaf itself). A number of operators have been proposed in the past. Some t-norm operators such as the "product" operator and the "minimum" operator are commonly used in this operation. If there is a rule weight, it is also included in this operation as well. The result could be fuzzy or crisp, depending upon whether the rule consequent is fuzzy or crisp (singleton). To simplify the calculation, a fuzzy rule consequent is often reduced to a singleton of its center value using some defuzzification method.

D. *Aggregation of rule results* – This step consolidates all the rule results (or leaf results in the case of fuzzy trees) into one. Any s-norm (or t-conorm) operator can be used for this operation. Among them, the "maximum" operator or the "sum" operator is often used. In the case that the rule consequent (or the leaf) is a crisp value (treated as singleton), the resultant fuzzy set simply comprises all singletons if the "sum" operator is used, or all dominant singletons if the "maximum" operator is used. The singleton could represent (i) the center value of a fuzzy set, or (ii) a constant denoting some class in a pattern recognition application.

E. *Defuzzification* – This step is used to determine the crisp output for the test datum. Many methods have been proposed for this operation. Among them, the centroid defuzzifier is the most popular. Let $\mu(y)$ be the aggregated fuzzy rule result for some fuzzy variable y. If $\mu(y)$ is a piecewise continuous membership function, then

$$y' = \frac{\int \mu(y) y \, dy}{\int \mu(y) \, dy}.$$

(1)

On the other hand, if $\mu(y)$ is discrete comprising singletons, then

$$y' = \frac{\sum_{i=1}^{N} y_i \mu(y_i)}{\sum_{i=1}^{N} \mu(y_i)}.$$

(2)

By dropping the denominator, Eq. (2) becomes a linear defuzzifier.

3.   GENERATION OF FUZZY IF-THEN RULES

Methods developed for the generation of Mamdani-like form of linguistic models can be roughly divided into six categories: grid partitioning, fuzzy clustering, genetic algorithms, neural networks, hybrid methods, and others. These methods differ in how each aspect of constructing a fuzzy model is accomplished. Each method has a fuzzy inference component for predicting the outcome of an unseen datum. All neural fuzzy systems build the network structures around the chosen fuzzy inference method. The fuzzy inference method employed might differ from one method to another. The commonly used ones have been reviewed in Section 2. The representative method in each category and concise summaries of subsequent improvements are discussed in detail below. Hybrid methods usually employ more than one method. Each of them is reviewed under the category of the primary method employed. Most methods consider only numeric attribute data with a few taking fuzzy data as input. Some methods can be easily modified to handle nominal attribute data as well by using the concept of fuzzy singleton, whereas others cannot be easily adapted and require a total different approach.

3.1 Grid Partitioning

The WM method, short for Wang and Mendel, is one famous grid partitioning method [Wang and Mendel, 1992]. It consists of five steps, as summarized below.

Step 1 – Divide the Input and Output Spaces into Fuzzy Regions

Given is a set of examples with multiple inputs and a single output, denoted as $(x_i^t; y^t)$ where $i = 1, ..., n$ and $t = 1, ..., N$ with n and N denote the number of variables and examples, respectively. Define the universe of discourse of each input variable as $[x_i^-; x_i^+]$ and the output variable as $[y^-; y^+]$. Divide each universe of discourse into m regions, which can be different for different variables. The lengths of the regions are usually set to be equal; and the shape of each membership function associated with each region that defines a fuzzy term is assumed triangular, denoted as (l, c, r) for (left bound, center, and right bound). Two special properties of fuzzy terms so defined are: (1) Adjacent terms have ½ overlap; and (2) For the middle terms, the left bound of term j is the center of term j-1 and the right bound of term j is the center of term j+1. Therefore, knowing term centers is sufficient to determine all the fuzzy triangular terms.

For implementation, the minimal and maximal values of each variable are often used to define its universe of discourse. That is, $[x_i^-; x_i^+] = [\min(x_i), \max(x_i)]$. They are also considered to be the center of the most-left term and the most-right term, respectively. That is, $c_{il} = \min(x_i)$ and $c_{im} = \max(x_m)$. Accordingly, the other term center, c_{ij}, can be computed as follows:

$$c_{ij} = \min(x_i) + (j\text{-}1)\,(\max(x_i) - \min(x_i))/(m\text{-}1), \text{ where } j = 2, ..., m\text{-}1. \qquad (3)$$

Step 2 – Generate Fuzzy Rules from the Given Examples

First, determine the membership degrees of each example belonging to each fuzzy term defined for each region, variable by variable (including the output variable). Secondly, associate each example with the term having the highest membership degree, variable by variable, denoted as md_i. Finally, obtain one rule for each example using the term selected in the previous step. The rules so generated are "and" rules, meaning that the antecedents of the if-part must be met simultaneously in order for the consequent of the rule to occur. Letting Tx_i be a term selected for variable x_i of an example, a rule could look like:

If x_1 is Tx_1 (with md_1) and x_2 is Tx_2 (with md_2) and ... and x_n is Tx_n
(with md_n) Then y is Ty (with md_y). $\qquad (4)$

Step 3 – Assign a Degree to Each Rule

The rule degree is computed as the product of the membership degree of all variables. Let D^t be the degree of the rule generated by example t. Mathematically,

$$D^t = \prod_{i=1,\dots n \text{ and } y} md_i^t. \tag{5}$$

The degree of a rule generated by an example indicates our belief of its usefulness.

Step 4 – Create a Combined Fuzzy Rule Base

When the number of examples is high, it is quite possible that the same rule could be generated by more than one example with different degrees: such rules are referred to as "redundant" rules. In addition, rules with the same if-part but a different then-part could also be generated; such rules are then called "conflicting" rules. The redundant and conflicting rules must be removed to maintain the integrity of the rule base. This is achieved by keeping only the rule with the highest degree for each fuzzy region. (The one with the highest degree is deemed most useful; therefore, it is kept.)

Up to this step, the fuzzy rule base is complete. Next, the usefulness of the rule base must be shown. This requires a fuzzy inference as given in the next step.

Step 5 – Determine a Mapping Based on the Combined Fuzzy Rule Base

To predict the output of an unseen example denoted as x_j, the centroid defuzzification formula is used. Accordingly, the predicted output, $\hat{y}$, is computed as

$$\hat{y} = \frac{\sum_{r=1}^{R} amd^r \cdot c^r}{\sum_{r=1}^{R} amd^r}, \tag{6}$$

where $amd^r = \prod_{i=1,n} md_i^r$; c^r is the center value of the consequent term of rule r; and R denotes the total number of rules after the combination operation.

The WM method assumes *a priori* knowledge about the number of variables, the number of fuzzy terms per variable, and the shape of fuzzy terms. The parameters of the fuzzy terms are determined based on the uniform grid-partition assumption. The if-part of each rule uses all input variables. The rule weight equals to the aggregated matching degree based on the "product" operator. Redundant rules are removed by keeping only the one with the highest rule weight.

Three improvements of the WM method have been reported. Chan *et al.* [1995] improved the accuracy of the WM method by incorporating a new concept called "virtual fuzzy set" in the then-part of the rule. A virtual fuzzy set is determined from the centroid of the consecutive fuzzy sets. Instead of processing all the examples in one pass, only one single data point is processed at one time. This method thus allows incremental learning when new samples become available. Cordón and Herrera [2000] suggested two ways to increase the accuracy: (i) by allowing a specific combination of antecedents to have two consequents, the first and second in importance (i.e., Step 4 of the WM method is modified), and (ii) by following the WM method with a genetic algorithm as a rule selection method to keep only those good cooperating rules. Our preliminary study indicates that the WM method could be improved by applying a fuzzy c-means variant algorithm [Liao *et al.* 2003] to derive a better partition of the domain space or by using a genetic algorithm to determine the optimal number of terms per variable, separately. A joint use is expected to improve more, but is hampered by the long computation time due to the iterative nature of both genetic and fuzzy c-means algorithms.

Another well-known grid partitioning method is the INT method developed by Ishibuchi *et al.* [1992] for classification problems in which the output variable takes on discrete values (or singletons in the sense of fuzzy sets). Consider a classification problem with M classes. The INT method has three steps, as described below.

Step 1 – Uniformly Partition the Input Space
This step is identical to the WM method, except that the output space is not partitioned.

Step 2 – Generate Fuzzy Rules from Given Examples
For each hyperspace cell, a fuzzy If-Then rule is defined as follows:

If x_1 is Tx_1 and x_2 is Tx_2 and ... and x_n is Tx_n Then y belongs to Class C* with CF.

For each rule, the class, C^*, and the grade of certainty, CF, must be determined. To identify C^*, one first calculates α_C, the sum of compatibility of all x's in class C, as follows:

$$\alpha_C = \sum_{x' \in C} \prod_{i=1}^{n} md_i^t . \tag{7}$$

C^* is determined as the class that has the maximal sum of compatibility. That is,

$$\alpha_{C*} = \max\{\alpha_1, ..., \alpha_C, ..., \alpha_M\}. \tag{8}$$

If two or more classes take the maximum value or all the α_C's are zero, the rule cannot be determined uniquely, and thus it is not induced. If a single class takes the maximum value, then the CF is determined as follows:

$$CF = (\alpha_{C^*} - \alpha) / \sum_{C=1}^{M} \alpha_C, \tag{9}$$

where

$$\alpha = \sum_{\substack{C=1 \\ C \neq C^*}}^{M} \alpha_C \bigg/ (M-1). \tag{10}$$

Step 3 – *Determine the Class for an Unseen Test Datum Based on the Fuzzy Rule Base*

Let R denote the set of rules. Each test datum, $x = \{x_1, \ldots, x_n\}$, is classified according to the following procedure:

1) Calculate β_C for each class C ($C = 1, \ldots, M$) as

$$\beta_C = \max_{C^*=C} \{\mu_{Tx1}(x_1) \cdot \mu_{Tx2}(x_2) \cdots \mu_{Txn}(x_n) \cdot CF\} \tag{11}$$

2) Find the class for the test datum, C', such that

$$\beta_{C'} = \max\{\beta_1, \ldots, \beta_C, \ldots, \beta_M\}. \tag{12}$$

If more than one class take the maximum value or $\beta_{C^*}=0$, then the test datum cannot be classified.

To cope with the difficulty in deciding the granularity of a fuzzy partition (or the number of fuzzy terms per variable), the concept of distributed fuzzy If-Then rules was proposed, where several partitions were simultaneously used. It was reported that high performance and its robustness with respect to the number of fuzzy terms in each axis are the main advantages of distributed fuzzy rules over ordinary fuzzy rules. However, one undesirable consequence is that the number of rules explodes quickly, especially when the dimension is high. To alleviate this problem, Ishibuchi *et al.* [1995] employed a genetic algorithm to remove the irrelevant and unnecessary rules. To increase the accuracy without increasing the number of rules, Nozaki *et al.* [1996] proposed an adaptive method that introduced an additional error-based procedure to adjust the grade of certainty of each rule according to its classification performance.

By allowing a variable to take on a "don't care" value (with membership of one for all values in the universe of discourse), Ishibuchi *et al.* [1997] were able to obtain rules using subsets of variables. The rule selection problem was formulated as a single objective and multi-objective problem, and was solved by genetic algorithms. They presented three ways to obtain a set of non-dominated rule subsets for the single objective case: employing variable weights, introducing a constraint condition on the number of rules, and introducing a constraint condition on the number of correctly classified patterns. Ravi *et al.* [2001] slightly modified the INT method by using some well-known aggregators such as the "compensatory and", "fuzzy and", and a convex combination of "min" and "max" operators in place of the traditional "min" and "product" operators to generate the initial set of rules. They then applied a modified threshold-accepting (TA) algorithm to find the smallest rule subset that maximizes the number of correctly classified patterns. They modified the original threshold accepting algorithm (a variant of the simulated annealing algorithm) proposed by Dueck and Scheuer [1990], by generating each neighborhood solution vector in a deterministic fashion from the given candidate solution vector, rather than chosen deterministically or randomly.

Ishibuchi *et al.* [1993] proposed a sequential subdivision method that starts with a rough partition and then refines only the subspace rule with low grade of certainty until 100% classification performance is attained or the maximum number of iterations is reached. Lin *et al.* [1997] partitioned the input space in a similar fashion, but added a fuzzy neural network, similar to a four-layer radial basis function network, to refine the parameters. Kbir *et al.* [2000] proposed a hierarchical fuzzy partition method based on 2^N-tree decomposition. The decomposition is controlled by the grade of certainty of the generated rules for each fuzzy subspace and the deeper hierarchical level allowed.

Abe and Lan [1995] defined fuzzy rules with variable regions by activation hyper-boxes which show the existence region of data for a class and by inhibition hyper-boxes which inhibit the existence of data for that class. These rules are extracted from numerical data by recursively resolving the overlaps between two classes. An input variable is deleted if the same rule set is obtained without it. Mikhailov *et al.* [1996] partitioned the input space into activation rectangles, corresponding to certain output intervals. Based on those activation rectangles, trapezoidal or triangular membership functions and fuzzy rules with no rule weight are generated. To remove the redundant rules generated this way, a real-valued genetic algorithm method was employed [Lekova *et al.*, 1998]. The values coded in the chromosome are the sensitivity parameters, defining the slope of the trapezoid or triangle.

Zhang and Knoll [1999] proposed a learning approach to designing fuzzy controllers based on the B-spline model. The B-spline basis functions are automatically determined after each input is partitioned with a pre-specified order of the B-spline functions. Learning of a fuzzy controller based on B-spline basis functions is then equivalent to the adaptation of a B-spline interpolator. They proposed to adapt the parameters of the controller output of each rule by using a gradient descent method. Optimal placements of the

B-spline basis functions for specifying each input is found by an algorithm working similarly to a self-organizing neural network.

Castro *et al.* [1999] proposed a procedure for generating fuzzy rules having a maximal structure from a set of examples, in the sense that fewer components are in the if-part of the rule and large numbers of examples are correctly identified. Starting from an empty set of definitive (maximal) rules and the set of examples, each example is first converted into one rule to form the initial set of rules based on a predefined set of fuzzy terms for each variable. Each initial rule is checked whether it is subsumed by some rule in the set of definitive rules. If yes, it is ignored; otherwise, perform a process of amplification in each variable. To reduce the number of rules, Castro *et al.* [2001] subsequently proposed two improvements to the above procedure: ordering the input variables in the training examples based on their correlation with the output variable and removing the noise present in the set of training examples based on two measures, the distance with respect to the examples of the same type and with the examples of different types. After the initial set of rules is obtained, a genetic algorithm is applied to generate a minimal set of maximal rules which identify the evident knowledge in the set of examples.

3. 2   Fuzzy Clustering

The paper by Sugeno and Yasukawa [1993] is probably the first fuzzy clustering-based modeling method. They proposed to apply the fuzzy c-means (FCM) algorithm to the output data only. The number of clusters, c, is determined so that $S(c)$ reaches a minimum as c increases, in which $S(c)$ is defined as:

$$S(c) = \sum_{t=1}^{N} \sum_{i=1}^{c} (\mu_{it})^m (\| x_t - v_i \|^2 - \| v_i - \bar{x} \|^2), \tag{13}$$

where μ_{it} is the membership grade of the t-th data belonging to the i-th

cluster; x_t is the t-th data vector, v_i is the i-th cluster center vector; and $\bar{x}$ is the average value of all data. Consequently, every output y is assigned a membership grade belonging to each fuzzy cluster B_k ($k = 1, ..., M$). By projecting B_k onto the input axes, one induces an input cluster for each axis. The projected input cluster is approximated with a convex fuzzy set. Each input and output cluster is then approximated with a fuzzy set of the trapezoidal type. For any data point in a cluster, we have $A_1(x_1') = A_2(x_2') = ... = A_n(x_n') = B_k(y')$. Thus, each cluster results in a fuzzy rule:

If x_1 is A_1 and x_2 is A_2 and ... and x_n is A_n, Then y is B_k . $\tag{14}$

In some special cases, one might have more than one fuzzy cluster in any dimension of the input space corresponding to one fuzzy cluster in the output space. Therefore, the number of rules might not be equal to the number of fuzzy clusters.

Emami *et al.* [1998] proposed a three-step structural identification and two-step parameter identification methodology. The first step of structural identification is done by using the FCM algorithm to derive the fuzzy partition of the output space from the data in order to obtain the required number of rules for explaining the system behavior. The optimal fuzzy weight and number of clusters were determined by an iterative process. An agglomerative hierarchical clustering algorithm was implemented as an introductory procedure to find properly identified hard-cluster centers as the initial locations of cluster prototypes in the FCM algorithm. The second step selects significant input variables using an overall measure of the non-significance of input variables. The third step employs a clustering technique called fuzzy line clustering to construct convex input membership functions from the output partitions one variable at a time. The first step of parameter identification specifies the "best" inference mechanism for the system with parameters optimized using the *constr* function of MATLAB, which is based on the sequential quadratic programming method. The second step tunes the parameters of input and output membership functions (trapezoidal) by applying the tuning algorithm of Segeno-Yasukawa [1993] with one modification, i.e., by using a variable adjustment value at each tuning step. Kilic *et al.* [2002] modified the above-mentioned methodology for modeling pharmacological data. The modifications include (i) selecting the cluster size contingent upon the training error, (ii) projecting the output clusters into *n*-dimensional input space and building input clusters without any assumptions of convexity, (iii) determining the similarity of the test data with respect to these input clusters via a k-nearest-neighbor search algorithm, and (iv) determining the significance of an input variable by degree in according with their weight in predicting the output, etc.

Klawonn and Kruse [1997] discussed how two modified fuzzy clustering algorithms could construct better fuzzy models from data than FCM. Other than the prototypes and the membership degrees for each cluster, each algorithm also computes a (positive-definite) diagonal covariance matrix. The two algorithms were applied to the input-output data, rather than the output data only, as done in [Sugeno and Yasukawa, 1993]. One rule was obtained from each cluster by projecting the fuzzy cluster to the one-dimensional coordinate spaces. To convert a discrete fuzzy set to a continuous one, the convex hull that covers all discrete data points is computed. The convex hull is then approximated to a trapezoidal function by using a heuristic algorithm that aims at minimizing the sum of quadratic errors. Hirota and Pedrycz [1996] proposed a directional clustering algorithm that takes the directionality requirement into account by incorporating the nature of the functional relationships as part of the objective function to guide the formation of the clusters. The clustering process is carried out in a bottom-up manner. The minimum number of clusters that does not lead to substantial performance degradation is taken as the "plausible" number of clusters. To generate the fuzzy model from pairs of input-output data, the original space is discretized using triangular membership functions with ½ overlap level between two consecutive terms. The modal values of these terms are situated at the cluster prototypes. Gómex-Skarmeta and Jiménez [1999] proposed a hybrid method that uses a fuzzy clustering method like the FCM to generate the initial fuzzy rules from pairs of input-output data and then applies a genetic algorithm to tune the rule parameters. Once the pre-specified number of clusters is found, fuzzy clusters in each domain are projected. Then the extensional hull of each projected fuzzy set is obtained, and approximated with a trapezoidal fuzzy set. Each individual in the GA is a rule set with each rule denoted by a sequence of four parameters associated with each trapezoidal fuzzy set in the if- or then-part of the rule. For comparison purpose, the GA can also be used alone to generate and refine rules from data with or without some priori information. More details about this version of GA are given in the next section.

Along the same line of generating fuzzy models from input-output data, Espinosa and Vandewalle [2000] presented an algorithm called the autonomous fuzzy rule extractor with linguistic integrity (AFRELI), which is complemented with the FuZion algorithm for merging consecutive membership functions while guaranteeing the distinguish ability between fuzzy sets. The AFRELI algorithm is a two-step approach to extracting rules, which allows the incorporation of *a priori* knowledge. The first step uses clustering and projection techniques to find good initial positions for the fuzzy sets in the input domains. Given pairs of input-output data, find the pre-specified number of clusters by using the mountain clustering method to initialize the centers and number of clusters and refine them using FCM. Taking the projected value of each prototype as the modal value of a triangular membership function together with two extreme values, construct the triangular membership functions with overlap of 1/2 for each variable. The second step reduces the complexity of the model (number of membership functions) using the concept of semantic integrity as a framework and the FuZion algorithm as the implementation tool. The FuZion algorithm is a routine that merges triangular membership functions whose modal values are "too close" to each other, determined by a preset minimum acceptable distance between modal values.

Yao *et al.* [2000] proposed an entropy-based fuzzy clustering (EFC) method and used it for fuzzy modeling. The EFC method calculates the entropy of each data point and selects the data point with minimum entropy as the first cluster center. Next, it removes all data points having similarity larger than a threshold β with the chosen cluster center. This process is repeated till all data points are removed. If outliers are present, another parameter γ is set (e.g., at 5% of the total number of data points). Before selecting a data point as a cluster center, count the number of data points that have similarity with this data point greater than β. If this number is less than γ, then the data point is deemed unfit to be a cluster center and is rejected. Once the cluster centers are found, they are used to obtain a fuzzy model with a collection of rules equal to the number of clusters. Each fuzzy set appeared in each rule is assumed to be defined as a standard deviation estimated by using a simple formula.

Delgado *et al.* [1997] presented different approaches to the problem of fuzzy rule extraction by using fuzzy clustering as the main tool. These approaches range from a pure approximate approach, which obtains more precise fuzzy rules in the form of "if x is A, then y is B", to a pseudo-descriptive one, which obtains more "linguistic" ones in the form of "if x_1 is A_1, x_2 is A_2, ..., and x_n is A_n, then y is B" in the sense that they can be interpreted by an expert. The x in "if x is A then y is B" is a Cartesian product of x_1, x_2, ..., and x_n while A denotes a multi-dimensional fuzzy set. These methods form clusters by working either with input-output data all together, input and output separately, or each individual variable one at a time.

3.3   Genetic Algorithms

Genetic algorithms (GAs) have been applied to fuzzy modeling in different modes: structural identification only, parameter identification only, and structural identification as well as parameter identification. Early works focused mainly on the parameter tuning of fuzzy inference systems used in control. Today, a genetic algorithm is often part of a hybrid fuzzy modeling method. Since the complete fuzzy modeling process addresses both structural identification and parameter identification, our review in this section will consider only those works addressing both issues. The sequential approach and the simultaneous approach are two general approaches often considered to address both structural identification and parameter identification. In either case, the GA approach considers the fuzzy modeling process as optimization or search processes in a high dimensional hyperspace. It should be noted that as part of their paper Carse *et al.* [1996] presented an overview of research that applied genetic algorithms to fuzzy rule based control. In addition, Cordón *et al.* [1997] provided a short review and gave a detailed bibliography on evolutionary fuzzy modeling up to 1996.

Generally speaking, genetic algorithms may be implemented for fuzzy modeling in three different ways: the Michigan, Pittsburg, and iterative rule learning (IRL) approach. In the Michigan approach, each chromosome encodes an individual rule and all rules are evolved as a whole, whereas in the Pittsburg approach, each chromosome encodes a complete rule set and only the best individual is considered as the solution. In the IRL approach, as in the Michigan one, each chromosome in the population represents a rule, but contrary to the Michigan one, only the best individual is taken as the solution, discarding the remaining chromosomes in the population. A covering method is thus necessary in order to generate a complete rule set. The papers reviewed below are grouped based on the implementation approach taken and whether the modeling task is done in stages or simultaneously.

3.3.1   Sequential Pittsburg approach

Cho *et al.* [1997] proposed a two-part procedure for rule generation: genetic learning of initial rules and genetic fine-tuning of fuzzy rules. The learning of initial rules determines the linguistic values of rules consequent under the assumption that the number (set at 7 in their study) and shape (triangular) of fuzzy terms for each variable is known. A fuzzy rule base is represented as a string, which consists of cells where each cell is further divided into a number of binary bits. The integer part of the decoded real number indicates a specific linguistic term. One-point crossover and a simple flip mutation scheme were employed as the genetic operators. The fine-tuning part adjusts the membership functions of the rules obtained in the previous step. The chromosome is a string having the length equal to the total number of parameters with each parameter value binary coded. Several cost functions were employed to select the best chromosome, including minimum rooted mean square error, improved controller response, smoother fuzzy rule base, and minimum control energy.

Heider and Drabe [1997] proposed a cascaded genetic algorithm, which is made up of two loops or cascades. An outer and an inner cascade alternatively determine and improve the structure and parameters of a fuzzy system. Each individual in the outer GA represents a complete fuzzy system structure consisting of flags for input and output fuzzy sets and of rules. The individuals from the inner GA represent only parameters of active (flagged) trapezoidal fuzzy sets. For the starting population, flags are set randomly. For the following populations activation or deactivation of rules and membership functions is determined by genetic operators. The individual fitness is measured according to the least-squares method. The routine is repeated until a global stopping criterion in the structure GA is fulfilled. The best individual is taken as the optimization result.

3.3.2   Sequential IRL+Pittsburg approach

Cordón and Herrera [1997] presented an evolutionary process based on genetic algorithms and evolution strategies for learning the fuzzy-logic-controller knowledge base from examples in three different stages. The first stage is an evolutionary process for generating fuzzy control rules, with two components. The fuzzy rule generation method finds the best rule in every run over the set of examples according to the features included in a fitness function. The iterative covering method allows the iterative use of the fuzzy rule generation method to obtain a set of fuzzy rules covering the set of examples. In each iteration the covering method runs the generation method for choosing the best fuzzy control rule, considers the relative covering value that this rule yields over the example set, and removes the examples with a covering value greater than a value provided. The second stage is a genetic simplification process for selecting rules, based on a binary-coded genetic algorithm. The individuals are selected based on the stochastic universal sampling procedure together with an elitist selection scheme, and the generation of the offspring population is put into effect by using the classical binary two-point crossover and uniform mutation operators. The third stage is a genetic tuning process, which has two variants differing in the coding scheme, depending upon whether the fuzzy model is approximate or descriptive. In either case, the GA uses real-coded chromosomes, stochastic universal sampling together with an elitist scheme as the selection procedure, Michalewicz's non-uniform mutation and the max-min arithmetical crossover operators.

Herrera *et al.* [1998] presented a three-stage genetic process for learning fuzzy rules from examples. The first stage is a fuzzy rule generating process based on an iterative rule learning approach. It consists of a rule generation method and an iterative covering method. The rule generation method is developed by means of a real coding GA (RCGA) that codes a single fuzzy rule (or each chromosome) as a vector of floating point numbers. The fitness function is defined with the objective to select fuzzy rules that (i) cover a lot of positive examples but a few negative examples, (ii) have small or fixed membership function width, and (iii) associate with highly symmetrical membership functions (the product operator was selected for combining all the above criteria). The evolution process uses the non-uniform mutation, the max-min-arithmetical crossover, and the stochastic universal sampling as the selection procedure. In each iteration, the covering method runs the RCGA to find the best chromosome (rule) over a set of examples, assigns the relative covering value to every example, and removes the examples with a covering value greater than ε (a set value). The second stage combines expert rules, if there are any, with those generated in the first stage, and removes the redundant rules. This process is based on a binary-coded GA. The fitness function considers the squared errors as well as the completeness property. The selection procedure is the same as in the first stage. The genetic operators used are two-point crossover and uniform mutation. The third stage is a tuning process for adjusting the membership functions of the fuzzy rules. In this stage, a fuzzy rule set is represented as a real coding chromosome. A rule is represented by a piece of chromosome with the number of positions equal to the number of rule parameters. The fitness function is the sum of the square errors of the associated rule set. The genetic operators and parameters are the same as in the generating process. The number of fuzzy terms (triangular or trapezoidal) for each variable was assumed.

Cordón *et al.* [1998] introduced a multistage genetic learning process to obtain linguistic fuzzy rule-based classification systems. It is based on a specific genetic learning methodology called MOGUL (*m*ethodology to *o*btain *g*enetic fuzzy rule-based systems *u*nder the iterative rule *l*earning approach). According to this methodology, the learning algorithm can be divided into three stages: an iterative rule learning process that obtains a set of linguistic classification rules from the training examples, a genetic multi-selection process that generates several simplified rule sets by selecting the rules that best cooperate from the initial fuzzy rule set and by selecting the best hedges for them, and a genetic tuning process that optimizes the parameters that define the triangular membership functions. Cordón and Herrera [2001] proposed a three-stage hybrid evolutionary algorithm for learning constrained approximate Mamdani-type knowledge bases from examples. The first stage is an evolutionary process for generating fuzzy rules with constrain-free semantics. The process has two components: a fuzzy rule generation method comprised of a hybrid GA-ES process which uses a phenotypic niche criterion to obtain the best possible cooperation among the fuzzy rule generated, and an iterative covering method identical to that employed by Herrera *et al.* [1998]. A chromosome encoding a candidate rule is composed of two parts with the first part encoding the composition of the fuzzy rule and the second part the membership functions associated with it. The fitness function is the product of four criteria. Other than mutation and crossover operations, an $(1+1)$-ES operator was also applied. The second stage is a genetic multi-simplification process for selecting rules, based on a binary coded GA with a Hamming distance-based genotypic sharing function and a measure of the system performance. The third stage is a genetic tuning process based on a real coding GA and the same performance measure used as the one in the second stage. It uses the same chromosome representation, selection procedure, and genetic operators as that used in the third stage of Herrera *et al.* [1998].

3.3.3   Simultaneous Pittsburg approach

Homaifar and McCormick [1995] studied the applicability of genetic algorithms in the simultaneous design of membership functions (only the base lengths of triangular fuzzy sets are determined, not the location of the peaks) and rule sets. They arbitrarily fixed the number of terms for input/output variables and the base length of the output variable. The chromosome is integer-based with the number of alleles equal to the number of rules plus the number of base lengths. The value of each allele is either one possible value of output fuzzy sets or one possible base length. To simplify the genetic operations, the same number of values was used for each allele. A procedure was used to decode base length values to the actual universe of discourse. For the fuzzy control applications shown in their study, two fitness functions were used at two different stages of the control process: the evolution stage and the refinement stage. The first stage intends to find a satisfactory controller whereas the second stage attempts to minimize the time needed. In developing a fuzzy model for control, Tarng *et al.* [1996] applied a GA to simultaneously determine the scaling factors, parameters of membership functions, and fuzzy rules under the assumption of known number and shape (trapezoidal) of membership functions. The chromosome is a long binary string because all real values are binary coded. A fuzzy rule is not selected if it takes on an empty set as its outcome. The fitness function is the difference between a large value and the summation of the square root errors due to the force error and the force error change, specially tailored for the subject application – adaptive force control in turning. Carse *et al.* [1996] proposed a Pittsburgh Fuzzy Classifier System #1 (P-FCS1), which is based on the Pittsburgh model of learning classifier systems and employs variable length rule-sets that simultaneously evolves fuzzy set membership functions and relations. Both rule and fuzzy set membership encodings are real-numbered rather than using bit strings. All membership functions were initialized randomly with the uniform distribution. The membership functions are encoded locally within individual rules, which could complicate linguistic interpretation if they are too many. They introduced a new crossover operator that respects the functional linkage between fuzzy rules with overlapping input fuzzy set membership functions. The mutation operator applies real-number creep to the centers as well as the widths of fuzzy set membership functions. The rule-set fitness was calculated as the inverse of the mean square error of the predicted outputs.

The GA developed by Gómex-Skarmeta and Jiménez [1999] for generating and refining rules is also a simultaneous approach for fuzzy modeling. A chromosome is represented as $R_1R_2...R_{MAX}d_1d_2...d_{MAX}$, where R_j = $\{A_1^jA_2^j...A_n^jB^j\}$ consists of fuzzy terms for n input variables and one output variable and d_j is a control digit corresponding to R_j, $j = 1, ..., MAX$. Each fuzzy term is assumed to be trapezoidal-shaped and is denoted by a four-tuple. The d_j value is binary with one (zero) indicating that the rule is active (inactive) in the rule set. Therefore, the number of rules is the number of ones in the d_j values. Due to the different representation, genetic operators used in the rule set are different from those used in the control set. Three crossover operators and two mutation operators are used for the rule set whereas simple binary crossover and mutation operators are used for the control set. The evaluation function was given as

$$eval = \begin{cases} \dfrac{1}{\sqrt{MSE + (Nr / MAX)}} & if \quad s = 0 \\ 0 & if \quad s \neq 0. \end{cases} \qquad (15)$$

In (15), s is the number of uncovered examples and Nr denotes the number of rules generated. The evaluation function is designed to choose a small and accurate set of rules that covers all examples.

Russo [1998] developed a fuzzy genetic neural system (FuGeNeSys) for fuzzy modeling from input-output data. Each individual in the population is made up of a set of user-specified R number of rules, each of which comprises I number of inputs and O number of outputs. The membership functions are assumed Gaussian denoted by two parameters: the center and the width (the inverse of sigma). For each antecedent it is thus necessary to code the two parameters with 16 bits each. An antecedent is considered irrelevant if the width value is zero. The consequents are coded in two different ways depending upon how the defuzzification is done. One consequent coding method uses two parameters: the center and the area of fuzzy set symmetrical with the center, both coded with 16 bits. The other method codes only the center using 16 bits. An apomictic, continuous, and fine-grain evolution algorithm was used. The populations were divided up into a certain number of subpopulations. Selection and crossover were local in an area with a pre-established radius. Other than a single-cut crossover operator and a simple mutation operator, a hill-climbing operator was introduced, which starts whenever an individual is generated with a fitness value higher than the best one obtained so far. The hill-climbing operation is done on a transformed neuro-fuzzy system with a backpropagation procedure. The trained system is then retransformed back into a genetic individual. The fitness function of an individual was derived based on four considerations, that we omit here for brevity; interested readers may refer to the original paper.

Subsequently, Russo [2000] introduced another hybrid learning algorithm called GEFREX, which stands for genetic fuzzy rule extractor. In this algorithm, the genetic coding involves only the premises of the rules. Each individual consists of two parts. The first part codes the Gaussians of all antecedents. The second part is dedicated to the enable bits for feature selection. As a result of this mixed coding (real part and binary part), additional genetic operators for real genes were introduced. The consequents are singletons derived through a least-squares solution of an over-determined system using the singular value decomposition algorithm. The fitness function was also modified by removing one consideration (out of the four mentioned above). If the fitness of the new individual improves the best fitness found so far, the new individual is transformed into a neuro-fuzzy system. Then the neuro-fuzzy system is trained. This neural-based genetic operator improves the performance of GEFREX with respect to learning speed and error. The premises extracted from the neuro-fuzzy system are retransformed into a genetic individual and reintroduced in the genetic population.

Shi *et al.* [1999] used a genetic algorithm to evolve the membership function shapes and types and the fuzzy rule set (including the number of rules). A total of six types of functions were used as the membership function candidates; each is represented by an integer from 1 to 6. A membership function was completely determined by three values: the start point, the end point, and the function type. The total length of each chromosome coding the entire fuzzy system is determined based on a given maximum number of rules in the rule set. A rule with a zero antecedent or consequent part is infeasible and is not included in the rule set. The fitness function is a relative error function. Each time an element is chosen to be mutated it is increased or decreased by one randomly within its range. The crossover and mutation rates of the evolutionary algorithm were adapted via a fuzzy system with eight fuzzy sets. This fuzzy system has three input variables: the best fitness, the number of generations for unchanged best fitness, and the variance of fitness. For simplicity, each variable has three possible fuzzy values: low, medium, and high. Surmann and Selenschtschitow [2002] used a genetic algorithm for the optimization of fuzzy rule-based systems with some initial structure. The membership functions were assumed to be Gaussian-like defined by two parameters if symmetrical, or three parameters if asymmetrical. Every chromosome contains all the fuzzy set parameters in the entire rule set. The fitness function has two parts. The first part, reflecting the model performance, is the maximization of the reciprocal of the mean square error. The second part, relating the structure and complexity of the resulting fuzzy system, has three items: the entropy of the system, the number of membership functions, and the number of membership functions never activated and always completely activated. Besides the well-known mutation and crossover operators, they introduced two new operators: *Set zero/one* is used to produce membership functions which are always one (activated) or always zero (not activated); *Set similar* selects randomly for each input/output variable a membership function and makes it equal to the membership function that is most similar to it.

Xiong and Litz [2002] employed a GA to learn the premises (or if-part) of rules together with fuzzy set membership functions at the same time in order to design an optimal fuzzy controller. The GA encodes each rule set as a hybrid string consisting of two substrings: binary coding of the premise structure of a rule base and integer coding of the membership functions of individual variables. The fitness value of each rule set is computed in consideration of its control performance and its consistency index. Each member in the population is given a probability proportional to its fitness value for being selected as parent. The selected parents then undergo the genetic operations (crossover and mutation) to produce their offspring. A three-point crossover is first used. One breakpoint of this operation is fixed to be the splitting point between both substrings, and the other two breakpoints can be randomly selected within the two substrings. For the binary substring, mutation is simply to inverse a bit. Each bit in the integer substring undergoes a disturbance with magnitude determined by a Gaussian distribution function. The rules with invalid premises are removed. There are two cases that could lead to an invalid rule premise when all the bits in the binary substring are all one (meaning "don't care") or they are all zero (meaning "empty").

Kang *et al.* [2000] used evolutionary programming to simultaneously evolve the structure and the parameters of a fuzzy rule base. The connection matrix representing the fuzzy rule base structure is a 2-D matrix with each element, m_{ij}, taking a positive real value indicating the relative importance of the j-th input variable in the i-th rule. Zero importance implies its irrelevance in the rule. Another 2-D matrix is used to represent the parameters for defining the membership functions within the fuzzy rule base. Trapezoidal or triangular functions were assumed for the input variables whereas fuzzy singletons for output variables. The mutation operation updates the original value in the structure and parameter matrices by adding a Gaussian random number adjusted in proportional to the fitness value. The fitness function is tailored to the control purpose by considering the modeling error, the control performance, and by penalizing the occurrence of null sets in the universe of discourse.

Nawa and Furuhashi [1999] proposed the bacterial evolutionary algorithm (BEA) for the discovery of the parameters of fuzzy systems from numeric data. Each chromosome encodes the rules of the fuzzy model as well as the membership functions of the variables. The isosceles triangular-shaped membership functions are assumed with each is encoded as a center-width pair. The length of chromosomes is not fixed, which means that the number of rules encoded by a chromosome could be varied. The encoding method provides a high degree of freedom in modeling the system, but results in non-uniformity of membership functions (every rule has a different set of membership functions to refer to), posing an interpretability problem. Considering both system performance and structural complexity, the chromosome performance index was defined as:

$$PI = \frac{1}{n}\sum_{i=1}^{n}\frac{|y_i - y_i'|}{y_i} + \frac{NumRules}{Num_{MAX}} * w_r, \qquad (16)$$

where n is the number of data; y_i and y_i' are the actual and predicted value of the i-th datum; *NumRules* and Num_{MAX} are the number of rules in the model and the maximum number allowed in a chromosome; and w_r is an assigned weight value. Two special genetic operators were applied: the bacterial mutation and the gene transfer operation, inspired by the processes that occur in the bacterial genetics level. The aim is to improve parts of the chromosome, instead of the whole chromosome.

Peña-Reyes and Sipper [2001] introduced a cooperative co-evolutionary approach to fuzzy modeling, named *Fuzzy CoCo*. In *Fuzzy CoCo*, the fuzzy modeling problem is solved by two coevolving, cooperating species. The individuals of the first species encode values which define completely all the membership functions for all system variables. The individuals of the second species define a set of rules of the Mamdani form. The relevant variables are searched for implicitly by letting the algorithm choose nonexistent membership functions as valid antecedents. A variable choosing a nonexistent membership function is considered irrelevant. The two evolutionary algorithms used to control the evolution of the two populations are instances of a simple genetic algorithm. The genetic algorithms apply the fitness-proportionate selection procedure to choose the mating pool and apply an elitist strategy with an elitism rate to allow some of the best individuals to survive into the next generation. The crossover and mutation operators employed are standard ones. An individual undergoing fitness evaluation establishes cooperation with one or more representatives of the other species, i.e., it is combined with individuals from the other species to construct a fuzzy model. The representatives, or cooperators, of either species are selected both fitness-proportionally and randomly from the last generation in which they were already assigned a fitness value. The fitness combines two criteria: classification performance and maximum number of variables in the longest rule. Fuzzy CoCo assumes that the number of membership functions and the number of rules are predefined.

3.4   Neural Networks

Several attempts have been made to integrate fuzzy systems and neural networks with a view to designing systems which are interpretable, robust, and learnable. Three groups of unification schemes can be generally classified: fuzzy neural systems, neural fuzzy systems, and cooperative systems. Fuzzy neural networks are neural networks capable of handling fuzzy information. The cooperation systems are those which use different paradigms (neuro or fuzzy) to solve various facets of the same problem. Neural fuzzy systems are fuzzy systems implemented by neural networks. It has been shown that under simple conditions a fuzzy inference system could be viewed as a neural network and vice versa. Therefore, neural fuzzy systems are the dominant form of fuzzy modeling. Mitra and Hayashi [2000] surveyed various neuro-fuzzy models used for rule generation (including rule extraction and rule refinement) and organized them, based on their level of integration, under a unified soft computing framework. In their paper, rule extraction refers to extracting knowledge from the artificial neural network, using the network parameters in the process. On the other hand, rule refinement pertains to extracting refined knowledge from the artificial neural network that was initialized using crude domain knowledge.

Without exception, the neural networks approach to fuzzy modeling attempts to take advantage of the adaptability and learning ability of neural networks. Various neural networks with regular or special tailored architectures have been applied in the past. To avoid redundancy as much as possible, the following review will focus more on the latest papers. Note that the training data could be real or fuzzy valued. However, no attempt was made to subdivide them further in order to minimize the number of subsections.

3.4.1   Fuzzy neural networks

Enbutsu *et al.* [1991] presented a three-stage procedure for fuzzy rule extraction using a three-layered neural network. The number of nodes in the input (output) layer equals the total number of fuzzy terms associated with all fuzzy input (output) variables. The membership function is used in the input nodes and conventional sigmoid functions are used in the hidden and output nodes. First, training data are learned by error backpropagation. Secondly, the acquired weights are used to calculate the "Causal Index" between each input node and output node, which was derived from the differential. Using the relative casual indices, the extraction of fuzzy rules is accomplished in three consecutive steps: selecting a fuzzy output variable, selecting a fuzzy term for the selected output variable, and selecting a fuzzy term for each input variable.

Mitra *et al.* [1997] proposed a new scheme of rule generation using a fuzzy multilayer perceptron (MLP) for classification problems. They formulated a methodology for encoding *a priori* initial knowledge in the fuzzy MLP in a way that both positive and negative rules can be generated. The network architecture, so encoded, is then refined by training on the pattern set supplied. The trained network is used for rule generation using two strategies described below. The first method treats the network as a black box and uses the training set input and network output to generate the if-part and then-part of rules. The second method backtracks along maximal weighted paths using the trained net and utilizes its input and output activations to obtain the antecedent and consequent clauses.

Li *et al.* [2002] proposed a feature-weighted detector (FWD) network, which consists of input (I), matching (M), detecting (D), and output (O) layers. It is capable of solving simultaneously two major problems in pattern recognition: pattern classification and feature selection. The activation functions in the M, D, and O layers are comparative, Gaussian (with fixed σ), and linear, respectively. In FWD networks, there are two types of learning when input is presented to the input layer. One is unsupervised memory learning based on the fuzzy learning law. It updates the memory vector associated with each neuron, i.e., the backward connection weights from the D layer to the neuron in the M layer. The other is supervised weight learning. It updates the connection weights between the M neurons and the D neurons based on the chain rule of differential calculus. A feature has no contribution to a cluster if the associated connection weight is zero. The trained network can be directly converted to fuzzy rules.

Huang and Xing [2002] presented an approach to represent continuous-valued input parameters using linguistic terms (discretization) and then extract fuzzy rules from the trained binary single-layer neural network. Their definition of linguistic terms is based on M number of equally divided crisp intervals, not based on the fuzzy set theory. Based on their scheme, the original problem with n continuous-valued input parameters is converted into a new problem with $n \cdot M$ binary input parameters. They developed an algorithm to extract the most dominant fuzzy rules, one from each neuron. The number of output nodes determines the number of rules to be extracted.

3.4.2   Neural fuzzy systems

The papers in this category are organized in three groups, following the similar idea of Nauck *et al.* [1997]: 1) the system starts without rules, and creates new rules as training patterns are learned; 2) the system starts with all possible rules and may delete those insignificant ones based on their performances; and 3) the system starts with an initial set of rules, given by domain experts or extracted by a unsupervised method, and then optimized by using some algorithm.

3.4.2.1. Starting empty

Lin and Lee (1991) proposed a fuzzy neural network model, called Falcon-ART, which effectively combines the fuzzy ART algorithm for structural learning (formulation of the fuzzy rules) and the backpropagation algorithm for parameter learning (tuning of the membership functions). The trained Falcon-ART network has five layers to represent fuzzy rules: input variable layer, input term layer, fuzzy rule layer, output term layer, and output variable layer. The input/output linguistic terms are represented as trapezoidal fuzzy sets. Prior to training, the Falcon-ART network has only the input layer and the output layer to represent the variables. The hidden layers for the input and output term nodes and the fuzzy rules are grown as the learning cycle progresses. The training data are the complementarily coded input-output vector. The Falcon-ART network has several shortcomings: (i) poor network performances when the classes of input data are closely similar to each other, (ii) weak resistance to noisy/spurious training data, (iii) strong dependence of the termination of network training process on a preset error parameter, and (iv) possible deterioration of learning efficiency as a result of using complementary coded training data. Quek and Tung (2001) modified the Falcon-ART (called Falcon-MART) in order to remove the above-mentioned shortcomings. The weighted averaging method was used to determine rule-firing strengths, which magnifies the membership value difference between the same attribute of different membership sets. A more progressive learning rule was adopted to minimize the effects of noisy data. To ensure the convergence, they introduced a new stopping criterion. The learning terminates when the change in the total error between two consecutive epochs is smaller than a preset small value. The problem of complementary coding was overcome by using absolute-valued data.

3.4.2.2 Starting full

Hiraga *et al.* [1995] described a procedure for acquiring a ship operator's control rules for collision avoidance using a fuzzy neural network with six-layer structure that realizes a simplified fuzzy inference method. Three sets of connection weights are adjusted by the BP algorithm. Two of them determine the positions and the gradients of the sigmoid functions, respectively. The third set corresponds to the singletons in the rule consequence. The tracks of the ship obtained from the simulations were used to train the FNN.

Lin and Cunningham [1995] introduced a four-layer fuzzy neural network for modeling a complex system from input-output data. The network has an N-$N \times R$-R-1 architecture (for N input nodes, $N \times R$ fuzzification nodes, R rule nodes, and 1 defuzzification node). The activation functions in the fuzzification, rule, and defuzzification layer are special-type fuzzy membership functions for input variables, multiplication functions, and weighted sum functions, respectively. A fuzzy curve was plotted for each variable using a procedure developed by the authors. The importance of input variables is ranked according to the range covered by their fuzzy curves (an input variable is insignificant if the fuzzy curve is flat, having a range of zero). The number of rules is estimated by the maximum and minimum points on the curve. The connection weights are initialized and adapted with a backpropagation technique. If a fuzzy membership function is always near zero over its input range, then the output of the rule using this fuzzy membership function is always near zero. Thus, this rule can be deleted. If a fuzzy membership function is always near one over its input range, then one can remove this node without affecting the performances.

Lin and Lu [1995] proposed a five-layered neural network similar to the one proposed by Lin and Lee [1991] for the connectionist realization of a fuzzy inference system that is capable of processing and learning the hybrid of numerical and linguistic information through the use of fuzzy singletons. They used α-level sets of fuzzy numbers to represent linguistic information. The inputs, outputs, and weights of the proposed network can be fuzzy numbers of any shape. An initial network structure is first constructed. It is then trained by a two-phase supervised learning algorithm. In phase one, a BP-based parameter learning scheme is used to adjust fuzzy weights connecting to fuzzy terms (between layers 1 & 2 and layers 3 & 4); In phase two, a two-part structure learning scheme is used. The first part merges the fuzzy terms of input/output linguistic variables, while the second part combines rules in order to reduce the number. A fuzzy reinforcement learning scheme was also developed for the same network, but not covered here because it learns by criticizing rather than by teaching.

Nauck and Kruse [1997] used NEFCLASS (a neuro-fuzzy model for pattern classification) to derive fuzzy classification rules together with the shape of triangular membership functions from a set of data that can be separated into different crisp classes. A NEFCLASS is a 3-layer fuzzy perceptron with some special characteristics. The first layer contains the input units representing the pattern features. The hidden layer holds rule units representing the fuzzy rules. The third layer consists of output units, one for each class. Each connection between an input unit and a rule unit is labeled with a linguistic term. The connections coming from the same input unit and having identical labels bear the same weight all the time (called shared weight) to ensure that for each linguistic value there is only one representative fuzzy set. A user has to define the number of initial fuzzy sets for partitioning the domains of the input features, and must specify the maximum number of rule nodes that may be created in the hidden layer. Compared to neural networks, NEFCLASS uses a much simpler learning strategy. Fuzzy rule creation can be seen as a selection from an initially given rule base, specified by a fuzzy grid in the input domain. The fuzzy sets are trained by a backprogagation-like algorithm that requires no gradient information.

Zhang and Kandel [1998] developed a crisp-fuzzy neural network (CFNN), a general fuzzy reasoning-oriented fuzzy neural network that is capable of extracting high level knowledge such as fuzzy If-Then rules from either crisp data or fuzzy data. A CFNN consists of five layers: input layer, compensation and linear combination layer (with two types of fuzzy neurons), fuzzy reasoning layer (the number of nodes in this layer corresponds to the number of fuzzy rules), summation layer (with a compensatory summation neuron and a fuzzy rule summation neuron), and output layer. To optimize the network, they proposed a knowledge discovery-based learning algorithm (KDBLA) based on heuristic gradient-descent learning. They assumed trapezoidal-type fuzzy sets and proposed a procedure to compress a CFNN with a big fuzzy rule base to a small one.

Su and Chang [2000] presented a class of fuzzy degraded hyper-ellipsoidal composite neural networks (FDHECNNs) that are trained by a real-valued genetic algorithm to generate If-Then rules on the basis of pre-selected meaningful features. A FDHECNN is a two-layer feedforward neural network. There is only one output node and the number of hidden nodes corresponds to the number of fuzzy sets (or fuzzy rules). The antecedent of each rule is an n-dimensional hyper-ellipsoid with three parameters. The term "degraded hyper-ellipsoidal" refers to a hyper-ellipsoid of which principal axes are parallel to the input coordinates. The rule consequent is a crisp value denoted by the connection weight between the hidden node and the output node. Each chromosome represents a vector which is composed of the parameters of the entire fuzzy rule set. Refer to the paper for the three main operators (reproduction, crossover, and mutation) used to manipulate real-valued parameters.

Chen and Chang [2000] presented a novel learning algorithm of fuzzy perceptron neural networks (FPNNs) for classifiers that utilize expert knowledge represented by fuzzy If-Then rules as well as numerical data as inputs. Owing to the quest for a nonlinear discriminant boundary rather than just a linear one, they used a second order perceptron neural network. In order to handle (symmetrical-triangular) fuzzy numbers, level sets of fuzzy input vectors are incorporated into perceptron neural learning. At different levels of the input fuzzy numbers, updating the weight vectors depends on the minimum of the output of the fuzzy perceptron neural network and the corresponding non-fuzzy target output that indicates the correct class of the fuzzy input vector. This minimum is computed efficiently by employing the modified vertex method to lessen the computational load and the training time required. Moreover, they introduced the fuzzy pocket algorithm into the learning scheme to solve the non-separable problems.

Azeem et $al.$ [2000] proposed a generalized fuzzy model (GFM) that encompasses both the Takagi-Sugeno (TS)-model and the compositional rule of inference (CRI)-model. They showed that the proposed GFM is functionally equivalent to a generalized radial basis function (GRBF) network. The basic function in GRBF is a generalized Gaussian function of three parameters (center, width, and power). The GRBF network is a three-layered architecture, where each node in layer 1 has exactly n inputs (from n-dimensional feature vector) and is a special type of radial basis function processor. Each node in layer 2 has m inputs, which is the weighted outputs of nodes in layer 1 with connection weights. The only one node in the output layer performs the summation of all the inputs weighted with the corresponding local models, which are functions of the input vector. They demonstrated through examples how an unnecessary rule from a rule base of the learned model could be eliminated and how an insignificant variable from a learned rule could be removed using the parameters of the learned GRBF network. They assumed that initial rules were obtained by using the fuzzy curve idea [Lin and Cunningham III, 1995].

Quek and Zhou [2001] proposed a Pseudo Outer-Product based Fuzzy Neural Network (POFNN) as an integrated fuzzy neural network that accomplishes the whole process from fuzzification, fuzzy inference to the defuzzification process. The POFNN network has five layers: layer 1 – the input layer, layer 2 – the condition layer, layer 3 – the rule-base layer, layer 4 – the consequence layer, and layer 5 – the output layer. The number of nodes in the input/output layer equals the size of numeric input/output feature vector. The number of nodes in the condition/consequence layer equals the number of (bell-shaped) linguistic labels for all input/output variables. The number of nodes in the rule-base layer is initially set to the product of the number of linguistic labels for each input variable. The network learning process consists of three phases. The Kohonen self-organization map is first used to initialize the membership functions of both the input and output variables by determining their centroids and widths; in the second phase, the Pseudo Outer-Product (POP) or Lazy Pseudo Outer-Product (LazyPOP) learning algorithm is performed to identify the fuzzy rules that are supported by the set of training data. Both algorithms remove irrelevant rules, but differ in starting with all the possible rules (POP) or not (LazyPOP). The derived structure and parameters are then fine-tuned using the backpropagation algorithm in the final phase.

Chakraborty and Pal [2001] proposed a neuro-fuzzy system that performs feature analysis and system identification in an integrated manner. The neural fuzzy system was realized as a five-layered network. Layer 1 is the input layer, with as many nodes as the number of input features. Each node in layer 2 represents the (bell shaped) membership functions of a linguistic value associated with an input feature (acts as the fuzzifier and also performs the feature analysis). To this end, a modulator function was defined, which has one tunable parameter, indicating whether the associated feature is good or not. Thus, layer 2 can be better realized using two layers of neurons, the first one for the computation of the membership value and second layer for the modulated output. All connection weights between the nodes in layers 1 and 2 are unity. Layer 3 is called the AND layer. Each node in this layer represents the if-part of a fuzzy rule. The "product" operator was chosen for the intersection (AND) operation. All connection weights between the nodes in layers 2 and 3 are unity. Layer 4 is the OR layer and it represents the then-part of the fuzzy rules. The connection weights between layers 3 and 4 represent the certainty factors of fuzzy rules. Every node of this layer picks up only one rule from all the associated rules based on the maximum agreement with facts in terms of the product of the firing strength and the certainty factor (i.e., realized by the "maximum" operator). The connection weights are modeled as the square of tunable parameters to ensure the positiveness of certainty factors. Layer 5 is the defuzzification layer. Each node in this layer represents an output linguistic variable and performs centroid defuzzification. All connection weights between the nodes in layers 4 and 5 are unity. The concept of backpropagation was used to train the network in three phases. Phase 1 is called the feature selection phase, where the training is done on the initial network with all possible nodes and links. Once phase 1 is completed, the redundant nodes are pruned and the modulation function is disabled. Phase 2 involves retraining the new reduced network. The incompatible rules are then removed and the network is again allowed to learn in this new architecture (phase 3). However, the parameters of different membership functions used were not tuned.

3.4.2.3 Starting with an initial rule base

Rutkowska [1998] mapped a fuzzy inference system into a 4-layer feedforward neural network. A hybrid procedure, consisted of two learning stages, was developed for training the neural network. In the first stage, a genetic algorithm is applied to find the near-optimal fuzzy rules and to learn the parameters of Gaussian membership functions. In the second stage, gradient descent procedures (i.e., error backpropagation) are used for final tuning of the membership functions. The number of fuzzy terms for each variable was assumed and allowed to vary from one variable to another.

Kaur and Lin [1998] built a neural network-based fuzzy logic control model trained by a two-phase process. The NN-FLC model has five layers with neurons in each layer implementing different functions of the fuzzy logic system. Layer one is the input layer. It transmits input signals to the next layer without any change. The link weight of this layer is set at one. Layer two is the input membership function layer. Each neuron in layer two performs a simple membership function. The link weight in this layer is learned. Layer three encodes the rules. Each neuron in this layer represents one rule. The links between this layer and the second layer are the antecedents of the rules. Each neuron in this layer performs a fuzzy AND operation such as "minimum". Layer four is the output membership function layer. Each neuron in this layer represents a simple membership function, usually identical to that in the second layer. The links at this layer perform the fuzzy OR operation, with link weights set at one. Layer five is the output layer. It transfers the fuzzy output to crisp signal used for control. The neurons and the links in this layer act as the defuzzifier of the FLC, performing the center-of-area defuzzification method based on the information of the output membership functions. To construct the network, the number and form of membership functions must be assumed before hand. The first phase of the learning process employs Kohonen's self-organizing feature maps learning to locate input and output membership functions (triangular) and competitive learning to find the correct consequence of each rule. In order to reduce the size of the fuzzy rule base, those rules which provide the same output are combined into one. The second phase uses backpropagation to adjust link weights between layers and to fine-tune the membership functions for desired output.

Yang *et al.* [1998] proposed a self-learning 4-layered fuzzy neural network for real-time stable control. They assumed that the antecedent fuzzy sets are bell-shaped membership functions with two parameters whereas the consequent fuzzy sets are fuzzy singletons. For fuzzy operations, they chose the product–inference logic and center-average defuzzifier. By assuming that the initial FNN controller is constructed from rough fuzzy If-Then rules provided by human experts and some arbitrary rules, a GA is then used to adjust the two parameters of antecedent fuzzy sets and the center of the consequent fuzzy sets, in search for the optimal fuzzy rules that satisfy the performance index specified by the designer. They used one byte real numbers that take a value between 0 and 1 to code the string in order to reduce its length. The fitness was defined as $1/(1+\int e(t)^2 dt)$, where e(t) is the tracking error important to the control task.

Chen and Likens [2001] proposed a systematic neural-fuzzy modeling framework for self generation of the initial fuzzy model, selection of significant inputs, partition validation, parameter optimization, and rule-based simplification. The fuzzy system model is represented as a three-layered RBF network with the number of hidden nodes equaling to the number of fuzzy rules. The fuzzy modeling procedure comprises of three main phases. First, a collection of fuzzy rules is created by a self-organizing network with each rule being represented by a cluster center. Second, important input variables are selected on the basis of the initial fuzzy model. The importance of the *i*-th input variable is defined as the change range of the corresponding output vector divided by the maximum change range among all input variables. An input variable is removed when its importance is less than the set threshold. The less important variable of closely related input variables is also removed. In addition, they used the FCM algorithm to determine the optimal number of fuzzy rules (hidden neurons) and the corresponding receptive fields based on the proposed validity measure that maximizes the compactness within clusters and minimizes the separation between clusters. Finally, the model optimization phase (including parameter learning and structure simplification) is executed on the basis of back-propagation learning and similarity analysis. If the similarity between two fuzzy sets characterized by Gaussian functions is higher than the set threshold, they are merged into one new fuzzy set. If the similarity between a fuzzy set and the universal set is higher than the set threshold, then it is removed from the antecedent.

Behloul *et al.* [2002] presented an efficient method to design 3-layered radial basis function neural networks for extracting rules with *n*-dimensional fuzzy sets. Advanced fuzzy clustering was used to design an optimal RBFN with smaller number of hidden nodes and to generate adequate shapes of kernel function that yields high accuracy. Each hidden node corresponds to a cluster and a fuzzy rule. The RBF centers correspond to the cluster prototypes; and the shape and width of the kernels are determined by the fuzzy covariance matrix of the corresponding cluster. The connection weights between the hidden layer and the output layer are considered as the truth degrees of the rules.

3.5   Hybrids

Many forms of hybrid fuzzy modeling methods have been proposed in the past. Unfortunately, there seems to be no widely accepted definition of what constitutes a hybrid method. We are not aware of any attempt made to classify different hybrid methods and have considered each hybrid method under the category of the primary method used.

Broadly speaking, three general categories of hybrid methods can be distinguished. One category of hybrid methods uses more than one technique at various stages of the fuzzy modeling process in sequence to generate the final model. The techniques used in such works, however, are not integrated. Another category of hybrid methods integrates more than one technique together. The neural-fuzzy approach reviewed in Section 2.5.2 that integrates the fuzzy model into the neural network framework falls into this category. The third category refers to those methods that use one technique to tune the parameters of another. For instance, genetic algorithms are popularly used to tune the parameters of membership functions after the structural identification is completed.

3.6   Others

The fuzzy modeling methods in this category are grouped according to whether the training data is numeric or fuzzy. For the sake of brevity, a detailed review of each method in this category is omitted. Interested readers may refer to the original papers to fully understand the uniqueness of each method.

3.6.1 From exemplar numeric data

Other techniques used to construct fuzzy models from numeric training data include evidence theory [Delgado and Gonzalez, 1993], fuzzy learning based on the α-cuts of equivalence relations and the α-cuts of fuzzy sets [Wu and Chen, 1999], utilization of an assumption-based truth maintenance system [Castro and Zurita, 1997], merging decision table first [Hong and Chen, 1999], merging membership function first [Hong and Chen, 2000], and so on.

3.6.2 From exemplar fuzzy data

Wang *et al.* [1999] proposed a fuzzy learning algorithm based on the PRISM learning strategy that learns fuzzy rules from "soft" instances. The "soft" instances differ from the conventional instances in that they have class membership values. Strictly speaking, they are not fuzzy data per se, but more like numeric data which have been matched with the relevant membership functions. Wang *et al.* [2001a] proposed a new approach called fuzzy extension matrix, which is a generalization of the concept of crisp extension matrix that was first proposed by Hong [1985] by incorporating the fuzzy entropy concept. They discussed paths of the fuzzy extension matrix and introduced a new heuristic algorithm for generating fuzzy rules.

4.   GENERATION OF FUZZY DECISION TREES

Many methods including the famous ID3 [Quinlan, 1986] have been developed for constructing a decision tree from a collection of examples with nominal or numeric attribute data [Safavian and Landgrebe, 1991]. There is no doubt that the decision trees generated by these methods are useful in building knowledge-based expert systems. However, they often suffer from inadequacy in expressing and handling the vagueness and ambiguity associated with human thinking and perception. To overcome this shortcoming, several different approaches have been proposed. This review groups them into two categories: those fuzzifying a crisp tree with discretized intervals, and variants of fuzzy ID3 methods.

4.1   Fuzzy   interpretation   of   crisp   trees   with   discretized intervals

This group of methods basically replaces the crisp cut points decided by a discretization method by some kind of curves (membership functions) serving as fuzzy borders. With these fuzzy borders, a value can then be classified into a few different intervals at the same time, with varying membership degrees.   Categorical data can be similarly handled using a fuzzy relation table. Following this idea, Chi and Yan [1996] fuzzified an ID3-derived tree to obtain a compact set of fuzzy rules. To derive the classification of a test datum, a defuzzification method was proposed and a two-layered perceptron was used to optimize defuzzification parameters (w_{ij} denoting the contribution of rule i to class j). Wu [1999] constructed and used the fuzzy borders at deduction time only when a "no match" occurs (no rule matches with the current conditions) in the crisp sense. They tried three different functions to fuzzify the borders, which include a linear function, a third-degree polynomial, and an arctangent function. Jeng *et al.* [1997] converted a decision tree induced by a regular method into a fuzzy decision tree in which the hurdle values for splitting branches and the classes associated with leaves are fuzzy. Major problems with their method are how to determine the optimum Yager's aggregator parameter w and how to choose a proper membership function for an attribute. Wang and Hong [1998] handled the fuzziness by revising the best cut point, which is computed as the cross point of two membership functions which describe two families (assuming binary partition). They proved that the decision tree generation does not depend on the selection of membership functions in a symmetrically distributed family.

Pal and Chakraborty [2001] proposed a method to construct a fuzzy rule-based classifier system from an ID3-type decision tree (DT) for real-valued data. Their method has three major steps: rule extraction using IRID3, genetic algorithm-based tuning of the rule-base, and performance-based pruning of the rule-base. IRID3 is an improved version of RID3, which in turn is an ID3-like DT that deals with real valued data. IRID3 employs a GA using the fitness function, $E = M + \eta L$, where M denotes that percentage of misclassification, L is the average depth of classification, and η is an adaptive parameter set high initially and decreased with the number of GA iterations.   To generate fuzzy rules from the tree, each tree node was associated with a membership function of Gaussian type.   The two parameters of all Gaussian functions were tuned by a gradient descent method to minimize a pre-defined error function. The performance-based pruning involves the deletion of rules that produce too few correct classifications or fewer correct classifications than incorrect classifications.

4.2   Fuzzy ID3 Variants

Methods in this category replace the heuristic algorithm used to derive a crisp tree with something that can handle the fuzzy concept. The heuristic algorithm contains two components: an attribute selection criterion for expanding the tree and an approximate reasoning mechanism.   Some methods in this category take crisp data of nominal-valued and real-valued examples as input whereas others deal with learning from fuzzy vector-valued examples.

4.2.1   From fuzzy vector-valued examples

Yuan and Shaw [1995] studied the fuzzy classification problem, in which both objects and classes are fuzzy. An object is said to be fuzzy if at least one of its features (attributes) is fuzzy. A class is fuzzy if it can be represented in fuzzy terms. Accordingly, the training data set is fuzzy in which each feature and class could have more than one linguistic value to a different membership degree.   Those membership degrees can be subjectively assigned or transferred from numeric values by a set of membership functions defined over the range of all numeric values. The self-organizing map method was used for the latter. The method used to construct a fuzzy decision tree is similar to the non fuzzy decision tree induction method such as ID3 where the use of information entropy as the heuristic induction criterion is replaced by the measurement of classification ambiguity.   The classification ambiguity directly measures the quality of classification rules at the decision node. The induction process is effectively controlled with the use of two parameters: significant level of evidence and truth level threshold. However, no guideline was given pertaining to their selection.

Wang *et al.* [2000] proved that the generation of an optimal fuzzy decision tree (with the minimum total number of leaves) is NP-hard and proposed a merging-branches (MB) algorithm for fuzzy decision tree generation. The experimental results showed that the size of each tree and the test accuracy of the MB algorithm were superior to that of the fuzzy ID3, but the training speed of the former algorithm was slightly slower than that of the latter.

Tsang *et al.* [2000] proposed a hybrid neural network (HNN) to refine the fuzzy decision tree (FDT) learnt from fuzzy vector-valued examples. This HNN, designed according to the generated FDT and trained by an algorithm derived by the authors, results in a FDT with parameters, thus called weighted FDT. A weighted FDT refers to a FDT in which several parameters are attached to each leaf node. These parameters include certainty factor (the degree of truth of the classification corresponding to the leaf node), local weights (the degree of importance of each segment in one path contributing to the classification of the leaf node), and global weights (the degree of importance of the leaf node contributing to the conclusion of classification). The local weights and global weights are refined by a HNN to improve the learning accuracy. To this end, the weighted FDT is first converted into an equivalent set of production rules and then it is mapped to a three-layer neural network comprising the term layer, the rule layer, and the classification layer. The local weights are regarded as the connection weights between the term layer and the rule layer whereas the global weights are regarded as the connection weights between the rule layer and the classification layer. The "minimum" operator and the "maximum" operator are used as the activity function in the rule layer and the classification layer, respectively. To modify the weights, a backpropagation algorithm was formulated for the HNN. The fuzzy reasoning mechanism is similarity based.

Wang *et al.* [2001b] analyzed and compared three heuristic algorithms for generating fuzzy decision trees: one using the fuzzy entropy of a possibilistic distribution, labeled 1st [Umanol *et al.*, 1994], another using the minimum classification ambiguity, labeled 2nd [Yuan and Shaw, 1996], and the third based on the degree of importance of attribute contributing to the classification, labeled 3rd [Yeung *et al.*, 1999]. The comparisons were two-fold. One was the analytic comparison based on the expanded attribute selection criterion and the reasoning mechanism. For the complexity, a non-rigorous relation was shown: $1^{st} \leq 2^{nd} \leq 3^{rd}$. For the comprehensibility, the relation was $1^{st} \leq 3^{rd} \leq 2^{nd}$. The max-min operator used in the 2nd method has worse reasoning accuracy than the sum-product operator used in the 1st and 3rd methods. The second comparison was experimental based on the size of trees (number of nodes and leaves), the learning accuracy (training and testing), and the robustness (prediction accuracy by dropping an attribute). The 3rd method was found to be better in terms of both learning accuracy and robustness.

Dong and Kothari [2001] proposed a fuzzy decision tree induction algorithm that utilizes look-ahead to produce smaller decision trees and as a result better generalization (test) performance. The algorithm is based on establishing the decision at each internal node by jointly optimizing the node splitting criterion (information gain or gain ratio) and the classifiability of instances along each branch of the node. The classifiability of instances is evaluated in terms of the smoothness of the class label surface of instances assigned to that branch, based on a modified co-occurrence matrix.

4.2.2   From nominal-valued and real-valued examples

While most methods require the partition of real-valued variables prior to tree construction, Janikow [1996] introduced a methodology that optimizes the partition of real-valued attributes while building the fuzzy tree. The optimization is based on genetic algorithms capable of processing constraints. All constraints are explicitly utilized to reduce the search space. Each chromosome is represented as a vector of four trapezoidal corners (parameters) denoting the fuzzy sets (values) of a known number of fuzzy attributes. The fuzzy tree quality is measured using the sum of squared errors between the acquired and the actual function on a dense sampling grid. Janikow [1998] proposed a tree building procedure same as that of ID3, but differing in that a training example can be found in a node to any degree. To calculate the number of examples falling to a node, norms used in fuzzy logic were adapted to deal with conjunctions of fuzzy propositions. To deal with missing attribute values, an example is evenly split into all children if the needed feature value is not available, and then to reduce the attribute's utilization by the percentage of examples with unknown value. He also defined a number of alternatives for knowledge inference based on rule-based systems and fuzzy control.

Chen and Yeh [1997] presented a fuzzy concept learning system (FCLS) algorithm for constructing a fuzzy decision tree from a relational database system. For attribute selection, the fuzziness of attribute (FA) concept was used. For every path from the root to a leaf in the fuzzy decision tree created by the proposed FCLS algorithm, if there are some null paths, then a hypothetical certainty factor (HCF) node is created for each null path to make the fuzzy decision tree complete.

Ichihashi *et al.* [1996] introduced the random set notion to the fuzzy ID3 in order to cope with expert's ignorance due to partial knowledge about the class information. The information entropy was defined using the evidence theory (instead of the Bayesian probability), and solved as a linear programming problem. The fuzzy attribute values were assumed to be B-spline functions of degree 2. The fuzzy decision tree which consists of B-spline membership functions was regarded as a three-layered neural network. They developed an algebraic learning method to tune the fuzzy rules. It varies the learning rate depending upon the square sum of compatibility degrees of the rules.

Boyen and Wehenkel [1999] described an algorithm able to infer fuzzy decision trees in domains where most of the input variables are numerical and the output information is best characterized as a fuzzy set. The algorithm is composed of three complimentary steps: growing (selecting relevant attributes and fuzzy thresholds), pruning (determining the appropriate tree complexity), and refitting (tuning the tree parameters in a global fashion). The fuzzy tree is grown in a top-down recursive partitioning approach, similar to growing a classical tree, using some ad hoc score function. At each step of the pruning procedure, a test-node is selected and the subtree starting at this node is replaced by a terminal node, and the resulting simpler tree is stored. The process terminates upon reaching the trivial single-node tree. The generalization capabilities of all the intermediate trees are evaluated on the independent pruning sample (not used for tree growing) and the best tree is chosen. The refitting step tunes the location values as well as the shape parameters of the test node discriminators (such as piecewise linear) and of the labels installed at the leaves using a mean square error type of criterion.

Chiang and Hsu [2002] defined a fuzzy entropy function based on the possibility concept and presented a learning algorithm for constructing a fuzzy classification tree (FCT) from a set of training instances containing real-valued attributes. The FCM algorithm was used to determine the membership function from a data set.

5.   APPLICATIONS

Previous fuzzy models were developed primarily for five major categories of applications: function approximation, classification, control, time series prediction, and other decision-making problems. The studies that address various problems in each category are summarized below. To save space, the data sets are not described. Interested readers may refer to the original papers for data sources and descriptions.

5.1   Function Approximation Problems
- Exclusive OR [Enbutsu et al., 1991]
- Seven-dimensional nonlinear function [Nawa and Furuhashi, 1999]
- Single-input single-output nonlinear system [Chan et al., 1995]
- Three-D functions [Cordón and Herrera, 2000], [Lin et al., 1997], [Zhang and Knoll, 1999], [Sugeno and Yasukawa, 1993], [Emami et al., 1998], [Kilic et al., 2002], [Klawonn and Kruse, 1997], [Delgado et al., 1997], [Cordón and Herrera, 1997], [Herrera et al., 1998], [Cordón et al., 1998], [Russo, 1998], [Russo, 2000], [Kang et al., 2000], [Lin and Cunningham, 1995], [Azeem et al., 2000], [Chakraborty and Pal, 2001]

5.2   Classification Problems
- 2-input functional classification [Ishibuchi et al., 1992], [Chen and Chang, 2000]
- Benchmark data such as iris [Li et al., 2002], [Ishibuchi et al., 1995], [Ishibuchi et al., 1997], [Ravi et al., 2001], [Ishibuchi et al., 1993], [Kbir et al., 2000], [Ishibuchi and Nakashima, 2001], [Abe and Lan, 1995], [Espinosa and Vandewalle, 2000], [Yao et al., 2000], [Russo, 2000], Shi et al. [1999], [Surmann and Selenschtschikow, 2002], [Peña-Reyes and Sipper, 2001], [Li et al.,

2002], [Huang and Xing, 2002], [Quek and Tung, 2001], [Nauck and Kruse, 1997], [Behloul *et al.*, 2002], [Castro and Zurita, 1997], [Wu and Chen, 1999], [Castro *et al.*, 1999], [Castro *et al.*, 2001], [Hong and Chen, 1999], [Hong and Chen, 2000], [Wang *et al.*, 1999], [Wu, 1999], [Jeng *et al.*, 1997], [Pal and Chakraborty, 2001], [Tsang *et al.*, 2000], [Wang *et al.*, 2001], [Dong and Kathari, 2001], [Chiang and Su, 2002]

- Recognition of handwritten numeral [Chi and Yan, 1996], handwritten Chinese characters [Wang *et al.*, 2000]
- Classification of radar returns from the Ionosphere [Surmann and Selenschtschikow, 2002], [Chiang and Su, 2002]
- License plate recognition [Abe and Lan, 1995]
- Medical diagnosis such as hepatobiliary disorders [Mitra *et al.*, 1997], diabetes mellitus [Su and Chang, 2000], Sleep states [Wang *et al.*, 2000]
- Rice taste evaluation [Cordón and Herrera, 2000], [Wang *et al.*, 2001], [Tsang *et al.*, 2000], [Wang *et al.*, 2001]
- Speech recognition [Mitra *et al.*, 1997], [Quek and Tung, 2001]
- Fault diagnosis of welds [Ravi *et al.*, 2001], turbine generators [Wang *et al.*, 2000]

5.3   Control Problems
- Backing a truck to a loading dock [Wang and Mendel, 1993], [Homaifar and McCormick, 1995], [Su and Chang, 2000]
- Cart-centering [Carse *et al.*, 1996]
- Cart-pole balancing [Heider and Drabe. 1997], [Lin and Lu, 1995], [Zhang and Kandel, 1998], [Kaur and Lin, 1998]
- Collision avoidance [Hiraga *et al.*, 1995]
- Inverse pendulum [Delgado *et al.*, 1997], [Gómex-Skarmeta and Jiménez, 1999], [Delgado *et al.*, 1998], [Xiong and Litz, 2002], [Rutkowska, 1998]
- Laser tracking [Zhuang and Wu, 2001]
- Machining operation [Tarng *et al.*, 1996]
- Mobile robot navigation [Russo, 1998]
- Network routing control [Carse *et al.*, 1996]
- Polymerization control [Sugeno and Yasukawa, 1993], [Russo, 2000], [Lin and Cunningham, 1995], [Chakraborty and Pal, 2001]
- Traffic intersection control [Lekova *et al.*, 1998]
- Water purification process control [Sugeno and Yasukawa, 1993]

5.4   Time Series Prediction Problems

- Box and Jenkins gas furnace data [Lin *et al.*, 1997], [Zhang and Knoll, 1999], [Sugeno and Yasukawa, 1993], [Emami *et al.*, 1998], [Delgado *et al.*, 1997], [Gómex-Skarmeta and Jiménez, 1999], [Delgado *et al.*, 1998], [Surmann and Selenschtschikow, 2002], [Kang *et al.*, 2000], [Lin and Cunningham, 1995]
- Health related monitoring such as plasma alprazolam concentrations [Kilic *et al.*, 2002]
- Stock prices [Lin *et al.*, 1997], [Sugeno and Yasukawa, 1993], [Lin and Cunningham, 1995], [Azeem *et al.*, 2000]
- The Mackey-Glass chaotic time series [Wang and Mendel, 1993], [Espinosa and Vandewalle, 2000], [Russo, 2000]
- Traffic flow [Quek and Tung, 2001], [Quek and Zhou, 2001]

5.5   Other Decision-Making Problems

- Electricity network length [Cordón and Herrera, 2001]
- Mechanical property prediction [Chen and Linkens, 2001]
- Power system transient stability [Boyen and Wehenkel, 1999]
- Surface roughness estimation [Ichihashi *et al.*, 1996]

6.   DISCUSSION

Among all the papers reviewed in this chapter, we are interested in those that satisfy all the four necessary conditions for a fuzzy model (either a set of fuzzy rules or a fuzzy decision tree) to be interpretable, as set forth in the Introduction. We will highlight only those studies satisfying all the four conditions or the first three in the case that there is no study satisfying all four in some category and point out possible topics for future study. Furthermore, some general comments about each category of fuzzy modeling methods will also be made.

None of the above-reviewed papers in the grid partitioning category satisfy all the four necessary conditions. Two studies satisfying the first three conditions are Ishibuchi *et al.* [1997] and Castro *et al.* [2001]. Both of them arbitrarily set the number of fuzzy partitions and did not attempt to optimize the parameters. One major difference between the two studies is that the latter allows a variable to have a subset of fuzzy terms as its value as a result of the amplification process in their rule generation algorithm. Future studies should investigate how to improve them by addressing the two shortcomings. The grid partitioning methods will work fine for a low-dimensional system, but not a high-dimensional system due to the explosion of the model size (i.e., the number of rules).

By nature, the fuzzy clustering methods that project to the Cartesian input-space will never be able to satisfy all the four conditions because the projected n-dimensional fuzzy sets are difficult to interpret. The work of Emami *et al.* [1998] loosely satisfies all the four necessary conditions. Their method could be more complete if a parameter tuning step is added. How the projected fuzzy sets are approximated seems to play a key role in determining the tradeoff between interpretability and performance.

Unfortunately, studies are lacking in this area. Recently it was showed how the fuzzy exponent, m, could affect the shape of membership function if fuzzy c-means [Liao *et al.*, 2003] or fuzzy c-medians [Liao, 2001] is used to define fuzzy concepts from data. Will the m value affect the way projected fuzzy sets should be approximated? Kilic *et al.* [2002] pointed out the potential problems of projecting one dimension at a time, especially for clusters with irregular shapes, such as ring-shaped clusters.

A more detailed examination of the problem identified by Kilic *et al.* is warranted as well. It is our opinion that such a study should also examine the effects of using various types of fuzzy clustering algorithm specially designed for non-spherical or other unique cluster shapes.   Generally speaking, fuzzy clustering methods are better suited for modeling high-dimensional systems than any other methods and can work with a small amount of training examples.

Six GA-based fuzzy modeling papers satisfy all the four necessary conditions. They include Heider and Drabe [1997], Shi *et al.* [1999], Xiong and Litz [2002], Kang *et al.* [2000], Nawa and Furuhashi [1999], Surmann and Selenschtschitow [2002].   Among them, the first one models the system in stages. Since membership functions and rule sets are co-dependent, the final model obtained by modeling the system in stages might not be really optimal. The other five took the simultaneous approach by allowing the GA to evolve fuzzy sets and rules at the same time.   The downside of the simultaneous approach is that it increases the size of the search space in the sense that there are more parameters to adapt. This makes modeling potentially more difficult and more training data might be needed. GAs are known to be computationally expensive.

The problem becomes much acute in modeling a high dimensional system. It is informative to conduct a comparative study of both approaches (sequential vs. simultaneous) for different problem sizes and training data sizes. Unlike the first three, the last three studies model the membership functions locally, meaning that each membership function defined for a particular variable is unique to each rule and not shared by other rules. This could complicate the interpretation task, especially when there are many membership functions defined in this way.   There is also a lack of comparative studies of different implementations of the simultaneous approach. Among the five methods cited above, which one is the best? A study that answers this question would definitely be useful.

In the neural network category the methods proposed by Azeem *et al.* [2000], Chakraborty and Pal [2001], Lin and Cunningham [1995], Lin and Lu [1995], Quek and Zhou [2001], and Chen and Linkens [2001] satisfy all the four conditions. The last method uses a modified competitive learning algorithm to construct the initial rule set whereas the rest start with all possible fuzzy rules. In some way, the last method works similarly to the fuzzy clustering methods, except that the fuzzy set parameters are optimized by backpropagation rather than by approximation. Each neural fuzzy system implements some fuzzy inference system. However, rarely there is a justification why such a fuzzy inference system is chosen. It is desirable to first figure out what is the best fuzzy inference system for a particular application (if not for all applications) and then design a corresponding neural fuzzy system. Without exception, the learning processes all take place in phases for each method mentioned above. The method of Lin and Lu and the method of Quek and Zhou identify parameters first whereas the other three methods identify the structure first. Therefore, they operate much like the sequential approach of genetic algorithm methods, but based on different learning principles: in fact, network learning could be done by GA. In this sense, it will be interesting to compare the final fuzzy models obtained by neural fuzzy systems versus those generated by genetic algorithms. A high-dimensional system generally cannot be handled well by the neural network approach because large network size could greatly hamper network learning.

By the nature of tree induction, all fuzzy decision tree generation methods use a subset of variables in some branches of the tree. Among all those reviewed, both the studies of Pal and Chakraborty [2001] and Boyen and Wehenkel [1999] satisfy all four conditions. The former method starts with inducing a crisp tree first, whereas the latter method induces a fuzzy tree directly. Once the tree is grown, the former method tunes the parameters first and then prunes the tree. The latter method does the opposite. It is unclear which order is preferable, and we are not aware of any study addressing this issue. In spirit, the fuzzy decision tree methods are closer to symbolic machine learning than other fuzzy modeling methods. It is interesting to know how fuzzy decision tree methods compare with crisp decision tree methods in terms of performance and computational cost. Another possible future study is to investigate the resulting interpretability/accuracy tradeoff if several attributes are combined at a test node.

Overall, there is a lack of information regarding the relative effectiveness and the efficiency of different fuzzy modeling methods across category. This seems to be a difficult task for a single researcher to undertake. A coordinated team effort from a group of researchers might be the best way to address this issue. The results are potentially useful to researchers so that their efforts can be better directed to advance the field. This information is also indispensable to potential users so that best results can be obtained with economic use of their resources.

Lastly, the bulk of the studies were shown to work by using relatively small amount of training data, from the perspective of data mining research. To the best of our knowledge, none of the fuzzy modeling methods reviewed in this chapter has been put to the test for any real-world data mining task. Such a task is what each one of these fuzzy modeling methods needs to pass for it to become a viable data mining tool. A conscientious effort is needed here. Some parallel versions of GAs have been proposed, but we are not aware of any use in fuzzy modeling yet. A similar development for each category of methods is desirable in order to scale up the methods for handling a large volume of data. The interactions between instance selection and fuzzy modeling also warrant investigations. For a high-dimensional system, attribute selection might be needed to reduce the dimensionality of the system before applying a fuzzy modeling method.

7. CONCLUSIONS

This chapter has given a review of fuzzy modeling methods proposed for the generation of human-understandable fuzzy If-Then rules or fuzzy decision trees. One common feature of these methods is that they all can handle imprecise and ambiguous data, an issue that is somewhat neglected by the data mining community at this juncture. The underlying principle is the fuzzy set theory first proposed by Zadeh in 1965. Even though Section 2 described some of the basic concepts, this chapter was written with the assumption that the readers already possess some basic knowledge about the fuzzy set theory. Moreover, readers are assumed to be familiar with the numerous technical terminologies mentioned in this review chapter.

Each fuzzy modeling method reviewed in this chapter was analyzed in view of the seven fuzzy modeling issues laid out in the Introduction. For easy comparison, a summary is also provided in Table 1. In addition, we introduced one more condition to complement the three conditions originally set forth by Guillaume [2001] for a fuzzy model to be interpretable. Those methods that satisfy all four conditions were identified in the Discussion. A number of possible topics for future study to advance those methods for data mining purpose were also identified. We sincerely hope that this review chapter will kindle greater interest in further advancement of fuzzy modeling for data mining and knowledge discovery in the future.

REFERENCES

1. Abe, S. and Lan, M.-S., "A method for fuzzy rules extraction directly from numerical data and its application to pattern recognition," *IEEE Trans. Fuzzy Systems*, 3(1), 1995, 18-28.

2. Azeem, M. F., Hanmandlu, M., and Ahmad, N., "Generalization of adaptive neuro-fuzzy inference systems," *IEEE Trans. Neural Networks*, 11(6), 2000, 1332-1346.

3. Behloul, F., Lelieveldt, B. P. F., Boudraa, A., and Reiber, J. H. C., "Optimal design of radial basis function neural networks for fuzzy rule extraction in high dimensional data," *Pattern Recognition*, 35, 2002, 659-675.

4. Boyen, X. and Wehenkel, L., "Automatic induction of fuzzy decision trees and its application to power system security assessment," *Fuzzy Sets and Systems*, 102, 1999, 3-19.

5. Carse, B., Fogarty, T. C., and Munro, A., "Evolving fuzzy rule based controllers using genetic algorithms," *Fuzzy Sets and Systems*, 80, 1996, 273-293.

6. Castro, J. L. and Zurita, J. M., "An inductive learning algorithm in fuzzy systems," *Fuzzy Sets and Systems*, 89, 1997, 193-203.

7. Castro, J. L., Castro-Schez, J. J., and Zurita, J. M., "Learning maximal structure rules in fuzzy logic for knowledge acquisition in expert systems," *Fuzzy Sets and Systems*, 101, 1999, 331-342.

8. Castro, J. L., Castro-Schez, J. J., and Zurita, J. M., "Use of a fuzzy machine learning technique in the knowledge acquisition process," *Fuzzy Sets and Systems*, 123, 2001, 307-320.

9. Chakraborty, D. and Pal, N. R., "Integrated feature analysis and fuzzy rule-based system identification in a neuro-fuzzy paradigm," *IEEE Trans. Systems, Man, Cybernetics- Part B: Cybernetics*, 31(3), 2001, 391-400.

10. Chan, K. C., Lin, G. C. I., and Leong, S. S., "A more accurate adaptive fuzzy inference system", *Computers in Industry*, 26, 1995, 61-73.

11. Chen, J.-L. and Chang, J.-Y., "Fuzzy perceptron neural networks for classifiers with numerical data and linguistic rules as inputs," *IEEE Trans. On Fuzzy Systems*, 8(6), 2000, 730-745.

12. Chen, M.Y. and Likens, D. A., "A systematic neuro-fuzzy modeling framework with application to material property prediction," *IEE Trans. Systems, Man, Cybernetics- Part B: Cybernetics*, 31(5), 2001, 781-790.

13. Chen, S.-M. and Yeh, M.-S., "Generating fuzzy rules from relational database systems for estimating null values," *Cybernetics and Systems*, 28, 1997, 695-723.

14. Chi, Z. and Yan, H., "ID3-derived fuzzy rules and optimized defuzzification for handwritten numeral recognition," *IEEE Trans. On Fuzzy Systems*, 4(1), 1996, 24-31.

15. Chiang, I.-J. and Hsu, J. Y., "Fuzzy classification trees for data analysis," *Fuzzy Sets and Systems*, 130, 2002, 87-99.

16. Cho, H.-J., Cho, K.-B., and Wang, B.-H., "Fuzzy-PID hybrid control: automatic rule generation using genetic algorithms", *Fuzzy Sets and Systems*, 92, 1997, 305-316.

17. Cordón, O. and Herrera, F., "A three-stage evolutionary process for learning descriptive and approximate fuzzy-logic-controller knowledge base from examples," *Int. J. of Approximate Reasoning*, 17, 1997, 369-407.

18. Cordón, O. and Herrera, F., "A proposal for improving the accuracy of linguistic modeling", *IEEE Trans. Fuzzy Systems*, 8(3), 2000, 335-344.

19. Cordón, O. and Herrera, F., "Hybridizing genetic algorithms with sharing scheme and evolution strategies for designing approximate fuzzy rule-based systems," *Fuzzy Sets and Systems*, 118, 2001, 235-255.

20. Cordón, O., Herrera, F., and Lozano, M., "On the combination of fuzzy logic and evolutionary computation: A short review and bibliography," in *Fuzzy Evolutionary Computation*, W. Pedrycz, Ed., Norwell, MA: Kluwer, 1997, 33-56.

21. Cordón, O., del Jusus, M. J., and Herrera, F., "Genetic learning of fuzzy rule-based classification systems cooperating with fuzzy reasoning methods," *Int. J. Intelligent Systems*, 13, 1998, 1025-1053.

22. Delgado, M., Gómez-Skarmeta, A. F., and Martín, F., "A fuzzy clustering-based rapid prototyping for fuzzy rule-based modeling", *IEEE Trans. Fuzzy Systems*, 5(2), 1997, 223-232.

23. Delgado, M. and Gonzalez, A., "An inductive learning procedure to identify fuzzy systems", *Fuzzy Sets and Systems*, 55, 1993, 121-132.

24. Dong, M. and Kothari, R., "Look-ahead based fuzzy decision tree induction," *IEEE Trans. On Fuzzy Systems*, 9(3), 2001, 461-468.

25. Dueck, G. and Scheuer, T., "Threshold accepting: A general purpose optimization algorithm appearing superior to simulated annealing," *J. Comput. Phys.*, 90, 1990, 161-175.

26. Emami, M. R., Türksen, I. B., and Goldenberg, A. A., "Development of a systematic methodology of fuzzy logic modeling", *IEEE Trans. Fuzzy Systems*, 6(3), 1998, 346-361.

27. Enbutsu, I., Baba, K., and Hara, N., "Fuzzy rule extraction from a multilayereed neural network", *Proc. Of IJCNN* '91, Seattle, 1991, II-461-465.

28. Espinosa, J. and Vandewalle, J., "Constructing fuzzy models with linguistic integrity from numerical data-AFRELI algorithm", *IEEE Trans. Fuzzy Systems*, 8(5), 2000, 591-600.

29. Gómez-Skarmeta, A. F. and Jiménez, F., "Fuzzy modeling with hybrid systems", *Fuzzy Sets and Systems*, 104, 1999, 199-208.

30. Guillaume, S., "Designing fuzzy inference systems from data: an interpretability-oriented review", *IEEE Trans. Fuzzy Systems*, 9(3), 2001, 426-443.

31. Heider H. and Drabe, T., "A cascaded genetic algorithm for improving fuzzy system design," *Int. J. Approximate Reasoning*, 17, 1997, 351-368.

32. Herrera, F., Lozano, M. and Verdegay, J. L., "A learning process for fuzzy control rules using genetic algorithms", *Fuzzy Sets and Systems*, 100, 1998, 143-158.

33. Hiraga, I., Furuhashi, T., Uchikawa, Y., and Nakayama, S., "An acquisition of operator's rules for collision avoidance using fuzzy neural networks," *IEEE Trans. Fuzzy Systems*, 3(3), 1995, 280-287.

34. Hirota, K. and Pedrycz, W., "Directional fuzzy clustering and its application to fuzzy modeling," *Fuzzy Sets and Systems*, 80, 1996, 315-326.

35. Homaifar, A. and McCormick, E., "Simultaneous design of membership functions and rule sets for fuzzy controllers using genetic algorithms", *IEEE Trans. Fuzzy Systems*, 3(2), 1995, 129-138.

36. Hong, J. R., "AE1: extension matrix approximate method for general covering problem," *Int. J. Comput. Inform. Sci.*, 14(6), 1985, 421-437.

37. Hong, T. P. and Chen, J.-B., "Finding relevant attributes and membership functions," *Fuzzy Sets and Systems*, 103, 1999, 389-404.

38. Hong, T. P. and Chen, J.-B., "Processing individual fuzzy attributes for fuzzy rule induction," *Fuzzy Sets and Systems*, 112, 2000, 127-140.

39. Huang, S. H. and Xing, H., "Extract intelligent and concise fuzzy rules from neural networks," *Fuzzy Sets and Systems*, 132, 2002, 233-243.

40. Ishibuchi, H., Murata, T., and Türksen, I. B., "Single-objective and two-objective genetic algorithms for selecting linguistic rules for pattern classification problems," *Fuzzy Sets and Systems*, 89, 1997, 135-150.

41. Ishibuchi, H., Nozaki, K., and Tanaka, H., "Distributed representation of fuzzy rules and its application to pattern recognition", *Fuzzy Sets and Systems*, 52, 1992, 21-32.

42. Ishibuchi, H., Nozaki, K., and Tanaka, H., "Efficient fuzzy partition of pattern space for classification problems", *Fuzzy Sets and Systems*, 59, 1993, 295-304.

43. Ishibuchi, H., Nozaki, K., Yamamoto, N. and Tanaka, H., "Selecting fuzzy If-Then rules for classification problems using genetic algorithms," *IEEE Trans. Fuzzy Systems*, 3(3), 1995, 260-270.

44. Ishihashi, H., Shirai, T., Nagasaka, K., and Miyoshi, T., "Neuro-fuzzy ID3: a method of inducing fuzzy decision trees with linear programming

for maximizing entropy and an algebraic method for incremental learning," *Fuzzy Sets and Systems*, 81, 1996, 157-167.

45. Janikow, C. Z., "A genetic algorithm method for optimizing fuzzy decision trees," *Information Sciences*, 89, 1996, 275-296.

46. Janikow, C. Z., "Fuzzy decision trees: issues and methods," *IEEE Trans. Systems, Man, and Cybernetics-Part B: Cybernetics*, 28(1), 1998, 1-14.

47. Jeng, B., Heng, Y.-M., and Liang, T. P., "FILM: a fuzzy inductive learning method for automated knowledge acquisition," *Decision Support Systems*, 21, 1997, 61-73.

48. Kang, S.-J., Woo, C.-H., Hwang, H.-S., Woo, K. B., "Evolutionary design of fuzzy rule base for nonlinear system modeling and control," *IEEE Trans. Fuzzy Systems*, 8(1), 2000, 37-44.

49. Kaur, D. and Lin, B., "On the design of neural-fuzzy control system", *Int. J. of Intelligent Systems*, 13, 1998, 11-26.

50. Kbir, M. A., Benkirane, H., Maalmi, K., and Benslimane, R., "Hierarchical fuzzy partition for pattern classification with fuzzy If-Then rules", *Pattern Recognition Letters*, 21, 2000, 503-509.

51. Kilic, K, Sproule, B. A., Türksen, I. B., and Naranjo, C. A., "Fuzzy system modeling in pharmacology: an improved algorithm," *Fuzzy Sets and Systems*, 130, 2002, 253-264.

52. Kim, C. J., "An algorithmic approach for fuzzy inference," *IEEE Trans. Fuzzy Systems*, 5(4), 1997, 585-598.

53. Klawonn, F. and Kruse, R., "Constructing a fuzzy controller from data", *Fuzzy Sets and Systems*, 85, 1997, 177-193.

54. Lekova, A., Mikhailov, L., Boyadjiev, D., and Nabout, A., "Redundant fuzzy rules exclusion by genetic algorithms", *Fuzzy Sets and Systems*, 100, 1998, 235-243.

55. Li, R. P., Mukaidono, M., and Türksen, I. B., "A fuzzy neural network for pattern recognition and feature selection," *Fuzzy Sets and Systems*, 130, 2002, 101-108.

56. Liao, T. W., "A fuzzy c-medians variant for the generation of fuzzy term sets," *Int. J. Intelligent Systems*, 17(1), 2001.

57. Liao, T. W., Celmins, A. K., and Hammell, R. J., II, "A fuzzy c-means variant for the generation of fuzzy term sets," *Fuzzy Sets and Systems*, 135, 2003, 241-257.

58. Lin, C.-T. and Lee, C. S. G., "Neural network-based fuzzy logic control and decision system", *IEEE Trans. Computing*, 40(12), 1991, 1320-1336.

59. Lin, C.-T. and Lu, Y.-C., "A neural fuzzy system with linguistic teaching signals," *IEEE Trans. Fuzzy Systems*, 3(2), 1995, 169-189.

60. Lin, Y. and Cunningham, G. A., II, "A new approach to fuzzy-neural system modeling," *IEEE Trans. Fuzzy Systems*, 3, 1995, 190-198.

61. Lin, Y., Cunningham, G. A., II, and Coggeshall, S. V., "Using fuzzy partitions to create fuzzy systems from input-output data and set the

initial weights in a fuzzy neural network", *IEEE Trans. Fuzzy Systems*, 5(4), 1997, 614-621.

62. Mamdani, E. H. and Assilian, S., "An experiment in linguistic synthesis with a fuzzy logic controller", *Int. J. Man-Mach. Stud.*, 7, 1975, 1-13.

63. Mikhailov, L., Lekova, A., and Nabout, A., "Method for fuzzy rule extraction from numerical data", *Complex Systems*, 1, 1996, 23-33.

64. Mitra, S., De, R. K., and Pal, S. K., "Knowledge-based fuzzy MLP for classification and rule generation", *IEEE Trans. Neural Networks*, 8(6), 1997, 1338-1350.

65. Mitra, S. and Hayashi, Y., "Neuro-fuzzy rule generation: survey in soft computing framework," *IEEE Trans. Neural Networks*, 11(3), 2000, 748-768.

66. Nauck, D., Klawonn, F., and Kruse, R., *Foundations of Neuro-Fuzzy Systems*. Chichester, U. K.: Wiley, 1997.

67. Nauck, D. and Kruse, R., "A neuro-fuzzy method to learn fuzzy classification rules from data," *Fuzzy Sets and Systems*, 89, 1997, 277-288.

68. Nawa, N. E. and Furuhashi, T., "Fuzzy system parameters discovery by bacterial evolutionary algorithm," *IEEE Trans. Fuzzy Systems*, 7(5), 1999, 608-616.

69. Nozaki, K., Ishibuchi, H., and Tanaka, H., "Adaptive fuzzy rule-based classification systems", *IEEE Trans. Fuzzy Systems*, 4(3), 1996, 238-250.

70. Pal, N. R. and Chakraborty, S., "Fuzzy rule extraction from ID3-type decision trees for real data," *IEEE Trans. On Systems, Man, and Cybernetics-Part B: Cybernetics*, 31(5), 2001, 745-754.

71. Pedrycz, W. "Fuzzy set technology in knowledge discovery," *Fuzzy Sets and Systems*, 98, 1998, 279-290.

72. Peña-Reyes, C. A. and Sipper, M., "Fuzzy CoCo: a cooperative-coevolutionary approach to fuzzy modeling", *IEEE Trans. On Fuzzy Systems*, 9(5), 2001, 727-737.

73. Quek, C. and Tung, W. L., "A novel approach to the derivation of fuzzy membership functions using the Falcon-MART architecture", *Pattern Recognition Letters*, 22, 2001, 941-958.

74. Quek, C. and Zhou, R. W., "The POP learning algorithms: reducing work in identifying fuzzy rules," *Neural Networks*, 14, 2001, 1431-1445.

75. Quinlan, J. R., "Induction of decision trees," *Machine Learning*, 1(1), 1986, 81-106.

76. Ravi, V., Reddy, P. J., and Zimmermann, H.-J., "Fuzzy rule base generation for classification and its minimization via modified threshold accepting", *Fuzzy Sets and Systems*, 120, 2001, 271-279.

77. Russo, M., "FuGeNeSys-A fuzzy genetic neural system for fuzzy modeling", *IEEE Trans. Fuzzy Systems*, 6(3), 1998, 373-388.

78. Russo, M., "Genetic fuzzy learning", *IEEE Trans. Evolutionary Computation*, 4(3), 2000, 259-273.

79. Rutkowska, D., "On generating fuzzy rules by an evolutionary approach", *Cybernetics and Systems*, 29, 1998, 391-407.

80. Safavian, S. R. and Landgrebe, D., "A survey of decision tree classifier methodology," *IEEE Trans. Systems Man Cybernet.*, 21, 1991, 600-674.

81. Shi, Y., Eberhart, R., and Chen Y., "Implementation of evolutionary fuzzy systems," *IEEE Trans. On Fuzzy Systems*, 7(2), 1999, 109-119.

82. Su, M.-C. and Chang, H.-T., "Application of neural networks incorporated with real-valued genetic algorithms in knowledge acquisition," *Fuzzy Sets and Systems*, 112, 2000, 85-97.

83. Sugeno, M. and Kang, G. T., "Fuzzy modeling and control of multiplayer incinerator", *Fuzzy Sets and Systems*, 18, 1986, 329-346.

84. Sugeno, M. and Yasukawa, T., "A fuzzy-logic-based approach to qualitative modeling", *IEEE Trans. Fuzzy Systems*, 1(1), 1993, 7-31.

85. Surmann, H. and Selenschtschitow, A., "Automatic generation of fuzzy logic rule bases: Examples I," *Proc. Of the NF2002: First Int. ICSC Conf. on Neuro-fuzzy Technologies*, Cuba, Jan. 16-19, 2002, 75-81.

86. Takagi, T. and Sugeno, M., "Fuzzy identification of systems and its application to modeling and control", *IEEE Trans. Syst. Man, Cybernet.*, 15, 1985, 116-132.

87. Tarng, Y. S., Yeh, Z. M., and Nian, C. Y., "Genetic synthesis of fuzzy logic controllers in turning", *Fuzzy Sets and Systems*, 83, 1996, 301-310.

88. Tsang, E. C. C., Wang, X. Z., and Yeung, D. S., "Improving learning accuracy of fuzzy decision trees by hybrid neural networks," *IEEE Trans. On Fuzzy Systems*, 8(5), 2000, 601-614.

89. Umanol, M., Okamoto, H., Hatono, I., Tamura, H., Kawachi, F., Umedzu, S., and Kinoshita, J., "Fuzzy decision trees by fuzzy ID3 algorithm and its application to diagnosis systems," in *Proc. IEEE Int. Conf. on Fuzzy Systems*, June 26-29, 1994, 2113-2118.

90. Wang, X. Z., Chen, B., Qian, G., and Ye, F., "On the optimization of fuzzy decision trees," *Fuzzy Sets and Systems*, 112, 2000, 117-125.

91. Wang, X. and Hong, J., "On the handling of fuzziness for continuous-valued attributes in decision tree generation," *Fuzzy Sets and Systems*, 99, 1998, 283-290.

92. Wang, C.-H., Liu, J.-F., Hong, T.-P., and Tseng, S.-S., "A fuzzy inductive learning strategy for modular rules," *Fuzzy Sets and Systems*, 103, 1999, 91-105.

93. Wang, L.-X. and Mendel, J. M., "Generating fuzzy rules by learning from examples", *IEEE Trans. Syst. Man Cybernet.*, 22(6), 1992, 1414-1427.

94. Wang, X. Z., Wang, Y. D., Xu, X. F., Ling, W. D., and Yeung, D. S., "A new approach to fuzzy rule generation: fuzzy extension matrix," *Fuzzy Sets and Systems*, 123, 2001a, 291-306.

95. Wang, X. Z., Yeung, D. S., and Tsang, E. C. C., "A comparative study on heuristic algorithms for generating fuzzy decision trees," *IEEE Trans. On Systems, Man, and Cybernetics-Part B: Cybernetics*, 31(2), 2001b, 215-226.

96. Wu, T.-P. and Chen, S.-M., "A new method for constructing membership functions and fuzzy rules from training examples", *IEEE Trans. Syst. Man, Cybernet.- Part B: Cybernetics*, 29(1), 1999, 25-40.

97. Wu, X., "Fuzzy interpretation of discretized intervals," *IEEE Trans. On Fuzzy Systems*, 7(6), 1999, 753-759.

98. Xiong, N. and Litz, L., "Reduction of fuzzy control rules by means of premise learning – method and case study," *Fuzzy Sets and Systems*, 132, 2002, 217-231.

99. Yang, Y., Xu, X., and Zhang, W., "Real-time stable self-learning FNN controller using genetic algorithm," *Fuzzy Sets and Systems*, 100, 1998, 173-178.

100.   Yao, J., Dash, M., Tan, S. T., and Liu, H., "Entropy-based fuzzy clustering and fuzzy modeling," *Fuzzy Sets and Systems*, 113, 2000, 381-388.

101.   Yeung, D. S., Wang, X. Z., and Tsang, E. C. C., "Learning weighted fuzzy rules from examples with mixed attributes by fuzzy decision trees," in *Proc. IEEE Int. Conf. on Systems, Man, and Cybernetics*, Tokyo, Japan, Oct. 12-15, 1999, 349-354.

102.   Yuan, Y. and Shaw, M. J., "Induction of fuzzy decision trees," *Fuzzy Sets and Systems*, 69, 1995, 125-139.

103.   Zadeh, L. A., "Outline of a new approach to the analysis of complex systems and decision processes", *IEEE Trans. Syst. Man, Cybernet.*, SMC-3, 28-44, 1973.Zadeh, L. A., "Fuzzy sets", *Information and Control*, 8, 1965, 338-353.

104.   Zhang, J. and Knoll, A., "Designing fuzzy controllers by rapid learning," *Fuzzy Sets and Systems*, 101, 1999, 287-301.

105.   Zhang, Y.-Q and Kandel, A., "Compression and expansion of fuzzy rule bases by using crisp-fuzzy neural networks," *Cybernetics and Systems*, 29, 1998, 6-34.

Appendix 1. A Summary of Grid Portioning Methods for Fuzzy Modeling.

Ref.	TPV	TS	IPMF/T	MV	RW	INOR/S
Abe and Lan [1995]	Assu.	Assu. Trap.	Hyper-boxes/No	Y	N	Iterative resolution of class overlaps/ No
Castro *et al.* [1999]	Assu.	Assu. Tri.	Assumed/No	Y	N	Proposed algorithm/ No
Castro *et al.* [2001]	Assu.	Assu. Tri.	Assumed/No	Y	N	Proposed algorithm/ GA
Chan *et al.* [1995]	Assu. One Value	Assu. Tri.	Uniform partition/No	N	Y	Modified WM/Yes
Cordón and Herrera [2000]	Assu. One Value	Assu. Tri.	Uniform partition/No	N	Y	Modified WM/GA
Ishibuchi *et al.* [1992]	Assu. Multi-Value	Assu. Tri.	Uniform partition/No	N	Y	I/No
Ishibuchi *et al.* [1995]	Assu. Multi-Value	Assu. Tri.	Uniform partition/No	N	Y	I/GA
Ishibuchi *et al.* [1997]	Assu. Multi-Value	Assu. Tri.	Uniform partition/No	Y	Y	I/GA
Ishibuchi *et al.* [1993]	Sequent. Sub-division	Assu. Tri.	Sequential subdivision/No	N	Y	Sequential subdivision/No
Kbir *et al.* [2000]	Hier. Partit.	Assu. Tri.	Hierarchical partition/No	N	Y	Hierarchical partition/ No
Lekova *et al.* [1998]	Assu. Multi-Value	Assu. Trap.	Activation rectangle/No	N	N	Activation rectangle/ GA
Lin *et al.* [1997]	Sequent. Sub-division	Assu. Trap.	Sequential subdivision/fuzzy NN	N	Y	Sequential subdivision/No
Mikhailov *et al.* [1996]	Assu. Multi-Value	Assu. Trap.	Activation rectangle/No	N	N	Activation rectangle/ No
Nozaki *et al.* [1996]	Assu. Multi-Value	Assu. Tri.	Uniform partition/No	N	Y$^{5.1}$	INT/No
Ravi *et al.* [2001]	Assu. Multi-Value	Assu. Tri.	Uniform partition/No	N	Y	Modified INT /Modified TA
Wang and Mendel [1992]	Assu. One Value	Assu. Tri.	Uniform partition/No	N	Y	WM/Yes
Zhang and Knoll [1998]	Assu.	Assu. NUBS	Initialized/Adaptation algorithm and gradient descent	N	N	Partitioning/No

Notes: a) TPV (number of terms per variable), TS, (term shape), IPMF/T (initial parameter of membership functions/parameter tuning), MV (missing variables), RW (rule weight), INOR/S (initial number of rules/rule selection)
b) 5.1 - adapted by performance

Appendix 2. A Summary of Fuzzy Clustering Methods for Fuzzy Modeling.

Ref.	TPV	TS	IPMF/T	MV	RW	INOR/S
Delgado et al. [1997]	# clusters w/wo project.	Appr. Trap.	Approximated/No	N	Y/N	Assumed # clusters/No
Emami et al. [1998]	# clusters & project.	Appr. Trap.	Approximated/No	Y	N	FCM with a validity index
Espinosa and Vandewalle [2000]	# clusters, project. & merging	Appr. Tri.	Approximated/fuzzy clustering	N	Y	AFRELI/FuZion
Gómex-Skarmeta and Jiménez [1999]	# clusters & project.	Appr. Trap.	Approximated/GA	N	N	Assumed # clusters/No
Hirota and Pedrycz [1996]	Assum.	Assu. Tri.	Directed clustering/No	N	N	Agglomeratively with an index
Kilic et al. [2002]	# clusters & n-d project.	Appr. Trap.	Approximated/Yes	Y	N	FCM with a validity index
Klawonn and Kruse [1997]	# clusters & project.	Conv. Hull/ Appr. Trap.	Approximated/No	N	N	Assumed # clusters/No
Sugeno and Yasukawa [1993]	# clusters & project.	Appr. Trap.	Approximated/No	N	N	FCM with a validity index
Yao et al. [2000]	# clusters & project.	Appr. Gaus.	EFC + Estimation/No	N	N	Entropy-based FC/No

Appendix 3. A Summary of GA Methods for Fuzzy Modeling.

Ref.	TPV	TS	IPMF/T	MV	RW	INOR/S
Carse et al. [1996]	GA-Varied	Assu. Tri.	GA	Y	N	GA/No
Cho et al. [1997]	Assu. One Value	Assu. Tri.	GA	N	N	GA/No
Cordón and Herrera [1997]	Assu.	Assu. Tri.	ES/GA	N	N	IRL-GA/GA
Cordón et al. [1998]	Assu.	Assu. Tri.	GA	N	Y	IRL-GA/GA
Cordón and Herrera [2001]	Assu.	Assu. Tri.	GA	N	N	GA-ES/GA
Gómex-Skarmeta and Jiménez [1999]	Assu. One Value	Assu. Trap.	GA	N	N	GA/Yes
Heider and Drabe [1997]	Assu.	Assu. Trap.	GA	Y	N	Cascaded GA/Yes
Herrera et al. [1998]	Assu.	Assu. Trap.	GA	N	N	IRL-GA/GA
Homaifar and McCormick [1995]	Assu.	Assu. Tri.	GA for inputs, assumed for output	N	N	GA/No
Kang et al. [2000]	EP-Varied	Assu. Trap.	EP	Y	N	EP/Yes
Nawa and Furuhashi [1999]	BEA-Varied	Assu. Tri.	BEA	Y	N	BEA/Yes
Peña-Reyes and Sipper [2001]	Assu. One Value	Assu. Tri.	Co-GA	Y	N	Co-GA/No
Russo [1998]	GA	Assu. Gaus.	GA/BP	Y	N	FuGeNeSys/No
Russo [2000]	GA	Assu. Gaus.	GA/BP	Y	N	GEFREX/No
Shi et al. [1999]	Assu. One Value	Assu. Mix of 6 Types	GA	Y	N	GA/Yes
Surmann and Selenschts-chitow [2002]	GA-Varied	Assu. Gaus.	GA	Y	N	Assumed/GA
Tarng et al. [1996]	Assu. One Value	Assu. Trap.	GA	N	N	GA/Yes
Xiong and Litz [2002]	Assu.	Assu. Tri.	GA	Y	N	GA/yes

Appendix 4. A Summary of Neural Network methods for Fuzzy Modeling.

Ref.	TPV	TS	IPMF/T	MV	RW	INOR/S
Azeem et al. [2000]	Assu.	Assu. Gaus.	Fuzzy curve/GRBF	Y	N	Fuzzy curve/GRBF
Behloul et al.[2002]	ERBFN (= # rules)	Assu. Gaus.	ERBFN	N	Y	ERBFN/No (rules with n-d input variables)
Chakraborty and Pal [2001]	Assu. Multi-Value	Assu. Gaus.	Backpropagation	Y	N	Neural fuzzy/Yes
Chen and Chang [2000]	Assu.	Assu. Sym. Tri.	Assumed/FPNN	N	N	FPNN/No
Chen and Linkens [2001]	Assu.	Assu. Gaus.	Modified competitive learning/Backpropagation	Y	N	Systematic neuro-fuzzy modeling
Enbutsu et al. [1991]	Assu.	Assu. Tri.	Assumed/No	N	N	NN/No
Hiraga et al. [1995]	Assu.	Assu. Sigm.	BP	N	N	FNN/No
Kaur and Lin [1998]	Assu.	Assu. Tri.	SOM/Backpropagation	N	N	Neural fuzzy/Combination
Li et al. [2002]	Assu.	Assu. Gaus.	FLL/No	Y	N	FWD network/No
Lin and Cunningham [1995]	Assu.	Assu. Special	Fuzzy curve/BP	Y	N	Proposed 4-step/Yes
Lin and Li [1991]	Assu.	Assu. Trap.	Assumed/BP	N	N	Falcon-ART/No
Lin and Lu [1995]	Assu.	Assu. Any	Randomly initialized/BP	Y	N	Two-phase/Yes
Mitra et al. [1997]	Assu.	Assu.	Assumed/No	N	N	Fuzzy MLP/No
Nauck and Kruse [1997]	Assu.	Assu. Tri.	Assumed/Backpropagation-like heuristic	N	N	NEFCLASS/Yes
Quek and Tung [2001]	Assu.	Assu. Trap.	Assumed/BP	N	N	Falcon-MART/No
Quek and Zhou [2001]	Assu.	Assu. Gaus.	SOM/Backpropagation	Y	N	POPFNN/Yes
Rutkowska [1998]	A ssu.	Assu. Gaus.	GA/Backpropagation	N	N	GA/No
Su and Chang [2000]	Assu. N-D	Degr. Hyper-Ellips.	GA/No	N	N	FDHECNN/No
Yang et al. [1998]	Assu.	Assu. Gaus.	Assumed/GA	N	N	Assumed +GA/No
Zhang and Kandel [1998]	Assu.	Assu. Trap.	KDBLA/No	N	N	CFNN/Yes by compression

Appendix 5. A Summary of Fuzzy Decision Tree Methods for Fuzzy Modeling.

Ref.	TPV	TS	IPMF/T	MV	RW	INOR/S
Boyen and Wehenkel [1999]	Assu.	Assu. Piece-wise Linear	Assumed/simple iteration	Y	N	Fuzzy ID3/Yes
Chen and Yeh [1997]	Assu.	Assu. Tri.	Assumed/No	Y	Y	Fuzzy ID3/No(completion)
Chiang and Hsu [2002]	Assu.	Un-defined	FCM/No	Y	N	FCT/No
Dong and Kothari [2001]	Assu.	Assu. Tri.	K-means/No	Y	N	Fuzzy ID3/No
Ichihashi *et al.* [1996]	Assu. 2nd order	Assu. B-spline	Neuro-fuzzy ID3/Yes	Y	N	Neuro-fuzzy ID3/No
Pal and Chakraborty [2001]	Fuzzy IRID3	Assu. Gaus.	Simple heuristic/gradient decent	Y	N	Fuzzy IRID3/Yes
Janikow [1996]	GA	Assu. Trap.	Assumed/GA	Y	N	Fuzzy ID3/No
Janikow [1998]	Assu.	Assu. Trap.	Assumed/No	Y	N	Fuzzy ID3/No
Tsang *et al.* [2000]	Assu.	Assu. Tri.	SOM/No	Y	Y	Fuzzy ID3/No
Wang *et al.* [2000]	Assu.	Un-defined	Undefined	Y	N	MB/No
Wang *et al.* [2001]	Assu.	Assu. Tri.	SOM/No	Y	Y	Fuzzy ID3/No
Yuan and Shaw [1995]	Assu.	Assu. Tri.	SOM/No	Y	N	Fuzzy ID3/No

AUTHOR'S BIOGRAPHICAL STATEMENT

Dr. **T. Warren Liao** received his Ph.D. from Lehigh University in 1990 in Industrial Engineering. Since then, he has been associated with the Department of Industrial and Manufacturing Systems Engineering, Louisiana State University (LSU). Currently, he is a Professor at LSU. His research interests include advanced materials and processes, intelligent manufacturing, soft computing and data mining. He has over 50 refereed journal publications appeared in IEEE Transactions, ASME Transactions, Int. J. of Machine Tools & Manufacture, Wear, J. of Intelligent Manufacturing, J. of Manufacturing Systems, Computers & IE, NDT&E International, Fuzzy Sets and Systems, Applied Artificial Intelligence, etc. Dr. Liao was on sabbatical with the Army Research Laboratory from September 2001 to August 2002. Since then, he has also been working on mining of time series data (particularly, those related to battle simulation data for military decision-making). Dr. Liao was a guest editor of several special issues, including Computers & IE, Journal of Intelligent Manufacturing, Applied Soft Computing, and International Journal of Industrial Engineering.

Chapter 16 [1]

DATA MINING FROM MULTIMEDIA PATIENT RECORDS

Adel S. Elmaghraby, Mehmed M. Kantardzic [2], and Mark P. Wachowiak
University of Louisville
Computer Engineering and Computer Science Department
J.B. Speed School of Engineering
Louisville, KY 40292
U.S.A.

Abstract: Most current patient records mining applications (for classification, prediction, and for other data mining objectives) are based on a standard representation in the form of structured records with numerical and/or categorical values. The significant advances in pre-processing, pattern recognition, and interpretation of medical images, texts and signals can, and should, be coupled with other data mining and knowledge discovery techniques, to increase the benefits of mining multimedia patient records. This integration is expected to greatly improve the results of patient records mining specifically when applied to a comprehensive set of data that includes description of the patient history and status. To achieve these objectives, careful selection of appropriate techniques is required, especially in the preprocessing phase following a specified methodology. In this chapter, the importance of preprocessing and feature extraction phases in mining large collections of multimedia patient records is emphasized. Selected techniques with illustrative examples are given showing the applicability of rule-based methodologies in the preparation phases of a data mining process.

Key Words: data mining, multimedia patient records, data transformation, feature extraction, rule-based techniques.

---

[1] Triantaphyllou, E. and G. Felici (Eds.), **Data Mining and Knowledge Discovery Approaches Based on Rule Induction Techniques**, Massive Computing Series, Springer, Heidelberg, Germany, pp. 551-595, 2006.

[2] Corresponding Author. E-mail: mmkant01@louisville.edu

1. INTRODUCTION

Health care is becoming increasingly data-driven. With the current rate of widespread use of medical information systems that include databases (which have recently experienced an explosive growth in size), health care providers, physicians and medical researchers are faced with the problem of making use of the stored data [Adibi, 2000]. These databases store a wide variety of data, including gene pools, patient's records, bedside monitoring information and physician diagnoses, and range in extent from physician office databases to hospital database management systems. Health care information is increasingly being made available on line. The rapid proliferation of vast amounts of data has led to a set of medical applications that manipulate massive amounts of dynamic, heterogeneous clinical data. Presently, physicians have at their disposal many different instruments, each providing a different *modality,* which provide complementary views of the patient. These modalities include ECG recordings, EMG, EEG and MEG signals, x-ray images, Doppler ultrasound, CAT- and PET-scans, and thus range from 1D to 4D datasets. While single modality views are sometimes sufficient to diagnose a patient (e.g., using x-rays to diagnose a simple fracture), many conditions require multi-modal information to enable a physician to diagnose a condition with confidence. When integration and fusion of data is necessary, the most suitable representation is that which can be manipulated by computer [Tang, 1999]. While the number of medical databases (and even more importantly, the amount of data within them) grows daily, both researchers and application developers have been responding to the problem of analysis and use of electronic data. Knowledge discovery and data mining in databases (KDD) is an area of common interest to researchers in machine learning, pattern recognition, statistics, intelligent databases, data visualization, high performance computing, but also signifies an important trend in medical informatics [Prather, 1997][Han, 2001].

Pattern-identification tasks, such as detecting associations between certain risk factors and outcomes, ascertaining trends in health care utilization, or discovering new models of disease in populations rapidly become daunting, even to the most experienced biomedical researcher or health care manager [Holmes, 2000]. In many systems, databases have become so large that they overwhelm traditional statistical approaches for performing these tasks. An alternative approach uses a variety of methods drawn from statistics and machine learning disciplines to mine databases for patterns that may be missed with traditional techniques. Until recently, much of the work of data mining has been the domain of a small number of computer scientists, programmers, database administrators, and management information specialists. With the amount of information and issues in healthcare industry (not to mention pharmaceutical industry and biomedical research), opportunities for data mining applications are extremely widespread, and benefits from the results are potentially enormous. The increasing development of electronic patient records and medical information systems allow a large amount of clinical data to be available online [Kohane, 1996]. Regularities, trends, and unexpected events extracted from these data by data mining methods are important in assisting clinicians to make informed decisions, and to thereby improve health services.

For medical domain understanding, the challenge is to continue developing more sophisticated techniques that can assist users in analyzing discovered knowledge easily and quickly. This paper has attempted to provide the reader with some issues of rule-based modeling techniques, an important approach to symbolic modeling. While some aspects of this technology have reached maturity and become stable, there are also many aspects that remain open. Symbolic modeling approaches are consistently robust across a wide variety of data sets, and they are based on very simple, readable, and accurate models. Therefore, they seem to be very appropriate methodologies for medical data mining.

Data mining is an iterative process with several important phases. While many researchers and practitioners recognize application of data mining tools in discovering new knowledge, less attention is given to careful and systematic preparation and integration of medical data as a source for data mining. Successful data mining applications, especially in medical domains with multimedia data, require clean, integrated medical records. In this review paper, the current methods and techniques for medical data preprocessing and integration will be reviewed. We describe characteristics of patient records, limitations, barriers, and technical challenges and successes in meeting the data requirements of a broad spectrum of clinical users employing data mining applications. Section 2 gives a brief explanation of the common phases in a data mining process. Basic characteristics and possible standards of an integrated patient record, as a source for data mining, are given in Section 3. Section 4 highlights patient record preprocessing, while Section 5 continues with methods and techniques for data transformation. Finally, Section 6 explains possibilities for dimensionality reduction in a database of patient records, and Section 7 describes some challenges and important research directions for successful preparation of patient records in a data mining process.

2.   THE DATA MINING PROCESS

The need for understanding large, complex, information-rich data sets is common to virtually all fields of business, science, and engineering. The ability to extract useful knowledge hidden in these data and to act on that knowledge is becoming increasingly important. The entire *process* of applying computer-based methodology, including new techniques for discovering various models, summaries and derived values from a given collection of data, is often called data mining [Hand, 2001]. The word "process" is very important here. Even in some professional environments, there is an apparent belief that data mining simply consists of picking and applying a computer-based tool to match the presented problem, and in obtaining a solution automatically. This is a misconception, based on an artificial idealization of the world. There are several reasons why this is incorrect.

First, the data mining is not simply a collection of isolated tools, each completely different from the other, that needs to be matched to the problem. Second, only very rarely is a research question stated with sufficient precision that a single, simple application of the method will suffice. In fact, in practice, data mining is an iterative process. One studies the data, examines it using some analytic technique, decides to look at it another way, perhaps modifying it, and then goes back to the beginning and applies another data analysis tool reaching either better (or different) results. The process can be repeated many times. Each technique is used to probe slightly different aspects of data – to ask a slightly different question of the data. What is essentially being described is a voyage of discovery. The general approach to data mining process involves the phases represented in Figure 1 [Han, 2001][Kantardzic, 2002].

Domain-specific knowledge and experience are usually necessary in order to formulate a meaningful problem statement in the first phase of a mining process. An observational data setting is assumed in most of data mining applications, where the amount of raw data is large. Typically, the sampling distribution for a data set is completely unknown after the data are collected, or it is partially given implicitly in the data collection procedure. Preprocessing includes several common tasks with a raw data set such as outlier detection (and perhaps removal), scaling, encoding, and feature selection. Generally, a good preprocessing method provides an enhanced representation for a data mining technique. Selection and implementation of an appropriate data mining technique is the main task in the phase of model estimation.

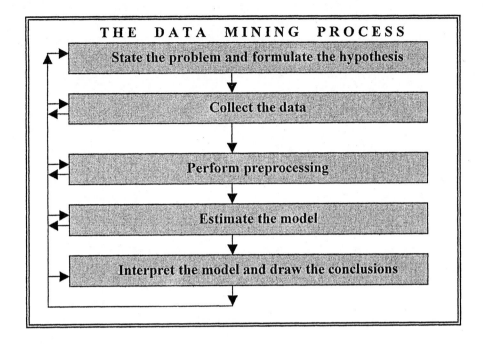

Figure 1. Phases of the Data Mining Process.

Although the potential advantages and disadvantages of utilizing each data mining method have been defined theoretically (given certain assumptions about data distribution, characteristics of the task, data-to-noise ratio etc.), it is often the case in practice that these assumptions cannot be verified. Under these circumstances, empirical comparison of data mining performances using standard metrics to describe discrimination and calibration is necessary. A final selection of the "best model" and corresponding data mining technique can only be concluded after considering the tradeoffs between algorithm performance, costs, and model interpretability. For example, for a typical mining task such as classification, we can compare the performance and results of methods such as k-nearest neighbor, logistic regression, artificial neural networks, and support vector machines. This task is not straightforward. Different approaches in verification and validation of models are available in the final phase of a data mining process assuming the trade-off between interpretability and complexity of the model.

Vast quantities of data are generated through the health care process. While technological advancements in the form of computer-based patient record software and personal computer hardware are making the collection of and access to health care data more manageable, new data mining techniques and tools are needed to evaluate and analyze large quantities of clinical data after it has been captured. Evaluation of stored clinical data may lead to the discovery of trends, patterns, and relationships hidden within the data that could significantly enhance our understanding of disease progression and management [Prather, 1997][Shortliffe, 2000].

The data mining process based on patient record data is focused on finding "interesting" and meaningful patterns within the multimedia data collection consisting of different texts, images, and laboratory data. It is assumed that a domain expert provides a distance function or a similarity function. The idea is to extract a few features out of every multimedia record, map it to a point in an n-dimensional space, and then to use fast searching methods based on available distances to discover patterns. A collection of multimedia patient records represents a specific problem for successful data mining. Extracting n features from multimedia documents has to preserve the distances between the original data. Therefore, when mapping the patents' records into points in a low n-dimensional space, the basic semantic relations between records should remain constant. This process of data transformation should be general and applicable not only for structured numerical features in patient records, but also to text documents, to time sequences (1D signals) or to 2D and 3D images which are an important part of multimedia representation. This entails transfer of the database from a comprehensive computer-based patient record system into a dataset suitable for analysis by extracting, cleaning, and preprocessing variables in the patient multimedia record.

3.   CLINICAL PATIENT RECORDS: A DATA MINING SOURCE

In today's multimedia-based environment with a huge Internet infrastructure, different types of data are generated and digitally stored. To prepare adequate data mining methods, we must analyze the basic types and characteristics of data sets. One can classify data, usually served as a source for a data mining process, into three classes [Kantardzic, 2002]:

1.   Structured data,
2.   Semi-structured data, and
3.   Unstructured data.

While structured data consist of well-defined fields with numeric or alphanumeric values, semi-structured data have only partial structure; parts are standard numeric or alphanumeric features, and the other parts are plain text, figures, or time domain signals. Examples of semi-structured data are laboratory reports, medical images, biosignal recordings, or physician reports. The majority of web documents also fall into this category. An example of unstructured data is a video recorded by a surveillance camera in an emergency room.

The complexity of the patient's record structure may be recognized by observing that these records include: encounters, historical data elements, individual lab results, subjective and physical findings, medical images, clinical laboratory, admit-discharge-transfer, pharmacy, discharge summaries, textual radiology reports, coded radiology findings, pathology, outpatient notes, and specific problems and procedures [Tang, 1999]. Obviously, some of the data are structured, but many very important components are represented in a semistructured or unstructured manner as represented in Figure 2. For example, some of the most valuable clinical data, such as admission notes, discharge summaries, progress notes, and radiology reports, are collected as a plain text. A large amount of clinical information stored in these narrative reports is inaccessible to automated data mining systems. To be useful, the information must be converted into a form that can be utilized effectively by any information system. Typically, the representation is in standardized codes, which represent not only information directly retrieved from the text, but also complex conclusions drawn from it.

The clinical laboratory assigns a unique code to all the tests it can perform. Most tests are grouped into batteries (panels) [Hripcsak, 1997]. A single patient specimen usually undergoes a battery of tests and the results are reported together. Examples of tests are the serum sodium test, a hemoglobin measurement, and a hepatitis B surface antibody titer. Examples of batteries are the chemistry panel (which includes the sodium test), an automated blood count (which includes the hemoglobin measurement), and a hepatitis panel (which includes the antibody titer). The laboratory distinguishes among tests with a very fine level of granularity. For example, a serum potassium test performed at the main medical center has a different code than an otherwise identical test performed at a satellite hospital. Whenever the machines that analyze the specimen change, a new code is assigned. The same test performed as part of two different batteries is usually (but not always) given two different codes. The codes stored in the database are defined in the institution's vocabulary. The vocabulary serves not only to define the codes, but also to map the central database codes to the codes used in local departments. It is difficult to predict which of the laboratory's many distinctions are clinically relevant. For example, a change of equipment may result in a change of normal levels, which is clinically relevant. Therefore, the central patient database maintains all the laboratory distinctions by a one-to-one mapping of the laboratory codes to distinct central MED codes [Hripcsak, 1997].

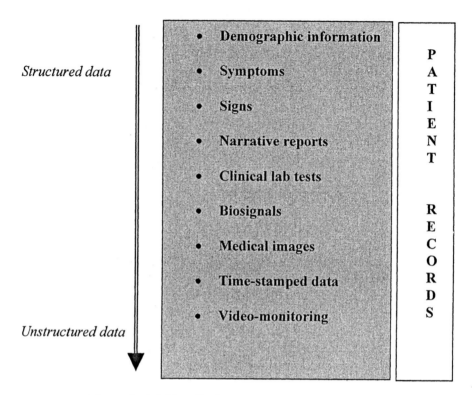

Figure 2. Multimedia Components of the Patient Record.

Medical images, including x-ray images, CAT scans, MRI scans, and ultrasound images, will be managed through the same patient record system for acquisition, storage, and transmission throughout the hearth-care environment. The goal of image integration is to develop an integrated patient record based system for archival, analysis and information distribution. Medical image database issues include image management, image retrieval and archival, image storage, image flow and image indexing in a large distributed and heterogeneous database environment. Additional software tools with corresponding standards will enable integrating this imaging information into "virtual patient folder" that contains the patient's demographic and other medical information, as well as relevant doctor's analyses in a text form [Wilcox, 1999].

Clinicians evaluate a patient's condition over time. The analysis of large quantities of time-stamped data will provide doctors with important information regarding the progression of the disease. Therefore, a patient record system should be capable of performing temporal abstraction because temporal reasoning becomes crucial in this context. Although the use of temporal reasoning methods require an intensive knowledge acquisition effort, they have found many successful medical applications, including data validation in intensive care, the monitoring of children's growth, analysis of diabetic patient's data, the monitoring of heart transplant patients, and intelligent anesthesia monitoring [Tang, 1999].

Medical research centers and other health care institutions should be interested in determining and developing data standards, vocabularies, and information infrastructure that will support mining of data collected through clinical trials. We need to understand the role of multimedia and image integration in health care, to gain a deeper understanding of the benefits of bringing these capabilities into their own clinical environments. To have access to real medical records that include images and text, and to perform data mining on these multimedia records requires a very difficult undertaking due to privacy issues and heavy bureaucratic hurdles [Mandl, 2001]. This chapter emphasizes aspects of imaging and multimedia integration that enhance the clinical records capabilities while ensuring continuity and integrity of patient information. Integration needs to be addressed at the levels of storage formats and schemas in databases. Also, we need efficient means of sharing integrated patient information across the research medical community.

Past efforts in this area have been limited primarily to epidemiological studies on administrative and claims databases [Porter, 1999]. These data sources lack the richness of information available in clinical databases. Clinical multimedia databases have accumulated large quantities of information about patients and their medical conditions in forms of medical images, lab and other measurements, narrative reports and explanations. Discovering relationships within this data may provide new medical knowledge.

To date, the burden of synthesizing different multimedia data into a single, consistent view (i.e., data fusion) is placed on the mental visualization capabilities of the physician. These processes of synthesis are extremely difficult, time-consuming, and error-prone tasks. It is a goal to develop computer-assisted methodologies and tools that increase the likelihood of a correct diagnosis and effective treatment strategy, and reduce the risk of a catastrophic misdiagnosis [Lavrac, 1999]. The next generation of datasets will incorporate higher-level relationships among the various information primitives that populate the database. To address these challenging problems for multimedia medical datasets, development of new multi-modal models based on semantically enriched data is necessary and can be achieved using new technologies.

3.1 Distributed Data Sources

Currently, most of the medical organizations have independent processes for collecting, analyzing, presenting and using clinical data. There is no systematic interaction or information sharing between different sources where the data are collected. The result is duplication of effort since some hospitals or even doctors might collect and analyze the same or similar information without realizing that the information exists elsewhere. Further, due to the independent nature of the research community, as the data are available and used locally, researchers lose the benefit of accessing data in other places. To share the data across the Internet, it is necessary to establish a system of standards that are also supported by software implementation of a schema translator. This software translates the site-internal data representation (database or file format) to the specified standards and vice-versa. The complexity of the translator includes resolving heterogeneity, autonomy, distribution and duplication issues in a distributed database of patient records. Heterogeneity needs to be addressed at three levels: storage formats, DBMS schema, and operating system [Kohane, 1996]. Concerning autonomy in patient records use, each site has the right to accept or reject requests for data or data by themselves, that are propagated from any other site. Making data available through the Internet, security cannot be compromised. Apart from the usual password protection, recent issues such as denial of service need to be addressed.

Building the infrastructure for distributed medical data mining is an important step in discovering new knowledge from medical records. It is necessary to evaluate different middleware strategies, which integrate clinical data from a variety of hospital-based data sources together with patient-reported health information, and present the data via a secure web interface [Collmann, 2001]. A promising trend in middleware organization is development of specialized Internet services that will take care not only of availability of data but also of quality, security and privacy

3.2 Patient Record Standards

A patients' medical records are generally fragmented across multiple treatment sites, posing an obstacle to clinical care, research, and public health efforts. Electronic medical records and the Internet provide a technical infrastructure on which to build longitudinal medical records that can be integrated across care sites. Choices about the structure and ownership of these records will have a profound impact on the accessibility and privacy of patient information [Tang, 1999]. The technology promising to unify the currently disparate pieces of a patient's medical record may actually threaten the accessibility of the information and compromise patients' privacy. Integrated computerized medical record should have the characteristics presented in Table 1 [Mandl, 2001].

Two main impediments stand in the way of these requirements. Firstly, patients are becoming increasingly anxious about the privacy of their medical records. Secondly, most healthcare institutions do not provide effective access for patients to their own data and, despite technical feasibility; they show little willingness to share data with their competitors [Mandl, 2001]. Therefore, many current systems fragment medical records by using incompatible means of acquiring, processing, storing, and communicating data. These incompatibilities may result from a failure to recognize the need for interoperability, or they may be deliberate, with the aim of locking consumers into using a particular system. Either way, the practice precludes sharing of data across different applications and institutions.

Patient record systems should be designed so that they can exchange all their stored data according to public standards and, at the same time, that patients should have control over access and permissions. Building software compliant with public standards will enable connectivity and interoperability even of diverse systems. Patients' control will allow protection of privacy according to individual preferences and help prevent some of the current misuses of personal medical information. However, views on the shape of standard records differ in emphasis: some anticipate records consisting of a collection of web documents, whereas others emphasize the importance of coded structured data that can be retrieved for aggregation, analysis, and decision support.

A standard in creation and maintenance of an electronic health record providing individual patient information when and where needed is underpinned by two principles: the need for public standards, and the need to respect patients' right to privacy. We refer to the efforts of HL7 (Health Level Seven) to develop public standards for health communication [Mandl, 2001]. The alternative to proprietary methods is the use of open standards. At minimum, open standards should be used in the exchange of information among different systems. For example, HL7 is a voluntary consensus standard for electronic data exchange in healthcare environments.

It defines standard message formats for sending or receiving data on patient admissions, registration, discharge, or transfer; queries; orders; results; clinical observations; and billing. Using an open messaging standard such as HL7 allows different health applications, including a laboratory system and a record system, to "talk" to each other. In May of 1999, the Computer-based Patient Record Institute (CPRI) published the "CPRI TOOLKIT: Managing Information Security in Health Care" [Cooper, 2001].

Table 1. Integrated Computerized Medical Record Characteristics.

CHARACTERISTICS OF INTEGRATED MEDICAL RECORD	Explanation
Comprehensiveness	Medical care is normally provided to a patient by different doctors, nurses, pharmacists, and ancillary providers, and, with the passage of time, by different institutions in different geographical areas. With integrated medical record, each provider must be able to know what others are currently doing and what has previously been done. Record systems should be able to accept data (historical, radiological, laboratory, etc) from multiple sources, including physician's offices, hospital computer systems, laboratories, and patients' personal computers. The records must also span a lifetime, so that a patient's medical and treatment history is available as a baseline and for retrospective analysis.
Accessibility	Data about patient may be needed at a patient's usual place of care or far from home. In addition, with patients' permission, these records should be accessible to and usable by researchers and public health authorities. Electronic medical record systems should be designed so that they can exchange all their stored data according to public standards.
Interoperability	Currently, many existing electronic medical record systems fragment medical records by adopting incompatible means of acquiring, processing, storing, and communicating data. Therefore, it will be necessary to develop standards and tools in which different computerized medical systems should be able to share records: they should be able to accept data (historical, radiological, laboratory, etc) from multiple sources, including doctors' offices, hospital computer systems, laboratories, and patients' personal computers.
Confidentiality	Patients should have the right to decide who can examine and alter parts of their medical records.
Accountability	Any access to or modification of a patient's record should be recorded and visible to the patient. Thus, data and judgments entered into the record must be identifiable by their source.
Flexibility	We believe that most people want to make data about themselves available to those genuinely trying to improve medical knowledge, the practice of medicine, the cost effectiveness of care, and the education of the next generation of healthcare providers. Patients should therefore be able to grant or deny study access to selected personal medical data.

That toolkit was designed to assist healthcare organizations address their needs in this area. The Toolkit describes requirements in each area of confidentiality and security. In Europe, CEN TC251 (European Committee for Standardization, Technical Committee for Health Informatics) undertakes similar activities, and a four part, preliminary standard on communication of electronic healthcare records was adopted in June 1999 [Markwell, 1999].

Other standards have been adopted for various other data exchanges: DICOM defines messages for encoding and exchanging medical images, and X12 is a recent set of standards for exchanging authorization, referral, and billing records [Mandl, 2001]. For different systems to share data effectively they must all use at least a common set of communication protocols and message formats and allow the import and export of all their data. Common data structures and open source programming can foster the possibility of effective data exchange among systems. Standards such as CorbaMED try to define universal object models that can be widely used among different interoperating systems. Programs that exchange data according to open standards may nevertheless store and use those data internally in proprietary ways.

4.   DATA PREPROCESSING

All raw data sets initially prepared for data mining process have the potential for being messy. One should expect missing values, distortions, misrecording, inadequate sampling, and so on in these initial data sets. Raw data, which do not exhibit any of these problems, should immediately arouse suspicion. The only real possibility for high quality is that the presented data have been cleaned and preprocessed before the application of any knowledge discovery technique.

It is very important to examine the data thoroughly before undertaking any further steps in formal data mining analysis. Traditionally, the analysts have to familiarize themselves with their data before beginning to model it or to apply data mining tools. However, with the large size of modern data sets, this is less feasible or even entirely impossible in many cases. Here we must rely on computer programs to check the data. The preparation of data is sometimes dismissed as a topic in data mining literature, and as a phase in a data mining process. In a real world of data mining applications, the situation is reversed. More effort is expended preparing data than applying data mining methods. There are two central tasks for the preparation of data [Han, 2001][Kantardzic, 2002]:

- To organize data into a standard form that is ready for processing by data mining and other computer-based tools, and

- To prepare data sets that lead to the best data mining performance.

Some analyses showed that most of evaluated medical databases contained erroneous, poorly organized, unstructured, inconsistently recorded and frequently dichotomous data elements. For patient records, with their multimedia components, adequate preprocessing is important for the success of the entire data mining process. A breakdown of reasons why data in patient records could not be used directly for standard data mining can be summarized through the counts of unusable value occurrences. Free text and images, representing 64% of data, account for the largest amount of unusable data for direct application of data mining techniques. Missing values, with 34%, account for the second largest unusable set of data, and incomplete data, with 4%, as the third largest [Prather, 1997]. The other causes of unprepared data include out of range values such as invalid heights, format discrepancies such as text in a numeric field, and data inconsistencies such as two different values for the birth date.

For structured elements of a patient record, standard data preprocessing techniques are used. As each variable (feature) is added to the dataset, it is cleansed of erroneous values, data inconsistencies, and formatting discrepancies. One of the most common processes is conversion of alphanumerical fields (coded values) into coded numerical quantities that permit more efficient data mining analyses. Data preprocessing also includes identifying missing values and prompting the user to either substitute them (for example with an average value for the variable), or to delete the record from the dataset. *Cleansing and scrubbing* are transformations concerned with ensuring consistent formatting and usage of a field or of related groups of fields [Prather, 1997] [Han, 2001]. This can include proper formatting of address information, for example. These transformations also include checks for valid values in a particular field, usually by range checking or by choosing from an enumerated list.

For text and especially for medical images, specific procedures have to be implemented. Many medical images are difficult to interpret directly, and a preprocessing phase is necessary to improve the quality of the images and to make the later feature extraction phase more reliable. Pre-processing is always a necessity whenever the images to be mined are noisy, inconsistent, or incomplete. This phase significantly improves the effectiveness of the data mining techniques applied later. Two typical techniques for image preprocessing are a *cropping operation*, and image *enhancement*. The former is employed in order to cut the background image area as well as the existing artifacts such as written labels, etc. For many medical images, a large percentage of the whole image (sometimes more than 50%) is comprised of a black background with a significant noise. Cropping should be performed prior to image enhancement to avoid additional noise from the non-data part of the image. Cropping is usually performed automatically by sweeping through the image and cutting horizontally and vertically the image segments with the mean and variance less than a specified threshold value [Antonie, 2001].

Image enhancement provides qualitative improvement in order to diminish the effect of over-bright or over–dark regions of the image, and also to accentuate the image features. One common technique to improve visual appearance is histogram equalization (HE). Applying HE increases the contrast range in an image by increasing the dynamic range of gray levels or colors [Lavrac, 1999][Adibi, 2000]. This improves directly the distinction of features of the image that are based on contours. The method proceeds by widening the peaks in the image histogram and by compressing the valleys.

In an effort to explore data mining from breast cancer databases of digitized mammography, a novel rule-based image segmentation algorithm for masking the breast region from the background in digital mammograms is proposed [Rickard, Tourassi and Elmaghraby, 2003]. The algorithm uses a self-organizing map (SOM) to obtain an initial segmentation. In image segmentation, each element is simply a pixel from the input image described with different features. Though hundreds of types of features are available in the literature, nine multiscale features have been used in the proposed approach. Multiscale features are created from combinations of images convolved with Gaussian partial derivatives. After the features were extracted to create a pattern matrix P, a training set P' was created by selecting one sample from each 16 x 16 subimage. After the SOM had been trained, the entire pattern matrix was presented to the SOM to determine each pixel's best matching unit (BMU), or, node.

SOMs may be visualized by methods such as the unified distance matrix (u-matrix) or using Sammon's mapping, but these visualizations only provide qualitative information about the underlying structure of the map. To obtain quantitative descriptions of data properties, the weight vectors of each SOM node were clustered by the K-means method. Several indices have been developed in an attempt to quantify the quality of clustering, and the Davies-Bouldin index DB(K) was selected [Rickard et al. 2003]. Originally proposed as a way of deciding when to stop clustering data, the Davies-Bouldin index is a function of the ratio between the sum of within-cluster distances and the between-cluster separation, which supposes that the minimum DB-index is for an optimal clustering. Given a partition of n objects into K clusters, the within-to-between cluster spread for all cluster pairs (j, k) is calculated as,

$$R_{j,k} = (e_j + e_k) / m_{j,k}$$

where e_j is the average error for the jth cluster and $m_{j,k}$ is the Euclidean distance between the centers of the jth and k^{th} clusters. The index for the kth cluster is:

$$R_k = \max_{j \neq k}\{R_{j,k}\}$$

and the Davies-Bouldin index of the K-cluster clustering is then,

$$DB(K) = \frac{1}{K} \sum_{k=1}^{K} R_k$$

The K value with the minimum DB-index, K_{DB}, was used for the final clustering and to create a corresponding segmented grayscale image with K_{DB} gray levels.

Knowledge-based refinement provides the final binary mask that segments the image. Rule-based analysis was performed to determine the breast orientation, remove the markers (such as information plates), remove unexposed film regions, and to smooth the final segmentation. For example, the breast orientation is determined by a simple histogram analysis of the original mammogram. When the image is split vertically down the center, one side will contain most of the breast while the other contains most of the background, regardless of the level of overlap. A histogram is accordingly calculated for both the right and left half of the original image. Without loss of generality, an orientation rule is defined in the form: if the right half contains more pixels in the high intensity range and the left half contains more pixels in the low intensity range, the breast is oriented on the right. Rules pertaining to identifying location and orientation of the breast are followed by rules to eliminate unwanted background clusters. Successful application of these rules enables focusing on the actual breast and eliminating nameplates and unnecessary background in the image.

The images used were obtained from 40 cases from the Digital Database for Screening Mammography (DDSM) [Heath, et al., 2000]. Each case contains four images, the medio-lateral oblique (MLO) and the cranio-caudal (CC) view of each breast, for a total of 160 images. Figure 3 (a) depicts an original mammogram with name plate and background noise, Figure 3 (b) shows the K_{DB}-clustering results, Figure 3 (c) shows an initial binary mask, and Figure 3 (d) shows results of applying the rules to eliminate unwanted segments and refine the breast mask to allow further study.

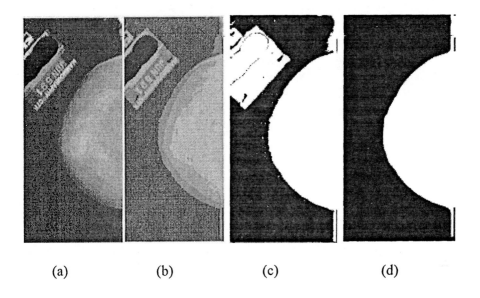

(a)   (b)   (c)   (d)

Figure 3.   Phases in Labels and Noise Elimination for Digitized
                 Mammography Images.

5.   DATA TRANSFORMATION

5.1   Types of Transformation

Most experts in data mining agree that one of the essential steps in a data mining process is the preparation and transformation of the initial data set. This task often receives little attention in the research literature, mostly because it is considered too application-specific. But in most data mining applications, some parts of a data preparation process, or sometimes even the entire process, can be described independently of an application and a data mining method.

Different transformations may be needed to produce medical records features more conducive to selected data mining methods such as prediction or classification. Counting in different ways, using different sampling sizes, taking important ratios, varying data window sizes for time-dependent data, and including changes in moving averages, may contribute to better data mining results. The computer will not find the best set of transformations without human assistance, and the transformations used in one data mining application are not necessarily best for another. Fundamental types of data transformations that are partially or totally independent on application may be classified as [Prather, 1997][Han, 2001]:

Simple transformations – These transformations are building blocks of all other more complex transformations. This category includes manipulations of data that is focused on one field at a time, without taking into account the values in related fields. Examples include changing the data type of a field or replacing an encoded field value with a coded value. Standard transformation procedures for numerical features in a patient record are: decimal scaling, min-max normalization, standard deviation normalization, and data smoothing. Processes for the replacement of *missing values*, and formatting of *time-dependent* data into standard windows belong to these elementary transformations.

Integration – This is the process of taking operational data from one or more sources and mapping it, field by field, onto a new data structure. The common identifier problem is one of the most important and difficult integration issues in building an integrated patient record. Essentially, this situation occurs when there are multiple system sources for the same entities and there is no clear way to identify those entities as the same. This is a challenging problem, and in many cases it cannot be solved in an automated fashion. It frequently requires sophisticated algorithms to pair up probable matches. Another complex data integration scenario occurs when there are multiple sources for the same data element. In reality, it is common that some of these values are contradictory, and resolving a conflict is not straightforward process. Just as difficult is the problem of having no value for a data element. All these problems and corresponding automatic or semiautomatic solutions are always domain dependent.

Aggregation and summarization – These are methods of condensing instances of data found in the operational environment into fewer instances in the data mining environment. Although the terms aggregation and summarization are often used interchangeably in the literature, we believe that they do have subtle differences in the data mining context. Summarization is a simple addition of values along one or more data dimensions. For example, adding up daily drug consumption to produce monthly total. Aggregation refers to the addition of different medical features into a common total; it is highly domain dependent.

Differences and ratios – These provide an additional methodology for data preprocessing. In many data mining applications, mining for changes can be more important than producing accurate models. Sometimes a model in itself, no matter how accurate, is a passive descriptor, and the only way of performing classification or prediction tasks is based on patterns mined in old data and compared with the new one to estimate the changes. These changes may follow a trend or may cause undesirable distortions in the trend. The analyst must understand that even in a relatively stable environment of data collection, changes are also inevitable, although at a slower pace, due to uncontrolled internal and external factors. Different types of changes could be detected, depending on the type of attributes in medical records. Common changes for medical images are boundary shift, join or split of regions, increasing/decreasing texture, and changes in a gray or color level. These techniques may also be included into the data transformation process, as they introduce new dimensions (features) of a data set based on initial features.

Feature composition – There are transformations of data that can have a surprisingly strong impact on results of data mining methods. In this sense, the composition of features is a greater determining factor in the quality of data mining results than the specific mining technique. In most instances, feature composition is dependent on knowledge of the application, and interdisciplinary approaches to feature composition tasks provide significant improvements in the preparation of data. For example, our experience has showed that composing patient features weight and height into a new feature called body mass index (BMI) improves classification results in an applicability analysis of laparoscopic techniques [Kantardzic et al., 2001].

The following normalization process is an example of methods that will assign equal emphasis to each component of the feature vector describing medical images [Kantardzic, 2002]. Different components within the vector may be of totally different physical quantities. Therefore, their magnitudes may vary drastically and therefore bias the similarity measurement significantly. One component may overshadow the others just because its magnitude is relatively too large. Assuming a Gaussian distribution of feature values for a set of images, we can obtain the mean μ_i and standard deviation σ_i for the ith component of the feature vector across the entire image data set. Then we can normalize the original feature values $A_{i,j}$ of the image into $A'_{i,j}$ values with the range of [-1, 1] as follows:

$$A'_{i,j} = (A_{i,j} - \mu_i) / \sigma_i .$$

It can easily be shown that the probability of an attribute value falling into the range [-1, 1] is 68%. In practice, the algorithm may map all the data into the required range by forcing the out-of-range values to be border values: either –1 or 1. Shifting the normalized values into the $A''_{i,j}$ value with the range [0, 1] is very simple and can be achieved by using the formula:

$$A''_{i,j} = (A'_{i,j} + 1) / 2 .$$

A feature vector may be weighted globally or locally. A global weight indicates the overall importance of the feature vector in the patient record. Therefore, the same global weighting is applied to an entire row. A local weight is applied to each element indicating the importance of the component within the vector. Common local weighting techniques include binary and log of term frequency, whereas common global weighting include entropy measures.

For structured, numerical parts of patient record, independent component analysis (ICA) is an effective method for removing artifacts and separating sources of the data from noise [Hand, 2001][Jung, 2001]. ICA is also a signal processing technique for modelling empirical data sets and for exploratory data analysis. It is particularly useful in blind source separation and feature extraction.

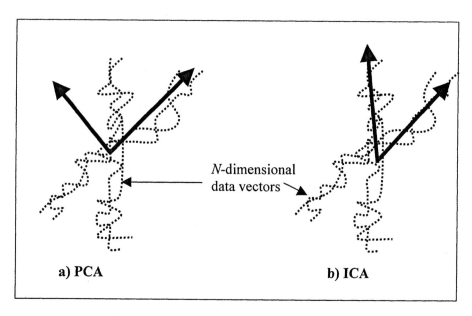

Figure 4. The Difference Between PCA and ICA Transforms.

At the same time data are transformed in this process and the number of dimensions (features) for a data set is reduced. Mathematically, the ICA problem is as follows: Given a collection of N-dimensional vectors $\mathbf{x}$, typically there are diffuse and complex patterns of correlation between the elements of the vectors. ICA, like principal component analysis (PCA), is a method to remove those correlations by multiplying vector $\mathbf{x}$ by a matrix $\mathbf{W}$ as follows:

$$U = W x .$$

We call the rows of W *filters* because they extract the independent components of the vector x. A matrix W is not an orthogonal transformation as it is a covariance matrix in the PCA method. While PCA only uses second-order statistics (the data covariance matrix), ICA uses statistics of higher order pursuing more ambitious objectives, and in general better results of transformation. The usefulness of a non-orthogonal transform sensitive to higher order statistics can be seen in Figure 4, where two main axes of maximum variance for N-dimensional data samples better fit the data if they are not orthogonal.

5.2 An Independent Component Analysis: Example of an EMG/ECG Separation

Some of the many applications of ICA include EEG signal processing and source localization [Vigário et al., 2000], suppressing noise and artifacts [Tong et al., 2001], and modelling retinal encoding [Milanova et al., 2001]. A recent application [Wachowiak et al., 2002a] addresses preprocessing issues of biosignals. Specifically, ICA was used to separate cardiac (electrocardiograph, or ECG) recordings from electromyography (EMG) signals. EMG tests the electrical activity of skeletal muscle. It is useful in detecting disorders that affect the muscles, and in diagnosing muscle problems caused by nerve dysfunction. EMG signals are collected with electrodes on the skin surface or by insertion of a needle electrode. Actual EMG data of the trunk and shoulder is the summation of the potential difference in muscle activity and ECG signal. For accurate clinical analysis, it is important to separate the mixture while retaining as much of the true EMG signal as possible. In ECG separation with ICA, three basic assumptions must be made: (1) EMG and ECG signals are independent and have non-Gaussian statistics; (2) EMG/cardiac mixtures are linear combinations of the true EMG and cardiac components; (3) It is possible to record at least two mixtures simultaneously from nearby locations.

To provide ground truth, experiments were performed on simulated mixtures of real EMG and ECG signals. The fixed-point ICA algorithm [Hyvärinen and Oja, 1997] was used to maximize negentropy as a measure of non-Gaussianity. The procedure is shown in Figure 5.

ICA was compared to high-pass filtering and noise removal with wavelet packets [Misiti et al., 1996]. For the latter two techniques, the two EMG signals used in each ICA trial were mixed only with ECG (not with each other), but in the same linear combination as for the ICA trials. Therefore, the EMG for both sets of experiments had the same degree of ECG artifact for corresponding trials. Three cardiac and 7 EMG signals from oblique muscles of a healthy male were collected. The signals were collected for 3 seconds at 1 KHz. Two time-synchronized EMG signals and one ECG signal were linearly combined with 3 × 3 mixing matrices that simulate realistic mixtures. One thousand EMG/ECG mixtures, each containing three signals, were generated from the EMG and ECG combinations and mixing matrices. The fixed-point ICA algorithm was applied to the mixtures to extract the EMG and ECG components.

The wavelet packets produced good results with low standard deviation, with transforms based on biorthogonal wavelets slightly outperforming the orthonormal filters. Also, the best results for high-pass filtering were obtained with a cut-off frequency of $f_c = 25$ Hz, as the dominant frequency power of ECG is at 20 Hz, and at 25-250 Hz for EMG. However, the ICA method was the best overall performer in mean SNR improvement and consistency.

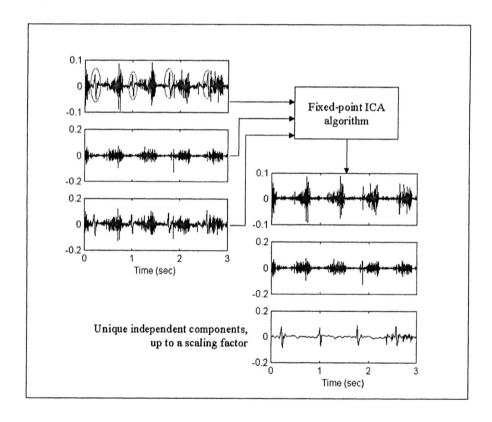

Figure 5. Three EMG/ECG Mixtures (left) Separated ino EMG and ECG Signals by ICA (right). Cardiac Artifacts in the EMG are Circled in Gray (upper left).

For ECG separation, ICA has the advantage that it is fully automatic. The method is robust with respect to choice of the specific non-Gaussian function being maximized. No thresholds (for wavelet packets) or filter order (for high-pass filtering) need to be chosen. Fixed-point ICA, although iterative, converges very rapidly. A disadvantage of the ICA approach is that at least as many signals, as independent components are required. Obtaining these signals in a localized area may be difficult, especially when needle electrodes are used [Wachowiak et al., 2002a].

ECG separation from EMG is an example of using ICA as a data preprocessing technique. In the data mining context, all separated source signals, or only sources considered to be relevant to the specific problem at hand, can be used in further data mining operations.

5.3 Text Transformation and Representation: A Rule-Based Approach

Electronic clinical information is typically stored either as structured, coded data or as images or full-text reports. Medical text reports represent a significant source of clinical data; especially data that are not available in other coded electronic forms. Recent studies found that coded information alone was not sufficient for different data mining tasks [Wilcox, 2000]. To be useful in data mining, the information, stored as narrative text, must be represented in such a way that it can be used effectively.

Different structured representations are used for medical text. The simplest possibility is a vector of the frequency of each word in the text, after removing stop words. Additionally, a vector of words may be associated with weights rather than with raw frequencies. Some studies use a limited form of natural language processing to identify concepts rather than individual words in the document. Another approach uses only those words and phrases that occur in a dictionary of relevant terms prepared by experts, and then they are mapped to specific codes representing concepts. Aronow et. al [1999] also mapped words and phrases to concepts, but also included a specific method to detect negation of these concepts. The CAPIS system, developed at Stanford University, extracts findings or observations from a text report, and assigns one out of several state values to each finding: instantiated-positive, instantiated-negative, or not-instantiated [Lin, 1991]. Instead of identifying all observations in a text, the system only identifies target findings specified by a user. In all previous methodologies the basic structured representation of the text is a vector of words with or without modifiers. From the described studies, there exist several standards in text structuring, as a prerequisite for implementation and evaluation of data mining methods. These are [Wilcox, 2000] as follows:

- *Text-keywords* - with weights,
- *Text-bin* – a vector of selected words without weights,
- *Concepts* - For each document vector of in-advance specified observations is set with a binary coding of whether they were instantiated in the document or not,
- *Modified concepts* - all concepts In the previous representation are with modifiers such as "low, "high" etc.,
- *No-concepts* – This is a slight variant of the concept representation that also includes negated concepts,
- *NLP-mod* - represents vector of natural language processed observations with modifiers,
- *NLP-ref* – a vector of observations with positive, negative, and not-occurring values,
- *NLP-neg* – similar representation to NLP-ref only negative and not-occurring values represent same state.

Based on these standard representations, some research tried to perform common data mining tasks, such as classification, to examine the quality of different structured representation of text [Wilcox, 1999]. Using Bayesian networks and decision trees, Chapman and Haug have analyzed classification of chest x-ray reports indicating pneumonia, where reports had different structures of the text [Chapman and Haug, 1998]. The analysis showed that each representation has advantages and disadvantages. Those that were based on raw text were easily implemented, and did not require natural language processing (*NLP*) [Wilcox, 2000]. However, those that use NPL could detect refuted concepts in the text and obtain better classification results.

Unlike traditional numeric, categorical, or Boolean data types, textual resources must first be transformed to an alternative representation with fewer dimensions, before a data-mining technique can be applied. A rule based approach is well suited for preprocessing documents with medical text because it causes drastic dimensionality reduction for large textual corpus. The basic requirements in this reduction process are that each individual feature should be informative; that is, it clearly captures some aspects of the problem described in the text. Therefore, the quality of features is described in terms of semantic richness. For example, breast cancer is a disease occurring in a particular part of the body. In a text-mining system, if this phrase is represented using two individual features breast and cancer, it would not capture the meaning of the phrase. We say that the concept feature breast cancer is semantically richer than the individual features breast and cancer. By increasing the semantic richness of features used to represent text it will correspond to an increase in the plausibility and usefulness of the model of data produced in the data mining process.

To identify semantic patterns in the text, one approach proposed the use of the popular data mining technique for generating association rules [Blake et al., 2001]. An association rule has the form:

$$A{\rightarrow}B,$$

which means that the presence of feature A in the text implies the presence of feature B in the same text. Each association rule has an associated level of support and confidence. The support is the probability that both A and B occur in a text. The confidence is the probability that B will occur in text given that A has already occurred. Selection of features in a text corpus is based on so-called "bi-directional association rules". The authors define a bi-directional association rule (indicated by A⇔ B) as one that satisfies the support and confidence in both directions (A→ B, and B→A), and they use a modified a priori algorithm to generate bi-directional association rules.

Significantly fewer features are required to represent medical text, compared with the number of isolated words. Bi-directional association rules may be generated based on word, keyword, and concept representation of the initial text features. Concept representation requires 90% fewer features than a word representation, and corresponding bi-directional association rules are more plausible and useful, because of their semantics, for further data mining process. Qualified physicians found only 25% of the rules based on word features to be useful and plausible, compared with 50% and 45% for keyword and concepts. The methodology is especially suitable for the large medical text corpus, such as that available on the Web.

5.4 Image Transformation and Representation: A Rule-Based Approach

In the data-preprocessing phase of medical images it is important to transform low-level features into a higher-level image description with meaning. While current database systems retrieve and process images based on low-level features, advanced applications such as data mining expect a more abstract notion of what is satisfactory. Therefore, standard definitions of similarity and measurement using low-level features generally will not produce good data mining results. In reality, the correspondence between application-based (and user-oriented) semantic concepts and system-based low-level features is many-to-many. That is, the same semantic concept may usually be associated with different sets of low-level image features. Also, for the same set of image features, different applications and users could easily find dissimilar images relevant to their needs [Antonie, 2001].

After cropping and enhancing the image, the next step is the most critical: to select the most important features for the given type of image, and how to extract the features from the cleaned image. The first part is highly subjective, and usually uses the knowledge from the corresponding medical domain, while the process of extraction is more often automated. The transformed data set now consists of feature set F_1, F_2,..., F_n, where new features are obtained by merging previously existing features (i.e., the type of the tissue, the position of the image etc.) with automatically generated features from the image. Common extracted features are standard statistical parameters such as mean, variance, skewness, and kurtosis, and entropy [Rushing, 2001]. Frequency domain features, including wavelet statistics, are also useful. These parameters may be calculated for the entire image as a unique value, or for the image segments as a vector of values.

While most features for medical images are based on structural, statistical, or spectral properties, a few methods extract image texture features that capture several of these. One of them, proposed recently, captures characteristics of a texture and automatically characterizes it as a set of association rules [Rushing et al., 2001]. The basic idea is to represent frequently occurring local intensity variation patterns in images as formalized association rules. An association rule has the form:

$$A_1 \wedge A_2 \wedge \dots \wedge A_m \Rightarrow A_{m+1} \wedge A_{m+2} \wedge \dots \wedge A_{m+n}$$

where:

- A_i represent triple (X_i, Y_i, I_i); X_i and Y_i are row and column offset of so called "*root pixel*", and I_i is the intensity of the pixel,
- $\wedge$ and $\Rightarrow$ are the standard logical operators for AND and IMPLICATION, respectively.

The root pixel is simply the pixel in the center of an n×n neighborhood; it represents a moving window through the image. There exist $(N-n+1)^2$ *root pixels* in an image of size $N \times N$.

Several characteristics are defined for this type of association rules. The *cardinality CA* of an association rule is the sum of the number of triples in the antecedent and the consequent parts of the rule. The *support S* for a rule is defined as the number of root pixels at which a rule appears, divided by the total number of root pixels. Finally, the *confidence C* of a rule is defined as the ratio of the number of root pixels at which all triples in the rule appear to the number of root pixels at which all triples in the antecedent appear. For example, consider the image shown in Figure 6 where the root pixel is defined with neighborhood 3×3. The total number of root pixels is $(5-3+1)^2$ = 9. The association rule of the form:

$$(0,0,2) \wedge (1,1,2) \Rightarrow (1,0,0)$$

has the following characteristics:

$$CA = 2 + 1 = 3,$$
$$S = 3 / 9 = 33.33\%,$$
$$\text{and } C = 3 / 5 = 60\%.$$

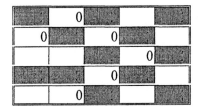

Figure 6. Sample of an Image of Size 5×5.

The objective of mining an image or a set of images for frequent association rules is to define the rules that satisfy user specified constraints. For a texture characterization application, the user may constrain the cardinality of the rules CA, the offset from the root pixel X and Y, the pixel values I, and minimum support S and confidence C levels. The rules with high support and confidence identified in images describe frequently occurring local image structures, which can be used for features characterizing texture.

Since the number of possible triples and their combinations as rules is very large, the brute force approach in discovering frequent association rules is not practical. Therefore, it is desirable to limit the number of triples and their combinations to be considered. This can be done by using the minimum support level specified by the user, and the fact that a combination of triplets is frequent only when all its subsets are also frequent. The algorithm uses an efficient iterative approach in which all frequent logical combinations of triples with cardinality CA are generated using the frequent combinations of cardinality CA -1. The approach is based on the adaptation of a well-known *Apriori* algorithm for the discovery of association rules in large data sets [Kantardzic, 2002]:

1. Find all frequent triples (support above a given threshold) of cardinality one.
2. Iteratively, find all frequent logical combinations (only AND operation) of triples with cardinality F that are:
   - generated from the frequent triples combinations of cardinality F-1, and
   - their support is above threshold value.

3. Using frequent triples find in Steps 1 and 2, generate association rules of cardinality F consisting of F-1 triples in the antecedent and one triple in the consequent which have confidence above a given threshold value.

For example, for the image given in Figure 6 assume that the minimum support level S is 0.3, the minimum confidence C is 0.8, and the offsets of interest are limited to points (0,0), (1,0), and (1,1). As results of the applied algorithm, frequent combinations of triples and corresponding association rules are given in Figure 7.

Triples	Support
(0,0,0)	3/9
(0,0,2)	5/9
(1,0,0)	3/9
(1,0,2)	4/9
(1,1,2)	5/9
(0,0,0) ∧(1,0,2)	3/9
(0,0,2) ∧ (1,0,0)	3/9
(0,0,2)∧(1,1,2)	5/9
(1,0,0)∧(1,1,2)	3/9
(0,0,2)∧ (1,0,0) ∧(1,1,2)	3/9

Association Rules	Confidence
(0,0,0) ⇒(1,0,2)	1.0
(1,0,0)⇒(0,0,2)	1.0
(0,0,2)⇒(1,1,2)	1.0
(1,0,0)⇒(1,1,2)	1.0
(0,0,2)∧(1,0,0) ⇒ (1,1,2)	1.0
(1,0,0)∧ (1,1,2)⇒(0,0,2)	1.0

a) Triples identified by mining the sample image in Figure 6

b) Association rules generated for the image in Figure 6

Figure 7. Feature Extraction for the Image in Figure 6 by Using the Association Rules Method.

Gray-level and color images pose a challenging problem for the use of the association rules approach to capture local image structure because of the large number of intensity values (I). Several algorithms for quantization exist, and one of the most promising is based on the computation of value distribution through root pixels. New values are based on the simple formula:

$$\text{New value} = \begin{cases} 0 & r \geq \mu - c\,\sigma \\ 1 & \mu - c\,\sigma < r < \mu + c\,\sigma \\ 2 & r \geq \mu + c\,\sigma \end{cases}$$

where:

- *c* is a positive constant in the range [0.1, 0.5],
- μ is the mean value for the distribution,
- σ is standard deviation for the distribution , and
- *r* is the old value for the pixel.

While rule-mining algorithms identify all of the rules that meet user-defined criteria, not all rules may provide discriminatory information necessary to describe texture and distinguish texture classes. Final reduction of a rule set for image classification problems may be based on one of two approaches, widely used in the area of pattern recognition:

a) For each texture class, one rule that best separates the class from remaining (*M*-1) classes is selected. This approach selects *M* rules, one for each class.

b) For each pair of texture classes, one association rule is selected. Thus, for an *M*-class problem, a significant rule-set for describing any texture contains $M(M-1)/2$ rules.

The association rule features are compared with other important methodologies for feature selection such as GLCM, GLRL, fractal dimension, Markov random field, and Gabor filter-base features [Rushing et al., 2001]. Experiments showed that association rule features are capable of distinguishing textures that other statistical methods cannot distinguish. They can even distinguish textures that are not discriminable by humans.

6. DIMENSIONALITY REDUCTION

6.1 The Importance of Reduction

For small or moderate data sets, the previously discussed preprocessing steps in preparation for data mining are usually sufficient. For very large data sets, there is an increased likelihood that an intermediate, additional step, data reduction, should be performed prior to applying the data mining techniques. As it will be explained below, aspects reduction may also be considered as preprocessing. Whereas large data sets have the potential for better mining results, there is no guarantee that better knowledge will be discovered than in small data sets. Given high-dimensional data, a central question is whether it can be determined, prior to searching for all data mining solutions in all dimensions, that the method has exhausted its potential for mining and discovery in a reduced data set. The main theme for simplifying the data in this step is dimension reduction, and the main question is: Can some of these prepared and preprocessed data be discarded without sacrificing the quality of the results? Also, can reduction potentially *improve* results in some cases?

The three main dimensions of preprocessed data set are: a) *columns* (features), b) *rows* (cases or samples), and c) *values* of the features [Kantardzic, 2002]. Therefore, three basic operations in a data reduction process are: delete a column, delete a row, and reduce the number of values in a column (smooth a feature). These operations attempt to preserve the character of the original data by deleting nonessential data. There are other operations that reduce dimensions, but the relationship between the new, reduced data and the original data set is not obvious. These operations are briefly mentioned here because they are highly application dependent. One approach is a replacement of a set of initial features with a new composite feature. For example, if samples in a data set have two features: person-height and person-weight, it is possible for some applications in a medical domain to replace these two features with only one: body-mass-index, which is proportional to the quotient of the initial two features. Final reduction of data does not reduce the quality of the results; some applications showed that the results of data mining are even improved [Porter, 1999]. The overall comparison involves the following parameters for analysis: *computing time, predictive/descriptive accuracy, and interpretability of the data mining model.*

The feature reduction process is especially important for databases with multimedia patient records, resulting in [Tang, 1999]:

1. Less data, so that the data mining algorithm can learn faster;
2. Higher accuracy of a data mining process, so that the model can generalize better from data;
3. Simpler results of a data mining process, so that they are easier to understand and to use; and
4. Fewer features, so that in the next round of data collection, redundant or irrelevant features can be removed.

A standard task associated with the production of a reduced set of features is termed feature selection. Based on the knowledge of the application domain and the goals of the mining effort, the human analyst may select a subset of the features found in the initial data set. The process of feature selection may be manual, or supported by automated procedures. Automated procedures are especially important for text-based and image-based documents because of the potentially extremely large number of features.

In order to make text data useable by data mining algorithms, it is necessary to flatten and model each text document as a vector of features representing the semantics of the document. To reduce the number of features in the vector and to select only those that are relevant, additional expert knowledge in the form of expert rules is necessary. Selker has recommended that the number of variables in the vector used should not exceed 10% of the total number of training samples (text documents) in a data set [Selker, 1993]. One method calculates the predictive accuracy of each attribute present in the training set of text documents. Accuracy is determined by adding the conditional probabilities for each attribute. All attributes are then ranked by accuracy, and the top N attributes are selected for the document vector.

There is an increasing demand for systems that can automatically analyze images and extract semantically meaningful information. The Latent Semantic Indexing (LSI) method, in conjunction with normalization and term weighting (which have been used for text retrieval for many years), is a promising technique for semantic description of images [Adibi, 2000][Kantardzic, 2002]. In the text environment, this technique determines clusters of co-occurring keywords, sometimes called concepts. To extract these co-occurrences in the image domain, a singular value decomposition (SVD) technique is performed on the feature-image-matrix, where the features could be extracted from quantized color histograms.

6.2 Data Fusion

Data fusion techniques are applied in many areas of biomedicine, and are important in many data mining contexts, as they facilitate both dimension reduction and extracting more information from different modalities. One of the most important applications is medical image fusion after registration, or alignment, of 2D images or 3D volumes from the same or different modalities. In fact, fusion is the end-goal of registration.

Decision fusion uses the output of data fusion as input to the decision-making process. *Model fusion* is the use of different models or modeling techniques to provide a better solution to a specific problem. An example from image processing is the edge detection problem, where numerical approaches, such as the well-known Canny algorithm, are combined with neural network techniques. In pattern recognition, mathematical models can be constructed at the pixel (picture element in a digital image) level with probabilistic approaches, combined with transforms, such as the Hough transform, that acts on the scene level. *Information fusion* is a combination of data fusion, decision fusion, and model fusion. It operates on a higher level than data fusion [Solaiman et al., 1999].

There are two main architectures for information fusion. In the *monosensor* architecture, data are obtained from a single sensor. New data sets are generated from the acquired set by utilizing probability theory or fuzzy set theory. *The multisensor* architecture is most commonly understood as acquiring data from multiple sources, or from different parameters (or orientations) of a single sensor [Solaiman et al., 1999].

In multimodal imaging, if the images have gray scale intensities, a simple and often effective way to combine information after registration is to assign a color band to each of the images. For example, if three images have been registered, then the gray scales of the images can represent the red, green, and blue components, and the result is a pseudo-color, fused image [Robb, 2000]. A potential problem with this method is that the images may be difficult to interpret. In addition, the contributions of each gray scale image are considered to be equal, when this need not be the case in all applications. In many cases, the different modalities provide different information – information not present in one image may be present in another. There are also instances when information is provided by more than one modality for a given voxel (volume element in a volume, or 3D image, generated either directly or by stacking slices of 2D images). Specifically, the problem is to decide which pixel/voxel, or which aggregation should be used to combine the registered multimodal images, under imprecise and uncertain information. For this reason, probabilistic, fuzzy, and Dempster-Shafer approaches have found utility in image fusion [Bloch and Maître, 1997] [Bloch et al., 1996][Bloch, 1996]. All three approaches are numerical (as opposed to symbolic). For the following discussion, the image fusion problem is stated as follows: given l images I_j consisting of heterogeneous data, a decision D_i is taken on an element x, where x denotes a pixel/voxel or extracted object. A number, denoted as $M_i^j, i \in \{1,...,n\}$, represents the information relating x to each possible decision D_i. Next, the measures related to each decision i are combined as $M_i = F\left(M_i^1, M_i^2,..., M_i^l\right)$, where $F\left(\cdot\right)$ denotes a fusion operator. A final, global, decision is taken on the set $\{M_i\}$ [Bloch and Maître, 1997].

Three of the most popular image fusion approaches are based on probability theory (Bayesian approaches), fuzzy methods, and those based on the Dempster-Schafer theory. In the Bayesian paradigm, the M_i^j denote conditional probabilities, which are computed as features extracted from the images, such as gray level or texture characteristics. Bayes' Theorem is used to combine image information. The most common decision rule is the maximum a posteriori probability. Other rules include maximum posterior marginal, maximum likelihood, maximum entropy, and minimum expected risk [Bloch and Maître, 1997].

In many medical applications, including biomedical imaging, it is important to represent imprecision. There is uncertainty in the spatial location of objects and whether those objects belong to a certain class. In particular, the *partial volume effect*, wherein different tissues may be included in a single voxel, must be taken into account. Approaches based on fuzzy logic can numerically represent such imprecision, and in this sense, can closely model reality [Bloch and Maître, 1997]. Using the notation and estimation-combination-decision schema described above, in the fuzzy logic paradigm, the M_i^j's represent degrees of membership to a fuzzy set: $M_i^j(x) = \mu_i^j(x)$, where the right-hand-side is the membership degree of x in class i from image j [Bloch and Maître, 1997]. Fuzzy set theory also provides many combination, or *aggregation* operators for fusion. These operators are classified as conjunctive (like a logical *or* operator), disjunctive (logical *and*), and compromise (between *or* and *and*). A decision is usually made from the maximum membership value that results after combination. Fuzzy aggregation operators are also discussed in [Smolikova and Wachowiak, 2002].

Classification has traditionally been the most popular application of the fuzzy paradigm to image fusion. It can also be used for preprocessing, such as combining contrast homogeneity measures to smooth regions while preserving or sharpening edges. Recently, fuzzy logic has also been combined with neural networks for learning capability, and for using several combination operations [Bloch and Maître, 1997]. The Dempster-Shafter (DS) theory has been popular in satellite image processing for many years. Like fuzzy logic, the DS theory can also represent imprecision and uncertainty. However, this uncertainty is modeled with *belief* and *plausibility* functions derived from a *mass function*, whose domain is a power set of a *discernment set D*. In image fusion, D may represent the set of all possible classes pertaining to the fused image, and any subset A may represent either one class (simple hypothesis) or a union of classes (compound hypothesis) [Bloch, 1996]. DS approaches can also be used where all information concerning a problem is known, as is the assumption with Bayesian techniques. More specific to multimodal image fusion, the DS theory may be used when a modality provides information concerning only a few of many classes, and when one modality can differentiate classes whereas others do not [Bloch and Maître, 1997]. Finally, the DS theory provides mechanisms to deal with the partial volume effect. Fuzzy logic and DS theory are primarily differentiated by the fact that the former is very flexible because of a wide range of aggregation operators, while the latter provides flexibility in modeling situations such as those just described [Bloch and Maître, 1997].

6.3   Example 1: Multimodality Data Fusion

As an example of multimodality data fusion, fusion of angiography and intravascular ultrasound (IVUS) images is presented [Wahle et al., 1999]. Both modalities are commonly utilized for the evaluation of atherosclerotic disease. The hypothesis is that data fusion can be used to determine correct IVUS image orientation in 3D space, which subsequently facilitates geometrically correct reconstruction of coronary vessels. Biplane quantitative coronary angiography (QCA) is a well-established standard for reconstructing any spatial structure visible in two different projections. However, QCA can only provide reconstructions of vessel lumen (the space inside vessels). IVUS, by contrast, permits analysis of the vascular wall and plaque deposits. However, because there is no available information about vessel curvature in IVUS, it lacks a correct 3D representation. Thus, the fusion of IVUS and biplane angiography is proposed to generate geometrically correct representations in 3D space, and to retain the relationships between image objects even in high-curvature vessels.

6.4   Example 2: Data Fusion in Data Preprocessing

In addition to providing a more integrated view from combining complementary imaging modalities, data and information fusion concepts can be applied to preprocessing operations, such as segmentation. In a recent study, data fusion was applied to detect the inner wall of the esophagus from ultrasound images [Solaiman et al., 1999]. An echo-endoscope, consisting of an endoscope and an ultrasound transducer, was used to collect image slices. The authors used two primary systems in their architecture: fuzzy modeling and dynamic modeling.

Data from different modalities can also be used to increase the usefulness of other modalities, although the data is not fused in the strict sense. An example is using statistical parameter maps to enhance the interpretation of 2D images [Smolikova et al., 2002]. Biomedical ultrasound is a popular modality for clinical diagnosis and treatment planning. In addition to low signal-to-noise ratio and numerous artifacts, ultrasound B-scans are characterized by speckle, which is also present in the ultrasound radio-frequency (RF) signal. Although speckle makes human and computerized analysis difficult, its statistical properties make it potentially useful for clinical applications. Therefore, analysis of the 1D RF signals can complement radiological analysis of the B-scans (brightness scans). Such approaches have been presented to characterize liver tissue and normal myocardial tissue [Molthen et al., 1998], and classify breast tissue [Shankar et al., 2001]. Additionally, B-scans can be segmented based on the statistics of the ultrasound RF signals. Such a technique is desirable, as speckle and other artifacts limit the usefulness of traditional segmentation methods based on gray levels. The new approach, based on using RF characteristics to segment B-scans may be used to complement B-scans to convey additional information from ultrasonographic data.

To illustrate, an envelope image, generated from simulated RF data, is shown in Figure 8a. The image was based on the MRI shoulder scan shown in Figure 8b. The data displayed as an image in Figure 8a has very low contrast and signal-to-noise ratio, and is difficult to interpret. Of course, a traditional ultrasound B-scan is generally of higher quality, but, as mentioned earlier, artifacts and especially speckle make processing and analysis difficult.

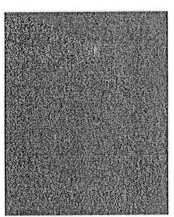   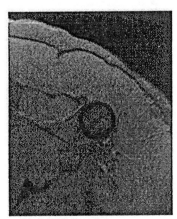

(a) Simulated ultrasound   **(b) MRI image.**
   envelope;

Figure 8. Shoulder Scan.

Much research has been performed into modelling scattering phenomena in ultrasound, manifested in B-scans as speckle patterns. It is now generally accepted that the amplitude of the RF signal of the ultrasound envelope (the logarithmic transformation of which results in the B-scan) follows specific statistical distributions, such as the Nakagami [Shankar, 2001], K [Molthen et al., 1998][Wachowiak et al., 2000][Smolikova et al., 2001][Wachowiak et al., 2002b], generalized K [Liu et al. 1997],

homodyned K [Dutt and Greenleaf, 1994][Hao et al., 2002], and generalized
Nakagami distributions [Shankar, 2002]. The parameters of such models
provide an indication of the density and regularity of tissue scatterers, which
is subsequently used to classify and characterize tissue.

Simple rules can be extracted from analyses of these parameters. For
example, the Nakagami distribution is specified by the shape parameter m
and the scale parameter Ω (also the second moment of the distribution). An
easy but robust method to estimate parameters from N samples x_i, $i = 1$,...,
N, is the inverse normalized variance estimator [Abidi and Kaveh, 2000]:

$$\hat{m} = \frac{\hat{\mu}_2^2}{\hat{\mu}_4 - \hat{\mu}_2^2}, \quad \Omega = \hat{\mu}_2, \quad \hat{\mu}_v = \frac{1}{N} \sum_{i=1}^{N} x_i^v$$

In ultrasound breast scans, malignant lesions are often characterized by
speculations that act as sharp boundaries, thereby increasing the average
level of the backscattered signal. The parameters are estimated in image
regions of interest corresponding to the suspected lesion ("site") and away
from the suspicious area ("away"). The differences in the parameters from
benign lesions and from normal tissue can be stated as *IF-THEN* rules
[Shankar et al., 2001]:

	IF	*THEN*
AND	$m_{site} < m_{away}$ $\Omega_{site} < \Omega_{away}$	images contain benign lesions
AND	$m_{site} > m_{away}$ $\Omega_{site} \ll \Omega_{away}$	images contain malignant lesions.

The rules can be further simplified by examining the two values $m_{norm} = m_{away}/m_{site}$, and $\Omega_{norm} = \Omega_{site}/\Omega_{away}$ (note the difference in the
denominators) [Shankar et al., 2001]. These rules, in combination with other
clinical tests, may be used to improve diagnosis and to better assess patient
response to therapy.

In addition, the numeric values of statistical parameters may be
substituted for image gray levels at corresponding spatial locations as a
segmentation mechanism. This approach, utilizing different parameter
estimation techniques for the Nakagami and K distributions, is shown in
Figure 9.

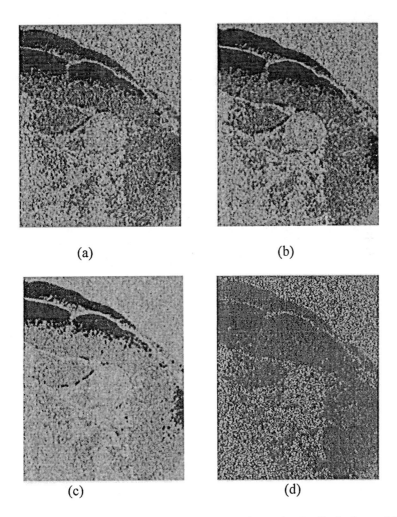

(a)   (b)

(c)   (d)

Figure 9.   Parameter Maps: (a) INV (Nakagami Distribution);   (b) TP
(Nakagami Distribution); (c) SNR Values (*K* Distribution);   (d)
Fractional SNR (*K* Distribution).

These results demonstrate that segmentation based on speckle model
parameters can provide an alternative view of ultrasound data that
complements B-scans. These parameter maps can highlight features not
normally visible in B-scans. Areas of homogeneous density not clearly
visible from the image are more apparent in the parameter maps. In a wider
sense, the preceding approach may be considered as data preprocessing (as
all segmentation is preprocessing) *and* as data reduction. Multiple
modalities are "fused" to generate a more informative set of data that can

potentially facilitate data mining tasks, and to increase the quality of the results from these tasks.

6.5   Feature Selection Supported By Domain Experts

Many of the concepts discussed above are illustrated in a recent application of data mining in a picture archiving and communication system (PACS) for computer-assisted diagnosis [Perner, 2002]. Here, knowledge for image analysis and diagnosis was obtained from descriptions in an image database, and data mining techniques were employed to gain additional knowledge about specific image features. Normally, statistical tests are applied to regions of interest (ROIs) extracted from a large number of images to determine the significance of various features [Megalooikonomou et al., 1999][Burl and Lucchetti, 2000]. Clustering is next utilized to determine groups of similar objects [Eklund et al., 2000]. Finally, patterns are identified using association rules [Perner, 2002][Burl and Lucchetti, 2000]. Another approach to an image representation and analysis is symbolic image description by experts. Domain experts often prefer this approach, as simple features (such as mean, standard deviation, entropy, etc.) cannot adequately describe complex objects. However, there are generally no standard vocabularies to provide such symbolic descriptions (the ARC-BIRADS code for analysis of mammograms is an attempt to standardize the vocabulary). Furthermore, a small number of relevant features, in contrast to a large, rich vocabulary, makes reasoning more effective [Perner, 2002]. To address these issues, a tool was developed at the Institute of Computer Vision and Applied Computer Sciences in Leipzig, Germany, to facilitate learning a compact vocabulary for diagnostic reasoning [Perner, 2002]. The tool was specifically used for HEp-2 cell classification, which is useful in the identification of antinuclear antibodies.

The entire image mining procedure consists of [Perner, 2002]: (1) Brainstorming, whereby the domain application is studied; (2) Interviewing, in which relevant attributes and their values are identified; (3) Collection of image descriptions into a database; (4) Conducting the actual data mining experiment, and (5) Review and analysis of the data mining results.

In this methodology, some features are derived from numerical ROI low-level statistical descriptions, such as mean, standard deviation, skewness, kurtosis, etc., features such as lines, edges, or blobs, and higher-level features derived from the lower-level features (data preprocessing and reduction). Experts determine symbolic features, representing the highest abstraction level. After a large number of images have been analyzed, a data mining tool performs decision-tree induction. A set of diagnostically relevant rules and image features are then learned. Thus, induction serves not only in knowledge discovery, but also in selecting relevant features [Perner, 2002].

As it is often difficult to describe particular features by automatic procedures, descriptions by experts are still required, and will be for the foreseeable future. Once the relevant features and rules are identified, fully automated systems for specific conditions can be developed to aid physicians in their diagnostic work.

7.   CONCLUSIONS

In the next few years, the pace of change for healthcare information management will accelerate substantially. Driven by the continuing increases in the cost of healthcare and the persistence of high rates of medical errors, the change will be aided by several factors such as:

- widespread application of the HIPAA (Health Insurance Portability and Accountability Act) on data privacy and security standards,
- the increasing penetration of sophisticated connectivity solutions, and
- the spread of intelligent computer-based medical devices and systems.

These factors will result in the electronic storage of more and more health data, leading ultimately to the increasing use of electronic patient records by hospitals, medical groups and health plans. New sources generate not only numeric and symbolic data about patients, but also text, images, signals, and sound, all of them integrated in an electronic multimedia patient record. The increase in sources of data is already allowing new types of analytical tools to be developed that will ultimately reshape the way of how the quality and cost of medical care is managed.

Applying data mining and knowledge discovery techniques to data from heterogeneous sources is often challenging. Difficulties are particularly apparent in the case of patient medical records, which consist of both descriptive and semi-structured qualitative information, and quantitative data, such as measurements, images, and a variety of biosignals. However, the quality and usefulness of data from quantitative sources are by no means easy to standardize, as they largely depend on the skill of medical personnel, acquisition equipment, and the specific data modality. Noise, imprecise measurements, and ambiguities in the representation of signals, text data and images underscore the importance of preprocessing, feature extraction and reduction in the preparatory phases of patient records data mining. In this chapter, we explained the importance of the preprocessing and feature extraction phases in mining a large collection of multimedia patient records.

Selected techniques with illustrative examples were given showing the applicability of rule-based methodologies in the preparation phases of a data mining process. Rule-based techniques are applicable not only for structured parts of patient records, but also for multimedia parts including medical images and medical texts. This approach tries to obtain a theoretical generalization automatically from the data by means of induction, deriving empirical models and learning from examples. The resultant theory, while maybe not expressed through fundamental physical laws, can yield a good understanding of the physical process and can have great practical utility. Various applications indicate that the rule-based algorithms offer numerous advantages over other approaches such as neural networks and regression analysis, namely:

- simplicity of representation and simplicity of interpretation of the discovered knowledge,
- relatively high accuracy of the rule-based models,
- low computational complexity, and
- model robustness with respect to missing and noisy data.

Although the first generation of data mining algorithms works well with the numeric and symbolic features, and although some learning algorithms are available for learning to classify images, or to classify text, the fact is that we currently lack effective methodologies for learning from data that are represented by a combination of these various media. As a result, the current state of the art in a medical outcome analysis is to ignore the image, text, and raw sensor portion of the medical record, or at best to summarize these in some oversimplified form (e.g., labeling the complex ultrasound image as simply "normal" or "abnormal"). However, it is intuitively clear that if interpretation could be based on the full medical record, we would expect much greater accuracy. Therefore, a topic of considerable current research interest is the development of algorithms that can learn regularities over rich, mixed media data. The important challenges and future research directions for the successful application of data mining techniques in medicine are:

- Electronic medical records consisting of different multimedia data, based on semantically clean and structured knowledge representation, are needed.

- New and/or improved techniques for automated capture of clinical data from speech, natural language text, images, laboratory measurements, or structured entry in a standard but semantically rich format, are also needed.

- Based on structured representation of clinical record, data should be universally accessible for different automated analysis. This includes solutions for standards and infrastructure for distributed databases with patient records.

- There is an expectation that new medical knowledge will be created with existing or improved data mining techniques, and here, the preprocessing phase will play an essential role. Having established the data infrastructure for clinical data, there will be unprecedented opportunities for gaining new knowledge.

The wealth of unstructured and distributed data presents enormous opportunities for research related to information extraction from patient records and other medical reports, and discovering associations, patterns, trends, complex multi-attribute correlations, and other difficult tasks involving discovering knowledge from data. Medicine is a data rich field, and also medicine is a knowledge rich field. The basic problems here involve the interaction of raw data and discovered knowledge, and producing more human centered methodologies that increase the trust and confidence of medical staff in using intelligent systems for a clinical practice.

REFERENCES

Aronow D.B., Fangfang F., Croft W.B., Ad hoc classification of radiology reports. *Journal of the American Medical Informatics Association*, 1999, 6(5), pp. 393-411.

Abdi A., Kaveh M., Performance Comparison of Three Different Estimators for the Nakagami *m* parameter using Monte Carlo Simulation, *IEEE Communications Letters*, Vol. 4, 2000, pp. 119-121.

Adibi J., Sheen W., A review on Data Mining Techniques and Applications in Health Care, *AMIA Tutorial*, Boston, MA, U.S.A., May 2000.

Antonie M., Zaiana O. R., Coman A., Application of Data Mining Techniques for Medical Image Classification, *Proceedings of the Second International Workshop on Multimedia Data Mining*, San Francisco, 2001, pp. 94-101.

Blake C., Pratt W., Better Rules, Fewer Features: A Semantic Approach to Selecting Features from Text, *IEEE Data Mining Conference*, San Jose, CA, U.S.A., 2001.

Bloch I., Some Aspects of Dempster-Shafer Evidence Theory for Classification of Multi-modality Medical Images Taking Partial Volume Effect Into Account, *Pattern Recognition Letters*, Vol. 17, 1996, pp. 905-919.

Bloch I., Sureda F., Pellot C., Herment A., Fuzzy Modeling and Fuzzy Mathematical Morphology Applied to 3D Reconstruction of Blood Vessels by Multimodality Data Fusion, in Dubois, D. et al., editors, *Fuzzy Set Methods in Information Engineering: A Guided Tour of Applications*, John Wiley & Sons, New York, NY, U.S.A., 1996, pp. 93-110.

Bloch I., Maître H., Fusion of Image Information under Imprecision, in Bouchon-Meunier, B., editor, *Aggregation and Fusion of Imperfect Information*, Physica Springer Verlag, 1997, pp. 189-213.

Burl M.C., Lucchetti D., Autonomous visual discovery. In: Dasarathy, B.V. (Ed.), Data *Mining and Knowledge Discovery: Theory, Tools, and Technology*, Vol. 4057. SPIE, Bellingham, Washington DC, U.S.A., pp. 240–250.

Chapman W.W., Haug P.J., Bayesian modeling for linking causally related observations in chest x-ray reports, *Proceedings of the AMIA Symposium*, 1998, pp. 587-591.

Collmann Jeff (Editor), CPRI's Comprehensive Toolkit for Health Care Security Management, April 2001, *http://www.himss.org/asp/cpritoolkit_homepage.asp*.

Dutt V., Greenleaf J.F., Ultrasound Echo Envelope Analysis Using a Homodyned K Distribution Signal Model, *Ultrasonic Imaging*, Vol. 16, 1994, pp. 265-287.

Eklund P.W., You J., Deer P., Mining Remote Sensing Image Data: An Integration of Fuzzy Set Theory and Image Understanding Techniques for Environmental Change Detection. In: Dasarathy B.V. (Ed.), Data *Mining and Knowledge Discovery: Theory, Tools, and Technology*, Vol. 4057. SPIE, Bellingham, Washington DC, U.S.A., 2000, pp. 265–273.

Han J., Kamber M., *Data Mining: Concepts and Techniques*, Academic Press, San Diego, CA, U.S.A., 2001.

Hand D., Mannila H., Smith P., *Principles of Data Mining*, The MIT Press, Cambridge, MA, U.S.A., 2001.

Hao X., Bruce C.J., Pislaru C., Greenleaf J.F., Classification of Normal and Infarcted Myocardium Based on Statistical Analysis of High Frequency Intracardiac Ultrasound RF Signal, *Proc. of SPIE Medical Imaging* 2002, Ultrasonic Imaging and Signal Processing, 2002, pp. 139-146.

Heath M., Bowyer K., Kopans D., Moore R., Kegelmeyer P. Jr., "The Digital Database for Screening Mammography", in *Proc. of the 5th International Workshop on Digital Mammography*, Toronto, Canada, June 2000. [Online]. Available: http:// marathon.csee.usf.edu/Mammography/Database.html.

Holmes J. H., Learning Classifier Systems Applied to Knowledge Discovery in Clinical Research Databases, In: Lanzi PL, Stolzmann W, and Wilson SW (eds.) Learning Classifier Systems: From Foundations to Applications. *Lecture Notes in Artificial Intelligence*, Volume 1813. Springer Verlag, Berlin, 2000, pp. 243-262.

Hripcsak G, Allen B, Cimino J, Lee R., Access to data: comparing AccessMed to Query by Review, *Proc AMIA Annu. Fall Symp* 1997, pp. 303-307.

Hyvärinen A., Oja E., A Fast Fixed-point Algorithm for Independent Component Analysis, *Neural Computation*, Vol. 9, 1997, pp. 1483-1492.

Jung T., Makeig S., McKeown M. J., Bell A. J., Lee T., Sejnowski T. J., Imaging Brain Dynamics Using Independent Component Analysis, *Proceedings of the IEEE*, Vol. 89, No. 7, July 2001, pp. 1107-1122.

Kantardzic M., R. P. Pasic, C. Templeman, R. Levine, "Data Mining Approach in a Selection of Laparoscopic Techniques", *Proceedings of the 10th International Conference on Intelligent Systems*, Arlington, VA, U.S.A., June 2001, pp. 1-4.

Kantardzic, M., Data *Mining: Concepts, Models, Methods, and Algorithms*, IEEE Press & John Wiley, November 2002.

Kohane I.S., Greenspun P., Fackler J., Cimino C., Szolovits P., Building National Electronic Medical Record Systems via the WWW, *Journal of the AMIA*, Vol. 3, No. 3, May/June 1996, pp. 191-207.

Lavrac N., Machine learning for data mining in medicine, *Proceedings of the Joint European Conference on Artificial Intelligence in Medicine and Medical Decision Making*, Springer Verlag, June 1999, pp. 47-62.

Lin R., Lenert L., Middleton B., Shiffman S., A free-text processing system to capture physical findings: Canonical Phrase Identification System (CAPIS), *Proc. Annual Symposium Computer App. Med. Care*, 1991, pp. 843-847.

Liu D.L., Waag R.C., Harmonic Amplitude Distribution in a Wideband Ultrasonic Wavefront After Propagation Through Human Abdominal Wall and Breast Specimens, *J. Acoustic Soc. Am.*, Vol. 2, 1997, 1172-1183.

Mandl K. D., Szolovits P., Kohane I. S., Markwell D., MacDonald R., Public standards and patients' control: how to keep electronic medical records accessible but private, *IBM Journal* 2001, Vol. 322, pp. 283-287.

Markwell D. C., Fogarty L., Hinchley A., Validation of a European message standard for electronic health records, In *"Medical Informatics Europe '99'"*, Kokol P. (ed.), IOPress, Amsterdam, 1999, pp.818-823.

Megalooikonomou K., Davatzikos C., Herskovits E., Mining Lesion-Defect Associations in a Brain Image Data Base, *Proceedings of the International Conference Knowledge Discovery and Data Mining* (KDD'99), San Diego, CA, U.S.A., 1999, pp. 347–351.

Milanova M. G., Wachowiak M. P., Rubin S., Elmaghraby A. S., Application of Information Theory for Encoding Objects in the Retina and in the Primary Visual Cortex Using Sequences of Natural Images, *Proceedings of the Conference on Mathematics and Engineering Techniques in Medicine and Biological Sciences*, Las Vegas, Nevada, June 25-28, 2001. pp. 311-317.

Misiti M., Misiti Y., Oppenheim G., Poggi J.-M., *Wavelet Toolbox User's Guide.* The Mathworks, Inc., 1996.

Molthen R.C., Shankar P.M., Reid J.M., Forsberg F., Halpern E.J., Comparisons of the Rayleigh and K-Distribution Models Using in Vivo Breast and Liver Tissue, *Ultrasound in Med. Biol.*, Vol. 24, No. 1, 1998, pp. 93-100.

Perner P., Image Mining: Issues, Framework, a Generic Tool and its Application to Medical-Image Diagnosis, *Engineering Applications of Artificial Intelligence*, Vol. 15, 2002, pp. 205-216.

Porter S. C., Mandl K. D., Data quality and the electronic medical record: a role for direct parental data entry, *Proc. AMIA Symp.* 1999, Vol. 1-2, pp. 354-8.

Prather, J. C., Lobach D. F., Goodwin L.K., Hales J.W., Hage M.L., Hammond W.E., Medical data mining: Knowledge discovery in a clinical data warehouse. *Proc AMIA Annul Fall Symposium* 1997, pp. 101-105.

Rickard H. E., G. D. Tourassi, and A. S. Elmaghraby, Self– Organizing Maps For Masking Mammography Images, *Proceedings of The 4th Annual IEEE Conference on Information Technology Applications in Biomedicine*, Birmingham, UK, April 2003, pp. 302-305.

Robb R. A., *Biomedical Imaging, Visualization, and Analysis*, Wiley-Liss, New York, NY, 2000.

Rushing J. A., Ranganath H. S., Hinke T. H., Graves S. J., Using Association Rules as Texture Features, *IEEE Transaction on Pattern Analysis and Machine Intelligence*, Vol. 23, No. 8, August 2001, pp. 845-858.

Selker H.P., Systems for comparing actual and predicted mortality rates: Characteristics to promote cooperation in improving hospital care. *Ann Intern Med*, 1993, Vol. 118, pp. 820-822.

Shankar P.M., Dumane V.A., Reid J.M., Genis V., Forsberg F., Piccoli C. W., Goldberg B.B., Classification of Ultrasonic B-mode Images of Breast Masses Using Nakagami Distribution, *IEEE Trans. Ultrasonics, Ferroelectrics, and Frequency Control*, Vol. 48, No. 2, 2001, pp. 569-580.

Shankar P.M., Ultrasonic Tissue Characterization Using a Generalized Nakagami Model, *IEEE Trans. Ultrasonics, Ferroelectrics, and Frequency Control*, Vol. 48, No. 6, 2001, pp. 1716-1720.

Shortliffe E. H., Perreault L. E., Wiederhold G., Fagan L. M.(ed.), *Medical Informatics: Computer Applications in Health Care and Biomedicine*, (2nd Edition), Springer Verlag, 2000.

Smolikova R., Wachowiak M. P., Zurada, J. M., Elmaghraby A. S., A Neural Network Approach for Estimating Large K Distribution Parameters, *IJCNN 2001*, Vol. 3, 2001, pp. 2139-2143.

Smolikova R., Wachowiak M.P., Zurada J.M., and Elmaghraby A.S., Segmentation of Ultrasound Images with Speckle Modeling, Analysis of Biomedical Signals and Images,

Proc. of IEEE EMBS/EUROSIP International Conference (Biosignal 2002), Eds. J. Jan, J. Kozumplik, I. Provaznik, 2002, pp. 316-319.

Smolikova R., Wachowiak M.P, Aggregation Operators for Selection Problems, (In Press), *Fuzzy Sets and Systems*, 2002, Elsevier.

Solaiman, B., Debon, R., Pipelier, F., Cauvin, J.-M., Roux, C., Information Fusion: Application to Data and Model Fusion for Ultrasound Image Segmentation, *IEEE Transactions on Biomedical Engineering*, Vol. 46, 1999, pp. 1171-1175.

Tang P. C., and Hammond W. E., A Progress Report on Computer-Based Patient Records in the United States, 1999, *http://www.nap.edu/html/computer/commentary.html*.

Tong S., Bezerianos A., Paul J., Zhu Y., Thakor N., Removal of ECG Interference from the EEG Recordings in Small Animals Using Independent Component Analysis, *Journal of Neuroscience Methods*, Vol. 108, 2001, pp. 11-17.

Vigário R., Särelä J., Jousmäki V., Hämäläinen M., Oja E., Independent Component Approach to the Analysis of EEG and MEG Recordings, *IEEE Transactions on Biomedical Engineering*, Vol. 47, 2000, pp. 589-593.

Wachowiak M.P., Elmaghraby A.S., Smolikova R, Zurada J.M, Classification and Estimation of Ultrasound Speckle Noise with Neural Networks, *IEEE Int. Symp. on Bio-Informatics & Biomedical Engineering (BIBE)*, Key Bridge , Nov. 8-10, 2000, pp. 245-252.

Wachowiak M.P., Smolikova R., Tourassi G.D., Elmaghraby A.S., Separation of Cardiac Artifacts from EMG Signals with Independent Component Analysis – Comparison with High-Pass and Wavelets Filtering, Analysis of Biomedical Signals and Images, *Proc. of IEEE EMBS/EUROSIP International Conference (Biosignal 2002)*, Eds. J. Jan, J. Kozumplik, I. Provaznik, 2002 (a), pp. 23-26.

Wachowiak M.P., Smolikova R., Zurada J.M., Elmaghraby A.S., Estimation of K Distribution Parameters Using Neural Networks, *IEEE Transactions on Biomedical Engineering*, Vol. 49, No.6, 2002 (b), pp. 617-620.

Wahle A., Prause G.P.M., von Birgelen C., Erbel R., Sonka M., Fusion of Angiography and Intravascular Ultrasound *in vivo*: Establishing the Absolute 3D Frame Orientation, *IEEE Transactions on Biomedical Engineering*, Vol. 46, 1999, pp. 1176-1180.

Wilcox A., Hripcsak G., Classification Algorithms Applied to Narrative Reports, *Proc. AMIA Symp.*, 1999, pp. 455-459.

Wilcox A., Hripcsak G., Medical Text Representations for Inductive Learning, *Proc. AMIA Symp.*, 2000, pp. 923-927.

Wloka M., Colleman J., Kuball S., Krishnan H., Johnson L., Bono P., Visualization and Registration of Multi-Modal Medical Data-Sets, 1998, http://www.cs.ucsd.edu/users/goguen/ courses/275/mmvr98.html.

AUTHORS' BIOGRAPHICAL STATEMENTS

Dr. Adel S. Elmaghraby is Professor and Chair of the Computer Engineering and Computer Science Department and the Director of the Multimedia Research Lab at the University of Louisville. He has also held appointments at the SEI - CMU, and the University of Wisconsin-Madison. His research is in Intelligent Multimedia Systems, Neural Networks, PDCS, Visualization, and Simulation with applications to biomedical computing, automation, and military war games. He is a member of editorial boards, and technical reviewer. He has been recognized for his achievements by several professional organizations including a Golden Core Membership Award by the IEEE Computer Society.

Dr. Mehmed Kantardzic received the B.S., M.S., and Ph.D. degrees in Computer Science from the University of Sarajevo, Bosnia. Until 1994, he was an Associate Professor at the University of Sarajevo, Faculty of Electrical Engineering. In 1995 he joined the Computer Engineering and Computer Science Department, University of Louisville as a visiting faculty, and since 2001 he is Associate Professor at the same Department, and Director of Data Mining Lab. His research interests are: data mining, soft computing, multimedia technologies on Internet, and distributed intelligent systems. He published in refereed journals and conference proceedings more than 120 articles, and his book on data mining is published by IEEE and John Wiley in 2002. Dr. Kantardzic is a member of IEEE, ISCA, SPIA, and he was Program Chair for ISCA '99 Conference in Denver, CO, and General Chair for ISCA-2001 Conference in Arlington, VA.

Dr. Mark P. Wachowiak obtained the Master of Science Degree from the University of Louisville in 1997, and the Ph.D. in Computer Science and Engineering from the same institution in 2002. He is currently with the Imaging Research Laboratories at the John P. Robarts Research Institute in London, Ontario, Canada. His research interests focus on biomedical computing and engineering, and include medical imaging, soft tissue modeling, surgery and therapy simulation, numerical analysis, and high-performance computing. Dr. Wachowiak is a member of the IEEE, the IEEE Engineering in Medicine and Biology Society, and SIAM.

Chapter 17 [1]

LEARNING TO FIND CONTEXT BASED SPELLING ERRORS

Hisham Al-Mubaid*, Klaus Truemper**

* *University of Houston - Clear Lake*
Department of Computer Science
email: hisham@cl.uh.edu

** *Department of Computer Science*
University of Texas at Dallas
Richardson, TX 75083-0688, U.S.A.
Email: truemper@utdallas.edu

Abstract: A context-based spelling error is a spelling or typing error that turns an intended word into another word of the language. For example, the intended word "sight" might become the word "site." A spell checker cannot identify such an error. In the English language—the case of interest here—a syntax checker may also fail to catch such an error since, among other reasons, the parts-of-speech of an erroneous word may permit an acceptable parsing. This chapter presents an effective method called *Ltest* for identifying the majority of context-based spelling errors. Ltest learns from prior, correct text how context-based spelling errors may manifest themselves, by purposely introducing such errors and analyzing the resulting text using a data mining algorithm. The output of this learning step consists of a collection of logic formulas that in some sense represent knowledge about possible context-based spelling errors. When, subsequently, testing text is examined for context-based spelling errors, the logic formulas and a portion of the prior text are used to analyze the case at hand and to pinpoint likely errors.

Tests conducted on different text samples indicate that the method is effective for the recognition of the majority of context-based spelling errors; Ltest found 68% of context-based spelling errors in large texts and 87% of such errors in small texts. These detection rates are relative to words for which training was possible using the prior text.

Keywords: Semantics of Natural Language, Algorithms, Learning Typing/Spelling Errors, Representation of Word Context, Data Mining, Learning Logic.

---

[1] Triantaphyllou, E. and G. Felici (Eds.), **Data Mining and Knowledge Discovery Approaches based on Rule Induction Techniques**, Massive Computing Series, Springer, Heidelberg, Germany, pp. 597-628, 2006.

1. INTRODUCTION

Finding a spelling or typing error is easy if the erroneous word is not part of the language, since then a spell checker can point out such a *non-word error.* The detection problem is harder if the erroneous word is part of the language. An example is the misspelling of the intended word "sight" as "site." Such an error can be detected by examining the context of the word. Accordingly, it has been called a *context-based spelling error* (Golding (1995), Golding and Roth (1996, 1999), Golding and Schabes (1996)).

It is convenient that throughout most of the chapter we make the following two assumptions. First, we assume that the event of a context-based spelling error is relatively rare, and that the user is unlikely to make the same mistake several times in the same document. For example, if the user misspells "sight" as "site," then this error is assumed to be due to a momentary lapse and not due to user ignorance regarding the spelling of "sight." Second, we assume that, for any erroneous word instance introduced by a context-based spelling error, the text also contains an instance of the correct word. The two assumptions are mostly but not always satisfied. For example, a person may confuse some words and make some errors repeatedly. For example, such confusion could exist about "its" versus "it's" or "complement" versus "compliment." As a second example, a word may occur just once in a text, and that single occurrence may be mistyped or misspelled. Toward the end of the chapter, in Sections 4 and 5, we describe extensions of the method that do not require the two assumptions.

In contrast to spell checkers, a syntax checker may possibly detect a context-based spelling error. However, there is no guarantee of such detection, since, among other reasons, the parts-of-speech of the erroneous word may permit an acceptable parsing of the sentence. For example, if "site" displaces "sight" in the sentence "It was a beautiful sight," then the resulting sentence "It was a beautiful site" has an acceptable parsing. Indeed, the latter sentence is meaningful and by itself gives no clue that the word "site" is out of place. Here are a few additional examples of intended and erroneous words: bay–pay, fair–fare, for–four, its–it's, lead–led, quiet–quite, them–then, there–three.

Error detection by a syntax checker likely is difficult if the text contains many special terms, symbols, formulas, or conventions whose syntactic contribution cannot be established without a complete understanding of the text; examples are mathematical TₑX or LATₑX texts. For such texts, as well as for texts that do not contain such complicating aspects, this chapter offers an effective technique for identifying the majority of context-based spelling errors without the need to fully understand the text. The main results are as follows.

(1) A new way of encoding, for a given occurrence of a word w, the structure of the neighborhood of the occurrence and the connection with other occurrences of w and their neighborhoods. The encoding uses the text under investigation as well as a second text that acts as a reference text.

(2) A new way of learning from prior, correct text how context-based spelling errors can be recognized. This step uses the encoding of (1) and an existing

data mining algorithm. It produces a set of logic formulas that contain insight into context-based spelling errors.

(3) A new way of employing the logic formulas of (2) to identify likely context-based spelling errors in testing texts. The scheme accepts both small and large testing texts, and it handles unusual cases such as erroneous words never seen in the learning phase.

The method is called *Ltest (Logic test)* as it uses logic formulas to test for errors. Ltest has been added to an existing spell and syntax checking system. We have conducted tests involving mathematical book chapters typeset in TEX, technical papers typeset in LATEX, and newspaper texts in two subject areas. For the learning step we randomly selected prior texts from the given domain. These texts averaged 30,012 word instances. The testing texts consisted of some large texts averaging 7,138 word instances and some small texts averaging 105 word instances. The latter texts were introduced to see if the method can find context-based spelling errors when a testing text does not provide much insight into the usage pattern of words. Although the average prior text had about four times the size of the average large testing text, roughly half the word usage in the testing texts was not sufficiently represented in the prior texts to allow learning of such usage and subsequent error checking. Such representation does not require much: If Ltest is to learn the difference between a given word and a given erroneous word, then both words must occur at least three times in both the *training text* and the *history text*, which Ltest obtains by splitting the prior text. Though this requirement is mild, for the average large text just 3,162 possible error cases out of a total of 7,360 possible error cases, or 43%, could be tested. For the average small text, 12 possible error cases out of a total of 28 possible error cases, or 43%, could be tested. It is shown later that these percentages can be boosted close to 100% by a suitable augmentation of the training text and the history text. We did not carry out such augmentation for the tests since such a change might have introduced a bias. Instead, we evaluated the performance of Ltest on the possible error cases for which the prior texts had allowed learning. We introduced such errors randomly into the testing texts. On average, Ltest detected 68% of these errors in large texts and 87% in small texts. The testing texts with the errors were also checked by the syntax checker of the system, in a separate step. The syntax checker, by itself, performed poorly, finding only 12% of the errors in large texts and 4% in small texts. Combined use of Ltest and the syntax checker—which is the way the entire process has been implemented—boosted the detection rate for large texts to 72%, but did not improve the rate of 87% for small texts. The difference in performance between samll and large texts is due to two factors:
– large texts normally involve numerous special terms, symbols, formulas, and conventions that make error detection more complicated than small texts, – small testing texts are examined by the classifiers that are created for large testing texts, so classifiers perform better on the small texts.

Define a diagnosis to be *false-positive* if the method estimates a correct word instance to be in error. Clearly, user acceptance of the method requires that

at most a few false-positive diagnoses are made. This requirement was satisfied in the test cases, since false-positive diagnoses occurred on average for 23
word instances, or 0.7% of the 3,162 tested instances of a large text, and for
1 word instance of a small text. The 1 false-positive diagnosis for the average
small testing text represents 8% of the tested instances, which is high but not
important since the number of such cases, which is 1, is small. We ran another
experiment on the method using texts for which the two leading prior methods,
which are *BaySpell* (Golding (1995)) and *WinSpell* (Golding and Roth (1999)),
had produced results. In the experiment, Ltest outperformed both methods
by classifying 95.6% of the considered word instances correctly. BaySpell and
WinSpell achieved 89.9% and 93.5% accuracy, respectively. Testing time is
very low in these experiments: in the order of 2 minutes for large texts, and in
order of 10 seconds for small texts, more details in Section 4 and in tables 3
and 6.

Taken together, the high detection rates and the low number of false-positive
diagnoses for both large and small texts make the method an effective tool.

The rest of the chapter proceeds as follows. Section 2 discusses previous
work. Section 3 describes the method. Section 4 discusses the implementation
of the method and the computational results. Section 5 outlines extensions.
Section 6 summarizes the main points of the chapter. Appendices A to D
contain technical details of some of the steps.

2.   PREVIOUS WORK

A number of methods have been developed for the detection of context-based
spelling errors. The research up to 1992 is covered in the survey by Kukich
(1992). The methods proposed since then use a Bayesian approach (Golding
(1995)) that may be combined with part-of-speech trigrams (Golding and Schabes (1996)), transformation-based learning (Mangu and Brill (1997)), latent
semantic analysis (Jones and Martin (1997)), differential grammars (Powers
(1997)), lexical chains (St-Onge (1995), Hirst and St-Onge (1995), Budanitsky
(1999), Budanitsky and Hirst (2001)), and Winnow-based techniques (Golding and Roth (1996, 1999), Roth (1998)). The two leading prior methods are
the statistics-based *BaySpell* (Golding (1995)) and the Winnow-based *WinSpell*
(Golding and Roth (1999)).

The Bayesian method (Golding (1995)) handles context-based spelling correction as a problem of ambiguity resolution. The ambiguity is modeled by
confusion sets. The Bayesian method uses decision lists to choose the proper
word from the confusion set. It also relies on classifiers for two types of features: context-words and collocations. The method learns these features from a
training corpus of correct text. The testing process starts with a list of features
sorted by decreasing strength and traverses the entire list to combine evidences
from all matching features in a given context and target word. In the experiment reported in Golding (1995), 18 confusion sets are used. The performance
ranges from 45% to 98% with an average of 82% of the words classified cor-

rectly. Golding uses 1-Million-Word Brown corpus and the 3/4-Million-Word corpus of the *Wall Street Journal.*

The *Winnow* approach of Golding and Roth (1996) uses a multiplicative weight update algorithm that achieves a good accuracy and handles a large number of features. The method learns large set of features with the corresponding weight. The method performs better than Bayesian. The multiplicative weight update algorithm represents the members of a confusion set as clouds of simple nodes corresponding to context words and collocation features. Winnow requires confusion sets to be known in advance. In the training phase, a feature extractor learns a set of features and produces a huge list of all features in the training text. Statistics of occurrence of features are also collected. Pruning is applied to eliminate unreliable features. The algorithm has been applied to 21 confusion sets taken from the list of "Words commonly confused" in the back of the Random House dictionary (Flexner (1983)).

3.   DETAILS OF Ltest

For a given domain of texts, Ltest carries out two steps called the *learning step* and the *testing step*. In the learning step, Ltest learns from *prior text* that is known to be error-free how context-based spelling errors may manifest themselves. Ltest splits the prior text into a *training text* and a *history text*. We cover the splitting process in a moment.

The idea of training text and history text is based on the following intuitive idea. Suppose we are not experts in some field, say in law. We are given some correct legal document to read. As we scan the text, we may not really understand the sense in which some words are used. But we can learn how words are used in connection with other words. Next, we are given another legal document and are asked to check it for errors. Strictly speaking, we cannot do so since we are not experts. But we can read the second text and see whether some words are used out of context, relative to the word usage in the first text.

In terms of this intuitive discussion, let us view the history text as the first document and the training text as the second one. The reader may object to the latter choice since the training text is correct, as is, of course, the history text. But that changes now. We introduce errors into the training text, one at a time, and try to see how we could locate that error using both the training text and the history text. Using data mining, we compress that knowledge about finding errors into logic formulas. Later, when a new text that is not known to be correct is tested for errors, we analyze that new text using these logic formulas. At that time, the new text plays the role of the training text, while the history text plays the same role as before.

Throughout this section, w is a word that by a typical spelling or typing error may become another word, which we denote by v. We call the correct word w the *intended* word, while any incorrect v that is produced instead of w by a typical spelling or typing error, is an *error word* for w. We collect the error words v for a given intended word w in the *confusion set* for w. For example, if the intended word w is *there*, then the possible error words v for w are *three* and *their*, and hence {*three, their*} is the confusion set for *there*.

We call the possible alteration of w to v a *substitution* and denote it by $v \leftarrow w$. The substitutions linking the just-mentioned correct *there* and the error words *their* and *three* are *three$\leftarrow$there* and *their$\leftarrow$there*. Other example substitutions are *must$\leftarrow$just* and *its$\leftarrow$it's*. To streamline the presentation, we skip here details of the construction of the substitutions. Those details are covered in Appendix A.

We employ the notation v_i to represent the ith instance of the word v in the given text. In connection with a given substitution $v \leftarrow w$, we use the adjectives *good* and *bad* in the obvious way. For example, if an instance v_i of v in a text was intended to be an instance w_j of w, then we say that the instance v_i is bad and that the instance w_j is good.

Next we discuss the learning step.

3.1 Learning Step

First, Ltest splits the prior text into a *training text* and a *history text* by assigning each sentence of the prior text to one of the two texts. The assignment is done by a heuristic method described in Appendix B. The method has the goal that, for each substitution $v \leftarrow w$ for which both v and w occur in the prior text, the training text and the history text contain about the same number of instances of v as well as w. Of course, that goal may not be reached for a particular v and w, due to the way these words may occur in the sentences of the prior text. But according to experiments, the method typically gets close to that goal.

With the training text and history text at hand, the learning step carries out the following process for each substitution $v \leftarrow w$. For each instance v_i of v in the training text, a *characteristic vector* is computed. The vector has a total of 18 ± 1 entries. The entries relate the words, parts-of-speech of words, punctuation marks, and special symbols near a given instance v_i in the training text to the words, parts-of-speech of words, punctuation marks, and special symbols near other instances v_j of v in either the training text or the history text. In terms of the earlier, intuitive discussion, the entries of the characteristic vector record the usage of the word v in the context of the training text and the history text.

For example, suppose that the instance v_i of v is preceded by two words p^1 and p^2, say in the sequence $p^2\ p^1\ v_i$. If some other instance v_j of v in the training text is preceded by the same two words, in the same sequence, that is, $p^2\ p^1\ v_j$, then the 4th entry of the characteristic vector is $+1$. If no such sequence $p^2\ p^1\ v_j$ exists in the training text, then the 4th entry is -1. Analogously, if the history text contains a sequence $p^2\ p^1\ v_j$, then the 13th entry of the characteristic vector is $+1$. If no such sequence exists in the history text, then that entry is -1. To unclutter the presentation, we omit here a detailed discussion of the remaining entries of the characteristic vector. Details are included in Appendix C.

The reader may wonder why we do not use 0 instead of -1 to record absence of the sequence $p^2 \; p^1 \; v_j$. The reason is the encoding convention of the data mining tool Lsquare introduced shortly. That tool interprets $+1$ to mean that a certain fact, say X, holds, -1 to mean that fact X does not hold, and 0 to mean that it is unknown whether fact X holds, Felici and Truemper (2002).

Suppose the characteristic vectors for each instance v_i of v have been computed. Then, for each instance w_j of w in the training text, w_j is replaced temporarily by an instance v_r of v, and a characteristic vector for that v_r is computed. Consistent with the earlier use of the terms *good* and *bad*, we are justified to call each v_i good and each v_r bad.

At this point, we have two classes of characteristic vectors. The first class consists of the vectors representing features of the good occurrences of v. Let us call this class $G(v)$. The second class consists of the vectors representing features of the bad occurrences of v generated from the occurrences of w in the text. Let us call the second class $B_{v \leftarrow w}(v)$. The subscript $v \leftarrow w$ in the notation $B_{v \leftarrow w}(v)$ is needed since the second class is the set of vectors of bad occurrences of v generated from occurrences of w according to the substitution $v \leftarrow w$.

With the two classes $G(v)$ and $B_{v \leftarrow w}(v)$ at hand, the learning step uses the data mining algorithm *Lsquare* to compute a set of logic formulas $L_{v \leftarrow w}(v)$ that correctly classify each characteristic vector as being in one of the two classes $G(v)$ or $B_{v \leftarrow w}(v)$. Details of Lsquare are given in Chapter 5 "Learning Logic Formulas and Related Error Distributions" included in this volume. Thus, we only sketch here the features of Lsquare needed for the situation at hand.

Lsquare accepts as input two sets A and B of $\{0, \pm 1\}$ vectors, all having the same length, say n. An entry $+1$ means that a certain fact, say X, is known to hold, -1 means that fact X is known not to hold, and 0 means that it is unknown whether fact X holds. For the cases considered in this chapter, the vectors are the above defined characteristic vectors, and thus do not contain any 0s and are $\{\pm 1\}$ vectors. Lsquare outputs a set of 20 disjunctive normal form (DNF) logic formulas and 20 conjunctive normal form (CNF) logic formulas, each of which uses some subset of logic variables $y_1, y_2, \ldots, y_n$. To classify an arbitrary $\{\pm 1\}$ vector x of length n, Lsquare first assigns *True/False* values to $y_1, y_2, \ldots, y_n$ according to the rule $y_i = True$ if $x_i = 1$ and $y_i = False$ if $x_i = -1$. The *True/False* values are used to evaluate each of the 20 DNF and 20 CNF formulas. If a formula evaluates to *True* (resp. *False*), then we say that the formula produces a vote of 1 (resp. -1). Summing up the 40 votes produced by the 40 logic formulas, we get a *vote-total* that is even and may range from -40 to 40. Lsquare guarantees that, for each vector x of A (resp. B), the vote-total is positive (resp. negative). When A and B are randomly drawn from two populations $\mathcal{A}$ and $\mathcal{B}$, then a vote-total for a record of $\mathcal{A} \cup \mathcal{B}$ close to 40 means that the vector is in $\mathcal{A}$ with high probability and thus is in $\mathcal{B}$ with very low probability. As the vote-total decreases from $+40$ and eventually reaches -40, the probability of membership in $\mathcal{A}$ decreases while that of membership in $\mathcal{B}$ increases.

We interrupt the discussion of the training step for a moment and sketch how the constructed logic formulas $L_{v \leftarrow w}(v)$ are used in the testing step. Suppose we have a testing text with instances of v and w. We want to know whether, relative to the substitution $v \leftarrow w$, an instance v_k of v is good or bad. We compute, for that instance, a characteristic vector $t(v_k)$ using the testing/history texts instead of the training/history texts, and apply to that vector the set of logic formulas of $L_{v \leftarrow w}(v)$. Suppose the vote-total exceeds an appropriately selected threshold. We then estimate the vector $t(v_k)$ to be in the class $G(v)$, which plays the role of $\mathcal{A}$ in the above discussion about Lsquare. Thus, we have evidence that the instance v_k may be good. On the other hand, if the vector $t(v_k)$ is declared to be in the class $B_{v \leftarrow w}(v)$, then this is evidence that the instance v_k may be bad.

We continue the discussion of the training step. So far, we have learned to differentiate between good and bad instances of v relative to the substitution $v \leftarrow w$. Next, the learning step trains how to classify the other word of the substitution, w, as good or bad. Analogously to the case of v, the training step constructs two classes of vectors for w. The first class, $G(w)$, contains one vector for each good occurrence of w in the training text. The second class, $B_{v \leftarrow w}(w)$, includes one vector for each bad occurrence of w generated from one occurrence of v in the training text. Once more, we use Lsquare to determine a set of 40 logic formulas $L_{v \leftarrow w}(w)$ that, using vote-totals, correctly assign the vectors to their sets $G(w)$ and $B_{v \leftarrow w}(w)$. One may employ $L_{v \leftarrow w}(w)$ for testing a text that contains both v and w, as follows. Take an instance v_k of v in the text. To see whether v_k was intended to be a w, temporarily replace v_k by an instance of w; let that instance be w_q. Compute a characteristic vector $f_{v \leftarrow w}(w_q)$ for w_q, and apply $L_{v \leftarrow w}(w)$ to the vector $f_{v \leftarrow w}(w_q)$. If $f_{v \leftarrow w}(w_q)$ is declared to be in $G(w)$ (resp. $B_{v \leftarrow w}(w)$) according to some appropriately selected threshold, then we have evidence that w_q likely is good (resp. bad) and thus v_k likely is bad (resp. good).

Here is an example, for the substitution $there \leftarrow three$. We assume that the training text contains instances of $there$ and instances of $three$. The learning step builds four classes of characteristic vectors: $G(there)$, $B_{there \leftarrow three}(there)$, $G(three)$, and $B_{there \leftarrow three}(three)$. Using the first two classes, Lsquare creates the set of logic formulas $L_{there \leftarrow three}(there)$. This set is used to classify new vectors of $there$ into the set $G(there)$ or $B_{there \leftarrow three}(there)$. Using the next two classes, namely $G(three)$ and $B_{there \leftarrow three}(three)$, Lsquare builds the set of logic formulas $L_{there \leftarrow three}(three)$. The latter set is used to classify vectors of $three$ into the set $G(three)$ or $B_{there \leftarrow three}(three)$. Note that the class $G(there)$ consists of the vectors of the good occurrences of $there$, while the class $B_{there \leftarrow three}(there)$ consists of the vectors of the bad occurrences of $there$ generated from the occurrences of $three$.

The above discussion several times explicitly or implicitly refers to appropriately selected thresholds for various vote totals. The computation of these thresholds is part of the testing step, which we cover next.

3.2 Testing Step

We assume that the testing text has been processed by a spell checker and that, therefore, it does not contain any illegal words. For each word v of the text, we find all possible words w that by misspelling or mistyping may become v. That is, we construct the confusion set for v. We process each substitution $v \leftarrow w$ so determined as follows. If the text does not contain w, we cannot test the instances v_k with respect to the substitution $v \leftarrow w$. So assume that at least one instance of w is present. The processing depends on how often v occurs in the testing text. Declare the case to be *regular* if v occurs at least twice in the testing text, and define it to be *special* otherwise. We first treat the regular case.

3.2.1 Testing regular cases

If we do not have both sets $L_{v \leftarrow w}(v)$ and $L_{v \leftarrow w}(w)$ of logic formulas, then the learning step did not provide sufficient insight into the relationship between v and w. Accordingly, we ignore each instance v_k of v in the testing text with respect to the substitution $v \leftarrow w$. We call each such ignored v_k instance relative to $v \leftarrow w$ a *discarded $v(v \leftarrow w)$ instance*.

Now suppose that both $L_{v \leftarrow w}(v)$ and $L_{v \leftarrow w}(w)$ are available. For each instance v_k of v in the testing text, we construct a characteristic vector $t(v_k)$ from the testing/history texts. For each instance w_l of w in the testing text, we replace w_l temporarily by v_p and construct a characteristic vector $f_{v \leftarrow w}(v_p)$. We handle each instance w_l of w in the testing text analogously to v_k. Thus, for each w_l, we construct a characteristic vector $t(w_l)$. For each v_k of the testing text, we replace v_k temporarily by w_q and construct a characteristic vector $f_{v \leftarrow w}(w_q)$. At this point, we have the characteristic vectors $t(v_k)$, $f_{v \leftarrow w}(v_p)$, $t(w_l)$, and $f_{v \leftarrow w}(w_q)$.

Let us assume that among the instances v_k in the testing text there is at most one in error. We make the corresponding assumption for w. Given these assumptions, we expect that, for all vectors $t(v_k)$ except at most one, the vote-total $r(t(v_k), L_{v \leftarrow w}(v))$ produced by $L_{v \leftarrow w}(v)$ is positive. Correspondingly, we expect that, for all vectors $f_{v \leftarrow w}(v_p)$ except at most one, the vote-total $s(f_{v \leftarrow w}(v_p), L_{v \leftarrow w}(v))$ computed via $L_{v \leftarrow w}(v)$ to be negative. Thus, we expect that there is a threshold value $\alpha_{v \leftarrow w}(v)$ such that almost all, if not all, vote-totals for the vectors $t(v_k)$ are greater than $\alpha_{v \leftarrow w}(v)$, and such that almost all, if not all, vote-totals for vectors $f_{v \leftarrow w}(v_p)$ are less than $\alpha_{v \leftarrow w}(v)$.

We calculate an odd-valued threshold $\alpha_{v \leftarrow w}(v)$ using the above considerations; the details of the computations are given in Appendix D. Given $\alpha_{v \leftarrow w}(v)$, we estimate an instance v_k of the testing text to be bad if its vote-total is less than the threshold, *i.e.*,
$r(t(v_k), L_{v \leftarrow w}(v)) < \alpha_{v \leftarrow w}(v)$ and estimate v_k to be good otherwise. In the former case, the difference $d_1(v_k)$ between the vote-total of $t(v_k)$ and the threshold is a reasonable measure of the likelihood that v_k is bad. That is, a large difference corresponds to a high likelihood.

We utilize $L_{v \leftarrow w}(w)$ in analogous fashion. Each instance v_k is temporarily replaced by an instance w_q of the word w, and we get the vote-total

$s(f_{v \leftarrow w}(w_q), L_{v \leftarrow w}(w))$ for the characteristic vector $f_{v \leftarrow w}(w_q)$ of the generated w_q. The vote-total is computed by $L_{v \leftarrow w}(w)$. If the vote-total is above the threshold $\alpha_{v \leftarrow w}(w)$, then the generated occurrence w_q likely is good, the instance v_k is estimated to be bad, and the difference $d_2(v_k)$ between the vote-total and the threshold is a measure of the likelihood that v_k is bad. If the vote-total is less than the threshold, then the generated occurrence w_q likely is bad, and thus the instance v_k is estimated to be good. Notice that the threshold $\alpha_{v \leftarrow w}(w)$ is computed analogously to $\alpha_{v \leftarrow w}(v)$ described above.

The tests involving the two thresholds may produce agreeing or conflicting estimates for a given instance v_k. If at least one of the two tests estimates v_k to be good, then we estimate v_k to be good. On the other hand, if both tests estimate v_k to be bad, then we estimate v_k to be bad and take the sum $d_s(v_k)$ of $d_1(v_k)$ and $d_2(v_k)$ to be a measure of the likelihood that the estimate of v_k being bad is indeed correct. Accordingly, we sort all such bad instances v_k using their $d_s(v_k)$ values. The v_k with the largest $d_s(v_k)$ is the most likely one to be bad. In the implementation of the method, that instance v_k is posed to the user as a questionable word. If the user declares v_k to be correct, we assume that the other instances of v that we estimated to be bad, are actually good as well. On the other hand, if the user agrees that the v_k with largest $d_s(v_k)$ is indeed bad, then we pose to the user the case of the v_k with the second largest $d_s(v_k)$ as potentially bad and apply the above rule recursively.

3.2.2 Testing special cases

We have completed the discussion of the regular case where each of v and w occurs at least twice in the testing text. Now, we discuss two special cases where v occurs exactly once in the testing text. Since v occurs just once, it may well be that this instance of v is bad. Hence, this situation calls for careful analysis. Here are the two cases.

Case (1) The word v occurs exactly once but w occurs at least twice in the testing text: We construct for each instance w_l the characteristic vector $t(w_l)$, apply $L_{v \leftarrow w}(w)$, and get the vote-total $r(t(w_l), L_{v \leftarrow w}(w))$. Next, we temporarily replace the single v_k by w_q, construct the characteristic vector $f_{v \leftarrow w}(w_q)$, and apply $L_{v \leftarrow w}(w)$. If the resulting vote-total $s(f_{v \leftarrow w}(w_q), L_{v \leftarrow w}(w))$ for the generated w_q is greater than the smallest of the $r(t(w_l), L_{v \leftarrow w}(w))$, then we estimate the w_q that replaced v_k to be good and thus estimate v_k to be bad; otherwise, we estimate v_k to be good.

Case (2) The word v occurs exactly once and w occurs only once in the testing text: We would like to construct a characteristic vector $t(v_k)$ for v_k as in the regular case, apply $L_{v \leftarrow w}(v)$, and make a decision based on the vote-total. However, the rules for construction of $t(v_k)$ demand that v_k occurs at least twice in the testing text, which does not hold here. Hence, $t(v_k)$ cannot be computed. We overcome this difficulty by a seemingly inappropriate step where the testing text is for the moment replaced by the history text appended by v_k and its neighborhood of the testing text. That temporary substitution allows computation of $t(v_k)$, since existence of $L_{v \leftarrow w}(v)$ implies that v occurs at least three times in the history text. We apply $L_{v \leftarrow w}(v)$ to the vector $t(v_k)$, get a vote-total $r(t(v_k), L_{v \leftarrow w}(v))$, and estimate v_k to be good or bad using a threshold of $\alpha_{v \leftarrow w}(v) = -19$. That is, if $r(t(v_k), L_{v \leftarrow w}(v)) < -19$, then v_k is estimated to be bad. Otherwise, it is estimated to be good. The threshold choice is driven by the consideration that vote-totals below -19 almost always show v_k to be bad.

3.2.3 An example

Let us discuss an example where the word *there* is examined in a given testing text. First, Ltest constructs the set of confusion words for *there*. Let that set be {*three, their*}. Thus, we have two substitutions involving *there*: *there←three* and *there←their*. Each occurrence of *there* is examined twice. Once, *there* is examined relative to the substitution *there←three*. The second time, *there* is examined relative to the substitution *there←their*. Let us discuss the first case. When *there* is examined relative to the substitution *there←three*, each occurrence *there$_k$* of *there* in the testing text is tested twice as follows:

(i) Compute the vector for *there$_k$*. Based on the testing technique described above, the occurrence *there$_k$* is estimated to be good or bad.

(ii) Replace *there$_k$* by an occurrence *three$_q$* of the word *three*, and construct a vector for that generated occurrence *three$_q$*. Then *three$_q$* can be classified as good (resp. bad), and thus the occurrence *there$_k$* is estimated as bad (resp. good). If the two tests (i) and (ii) estimate *there$_k$* as bad, then the occurrence *there$_k$* is declared bad; otherwise *there$_k$* is declared good.

Declare each instance of v that in the testing step is ignored relative to a substitution $v \leftarrow w$ to be a *discarded* $v(v \leftarrow w)$ *instance*. If an instance of v is not discarded relative to a substitution $v \leftarrow w$, declare it to be a *tested* $v(v \leftarrow w)$ *instance*. By these definitions, an instance of v may be discarded relative to a substitution $v \leftarrow w$ and may be tested relative to another substitution $v \leftarrow z$.

Let N_d (resp. N_t) be the total number of discarded (resp. tested) $v(v \leftarrow w)$ instances encountered in all iterations through the testing step. If the ratio $N_t/(N_d + N_t)$ is close to 1, then the learning step has produced most of the logic formulas needed for checking the given testing text. On the other hand, a ratio close to 0 implies that the learning step has produced few of the logic formulas that are relevant for the testing text. For this reason, we call the ratio $N_t/(N_d + N_t)$ the *relevance ratio* of the given prior text and the given testing text. Section 5 shows that relevance ratios close to 1 can be achieved by a suitable augmentation of the given training and history texts.

4.   IMPLEMENTATION AND COMPUTATIONAL RESULTS

The learning step and the testing step of Ltest have been added to an existing software system for spell and syntax checking called *Laempel*. In this section, we review that system, describe how the method has been inserted, and report computational results that include a comparison with the prior methods BaySpell and WinSpell.

The spell checker of Laempel is described in Zhao and Truemper (1999). The key feature setting it apart from other spell checkers is the high probability with which Laempel suggests correct replacement words for misspelled words (96% for the top-ranked replacement word) and recognizes correct words that are not in the dictionary, as correct (82%). Laempel achieves this performance by learning user behavior and using that insight to make decisions.

The syntax checker of Laempel is covered in Zhao (1996). It consists of three steps. In the first step, the given text is cleaned up by a screening process. In the second step, two logic modules check the cleaned text for local syntactic errors. A total of 27 different cases are considered. The third step is applied to each sentence that does not contain any local syntactic errors. A reasoning process involving 18 logic modules analyzes each such sentence for global syntactic errors. If no such error is determined, the process attempts to parse the sentence. We say "attempts" since the process gives up on parsing if the sentence is so complex that the 18 logic modules become bogged down in the parsing process. In tests, the percentage of sentences that were parsed by the syntax checker ranged from 100% for simple texts and 76% for a mathematical text to 61% for a TV network news text. For the sentences that have been parsed, Laempel records for each word the assigned part-of-speech. That information is utilized later to estimate whether a given word has a dominant part-of-speech.

We are ready to discuss the implementation of the learning step of Ltest. Recall that the learning algorithm splits the prior text into a training text and a history text, and then deduces from these two texts a collection of logic formulas. Prior to the computation of the formulas, Laempel carries out spell checking and syntax checking for the two texts and asks the user to make corrections as needed. The learning algorithm processes the corrected texts to obtain the collection of logic formulas.

We turn to the implementation of the testing step of Ltest. Let a testing text be given. Laempel first checks the text for spelling and syntax errors. Once the user has made appropriate corrections, the testing algorithm searches the text for context-based spelling errors. Whenever the algorithm has produced a list of likely errors for a substitution $v \leftarrow w$, Laempel poses the top-ranked instance of the list to the user as possibly in error. If the user declares the instance to be correct, Laempel assumes that all other instances of the list are correct as well. On the other hand, if the user declares the instance to be in error, Laempel records that fact, removes the instance from the list, and applies the above rule recursively; that is, Laempel poses the currently top-ranked instance to the user as possibly being in error, and so on. Once a testing text has been checked for context-based spelling errors, Laempel records all sentences that do not contain any error acknowledged by the user. When the text is processed again after changes by the user, those sentences are presumed to be correct, and checking focuses on modified or new sentences. This rule reduces subsequent processing times of the testing file.

We have evaluated the performance of Ltest. The texts consisted of mathe-

Table 1. Text statistics.

Text	Used for	Type	Number of different words	Number of word instances
1–1	training	math book	1,922	2,4581
1–2	history	chapters	1,143	8,291
1–3	history	in	1,827	1,6443
1–4	testing	TEX	1,100	9,744
2–1	training	math book	1,826	1,6444
2–2	history	chapters in	1,715	1,5098
2–3	testing	TEX	1,216	6,491
3–1	training	technical	2,029	1,8773
3–2	history	papers in	2,817	2,5881
3–3	testing	LATEX	1,318	6,456
4–1	training	newspaper	1,968	6,645
4–2	history	articles about	1,925	5,854
4–3	testing	health	1,334	4,667
5–1	training	newspaper	2,054	8,837
5–2	history	articles about	2,086	8,645
5–3	testing	politics	1,590	5,726

matical book chapters formulated in TEX, technical papers in LATEX, and newspaper texts covering health and politics. Table 1 tells the number of words, the number of word instances of the texts, and the classification as training, history, or testing text. Note that the first group of texts consisting of texts 1–1 to 1–4 contains two history texts 1–2 and 1–3. The smaller of the two history texts, 1–2, has 8,291 word instances, while the larger history text, 1–3, has 16,443 instances. We see in a moment how the difference in size of the two history texts affects the learning of logic formulas.

Recall from the learning step that for a given substitution $v{\leftarrow}w$ we attempt to derive two sets $L_{v\leftarrow w}(v)$ and $L_{v\leftarrow w}(w)$ of logic formulas, by first replacing each instance of w by v, and then replacing each instance of v by w. Denote the first replacement by $v{-}w$ and the second one by $w{-}v$. We need this notation for the next table, which summarizes the results of applying the learning algorithm to the combinations of training/history texts shown in Table 4. The statistics include the number of replacements $v{-}w$ evaluated, the distribution of the number of instances of v in the training text connected with the replacements $v{-}w$, the total number of logic formulas learned from the texts, and the execution time. Computations were done on a Sun Ultra 1 (167 MHz) workstation, which by current standards is slow.

The training time ranges from 1h 17m to 6h 14m, with an average of 3h 43m, mostly is required to compute the logic formulas by Lsquare. On present day computers, say with 1000 MHz, training time would be at most 1h.

Table 2. Learning cases.

Texts		Number of re-placements $v-w$	Distribution of number of instances of v in training text for replacements (%) $v-w$						Number of logic formulas learned	Training time
Train-ing	Hist-ory		3 to 10	11 to 20	21 to 50	51 to 100	101 to 200	>200		
1–1	1–2	119	11	13	17	27	18	14	4,760	4h 3m
1–1	1–3	176	27	16	15	18	13	11	7,040	5h 58m
2–1	2–2	178	24	16	21	19	12	8	7,120	3h 4m
3–1	3–2	250	31	19	15	18	6	10	10,000	6h 14m
4–1	4–2	48	40	15	33	2	6	4	1,920	1h 17m
5–1	5–2	64	30	23	25	8	11	3	2,560	1h 40m
Avrg.		139	27	17	21	15	11	8	5,567	3h 43m

Line 1 of Table 4 shows that training text 1–1 and history text 1–2 led to learning of 4,760 logic formulas for 119 replacements. In contrast, the same training text paired with history text 1–3 results in learning 7,040 logic formulas for 176 replacements, an increase of 48%. The large increase in learned information is due to the larger size of history text 1–3 compared with history text 1–2. Note that on average 27% of the training samples contained 3 to 10 instances of v in the training text, while 17% of the training samples contained 11 to 20 instances. Thus, roughly half of the training samples had at most 20 instances.

Once training was completed, the testing algorithm was applied to both large and small testing texts in the domains of the training/history texts. The cases of large testing texts are given in Table 3. For each testing text, the table includes the related training/history texts, the number of discarded and tested $v(v \leftarrow w)$ instances, and the number of false-positive diagnoses incurred when algorithm processes the text. The percentage given with the number of tested $v(v \leftarrow w)$ instances is the relevance ratio, which in Section 3 is defined to be the number of tested $v(v \leftarrow w)$ instances divided by the total number of discarded and tested $v(v \leftarrow w)$ instances. For testing text 1–4, the relevance ratio is 46% when 1–1/1–2 are used as training/history texts. The ratio increases to 54% when 1–1/1–3 are used instead. The improvement is due to the fact that history text 1–3 leads to increased learning when compared with history text 1–2, as discussed in connection with Table 4. The average relevance ratio, which is 43%, is an undesirably small number that results from the random selection of training and history texts. In Section 5 it is described how relevance ratios close to 1 can be achieved by an appropriate augmentation of the training texts and history texts. We did not carry out such manipulation for the tests of this section so that the test results are unbiased.

The percentage listed in Table 3 with the number of false-positive diagnoses is the ratio of that number divided by the number of tested $v(v \leftarrow w)$ instances.

Table 3. Large testing text cases.

Texts			Number of discarded $v(v \leftarrow w)$ instances	Number of tested $v(v \leftarrow w)$ instances	Number of false-positive diagnoses	Testing time
Testing	Training	History				
1–4	1–1	1–2	5,324	4,610 (46%)	18(0.4%)	2m 0s
1–4	1–1	1–3	4,535	5,399 (54%)	24(0.4%)	2m 35s
2–3	2–1	2–2	3,777	3,061 (45%)	28(0.9%)	2m 2s
3–3	3–1	3–2	2,911	3,258 (53%)	33(1.0%)	2m 32s
4–3	4–1	4–2	3,404	891 (21%)	20 (2.2%)	1m 6s
5–3	5–1	5–2	5,239	1,756 (25%)	17 (1.0%)	1m 25s
Average			4,198	3,162 (43%)	23.4(0.7%)	1m 57s

Table 4. Error detection for large testing texts.

Texts			Number of errors generated	Number of errors detected by		
				syntax checker alone	Ltest alone	syntax checker and Ltest
Testing	Training	History				
1–4	1–1	1–2	37	3 (8%)	26 (70%)	26 (70%)
1–4	1–1	1–3	163	16 (10%)	114 (70%)	120 (74%)
2–3	2–1	2–2	47	7 (15%)	34 (72%)	35 (74%)
3–3	3–1	3–2	53	9 (17%)	38 (72%)	39 (74%)
4–3	4–1	4–2	47	5 (11%)	27 (57%)	32 (68%)
5–3	5–1	5–2	33	5 (15%)	20 (61%)	22 (67%)
Average			63.3	7.5 (12%)	43.2 (68%)	45.7 (72%)

That percentage is small and ranges from 0.4% to 2.2%, with an average of
0.7%. Much more important from a user standpoint is the fact that the number
of false-positive diagnoses is uniformly small, ranging from 17 to 33, with an
average of about 23. The testing time is on the order of 2m for each case. On
current computers, that time would be on the order of 20s.

Into each large testing text of Table 3, we randomly introduced context-based
spelling errors and, for each such error, checked if the syntax checker or Ltest
detected that error and posed it to the user as top-ranked candidate. Thus,
the results characterize the error detection capability of Ltest for cases where
learning is possible from the training/history texts. Table 4 summarizes the
performance. The percentage figures in parentheses represent the portion of
generated errors detected by the syntax checker or Ltest, as applicable. Note
that the syntax checker on average found only 12% of the errors, while Ltest
identified 68%. Combined, the two checks located 72% of the errors.

We extracted several small testing texts consisting of at most a few sentences
from the large testing texts. Table 5 contains the statistics about these small
testing texts. The names of the texts are derived from those of the large ones
by adding one or two primes. For example, the small testing texts 1–4' and

Table 5. Small testing texts.

Text	Number of different words	Number of word instances
1–4′	81	184
1–4″	58	110
2–3′	36	50
3–3′	51	80
4–3′	78	106
5–3′	85	102

Table 6. Small testing text cases.

Texts			Number of discarded $v(v{\leftarrow}w)$ instances	Number of tested $v(v{\leftarrow}w)$ instances	Number of false-positive diagnoses	Testing time
Testing	Training	History				
1–4′	1–1	1–2	43	32 (43%)	0 (0%)	12s
1–4″	1–1	1–3	11	20 (65%)	1 (5%)	7s
2–3′	2–1	2–2	3	3 (50%)	2 (67%)	4s
3–3′	3–1	3–2	7	4 (36%)	1 (25%)	5s
4–3′	4–1	4–2	23	7 (23%)	2 (29%)	3s
5–3′	5–1	5–2	7	7 (50%)	0 (0%)	5s
Average			16	12 (43%)	1 (8%)	6s

1–4″ are derived from the large testing text 1–4.

Table 6 lists the training/history texts used in conjunction with the small testing texts and provides statistics analogously to Table 3. The average relevance ratio is 43% and thus equal to that for large testing texts. The number of false-positive diagnoses ranges from 0 to 2, with an average of 1. The average false-positive rate is 8%. That percentage may seem high, but this is not important since the number of false-positive diagnoses is small. The execution times of Table 6 are far below the roughly 2m required for large testing texts and average 6s. On current (2001) computers, the average time would be about 1s.

As for the cases of large testing texts, we randomly inserted context-based spelling errors and determined how many of these errors were identified by the syntax checker or by Ltest. Table 7 contains the results. On average, the syntax checker finds only 4% of the errors, while Ltest locates 87%. In contrast to the large testing texts, the syntax checker does not help at all since Ltest finds all errors determined by the syntax checker.

Table 8 summarizes the performance of the leading prior methods BaySpell (Golding (1995)) and WinSpell (Golding and Roth (1999)) and Ltest on the same prior text and testing text. D. Roth kindly made these texts available. They were obtained by a 80/20 split of the 1-Million-Words Brown corpus

Table 7. Error detection for small testing texts.

Texts			Number of	Number of errors detected by		
			errors	syntax	Ltest	syntax checker
Testing	Training	History	generated	checker alone	alone	and Ltest
1–4′	1–1	1–2	8	0 (0%)	6 (75%)	6 (75%)
1–4″	1–1	1–3	10	2 (20%)	10 (100%)	10 (100%)
2–3′	2–1	2–2	8	0 (0%)	6 (75%)	6 (75%)
3–3′	3–1	3–2	6	0 (0%)	5 (83%)	5 (83%)
4–3′	4–1	4–2	6	0 (0%)	6 (100%)	6 (100%)
5–3′	5–1	5–2	2	0 (0%)	2 (100%)	2 (100%)
Average			6.7	0.3 (4%)	5.8 (87%)	5.8 (87%)

(Kučera and Francis (1967)). The figures in the table represent the percentages of correctly classified word instances for the specified confusion sets. On average, Ltest achieved the best performance with 95.4% accuracy, compared with 89.9% for BaySpell and 93.5% for WinSpell. The testing times used by Ltest for the cases in Table 8 are comparable and very close to those reported in Table 3.

The detection rate of 95.4% for Ltest is much higher than the 68% found earlier for large texts. How is this possible? First, the two rates concern different statistics. The 95.4% rate covers classification of correct words as correct and of erroneous words as incorrect. The 68% rate covers only the detection of erroneous words as incorrect. If we are to compare numbers, we must combine the 68% rate with the rate for classifying correct words as correct. The latter rate is $1 -$ (false-positive rate) $= 1 - 0.007 = 99.3\%$. Using a 50/50 weighting to combine rates, we see that $(0.68 + 0.993)/2 = 83.7\%$ should be compared with 95.4%. From our computational experience with Ltest, the gap between 83.7% and 95.4% is due to four factors:

– First, the test using the Brown corpus relies on much larger training texts than we used in the earlier tests.

– Second, most confusion words of Table 8 are *content* words—that is, nouns, verbs, adjectives, and adverbs. We have found confusion sets involving such words to be much easier to handle than sets involving *function* words such as prepositions, connectives, and articles. Such words were part of the earlier tests. Indeed, the tests even check for some errors in mathematical formulas such as misspelled mathematical variables.

– Third, some of the large testing texts considered earlier involve numerous special terms, symbols, formulas, and conventions, which complicate the search for errors.

– Fourth, the constraint of very low false-positive rate imposed on Ltest makes detection of errors much more difficult. It would be interesting to see how the two leading prior methods perform when they are adapted so that they take all of these aspects into account.

The experiments reported show that Ltest finds the majority of context-

Table 8. Performance of Ltest compared with BaySpell and WinSpell.

Confusion set	BaySpell	WinSpell	Ltest
accept, except	92.0	96.0	94.0
affect, effect	98.0	100	97.9
being, begin	95.2	97.9	98.7
cite, sight	73.5	85.3	81.3
country, county	91.9	95.2	94.1
its, it's	95.9	97.3	98.3
lead, led	85.7	91.8	98.0
passed, past	90.5	95.9	94.7
peace, piece	92.0	88.0	92.6
principal, principle	85.3	91.2	94.7
quite, quiet	89.4	93.9	98.5
raise, rise	87.2	89.7	98.2
weather, whether	98.4	100	98.7
your, you're	90.9	97.3	95.9
average	89.9	93.5	95.4

based spelling errors, provided the error instances v_k can be tested. This is so if two conditions are satisfied: (1) For each erroneous instance v_k, the correct word must occur in the testing text. (2) Logic formulas for the applicable substitutions $v \leftarrow w$ must have been learned.

The first condition is typically met in large testing texts, but is not necessarily satisfied in small testing texts. There is a simple way to avoid this shortcoming for small testing texts. We take an additional, large text in the same domain area, test it, and correct it if necessary. Let us call the resulting text the *core text*. Whenever a small text is to be tested, we adjoin it to the core text and test the resulting large *expanded text*. If an instance of v occurs in the small text portion, and if an instance of w occurs anywhere in the expanded text, then v is tested for possibly being the result of a context-based spelling error. As a result, almost any v that should be tested is indeed tested.

The second condition is satisfied if the training/history texts are representative of the testing texts. This is not the case for the above tests due to our random selection of training/history texts. In the next section, we see how representative texts can be obtained, as part of several extensions.

5.   EXTENSIONS

Significant improvements in the error detection rate can be attained by a better syntax checker, since, in our tests, quite a few context-based spelling errors resulted in syntactically incorrect sentences that were not flagged by the Laempel syntax checker. A better syntax checker would also lower the false-positive rate, for the following reason. Let $v \leftarrow w$ be the currently processed substitution in the testing step. Suppose the testing step tentatively replaces an instance of v by w. If the syntax checker determines that the modified sentence is syntactically incorrect, then we need not consider v as a possibly misspelled or mistyped w, and thus eliminate a potential false-positive diagnosis. We tried this idea using the Laempel syntax checker and found that it reduced the number of false-positive diagnoses insignificantly. A better syntax checker should produce substantially better results.

Another improvement produces a relevance ratios very close to 1. Suppose we have sufficient text to determine the entire vocabulary used in the given domain. We compute the confusion set for each word of that vocabulary. Given a training text and a history text, we check if each of these texts contains, for each word occurring in one of the confusion sets, at least three instances each. If this is not the case for a given word, we add sentences from general text material to the training or history text, as needed, until each word is reasonably represented, say, by 10-20 instances. When training is done using the expanded training and history texts, then logic formulas are produced for each word of each confusion set. Accordingly, testing achieves a relevance ratio of close to 1.

It is possible that a person makes an error repeatedly, for example, by confusing "its" and "it's" or "complement" and "compliment." Such behavior is contrary to one of the two assumptions made in Section 1, and it affects the reliability with which errors are detected via thresholds. One may remedy this shortcoming of Ltest as follows. Whenever an error involving a given substitution $v \leftarrow w$ is found to occur more than once in a testing text, then that case is recorded as part of the *performance history* of the person who created the text. In subsequent tests, that fact is taken into account when characteristic vectors are constructed in connection with the substitution $v \leftarrow w$ and evaluated via logic formulas. Space constraints prevent a detailed discussion, but the main idea is that, for the evaluation of $v \leftarrow w$, each sentence with an instance of v is viewed as separate small text, and that v is tested for correctness as described in Section 4 using a core text. The use of a performance history of a person may seem far-fetched. But the spell and syntax checker of the Laempel System, of which Ltest is now part, already uses such history information, with good results.

This section discussed some of the future research directions which can be summarized as follows: –Improving the syntax checker to reduce the number of false-positive cases as mentioned earlier in this section. –Devise methods to derive certain *generic* formulas to be used whenever training is not possible due to small number instances. –Explore the usage of some *core* good text (see the last two paragraphs in section 4) to be adjoined to small testing texts where there may not be enough word instances to collect sufficient features of these words in the characteristics vector.

6.   SUMMARY

The chapter describes the method Ltest for finding context-based spelling errors. The key elements are as follows.

(1)   An encoding of the relationships of an instance of a word to other instances of that word, using the text under investigation and a history text that acts as a reference text for both training and testing. The encoding is based on neighborhoods of word instances and, if applicable, on the dominant parts-of-speech of such instances.
(2)   Representation of   the   relationships   between words instances   and correct/incorrect use by logic formulas that are extracted by a data mining algorithm.
(3)   A voting system based on the logic formulas.
(4)   A calibration of the voting system via thresholds for each testing text.

Ltest has been added to an existing system for checking spelling and syntax errors. A number of tests have proved that the resulting system is effective and robust. It detects the majority of context-based spelling errors while committing few false-positive diagnoses. Execution times of the system are moderate for the learning step and are small for testing even large texts.

REFERENCES

Al-Mubaid, H., Identifying Inadvertent Semantic Errors in English Texts, Ph.D. Thesis, University of Texas at Dallas, 2000.

Bruce, R., and Wiebe, J., Word-sense disambiguation using decomposable models, Proceedings of the 32nd Annual Meeting of the Association for Computational Linguistics (ACL-94), 1994, 139–146.

Bruce, R., and Wiebe, J., Decomposable modeling in natural language processing, Computational Linguistics, 25 (1999) 195–207.

Budanitsky, A., Lexical semantics relatedness and its application in natural language processing, Technical Report CSRG-390, University of Toronto, 1999.

Budanitsky, A., and Hirst, G., Semantic distance in WordNet: An experimental, application-oriented evaluation of five measures, Workshop on WordNet and Other Lexical Resources, Second Meeting of the North American Chapter of the Association of Computational Linguistics, Pittsburgh, June, 2001.

Felici, G., Sun, F., and Truemper, K., A method for controlling errors in two-class classification, Proceedings of the 23rd Annual International Computer Software & Applications Conference COMPSAC 99, Phoenix, AZ, 1999, 186–191.

Felici, G., and Truemper, K., A Minsat approach for learning in logic domains, INFORMS Journal on computing, 14(1) 2002, 20–36.

Golding, A. R., A Bayesian hybrid method for context-sensitive spelling correction, Proceedings of the Third Workshop on Very Large Corpora, Cambridge, MA, 1995, 39–53.

Golding, A. R., and Roth, D., Applying Winnow to context-sensitive spelling correction, Machine Learning: Proceedings of the Thirteenth International Conference, San Francisco, CA, 1996, 182–190.

Golding, A. R., and Roth, D., A Winnow-based approach to context-sensitive spelling correction, Machine Learning, Special Issue on Machine Learning and Natural Language Processing, (34) 1999 107–130.

Golding, A. R., and Schabes, Y., Combining Trigram-based and feature-based methods for context-sensitive spelling correction, Proceedings of the 34th Annual Meeting of the Association for Computational Linguistics, Santa Cruz, CA, 1996, 71–78 .

Hirst, G., and St-Onge, D., Lexical chains as representations of context for the detection and correction of malapropisms, Christaine Felbaum, editor, WordNet, MIT Press, MA, 1995.

Jones, M. P., and Martin, J. H., Contextual spelling correction using latent semantic analysis, Proceedings of the 5th Conference on Applied Natural Language Processing, Washington, DC, 1997.

Kučera, H., and Francis, W. N., *Computational Analysis of Present-Day American English*, Brown University Press, Providence, RI, 1967.

Kukich, K., Techniques for automatically correcting words in text, ACM Computing Survey, 24 (1992) 377–439.

Mangu, L., and Brill, E., Automatic rule acquisition for spelling correction, Proceedings of the International Conference on Machine Learning, 1997, 734–741.

Pedersen, T., Search techniques for learning probabilistic models of word sense disambiguation, Working Notes of the AAAI Spring Symposium on Search Techniques for Problem Solving Under Uncertainty and Incomplete Information, Palo Alto, CA, 1999.

Pedersen, T., and Bruce, R., Knowledge lean word-sense disambiguation, Proceedings of the Fifteenth National Conference on Artificial Intelligence (AAAI-98), Madison, WI, 1998.

Pedersen, T., Bruce, R., and Wiebe, J., Sequential model selection for word sense disambiguation, Proceedings of the 1997 Conference on Applied Natural Language Processing (ANLP-97). Washington, DC, 1997, 388–395.

Powers, D., Learning and application of differential grammars, Proceedings of the ACL Special Interest Group in Natural Language Learning, Madrid, 1997.

Roth, D., Learning to resolve natural language ambiguities: A unified approach, Proceedings of National Conference on Artificial Intelligence, 1998, 806–813.

St-Onge, D., Detecting and correcting malapropisms with lexical chains, MS Thesis, University of Toronto, Department of Computer Science, 1995.

Webster's Ninth Collegiate Dictionary, Merriam-Webster, Inc., and Highlighted Data, Inc., Macintosh CD-ROM edition, 1989.

Zhao, Y., Intelligent text processing, Ph.D. Thesis, University of Texas at Dallas, 1996.

Zhao, Y., and Truemper, K., Effective spell checking by learning user behavior, Applied Artificial Intelligence, 13 (1999) 725–742.

Appendix A: Construction of substitutions

Recall that the substitution $v \leftarrow w$ represents that the word w may by misspelling or mistyping become v. In this appendix, we summarize how, given v, all words w that may give rise to a substitution $v \leftarrow w$ are computed. For complete details of the construction rules, see Al-Mubaid (2000).

We collect the misspelling cases in four groups that involve the following situations. For each situation, we include some examples.

- vowel combinations producing similar sounds: by↔buy, fair↔fare, week↔weak.

- consonants having similar sounds: bay↔pay, cine↔sine, hid↔hit.

- silent characters and substrings: knee↔nee, right↔rite, sight↔site, where↔were.

- apostrophe use: he's↔his, it's↔its, let's↔lets, they're↔there.

A total of 61 rules create all cases of these four groups. We determined these rules as follows. First, in a combination of manual and computer search, we extracted from Webster's Ninth Collegiate Dictionary (1989) a number of classes of different words with identical or nearly identical pronunciation. Second, we manually eliminated rare words. Third, we represented the remaining classes by rules. It turned out that 61 rules suffice to represent those classes. Due to space constraints, we omit a detailed listing of the rules; they are included in Al-Mubaid (2000). We use the shorthand notation $v \leftrightarrow w$ for the substitutions $v \leftarrow w$ and $w \leftarrow v$.

The mistyping cases are taken from Zhao and Truemper (1999). Define a *neighbor letter* to be any letter that on the keyboard is close to a given letter. Then the typing errors considered in the cited reference are as follows: transposing two letters, repeating a letter, omitting a letter, inserting a letter that is a neighbor of a given letter, and typing an incorrect letter that is a neighbor of the required letter. Here are some examples for each type of error.

1. Transposing two letters: bye↔bey, form↔from, goal↔gaol, trial↔trail.
2. Repeating a letter: latter←later, tiller←tiler.
3. Omitting a letter: cam←scam, met←melt, see←seem, tale←table.
4. Inserting a letter that is a neighbor of a given letter: defined←define, care←car,
   trash←rash.
5. Typing an incorrect letter that is a neighbor of the required letter: for↔foe, high↔nigh, into↔onto, just↔must.

Appendix B: Construction of training and history texts

Suppose we have a database of correct texts for the given domain. For example, the database may consist of a large number of working papers on graph theory, or of papers published in a combinatorics journal, or of some books on matrix algebra, or of a large collection of legal documents in one area of law. We assume that the words used in the database constitute the entire or almost entire vocabulary of the testing texts we intend to process in the same domain area. From the database, we want to derive reasonably sized training and history texts so that the learning step applied to them produces the logic formulas needed in subsequent testing of texts. The construction of the training text and history text from the given database proceeds as follows.

Construction of training/history texts

INPUT: A database of texts for the given domain area.

OUTPUT: Training/history texts for the domain area.

1. Initialize the training text and history text as empty texts. Determine the number $n(v)$ of instances of each word v in the database.

2. Derive all substitutions $v \leftarrow w$ for which both v and w occur in the database, and collect the words v and w of these $v \leftarrow w$ in a set V. Sort the words of V using the counts $n(\cdot)$ so that the topmost word has the smallest $n(\cdot)$ value.

3. Process the words v of V one by one and in the order determined in Step 2, as follows. Randomly select sentences of the database that contain at least one instance of v, and assign each selected sentence to the training text or the history text, whichever has at that time the fewest number of instances of v. Stop the processing of v when all sentences of the database containing instances of v have been assigned, or when both the training text and the history text contain at least 1,000 instances of v each.

4. Output the training/history texts on hand, and stop.

Appendix C: Structure of characteristic vectors

Both the learning step and the testing step use characteristic vectors to encode the relationships connecting a given word instance with other instances of the same word. The characteristic vectors are based on two texts. The first text is the training text or testing text, depending on whether we are in the learning step or in the testing step, respectively. We denote either one of the two texts by T. The second text is the history text, regardless of whether we are in the learning step or in the testing step. We denote that text by H. It acts as a correct reference text during both the learning step and the testing step.

Define a *non-word token* to be any symbol that occurs in text T or H that is not a word. Examples are the period, comma, exclamation mark, question mark, semicolon, colon, forward and backward slash, plus, minus, ampersand, and the signs for pound and dollar.

Define the *neighborhood* of an instance x_m of a word x in text T or H to consist of the two words or tokens immediately preceding x_m and of the two words or tokens immediately following x_m. Let p^1, p^2, f^1, and f^2 denote words or tokens. Then x_m and its neighborhood in the text T or H may be depicted as a sequence $p^2\ p^1\ x_m\ f^1\ f^2$ of words or tokens in the text. The neighborhood definition is modified in the obvious way if x_m occurs at or near the beginning or end of the text. That is, p^1 and p^2, or just p^2, or f^1 and f^2, or just f^2 are then absent from the sequence.

Define a part-of-speech of a word to be the *dominant* part-of-speech of the word if in past usage of the word in the given domain that part-of-speech was the correct syntactic interpretation at least 90% of the time. In our implementation, we use the output of the Laempel syntax checker to estimate whether a part-of-speech is dominant. Below, we assume that we have that estimate available.

Both the learning step and the testing step require characteristic vectors for instances x_m of words x in text T. Such a vector, denoted by Z^{x_m}, has 18 entries encoding 18 different features of that particular instance. The first half of the entries is produced from text T, while the second half is generated from text H. All but four of the entries of Z^{x_m} relate tokens of the neighborhood of the instance x_m of a given word x to the tokens of the neighborhood of other instances x_n of x. The remaining four entries of Z^{x_m} link the parts-of-speech of words in the neighborhood of x_m to the parts-of-speech of words in the neighborhood of instances x_n. The 18 features are the result of a long series of experiments involving many different rule sets. In those experiments, we started out with elaborate rule sets. We discovered that such sets tend to produce erratic detection results and are unsuitable when both large and small texts are to be processed. By gradual simplification we arrived at the current rule set. Here are the details.

Construction of the characteristic vector

Each of the entries Z_1^{xm}, Z_2^{xm}, ... Z_{18}^{xm} is equal to ± 1. The rules below list explicitly for each entry the condition under which an entry takes on the value 1. If that condition is not satisfied, then the entry implicitly has the value -1. We use the above notation for neighborhoods—that is, p^2 p^1 x_m f^1 f^2—to denote the tokens immediately preceding or following a given instance x_m in a sentence. Here are the definitions.

1. (p^1 or p^2 in text T, word case) Define $Z_1^{xm} = 1$ if (a) or (b) below hold.
   (a) p^1 is a word and, for another instance x_n of x, the sequence p^1 x_n occurs in text T.
   (b) p^1 is a non-word token and p^2 is a word, and, for another instance x_n of x and for another non-word token q, the sequence p^2 q x_n occurs in text T.

2. (f^1 or f^2 in text T, word case) Define $Z_2^{xm} = 1$ if (a) or (b) below hold.
   (a) f^1 is a word and, for another instance x_n of x, the sequence x_n f^1 occurs in text T.
   (b) f^1 is a non-word token and f^2 is a word, and, for another instance x_n of x and for another non-word token q, the sequence x_n q f^2 occurs in text T.

3. (p^1 and f^1 in text T, word case) Define $Z_3^{xm} = 1$ if both p^1 and f^1 are words and if, for another instance x_n of x, the sequence p^1 x_n f^1 occurs in text T.

4. (p^1 and p^2 in text T, word case) Define $Z_4^{xm} = 1$ if both p^1 and p^2 are words and if, for another instance x_n of x, the sequence p^2 p^1 x_n occurs in text T.

5. (f^1 and f^2 in text T, word case) Define $Z_5^{xm} = 1$ if both f^1 and f^2 are words and if, for another instance x_n of x, the sequence x_n f^1 f^2 occurs in text T.

6. (p^1 in text T, non-word token case) Define $Z_6^{xm} = 1$ if p^1 is a non-word token and if, for another instance x_n of x, the sequence p^1 x_n occurs in text T.

7. (f^1 in text T, non-word token case) Define $Z_7^{xm} = 1$ if f^1 is a non-word token and if, for another instance x_n of x, the sequence x_n f^1 occurs in text T.

8. (p^1 in text T, part-of-speech case) Define $Z_8^{xm} = 1$ if the following two conditions are satisfied. First, p^1 must be a word and is estimated to have a dominant part-of-speech. Second, a sequence q x_n must occur in text T where x_n is another instance of x and where q is a word having an estimated dominant part-of-speech equa

9. (f^1 in text T, part-of-speech case) Define $Z_9^{xm} = 1$ if the following two conditions are satisfied. First, f^1 must be a word and is estimated to have a dominant part-of-speech. Second, a sequence x_n q must occur in text T

where x_n is another instance of x and where q is a word having an estimated dominant part-of-speech equal to that estimated for f^1.

10.–18. (Text H) Define $Z_{10}^{x_m}-Z_{18}^{x_m}$ like $Z_1^{x_m}-Z_9^{x_m}$ except that, in each case, the specified sequences must be in text H instead of text T.

The characteristic vectors of the sets $G(v)$, $B_{v \leftarrow w}(v)$, $G(w)$, and $B_{v \leftarrow w}(w)$ are constructed by the above rules when one takes x_m of the above rules to be v_i, v_j, w_j, and w_i, respectively, and selects the applicable texts. The characteristic vectors needed in the testing step are constructed analogously.

Some previous work in word sense disambiguation (for example, see Bruce and Wiebe (1994, 1999), Pedersen, Bruce, and Wiebe (1997), Pedersen and Bruce (1998), Pedersen (1999)) uses similar encodings where words, parts-of-speech, and morphological features near a given word instance are recorded. Here, our list of parts-of-speech has 46 items that accommodate all morphological subcases. Ignoring that minor variation, the main difference between the cited methods and the one proposed here is the use of dominant parts-of-speech instead of just parts-of-speech, the use of a reference text for both learning and testing, and the way the characteristic vectors are evaluated.

Appendix D: Classification of characteristic vectors

We describe how the set $L_{v \leftarrow w}(v)$ (resp. $L_{v \leftarrow w}(w)$) is used to estimate whether a given characteristic vector is in $G(v)$ or $B_{v \leftarrow w}(v)$ (resp. $G(w)$ or $B_{v \leftarrow w}(w)$). It suffices to examine how $L_{v \leftarrow w}(v)$ is applied to the characteristic vector $t(v_k)$ of an instance v_k of v. The set $L_{v \leftarrow w}(v)$ consists of 20 disjunctive normal form (DNF) logic formulas and 20 conjunctive normal form (CNF) logic formulas. Each of the 40 formulas produces for $t(v_k)$ a *vote* of $+1$ or -1. A $+1$ (resp. -1) indicates that the logic formula estimates $t(v_k)$ to be in $G(v)$ (resp. $B_{v \leftarrow w}(v)$). Let the sum of these 40 votes be the *vote-total* $r(t(v_k), L_{v \leftarrow w}(v))$. Since each vote is equal to $+1$ or -1, the vote-total $r(t(v_k), L_{v \leftarrow w}(v))$ is even and may range from -40 to 40. Furthermore, if $r(t(v_k), L_{v \leftarrow w}(v))$ is close to 40 (resp. -40), then $t(v_k)$ is likely to be in $G(v)$ (resp. $B_{v \leftarrow w}(v)$). For example, a vote-total $r(t(v_k), L_{v \leftarrow w}(v))$ equal to 40 means that all of the 40 formulas has estimated $t(v_k)$ to be in $G(v)$. But how are positive or negative vote-totals near 0, or 0 itself, to be interpreted? The data mining algorithm Lsquare estimates probability distributions for the vote-totals that one may be tempted to use for the answer. But such use assumes that the testing text comes, statistically speaking, from the same population as the training text. But we only know that these two texts are in the same domain area. Thus, the two texts are not guaranteed to satisfy the assumption. A few test cases have confirmed that the assumption may indeed not be satisfied. For this reason, we do not make use of the probability distributions. Instead, we compute from the testing text an odd integer *threshold* $\alpha_{v \leftarrow w}(v)$, $-40 < \alpha_{v \leftarrow w}(v) < 40$, to decide if $t(v_k)$ should be declared to be in $G(v)$ or $B_{v \leftarrow w}(v)$. Recall that $r(t(v_k), L_{v \leftarrow w}(v))$ is even, so $r(t(v_k), L_{v \leftarrow w}(v)) = \alpha_{v \leftarrow w}(v)$ is not possible. We estimate $t(v_k)$ to be in $G(v)$, and thus to be good, if $r(t(v_k), L_{v \leftarrow w}(v)) > \alpha_{v \leftarrow w}(v)$, and estimate $t(v_k)$ to be in $B_{v \leftarrow w}(v)$, and thus to be bad, if $r(t(v_k), L_{v \leftarrow w}(v)) < \alpha_{v \leftarrow w}(v)$. The computation and use of $\alpha_{v \leftarrow w}(w)$ mimics that of $\alpha_{v \leftarrow w}(v)$, so we only discuss the case of $\alpha_{v \leftarrow w}(v)$.

Given a substitution $v \leftarrow w$, for each instance v_k of a word v in the given testing text, the testing step determines a characteristic vector $t(v_k)$. Furthermore, for each instance w_l of a word w in the given testing text, w_l is temporarily replaced by v_p and a characteristic vector $f_{v \leftarrow w}(v_p)$ is computed. Finally, the testing step applies $L_{v \leftarrow w}(v)$ to each $t(v_k)$ and to each $f_{v \leftarrow w}(v_p)$, getting vote-totals $r(t(v_k), L_{v \leftarrow w}(v))$ and $s(f_{v \leftarrow w}(v_p), L_{v \leftarrow w}(v))$, respectively. The threshold is derived from these vote-totals. Before we describe the computations, let us try to predict the behavior of the vote-totals.

Suppose no instance v or w in the testing text involves a context-based spelling error. Then the instances v_k are good, and the instances v_p, which are derived from instances w_l, are bad. The learning step has created logic formulas that produce positive vote-totals for good instances and negative vote-totals for bad instances. Assuming that the testing text is similarly structured as the training text, we therefore expect that the vote-totals $r(t(v_k), L_{v \leftarrow w}(v))$ for the instances v_k are positive and that the vote-totals $s(f_{v \leftarrow w}(v_p), L_{v \leftarrow w}(v))$ for the instances v_p are negative. Of course, this need not be so. But at least one may reasonably expect that most if not all $r(t(v_k), L_{v \leftarrow w}(v))$ values are greater than most if not all $s(f_{v \leftarrow w}(v_p), L_{v \leftarrow w}(v))$ values.

The above discussion supposes that no v or w involves a context-based spelling error. In Section 1, we assumed that such errors are rare, so we may suppose rather reasonably that at most one instance of v and at most one instance of w is involved in a context-based spelling error. Regardless of the specific situation, any such error most likely involves a v_k with smallest vote-total $r(t(v_k), L_{v \leftarrow w}(v))$ or a v_p with largest vote-total $s(f_{v \leftarrow w}(v_p), L_{v \leftarrow w}(v))$. Of course, we do not know if such an error is present. But we do not want the threshold computations to be affected by such errors. So, as a precautionary measure, we delete the smallest vote-total from the list of $r(t(v_k), L_{v \leftarrow w}(v))$ and sort the remaining entries. We end up with a sorted list of vote-totals, say, r_1, r_2, ... r_m with r_1 largest, and know that these vote-totals very likely correspond to good instances of v. Similarly, we delete the largest vote-total from the list of $s(f_{v \leftarrow w}(v_p), L_{v \leftarrow w}(v))$ and sort the remaining entries. We end up with a sorted list of vote-totals, say, s_1, s_2, ... s_n with s_1 largest, and know that these vote-totals very likely correspond to bad instances of v. Note that the above arguments crucially depend on the assumption of Section 1 that errors involving a given word are rare. There may be situations where a person makes the same error repeatedly. For example, the person may repeatedly confuse "it" and "it's" or "complement" and "compliment." In that case, the threshold computed next may still allow such errors to be caught. But the probability that this will take place is reduced. In Section 5, a modification of Ltest is described that, over time, leads to improved detection of such systematic errors.

Recall that the testing step estimates an instance of v to be good (resp. bad) if the vote-total is above (resp. below) the threshold $\alpha_{v \leftarrow w}(v)$. Hence, if the smallest r_i, which is r_m, is larger than the largest s_j, which is s_1, then we pick $\alpha_{v \leftarrow w}(v)$ about halfway between r_m and s_1. If $r_m \leq s_1$, we want a compromise value for $\alpha_{v \leftarrow w}(v)$ that minimizes the sum of the number of r_i below $\alpha_{v \leftarrow w}(v)$ and the number of s_j above $\alpha_{v \leftarrow w}(v)$. The computations below reflect these ideas, but also rely on the notion that, in case several threshold values equally well achieve the stated goal, then, among these, the threshold value closest to 0 is preferred.

The above computations can be carried out only if each of the words v and w occurs at least twice in the testing text. In the situations where the testing step requires thresholds, two instances of v are guaranteed to exist. However, w may occur just once, and thus the vote-totals s_1, s_2, ... s_n may not exist. In that exceptional case, the single instance of w may itself constitute a context-based spelling error, and we are reluctant to rely on that instance to make decisions regarding the instances of v. Instead, we define the threshold $\alpha_{v \leftarrow w}(v)$ to be equal to -39. This means that we are very conservative in estimating an instance of v to be in error and that we do so only if the vote-total is equal to -40.

Computation of threshold

INPUT: Sorted vote-totals $r_1, r_2, \ldots r_m$ and possibly $s_1, s_2, \ldots s_n$.

OUTPUT: Threshold $\alpha_{v\leftarrow w}(v)$.

1. If $s_1, s_2, \ldots s_n$ do not exist, define $\alpha_{v\leftarrow w}(v) = -39$, and stop.

2. If $r_m > s_1$: Define $\alpha_{v\leftarrow w}(v) = (r_m + s_1)/2$. Reduce (resp. increase) $\alpha_{v\leftarrow w}(v)$ by 1 if $(r_m + s_1)/2$ is even and greater than (resp. less than or equal to) 0. Stop.

3. $(r_m \leq s_1)$ Select an odd-valued $\alpha_{v\leftarrow w}(v)$ so that the number of r_i below $\alpha_{v\leftarrow w}(v)$ plus the number of s_j above $\alpha_{v\leftarrow w}(v)$ is minimum. If there is a choice, pick among them the value closest to 0. Stop.

AUTHORS' BIOGRAPHICAL STATEMENTS

Dr. **Klaus Truemper** is Professor of Computer Science at the University of Texas, Dallas. Dr. Truemper received his doctorate in Operations Research from Case Western Reserve University in 1973. In 1988, he received the prestigious Senior Distinguished U.S. Scientist Award from the Alexander von Humboldt Foundation (Germany). Dr. Truemper's work includes the books Matroid Decomposition and Effective Logic Computation, and the Leibniz System software.

Dr. **Hisham Al-Mubaid** has received MS and Ph.D. degrees in Computer Science from the University of Texas at Dallas in 1997 and 2000 respectively. Then, he worked one year at the State University of New York at Geneseo. Currently, Dr. Al-Mubaid is an assistant professor of Computer Science at the University of Houston - Clear Lake, in Houston, Texas. His main research interests include natural language processing, machine learning, text-mining, and data mining.

Chapter 18 [1]

INDUCTION AND INFERENCE WITH FUZZY RULES FOR TEXTUAL INFORMATION RETRIEVAL

Jianhua Chen*, Donald H. Kraft*, Maria J. Martin-Bautista*, and Maria-Amparo Vila**

* *Computer Science Department*

Louisiana State University
Baton Rouge, LA 70803-4020, USA
e-mail: {jianhua, kraft}@bit.csc.lsu.edu

** *Department of Computer Science and AI*

University of Granada
Granada, 18071 SPAIN
e-mail: {mbautis, vila}@decsai.ugr.es

Abstract: In this chapter we present a unified framework that combines fuzzy rule induction and inference with textual information retrieval using user profiles. Fuzzy rules are extracted from the fuzzy clusters discovered by the fuzzy C-means clustering method. These rules can be used to characterize the semantical connections between keywords in a set of textual documents, and thus the rules can be used to improve the user queries for better retrieval performance. The fuzzy rules and fuzzy clusters are also useful for modeling user profiles that describe the groups of textual documents in which the user is interested. We apply fuzzy rules to adapt user queries by fuzzy inference within a sound and complete fuzzy logic system. We show some empirical results indicating that using our unified framework, the induction and application of fuzzy rules produces a more effective textual information retrieval system.

Keywords: Information Retrieval, Fuzzy Rules, Rule Induction, Fuzzy Clustering, Query Expansion, User Profiles.

---

[1] Triantaphyllou, E. and G. Felici (Eds.), **Data Mining and Knowledge Discovery Approaches based on Rule Induction Techniques**, Massive Computing Series, Srpinger, Heidelberg, Germany, pp. 629-654, 2006.

1.   INTRODUCTION

Information Retrieval (IR) has been a subject of active study for quite some time. Today, with the advent of the information age and the explosive growth of the Internet and the World Wide Web, users of information retrieval systems are faced with an ever increasing flood of information. In particular, Web retrieval poses great challenges and opportunities to information retrieval research. Everyday, millions of people all over the world surf the Web for their information needs. The Web can be seen as a huge database of textual documents, with each Web page considered as a textual document. Web users use various search engines to retrieve information from this huge database. The challenges for Web/online retrieval come from the facts that the Web and online information sources are huge, complex, and dynamically changing, and that the users of online retrieval systems vary widely in terms of search interests and experiences with Web retrieval. On the other hand, the instantaneous, interactive nature of the Web greatly enhances the possibility for Web retrieval systems to quickly adapt to a user's needs. Besides general search engines for searching the entire Web, we also need specialized retrieval software that supports queries for document databases of specific topics and features. There is a great need for powerful, automated information retrieval systems to address these challenges and opportunities.

We will consider textual information retrieval in general and Web retrieval in particular in this chapter. The two major components of a typical textual retrieval system are: a text database which is a set of texts (often called documents), and a retrieval (query-answering) engine. A user of the retrieval system presents queries describing the documents desired. The retrieval engine matches the queries with the documents in the text database, and returns to the user a (ranked) list or collection of the documents which are "best matches". Obviously, uncertainty is quite common in both the document description (namely, what a document is "about") and the query specification (what kind of documents for which the user is looking). For example, a document may be primarily about "Fuzzy Logic" and "Rule Induction", but it could also be relevant to "Humanity" and "Business". A query may target primarily documents on "Information Technology" and "Online Textual Retrieval", yet the user may also desire documents somewhat relevant to "Social Changes" and "Music". Given the fuzziness in specification of both user queries and document descriptions, the application of fuzzy set theory in information retrieval is quite natural [Kraft and Buell, 1983, Kraft et. al., 1999]. Fuzzy clustering and fuzzy rules are useful methods for handling textual document representation and user query adaptation for improved textual retrieval performance.

In our work [Chen et. al., 1998, Kraft and Chen, 2000], we use fuzzy C-means and hierarchical clustering methods to group textual documents into clusters. The clusters are useful for characterizing the documents and for answering subsequent queries. Fuzzy rules are then extracted from the cluster centers. These rules are then used to modify user queries according to a fuzzy inference method [Chen and Kundu, 1996], which is found to be sound and complete. Other researchers [Akrivas et. al., 2002] have also developed methods of applying to text retrieval. User profiles provide valuable information about the users of a retrieval system. In the Web retrieval setting, the construction and utilization of user profiles may be even more important for good retrieval performance, i.e., user satisfaction with the retrieval results. Moreover, user profiles are very important for targeted advertisement and marketing in electronic commerce.

The application of user profiles has received tremendous amount of attention recently with the advent of data mining technologies and the rapid expansion of the Web. [Pazzani and Billsus, 1997] develop a method for learning user profiles based on Naive Bayes classifier.

The WEBKDD workshop [Masand and Spiliopoulou, 1999] is devoted to the issue of Web usage mining and user profiling. [Fu et. al., 1999] investigate the discovery of user groups characterized by similar access patterns. They use a hierarchical clustering approach to cluster Web access sessions generalized according to Web page generalization hierarchy. [Chan, 1999] considers the issue of user profiling with page interest estimators and Web access graphs. [Nasraoui et. al., 2000] use a fuzzy clustering approach to mine Web log files for user profiles. We have proposed to use a fuzzy clustering method combined with fuzzy inference for constructing user profiles already discussed in the paper by [Martin-Bautista et. al., 2002, Kraft et. al., 2002].

To a Web retrieval system (be it a search engine or a specialized information retrieval system), a user profile is generally the knowledge about the user's interests and characteristics acquired and maintained by the system. We can distinguish two types of profiles [Korfhage, 1997]. *Simple profiles* are essentially a set of keywords (document indexing terms) extracted from documents deemed interesting to the user. These terms represent the user's main interests in the relevant topics. On the other hand, *extended profiles* include other information about the user in addition to the knowledge in a simple profile. The additional information in extended profiles may include demographic information such as age group, education level, income, or location. A user's prior Web navigation patterns can also be included in the user profile. Profiles could be based on user queries or similar user queries or user characterizations. The imprecision of knowledge in both simple and extended profiles can be handled by fuzzy logic based approaches. In this chapter, we present an integrated approach to textual information retrieval with user profiles. Fuzzy clustering, fuzzy rule extraction and fuzzy inference are combined with conventional IR techniques in order to achieve optimal retrieval performance. The conventional IR techniques used are term frequency-inverted document frequency (TFIDF) measures as a basis for document vector representations, and the cosine measure for query-document similarity [Salton, 1989]. Fuzzy clustering methods are applied in two cases: (1) application of fuzzy clustering to documents in the database serves the purpose of characterization and grouping of documents; (2) application of fuzzy clustering to subsets of documents related to user interests helps to build user profiles. The clusters are subsequently used for query-answering and for rule discovery. Fuzzy logic rules are extracted from the fuzzy cluster centers.

These rules capture the semantical connections among index terms. We use the fuzzy logic system generated by [Chen and Kundu, 1996], which is sound and complete, for fuzzy inferencing in order to derive useful modifications of the initial query, and use the modified query to guide the search for relevant documents. Moreover, user profiles constructed by fuzzy clustering methods can be used to influence the retrieval results. The advantage of our approach is that semantic information embedded in the rules and the user profile information have been utilized, which should lead to superior retrieval performance.

Several preliminary experiments have been performed using the Air Force EDC database [Boff and Lincoln, 1988] and a Web retrieval dataset. We have also gotten evaluations for the clustering results from experts as reported in [Lincoln and Monk, 1997], and all results have shown that the method is promising.

The chapter is organized as follows. In Section 2, we present a preliminary background for the vector space approach to information retrieval, for fuzzy set theory and the fuzzy clustering methods used in this study. In Section 3, we describe the application of the two clustering algorithms to document clustering and fuzzy rule discovery, illustrated through our experiments using the documents from the US Air Force *Engineering Data Compendium* (EDC) database [Boff and Lincoln, 1988]. The fuzzy logic inference method for deriving new queries is also presented in this section. The application of user profiles via fuzzy clustering to Web retrieval is presented in Section 4, along with the preliminary experimental results using a collection of tourist Web pages. Conclusions are drawn in Section 5.

2.   PRELIMINARIES

We briefly describe the (traditional) vector space approach to IR, the basic concepts of fuzzy sets theory, and the fuzzy clustering methods used. Throughout the chapter, we consider a finite set of textual documents
$D = \{D_1, D_2, ..., D_N\}$, and a finite set of index terms $T = \{t_1, t_2, ..., t_s\}$.

2.1.   The Vector Space Approach To Information Retrieval

The vector space model is a representative of the ranked, "best-match" retrieval models. In this model, each document D_i is represented as a vector of dimension s, the number of terms:

$$D_i = \langle w_{i1}, w_{i2}, ..., w_{is} \rangle \tag{1}$$

Here, each w_{ij} is a real number (typically positive), characterizing the *weight* of the term t_j in D_i. These weights, called indexing weights, can be computed from the frequencies of occurrence of the terms as follows:

$$w_{ij} \; = \; f_{ij} * \log(N/N_j) \tag{2}$$

where f_{ij} is the frequency with which term t_j occurs in document D_i, N is the number of documents in the collection, and N_j is the number of documents in which the term t_j occurs at least once. Equation (2) is called the term frequency-inverted document frequency (TFIDF) model. Moreover, terms can be generated from the text itself as keywords; one can remove words that are too common and non-content bearing (e.g., "a", "the", "however") from the natural language of the texts, and can then stem the remaining words (e.g., "work", "worker", "worked", "working" all converted to "work"), before doing the frequency analysis [Salton, 1989].

A query q is represented in the same way as an s-dimension vector:

$$= \; \langle w_{q1}, w_{q2}, \; ..., \; w_{qs} \rangle \tag{3}$$

Here, the weights w_{qj} are called *query weights*.

The degrees of match between a query and the documents are obtained by comparing the vectors and computing similarity levels. For a given query, a ranked collection of "best match" documents according to the similarity measure will be returned to the user. [Salton, 1989] suggests using the cosine measure as the criterion for document and query similarity. Given a document D_i and a query q, as represented above in equation (1) and equation (3), the cosine similarity measure SIM(D_i, q) is defined to be:

$$SIM(D_i, \; q) \; = \; \frac{\sum_{j=1}^{s} w_{ij} * w_{qj}}{\sqrt{\sum_{j=1}^{s} {w_{ij}}^2} \sqrt{\sum_{j=1}^{s} {w_{qj}}^2}} \tag{4}$$

[Kraft and Boyce, 1995] propose a generalized retrieval scheme as follows. Given D, the set of textual documents in the database, and T, the set of index terms, the indexing function W is

$$W : \; D \times T \; \mapsto \; [0, 1].$$

Note that an W of 1 implies that a document is in the set of documents about the concept(s) of a term, an W of 0 implies that the document is not in the set, and values in the middle, if allowed, represent partial or weighted membership. One could subjectively estimate the W values; or one could use term frequency models, such as the TFIDF model described by equation (2). Of course, to make the W values occur in [0,1], we have to normalize each of the document vectors by dividing each w_{ij} by the maximum weighty w_{ik} for each document D_i. Moreover, consider Q = the set of user queries for information from the database, so that

$$a : \; Q \times T \; \mapsto \; [0, 1]$$

is the query term weighting function. To process queries, we have

$$g : \; W \times a \; \mapsto \; [0, 1]$$

to evaluate a given document along the dimensions of a single given keyword. Various forms for g have been developed, based on the query term weighting function a being representative of term importance, or being a term threshold, or viewing the query as an ideal document, or hybrids of these forms [Kraft and Boyce, 1995]. Finally,

$$e : g_1 \times g_2 \times ... \times g_s \mapsto [0,1]$$

is the retrieval status value (RSV), the evaluation of the relevance of the given document based on the Boolean structure of the entire query. Often, the Max function is used for OR, the Min function for AND, and the $1-$ (one minus) function for NOT.

2.2. Fuzzy Set Theory Basics

The theory of fuzzy sets was developed by [Zadeh, 1965]. A fuzzy subset A of a (crisp) set U is defined by a membership function:

$$\mu_A : U \mapsto [0,1]$$

where $\mu_A(x)$, for $x \in U$, defines x's degree of belonging to the fuzzy set A. Obviously, fuzzy sets are a generalization of the ordinary notion of sets. The set-theoretic operations, *union, intersection, complementation, and Cartesian product*, have been naturally extended to fuzzy sets. A number of fuzzy logics based on fuzzy sets have been defined in the literature [Chen and Kundu, 1996, Dubois et. al., 1997, Klir and Yuan, 1995, Klir and Folger, 1988].

2.3. Fuzzy Hierarchical Clustering

By fuzzy hierarchical clustering we mean agglomerative hierarchical clustering (AHC) [Miyamoto, 1990, Rasmussen, 1992, Salton, 1989] based on a weighted similarity measure. The idea behind AHC is fairly simple. We start with the set of objects to be clustered and a similarity measure $SIM(O_i, O_j)$ for any pair of objects (O_i, O_j) in the data set. The AHC algorithm will initially make every object a cluster. Then, the algorithm will repeatedly merge the two "most similar" clusters into one cluster until the similarity between any two clusters falls below some heuristic threshold. The measurement of similarity between two clusters can be done in a number of ways. For example, one can take the minimum of the similarities between any pair of objects, one from each cluster. This is the so-called *complete link clustering* (CLC) [Salton, 1989]. One can also use the maximum, or the average, pair-wise similarity measures. In the experiments done in this work, we use the CLC approach.

2.4. Fuzzy Clustering by the Fuzzy C-means Algorithm

The fuzzy C-means algorithm [Bezdek, 1980, Bezdek et. al., 1987] is a family of algorithms which form fuzzy clusters iteratively through optimizing an objective function. Given a set of n sample data points $p_i = \langle x_{i1}, x_{i2}, ..., x_{is} \rangle$:

$1 \le i \le n$, and the desired number of clusters C (≥ 2), the fuzzy C-means algorithm produces C fuzzy clusters, A_k, $1 \le k \le C$, by finding the membership values $\mu_{ki} = \mu_k(p_i)$ for each point p_i and cluster A_k. The algorithm chooses the μ_{ki} and v_k so that the following objective function (where $m > 1$ is a parameter heuristically selected) is minimized:

$$J_m = \sum_{k=1}^{C} \sum_{i=1}^{n} (\mu_{ki})^m \|p_i - v_k\|^2 \tag{5}$$

This is subject to the constraints that $\sum_k \mu_{ki} = 1$ for each i, and that every $\mu_{ki} \ge 0$. Here, v_k is visualized as the center of the cluster A_k. Moreover, $\|p_i - v_k\|$ denotes the Euclidean distance between the points p_i and v_k. The equations for determining the μ_{ki} that minimize J_m are given by:

$$\mu_{ki} = \frac{[\|p_i - v_k\|^2]^{\frac{-1}{(m-1)}}}{\sum_{j=1}^{C} [\|p_i - v_j\|^2]^{\frac{-1}{(m-1)}}}, \quad 1 \le k \le C \text{ and } 1 \le i \le n. \tag{6}$$

together with the following equations for v_k (which are to be considered coordinate-wise for p_i and v_k):

$$v_k = \frac{\sum_{i=1}^{n} (\mu_{ki})^m p_i}{\sum_{i=1}^{n} (\mu_{ki})^m}, \quad 1 \le k \le C. \tag{7}$$

The actual computation of μ_{ki} begins by initializing the μ_{ki} values randomly, subject to $\mu_{ki} \ge 0$ and $\sum_k \mu_{ki} = 1$ for each i. One then iteratively uses equation (7) to first compute the v_k values, and then uses those values in equation (6) to update the μ_{ki} values. The process continues until the maximum of the absolute difference in the membership values (and the centers) in the current iteration and those in the previous iteration falls below some convergence threshold $\delta > 0$. The convergence proofs of the C-means algorithm are presented in [Bezdek, 1980, Bezdek et. al., 1987].

3. FUZZY CLUSTERING, FUZZY RULE DISCOVERY AND FUZZY INFERENCE FOR TEXTUAL RETRIEVAL

We apply the Fuzzy C-means and hierarchical clustering methods described in the previous section to the Airforce EDC database and obtain very good results. Both methods give meaningful clusters which roughly correspond to the sections within the EDC database. We will present a method for extracting fuzzy rules from the cluster centers obtained by Fuzzy C-means. A fuzzy logic inference method is also described, which uses discovered fuzzy rules to derive modified user queries for better retrieval performance. This combination of fuzzy clustering, fuzzy rule extraction and fuzzy inference for retrieval is tested on the Airforce EDC database.

Table 1. Portions of the EDC database Used in This Study

Sec. 2 Audit. Acqui. of Info	Subsec. 2.1 Measurement of Sound
Sec. 2 Audit. Acqui. of Info	Subsec. 2.2 Physiology of the Ear
Sec. 2 Audit. Acqui. of Info	Subsec. 2.3 Detection
Sec. 2 Audit. Acqui. of Info	Subsec. 2.4 Discrimination
Sec. 2 Audit. Acqui. of Info	Subsec. 2.5 Temporal Resolution
Sec. 2 Audit. Acqui. of Info	Subsec. 2.6 Loudness
Sec. 2 Audit. Acqui. of Info	Subsec. 2.7 Pitch
Sec. 2 Audit. Acqui. of Info	Subsec. 2.8 Localization
Sec. 6 Perceptual Organiz.	Subsec. 6.4 Audit. Perceptual Organiz.
Sec. 8 Human Lang. Proc.	Subsec. 8.3 Intelligibility of Speech
Sec. 8 Human Lang. Proc.	Subsec. 8.4 Intelligibility of Alt. Speech
Sec. 10 Effects of Env. Stress.	Subsec. 10.3 Noise

3.1. The Air Force EDC Data Set

The Air Force EDC data set [Boff and Lincoln, 1988] is a text database, which is a part of the US Air Force's multimedia ergonomics database system, CASHE:PVS (Computer Aided Systems Human Engineering: Performance Visualization System). The CASHE:PVS system consists of the complete Engineering Data Compendium (EDC) data set [Boff and Lincoln, 1988], the military standard (MIL-STD-1472D) Human Engineering Design Criteria for Military Systems, Equipment, and Facilities [DoD, 1994], and a unique visualization tool, the Perception and Performance Prototyper (P^3).

CASHE:PVS has been produced to define new approaches to communicate human factors data and to provide access to technical information relevant to human performance design problems. The goal is to enable ergonomics to be supported as a full partner among other design disciplines within a computer-aided environment [Boff et. al., 1991a, Boff et. al., 1991b]. For example, a designer interested in the intelligibility of speech in a noisy environment, such as the cockpit of an airplane, can look up the appropriate data in CASHE:PVS and peruse them. However, to gain a deeper understanding of what the data really means, that designer can also use the P^3 visualization tool to experience the data. Sample speech signals can be heard in varying amounts of background noise, different noises can be used, and techniques to improve speech intelligibility are demonstrated. The reference data, coupled with interactive visualization, provide the designer with a synthesis and analysis capability for working with other designers.

The EDC data set consists of 1136 documents containing engineering design and human factor data. A subset of the EDC related to audio topics has been selected in order to keep the dataset to a manageable size for this study. Table 1 illustrates the portion of the EDC which was used for this study. This represents N = 114 entries out of the 1136 in the entire EDC.

3.2.   Clustering Results

We have performed several experiments using these two clustering algorithms on the chosen subset of the EDC database. Before applying these clustering algorithms, some pre-processing has to be performed to extract the vector space representations. First, as noted above, stop words have to be eliminated, as they provide no useful characterization of the document. Subsequently, we need to apply a stemming algorithm to find the root form of the words. We use the stemming algorithm in [Frakes, 1992] for this task. Newly encountered words are added to a global word list, and the word frequency count is calculated for each word in each document. The 114 documents from the EDC database yield 2857 keywords after using a stoplist and stemming. Finally, we need to reduce this list of terms to an even smaller size in order to be amenable to clustering. This is done by choosing the top s maximal-weighted keywords from the data set. The maximal weight w_j of term t_j is obtained by taking the maximal weight of t_j over all 114 documents, i.e., $w_j = max_{i=1}^{114} w_{ij}$. After finding w_j for each of the 2857 terms, we choose the top s terms from the term list when sorted in descending order of the w_j values. Here, for our experiment, s is set to be 100. Thus, after pre-processing, each of the 114 documents is represented as a vector of dimensionality of 100.

We conduct two experiments on fuzzy hierarchical clustering: one uses word frequency counts as weights in the vector space representation, and the other uses inverted document frequencies. The heuristic threshold for the minimum similarity (above which to merge two clusters) was heuristically set to 0.01 for the inverted document frequency case, and it was set to 0.1 for the word frequency case. In both cases, the algorithms formed 12 clusters out of the 114 documents and the clusters obtained by the two experiments differ only slightly.

In applying the fuzzy C-means algorithm, we set the convergence threshold δ to 0.001, and the number of clusters, C, to 12. This choice of C reflects our intention to show that fuzzy C-means algorithm can also find natural clusters in documents, just like the hierarchical clustering method can. The fuzzy C-means algorithm will produce "fuzzy" clusters in the sense that μ_{ki}, the membership of document D_i in cluster A_k, is a value in the interval [0,1]. "Hardening" is performed to the fuzzy clusters obtained by the fuzzy C-means algorithm. That is, for each document D_i, we find the cluster index k (for cluster A_k) such that μ_{ki} is maximal over the μ_{ji} for all clusters A_j; we then set μ_{ki} to 1 and the other μ_{ji} values to 0 for $j \neq k$.

We have performed several experiments with the C-means algorithm, varying the values of the parameter $m > 1$ in equation (5). We found that for the subset of EDC database, when $m = 2.0$ or $m \geq 1.5$, the cluster centers take on the same, or nearly the same value, so that the clusters look identical, and each document belongs to each of the 12 clusters with essentially the same membership value. Therefore, after "hardening", the clusters obtained are chaotic. On the other hand, for $m \leq 1.4$, the crisp clusters obtained after hardening seem to be more correct. This was verified by the experts

[Lincoln and Monk, 1997], when they were given the results of two fuzzy C-means clusterings, one with $m = 2.0$ and the other with $m = 1.1$. Of course, the experts were also given the two hierarchical clustering results.

The experts [Lincoln and Monk, 1997] indicate that in evaluating clusters, they considered both:

1. Whether the entries within a given cluster were related enough to make a valid cluster, and

2. Whether other entries that are equally related were missing from the cluster.

They comment that "Both of the hierarchical methods did a much better job of clustering the entries than did the original fuzzy clustering method. Clustering using inverted frequency may have been a little bit better than clustering that considered the number of occurrences in each entry, but the difference was very slight ... Modified fuzzy clustering (C-means with m = 1.1) was at least as good as hierarchical clustering. It tended to generate fewer large, heterogeneous clusters (though it did have one extremely mixed, 39-member cluster!) ... The hierarchical/inverted matrix method was the best at avoiding outliers (items off the topic of the other cluster entries), but the modified fuzzy method also did a pretty good job at this. Both hierarchical methods (but not the fuzzy methods) also managed to create at least one "perfect" cluster (no misses and no outliers)."

3.3.   Fuzzy Rule Extraction from Fuzzy Clusters

After finding the document clusters by the fuzzy C-means algorithm (with hardening), we can construct fuzzy rules of the form

$$[t_i \geq w_i] \to [t_j \geq w_j] \tag{8}$$

from the clusters and their centers obtained by the fuzzy C-means algorithm. Here, t_i and t_j are terms, and w_i and w_j are positive real weights in the interval (0,1]. The intuitive meaning of the rule is that whenever term t_i's weight (in a document or query) is at least w_i, the related term t_j's weight (in the same document or query) should be at least w_j. These rules can be applied to derive useful modifications of the user's original query.

The current implementation of our method uses the *centers* (centroids) obtained by the fuzzy C-means algorithm to construct the fuzzy logic rules. Our method proceeds as follows: First, we normalize the vectors representing the cluster centers. Then for each cluster center, we sort the terms in descending order of term weights and focus on the first K (≥ 2) terms in this sorted list. Here the value of K is determined by trial and error. Subsequently, build term pairs from the chosen terms in each cluster center in the form of $\langle [t_i, w_i], [t_j, w_j] \rangle$. Moreover, multiple occurrence of the same pairs with different weights (obtained from different cluster centers) will be merged by selecting the minimal weight for each term over all pair occurrences. Finally, from the pair of the form $\langle [t_i, w_i], [t_j, w_j] \rangle$, we build two rules: $[t_i \geq w_i] \rightarrow [t_j \geq w_j]$ and $[t_j \geq w_j] \rightarrow [t_i \geq w_i]$.

3.4. Application of Fuzzy Inference for Improving Retrieval Performance

The fuzzy logic rules obtained by fuzzy clustering and rule discovery (as described in Section 3.3) can be used to modify a user's original query, using the sound and complete fuzzy logic system [Chen and Kundu, 1996]. We note that each fuzzy rule extracted is of the form as in equation (8), which is a well-formed formula in the fuzzy logic defined in [Chen and Kundu, 1996], where formulas are formed by using logical connectives $\{\vee, \wedge, \neg, \rightarrow\}$. the logical constant $\perp$ (= false), and propositions of the form $[A \leq \alpha]$, or of the form $[A \geq \alpha]$, where A is an ordinary atom in a propositional logic and $\alpha \in [0, 1]$. The rule in equation (8) is used to modify a user's query q as follows. Given the query q in the form

$$q = \langle w_{q1}, w_{q2}, ..., w_{qs} \rangle, \tag{9}$$

the rule is applicable to q if $w_{qi} \geq w_i$ and $w_{qj} < w_j$. The application of this rule to q will yield q^*, which coincides with q on each dimension except $w_{q^*j} = w_j$. Note that this application step precisely corresponds to the modus-ponens inference in the fuzzy logic in [Chen and Kundu, 1996], namely,

$$From \ [t_i \geq w_i] \rightarrow [t_j \geq w_j] \ And \ [t_i \geq w_i] \ Infer \ [t_j \geq w_j].$$

Let R = $\{r_1, r_2, ..., r_z\}$ be the set of all fuzzy rules extracted and query q be as in defined by equation (9). The final modified query q' is obtained from q by repeatedly applying the rules in R until no more applicable rules can be found. The modified query q' will be used to search for relevant documents.

We have implemented the query modification method and performed several experiments with it. The preliminary results obtained in the experiments suggest that the modified queries are helpful to improve precision in most of the cases. For example, suppose we want to get documents regarding the topics of "pitch" and "adaptation", with more emphasis on "pitch". This is modeled by the query q_1 with weight for the term "adapt" set to 0.4, and the weight for "pitch" set to 0.8, and weights for all other terms set to 0. Here we did not use a weight of 1.0 for "pitch" because in the fuzzy retrieval setting, a term weight of 0.8 in a document already indicates quite a high degree of relevance of the document for the term. The term weight 0.4 for "adopt" is chosen to be half of the weight for "pitch". The intended target set of documents is for those in subsection 2.7 (with 11 documents), which is essentially captured by a cluster obtained by fuzzy clustering with $m = 1.10$, which is judged by the experts [Lincoln and Monk, 1997] as a "pretty good cluster". Starting with q_1, we apply the query modification method and get the modified query q'_1, which has the same weights for "adapt" and "pitch" as in q_1 and several additional terms with positive weights: term "interrupt" got weight 0.2029, term "modul" (root of "modulate", "modulation", etc.) got weight 0.2399 and term "tone" got weight 0.6155. Using both queries q_1 and q_1' for the retrieval task, we have the following observations on the query results:

(1)

If we compare the top M documents obtained by query q_1 (according to their similarity to q_1) versus the top M documents obtained by q_1', where M is a fixed number (say M = 10), then q_1' fares better (or comparable) in both precision and recall. For example, when M = 11, q_1 produces 9 documents out of the 11 documents in the cluster, giving rise to a 81.8 percent recall and precision; while q_1' captures exactly the 11 documents in the cluster, resulting in a 100 percent recall and precision.

(2)

If we compare the documents obtained by q_1 with similarities above some threshold $0 < \delta < 1$ versus those obtained by q_1' with the same similarity threshold, then q_1' gives better precision with a comparable or slightly inferior recall. For example, for $\delta = 0.1$, q_1 produces 17 documents which contains all the 11 relevant documents, resulting in a 100 percent recall but a 68.7 percent precision; while q_1' produces 12 documents including all 11 relevant ones, thus giving rise to a 100 percent recall and 91 percent precision. When we take $\delta = 0.15$, q_1 presents 15 documents with 100 percent recall and 73 percent precision; while q_1' presents 8 documents with 72 percent recall and 100 percent precision.

The experiments we have performed on using the query modification method are still quite limited and the nature of the results reported here on the performance of the modified query should be considered *preliminary*. Further studies are needed to validate the query modification method. We would like to point out that some researchers [Horng et. al., 2002] further extended our approach of fuzzy clustering and fuzzy inference for textual retrieval, and experimented with our method on a larger dataset (with 200+ documents). Their results also indicate that our method may improve precision in textual retrieval.

4.   FUZZY CLUSTERING, FUZZY RULES AND USER PROFILES FOR WEB RETRIEVAL

In this section, we present a fuzzy logic based approach to Web retrieval with user profiles. The method described in Section 3 that combines algorithms and fuzzy rule extraction is applied to construct user profiles for textual retrieval. One main difference is that fuzzy C-mean clustering is applied separately to documents deemed interesting and uninteresting by a user. From the cluster centers, a *simple user profile* is constructed which indicates the user's general preference with respect to various terms. Fuzzy logic rules are also extracted from the cluster centers or from the user profiles. The user profiles and the fuzzy rules are subsequently used in personalized retrieval for better retrieval performance. We present some preliminary experimental results on a Web retrieval task. Additional non-topical information (demographic, navigational behavior patterns) about the user can be added to form *extended profiles*. Moreover, fuzzy clustering can be applied to extended profiles of many users to extract knowledge about different user groups. The extracted knowledge is potentially useful for personalized marketing on the Web.

4.1.   Simple User Profile Construction

User profiles provide useful information that can be exploited for better information retrieval results. The consideration of user profiles is even more important for Web-page retrieval, because of the typical low precision of Web search partly due to the huge size of the Web. A classical or simple user profile for IR is a set of (possibly unweighted) terms extracted from the set of documents relevant to a user. In dealing with fuzzy retrieval systems, we would like to consider fuzzy user profiles. Let $P = \{p_1, ..., p_m\}$ be the set of all profiles. The profile function G is defined by $G: P \times T \mapsto [0, 1]$. Here recall that T is the set of index terms of the form $T = \{t_1, t_2, ... , t_s\}$.

Again, analogous to the indexing function F, the function G defines fuzzy membership functions μ_p: for all $p \in P$ and $t \in T$, $G(p, t) = \mu_p(t)$. The value $G(p, t)$ denotes the degree of membership of the term t in profile p, which can be seen as the strength of the user interests in topics related to this term. Some existing works related to this topic of user profiles with fuzzy and genetic algorithm techniques include [Martin-Bautista et. al., 1999] and [Martin-Bautista et. al., 2000]. In [Martin-Bautista et. al., 1999], an intelligent agent for constructing adaptive user profiles using genetic algorithms and fuzzy logic is presented.

The method to combine fuzzy clustering and fuzzy rule construction described in Section 3 of this chapter is also applied here to extract fuzzy user profiles. We first collect a number of queries and documents deemed relevant by a specific user. The number of such relevant documents should be reasonably large to avoid accidental patterns being extracted. Fuzzy clustering is applied to the document collection. A user profile is constructed from the cluster centers. Fuzzy rules are extracted either from the cluster centers or from the final user profile. The user profiles and fuzzy rules can be used to rank and filter retrieved documents and to expand user queries, with the objective of better reflecting the user preferences and habits.

In this work, we use the fuzzy C-means method [Bezdek, 1980] to discover simple user profiles from a set of documents relevant to a particular user. The input to the fuzzy C-means algorithm is the set of document vectors in either word frequency representation or inverted document frequency representation. The output of the fuzzy C-means algorithm consists of C clusters where each cluster A_k is characterized by the cluster center (prototype) v_k. We can derive a simple user profile from these clusters in two possible ways. One way is to simply consider the set of all these cluster centers $v_1, ..., v_C$ as the user's profile with respect to various query terms, where each center v_k describes a topic of interest to the user. This is reasonable because a user may be interested in several topics. Such a profile is called *union simple profile*. The other way to obtain a simple user profile is by combining all the cluster centers into one prototype. This can be done by taking, for example, the vector sum of all the v_k's and then normalizing the resulted vector. We call such a user profile *aggregated simple profile*. Other ways of deriving the aggregated simple user profile can also be tried.

From cluster centers $\{v_1, ..., v_C\}$, fuzzy rules of the form

$$[t_i \geq w_i] \rightarrow [t_j \geq w_j]$$

are constructed, as described in Section 3 of this chapter. These rules can be applied to derive useful modifications of the user's original query. We can also use the aggregated simple user profile to construct the fuzzy logic rules. This can be done because a user profile is essentially of the same structure as the cluster centers.

Once we establish profiles for many users, we can also apply the fuzzy C-means clustering algorithm to cluster these profiles. This will lead to fewer number of user profiles being maintained. Moreover, fuzzy rules can be extracted from the profile cluster centers, which represent valuable knowledge about groups of users. The fuzzy clustering method can also be applied to a set of *uninteresting* Web documents with respect to a user. The fuzzy clusters obtained characterize the types of Web pages that are not relevant to the user. In a more general setting, we can include information from these clusters in a simple user profile.

4.2. Application of Simple User Profiles in Web Information Retrieval

There are several ways in which we can apply the simple user profiles in Web information retrieval.

4.21. Retrieving Interesting Web Documents

Consider the scenario in which a user is surfing a Web site for some information-seeking purpose. Assume that the adaptive IR system on the Web server has constructed a union simple user profile V based on some previous interaction with the user. Here $V = \{v_1, ..., v_C\}$ is the set of prototypes for the user's relevant documents. Moreover, we also assume that the IR system has a set $N = \{n_1, ..., n_p\}$ of prototypes for the user's irrelevant documents. Given the current user profile information V and N, the adaptive IR system can push or suggest "interesting", unvisited Web documents to this user. For each document d_i, we define the interestingness of the document with respect to this user u by

$$I(d_i, u) = \sum_{j=1}^{C} SIM(d_i, v_j) - \sum_{j=1}^{p} SIM(d_i, n_j) \qquad (10)$$

This measure captures the degree of interest of the user u in document d_i. The intuition is that documents closer to the prototypes of known relevant ones and farther from prototypes of known irrelevant ones should be more likely to be more interesting to the same user. All the unvisited Web documents can be ranked by this interestingness measure, and those above some pre-defined threshold can be suggested to the user in decreasing order of the I measure. Another variation of this method is to classify a Web document as interesting/uninteresting based on a *nearest neighbor* method: a document d is considered interesting if the nearest neighbor of d to all the prototypes $V \cup N$ is from V; otherwise d is considered uninteresting. Here a distance measure can be easily defined as the inverse of the SIM measure. Again, all the interesting documents can be ranked. The union simple profiles can also be used to rank or filter retrieved documents with respect to a user's given query.

In [Martin-Bautista et. al., 2000, Martin-Bautista et. al., 2001b], we have investigated the issue of document classification by extracting *"discrimination terms"* using techniques inspired by the feature selection problem in machine learning. The general idea is to include in the profile information related to the user preferences, both about relevant and irrelevant documents, reflecting what the user likes or does not like. We use extensions of the Jaccard score and Dice score in order to calculate the discrimination power of the terms. By using a Genetic Algorithm, the most discriminatory terms are kept in the first chromosomes. These most discriminatory terms are subsequently used to classify new documents into relevant and irrelevant categories.

4.22. User Profiles for Query Expansion by Fuzzy Inference

User profiles and the fuzzy logic rules extracted from them are used in this study to expand the user's original queries, with the expectation to improve retrieval performance, in particular, precision. The user's original queries will be modified using the fuzzy rules extracted from the user profile. This process is essentially the same as described in Section 3 of this chapter for modification of user queries based on rules extracted from document clusters.

In this current study, we perform a number of experiments for user profile construction and its use in Web textual information retrieval. We compare the effectiveness of rules constructed from the aggregate simple profiles and rules constructed from the union simple profiles. We experiment with several different ways to build the aggregate simple profile from the cluster centers of the user's relevant documents. It would also be interesting to study the new form of rules which characterize the "negative" correlation among terms, i.e., when a term t_i's weight is at least w_i, another term t_j's weight can be at most w_j - this may need information from prototypes of documents deemed uninteresting to a user. Different ways of using user profiles will be explored as well.

4.3.   Experiments of Using User Profiles

We have performed some preliminary experimental studies for user profile construction and its use in Web textual information retrieval. Due to time constraint, we have not yet tested our method on many datasets. Instead, we tested our ideas on one dataset, which consists of 103 Web pages obtained from Web search with the search engine "looksmart" by using the keyword "yellowstone". The user in our study is a colleague of the authors. The Web search actually returned 500 pages, but the specific user in our study marked only those pages as the most typical "interesting/uninteresting" ones. Among the 103 Web pages, 62 Web pages are marked as intersting and the rest 41 are marked as uninteresting. The user explained to us that the intersting Web pages match his needs to plan this summer's trip to the Yellowstone National Park, whereas the uninteresting ones do not match his desired ways to explore Yellowstone. For example, some of the pages classified as "uninteresting" mainly describe guided tours or backcountry hiking that are not suitable for the specific user's plans.

We first run the text processing program for lexical analysis and stemming on the Web page files with a stop word list containing the most common non-meaning-bearing words. The stop word list also contains common html commands. This processing step produces 4878 keywords, which is too big for indexing the Web pages. So we use the most frequent 150 keywords to index these 103 files. To construct simple user profiles, we apply the fuzzy C-means algorithm to the 62 interesting Web pages. The number of clusters is set to be 3 after trial and error. The three clusters do share a number of common keywords in addition to the distinctive features in each. Each of the three clusters contains some Web pages for the common topic "general introduction to Yellowstone". Cluster1 has more pages on "wildlife". Cluster2 contains most of the pages on "geysers". And Cluster3 has more pages on "lodging" and "transportation". We have also applied the fuzzy C-means algorithm to the 41 uninteresting Web pages, with the number of clusters being equal to 2. The two clusters respectively focus on "hiking and trails" and "flyfishing". They also share common features such as pages describing guided tours and travel packages.

From the cluster centers, simple user profiles are constructed. As we discussed in Section 4.1, a *union simple profile* is just the collection of cluster centers from the interesting class. As to *aggregate simple profiles*, we tried three ways to construct the aggregate simple profiles: the sum, max, and weighted-sum. Since the cluster centers share a number of common features, the above three ways to create an aggregate simple profile do not make much difference. Fuzzy rules are then extracted from the union simple profile, which is essentially the collection of cluster centers of interesting Web pages. We also tried to extract rules from aggregate profiles.

As we discussed in Section 4.1, simple profiles obtained from cluster centers can be used to classify Web pages not visited by the user. In our experiments, we tried to predict the interestingness of a Web page. A subset of the 103

Table 2. The prediction of interestingness of unseen Web pages

Number of training examples	50	60	70	80
Prediction accuracy	72.2%	74.0%	83.5%	87.5%

Table 3. The precisions of queries vs number of top Web pages

Number of top Web pages considered	10	20	30	40
Precision of q_1	90%	75%	71%	67.5%
Precision of q_1'	100%	90%	77%	70%

Web pages was used as the training data and the remaining pages were used as testing data. We varied the size of the training data sets for constructing the simple profiles, and then applied these profiles to classify the remaining Web pages. The results are quite encouraging. With 50 pages as the training set and using simple profiles constructed from both interesting and uninteresting Web pages, the prediction accuracy on the test data set is approximately 72 percent. We tested training data sets of size 60, 70 and 80. The results are summarized in Table 2. One can see that the prediction accuracy is increased with the increase of training data set size. The prediction accuracy shown in Table 2 presents results using the nearest neighbor method. A new Web page is classified as interesting/uninteresting according to whether the page's nearest neighbor (using the similarity measure (4)) is a cluster center of either class. Several other measures for this prediction task were tested, including the I measure in Section 4.2, the nearest neighbor between the Web page and the interesting/uninteresting prototypes in the aggregate profile. The prediction accuracies with these alternative measures are quite similar to the ones presented in Table 2.

We indicated in Section 4.2 that simple user profiles and the fuzzy rules extracted from them can be used to expand user queries for better performance. We experimented with query expansion using union simple profiles with the Yellowstone data set. We ran a number of queries which were intended for a subset of the interesting class Web pages. We observed that expanded queries seem to result in better precision with comparable recall. For example, consider the user's query q_1 with "airline" weighted 0.8, "gen-info" weighted 0.6 and "hotel" weighted 0.8, "lodge" weighted 0.9, and all other keywords weighed 0. The expanded query q_1' identified several additional keywords with positive weights: "road" weighted 0.554, "entrance" weighted 0.351, "geyser" weighted 1.0, etc. This query is intended for general information about the Yellowstone Park, the airlines that serve the areas near Yellowstone, and more importantly, the lodgings at Yellowstone. According to the user, there are 30 Web pages among the 62 interesting ones relevant to this query. The modified query q_1' is seen to give better precision compared with q_1, when we focus on the top M Web pages returned by both queries. Table 3 shows the precision of both queries vs. the number M of top Web pages returned.

Note that the precision goes down when the number of top Web pages considered goes up for both q_1 and q'_1. This is actually not counter-intuitive, because when one considers more Web pages returned (say considers the top 40 pages instead of the top 30 pages), it is more likely that the additional top pages (in this case, the pages ranked 31 through 40) would include more non-relevant documents, and thus the precision goes down.

4.4. Extended Profiles and Fuzzy Clustering

We have defined [Martin-Bautista et. al., 2002] an *extended user profile* as a tuple $e_i = \langle G_i, L_i, K_i, z'_i \rangle$, where $1 \leq i \leq h$, with h being equal to the number of the user's sessions considered. Here $G_i = (g_{i1}, g_{i2}, ..., g_{ib})$ is a set of demographic variables such as age educational level, or gender. $L_i = (l_{i1}, l_{i2}, ..., l_{ic})$ is the set of identification variables such as the host (domain name or IP address), or user agent (name and version of the browser). $K_i = (k_{i1}, k_{i2}, ..., k_{ir})$ is the set of clickstream variables that represent the weights associated with each of the Web pages by the specific user during a session, typically represented as the elapsed time the user has spent on the Web page. And $z'_i = (t_{i1}, t_{i2}, ..., t_{ip})$ is a session simple user profile, with each $t_{ij} \in T$, indicating the interests of the user in these keywords during a session.

We can apply the method of fuzzy clustering and fuzzy rule extraction to derive more general extended profiles for groups of users. The resulting extended profiles are *not* session-specific. This can be achieved by applying fuzzy clustering (either C-means or hierarchical) to the (session-specific) extended profiles collected from the Web log files. The input to the fuzzy clustering algorithms typically omits the identification variables, because the main objective here is to discover the clusters in Web page access patterns, clusters in topical keywords, and the connection between these clusters to demographic classes. We have studied a general method of clustering [Gomez-Skarmeta et. al., 1999] applied to this task. We are in the process of performing more extensive experiments to validate the effectiveness of the fuzzy clustering and fuzzy rule extraction method for user profile construction and usage.

5. CONCLUSIONS

In this chapter, we present an integrated approach to information retrieval which combines fuzzy clustering and fuzzy rule discovery for fuzzy inference with user profiles in textual document retrieval. Fuzzy clustering and hierarchical clustering methods are applied for document classification and for finding natural clusters in documents. Fuzzy C-means clustering is also used to extract simple user profiles. From the fuzzy clusters, fuzzy logic rules are constructed in an attempt to capture semantic connections between index terms. The fuzzy rules are subsequently used in fuzzy inference within a fuzzy logic system to modify user's queries in retrieval. Two sets of experiments, one for document clustering and query expansion with the Airforce EDC database

[Boff and Lincoln, 1988], in conjunction with expert evaluations (described in Section 3), the other for user profile construction and query expansion on a Web retrieval dataset (described in Section 4), have been conducted to validate our method.

The experiments with clustering methods using the Air Force EDC data set show that both clustering methods can find reasonable natural clusters in documents. However, neither method is perfect, as judged by experts [Lincoln and Monk, 1997]. This is not surprising, considering the fact that only very primitive statistical information (word frequency or TFIDF) is used in the clustering methods, and no semantic information (e.g.word meaning and connections between words) is available. Nevertheless, the preliminary results obtained in fuzzy rule construction and fuzzy inference for query modification show good promise for retrieval precision improvement.

User profiles provide useful information that should be exploited for better retrieval performance within a Web framework. We present our method using fuzzy clustering and fuzzy rule discovery for user profile extraction and usage in Web textual information retrieval. The preliminary experiments performed in this study indicate that simple user profiles are helpful for predicting the degree of user interest of unseen Web pages, and for improving retrieval precision.

One limitation of the current work is that the experiments performed are on small datasets, and thus the results are preliminary in nature. More studies and experiments are needed to further validate or perhaps refine the proposed approach.

We see several areas of future research related to the current work. As just mentioned, no semantic information is available or utilized in constructing the fuzzy clusters. One possible future research direction is to consider incorporating semantic information in the clustering process. This may require some limited form of a natural language processing method. The challenge is to find a good balance between utilization of semantical information and computational efficiency. Another future goal is to study fuzzy clustering and rule extraction for constructing extended user profiles using a combination of user session data, clickstream data, as well as user demographic data if available. The profiles we constructed so far are "flat" profiles without hierarchies. Fuzzy hierarchical clustering can be considered for building user profiles which have a hierarchical structure, and thus possibly better capture user characteristics at different levels of abstraction.

ACKNOWLEDGEMENTS

The authors are grateful to Janet Lincoln and Don Monk at the US Air Force for offering their expert evaluations on the experimental results in this work, and for allowing us to use the Air Force's EDC data set. We would also like to thank Sukhamay Kundu for allowing us to use his implementation of the fuzzy C-means algorithm. Dr. Chen's work was partially supported by the National Science Foundation under contract ITR-0326387, and by the Louisiana Education Quality Support Fund under contract LEQSF(2001-04)-RD-A-03.

REFERENCES

[Akrivas et. al., 2002] G. Akrivas, M. Wallace, G. Satmou, S. Kollias, (2002). Context-Sensitive Query Expansion Based on Fuzzy Clustering of Index Terms. *Proc. of the Fifth International Conference on Flexible Query Answering Systems (FQAS)*, Copenhagen, Denmark.

[Berzal et. al., 2001] F. Berzal, H.L. Larsen, M.J. Martin-Bautista, M.A. Vila, (2001). Computer with Words in Information Retrieval, *Proc. of IFSA/NAFIPS International Conference*, Vancouver, Canada.

[Bezdek, 1980] J.C. Bezdek, (1980). A convergence theorem for the fuzzy ISODATA clustering algorithms, *IEEE Transactions on Pattern Analysis and Machine Intelligence* (2), pp. 1-8.

[Bezdek et. al., 1987] J.C. Bezdek, R.J. Hathaway, M.J. Sabin, and W.T. Tucker, (1987). Convergence theory for fuzzy c-Means: counterexamples and repairs, *IEEE Transactions on Systems, Man, and Cybernetics* (17), pp. 873-877.

[Boff and Lincoln, 1988] K.R. Boff, J.E. Lincoln (Eds), (1988). *Engineering Data Compendium: Human Perception and Performance* v I, II, and III (Wright-Patterson Air Force Base, OH: Human Engineering Division, Harry G. Armstrong Medical Research Laboratory).

[Boff et. al., 1991a] K.R. Boff, D.L. Monk, W.J. Cody (1991). Computer Aided Systems Human Engineering: A Hypermedia Tool, Space Operation Applications and Research (SOAR), Houston: NASA.

[Boff et. al., 1991b] K.R. Boff, D.L. Monk, S.J. Swierenga, C.E. Brown, W.J. Cody, (1991). Computer-Aided Human Factors for Systems Designers, (San Francisco: Human Factors Society annual meeting).

[Chan, 1999] P.K. Chan (1999). Constructing Web User Profiles: A Non-invasive Learning Approach, *International WEBKDD'99 Workshop*, San Diego, CA, USA, pp. 39-55.

[Chen and Kundu, 1996] J. Chen, S. Kundu, (1996). A sound and complete fuzzy logic system using Zadeh's implication operator, *Foundations of Intelligent Systems: Lecture Notes in Computer Science 1079*, pp. 233-242.

[Chen et. al., 1998] J. Chen, A. Mikulcic, D. Kraft, (1998). An Integrated Approach to Information Retrieval with Fuzzy Clustering and Fuzzy Inferencing, in Pons, O., Amparo Vila, M., and Kacprzyk, J. (eds.), *Knowledge Management in Fuzzy Databases*, Heidelberg, Germany: Physica-Verlag.

[Chau and Yeh, 2000] R. Chau and C.H.Yeh, (2000). Explorative multilingual text retrieval based on fuzzy multilingual keyword classification. In Proc. of the fifth international workshop on Information Retrieval with Asian Languages, pp.33-49, Hong Kong, China.

[Delgado, 1996] M. Delgado, A.F. Gomez-Skarmeta, M.A. Vila, (1996). On the Use of Hierarchical Clustering in Fuzzy Modeling, *International Journal of Approximate Reasoning*, 14, pp. 237-257.

[DoD, 1994] Department of Defense, *Human Engineering Design Criteria for Military Systems, Equipment, and Facilities* (MIL-STD-1472D), Notice 3, Washington, DC.

[Dubois et. al., 1997] D. Dubois, H. Prade, R.R. Yager (Eds), (1997). *Fuzzy Information Engineering: A Guided Tour of Applications*, New York, NY: Wiley.

[Frakes, 1992] W. B. Frakes, (1992). Stemming algorithms, In: W. B. Frakes, R. Baeza-Yates (Eds), *Information Retrieval: Data Structures & Algorithms*, Prentice Hall.

[Fu et. al., 1999] Y. Fu, K. Sandhu, M-Y. Shih, (1999). A Generalization-Based Approach to Clustering of Web Usage Sessions, *International WEBKDD'99 Workshop*, San Diego, CA, USA, pp. 21-38.

[Gomez-Skarmeta et. al., 1999] A.F. Gomez-Skarmeta, M. Delgado, M.A. Vila, (1999). About the Use of Fuzzy Clustering Techniques for Fuzzy Model Identification, *Fuzzy Sets and Systems* 106: pp.194-216.

[Horng et. al., 2002] Y.J. Horng, S.M. Chen, C.H. Lee, (2002). Fuzzy Information Retrieval Using Fuzzy Hierarchical Clustering and Fuzzy Inference Techniques. *Proceedings of the 13th International Conference on Information Management*, Taipei, Taiwan, pp.215-222.

[Klir and Folger, 1988] G.J. Klir, T.A. Folger, (1988). *Fuzzy Sets, Uncertainty, and Information*, Englewood Cliffs, NJ: Prentice-Hall.

[Klir and Yuan, 1995] G.J. Klir, B. Yuan, (1995). *Fuzzy Sets and Fuzzy Logic: Theory and Applications*, Upper Saddle Rive, NJ: Prentice-Hall.

[Korfhage, 1997] R.R. Korfhage, (1997). *Information Storage and Retrieval*, New York: NY: John Wiley & Sons.

[Kraft and Buell, 1983] D.H. Kraft and D.A. Buell, (1983). Fuzzy Sets and Generalized Boolean Retrieval Systems, *International Journal of Man-Machine Studies*, v. 19, pp. 45-56; reprinted in D. Dubois, H. Prade, and R. Yager, (Eds), *Readings in Fuzzy Sets for Intelligent Systems*, San Mateo, CA: Morgan Kaufmann Publishers, 1992.

[Kraft et. al., 1999] D.H. Kraft, G. Bordogna, G. Pasi, (1999). Fuzzy Set Techniques in Information Retrieval, In D. Dubois, H. Prade (Eds.), *Handbook of Fuzzy Sets (Vol. 3): Approximate Reasoning and Information Systems.* Kluwer Academic Publishers, The Netherlands, pp. 469-510.

[Kraft and Chen, 2000] D.H. Kraft, J. Chen, (2000). Integrating and Extending Fuzzy clustering and inferencing to improve text retrieval performance, in *Flexible Query Answering Systems: Recent Advances, Proceedings of the 4th International Conference on Flexible Query Answering Systems*, Warsaw, Poland, Heidelberg, Germany: Physica-Verlag, pp. 386-395.

[Kraft, 1994] D.H. Kraft, (1994). An exploratory study of weighted fuzzy keyword retrieval With hypertext links for the CASHE:PVS system, *Final report for the Summer faculty research associate program*, Wright-Patterson AFB, OH.

[Kraft and Barry, 1994] D.H. Kraft, C. Barry, (1994). Relevance in textual Retrieval, American Association for Artificial Intelligence (AAAI), AAAI-94 Fall Symposium - Relevance, New Orleans, LA, Working Notes.

[Kraft et. al., 1995] Kraft, D. H., Bordogna, G., and Pasi, G., (1995). An Extended Fuzzy Linguistic Approach to Generalize Boolean Information Retrieval, *Information Sciences*, (2), pp. 119-134.

[Kraft and Boyce, 1995] D.H. Kraft, B.R. Boyce, (1995). Approaches to Intelligent Information Retrieval, in F.E. Petry, M.L. Delcambre (Eds), *Advances in Databases and Artificial Intelligence*, volume 1: Intelligent Database Technology: Approaches and Applications, Greenwich, CT: JAI Press, pp. 243-261.

[Kraft et. al., 2002] D. Kraft, J. Chen, M.J. Martin-Bautista, M.A. Vila, (2002). Textual Information Retrieval with User Profiles Using Fuzzy Clustering and Inferencing, *Intelligent Exploration of the Web*, Piotr Szczepaniak, J. Segovia, J. Kacprzyk, L. Zadeh (Eds.), Springer-Verlag, pp.152-165.

[Kraft and Monk, 1997] D.H. Kraft, D. Monk, (1997). Applications of Fuzzy Computation - Information Retrieval: A Case Study with the CASHE:PVS System, In E. Ruspini, P. Bonissone, W. Pedrycz (Eds), *Handbook of Fuzzy Computation*, Information Science, New York, NY: Oxford University Press and Institute of Physics Publishing.

[Kraft et. al., 1995] D.H. Kraft, F.E. Petry, B.P. Buckles, T. Sadasivan, (1995). Applying Genetic Algorithms to Information Retrieval Systems Via Relevance Feedback, in P. Bosc, J. Kacprzyk, (Eds), *Fuzzy Sets and Possibility Theory in Database Management Systems*, Studies in Fuzziness Series, Heidelberg, Germany: Physica-Verlag, pp. 330-344.

[Kundu and Chen, 1994] S. Kundu, J. Chen, (1994). Fuzzy linear invariant clustering for applications in fuzzy control, *Proceedings of NAFIPS/IFIS/NASA'94*, San Antonio, TX.

[Lincoln and Monk, 1997] J. Lincoln, D. Monk, (1997). private communications.

[Martin-Bautista et. al., 2002] M. Martin-Bautista, D.H. Kraft, M.A. Vila, J. Chen, J. Cruz, (2002). User Profiles and Fuzzy Logic for Web Retrieval Issues. Soft Computing, vol. 6, pp. 365-372.

[Martin-Bautista et. al., 2001a] M.J. Martin-Bautista, M.A. Vila, D.H. Kraft, J. Chen, (2001). User Profiles in Web Retrieval, *FLINT'2001*, Berkeley, CA.

[Martin-Bautista et. al., 2001b] M.J. Martin-Bautista, M.A. Vila, D. Sanchez, H.L. Larsen, (2001). Intelligent filtering with genetic algorithms and fuzzy logic. In B. Bouchon-Meunier, J. Gutierrez-Rios, L. Magdalena, R.R. Yager (eds.) Technologies for Constructing Intelligent Systems. Springer-Verlag, pp. 351-362.

[Martin-Bautista et. al., 2000] M.J. Martin-Bautista, M.A. Vila, H.L. Larsen, (2000). Building adaptive user profiles by a genetic fuzzy classifier with feature selection. Proceedings of the IEEE Conference on Fuzzy Systems vol.1, pp. 308-312, San Antonio, Texas.

[Martin-Bautista et. al., 1999] M.J. Martin-Bautista, M.A. Vila, H.L. Larsen, (1999). A Fuzzy Genetic Algorithm Approach to An Adaptive Information Retrieval Agent, *Journal of the American Society for Information Science*, 50(9), pp. 760-771.

[Masand and Spiliopoulou, 1999] B. Masand, M. Spiliopoulou, (Eds.), (1999). Web Usage Analysis and User Profiling, *International WEBKDD'99 Workshop*, San Diego, CA, USA.

[Mikulcic and Chen, 1996] A. Mikulcic, J. Chen, (1996). Experiments on using fuzzy linear clustering from fuzzy control system design, *Proceedings of IEEE/FUZZ'96*, New Orleans.

[Miyamoto, 1990] S. Miyamoto, (1990). *Fuzzy Sets in Information Retrieval and Cluster Analysis*, Boston, MA: Kluwer Academic Publishers.

[Nasraoui et. al., 2000] O. Nasraoui, H. Frigui, R. Krishnapuram, A. Joshi, (2000). Extracting Web User Profiles Using Relational Competitive Fuzzy Clustering, *International Journal on Artificial Intelligence Tools*, 9(4), pp. 509-526.

[Pazzani and Billsus, 1997] M. Pazzani, D. Billsus, (1997). Learning and revising User profiles: The identification of Interesting Web Sites, *Machine Learning* 27, pp. 313-331.

[Petry, 1996] F.E. Petry, (1996). *Fuzzy Databases: Principles and Applications*, Norwell, MA: Kluwer Academic Publishers, with contribution by P. Bosc.

[Rasmussen, 1992] E. Rasmussen, (1992). Clustering Algorithms, In W.B. Frakes, R. Baeza-Yates (Eds), *Information Retrieval: Data Structures & Algorithms*, Englewood Cliffs, NJ: Prentice Hall.

[Salton, 1989] G. Salton, (1989). *Automatic Text Processing: The Transformation, Analysis, and Retrieval of Information by Computer*, Reading, MA, Addison Wesley.

[Salton and Buckley, 1985] G. Salton, C. Buckley, (1985). Improving retrieval performance by relevance feedback, *Journal of the American Society for Information Science*, vol. 36, pp. 200-210.

[Salton et. al., 1985] G. Salton, E.A. Fox, and E. Voorhees, (1985). Advanced Feedback Methods in Information Retrieval, *Journal of the American Society for Information Science*, v. 36, pp. 200-210

[Srinivasan et. al., 2001] P. Srinivasan, M.E. Ruiz, D.H. Kraft, J. Chen, (2001). Vocabulary Mining for Information Retrieval: Rough Sets and Fuzzy Sets, *Information Processing and Management*, 37, pp. 15-38.

[Zadeh, 1965] L.A. Zadeh, (1965). Fuzzy sets, *Information and Control* (8), pp. 338-353.

AUTHORS' BIOGRAPHICAL STATEMENTS

Dr. **Jianhua Chen** received her M.S. and Ph.D. in Computer Science from Jilin University, China, in 1985 and 1988 respectively. She is currently an associate professor in the Computer Science Department of Louisiana State University, USA. Her research interests include knowledge representation and reasoning, logic foundations of Artificial Intelligence, machine learning and data mining, fuzzy logic and fuzzy systems with applications to information retrieval and intelligent databases. Her most recent research works focus on applications of AI and machine learning techniques for cyber security.

Dr. **Donald H. Kraft** holds the BSIE, MSIE, and Ph.D. degrees in industrial engineering with a specialization in operations research from Purdue University. He is currently a professor of computer science and adjunct professor of library and information science at Louisiana State University, USA. Prior to his coming to LSU, he was at the University of Maryland, and has been a visiting professor at Indiana University, the University of California, Berkeley, and the University of California, Los Angeles. His research has focused on the modeling of information retrieval systems, of late incorporating fuzzy sets, genetic programming, and rough sets. He has been given several honors for his work, including being named an IEEE Fellow, an AAAS Fellow, an Honorary Member of the Beta Phi Mu honorary society, and a recipient of the ASIST Research Award. He has served as chairman of his department, is currently Editor of the Journal of the American Society for Information Science and Technology (JASIST) and an Associate Editor of IEEE Transactions on Fuzzy Systems. He is also a Past President of the American Society for Information Science and Technology (ASIST). He also was awarded the ASIST Watson Davis Award for service to that society.

Dr. **Mara J. Martn-Bautista** received her M.S. and Ph.D. degree in Computer Science and Artificial Intelligence from the University of Granada, Spain, in 1995 and 2000, respectively. Her current research interests include intelligent information systems, information retrieval, classification problems with fuzzy sets and genetic algorithms, as well as data, text and web mining. She belongs to the Intelligent Databases and Information Systems researching group of the Computer Science and Artificial Intelligence Department at University of Granada, where she is currently an Associate Professor. She belongs to the European Society for Fuzzy Logic and Technology since 2001.

Dr. **Mara-Amparo Vila** received her M.S. degree in Mathematics in 1973 and her Ph.D. in Mathematics in 1978, both from the University of Granada, Spain. She was assistant professor in the department of Statistics until 1982, associate professor in the same department until 1986, and associate professor in the department of Computer Science and Artificial Intelligence until 1992. Since 1992 she is a professor in the same department. Since 1997 she is also head of the department and the IDBIS research group. Her research activity is centered around the application of soft computing techniques to different areas of Computer Science and Artificial Intelligence, such as theoretical aspects of fuzzy sets, decision and optimization processes in fuzzy environments, fuzzy databases including relational, logical and object-oriented data models, and information retrieval. Currently she is interested in the application of soft computing techniques to data, text and web mining. She has been responsible of ten research projects and advisor of seven Ph.D. theses. She has published more than fifty papers in prestigious international journals, more than sixty contributions to international conferences, and many book chapters.

Chapter 19 [1]

STATISTICAL RULE INDUCTION IN THE PRESENCE OF PRIOR INFORMATION: THE BAYESIAN RECORD LINKAGE PROBLEM

Dean H. Judson[2]
U.S. Census Bureau
Washington, D.C. 20233
U.S.A.
Email: *Dean.H.Judson@census.gov*

Abstract: This chapter applies the theory of Bayesian logistic regression to the problem of inducing a classification rule. The chapter first describes the classification rule as a decision to link or not to link two records in different databases in the absence of a common identifier. When a training data set of classified cases is available, developing a rule is easy; this chapter expands the application of the technique to situations where a training data set of classified cases is *not* available. The steps are conceptually simple:first fit a logistic regression with latent dependent variable using Bayesian methods, then use the parameter estimates from the best fitting model to derive the equivalent record linkage rule. This chapter first describes the application area of record linkage, followed by a description of the Fellegi-Sunter model of record linkage. The chapter then shows how to estimate the appropriate Bayesian generalized linear model with latent classes, and, using the posterior kernels, determine the final decision rule.

Key Words: Bayesian record linkage, concept learning, latent class analysis, unsupervised learning, Fellegi-Sunter model.

---

[1] Triantaphyllou, E. and G. Felici (Eds.), **Data Mining and Knowledge Discovery Approaches Based on Rule Induction Techniques**, Massive Computing Series, Springer, Heidelberg, Germany, pp. 655-694, 2006.

[2] This chapter reports the results of research and analysis undertaken by Census Bureau staff. It has undergone a more limited review by the Census Bureau than its official publications. This chapter is released to inform interested parties and encourage discussion.

1.   INTRODUCTION

Imagine two databases, database A and database B, each of which contain information on individual persons. (We note for the record that it is not important that the object of the database is a person; it could be housing units or establishments or any other object of interest.) Suppose that each of these databases contains some information not contained in the other. If the databases refer to the same population, it would be of some analytic value to combine the separate information on each person into a single record. Presumably, we can then tabulate data from the first database with data from the second, and we are able to make broader inferences from the joint database than we could make from either separately.

In order to construct the single record for each person, however, we must first find a way to associate that person in database A with the same person in database B. On the surface, if the databases contain identifier information such as a person's Social Security Number (SSN), this appears to be a simple problem: We merely merge the two databases, using the SSN as the merge field. However, suppose that some SSNs are collected with error, that is, errors in the SSN field are distributed throughout database A, and, independently or with some correlation, errors in the SSN field are also distributed throughout database B. Now the problem is more challenging.

Suppose further that each database does not contain a unique identifier--there is no SSN or comparable field in each database, but suppose that there are several fields which, *when used together*, might be sufficient to uniquely link cases. (Notably, this is the same problem as that of protecting the identity of an individual person in a microdata file release [Jabine, 1993], only in reverse--we *want* to identify the person uniquely.) Using just the fields in the two databases, rather than a unique identifier, can we identify which person records in database A should be associated with which records in database B so as to construct a merged database C consisting of all the information we have on that person?

The most natural approach to linking records without a common identifier is to construct some sort of "decision rule" for linking, e.g., declare two records "linked" if the first name and the last name match. This immediately invites us to consider three questions [Leenen, Van Mechelen, and Gelman, 2000]:

1) Can this rule be chosen in some optimal way?
2) Can the statistical properties of this rule be established? and
3) Can experts' prior knowledge about individual fields (e.g. sex is not very useful, but middle initial can be) be incorporated into this rule

construction?

This chapter attempts to summarize research into these three questions. This chapter will proceed in five major parts:

- We shall first describe some of the challenges of the record linkage problem, followed by the standard Fellegi-Sunter model for record linkage, and show how estimating Fellegi-Sunter weights is equivalent to constructing a decision rule.
- Second, we will cast the entire problem as a logistic regression problem, which will reveal the deep links between the Fellegi-Sunter model and logistic regression, and continue to show how to construct a decision rule.
- Third, we will show that this logistic regression framework can be used even for unlabeled data, that is, in the unsupervised learning situation.
- Fourth, we will illustrate with an example how this framework can be used and interpreted in the unsupervised learning situation.
- Fifth, we will make recommendations for future research in this area.

2.   WHY IS RECORD LINKAGE CHALLENGING?

Record linkage can be considered simply an application of pattern classification [Duda, Hart, and Stork, 2001], concept learning [Davey and Priestly, 1990: 221-231] or, even more simply, finding a subset (all the pairs which we will declare linked) of a set (all possible pairs). The fundamental object in a record linkage problem is a *pair* of records - to fix ideas, they could be considered a randomly drawn pair, one from each database. However, record linkage problems are particularly challenging for two reasons:

First, as the number of records in either file increase, the number of possible comparisons increases as the product of the two file sizes. However, even assuming that neither file contains duplicate records, the number of matched pairs increases only as the minimum of the size of each file.

Thus, for any reasonably-sized record linkage problem, the size of the target subset becomes proportionally smaller and smaller relative to the size of the search space. Imagine the two databases lined up in order:

Record #	1	2	3	4	5	...	n
1	M						
2		M					
3			M				
4				M			
5					M		
⋮						⋱	
n							M

In practice, of course, the records are not lined up:

Record #	3	5	4	27	2	...	n
1							
2					M		
3	M						
4			M				
5		M					
⋮						⋱	
n							M

It should be clear from these two tables that the target subset (the M's) are a small subset of the total search space, that as the file sizes increase the proportion of blank (non M) cells increases very fast, and that the goal of record linkage is to find the characteristics of record pairs that predict whether the two records are a match or not.

Second, in practice, one often does *not* have a labeled training data set. In machine learning language, this is an unsupervised learning problem. In statistical language, this means that the problem is fundamentally a latent class problem, with the two latent classes being those pairs that are indeed a match, and those that are not [Thibaudeau, 1993]. However, we do not have a data set of pairs marked with those labels - it is up to us to find the appropriate way to label pairs of records.

3.   THE FELLEGI-SUNTER MODEL OF RECORD LINKAGE

We begin with terminology. A record can be considered as a collection of data about an external object in the empirical world. Fields in the record refer to individual items of information about the external object (e.g., first name, sex, street name, FIPS code). In the population of all possible record pairs, we shall say that two records match if they *refer to the same external object, even if they do so with error or variation*; otherwise the two records are a non-match. After analyzing a pair of records, we shall declare the records linked if we decide that they are most likely a match, possibly linked if they might be a match, and non-linked if we decide that they are most likely not a matched pair. (Note that this terminology distinguishes matches in the population from link and nonlink decisions, which we make about record pairs.)

The Fellegi-Sunter model [1969; hereafter F-S; see also Winkler, 1995] is framed as a hypothesis test when two records are compared. The separate fields are compared on a field-by-field basis, and the F-S model uses information about the relative frequency of those fields to output one of three decisions: The records are declared to be a positive link; the records are declared to be a positive nonlink, or the decision possible link is returned. The possible link region is then sent to presumably expensive clerical review and resolution. If we (arbitrarily) label positive link with 1, possible link with 2, and positive nonlink with 3, and consider the set A to be all records in the first file, while the set B is all records in the second file, then the Fellegi-Sunter model is a function from the space $A \times B$ into the space $\{1,2,3\}$.

In the general F-S model, the problem is framed as an ordering of configurations by their "weight." For any collection of N individual fields $\vec{x}$, that configuration gets a ratio of match weight and non-match weight, $w(\vec{x}) = m(\vec{x}) / u(\vec{x})$. The configurations are presumed ordered by this ratio (ties broken arbitrarily), indexed in order from highest weight to lowest weight, and cutoffs are chosen by defining a function $f(\vec{x})$ as:

$$f(\vec{x}) = \begin{cases} Positive\ link & if\ index\ for\ \vec{x} \geq upper\ cutoff \\ Positive\ nonlink & if\ index\ for\ \vec{x} \leq lower\ cutoff \\ Possible\ link & if\ upper\ cutoff > index\ for\ \vec{x} > lower\ cutoff \end{cases}$$

(Here we are using Fellegi and Sunter's corollary 1 to ignore randomized choices falling exactly on a boundary.)

The only remaining task is to define the weights w. In the standard F-S model, denoting the event the records are in fact a match by M and the records are in fact a non-match by $\tilde{M}$, these weights are defined likelihood ratios, viz.,

$$w(\vec{x}) = \frac{P[\vec{x}\ configuration \mid M]}{P[\vec{x}\ configuration \mid \tilde{M}]}$$

The F-S paper [1969] demonstrated that these weights are optimal in the sense that, for a fixed false link rate α and fixed false non-link rate μ, this decision rule, using these weights, minimizes the clerical review region.

Typically, in practice researchers make the conditional independence assumption. This assumption allows the weights in the equation above to be factored into:

$$w(\vec{x}) = \frac{P[x_1=1|M]}{P[x_1=1|\widetilde{M}]} \frac{P[x_2=1|M]}{P[x_2=1|\widetilde{M}]} \cdots \frac{P[x_N=1|M]}{P[x_N=1|\widetilde{M}]} .$$

When logarithms are taken, as is typically done in practice, this becomes a sum:

$$w^*(\vec{x}) = \ln \frac{P[x_1=1|M]}{P[x_1=1|\widetilde{M}]} + \ln \frac{P[x_2=1|M]}{P[x_2=1|\widetilde{M}]} + \ldots + \ln \frac{P[x_N=1|M]}{P[x_N=1|\widetilde{M}]}.$$

The term $P[x_i=1|M]$ is typically called a match weight or m-probability; the term $P[x_i=1|\widetilde{M}]$ is typically called a non-match weight or u-probability, and these terms are summed to construct a total score, compared to upper and lower (user-defined) cutoffs, and a decision is made.

4.   HOW ESTIMATING MATCH WEIGHTS AND SETTING THRESHOLDS IS EQUIVALENT TO SPECIFYING A DECISION RULE

If we temporarily ignore the ``don't know" category of the F-S model, then the upper cutoff equals the lower cutoff and the F-S model partitions the data space into two zones, ``linked" and ``non-linked." In practice, the mechanism by which this is done is the sum of the logarithms of match weights and non-match weights. Under the (usual) conditional independence assumption, the F-S model postulates that if the sum of the ``match weights" minus the "non-match weights" is greater than the upper cutoff, then the cases match, otherwise they do not. That is, if

$$\sum_{i=1}^{N} \ln w_i x_i + \ln u_i (1 - x_i) \geq UPPER$$

or

$$\sum_{i=1}^{N} (\ln u_i) + \sum_{i=1}^{N} (\ln w_i - \ln u_i) x_i \geq UPPER$$

or

$$\sum_{i=1}^{N} (\ln w_i - \ln u_i) x_i \geq UPPER - \sum_{i=1}^{N} (\ln u_i)$$

where:

N = number of matching fields;

x_i = the result of the comparison on the i-th matching field, 1 = matches, 0=non-match;

w_i = the match weight (m-probability) associated with the i-th matching field;

u_i = the non-match weight (u-probability) associated with the i-th matching field; and

$UPPER$ = the cutoff for the "match" threshold in the F-S model.

The conditional independence model fits the definition of a linear threshold: Based on the sum of the results of individual record comparisons, we either add weights (if fields match in the two databases) or subtract non-match weights (if they do not) to the sum. If the sum is less than the pre-specified cutoff point UPPER (shifted for the sum of non-match weights), we declare the comparison a positive non-match and do not link the records. If the sum is greater than the lower cutoff but less than the higher cutoff, we declare a "don't know" case. If the sum is greater than the upper cutoff, we declare a positive match and link the records. This is a decision rule.

5. DEALING WITH STOCHASTIC DATA: A LOGISTIC REGRESSION APPROACH

The problem we are examining is to learn the optimal decision rule given data that provide evidence toward one or more decisions. Several authors (for instance, see [Judson, Bagchi and Quint, 2005, Boros, et. al., 2000, Boros, et. al., 1996, and Triantaphyllou, et. al., 1997]) focus on the problem of learning a single structure given data about that structure. However, in the record linkage problem, the problem is generalized.

Previous authors have imagined a *single* deterministic structure in which we have an active agent deciding which configuration to test next until we have learned the entire structure. We now presume that we are sampling from a population of record linkage decisions (thus our training data set is "passive" rather than "active"), and we wish to infer the structure that best represents this population of record linkage decisions. That is, the outcome of the record linkage decision is now a random variable. We will begin with notation about linkage decisions and field matches:

Definition 1: Let Y be the record linkage decision, $Y \in \{0,1\}$, where 1 denotes the "link" decision that the two records are matching, and 0 denotes the "nonlink" decision that the two records are not matching.

Note: We will ignore "possible link" decisions in this chapter - the extension for link/nonlink to link/possible/nonlink is straightforward.

Definition 2: Let $\vec{X}$ be a table of field match values, with a 1 in the i-th position denoting that the i-th field matches between two records, and a 0 in the i-th position denoting that the i-th field does not match between two records, or is missing on one or both.

Therefore, $X_i =$ the i-th comparison field between the two records, taking on the value 1 if the i-th field matches between the two records, otherwise 0 if the i-th field does not match between the two records. We will illustrate this definition with an example. Suppose records consist of five fields: First name, middle initial, last name, generational suffix (i.e. jr/sr/II/III, etc.), and age. Suppose we have two records in the following form:

Table 1. An illustration of the comparison between two records.

Record 1	Record 2	$\vec{X}$
Arthur	Arthur	1
F.		0
Jones	Jones	1
	Jr.	0
32	33	0

There are N=5 matching fields $X_1 = X_3 = 1$ and $X_2 = X_4 = X_5 = 0$, and the third column provides the values of the vector $\vec{X}$. In the machine learning literature, this is referred to as a "feature vector" or sometimes a "bit pattern". We will also use the term "comparison vector".

The decision rule that yields the decision $Y = 1$ (these records refer to the same person) or $Y = 0$ (these records do not refer to the same person) remains to be determined.

We shall denote the probability $P[Y = y]$ by π_y. Similarly, we shall use the notation $\pi_{x|y} = P[X = x | Y = y]$, and $\pi_{\vec{x}|y} = P[\vec{X} = \vec{x} | Y = y]$.

Definition 3: We shall assume that N is the number of fields being compared. We form a $2 \times 2 \times \ldots \times 2$ cross-classification table of the N field matches.

We index a cell in this table by $\vec{x}$. The (full) likelihood of a case falling in the $\vec{x}$ cell in this table is:

$$P[\vec{X} = \vec{x}] = \sum_{y \in \{0,1\}} \pi_y \pi_{x_1|y} \pi_{x_2|x_1, y} \ldots \pi_{x_N|x_1,\ldots,x_{N-1}, y}.$$

Obviously, there are far more parameters than can be identified (in the statistical sense; see, e.g., [Kaufman, 2001]). By placing constraints on the table, statistical identification can be achieved. The typical constraint is the "conditional independence" assumption, which can be represented as:

$$P[\vec{X} = \vec{x}] = \sum_{y \in \{0,1\}} \pi_y \pi_{x_1|y} \pi_{x_2|y} \ldots \pi_{x_N|y}, \text{where each random variable is}$$

independent of the next, conditional on the record's true latent status.

Suppose that we construct a $2 \times 2 \times \ldots \times 2$ cross classification table, where each margin takes on the value 0 or 1 if the corresponding match field is a non-match or a match, respectively. We wish to note that our space $\{0,1\}^N$, and this cross-classification table are equivalent (strictly speaking, there is a set isomorphism between them).

We will presume that we have a sampled collection of data in which we know the field match status for each field in the data; however, we do not know the record linkage status for each pair of records in the data. We will presume that all are drawn consistently from a population with a correct decision rule. But instead of observing the record linkage structure deterministically, we will assume that we observe the record linkage structure under a stochastic process. Judson [2001] showed that one could fit a generalized linear model (GLM, see [McCullagh and Nelder, 1989]) that represents this decision rule, then demonstrated a Bayesian GLM that could also be fit to represent the rule.

Our strategy for inferring the best fitting record linkage structure from a collection of observations of structures takes the following steps:

1) We sample a collection of candidate pairs of records from the space of all possible record pairs.
2) For each cell in the $2 \times 2 \times ... \times 2$ cross-classification table, we will increment the count in that cell by one if the two records being compared have that particular field match configuration. This table will be the data from which inference shall be made.
3) Using background (or expert) information, we first set priors on each individual parameter in the GLM for the given cross-classification table.
4) Finally, using Markov-Chain Monte Carlo Gibbs sampling (hereafter, MCMC) methods and the data set, we generate parameter estimates from the best fitting posterior GLM.
5) The posterior parameter estimates are used to define our best fitting record linkage rule.

Definition 4: Let $\vec{x}$ be a boolean vector of length N, and $Y_{\vec{x}} \in \{0,1\}$ be a random variable indexed by $\vec{x}$.

Given a collection of N fields on which we wish to match, there will be 2^N possible configurations of field matches or non-matches. For a particular configuration of field match/non-match results, we can presume that there exists some probability $p_{\vec{x}}$ that the record linkage rule will declare that the two records are a match. Again, we index by $\vec{x}$.

Now, if each record linkage decision is independent of the next, then the decisions for the i-th configuration will form a sequence of Bernoulli trials, each with probability $p_{\vec{x}}$ of returning a match result. Clearly, $Y_{\vec{x}} \sim BINOMIAL(1, p_{\vec{x}})$. This is true for each and every configuration, for all 2^N $\vec{x}$ configurations. Thus, let $Y_{\vec{x}} \sim BINOMIAL(1, p_{\vec{x}})$. for $p_{\vec{x}} \in [0,1]$.

Obviously, $P[Y_{\vec{x}} = y] = p_x^y (1 - p_{\vec{x}})^{1-y}$. However, we believe that the probability of the two records being declared a match is a (generally monotonic) function of how many, and in what combination, the individual matching fields match. What we need at this point is a link between these two notions.

For generalized linear models, the canonical link function for a dependent binomial random variable and a collection of independent variables is the logit link, $\ln\left(\frac{p_{\vec{x}}}{1-p_{\vec{x}}}\right) = \vec{x}\vec{\beta}$, which of course implies that $\left(\frac{p_{\vec{x}}}{1-p_{\vec{x}}}\right) = e^{\vec{x}\vec{\beta}}$, which implies that $p_{\vec{x}} = \frac{e^{\vec{x}\vec{\beta}}}{1+e^{\vec{x}\vec{\beta}}}$, which is exactly what we are looking for (Harville and Moore [1999] developed a similar approach for business linkages). For the remainder of this chapter, we shall assume that

$p_{\vec{x}}$ is related to the boolean vector $\vec{x}$ in such a fashion.

5.1   Estimation of the model

As specified, our generalized linear model consists of:

1) The structural component $\vec{x}\vec{\beta}$;
2) the stochastic specification that $Y_{\vec{x}} \sim BINOMIAL(1, p_{\vec{x}})$;
3) the link $p_{\vec{x}} = \frac{e^{\vec{x}\vec{\beta}}}{1+e^{\vec{x}\vec{\beta}}}$, and
4) the latent class assumption that $Y_{\vec{x}}$ is in fact unobserved.

With the exception of the last component, the problem is a standard logistic regression estimation problem.

5.2   Finding the implied threshold and interpreting coefficients

After estimating the conditional independence logistic regression equation, we have estimated parameters $\hat{\beta}_0, \hat{\beta}_1, \hat{\beta}_2, ..., \hat{\beta}_N$. The parameters may be considered voting weights in a voting (record linkage) rule. Obviously, the definitions given above imply that, with some collection of data drawn from the population and obeying the proposed logistic regression relationship, we can estimate β_k for all $k \in \{1, 2, ..., N\}$. But, at this point we ask, what do the β_k mean in this context? It is the answer to this question that illustrates how we can use the logistic regression model to estimate Fellegi-Sunter weights.

For any collection of data drawn from a population satisfying the logistic regression model above, for $k = 2, ..., N$,

$$e^{\beta_k} \propto \frac{P[the\ i\text{-}th\ field\ \ matches\,|\,Records\ \ are\ \ a\ \ match]}{P[the\ i\text{-}th\ field\ \ matches\,|\,Records\ \ are\ \ a\ \ non\text{-}match]},$$

that is, the regression coefficients are proportional to Fellegi-Sunter weights.

Fix any $k \in \{2, ...N\}$.
We let the event M = {the i-th record is declared a match},
with $\widetilde{M}$ = {the i-th record is declared a non-match}.
By assumption, $\ln\frac{p_i}{1-p_i} = \vec{x}_i\vec{\beta}$, holds in the population, thus

$$\frac{P[M\,|\,\vec{x}\vec{\beta}]}{P[\widetilde{M}\,|\,\vec{x}\vec{\beta}]} = \exp(\beta_0 + \beta_1 x_1 + ... + \beta_N x_N)$$

$$= \exp(\beta_0)\exp(\beta_1 x_1)...\exp(\beta_N x_N).$$

We may set $x_k = 1$ and $x_j = 0$ for all $j \neq k$. Then:

$$\frac{P[M \mid x_k]}{P[\tilde{M} \mid x_k]} = \exp(\beta_0)\exp(\beta_k x_k).$$

We solve for β_k, and obtain:

$$\ln\left[\frac{P[M \mid \{x_k\}]}{P[\tilde{M} \mid \{x_k\}]}\left(\frac{1}{\exp(\beta_0)}\right)\right] = \beta_k.$$

Now, by using the Bayes theorem, we may rewrite $P[M \mid \vec{x}\vec{\beta}]$ and $P[\tilde{M} \mid \vec{x}\vec{\beta}]$.

$$P[M \mid x_k] = \frac{P[x_k \mid M]P[M]}{P[x_k \mid M]P[M] + P[x_k \mid \tilde{M}]P[\tilde{M}]}.$$

Similarly,

$$P[\tilde{M} \mid x_k] = \frac{P[x_k \mid \tilde{M}]P[\tilde{M}]}{P[x_k \mid M]P[M] + P[x_k \mid \tilde{M}]P[\tilde{M}]}.$$

At this point we merely substitute and obtain:

$$\ln \frac{\frac{P[x_k|M]P[M]}{P[x_k|M]P[M]+P[x_k|\tilde{M}]P[\tilde{M}]}}{\frac{P[x_k|\sim\tilde{M}P[\tilde{M}]}{P[x_k|M]P[M]+P[x_k|\tilde{M}]P[\tilde{M}]}}\left(\frac{1}{\exp(\beta_0)}\right) = \beta_k.$$

And, canceling equivalent denominators,

$$\ln\left[\frac{P[x_k \mid M]}{P[x_k \mid \tilde{M}]}\left(\frac{P[M]}{P[\tilde{M}]}\right)\left(\frac{1}{\exp(\beta_0)}\right)\right] = \beta_k.$$

By exponentiating both sides, the theorem is proved. $e^{\beta_k} \propto \frac{P[x_k|M]}{P[x_k|\tilde{M}]}$, the Fellegi-Sunter weight.

In this context, certain additional information is provided by parameter relationships. Obviously, if we set $\exp(\beta_0) = \frac{P[M]}{P[\tilde{M}]}$, we obtain strict equality between β_k and the Fellegi-Sunter weight

($\beta_k = \ln P[x_k \mid M] - \ln P[x_k \mid \tilde{M}]$). Clearly exp (β_0) is an estimate of the prior odds ratio of a record being declared a match under the condition that $x_1 = x_2 = \ldots = x_N = 0$. In most populations, we would assume that $exp(\beta_0)$ is far less than one, indeed it approaches zero. Additionally, we can call $\vec{F}$ the vector representing some configuration of field match values, $\vec{F} = (F_1, \ldots, F_N)$ for $F_i \in \{0,1\}$, $i = 1, 2 \ldots, N$. Since β_k represents the Fellegi-Sunter weight under the configuration $F_k = 1$, $F_j = 0$ for $j \neq k$, we can use the same methods to derive the following immediate corollary.

Corollary: Given any vector of field match values $\vec{F} = (F_1, \ldots, F_N)$ for $F_i \in \{0,1\}$, $i = 1, 2 \ldots, N$, $\frac{P[\vec{F}\mid M]}{P[\vec{F}\mid \tilde{M}]} \propto e^{\beta_1 F_1 + \ldots + \beta_K F_N}$.

This corollary implies that, if we have a particular configuration $\vec{F}$ of match fields and we wish to evaluate their total weight toward a positive record linkage decision, then, consistent with the Fellegi-Sunter model, we merely sum the coefficients associated with fields that match, and exponentiate the sum. Again, for models containing no interaction terms, this is consistent with the original record linkage theory under conditional independence.

Finally, how should the intercept be interpreted? The parallel question is: How to find the threshold? The answer to both questions is given in the following proposition.

Proposition: After estimating the model $\ln\left(\frac{p}{1-p}\right) = \vec{x}\hat{\vec{\beta}}$, fix p = 0.50.

Assume that we desire misclassification (false negative and false positive) rates to be equal. Then $r = -\hat{\beta}_0$ is the optimally predictive threshold for the nonlinear threshold record linkage rule, within the sample data.

Proof: We begin by noting that p = 0.50 $\Rightarrow \vec{x}\hat{\vec{\beta}} = 0$ and p = 0.50 is our optimal cutoff for classification under the logistic regression model. Thus, optimally, we make the decision to call the pair a match if $0 > \hat{\beta}_0 + \hat{\beta}_1 x_1 + \ldots + \hat{\beta}_N x_N$, and not if $0 < \hat{\beta}_0 + \hat{\beta}_1 x_1 + \ldots + \hat{\beta}_N x_N$. Both inequalities imply that $-\hat{\beta}_0$ is the optimal split between link and non-link decision, as desired.□

6.   DEALING WITH UNLABELED DATA IN THE LOGISTIC REGRESSION APPROACH

Up to this point, development of the model implicitly assumed that a labeled training data set was available, and adopted no explicit Bayesian framework or method. In this section, and henceforth, we will make two changes: 1) We will adopt an explicitly Bayesian point of view (see, e.g., Fortini, et. al. [2001], for what we believe to be the first analysis of record linkage from a fully Bayesian perspective), and 2) We will explicitly *not* assume that we have training data, thus transforming the problem into a latent class problem. Following Congdon [2001], we specify the model we will estimate as a two-class latent class model, and show that the latent class model we estimate is equivalent to the logistic regression model with latent dependent variable.

The immediate question in this specification is: How does the latent class construction here relate to the logistic regression construction described above? Haberman [1979] demonstrated that the latent class model above is equivalent to the hierarchical log-linear model:

$$\ln m_{y,\vec{x}} = \mu + \mu_y^Y + \mu_{x_1}^{X_1} + \mu_{x_2}^{X_2} + ... + \mu_{x_N}^{X_N} + \mu_{yx_1}^{YX_1} + \mu_{yx_2}^{YX_2} + ... + \mu_{yx_N}^{YX_N}, \text{ where}$$

$m_{y,\vec{x}}$ is the expected cell count in the $y, \vec{x}$ cell under the right hand side model, and the terms on the right hand side are log-linear parameter estimates on the full table including the latent variable. The conditional independence assumption is imposed on the model by the exclusion of all interaction terms among the observed variables $X_1, ... X_N$. Typically, such a model would be estimated using some variation of the Expectation-Maximization (EM) algorithm [Winkler, 1989; McLachlan and Krishnan, 1997], by generating an expected table and then fitting a loglinear model by maximizing a Poisson or multinomial likelihood. In our application, of course, we will use Bayesian simulation methods rather than EM.

Given this rewriting of the latent class model, the following theorem relates the conditional independence latent class model to the logistic regression model without interaction terms.

Theorem: For any collection of data drawn from a population satisfying the logistic regression model above without interaction terms and the latent class conditional independence model, for $i=1,...,N$ fields, $\beta_i = \mu^{Y=1,X_i} - \mu^{Y=0,X_i}$, where $\mu^{Y=y,X_i} = \ln P[X_i = 1 | Y = y]$.

Proof: First, we note that we can write:

$$\ln m_{y=0,\vec{x}} = \mu + \mu_{y=0}^Y + \mu_{x_1}^{X_1} + \mu_{x_2}^{X_2} + ... + \mu_{x_N}^{X_N} + \mu_{y=0,x_1}^{YX_1} + \mu_{y=0,x_2}^{YX_2} + ... + \mu_{y=0,x_N}^{YX_N}$$

and

$$\ln m_{y=1,\bar{x}} = \mu + \mu_{y=1}^{Y} + \mu_{x_1}^{X_1} + \mu_{x_2}^{X_2} + ... + \mu_{x_N}^{X_N} + \mu_{y=1,x_1}^{YX_1} + \mu_{y=1,x_2}^{YX_2} + ... + \mu_{y=1,x_N}^{YX_N}.$$

Second, we recall that, if $\exp(\beta_0) = \frac{P[M]}{P[\tilde{M}]}$,

$$\beta_i = \ln P[X_i = 1 | Y = 1] - \ln P[X_i = 1 | Y = 0].$$

Now, as is well known (see, e.g. Long, 1997: 261-263), using the loglinear model above, we can write an equivalent logistic regression equation:

$$\ln\left(\frac{m_{y=1,\bar{x}}/M^S}{m_{y=0,\bar{x}}/M^S}\right)$$

$$= \mu + \mu_{y=1}^{Y} + \mu_{x_1}^{X_1} + \mu_{x_2}^{X_2} + ... + \mu_{x_N}^{X_N} + \mu_{y=1,x_1}^{YX_1} + \mu_{y=1,x_2}^{YX_2} + ... + \mu_{y=1,x_N}^{YX_N}$$

$$- (\mu + \mu_{y=0}^{Y} + \mu_{x_1}^{X_1} + \mu_{x_2}^{X_2} + ... + \mu_{x_N}^{X_N} + \mu_{y=0,x_1}^{YX_1} + \mu_{y=0,x_2}^{YX_2} + ... + \mu_{y=0,x_N}^{YX_N})$$

$$= (\mu_{y=1}^{Y} - \mu_{y=0}^{Y}) + (\mu_{y=1,x_1}^{YX_1} - \mu_{y=0,x_1}^{YX_1}) + ... + (\mu_{y=1,x_N}^{YX_N} - \mu_{y=0,x_N}^{YX_N})$$

Since our earlier logistic regression specification is:

$$\ln\left(\frac{P[Y=1|\bar{x}]}{P[Y=0|\bar{x}]}\right) = \beta_0 + \beta_1 x_1 + ...\beta_N x_N,$$

it is apparent by equating like terms that

$$\beta_0 = (\mu_{y=1}^{Y} - \mu_{y=0}^{Y}), \qquad \beta_1 = (\mu_{y=1,x_1}^{YX_1} - \mu_{y=0,x_1}^{YX_1}), ..., \beta_N = (\mu_{y=1,x_N}^{YX_N} - \mu_{y=0,x_N}^{YX_N})$$

and since

$$\beta_i = \ln P[X_i = 1 | Y = 1] - \ln P[X_i = 1 | Y = 0],$$

$$\mu_{y=i,x_i}^{YX_i} = \ln P[X_i = 1 | Y = i], \quad \text{as desired.}$$

7. BRIEF DESCRIPTION OF THE SIMULATED DATA

This section will report results from two sets of data: One, simulated record linkage data generated to test the ability of the logistic regression with latent classes approach to reconstruct "known" data, and a second involving a "real world" record linkage project.

Judson [2001] developed simulated record linkage data following the ideas introduced by Belin [1993]. We take a similar approach with this simulated data set. First we establish the total number of simulated "pairs" we wish to consider, and what fraction of them will be considered to be matches in the "true" data. For example, if we fix 200 records in file A, and 10,000 in file B (assuming no duplication in either file), then there are 2,000,000 pairs to consider, and using a calculation based on section two, we expect that about 200/2,000,000=.01% of the pairs will be matches, the rest non-matches. (In the actual sample, 177 such pairs were true matches, leaving the remainder non-matches.)

Starting with this "true" data set, consisting of about 200 matching pairs, and 1,999,800 non-matching pairs, we first fix the true field matches to all ones for the matching pairs, and all zeros for the non-matching pairs. We then "perturb" the field match values with various levels of error. For the purposes of this demonstration, we perturbed the field match values using the following table of probabilities.

Table 2. Parameters for the simulated data.

	$P[X_i = 1 \mid Y = 1]$	$P[X_i = 1 \mid Y = 0]$	Ratio	ln Ratio
	[a]	[b]	[a]/[b]	ln [a]/[b]
X_1	0.8	0.1	8	2.08
X_2	0.7	0.1	7	1.95
X_3	0.3	0.1	3	1.10
X_4	0.5	0.1	5	1.61

Finally, to reflect the "real world" limitation that we cannot compare all possible pairs in data sets of realistic size, we subsample the space of all possible pairs. In this study, our subsample consists of 20,086 individual record pairs, chosen randomly.

The main advantage of using these simulated data is to demonstrate, if possible, that the Bayesian logistic regression with latent classes method can successfully reconstruct a *known* set of parameters, under various levels of error.

8.   BRIEF DESCRIPTION OF THE CPS/NHIS TO CENSUS RECORD LINKAGE PROJECT

The second data set used for this analysis comes from a "real world" project known as the CPS/NHIS to Census record linkage project. In fall of 1999, the CPS/NHIS to Census record linkage project began. Its goal was to link addresses and persons from the CPS (Current Population Survey) and NHIS (National Health Interview Survey) surveys into the decennial census files, with the goal of comparing responses at the household level and within-household coverage.

The CPS is a monthly labor force survey, covering the civilian non-institutionalized population of the U.S. The NHIS is a monthly health conditions survey, also covering the civilian non-institutionalized population of the U.S. Space precludes a detailed exposition of the characteristics of each survey, but in summary, the selected data sets contained 100,000 unique address records and 250,000 unique person records (for the CPS), and 52,000 unique address records and 100,000 unique person records (for the NHIS).

These two sets of files were computer linked to the set of 100% Census Unedited File (also known as HCUF). The HCUF consisted of about 290,000,000 person records and about 120,000,000 address records, including both residential and Group Quarters addresses but excluding commercial addresses. The HCUF file set is merely one step in the series of processing steps that lead from original census forms to final decennial census tabulations, but it was chosen for this project because it is sufficiently "close" to raw census data, yet sufficiently processed so as to make the file set amenable to computer matching. We chose a single state for this test of address matching. (The specific state shall remain nameless, for confidentiality protection purposes.)

For purposes of the project, these files were pre-edited (to standardize name and address components, and clean certain anomalies in each data set), and linked using "standard" probabilistic techniques with the

commercial package Automatch.   However, for the purposes of testing the Bayesian approach, the files were also linked using the methods described here. A brief discussion of the specifics of the matching fields is in order.

Addresses are an interesting object: The U.S. Census Bureau has several versions of address "standardizers" that will take as input a string representing an address and parse it into components. The components used in this project include: House Number Prefix, House Number 1, House Number Prefix 2, House Number 2, House Number Suffix, Prefix Directional, Prefix Type, Street Name, Suffix Type, Street Extension, Within structure identifier, State FIPS code, County FIPS code, and Zip5 (five digit zip code).

For example, Table 3 illustrates three (completely fictional) parsings of records one, two, and three, and an illustration of the comparison vector that would occur if we compared records one and two on a field by field basis.

As can be seen, addresses take a wide variety of forms, making them exquisitely difficult to parse and unduplicate properly. For our purposes, we assume that they have been standardized, cleaned, and pre-parsed, and we merely concern ourselves with the field by field comparison vector $\overset{\leftrightarrow}{x}$, consisting of zeros (where fields do not match or are missing on either or both files) and ones (where fields are nonmissing and declared matched). Note that in this application, if a field is missing on both records (e.g., neither address has an apartment number), then by convention the comparison vector is set to zero. This is merely a convention, and the opposite convention (e.g. both missing implies the field match is set to one) could be adopted in particular applications.

Table 3. Three fictional address parsings, and the comparison vector between record one and record two.

Field	One	Two	Three	Four	Comparison vector (Col 1 to 2)
House number prefix				A	0 (1)
House number 1	45	45	101	1201	1
House number 2	2	2			1
House number suffix		A			0
Prefix directional	N		N		0
Prefix type		HWY			0
Street name	101st	97	South Temple	FISHPATTY	0
Suffix type	ST		ST		0
Suffix directional			E		0 (1)
Street extension			EXT		0 (1)
Within structure Descriptor	APT	STE	PISO	#	0
Within structure ID	1	2	1	BSMT	0
State FIPS code	01	01	02	02	1
County FIPS code	001	001	023	510	1
Zip5	12345	12345	12345	12345	1

9.   RESULTS OF THE BAYESIAN LATENT CLASS METHOD WITH SIMULATED DATA

We now present results of an approach using Markov-Chain Monte Carlo methods to generate posterior densities under a latent class model [Gelfand and Smith, 1990, Gelman and Rubin, 1992, Geyer, 1992]. In these analyses, implemented with the software package BUGS [Speigelhalter,

Thomas, and Best, 1999], we developed two models: One with relatively uninformative prior information, and a second with highly informative prior information. We compare the posterior results from these two sets of priors. Further information on MCMC methods for estimating Bayesian models can be found in Jackman [2000]. Computer notation relates to mathematical notation as follows (For programming reasons, the computer notation uses a 1,2 index rather than a 0,1 index for Y).

Table 4. Parameters, computer notation, and their interpretation for the simulated data.

Parameter	Computer Notation	Interpretation
$\mu_{1,1}^{YX_1}$	mu[1,1]	$\ln P\big[x_1 = 1 \mid Y = 1 \,(\text{non - match})\big]$
$\mu_{2,1}^{YX_1}$	mu[2,1]	$\ln P\big[x_1 = 1 \mid Y = 2 \,(\text{match})\big]$
$\mu_{1,2}^{YX_2}$	mu[1,2]	$\ln P\big[x_2 = 1 \mid Y = 1 \,(\text{non - match})\big]$
$\mu_{2,2}^{YX_2}$	mu[2,2]	$\ln P\big[x_2 = 1 \mid Y = 2 \,(\text{match})\big]$
$\mu_{1,3}^{YX_3}$	mu[1,3]	$\ln P\big[x_3 = 1 \mid Y = 1 \,(\text{non - match})\big]$
$\mu_{2,3}^{YX_3}$	mu[2,3]	$\ln P\big[x_3 = 1 \mid Y = 2 \,(\text{match})\big]$
$\mu_{1,4}^{YX_4}$	mu[1,4]	$\ln P\big[x_4 = 1 \mid Y = 1 \,(\text{non - match})\big]$
$\mu_{2,4}^{YX_4}$	mu[2,4]	$\ln P\big[x_4 = 1 \mid Y = 2 \,(\text{match})\big]$
$\mu^{Y=0}$	Y[1]	$P[Y = 1 \;(\text{non-match})$ ⁻
$\mu^{Y=1}$	Y[2]	$P[Y = 2 \;(\text{match})$ ⁻

Case 1: Uninformative

Prior densities for all μ coefficients except the intercept were chosen to be $N(0,1)$. The hyperparameter mean of 0 indicates a prior centered on $\ln P\big[x_{ijkl} = 1 \mid M\big] = \ln P\big[x_{ijkl} = 1 \mid \tilde{M}\big]$ indicating a field that provides no information. (By choosing all the priors to be the same and centered on zero, this is a relatively uninformative prior- it does nothing to help distinguish the predictive power of the four fields). For the (intercept) term $\mu^{Y=1} - \mu^{Y=0}$, a Dirichlet $(2,1)$ (corresponding to a beta distribution when only two classes exist) prior was used, although one should expect that the posterior of the intercept will be substantially negative when converted to the logarithmic scale[1]. Two chains were simulated, and the Brooks-Gelman-Rubin (non)convergence diagnostics [Gelman and Rubin, 1992; Geyer, 1992] were performed, as well as visual examination of the time series. After a "burn-in" of 10,000 iterations, 32,000 simulated draws from the conditional distributions were performed.

Results for the simulated data set are presented in Table 5. Note that in this table, $\phi[Y,i] = \frac{e^{\mu[Y,i]}}{1+e^{\mu[Y,i]}}$. It can be considered an estimate of the probability that $X_i = 1$ conditional on $Y = y$ (1 or 2). (Recall that for programming reasons, a result of Y=2 is a match, and a result of Y=1 is a non-match.)

As can be seen, the $\mu[1,i]$ parameters are approximately recovering the structure that we specified in the simulation: exp(-2.221)=0.1085, which is very close the correct value, 0.10. The same holds for all $\mu[1,i]$.

Correctly, the latent class analysis discovers that it is far more likely that a pair of records belongs to class 2 (the non-matches) than class 1 (the matches), conditional on all the fields not matching (recall that $(\ln Y[2] - \ln Y[1])$ represents the intercept term in the logistic regression model.) Also correctly, the exponentiated $\mu[1,i]$ and $\mu[2,i]$ parameter estimates for the i-th field (i=1,...,4) are in the appropriate direction. However, the recovered $\mu[2,i]$ values are not on their population setting, and the likelihood ratios $P[x_i = 1 | M] / P[x_i = 1 | \tilde{M}] = e^{\mu[2,i] - \mu[1,i]}$ are not reproducing their population values, indicating that the latent class method, with relatively non-informative priors, is not able to differentiate the varying predictive power of each field separately.

---

[1]This occurs for two reasons: First, Judson [2001] demonstrated that, treating the estimated model as a decision making voting rule, one should consider the intercept to be the negative of the voting threshold. As we expect the coefficients of the model to satisfy monotonicity constraints, this implies that the voting threshold should be positive and the intercept negative. Second, considering the space of all possible pairs, it is incredibly unlikely that a pair of records matching on *no* fields should in fact be declared a match. This implies that the intercept should be negative, as well.

Table 5. Results from the MCMC (Gibbs sampling) estimation of posterior distributions of simulated parameters.

parameter	post. mean	post. sd	post. 2.50%	post. median	post. 97.50%	MCMC start	MCMC sample
Y[1]	0.9786	0.0375	0.8581	0.9934	0.9994	10001	32000
Y[2]	0.02137	0.0375	0.0006	0.0066	0.1419	10001	32000
mu[1,1]	-2.221	0.0388	-2.315	-2.216	-2.165	10001	32000
mu[1,2]	-2.193	0.0490	-2.325	-2.185	-2.132	10001	32000
mu[1,3]	-2.243	0.0510	-2.363	-2.234	-2.179	10001	32000
mu[1,4]	-2.237	0.0408	-2.334	-2.232	-2.18	10001	32000
mu[2,1]	-1.026	0.8297	-2.132	-1.191	0.9448	10001	32000
mu[2,2]	-0.8082	0.8624	-2.067	-0.9245	1.155	10001	32000
mu[2,3]	-0.6417	0.9159	-2.061	-0.7321	1.379	10001	32000
mu[2,4]	-0.9158	0.8789	-2.142	-1.047	1.11	10001	32000
phi[1,1]	0.09792	0.0033	0.0899	0.0983	0.1029	10001	32000
phi[1,2]	0.1005	0.0042	0.0891	0.1011	0.106	10001	32000
phi[1,3]	0.09602	0.0042	0.0861	0.0967	0.1017	10001	32000
phi[1,4]	0.09654	0.0034	0.0884	0.0969	0.1016	10001	32000
phi[2,1]	0.286	0.1666	0.1061	0.2331	0.7201	10001	32000
phi[2,2]	0.3282	0.1779	0.1123	0.284	0.7605	10001	32000
phi[2,3]	0.363	0.1902	0.1130	0.3247	0.7989	10001	32000
phi[2,4]	0.3084	0.1775	0.1050	0.2598	0.7522	10001	32000

Note: Parameter estimates are taken to be posterior medians output from MCMC (Gibbs Sampling) methods. N=20086 simulated pairs from a population of 2,000,000 simulated pairs. Uninformative priors N(0,1) are used for μ parameters, Dirichlet(2,1) for Y parameters. MCMC specifications: 10,000 burn-in iterations, 32,000 samples after burn-in.

Nonetheless, a record linkage structure for decision making *is* being constructed. The following table calculates $P[\hat{Y}=1|\vec{x}]$ by transforming these parameter estimates into their logistic regression equivalents, extracting their posterior medians from the MCMC output, and then recovering

$$P[\hat{Y}=1|\vec{x}] = \frac{e^{\vec{x}\vec{\beta}}}{1+e^{\vec{x}\vec{\beta}}}.$$

Thus, the prediction equation is:

$\ln(P[Y=1|X]/1-P[Y=1|X]) =$

$\ln(Y[2]-\ln Y[1]) + (mu[2,1]-mu[1,1]) +$

$(mu[2,2]-mu[1,2]) + (mu[2,3]-mu[1,3]) + (mu[2,4]-mu[1,4]),$

where:

$$ln(Y[2] - lnY[1]) = -5.0141;$$
$$(mu[2,1] - mu[1,1]) = 1.025;$$
$$(mu[2,2] - mu[1,2]) = 1.2605;$$
$$(mu[2,3] - mu[1,3]) = 1.502; \text{ and}$$
$$(mu[2,4] - mu[1,4]) = 1.185.$$

Table 6. Estimated posterior probability that the records are a match, for all possible field configurations and the estimated logistic regression parameters - Relatively uninformative priors condition.

P[Y=1 | X]	x1	x2	x3	x4
0.007	0	0	0	0
0.021	0	0	0	1
0.029	0	0	1	0
0.089	0	0	1	1
0.023	0	1	0	0
0.071	0	1	0	1
0.095	0	1	1	0
0.256	0	1	1	1
0.018	1	0	0	0
0.057	1	0	0	1
0.077	1	0	1	0
0.214	1	0	1	1
0.061	1	1	0	0
0.176	1	1	0	1
0.227	1	1	1	0
0.490	1	1	1	1

Note: Parameter estimates are taken to be posterior medians output from MCMC (Gibbs Sampling) methods. N=20086 simulated pairs from a population of 2,000,000 simulated pairs. Uninformative priors (N(0,1) are used for μ parameters, Dirichlet(2,1) for Y parameters. MCMC specifications: 10,000 burn-in iterations, 32,000 samples after burn-in.

The appropriate comparison in this table is the partial ordering implied by the $\bar{x}$'s themselves. As can be verified in the table, as the number of field matches increase, the posterior probability that the records are a match increases to its maximum of 0.490.

9.2   Case 2: Informative

In the informative case, we take the prior density for the *mu[j,i]* coefficient (except for the one representing the intercept) were chosen to be $N(\ln P[X_i = 1 \mid Y = j], 1)$. That is, we center the prior information exactly where the simulation started. For the intercept term $\mu^{Y=1} - \mu^{Y=0}$, again we choose Dirichlet(2,1). Based on centering the μ priors we would expect this case to more accurately reproduce the population parameters. Results for the simulated data set are presented below. Note that in this case, after a "burn-in" if 10,000 iterations, only 22,000 simulated draws from the conditional distributions were performed.

Table 7. Results from the MCMC (Gibbs sampling) estimation of posterior distributions of simulated parameters.

Parameter	post. mean	post. sd	post. 2.50%	post. median	post. 97.50%	MCMC start	MCMC sample
Y[1]	0.929	0.087	0.724	0.985	0.999	10001	22000
Y[2]	0.072	0.087	0.0003	0.0152	0.276	10001	22000
mu[1,1]	-2.25	0.078	-2.45	-2.23	-2.17	10001	22000
mu[1,2]	-2.23	0.105	-2.51	-2.20	-2.14	10001	22000
mu[1,3]	-2.26	0.076	-2.48	-2.24	-2.18	10001	22000
mu[1,4]	-2.26	0.071	-2.45	-2.24	-2.18	10001	22000
mu[2,1]	-1.20	0.888	-2.18	-1.46	1.00	10001	22000
mu[2,2]	-1.11	0.878	-2.13	-1.36	1.02	10001	22000
mu[2,3]	-1.40	0.662	-2.18	-1.59	0.269	10001	22000
mu[2,4]	-1.36	0.777	-2.19	-1.62	0.641	10001	22000
phi[1,1]	0.096	0.006	0.080	0.097	0.103	10001	22000
phi[1,2]	0.098	0.008	0.076	0.100	0.106	10001	22000
phi[1,3]	0.094	0.006	0.077	0.096	0.102	10001	22000
phi[1,4]	0.095	0.006	0.080	0.096	0.101	10001	22000
phi[2,1]	0.26	0.173	0.102	0.188	0.731	10001	22000
phi[2,2]	0.27	0.175	0.106	0.204	0.735	10001	22000
phi[2,3]	0.22	0.124	0.102	0.170	0.567	10001	22000
phi[2,4]	0.23	0.148	0.100	0.166	0.655	10001	22000

Note: Parameter estimates are taken to be posterior medians output from MCMC (Gibbs Sampling) methods. N=20086 simulated pairs from a population of 2,000,000 simulated pairs. Informative priors (N(t,1)) are used for μ parameters, Dirichlet(2,1) for Y parameters, where t = true value. MCMC specifications: 10,000 burn-in iterations, 22,000 samples after burn-in.

As can be seen, again the $\mu[1,i]$ parameters are approximately recovering the structure that we specified in the simulation. Again, however, the recovered $\mu[2,i]$ values are not on their population setting, and the likelihood ratios $P[x_i = 1 | M] / P[x_i = 1 | \tilde{M}] = e^{\mu[2,i]-\mu[1,i]}$ are not reproducing their population values, indicating that the latent class method, with highly *informative* priors, is still not able to differentiate the varying predictive power of each field separately.

However, as with the noninformative case, the record linkage decision making structure is being constructed. These tables are mates, using posterior medians as point estimates, with informative priors. The prediction equation is equivalent in form as before.

Table 8. Estimated posterior probability that the records are a match, for all possible field configurations and the estimated logistic regression parameters - Informative priors condition.

P[Y=1	X]	x1	x2	x3	x4
0.015	0	0	0	0
0.028	0	0	0	1
0.029	0	0	1	0
0.053	0	0	1	1
0.034	0	1	0	0
0.062	0	1	0	1
0.064	0	1	1	0
0.113	0	1	1	1
0.032	1	0	0	0
0.058	1	0	0	1
0.060	1	0	1	0
0.106	1	0	1	1
0.071	1	1	0	0
0.125	1	1	0	1
0.128	1	1	1	0
0.216	1	1	1	1

N=20,086 simulated pairs from a population of 2,000,000 simulated pairs.
Note: Parameter estimates are taken to be posterior medians. Output from MCMC (Gibbs Sampling) methods. Informative priors (N(t,1)) are used for μ parameters, Dirichlet(2,1) for Y parameters, where t is the true population value. MCMC specifications: 10,000 burn-in iterations, 22,000 samples after burn-in.

9.3　False link and non-link rates in the population of all possible pairs

A final test of this method with simulated data is to use the record linkage decision rule we have just estimated, apply that rule to our population of all possible pairs, and assess false link and false non-link rates in the population. As noted above, if we assume that we desire the false link and the false non-link rates to be equal, then we can simply use the estimated intercept term as a threshold.

However, such a formula would be heavily weighted toward choosing a non-link decision, because in the population the frequency of non-matches far exceeds the frequency of matches, and this is reflected in the intercept term. Instead, we would rather shift the threshold by adding or subtracting a constant from it, thus allowing ourselves to tune the threshold and not be swamped by the overwhelming prevalence of non-matches in the population of all possible pairs. In any case, in practice, the setting of the shift term would take the equivalent role of threshold setting in traditional (Fellegi-Sunter based) methods, and, like traditional methods, more than one shift could be defined (a link shift for positive matches and a lower possible link shift for clerical review, for example).

The formula for implementing the threshold is as follows:

$$\begin{cases} \text{Declare pair "LINKED" if } \sum_{i=1}^{4} (\mu_{2,i} - \mu_{1,i})x_i \geq -(ln\,Y[2] - ln\,Y[1]) \pm shift; \\ \text{Otherwise, declare pair "NOT LINKED".} \end{cases}$$

10.   RESULTS FROM THE BAYESIAN LATENT CLASSS METHOD WITH REAL DATA

The proposed tool (Bayesian latent class analysis) requires several data processing steps to implement.

10.1   Steps in preparing the data

In this implementation, we first used an internal program, "Bigmatch" [Yancey, 2002] to extract a set of about 27,000 Census addresses from the space of all possible Census addresses (about 2 million). This subset was chosen based on "blocking criteria" that limit the number of addresses extracted [Yancey, 2002].

Next we compared each CPS address with each address in this subset of probable links. (Note that we have reduced the search space considerably at this point.) For each comparison, we generate a Boolean feature vector - a 15 component vector with each element taking on the value 1 if the corresponding fields match, and 0 if either is missing or the fields do not match (the 15 components are described earlier). This Boolean feature vector is passed to our Bayesian data analysis program (WinBUGS).

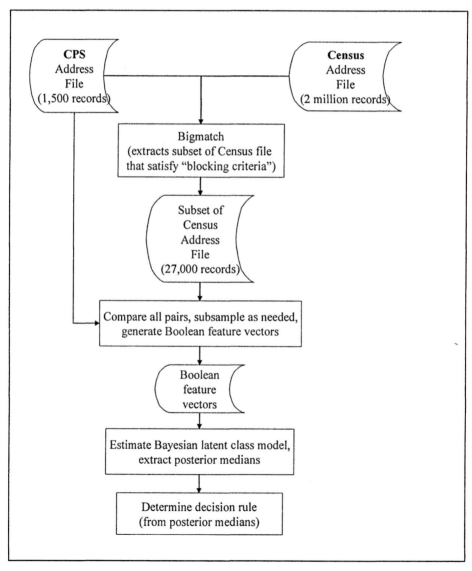

Figure 1. File processing flowchart for Bayesian record linkage.

This program uses priors applied to the μ parameters, updates the priors using the feature vector, and puts out posterior kernel densities and medians. As with the simulated data, the posterior medians are used to construct the decision rule.

10.2   Priors and constraints

For this analysis, we have 15 matching fields. Because the simulated results suggested that statistical identifiability was a potential problem, for each field i, we fixed the associated matching parameter $\mu_{2,i}^{YX_i}$ to zero. This constraint implies that we are not, strictly speaking, estimating the quantity $\ln P\left[x_i = 1 \mid Y = 1 \, (\text{non - match})\right]$ with $\mu_{1,i}^{YX_i}$, but the *difference* $\ln P\left[x_i = 1 \mid Y = 1 \, (\text{non - match})\right] - \ln P\left[x_i = 1 \mid Y = 2 \, (\text{match})\right]$. However, if we take care in interpretation, recalling that $P\left[x_i = 1 \mid Y = 2 \, (\text{match})\right]$ is not exactly equal to one, we can then say that $\mu_{1,i}^{YX_i}$ is *approximately* $\ln P\left[x_i = 1 \mid Y = 1 \, (\text{non - match})\right]$.

The reader should be aware that these are somewhat tricky to interpret, because they are logarithms of probabilities; thus, they will always be negative. Further, because they represent probabilities $\ln P\left[x_i = 1 \mid Y = 1 \, (\text{non - match})\right]$, we expect them to be substantially negative, as the probability that a field will match in two randomly chosen pairs should be relatively small for most fields. As we shall see, a highly discriminating field will have a very negative estimate, while a less discriminating field will have only a moderately negative estimate. (Note that $\ln(.5)$ is about -0.693)

For this analysis, we chose the following prior distributions. Since this is a Bayesian approach, we are making use of prior experience to choose these values. For example, for addresses that contain a within-structure identifier (e.g. an apartment number), that field is usually of quite crucial importance in address matching, so we give it a prior with a large negative mean. Similarly, many addresses have the same ZIP code, so it is not as important in address matching, so we give its prior a more moderate negative mean. In order to give the data greater weight than our priors, the standard deviations in our prior distributions are quite large, thus expressing our prior uncertainty regarding what the true values *should* be. The table below shows the parameter associated with each matching field.

Table 9. Associated matching fields, parameters, computer notation, and their interpretation for CPS address data.

Field type	Parameter for this field	Computer Notation	Prior	Implied mean: $P[X_i = 1 \mid Y = 1] =$ exp(prior mean)
House Number Prefix	$\mu_{1,1}^{Y,X_1}$	mu[1,1]	N(-1,10)	.37
House Number 1	$\mu_{1,2}^{Y,X_1}$	mu[1,2]	N(-1,10)	.37
House Number Prefix 2	$\mu_{1,3}^{Y,X_1}$	mu[1,3]	N(-2,10)	.13
House Number 2	$\mu_{1,4}^{Y,X_1}$	mu[1,4]	N(-2,10)	.13
House Number Suffix	$\mu_{1,5}^{Y,X_1}$	mu[1,5]	N(-.693,10)	.50
Prefix Directional	$\mu_{1,6}^{Y,X_1}$	mu[1,6]	N(-.693,10)	.50
Prefix Type	$\mu_{1,7}^{Y,X_1}$	mu[1,7]	N(-1,10)	.37
Street Name	$\mu_{1,8}^{Y,X_1}$	mu[1,8]	N(-3,10)	.05
Suffix Type	$\mu_{1,9}^{Y,X_1}$	mu[1,9]	N(-.693,10)	.50
Suffix Directional	$\mu_{1,10}^{Y,X_1}$	mu[1,10]	N(-.693,10)	.50
Street Extension	$\mu_{1,11}^{Y,X_1}$	mu[1,11]	N(-3,10)	.05
Within Structure ID	$\mu_{1,12}^{Y,X_1}$	mu[1,12]	N(-5,10)	.007
FIPS State	$\mu_{1,13}^{Y,X_1}$	mu[1,13]	N(-.01,10)	.99
FIPS County	$\mu_{1,14}^{Y,X_1}$	mu[1,14]	N(-.1,10)	.91
ZIP5	$\mu_{1,15}^{Y,X_1}$	mu[1,15]	N(-.2,10)	.82

10.3   Results

Results from the Bayesian data analysis are given below. After a burn-in of 1,000 samples, we generated two chains (with different start values) of 5,000 samples each, and combine them. First, we display graphs of selected posterior kernel densities derived from the Gibbs sampler. Then, we provide summary statistics on these posterior densities.

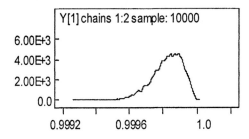

Figure 2. Posterior kernel for Y[1].

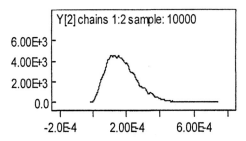

Figure 3. Posterior kernel for Y[2].

As can be seen, while we started with a Dirichlet prior of beta(2,1), the posterior densities are heavily weighted toward what they should be: The marginal probability of a pair being a match in the population of pairs is very small (Y[2] is close to zero).

As an example of two posterior densities, we present the posterior kernels for *mu*[1,12] (the parameter associated with the important field, within-structure identifier) and for *mu*[1,15] (the parameter associated with the relatively unimportant field, zip code).

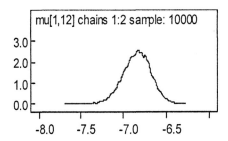

Figure 4. Posterior kernel for *mu*[1,12].

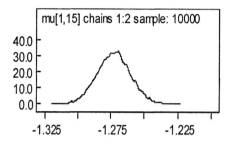

Figure 5. Posterior kernel for *mu*[1,15].

Finally Table 10 presents the posterior statistics associated with these parameters.

Table 10. Results from the MCMC (Gibbs sampling) estimation of posterior distributions of CPS address field parameters.

Parameter	post. mean	post. sd	post. 2.50%	post. median	post. 97.50%	MCMC start	MCMC sample
Y[1]	0.9997	0.0001	0.9994	0.9997	.9999	1001	10000
Y[2]	0.0003	0.0001	0.0001	0.0003	0.0006	1001	10000
mu[1,1]	-11.02	1.12	-13.67	-10.87	-9.27	1001	10000
mu[1,2]	-4.98	0.06	-5.11	-4.98	-4.86	1001	10000
mu[1,3]	-11.15	1.18	-13.91	-11.00	-9.34	1001	10000
mu[1,4]	-11.16	1.17	-13.91	-10.99	-9.31	1001	10000
mu[1,5]	-8.04	0.28	-8.64	-8.02	-7.52	1001	10000
mu[1,6]	-5.71	0.09	-5.89	-5.71	-5.54	1001	10000
mu[1,7]	-3.33	0.03	-3.38	-3.33	-3.28	1001	10000
mu[1,8]	-2.46	0.02	-2.49	-2.46	-2.42	1001	10000
mu[1,9]	-0.0001	0.0001	-0.0005	-0.0001	0.0000	1001	10000
mu[1,10]	-3.05	0.03	-3.1	-3.05	-3.00	1001	10000
mu[1,11]	-11.30	1.24	-14.24	-11.13	-9.40	1001	10000
mu[1,12]	-6.91	0.17	-7.26	-6.91	-6.59	1001	10000
mu[1,13]	-.00005	.00005	-.00002	-.00004	-.00000	1001	10000
mu[1,14]	-1.03	0.01	-1.05	-1.03	-1.005	1001	10000
mu[1,15]	-1.27	0.01	-1.30	-1.27	-1.249	1001	10000

As an aid to interpretation, we can exponentiate these posterior medians, to provide information on the relative importance of different matching fields. Recalling that this are approximate, we see an estimate of the probability that particular fields will match, even if the records are not matching - this is the probability that fields match "by chance" in this selected subset.

Table 11. Posterior median estimates converted to *approximate* probabilities.

Field:	Posterior Median $\ln P[X=1 \mid Y=0]$	Posterior Median $P[X=1 \mid Y=0]$
P[Y=1]	almost zero	.9998
House Number Prefix	-11.02	exp(-11.02)=.00002
House Number 1	-4.98	exp(-4.98)=.0069
House Number Prefix 2	-11.16	exp(-11.16)=.00001
House Number 2	-11.16	exp(-11.16)=.00001
House Number Suffix	-8.04	exp(-8.04)=.0003
Prefix Directional	-5.71	exp(-5.71)=.0033
Prefix Type	-3.33	exp(-3.33)=.036
Street Name	-2.46	exp(-2.46)=.085
Suffix Type	-.0001	exp(-.0001)=0.9999
Suffix Directional	-3.05	exp(-3.05)=.047
Street Extension	-11.3	exp(-11.3)=.000012
Within Structure ID	-6.91	exp(-6.91)=.00099
FIPS State	-.000005	exp(-.000005) ≈ 1.0000
FIPS County	-1.03	exp(-1.03)=0.36
ZIP5	-1.27	exp(-1.27)=0.28

It is clear that these posterior medians make intuitive sense (they represent the probability of a matching field, *conditional on the two records being from different addressees,* and construct a decision rule. The equation below gives the rule, and the posterior probability that a pair with the given feature vector is indeed a match in the reduced space of candidate pairs is

merely $\quad P[\hat{Y}=1 \mid \vec{x}] = \dfrac{e^{\vec{x}\vec{\beta}}}{1+e^{\vec{x}\vec{\beta}}}$ as before. As with the simulated data, the

posterior probabilities are small, in that the prior likelihood of any particular pair being a match is small, and this base rate affects the posterior probability. However, here is where the user-defined shift component, discussed earlier, is used. We move the threshold for declaring a pair of records to be linked up or down, so as to not be deterred by the low base rate of matched pairs. Confidentiality restrictions prohibit displaying the record-level data here, but with a shift component, the effective decision rule is:

$$\begin{cases} \text{Declare pair "LINKED" if } \sum_{i=1}^{15}(\mu_{2,i} - \mu_{1,i})x_i \geq -(ln\,Y[2] - ln\,Y[1]) \pm \text{shift}; \\ \text{Otherwise, declare pair "NOT LINKED",} \end{cases}$$

which in our case translates into comparing:

$-(ln(.0003082) - ln(.99969)) \pm \text{ shift } = 8.085 \pm \text{ shift}$

versus

$11.02x_1 + 4.98x_2 + 11.16x_3 + 11.16x_4 + 8.04x_5 + 5.71x_6 + 3.33x_7$

$+ 2.46x_8 + .0001x_9 + 3.05x_{10} + 11.3x_{11} + 6.91x_{12} + .000005x_{13} + 1.03x_{14} + 1.27x_{15},$

and declare the pair of records a link when this sum exceeds 8.085 ± the user-defined shift value.

Table 12 calculates the posterior probabilities $P[Y=1|X\hat{\beta}]$ using posterior medians for point estimates and a table of actual comparison vectors from the data set used in this analysis. The individual components are labeled, thus, as can be seen in the first row, a pair of addresses that match only in the ZIP code field, and no other field (recalling that a missing value on one or both records is by convention treated as a non-match), have a probability of almost zero of referring to the same address in the population of address pairs. (The specific probability is 0.00059, rounding to .00 in two decimal places.)

There are 4,793 such address pairs. Similarly, row number 11 (in bold) indicates that 1,155,256 pairs matched only in the suffix type field (Rd., Ln, etc.), and no other field matched; these pairs also have a posterior probability of almost zero of referring to the same address in the population. Alternatively, row 87 (bold) indicates that a pair of two address records that matches in the house number, street name, suffix type, suffix directional, county code and ZIP code have a probability of 0.99 of referring to the same address in the population, and there are 1,781 such pairs of records.

In calculating these posterior probabilities, we did not make use of the shift value - if we were to pick a particular threshold, for example 0.95, and declare pairs with a posterior probability of 0.95 or higher to be linked, we would be, in effect, using the shift. Because there are 99 unique comparison vectors in the data set, we split this table across three pages.

Table 12. Posterior probability calculations for all obtained comparison vectors.

Row Num	HSNPFX	HSN1	HSNPFX2	HSN2	HSNSFX	PFXDIR	PFXTYPE	STRNAME	SFXTYPE	SFXDIR	STREXT	W/INSTRID	FIPST	FIPSCTY	ZIP5	N	%	Posterior P[Y=1|X]
1	0	0	0	0	0	0	0	0	0	0	0	0	1	0	1	4,793	0.3	0.00
2	0	0	0	0	0	0	0	0	0	0	0	0	1	1	1	353K	18.6	0.00
3	0	0	0	0	0	0	0	0	0	0	0	1	1	0	0	1,024	0.1	0.24
4	0	0	0	0	0	0	0	0	0	0	0	1	1	1	0	73	0.0	0.46
5	0	0	0	0	0	0	0	0	0	0	0	1	1	1	1	69	0.0	0.76
6	0	0	0	0	0	0	0	0	0	1	0	0	1	0	0	45,182	2.4	0.01
7	0	0	0	0	0	0	0	0	0	1	0	0	1	1	0	7,948	0.4	0.02
8	0	0	0	0	0	0	0	0	0	1	0	0	1	1	1	7,331	0.4	0.06
9	0	0	0	0	0	0	0	0	0	1	0	1	1	0	0	8	0.0	0.87
10	0	0	0	0	0	0	0	0	0	1	0	1	1	1	0	28	0.0	0.95
11	**0**	**0**	**0**	**0**	**0**	**0**	**0**	**0**	**1**	**0**	**0**	**0**	**1**	**0**	**0**	**1.16M**	**61.0**	**0.00**
12	0	0	0	0	0	0	0	0	1	0	0	0	1	0	1	63	0.0	0.00
13	0	0	0	0	0	0	0	0	1	0	0	0	1	1	0	67,079	3.5	0.00
14	0	0	0	0	0	0	0	0	1	0	0	0	1	1	1	15,310	0.8	0.00
15	0	0	0	0	0	0	0	0	1	0	0	1	1	0	0	94	0.0	0.24
16	0	0	0	0	0	0	0	0	1	0	0	1	1	1	0	1	0.0	0.46
17	0	0	0	0	0	0	0	0	1	0	0	1	1	1	1	4	0.0	0.76
18	0	0	0	0	0	0	0	0	1	1	0	0	1	0	0	11,569	0.6	0.01
19	0	0	0	0	0	0	0	0	1	1	0	0	1	1	0	2,486	0.1	0.02
20	0	0	0	0	0	0	0	0	1	1	0	0	1	1	1	3,979	0.2	0.06
21	0	0	0	0	0	0	0	0	1	1	0	1	1	1	0	32	0.0	0.95
22	0	0	0	0	0	0	0	0	1	1	0	1	1	1	1	4	0.0	0.98
23	0	0	0	0	0	0	0	1	0	0	0	0	1	0	0	94,210	5.0	0.00
24	0	0	0	0	0	0	0	1	0	0	0	0	1	0	1	1	0.0	0.01
25	0	0	0	0	0	0	0	1	0	0	0	0	1	1	0	5,498	0.3	0.01
26	0	0	0	0	0	0	0	1	0	0	0	0	1	1	1	1,479	0.1	0.03
27	0	0	0	0	0	0	0	1	0	0	0	1	1	0	0	9	0.0	0.78
28	0	0	0	0	0	0	0	1	0	1	0	0	1	0	0	515	0.0	0.07
29	0	0	0	0	0	0	0	1	0	1	0	0	1	1	0	204	0.0	0.18
30	0	0	0	0	0	0	0	1	0	1	0	0	1	1	1	270	0.0	0.43
31	0	0	0	0	0	0	0	1	0	1	0	1	1	1	0	24	0.0	1.00
32	0	0	0	0	0	0	0	1	1	0	0	0	1	0	0	22,077	1.2	0.00
33	0	0	0	0	0	0	0	1	1	0	0	0	1	0	1	11	0.0	0.01
34	0	0	0	0	0	0	0	1	1	0	0	0	1	1	0	1,070	0.1	0.01
35	0	0	0	0	0	0	0	1	1	0	0	0	1	1	1	9,204	0.5	0.03

Table 12, continued. Posterior probability calculations for all obtained comparison vectors.

Row Num	HSNPFX	HSN1	HSNPFX2	HSN2	HSNSFX	PFXDIR	PFXTYPE	STRNAME	SFXTYPE	SFXDIR	STREXT	W/INSTRID	FIPST	FIPSCTY	ZIP5	N	%	Posterior P[Y=1|X]
	Comparison vector															N	%	Posterior P[Y=1|X]
36	0	0	0	0	0	0	0	1	1	0	0	1	1	0	0	8	0.0	0.78
37	0	0	0	0	0	0	0	1	1	0	0	1	1	1	1	40	0.0	0.97
38	0	0	0	0	0	0	0	1	1	1	0	0	1	0	0	178	0.0	0.07
39	0	0	0	0	0	0	0	1	1	1	0	0	1	1	0	4	0.0	0.18
40	0	0	0	0	0	0	0	1	1	1	0	0	1	1	1	2,494	0.1	0.43
41	0	0	0	0	0	0	0	1	1	1	0	1	1	1	1	40	0.0	1.00
42	0	0	0	0	0	0	1	0	0	0	0	0	1	0	0	52,212	2.8	0.01
43	0	0	0	0	0	0	1	0	0	0	0	0	1	0	1	7	0.0	0.03
44	0	0	0	0	0	0	1	0	0	0	0	0	1	1	0	4,955	0.3	0.02
45	0	0	0	0	0	0	1	0	0	0	0	0	1	1	1	1,549	0.1	0.08
46	0	0	0	0	0	0	1	0	0	1	0	0	1	0	0	138	0.0	0.15
47	0	0	0	0	0	0	1	1	0	0	0	0	1	0	0	2,470	0.1	0.09
48	0	0	0	0	0	0	1	1	0	0	0	0	1	0	1	2	0.0	0.26
49	0	0	0	0	0	0	1	1	0	0	0	0	1	1	0	308	0.0	0.22
50	0	0	0	0	0	0	1	1	0	0	0	0	1	1	1	1,755	0.1	0.50
51	0	0	0	0	0	0	1	1	0	1	0	0	1	1	1	80	0.0	0.95
52	0	0	0	0	0	1	0	0	0	0	0	0	1	0	0	3,002	0.2	0.09
53	0	0	0	0	0	1	0	0	0	0	0	0	1	1	0	165	0.0	0.21
54	0	0	0	0	0	1	0	0	0	0	0	0	1	1	1	165	0.0	0.48
55	0	0	0	0	0	1	0	0	1	0	0	0	1	0	0	1,568	0.1	0.09
56	0	0	0	0	0	1	0	0	1	0	0	0	1	1	0	16	0.0	0.21
57	0	0	0	0	0	1	0	0	1	0	0	0	1	1	1	245	0.0	0.48
58	0	0	0	0	0	1	0	1	0	0	0	0	1	0	0	38	0.0	0.52
59	0	0	0	0	0	1	0	1	0	0	0	0	1	1	0	3	0.0	0.75
60	0	0	0	0	0	1	0	1	1	0	0	0	1	0	0	71	0.0	0.52
61	0	0	0	0	0	1	0	1	1	0	0	0	1	1	1	317	0.0	0.92
62	0	0	0	0	1	0	0	0	0	0	0	0	1	0	0	243	0.0	0.49
63	0	0	0	0	1	0	0	0	0	0	0	0	1	1	0	30	0.0	0.73
64	0	0	0	0	1	0	0	0	1	0	0	0	1	0	0	53	0.0	0.49
65	0	0	0	0	1	0	0	0	1	0	0	0	1	1	0	8	0.0	0.73
66	0	0	0	0	1	0	0	0	1	0	0	0	1	1	1	1	0.0	0.90
67	0	0	0	0	1	0	0	1	0	0	0	0	1	0	0	16	0.0	0.92
68	0	0	0	0	1	0	0	1	1	0	0	0	1	0	0	1	0.0	0.92
69	0	1	0	0	0	0	0	0	0	0	0	0	1	0	0	2,780	0.2	0.04
70	0	1	0	0	0	0	0	0	0	0	0	0	1	1	0	284	0.0	0.11

Table 12, continued. Posterior probability calculations for all obtained comparison vectors.

Row Num	HSNPFX	HSN1	HSNPFX2	HSN2	HSNSFX	PFXDIR	PFXTYPE	STRNAME	SFXTYPE	SFXDIR	STREXT	W/INSTRID	FIPST	FIPSCTY	ZIP5	N	%	Posterior P[Y=1|X]
	Comparison vector																	
71	0	1	0	0	0	0	0	0	0	0	0	0	1	1	1	75	0.0	0.31
72	0	1	0	0	0	0	0	0	0	0	0	1	1	1	1	2	0.0	1.00
73	0	1	0	0	0	0	0	0	0	1	0	0	1	1	1	28	0.0	0.90
74	0	1	0	0	0	0	0	0	1	0	0	0	1	0	0	567	0.0	0.04
75	0	1	0	0	0	0	0	0	1	0	0	0	1	1	0	49	0.0	0.11
76	0	1	0	0	0	0	0	0	1	0	0	0	1	1	1	742	0.0	0.31
77	0	1	0	0	0	0	0	0	1	0	0	1	1	1	1	10	0.0	1.00
78	0	1	0	0	0	0	0	0	1	1	0	0	1	1	1	398	0.0	0.90
79	0	1	0	0	0	0	0	1	0	0	0	0	1	0	0	54	0.0	0.34
80	0	1	0	0	0	0	0	1	0	0	0	0	1	1	0	3	0.0	0.59
81	0	1	0	0	0	0	0	1	0	0	0	0	1	1	1	74	0.0	0.84
82	0	1	0	0	0	0	0	1	0	1	0	0	1	1	1	21	0.0	0.99
83	0	1	0	0	0	0	0	1	1	0	0	0	1	0	0	3	0.0	0.34
84	0	1	0	0	0	0	0	1	1	0	0	0	1	1	0	15	0.0	0.59
85	0	1	0	0	0	0	0	1	1	0	0	0	1	1	1	3,876	0.2	0.84
86	0	1	0	0	0	0	0	1	1	0	0	1	1	1	1	328	0.0	1.00
87	**0**	**1**	**0**	**0**	**0**	**0**	**0**	**1**	**1**	**1**	**0**	**0**	**1**	**1**	**1**	**1,781**	**0.1**	**0.99**
88	0	1	0	0	0	0	0	1	1	1	0	1	1	1	1	252	0.0	1.00
89	0	1	0	0	0	0	1	0	0	0	0	0	1	0	0	16	0.0	0.56
90	0	1	0	0	0	0	1	1	0	0	0	0	1	0	1	1	0.0	0.98
91	0	1	0	0	0	0	1	1	0	0	0	0	1	1	0	3	0.0	0.98
92	0	1	0	0	0	0	1	1	0	0	0	0	1	1	1	380	0.0	0.99
93	0	1	0	0	0	0	1	1	0	0	0	1	1	1	1	8	0.0	1.00
94	0	1	0	0	0	0	1	1	0	1	0	0	1	1	1	40	0.0	1.00
95	0	1	0	0	0	1	0	0	0	0	0	0	1	1	1	3	0.0	0.99
96	0	1	0	0	0	1	0	0	1	0	0	0	1	1	1	62	0.0	0.99
97	0	1	0	0	0	1	0	1	1	0	0	0	1	1	1	208	0.0	1.00
98	0	1	0	0	0	1	0	1	1	0	0	1	1	1	1	8	0.0	1.00
99	0	1	0	0	1	0	0	1	1	0	0	0	1	1	1	16	0.0	1.00

11.   CONCLUSIONS AND FUTURE RESEARCH

Based on the ability of the Bayesian logistic regression with latent variables (Bayesian latent class) method to reconstruct appropriate *decision rules* in our sample of simulated record linkage data, and generate parameter estimates that make intuitive sense in the real record linkage data, we conclude that these results are promising. These results support further consideration of these methods, and development with an eye toward practical (that is, *operational*) applications.

There are several directions that future research might take:

- The particular strength of the Bayesian approach is that it allows us to incorporate information from previous record linkage studies into current record linkage work, thus incrementally improving our ability to develop record linkage rules for new data sets. More can be done with this notion, particularly since "expert opinion" can be elicited in modern ways [Meyer and Booker, 1991] and used directly. We envision formally incorporating "local knowledge" into our regression model via the tuning of priors on matching coefficients to reflect local conditions and via the incorporation of indicator variables much like fixed- and random-effects models.

- Evaluating false positive and false negative error rates has been a challenging dilemma for record linkage researchers [see, e.g., Rogot, Sorlie and Johnson, 1986; Belin, 1991; Belin and Rubin, 1995], and a general statistical approach has not yet been found to outperform clerical review evaluation methods. Yet, false positives and false negatives have the potential to have a very biasing effect on analyses using the linked data set [Scheuren and Winkler, 1993; 1997]. The development of methods to estimate these quantities should be given high priority.

- One of the vexing problems with the record linkage problem is that the space of matching pairs of records is a very small subset of the space of all possible pairs. The approach taken here, to sample from the space of all possible pairs, is conceptually simple, but annoyingly inefficient. King and Zeng [2001] faced a similar problem in their data sets, and developed "rare events logit" modelling to overcome it, in a maximum-likelihood framework. In their case, however, they had observed data rather than latent data. Can their framework be adapted to the Bayesian latent variable logistic regression modelling proposed here? If so, massive efficiency gains in improving the search space could be achieved.

- Finally, the difficulty we had recovering the $P[X_i = 1 | Y = 1]$ structure in the simulated data situation suggests that one of the two parameters, $P[X_i = 1 \mid Y = 1]$ and $P[X_i = 1 \mid Y = 0]$, is not estimable-perhaps the best that we can hope for is that the *difference* of the two parameters *is* estimable. Implicitly, we used that attempt in constraining our $P[X_i = 1 \mid Y = 1]$ values to one. Fortunately, we can construct an appropriate decision rule in either case.

REFERENCES

Belin, T. R. (1991). Using Mixture Models to Calibrate Error Rates in Record-Linkage Procedures, with Applications to Computer Matching for Census Undercount Estimation. Ph.D. Thesis, Harvard University Department of Statistics, Boston, MA, USA.

Belin, Thomas R. (1993). Evaluation of sources of variation in record linkage through a factorial experiment. Survey Methodology, 19:13-29.

Belin, Thomas R., and Rubin, Donald B. (1995). A method for calibration of false-match rates in record linkage. Journal of the American Statistical Association, 90: 694-707.

Boros, E., Hammer, P. L., Ibaraki, T., Kogan, A., Mayoraz, E., and Muchnik, I. (2000). An implementation of logical analysis of data. IEEE Transactions on Knowledge and Data Engineering, 12: 292-306.

Boros, E., Ibaraki, T., and Makino, K. (1996). Boolean analysis of incomplete examples. In: Algorithm Theory - Proceedings of the 5th Scandinavian Workshop on Algorithm Theory (SWAT'96), (Rolf Karlsson and Andrzej Lingas, eds., Reykjavik, Iceland, July 3-5,1996). Lecture Notes in Artificial Intelligence 1097 (1996) pp. 440-451. Berlin: Springer Verlag.

Congdon, Peter J. (2001). Bayesian Statistical Modelling. New York, NY: John Wiley and Sons, Inc.

Davey, B.A., and Priestly, H.A. (1990). Introduction to Lattices and Order. Cambridge, UK: Cambridge University Press.

Duda, Richard O., Hart, Peter E., and Stork, David G. (2001). Pattern Classification, Second Edition. New York, NY: John Wiley and Sons, Inc.

Fellegi, Ivan P., and Sunter, A. B. (1969). A theory for record linkage. Journal of the American Statistical Association, 64: 1183-1210.

Fortini, M., Liseo, B., Nuccitelli, A., and Scanu, M. (2001). On Bayesian Record Linkage. ISBA.

Gelfand, A. and Smith, A.F.M. (1990). Sampling-based approaches to calculating marginal densities. Journal of the American Statistical Association, 85:398-409.

Gelman, A., and Rubin, D.B. (1992). Inference from iterative simulation using multiple sequences. Journal of the American Statistical Association, 7:457-472.

Geyer, C.J. (1992). Practical markov chain monte carlo. Statistical Science, 7:473-483.

Haberman, S. (1979). Analysis of Qualitative Data, Vol. 2, New Developments. New York, NY: Academic Press.

Harville, D.S., and Moore, R.A. (1999). Determining record linkage parameters using an iterative logistic regression approach. Paper presented at the 1999 Joint Statistical Meetings, Baltimore, MD, August 11, 1999.

Jabine, T. (1993). Procedures for restricted access. Journal of Official Statistics, 9:537-590.

Jackman, S. (2000).Estimation and inference via Bayesian simulation: An introduction to markov chain monte carlo. American Journal of Political Science, 44:369-398.

Judson, D.H., Bagchi, Sitadri, and Quint, Thomas C. (2005). On the Inference of Semi-Coherent Structures from Data. Computers and Operations Research, 32:2853-2874.

Judson, D.H. (2001). A partial order approach to record linkage. Proceedings of the 2001 meetings of the Federal Committee on Statistical Methodology. Washington, DC: Federal Committee on Statistical Methodology.

Kaufman, G.M. (2001). Statistical identification and estimability. In Neil J. Smelser and Paul B. Baltes (Eds.), International Encyclopedia of the Social and Behavioral Sciences. Amsterdam: Elsevier.

King, Gary, and Zeng, Langche (2001). Logistic regression in rare events data. Political Analysis, 9:1-27.

Long, J. Scott (1997). Regression Models for Categorical and Limited Dependent Variables. Thousand Oaks, CA: Sage Publications.

Leenen, Iwin, Van Mechelen, Iven, and Gelman, Andrew (2000). Bayesian probabilistic extensions of a deterministic classification model. Computational Statistics, 15: 355-371.

Meyer, Mary and Booker, Jane (1991). Eliciting and Analyzing Expert Judgment: A Practical Guide. Knowledge Acquisition for Knowledge-Based Systems series, vol. 5. London, United Kingdom: Academic Press.

McLachlan, G.J, and Krishnan, T. (1997). The EM Algorithm and Extensions. New York, NY: Wiley.

McCullagh, P., and Nelder, J.A. (1989). Generalized Linear Models, 2nd ed. London: Chapman and Hall.

Rogot, E., Sorlie, P.D., and Johnson, N.J. (1986). Probabilistic methods in matching census samples to the national death index. Journal of Chronic Diseases, 39: 719-734.

Scheuren, Fritz, and Winkler, William E. (1993). Regression analysis of data files that are computer matched. Survey Methodology, 19:39-58.

Scheuren, Fritz, and Winkler, William E. (1997). Regression analysis of data files that are computer matched - Part II. Survey Methodology, 23:157-165.

Spiegelhalter, D.J., Thomas, A., and Best, N.G. (1999). WinBUGS Version 1.4 User Manual. MRC Biostatistics Unit.

Thibaudeau, Yves (1993). The discrimination power of dependency structures in record linkage. Survey Methodology, 19:31-38.

Triantaphyllou, E., Kovalerchuk, B., and Deshpande, A. (1997). Some recent developments of using logical analysis for inferring a boolean function with few clauses, pp. 215-236 in Barr, R., Helgason, R., and Kennington, J (Eds.), Interfaces in Computer Science and Operations Research: Advances in Metaheuristics, Optimization, and Stochastic Modelling Technologies. Boston, MA: Kluwer Academic Publishers.

Winkler, William E. (1989). Near automatic weight computation in the Fellegi-Sunter model of record linkage. Proceedings of the Fifth Annual Research Conference, U.S. Census Bureau: Washington, D.C.

Winkler, William (1995). Matching and record linkage. In: B.G. Cox, et. al., Eds., Business Survey Methods. New York, NY: John Wiley.

Yancey, William (2002). Bigmatch: A Program for Extracting Probable Matches from a Large File for Record Linkage. Statistical Research Report Series RRC2002/01. U.S. Census Bureau: Washington, D.C.

AUTHOR'S BIOGRAPHICAL STATEMENT

Dr. Dean H. Judson is a Special Assistant for Administrative Records Research at the U.S. Census Bureau. In that role, he has worked on large scale record linkage projects and developed enhancements to existing methods for linking records across databases. Formerly, he was the Nevada State Demographer and has worked as a private consultant for Decision Analytics, Inc. Dr. Judson received his M.S. in Mathematics from the University of Nevada and his M.S. and Ph.D. in Sociology from Washington State University.

Chapter 20 [1]

SOME FUTURE TRENDS IN DATA MINING

Xiaoting Wang*, Peng Zhu*, Giovanni Felici**, and Evangelos Triantaphyllou***

*:   *Department of Industrial Engineering*
         3128 CEBA Building
         Louisiana State University
         Baton Rouge, LA 70803-6409, U.S.A.
         E-mail: {xwang8, pzhu1 } @lsu.edu
**:   *Istituto di Analisi dei Sistemi ed Informatica "A. Ruberti"*
         Consiglio Nazionale delle Ricerche
         Viale Manzoni 30, 00185 Rome, Italy
         E-mail: felici@iasi.cnr.it
***:   *Department of Computer Science*
         298 Coates Hall
         Louisiana State University
         Baton Rouge, LA 70803-6409, U.S.A.
         E-mail: trianta@lsu.edu

Abstract: This chapter considers four key data mining areas which seem to have a promising future. These areas are: web mining, visual data mining, text data mining, and distributed data mining. The reason of their importance is to be found in the valuable applications they can support but also in the proliferation of the web and in the dramatic improvements in computing and storage media. Although they are currently limited by certain impediments, their future looks very exciting.

Key Words: Data Mining, Web Mining, Visual Data Mining, Text Data Mining, Distributed Data Mining, Obstacles in Data Mining Research and Applications.

---

[1] Triantaphyllou, E. and G. Felici (Eds.), **Data Mining and Knowledge Discovery Approaches Based on Rule Induction Techniques**, Massive Computing Series, Springer, Heidelberg, Germany, pp. 695-716, 2006.

1.   INTRODUCTION

Data Mining (DM) is the extraction of new knowledge from large databases. Many techniques are currently used in this fast emerging field, including statistical analysis and machine learning based approaches. With the rapid development of the World Wide Web and the fast increase of unstructured databases, new technologies and applications are continuously coming forth in this field. The purpose of this chapter is to offer a brief survey of some of the latest branches in data mining that can be regarded to have some potential on the present and the future of this discipline. These areas are Web mining, text mining, distributed data mining, and visual data mining. Of these four areas, the first two can be viewed as directly related to the Internet and the Web, while the other two are more related to new computational methods for carrying out data mining searches.

This chapter is organized as follows. The second section is devoted to Web mining. It further splits into three subsections: Web content mining, Web usage mining, and Web structure mining. The third section describes the essentials of mining text documents. The fourth section discusses the basics of visual data mining, while the fifth section describes the main issues of distributed data mining. Some comments regarding current impediments and future possibilities for each area are discussed at the end of each section. The last section provides some concluding remarks.

2.   WEB MINING

Since its advent the Internet and the World Wide Web have allowed people from all over the world to get closer together in search of new information and also in publishing new information. Resources on one side of the world can be shared by anyone on the other side of the world through the Internet and the Web.

However, the accumulation of vast amounts of data on the Web often makes searching for the right answer too cumbersome. At the same time, it is also too often the case that the right answer is available but it may remain hidden because of the presence of lots of peripheral data and the inability of current search engines to adequately find what a user really wants.

A new type of data mining techniques, as it applies to Web applications, may be the solution to some of the above problems. These techniques are known as "Web mining". Enabling people to access the vast information resources of the Web efficiently and effectively and, at the same time, attracting even more users, are the main goals of Web mining.

Web mining techniques can be classified into three categories [Madria, *et al.*, 1999]: Web *content* mining, Web *usage* mining, and Web *structure* mining. Due to the network nature of the Internet, Web resources are distributed all over the world and the only way to organize and explore them efficiently is by using Web mining. Based on the goals of Web mining, several tools and techniques can be used for each one of the above three Web mining categories. For instance, Web usage mining may use association rules to better understand the behavior of Web users. Web structure mining may use statistical analysis to identify the potential relationships among hyperlinks, etc. In general, Web mining is one of the most promising areas in the general data mining field. Extracting unseen but potentially useful patterns from the Web in order to provide implicit information is becoming one of the hot research tasks in this field.

2.1 Web Content Mining

Web content mining is the process of automatically extracting content patterns that may be hidden in the Web. Such Web content patterns may help users to easier retrieve information that they are interested in. Furthermore, Web content is much more complex than the data in regular and structured databases. Thus, the extracted patterns may better facilitate a user to search what he/she needs by applying regular queries on these patterns.

Ordinary Web content includes HTML or ASP pages, addresses of emails and even image and video files (this is also the objective of multimedia data mining). So far, widely used technologies are limited to determining key phrase frequency in target pages [Frank, *et al.*, 1999] and statistical analysis. However, some new methods may be more complicated. For instance, in [Turney, 2003] a more complex approach is discussed for mining coherent key phrases from Web pages, while Caramia, Felici, and Pezzoli in [2004] proposed a combined use of clustering techniques and a genetic algorithm to improve search results.

There are two main approaches to Web content mining: the agent based approach and the database based approach [Cooley, *et al.*, 1997]. The agent based approach for Web mining is aiming at building automatically or semi-automatically systems to discover and organize Web-based information on behalf of certain users. For example, the search engine *Google.com* uses this approach. Some other algorithms, such as Occam, have been developed to generate plans to gather and interpret information from agents [Kwok and Weld, 1996].

The database approach, which was developed to mine semi-structured documents, uses many of the same techniques as the ones used for unstructured documents. However, this approach now reorganizes the semi-structured files into a structured database such that standard queries can be used next. For example, in [Han, *et al.*, 1995] a multi-layered database is used in which each layer is obtained via generalization and transformation operations performed on the lower layers. Also, in [Zhu and Triantaphyllou, 2004] a multi-query engine was built for extracting publication patterns from the *Citeseer* digital library.

2.2   Web Usage Mining

Web usage mining involves the automatic discovery of pattern related to user access behaviors from one or more Web servers [Cooley, *et al.*, 1997]. As one of the most direct methods to mine users' information that best corresponds to their needs and behaviors, Web usage mining may offer extremely valuable information to businesses. Data filtering has been widely used to track the reports of a user's behavior such as the project of "Open web market reporter" carried by Open Market Inc. [1996]. Web servers usually record and accumulate data about their users' interactions whenever requests for resources are received. Then, Web usage mining tools analyze web access logs to better understand the users' behaviors.

Based on the information gathered interactively from users, the Web resources will be redesigned and reallocated. Some of the tools are used to accumulate data and provide reports such as a CGI script that mainly counts the number of users and records user registration information. This type of tools also includes some DBMS (Database Management Systems) such as Oracle and SQL-Sever to track users' behavior and log accessing files for extracting knowledge. Other emerging tools are used to monitor and analyze the users' behavior. Mobasher, *et al.*, in [1996] constructed a framework for Web usage mining which provided an engine named Webminer to automatically extract patterns such as association rules from log files. It also utilized an SQL like system to analyze the data. In general, such tools implement recording and basic analysis of the interaction between users and Web resources.

2.3   Web Structure Mining

Web structure mining is a type of mining activity that focuses on using the analysis of structures of links and hyperlinks on Web documents to identify the most preferable documents. Through the analysis of such Web structures, some more efficient Web schema may be constructed. Madria, *et al.*, in [1999] proposed some detailed descriptions on how to facilitate navigation by using a reference schema which is based on a tree structure. In this way, extracting any structural pattern hidden among hyperlinks may become the main goal of structure mining. In [1998] Page, *et al.*, described a method named *PageRank*, which is used for rating Web pages and structures objectively and systematically in order to reflect human interest and attention. The intuitive explanation for Web structure mining is that a hyperlink from a keyword *A* to a keyword *B* implies that there might be some potential relation between keyword *A* and keyword *B* (http://www.cs.ualberta.ca/ ~tszhu/webmining.htm).

Usually, mining of Web structures is executed as a two-step process. First, such a method extracts patterns from Web transactions including the users' registration information. This step applies the most commonly used data mining techniques such as data preprocessing, clustering and the derivation of association rules. The second step analyzes structure patterns and it involves some more specific methods, depending on the nature of the Web files. Based on the database mechanism, the OLAP (for Online Analysis Processing) approach is one of the emerging tools for online databases analysis. Dyreson, in [1997] provided an approach that uses OLAP techniques on data warehouses and data cubes to simplify the analysis of Web usage statistics from server logs. Furthermore, some visualization techniques and standard database querying can be of powerful assistance in this direction as well.

2.4   Current Obstacles and Future Trends

Although the Web has invaded many aspects of modern life, it still lacks standardization. Some major companies (such as *Microsoft* and *Sun Microsystems*) are competing for whose standards should be accepted by the rest. The above flexibility and freedom provided a great impetus for large and small players to offer innovation and plurality in developing this new communication medium. At the same time, however, the lack of standards acceptable by Web developers creates a "Babel syndrome" that may hinder the rate of future developments. Standardization on the structures of Web pages will make it easier for search engines and computerized mobile agents to analyze them and locate context of potential interest to users. Furthermore, computer viruses, hacker attacks, security issues, and spam mailings, add more impediments for a wider and faster use of the Web. Better protection against hacker attacks and computer viruses will make access to the Web sources be more efficient by allowing the exchange of information to be both ways: from and to Web servers and also the end users.

Some other key research problems are how to differentiate between legitimate and illegitimate computer users and also detect potentially fraudulent computer transactions. Better understanding the usage profiles of particular users is a typical data mining task and may allow for a better design of Web pages with dynamic characteristics.

Solving the above problems requires more time to reach maturity, more technological developments, and also new legislations. It also requires cooperation at the national and international levels. Data mining already plays a critical role in identifying unauthorized computer intruders (hackers) and also credit card fraud. One method for detecting fraud is to check for suspicious changes in users' behavior. Dokas, *et al.*, in [2002] developed an Intrusion Detection System for cyber threat analysis by using the models of misuse detection and anomaly detection. Many of these data mining problems require a deep understanding of the phenomena under study, thus motivating the use of rule induction based methods. A rule-learning program has been used to uncover indicators of fraudulent behavior from a large database of customer transactions [Fawcett and Provost, 1997]. New methods for searching and analyzing multimedia content are also needed for a better utilization of the Web resources.

3.   TEXT MINING

General data mining methods focus on the discovery of patterns and unknown knowledge from structured data, such as databases, data warehouses, etc. However, in reality there are huge amounts of unstructured or semi-structured data, such as text documents. Like any other information source, text data also includes vast and rich information. However, it is hard to analyze and get the information from text data in their original format. So the sub field of text mining was introduced to solve the problem.

Text mining, also known as text data mining (or TDM) [Hearst, 1997] or knowledge discovery from textual databases [Feldman and Dagan, 1995], generally refers to the process of extracting interesting and non-trivial patterns or knowledge from unstructured text documents. Text mining is a nascent field and can be viewed as an extension of data mining or knowledge discovery from structured databases [Fayyad, *et al.*, 1996]. Its goal is to look for nuggets of new knowledge in the mountains of text [Hearst, 1999].

3.1   Text Mining and Information Access

It is necessary to firstly differentiate between information access (or information retrieval) and text mining. Text mining focuses on how to use a body of textual information as a large knowledge base from where one can extract new, never-before encountered, information [Craven, *et al.*, 1998]. While the goal of information access is to help users find the information that is currently of interest to them since there may be various types of information in a collection of documents. As it was pointed out by Hearst [1999], the fact that an information retrieval system can return a document that contains the information a user requested does not imply that a new discovery has been made. For a more detailed comparison between information retrieval and text mining, we refer to [Hearst, 1997].

3.2   A Simple Framework of Text Mining

Text mining can be viewed as comprised of two phases. The first is text refining, which transforms free-form text documents into a chosen intermediate form. The second is knowledge distillation, which deduces patterns or knowledge from the intermediate form [Tan, 1999]. The intermediate form (or IF) can be semi-structured such as the conceptual graph representation, or structured such as the relational data representation. At the same time, the intermediate form can also be document-based (in which each entity represents a document) or concept-based, in which each entity represents an object or concept of interest in a specific domain

3.3   Fields of Text Mining

The main fields of text mining include feature extraction, text categorization, and text clustering. These three fields are briefly described in the following paragraphs.

Feature extraction (or selection) attempts to find significant and important vocabulary from within a natural language text document [Hsu, 2003]. Usually, it is the first step of text categorization which improves categorization effectiveness and reduces computational complexity by removing non-informative words from documents. Feature extraction has been proven to be a valuable technique in supervised learning for improving predictive accuracy while reducing the number of attributes considered in a task [Devaney and Ram, 1997]. Yang and Pedersen, in [1997] made an evaluation of five feature selection methods: Document Frequency Thresholding, Information Gain, χ^2-Statistic, Mutual Information, and Term Strength. They found that the first three were the most effective in their experiment. Smith, *et al.*, in [1994] introduced a genetic feature selection for clustering and classification.

Text categorization is the assignment of free text documents to one or more pre-determined categories based on their content. It belongs to the broader category of supervised data mining. A number of statistical classification and machine learning techniques have been applied to text categorization. Such techniques include regression models [Yang and Pedersen, 1997], nearest neighbor classifiers [Yang and Pedersen, 1997], decision trees [Lewis and Ringuette, 1994], Bayesian classifiers [Lewis and Ringuette, 1994], support vector machines (SVMs) [Joachims, 1998], rule learning algorithms [Cohen and Singer, 1996], relevance feedback [Rocchio, 1971], voted classification [Apte, *et al.*, 1999], and neural networks [Wiener, *et al.*, 1993]. A comparative study about fourteen commonly used text categorization methods is provided in [Yang, 1999]. Aas and Eikvil, in [1999] offered a detailed survey on text categorization.

General text categorization does not lead itself to the discovery of new knowledge. However, there are two recent areas of inquiry that make use of text categorization to discover trends and patterns within textual data for more general purpose usage [Hearst, 1999]. One of them uses text category labels to find "unexpected patterns" among text articles [Feldman and Dagan, 1995], [Dagan, *et al.*, 1996], and [Feldman, *et al.*, 1997]. Another contribution is that of the DARPA Topic Detection and Tracking initiative [Allan, *et al.*, 1998]. This project describes an interesting mechanism called On-line New Event Detection, whose focus is on the discovery of the beginning of a new theme or trend [Hearst, 1999].

Compared to categorization, clustering is the process of grouping documents with similar contents into dynamically generated clusters. It is also part of the broader category of unsupervised data mining. Agglomerative hierarchical clustering and K-means are two widely used clustering techniques for text clustering. A study of these two clustering approaches and their variants can be found in [Steinbach, *et al.*, 2000].

3.4   Current Obstacles and Future Trends

Though people have made some progress in text mining, and some real-life projects are on their way, there are still many issues that are waiting to be solved before this young area becomes mature. Some examples are automatic natural language processing by computer and copyright of text documents.

Similar to Web mining, text mining also involves the analysis of published documents; text documents in this case. A typical Web page has special markers to denote its title, key words, links, etc. In this way, a text document may be considered more unstructured than a Web page. Furthermore, many text documents were generated long time before the advent of the Web or even computers. This creates special problems regarding optical character recognition (OCR) [Mori, *et al.*, 1999] and natural language processing (as some human languages change over time) [Jackson and Moulinier, 2002], just to name a few. The problems are also compounded with the legal aspects regarding copyright issues.

Optical character recognition is itself a typical pattern recognition problem, thus data mining can play a pivotal role here as well. Understanding a natural language is based on parsing a text document or speech in terms of some human grammar, which is nothing but a collection of rules (grammar rules) designed to govern a particular language. Therefore, data mining approaches based on rule induction are the natural way for developing better natural language processors for better text mining and also Web context mining.

4. VISUAL DATA MINING

As one of the most popular areas of knowledge discovery, visual data mining is a collection of interactive and reflective methods that support exploration of data sets by dynamically adjusting parameters to see how they affect the information being presented [Thearling, *et al.*, 2001]. Visual data mining is the combination of data mining and visualization techniques which can help introduce user insights, preferences, and biases in earlier stages of the data mining life cycle to reduce its overall computation complexity and reduce the set of uninteresting patterns in the product [Ganesh, *et al.*, 1996].

This emerging area of data analysis and mining is based on the integration of graphics, visualization metaphors and methods, information and scientific data visualization. It offers machine learning and data mining communities some powerful tools for the analysis of large and complex data sets that can assist in uncovering patterns and trends that are likely to be missed with other non-visual data mining methods. Keim, *et al.*, in [1995] developed a visual data mining and databases exploration system that supported the exploration of large databases by implementing some visual data mining techniques.

As it was pointed out by John W. Tukey, seeing may be believing or disbelieving [Tukey, 1965]. However, seeing is the key to knowing [Wong, *et al.*, 1999] and leads to believing and understanding. The main purpose of visualization is to offer simplicity and make any vagueness in data easier to understand. Visualization methods use 2-D, 3-D graphics or just tabular forms for data analysis and prediction of the future. Visualization and data mining techniques can be combined together in order to extract any explicit knowledge from vague data structures.

4.1   Data Visualization

Most of the data types in real world applications lack the ability to be directly illustrated by 2-D or 3-D graphics. There are several techniques that have been commonly used to visualize data types including point plots and histograms. However, these traditional techniques are too limited for analyzing highly dimensional data. During the last decade, a number of novel techniques have been developed and classified into the following types [Keim, 2002]:

1. Geometrically transformed displays, such as landscapes and parallel coordinates as in scalable framework (see also Figure 1).
2. Icon-based displays, such as needle icons and star icons.
3. Dense pixel displays, such as the recursive pattern, circle segments techniques and the graph sketches (see, for instance, Figure 2).
4. Stacked displays, such as tree maps or dimensional stacking (see, for instance, Figure 3).

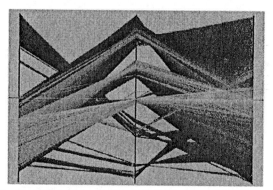

Figure 1. Parallel Coordinate Visualization [Keim, 2002].

Figure 2. Dense Pixel Displays [Keim, 2002].

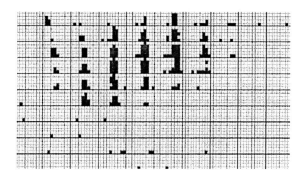

Figure 3. Dimensional Stacking Visualization
[Keim, 2002].

4.2 Visualizing Data Mining Models

A number of well developed data mining methods can be applied to visualize data mining models. Basically, there are two issues involved in visual data mining: understanding and trust [Thearling, *et al.*, 2001]. Understanding newly discovered patterns is definitely the most fundamental motivation behind visualizing a model. Therefore, whether a given visualization is effective depends on the users' understanding of the visualized data mining model. For instance, clearly knowing the customer distribution might be the most important parameter in designing a local retail store. Moreover, visualizing a model could allow users to discuss and explain the logic behind the model with colleagues, customers, and other users based on trust.

Kriegel in [2001] describes several projects which focused on integrating users in the KDD (knowledge discovery from databases) process in terms of effective and efficient visualization techniques, interaction capabilities, and knowledge transfer. The Interactive Data Mining (IDM) project constructed decision trees for users by using the PBC (Perception-Based Classification) system (http://www.dbs.informatik.unimuenchen.de/ Forschung/KDD/VisualDM/). A new technique for visual data mining called Independence Diagrams is proposed in [Berchtold, *et al.*, 1998]. That approach divides a given attribute into ranges and defines a grid to store a number of data items such that it could recognize the complexity between various attributes.

4.3 Current Obstacles and Future Trends

More visual data mining algorithms need to be developed since traditional data mining algorithms are not perfectly matched with the requirement of data visualization [Joshi, 1997]. Visual data mining is still a young field. One of the challenges to better interpret visual patterns calls for matching such visual patterns with the etiology behind the behavior of the system under study [Zhu, 2003].

Meanwhile, being able to deal with highly dimensional datasets is another concern. Some artificial intelligence research laboratories have begun adjusting the focus to this issue [Cook and Buja, 1997]. Special care should be given such that not to overwhelm the end user with visual effects and *"miss the forest for the trees."*

New methods in this area should offer a two-way analysis. First, be able to interpret any visual findings into terms that explain the etiology of the behavior of the system under study. Second, be able to transfer any known or newly derived rules that govern the behavior of the system under study, into visual effects. This two-way approach may offer a better understanding of any newly derived knowledge.

With the need for simplicity of data mining from non-professional users, visualization is becoming more and more popular in the field of data mining. Due to the research developments in techniques and methods especially for visualization, they have helped verify many of the research directions and business decision making in a variety of fields, including visual methods for data analysis, visual DM process models, etc. Some software packages have also been developed for visualizing data mining models such as the Tiberius system (http://www.philbrierley.com/).

Visual data mining is also connected with many other research areas, which comprehend the study of domain knowledge in visual reasoning, in virtual environments, visual analysis of large databases, and in generic system architectures and methods for visualizing semantic content [Han and Kamber, 2001]. With visual data mining, KDD is becoming more valid, useful and understandable to researchers and end-users alike.

5.   DISTRIBUTED DATA MINING

Another important and attractive area of data mining is distributed data mining. Traditionally, most of data mining work is done at a database or data warehouse which is physically located at one place. However, often times data may be located at different places or at different physical locations. The mining of such distributed data that are located at heterogeneous sites is known as distributed data mining (DDM).

5.1 The Basic Principle of DDM

When faced with distributed data, an obvious solution is to gather all the data at a central site which has enough storage capacity and apply some algorithms on these data. However, such an approach may not be feasible or efficient for some applications where the data are inherently distributed but global insights are required. For example, each site of a multinational company may manage its own operational data locally, but the data may also need to be analyzed for global patterns to allow company-wide activities such as planning, marketing, and sales to take place. Furthermore, centralized data mining may be associated with some other challenges. For instance, sometimes it may be too expensive to transfer all the required data to a central site. Also, the distributed data sets may not be transferable to a central site when considering the security and privacy of the individual data sources [Clifton, 2001].

In cases like the above ones, current research in DDM is more interested in developing new algorithms that can effectively combine data mining results from different local mining operations in an effort to gain a global perspective of the data. In more specific terms, this is defined as performing local data analysis for generating partial data models, and combining the local data models from different data sites in order to develop the global model [Hsu, 2003]. However, such a global model may become inaccurate when the individual data sources have data that are heterogeneous [Hsu, 2003].

Distributed data mining has attracted more interest in recent years. Many distributed approaches have been developed for classification [Guo and Sutiwaraphun, 2000], clustering [Johnson and Kargupta, 2000], and deriving association rules from transactional databases [Cheung, *et al.*, 1996]. DDM has also gained wide applicability for many real life problems. For instance, credit card fraud detection [Chan, *et al.*, 1999], facility management [Ariwa and Gaber, 2003], and distributed data mining management for e-commerce [Krishnaswamy, *et al.*, 2000] etc.

5.2 Grid Computing

An emerging technique, Grid computing, is worth mentioning as for the development of distributed data mining. The development of high-speed Internet and powerful computers brought out the possibility of using distributed computers as a unified computing resource known as Grid computing. The concept of Grid computing started as a project to link geographically dispersed supercomputers, but now it has grown far beyond its original intent [Baker, *et al.*, 2002]. Buyya in [2002] defines Grid as "a type of parallel and distributed system that enables the sharing, selection, and aggregation of geographically distributed "autonomous" resources dynamically at runtime depending on their availability, capability, performance, cost, and users' quality-of-service requirements." The Grid can play a significant role in providing an effective computational support for knowledge discovery applications [Cannataro, et al., 2002]. Thus Grid computing can contribute a lot to distributed data mining. In [2002] Cannataro, et al., discuss how one kind of software architecture called "KNOWLEDGE GRID" which is based on computational grid mechanisms can be used to implement distributed data mining services.

5.3   Current Obstacles and Future Trends

As a newly emerging area, the field of distributed data mining still has many problems waiting to be solved. Since the essence and main task of distribute data mining is to mine large and distributed data sets, the efficiency of distributed data mining has been an attractive challenge for some researchers in the field. One case is to study how to reduce the response time of the DDM based on some kind of cost model [Krishnaswamy, et al., 2002]. Some other potential works include developments of new algorithms, design of better standardization among distributed databases for uniform / easier processing [Grossman, et al., 2002], better protection strategies against hackers, computer viruses, industrial espionage etc, and better identification of distributed computing resources.

Meanwhile, the networked PC will be pervasive with the liberation of the confines of the individual PC and especially with the rapid emergence of Wi-Fi technologies [Battiti, et al., 2003]. In this way a user may have access to virtually unlimited computing resources from many different locations. Such development necessitates the need for developing new authentication protocols that can allow for the proper use of distributed computing resources by legitimate users.   An excellent survey of distributed data mining techniques and a discussion of some other issues about DDM can be found in [Fu, 2001].

6.   SUMMARY

This chapter discussed four fast emerging and promising areas of data mining: Web mining, text mining, distributed data mining and visual data mining, including their technologies, applications, impediments and future trends. These four areas focus on different aspects of data mining.   Web mining and text mining all deal with unstructured data.   The first area aims at hypertext data, HTML resources and other issues with general text documents. Therefore, they have some common issues to solve, like privacy of the data and their security. Similarly, such problems may also need to be solved in a distributed data mining setting which can offer tools for people to utilize distributed data and computing resources effectively.

Data visualization can help end-users to analyze data from various resources. For instance, data obtained from a text document can include word frequency, relative frequency, time sequence, etc. An interactive data visualization process can greatly help users to find useful facts from various data mining analyses.

Although it is a rapidly growing field, data mining is still a young field an as such it faces many challenges. The complexity of structured and unstructured databases urges more and more data mining technologies to be developed in related areas such as multimedia data mining, hypertext and hypermedia data mining, spatial, and geographic data mining. Meanwhile, it is still necessary to perform dedicated studies that could aim at developing new data mining algorithms and methods. In conclusion, the power of data mining in both research and industrial fields indicates, with strong evidence, that it has a bright and promising future.

REFERENCES

Aas, K., and L. Eikvil, (1999), Text Categorisation: A Survey, *Report No. 941*, June, ISBN 82-539-0425-8.

Allan, J., J. Carbonell, G. Doddington, J. Yamron, and Y. Yang, (1998), "Topic Detection and Tracking Pilot Study: Final Report," *Proceedings of the DARPA Broadcast News Transcription and Understanding Workshop*, pp. 194-218.

Apte, C., M. S. Weiss, and F. J. Damerau, (1999), "Maximizing Text Mining Performance," *IEEE Intelligent Systems*, July/August, pp. 3-8.

Ariwa, E., and M. M. Gaber, (2003), "Information Systems and Application of Distributed Data Mining to Facilities Management," *The Second Annual Conference: Hawaii International Conference on Statistics and Related Fields*, Hawaii, USA.

Baker, M., R. Buyya, and D. Laforenza, (2002), "Grids and Grid Technologies for Wide-Area Distributed Computing," *Software: Practice and Experience*, Vol. 32-15, pp. 1437-1466, Wiley Press, USA.

Battiti, R., M. Conti, E. Gregori, and M. Sabel, (2003), "Price-Based Congestion-Control in Wi-Fi Hot Spots," *Proceedings of WiOpt'03*, Sophia-Antipolis, France, Vol. 3-5, March.

Berchtold, S., H. V. Jagadish, and K. A. Ross, (1998), "Independence Diagrams: A Technique for Visual Data Mining," *Proceedings of the 4th Int. Conf. Knowledge Discovery and Data Mining, KDD*.

Buyya, R., (2002), Grid Computing Information Center, http://www.gridcomputing.com.

Cannataro, M., D. Talia, and P. Trunfio, (2002), "Distributed Data Mining on the Grid," *Future Generation Computer Systems*, Vol. 18-8, pp. 1101-1112.

Caramia, M., G. Felici, and A. Pezzoli, (2004), "Improving Search Results with Data Mining in a Thematic Search Engine", *Computers and Operations Research*, Vol. 31, pp. 2387-2404.

Chan, P., W. Fan, A. Prodromidis, and S. Stolfo, (1999), "Distributed Data Mining in Credit Card Fraud Detection," *IEEE Intelligent Systems*, Vol. 14-6, pp. 67-74.

Cheung, D., V. Ng, A. Fu, and Y. Fu, (1996), "Efficient Mining of Association Rules in Distributed Databases," *IEEE Trans. on Knowledge and Data Engineering*, Vol. 8, pp. 911-922.

Clifton, C., (2001), "Privacy Preserving Distributed Data Mining," Department of Computer Sciences, Purdue University, November 9.

Cohen, W. J., and Y. Singer, (1996), "Context-Sensitive Learning Methods for Text Categorization," *Proceedings of 19th Annual Int. ACM SIGIR*

Conf. on Research and Development in Information Retrieval, pp. 307-315.

Cook, D., and A. Buja, (1997), "Manual Controls for High-Dimensional Data Projections," *Journal of Computational and Graphical Statistics*, Vol. 6-4.

Cooley, R., B. Mobasher, and J. Srivastava, (1997), "Web Mining: Information and Pattern Discovery on the World Wide Web," *Proceedings of the 9th IEEE International Conference on Tools with Artificial Intelligence (ICTAI'97).*

Craven, M., D. DiPasquo, D. Freitag, A. McCallum, T. Mitchell, K. Nigam, and S. Slattery, (1998), "Learning to Extract Symbolic Knowledge from the World Wide Web," *Proceedings of the Fifteenth National Conference on Artificial Intelligence (AAAI 98)*, pp. 509-516.

Dagan, I., R. Feldman, and H. Hirsh, (1996), "Keyword-Based Browsing and Analysis of Large Document Sets," *Proceedings of the Fifth Annual Symposium on Document Analysis and Information Retrieval (SDAIR)*, Las Vegas, NV, USA.

Devaney, M., and A. Ram, (1997), "Efficient Feature Selection in Conceptual Clustering," *Proceedings of the Fourteenth International Conference on Machine Learning (ICML-97).*

Dokas, P., L. Ertoz, V. Kumar, A. Lazarevic, J. Srivastava, and P.-N. Tan (2002), "Data Mining for Network Intrusion Detection," *Proceedings of NSF Workshop on Next Generation Data Mining*, Baltimore, MD, USA

Dyreson, C., (1997), "Using an Incomplete Data Cube as a Summary Data Sieve," *Bulletin of the IEEE Technical Committee on Data Engineering*, pp. 19--26, March.

Fayyad, U., G. Piatesky-Shapiro, and P. Smyth, (1996), "From Data Mining to Knowledge Discovery: An Overview," Advances in Knowledge Discovery and Data Mining, U. Fayyad, G. Piatetsky-Shapiro, P. Smyth, and R. Uthurusamy, editors, pp. 1-36, *MIT Press*, Cambridge, Mass, USA.

Fawcett, T., and F. J. Provost, (1997), "Adaptive Fraud Detection," *Data Mining and Knowledge Discovery*, Vol. 1-3, pp. 291-316.

Feldman, R., and I. Dagan, (1995), "Knowledge Discovery in Textual Databases (KDT)," *Proceedings of the First International Conference on Knowledge Discovery and Data Mining (KDD-95)*, Montreal, Canada, August 20-21, AAAI Press, pp. 112-117.

Feldman, R., W. Klosgen, and A. Zilberstein, (1997), "Visualization Techniques to Explore Data Mining Results for Document Collections," *Proceedings of the Third Annual Conference on Knowledge Discovery and Data Mining (KDD)*, Newport Beach, CA, USA.

Frank, E., G. W. Paynter, I. H. Witten, C. Gutwin, and C. G. Nevill-

Manning, (1999), "Domain-specific Keyphrase Extraction," *Proceedings of the Sixteenth International Joint Conference on Artificial Intelligence (IJCAI-99)*, pp. 668-673, CA, USA, Morgan Kaufmann.

Fu, Y., (2001), "Distributed Data Mining: An Overview," *Newsletter of the IEEE Technical Committee on Distributed Processing*, pp. 5-9.

Ganesh, M., E. Han, V. Kumar, S. Shekhar, and J. Srivastava, (1996), "Visual Data Mining: Framework and Algorithm Development," Technical Report, TR-96-021, Department of Computer Science, University of Minnesota, Minneapolis, MN, USA.

Grossman, R., M. Hornick, and G. Meyer, (2002), "Data Mining Standards Initiatives," *Communications of the ACM*, Vol. 45-8, pp. 59-61.

Guo, Y., and J. Sutiwaraphun, (2000), "Distributed Classification with Knowledge Probing," In H. Kargupta and P. Chan, Editors, Advances in Distributed and Parallel Knowledge Discovery, *AAAI Press*.

Han, J., O. R. Zaiane, and Y. Fu, (1995), "Resource and Knowledge Discovery in Global Information Systems: A Multiple Layered Database Approach", *Proceedings of A Forum on Research and Technology Advances in Digital Library*, McLean, VA, USA.

Han, J., and M. Kamber, (2001), Data Mining: Concepts and Techniques, San Mateo, CA, USA, *Morgan Kaufmann*.

Hearst, M. A., (1997), "Text Data Mining: Issues, Techniques, and the Relationship to Information Access," Presentation notes for UW/MS workshop on data mining.

Hearst, M. A., (1999), "Untangling Text Data Mining," *Proceedings of ACL'99: the 37th Annual Meeting of the Association for Computational Linguistics*, University of Maryland, MD, USA.

Hsu, J., (2003), "Chapter XX: Critical and Future Trends in Data Mining: a Review of Key Data Mining Technologies/Applications," Data mining: opportunities and challenges, *Idea Group Publishing*, Hershey, PA, USA.

Jackson, P, and I. Moulinier, (2002), Natural Language Processing for Online Applications, *John Benjamins*, Natural Language Processing Series.

Joachims, T., (1998), "Text Categorization with Support Vector Machines: Learning with Many Relevant Features," In C. Nedellec and C. Rouveirol, Editors, Proceedings of ECML-98, 10th European Conference on Machine Learning, *Springer-Verlag*, Heidelberg, Germany.

Johnson, E., and H. Kargupta, (2000), Collective, Hierarchical Clustering from Distributed, Heterogeneous Data, In M. Zaki and C. Ho, editors, Large-Scale Parallel KDD Systems, Vol. 1759, *Springer-Verlag*.

Joshi, K. P., (1997), Analysis of Data Mining Algorithms, Copyright Karuna Pande Joshi.

Keim, D. A., (2002), "Information Visualization and Visual Data Mining,"

IEEE Transactions on Visualization and Computer Graphics, Vol. 7-1, pp. 100-107, January-March.

Keim, D. A., and H.-P. Kriegel, (1995), "Issues in Visualizing Large Databases," *Proceedings of Conference on Visual Database Systems (VDB'95)*, Lausanne, Switzerland.

Kriegel, (2001),http://www.dbs.informatik.unimuenchen.de/Forschung/KDD /VisualDM/.

Krishnaswamy, S., A. Zaslavsky, and W. S. Loke, (2000), "An Architecture to Support Distributed Enterprise Data Mining Services in E-Commerce Environments," *In Workshop on Advanced Issues of E-Commerce and Web Based Information Systems*, pp. 239-246.

Krishnaswamy, S., W. S. Loke, and A. Zaslavsky, (2002), "Supporting the Optimization of Distributed Data Mining by Predicting Application Run Times," In M. Piatting, J. Filipe, and J. Braz, editors, Enterprise Information Systems IV, *Kluwer Academic Publishers*, ISBN 1-4020-1086-9. Hingham, MA, USA.

Kwok, C., and D. Weld, (1996), "Planning to Gather Information," *Proceedings of 14th National Conference on AI*.

Lewis, D., and M. Ringuette, (1994), "A Comparison of Two Learning Algorithms for Text Classification," *In Third Annual Symposium on Document Analysis and Information Retrieval*, pp. 81-93.

Madria, S. K., S. S. Rhonwmich, W. K. Ng, and F. P. Lim, (1999), "Research Issues in Web Data Mining," *Proceedings of Data Warehousing and Knowledge Discovery, First International Conference. DaWak'*, pp. 303-312.

Mobasher, B., N. Jain, E. Han, and J. Srivastava, (1996), "Web Mining: Pattern Discovery from World Wide Web Transactions," *Technical Report TR 96-050*, University of Minnesota, Dept. of Computer Science, Minneapolis, MN, USA.

Mori, S., H. Nishida, and H. Yamada, (1999), Optical Character Recognition, *John Wiley & Sons*, NY, USA.

Open Market Inc. Open Market Web Reporter, (1996), http://www.openmarket.com.

Page, L., S. Brin, R. Motwani, and T. Winograd, (1998), "the PageRank Citation Ranking: Bring Order to the Web," Stanford Digital Library Technologies Project.

Rocchio, J., (1971), Relevance Feedback in Information Retrieval, the SMART Retrieval System: Experiments in Automatic Document Processing, pp. 313-323, *Prentice-Hall Inc*.

Smith, J. E., T. C. Fogarty, and I. R. Johnson, (1994), "Genetic Feature Selection for Clustering and Classification," *Proceedings of the IEE Colloquium on Genetic Algorithms in Image Processing & Vision*,

London, pp. 130-136.

Steinbach, M., G. Karypis, and V. Kumar, (2000), "A Comparison of Document Clustering Techniques," *Text Mining Workshop*, KDD 2000.

Tan, A.-H., (1999), "Text Mining: The State of the Art and the Challenges," *Proceedings of PAKDD'99 Workshop on Knowledge discovery from Advanced Databases (KDAD'99)*, Beijing, pp. 71-76.

Thearling, K., B. Becker, D. DeCoste, B. Mawby, M. Pilote, and D. Sommerfield, (2001), "Visualizing Data Mining Models," In U. Fayyad, G. Grinstein and A. Wierse, editors, Information Visualization in Data Mining and Knowledge Discovery, *Morgan Kaufman*.

Tukey, J. W., and M. B. Wilk, (1965), "Data Analysis and Statistics: Techniques and Approaches," *Proceedings of the Symposium on Information Processing in Sight Sensory Systems*, pp. 7-27, California Institute of Technology, Pasadena, CA, USA.

Turney, P., (2003), "Coherent Keyphrase Extraction via Web Mining," *Proceedings of the Eighteenth International Joint Conference on Artificial Intelligence (IJCAI-03)*, pp. 434-439, Acapulco, Mexico.

Wiener, E., J. O. Pedersen, and A. S. Weigend, (1993), "A Neural Network Approach to Topic Spotting," *Proceedings of 4th annual symposium on document analysis and information retrieval*, pp. 22-34.

Wong, P-C., P. Whitney, and J. Thomas, (1999), "Visualizing Association Rules for Text Mining," *INFOVIS*, pp. 120-123.

Yang, Y., (1999), "An Evaluation of Statistical Approaches to Text Categorization," *Journal of Information Retrieval*, Vol. 1-1/2, pp. 67-88.

Yang, Y., and J. P. Pedersen, (1997), "Feature Selection in Statistical Learning of Text Categorization," *Proceedings of the 14th Int. Conf. on Machine Learning*, pp. 412-420.

Zhu, P., and E. Triantaphyllou, (2004), "Identifying New Trends in Knowledge Discovery by Analyzing Patterns in Research Publication Records", *Proceedings of the IIE 2004 Annual Conference*, on the Conference's CD, May 2004, Houston, TX, USA.

Zhu, S., (2003), "Statistical Modeling and Conceptualization of Visual Patterns," *IEEE Transactions on Pattern Analysis and Machine Intelligence*, Vol. 25-6, pp. 691-712.

AUTHORS' BIOGRAPHICAL STATEMENTS

Xiaoting Wang received her B.S. degree in Mechatronics Engineering at Nanchang Institute of Aeronautical Technology, Nanchang, China, in 1999, and M.S. degree in Mechatronics Engineering at Northwestern Polytechnic University, Xi'an, China, in 2002. Currently, she is a Ph.D. candidate in Industrial and Manufacturing Systems Engineering department, Louisiana State University. Her current research activities mainly focus on the theory and applications of Multi-Criteria Decision Making and Data Mining. More details of her research work can be found in her web site (http://www.csc.lsu.edu/~xiaoting).

Peng Zhu received the B.S. in Management Information System from Beijing Technology and Business University, Beijing, China. He is currently an MS candidate in Industrial and Manufacturing Systems Engineering department at Louisiana State University. His research interests focus on data mining and knowledge discovery, especially identification of scientific discovery from bibliographic databases.

Dr. Felici graduated in Statistics at the University of Rome "La Sapienza". He received his M.Sc. in Operations Research and Operations Management at the University of Lancaster, UK, in 1990, and his Ph.D. in Operations Research at the University of Rome "La Sapienza" in 1995. He is presently a permanent researcher in IASI, the Istituto di Analisi dei Sistemi ed Informatica of the Italian National Research Council (CNR), where he started his research activity in 1994 working on research projects in logic programming and mathematical optimization. His current research activity is mainly devoted to the application of optimization techniques to data mining problems, with particular focus on integer programming algorithms for learning in logic and expert systems.

Dr. Triantaphyllou did his graduate studies at Penn State University from 1984 to 1990. While at Penn State, he earned a Dual M.S. degree in Environment and Operations Research (OR), an M.S. degree in Computer Science and a Dual Ph.D. degree in Industrial Engineering and Operations Research. Since the spring of 2005 he is a Professor in the Computer Science Department at the Louisiana State University (LSU) in Baton Rouge, LA, U.S.A., after he has served for 11 years as an Assistant, Associate, and Full Professor in the Industrial Engineering Department at the same university. He has also served for one year as an Interim Associate Dean for the College of Engineering at LSU.

His research is focused on decision-making theory and applications, data mining and knowledge discovery, and the interface of operations research and computer science. Since the years he was a graduate student, he has developed new methods for data mining and knowledge discovery and also has explored some of the most fundamental and intriguing subjects in decision making. In 1999 he has received the prestigious IIE (Institute of Industrial Engineers), OR Division, Research Award for his research contributions in the above fields. In 2005 he received an LSU Distinguished Faculty Award as recognition of his research, teaching, and service accomplishments. Some of his graduate students have also received awards and distinctions including the Best Dissertation Award at LSU for Science, Engineering and Technology for the year 2003. In 2000 Dr. Triantaphyllou published a bestseller book on multi-criteria decision-making. Also, in 2006 he published a monograph on data mining and knowledge discovery, besides co-editing a book on the same subject.

He always enjoys sharing the results of his research with his students and is also getting them actively involved in his research activities. He has received teaching awards and distinctions. His research has been funded by federal and state agencies, and the private sector. He has extensively published in some of the top refereed journals and made numerous presentations in national and international conferences.

Dr. Triantaphyllou has a strong inter-disciplinary background. He has always enjoyed organizing multi-disciplinary teams of researchers and practitioners with complementary expertise. These groups try to comprehensively attack some of the most urgent problems in the sciences and engineering. He is a strong believer of the premise that the next round of major scientific and engineering discoveries will come from the work of such inter-disciplinary groups. More details of his work can be found in his web site (*http://www.csc.lsu.edu/trianta/*).

SUBJECT INDEX

AUTHOR INDEX

LIST OF CONTRIBUTORS

Abbass, Hussein A.
Artificial Life and Adaptive Robotics Lab
School of Information Technology & Electrical Engineering
University of New South Wales at ADFA
Canberra, ACT 2600
AUSTRALIA
Email: h.abbass@adfa.edu.au
Web: http://www.itee.adfa.edu.au/~abbass

Al-Mubaid, Hisham
University of Houston at Clear Lake
Department of Computer Science
Clear Lake, TX
USA
Email: hisham@cl.uh.edu

Bartnikowski, Stephen
Department of Computer Science EC31
University of Texas at Dallas
Box 830688
Richardson, TX 75083-0688
U.S.A.
Email: sjbart@utdallas.edu

Chen, Guoqing
School of Economics and Management
Tsinghua University
Beijing 100084, CHINA
Email: chengq@em.tsinghua.edu.cn

Chen, Jianhua
Department of Computer Science
Louisiana State University
Baton Rouge, LA 70803-4020
U.S.A.
Email: jianhua@bit.csc.lsu.edu

De Angelis, Vanda
Facoltà di Scienze Statistiche
Università degli studi di Roma "La Sapienza"
Piazzale A. Moro 5
00185 Rome
ITALY
          Email: vanda.deangelis@uniroma1.it

Elmaghraby, Abel S.
University of Louisville
Department of Computer Engineering and Computer Science
J.B. Speed Scientific School
Louisville, KY 40292, U.S.A.

Felici, Giovanni
Istituto di Analisi dei Sistemi ed Informatica
Consiglio Nazionale delle Ricerche
Viale Manzoni 30
00185 Rome
ITALY
          Email: felici@iasi.cnr.it

Fok, Sai-Cheong
Faculty of Engineering & Surveying
University of Southern Queensland
Toowoomba, Qld 4350, AUSTRALIA
          Email: foksai@usq.edu.au
          Web: http://www.usq.edu.au/users/foksai/

Freitas, Alex A.
Computing Laboratory, University of Kent
Canterbury
Kent, CT2 7NF
UK
          Email: A.A.Freitas@kent.ac.uk
          Web: http://www.cs.kent.ac.uk/people/staff/aaf

Granberry, Matthias
Department of Computer Science EC31
University of Texas at Dallas
Box 830688
Richardson, TX 75083-0688
U.S.A.
          Email: matthias@utdallas.edu

Judson, Dean H.
U.S. Census Bureau
4700 Silver Hill Road
Suitland, MD 20746
U.S.A.
　　　Email: Dean.H.Judson@census.gov

Kantardzic, Mehmet M.
University of Louisville
Department of Computer Engineering and Computer Science
J.B. Speed Scientific School
Louisville, KY 40292, U.S.A.
　　　Email: mmkant01@athena.louisville.edu

Kerre, Etienne E.
Department of Applied Mathematics and Computer Sciences
University of Gent
Krilgslaan 281/S9
9000 Gent
BELGIUM
　　　Email: eekerre@gent.edu.be

Khoo, Li-Pheng
School of Mechanical & Production Engineering
Nanyang Technological University
50 Nanyang Avenue
SINGAPORE 639798
　　　Email: mlyzhai@ntu.edu.sg, mlpkhoo@ntu.edu.sg
　　　Web: http://www.ntu.edu.sg/mpe/Admin

Kirley, Michael
School of Environmental & Information Sciences
Charles Stuart University
Thurgoona Campus, PO Box 789
Albury, NSW2640
AUSTRALIA
　　　Email: mkirley@unimelb.edu.au

Kraft, Donald H.
Department of Computer Science
Louisiana State University
Baton Rouge, LA 70803-4020
U.S.A.
　　　Email: kraft@bit.csc.lsu.edu

Kusiak, Andrew
Intelligent Systems Laboratory
Mechanical and Industrial Engineering
2139 Seamans Center
The University of Iowa
Iowa City, Iowa 52242 – 1527
U.S.A.
>   Email: andrew-kusiak@uiowa.edu
>   Web: http://www.icaen.uiowa.edu/~ankusiak

Lee, Jun-Youl
Iowa State University
2019 Black Engineering
Ames, IA 50010, U.S.A.

Liao, T. Warren
Department of Industrial & Manufacturing Systems Engineering
3128 CEBA Building
Louisiana State University
Baton Rouge, LA 70803
U.S.A.
>   Email: ieliao@lsu.du
>   Web: http://www.imse.lsu.edu/liao

Mancinelli, Gabriella
Facoltà di Scienze Statistiche
Università degli studi di Roma "La Sapienza"
Piazzale A. Moro 5
00185 Rome, ITALY

Martin-Bautista, Maria J.
University of Granada
Granada 18071
SPAIN
>   Email: mbautis@decsai.ugr.es

McKay, Robert (Bob) I.
School of Information Technology & Electrical Engineering
University of New South Wales at ADFA
Canberra, ACT 2600
AUSTRALIA
>   Email: rim@cs.adfa.edu.au
>   Web: http://www.itee.adfa.edu.au/~rim

Mugan, Jonathan
Department of Computer Science EC31
University of Texas at Dallas
Box 830688
Richardson, TX 75083-0688
U.S.A.
Email: jwm016000@utdallas.edu

Naidenova, Xenia
Military Medical Academy
Saint Petersburg
196046 Lebedev Street, 6
RUSSIA
Email: naidenova@mail.spbnit.ru

Noda, Edgar
School of Electrical & Comp. Eng.(FEEC)
State University of Campinas (UNICAMP)
Campinas –SP
BRAZIL
Email: edgar@dt.fee.unicamp.br

Olafsson, Sigurdur
Iowa State University
2019 Black Engineering
Ames, IA 50010, U.S.A.
Email: olafsson@iastate.edu
Web: http://www.public.iastate.edu/~olafsson

Orsenigo, Carlotta
Politecnico di Milano
P.za Leonardo da Vinci 32
I20133 Milano
ITALY
Email: carlotta.orsenigo@polimi.it
Web: http://www.dep.polimi.it/eng/comunita/cl.php?id=70

Sun, Fushing
Department of Computer Science
Ball State University
Muncie, IN 47306
U.S.A.
Email: fsun@cs.bsu.edu

Torvik, Vetle I.
University of Illinois at Chicago
Department of Psychiatry
MC 912, 1601 W Taylor St
Chicago, IL 60612
U.S.A.
   Email: vtorvik@uic.edu
   Web: http://arrowsmith2.psych.uic.edu/torvik

Triantaphyllou, Evangelos
Department of Computer Science
298 Coates Hall
Louisiana State University
Baton Rouge, Louisiana 70803
U.S.A.
   Email: trianta@lsu.edu
   Web: http://www.csc.lsu.edu/trianta

Truemper, Klaus
Department of Computer Science EC31
University of Texas at Dallas
Box 830688
Richardson, TX 75083-0688
U.S.A.
   Email: truemper@utdallas.edu

Vercellis, Carlo
Politecnico di Milano
P.za Leonardo da Vinci 32
I20133 Milano
ITALY
   Email: carlo.vercellis@polimi.it
   Web: http://www.dep.polimi.it/eng/comunita/cl.php?id=70

Vila, Maria-Amparo
University of Granada
Granada 18071, SPAIN
   Email: vila@decsai.ugr.es

Wachowiak, Mark P.
University of Louisville
Department of Computer Engineering and Computer Science
J.B. Speed Scientific School
Louisville, KY 40292, U.S.A.

Wei, Qiang
School of Economics and Management
Tsinghua University
Beijing 100084
CHINA

Wang, Xiaoting
Department of Industrial & Manufacturing Systems Engineering
3128 CEBA Building
College of Engineering
Louisiana State University
Baton Rouge, Louisiana 70803
U.S.A.
      Email: xwang8@lsu.edu
      Web: http://www.csc.lsu.edu/~xiaoting

Zakrevskij, Arkadij
United Institute of Informatics Problems
of the National Academy of Sciences of Belarus
Surganova Str. 6
220012 Minsk
BELARUS
      E-mail: zakr@newman.bas-net.by

Zhai, Lian-Yin
School of Mechanical & Production Engineering
Nanyang Technological University
50 Nanyang Avenue
SINGAPORE 639798
      Email: mlyzhai@ntu.edu.sg, mlpkhoo@ntu.edu.sg
      Web: http://www.ntu.edu.sg/mpe/Admin

Zhu, Peng
Department of Industrial & Manufacturing Systems Engineering
3128 CEBA Building
College of Engineering
Louisiana State University
Baton Rouge, Louisiana 70803
U.S.A.
      Email: pzhu1@lsu.edu

ABOUT THE EDITORS

Dr. Triantaphyllou did his graduate studies at Penn State University from 1984 to 1990. While at Penn State, he earned a Dual M.S. degree in Environment and Operations Research (OR), an M.S. degree in Computer Science and a Dual Ph.D. degree in Industrial Engineering and Operations Research. Since the spring of 2005 he is a Professor in the Computer Science Department at the Louisiana State University (LSU) in Baton Rouge, LA, U.S.A., after he has served for 11 years as an Assistant, Associate, and Full Professor in the Industrial Engineering Department at the same university. He has also served for one year as an Interim Associate Dean for the College of Engineering at LSU.

His research is focused on decision-making theory and applications, data mining and knowledge discovery, and the interface of operations research and computer science. Since the years he was a graduate student, he has developed new methods for data mining and knowledge discovery and also has explored some of the most fundamental and intriguing subjects in decision making. In 1999 he has received the prestigious IIE (Institute of Industrial Engineers), OR Division, Research Award for his research contributions in the above fields. In 2005 he received an LSU Distinguished Faculty Award as recognition of his research, teaching, and service accomplishments. Some of his graduate students have also received awards and distinctions including the Best Dissertation Award at LSU for Science, Engineering and Technology for the year 2003. In 2000 Dr. Triantaphyllou published a bestseller book on multi-criteria decision-making. Also, in 2006 he published a monograph on data mining and knowledge discovery, besides co-editing a book on the same subject.

He always enjoys sharing the results of his research with his students and is also getting them actively involved in his research activities. He has received teaching awards and distinctions. His research has been funded by federal and state agencies, and the private sector. He has extensively published in some of the top refereed journals and made numerous presentations in national and international conferences.

Dr. Triantaphyllou has a strong inter-disciplinary background. He has always enjoyed organizing multi-disciplinary teams of researchers and practitioners with complementary expertise. These groups try to comprehensively attack some of the most urgent problems in the sciences and engineering. He is a strong believer of the premise that the next round of major scientific and engineering discoveries will come from the work of such inter-disciplinary groups. More details of his work can be found in his web site (http://www.csc.lsu.edu/trianta/).

Dr. Giovanni Felici graduated in Statistics at the University of Rome "La Sapienza" in 1991. While completing his graduate studies, he won an Erasmus scholarship to attend the Master of Science in Operations Research and Operations Management course at the University of Lancaster, UK, where he was awarded the M.Sc. title in 1990. He was then enrolled in the Ph.D. program in Operations Research at the University of Rome "La Sapienza", where he successfully defended his dissertation on Classification and Recognition algorithms in 1995. He is presently a permanent researcher in IASI, the Istituto di Analisi dei Sistemi ed Informatica of the Italian National Research Council (CNR), where he started his research activity in 1994 working on research projects in Logic Programming and Mathematical Optimization, both publicly and privately funded. In 1995 and 1996 he was research assistant of Professor Klaus Truemper at the University of Texas at Dallas, TX, where he developed new algorithmic approaches for Data Mining in logic settings.

His current research activity is mainly devoted to the application of Optimization Techniques to Data Mining problems, with particular focus on Integer Programming algorithms for Learning in Logic and Expert Systems, but he is also active in the field of Operations Research techniques for large-scale logistics and production problems; he published papers in international refereed journals and edited books and presented his researches in many international conferences.

He is also involved in education and teaching, holding graduate and post-graduate courses in Operations Research and Data Mining in two Roman universities and hosting and tutoring students in the Optimization Laboratory for Data Mining (OLDAM), that he co-founded in IASI with some colleagues in 2002.

He is one of the members of the board of the Italian Operations Research Association, playing an active role in the organization of scientific events and in the relations with the Operations Research International community.

Dr. Felici's strong interest in Data Mining and in the cross-fertilization between this research area and Mathematical Optimization is driven by the belief that the amazing progress made in the last decades in the field of mathematical programming can provide enormous benefits if it is applied to the construction of intelligent systems with recognition, learning, and rule induction capabilities.